the architects and architecture of London

For Alex, 18th happy birthday to you.

Margaret

"It's the quality, not the vintage ..."

For Victoria.
And with apologies for the dozens of London architects and
fine London works there has not been space to celebrate.

Architectural Press is an imprint of Routledge
2 Park Square, Milton Park, Abingdon, Oxon OX14 4RN
711 Third Avenue, New York, NY 10017, USA

Routledge is an imprint of the Taylor & Francis Group, an informa business

First published 2008 (Ken Allinson)
Revised 2009.
Book design, all photos and drawings by Ken Allinson except as noted.
Copyright © 2008, Ken Allinson.
Published by Taylor & Francis. All rights reserved.
Minor revisions and corrections made 2009.

Notice:
No responsibility is assumed by the publisher for any injury and/or damage to persons or property as a matter of products liability, negligence
or otherwise, or from any use or operation of any methods, products,
instructions or ideas contained in the material herein. Because of rapid
advances in the medical sciences, in particular, independent verification
of diagnoses and drug dosages should be made.

British Library Cataloguing in Publication Data
A catalogue record for this book is available from the British Library
ISBN-978-0-7506-8337-1

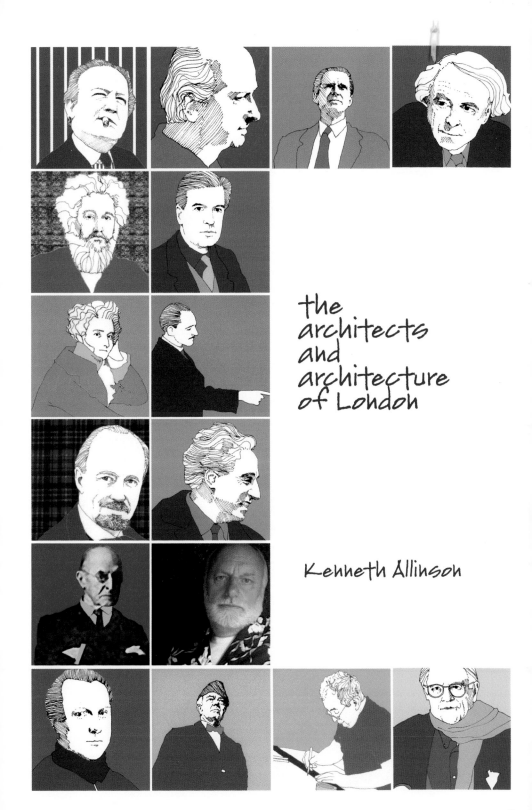

the architects and architecture of London

Kenneth Allinson

contents

RIBA Royal Gold Medal winners

The Institute of British Architects was founded in 1834 and obtained its royal charter in 1837. The first Gold Medal was awarded by Queen Victoria in 1848. Names in bold are featured in this text.

1848 **Charles Robert Cockerell, RA**
1849 *Luigi Canina, Italy*
1850 **Charles Barry, RA**
1851 **Thomas L. Donaldson**
1852 *Leo von Klenze, Austria*
1853 **Sir Robert Smirke, RA**
1854 **Philip Hardwick, RA**
1855 *J. I. Hittorff, France*
1856 **William Tite**
1857 **Owen Jones**
1858 *August Stuler, Germany*
1859 **George Gilbert Scott, RA**
1860 **Sydney Smirke, RA**
1861 *J.B. Lesueur, France*
1862 *Rev. Robert Willis*
1863 **Anthony Salvin**
1864 *E. Viollet-le-Duc, France*
1865 **James Pennethorne**
1866 **Sir M. Digby Wyatt**
1867 *Charles Texier, France*
1868 *Sir Henry Layard*
1869 *C. R. Lepsius, Germany*
1870 **Benjamin Ferrey**
1871 *James Fergusson*
1872 *Baron von Schmidt, Austria*
1873 **Thomas Henry Wyatt**
1874 **George Edmund Street, RA** *(the year John Ruskin turned down the honour)*
1875 *Edmund Sharpe*
1876 *Joseph Louis Duc, France*
1877 **Charles Barry**
1878 **Alfred Waterhouse, RA**
1879 *Marquis de Vogue, France*
1880 *John L. Pearson, RA*
1881 **George Godwin**
1882 *Baron von Ferstel, Austria*
1883 *Francis Cranmer Penrose*
1884 **William Butterfield**
1885 *H Schliemann, Germany*
1886 *Charles Garnier, France*

1887 *Ewan Christian*
1888 *Baron von Hansen, Austria*
1889 *Sir Charles T. Newton*
1890 *John Gibson*
1891 **Arthur Blomfield, ARA**
1892 *César Daly, France*
1893 *Richard Morris Hunt, USA*
1894 *Lord Leighton, RA*
1895 **James Brooks**
1896 **Ernest George, RA**
1897 *Dr P. J. H. Cuypers, Holland*
1898 *George Aitchison, RA*
1899 **George Frederick Bodley, RA**
1900 *Professor Rodolfo Amadeo Lanciani, Italy*
1901 *(Not awarded, owing to the death of Queen Victoria.)*
1902 **Thomas Edward Collcutt**
1903 *Charles F McKim, USA*
1904 *Auguste Choisy, France*
1905 **Sir Aston Webb, PPRA**
1906 *Sir L. Alma-Tadema, RA*
1907 **John Belcher, RA**
1908 *Honoré Daumet, France*
1909 *Sir Arthur John Evans, FRS, FSA*
1910 *Sir Thomas Graham Jackson*
1911 *Wilhelm Dorpfeld, Germany*
1912 **Basil Champneys**
1913 **Reginald Blomfield, RA, FSA**
1914 *Jean Louis Pascal, France*
1915 *Frank Darling, Canada*
1916 *Sir Robert Rowand Anderson, FRIAS*
1917 *Henri Paul Nenot, France*
1918 **Ernest Newton, RA**
1919 *Leonard Stokes*
1920 *Charles Louis Girault, France*
1921 **Sir Edwin Landseer Lutyens, OM, KCIE, RA, FSA**
1922 *Thomas Hastings, USA*
1923 **Sir John James Burnet, FRIAS, RA, RSA**
1924 *Not awarded*
1925 **Sir Giles Gilbert Scott, OM, DCL, RA**
1926 *Professor Ragnar Ostberg, Sweden*
1927 **Sir Herbert Baker, KCIE, RA**
1928 *Sir Guy Dawber, RA, FSA*
1929 *Victor Alexandre Frederic Laloux, France*
1930 *Percy Scott Worthington, FSA*
1931 **Sir Edwin Cooper, RA**
1932 *Dr Hendrik Petrus Berlage, Holland*
1933 *Sir Charles Reed Peers, CBE, PPSA*
1934 **Henry Vaughan Lanchester, PPTPI**
1935 *Willem Marinus Dudok, Holland*
1936 **Charles Henry Holden, MTPI**

1937 Sir Raymond Unwin
1938 Professor Ivar Tengbom, Sweden
1939 Sir Percy Thomas, OBE, JP, MTPI
1940 **Charles Francis Annesley Voysey**
1941 Frank Lloyd Wright, USA
1942 **William Curtis Green, RA**
1943 Professor Sir Charles Herbert Reilly, OBE
1944 Sir Edward Maufe, RA
1945 Victor Vessnin, USSR
1946 Professor Sir Patrick Abercrombie FSA, PPTPI, FILA
1947 **Professor Albert Edward Richardson, RA, FSA**
1948 Auguste Perret, France
1949 Sir Howard Robertson, MC, ARA, SADG
1950 Eliel Saarinen, USA
1951 **Emanuel Vincent Harris, OBE, RA**
1952 **George Grey Wornum**
1953 Le Corbusier (C. E. Jeanneret), France
1954 Sir Arthur George Stephenson, CMG, AMTPI, Australia
1955 John Murray Easton
1956 Dr Walter Adolf Georg Gropius, USA
1957 Hugo Alvar Henrik Aalto, Finland
1958 Robert Schofield Morris, FRAIC, Canada
1959 Professor Ludwig Mies van der Rohe, USA
1960 Professor Pier Luigi Nervi, Italy
1961 Lewis Mumford, USA
1962 Professor Sven Gottfried Markelius, Sweden
1963 The Lord Holford, ARA, PPTPI, FILA
1964 **E. Maxwell Fry, CBE**
1965 Professor Kenzo Tange, Japan
1966 Ove Arup, CBE, MICE, MIStructE
1967 Sir Nikolaus Pevsner, CBE, FBA, FSA, Hon ARIBA
1968 Dr Richard Buckminster Fuller, FRSA, Hon AIA, USA
1969 Jack Antonio Coia, CBE, RSA, AMTPI, FRIAS
1970 **Professor Sir Robert Matthew, CBE, ARSA, FRIAS**
1971 Hubert de Cronin Hastings
1972 Louis Kahn, USA
1973 **Sir Leslie Martin**
1974 **Powell & Moya**
1975 Michael Scott, Ireland
1976 Sir John Summerson, CBE, FBA, FSA
1977 **Denys Lasdun, CBE**
1978 Jørn Utzon, Denmark
1979 The Office of Charles and Ray Eames, USA

1980 **James Stirling**
1981 Sir Philip Dowson, CBE
1982 **Berthold Lubetkin**
1983 **Norman Foster**
1984 Charles Correa, India
1985 **Richard Rogers**
1986 Arata Isozaki, Japan
1987 Ralph Erskine, CBE
1988 Richard Meier, USA
1989 Renzo Piano, Italy
1990 Aldo van Eyck, Holland
1991 Colin Stansfield Smith, CBE
1992 Peter Rice, DIC(IC), MICE
1993 Giancarlo de Carlo, Italy
1994 **Michael and Lady Patricia Hopkins**
1995 Colin Rowe, USA
1996 Harry Seidler, Australia
1997 Tadao Ando, Japan
1998 Oscar Niemeyer, Brazil
1999 The City of Barcelona, Spain
2000 Frank Gehry, USA
2001 Jean Nouvel, France
2002 **Archigram**
2003 Rafael Moneo, Spain
2004 Rem Koolhaas, The Netherlands
2005 Frei Otto, Germany
2006 Toyo Ito, Japan
2007 Herzog & de Meuron, Switzerland
2008 **Edward Cullinan**

By way of introduction : heroes and things . . .

One could say this is a book about heroes: those salient architects whose London works have made them significant in the life of the metropolis. On the other hand, the surreptitious principal among the *dramatis personae* in the book is London itself. To accept this is perhaps to lend a strange characterisation to a two-thousand-year urban phenomenon that has long been one of Europe's more peculiar and dominant cities. By 1750, for example, when England was at the forefront of the Industrial Revolution and the focus of a burgeoning empire, London was the largest city in Europe, twice the size of that great European cultural focus: Paris; and so it continued, throughout the nineteenth century. To do so can also be read as an idiosyncratic manoeuvre that courts a charge of sentimentality and romanticism. The historian who deals with London's apparent vitality as a living spirit to which (like Peter Ackroyd) they lend a 'biography', is entering a dark territory where such a characterisation is similar to the manner in which the eighteenth century Adam Smith's 'hidden hand' of market economics was employed as a useful but opaque short-hand in order to allude to what is convenient to construe but cannot be explained.

Nevertheless, like Smith faced with the self-evident reality of markets and their awesome co-ordinative capacity, anyone who has lived in London and studied its dynamics can surely be forgiven for resorting to such a ploy. The metropolis certainly *appears* to have a life of its own, regardless of its inhabitants' intentions – a life that outlives those of individuals abiding there, their longings, dreams and scheming; a life that, as if animated by some Hegelian spirit, determines epochal character and, as a spirit of place, is attributed with physiognomic character and an active intelligence that ostensibly informs the city with a purpose underlying its continuities. Those who dwell within this place have lives that are grist to its mill, energy to its metabolism.

Such a rationale is possibly absurd, although one detects it at the root of perspectives on urban life that informed, for example the 1960s Non-Plan put forward by an otherwise hard-headed and entirely unsentimental London architect, Cedric Price (see page 392), an architect thoroughly disillusioned by the planning regime. One also has to admit that it is a useful way to deal with something in terms of 'as if', assisting us to make sense of our experiences. If Adam Smith could satisfy hard-headed economists with references to 'a hidden hand', then surely it is legitimate for architects and urban planners to look upon London's dynamics in similar terms?

Certainly, such a viewpoint lends a convenient unifying basis to the constructions one necessarily puts upon historical dynamics. For example, London possesses a consistent dynamic patterning that can be traced back to its Roman foundation, subsequent Saxon inhabitation and later Norman conquest. And a constant factor throughout that patterned history is a central feature also suffering occasional characterisation: the River Thames. Cultivated, encultured, rudely utilised and crudely abused, the Thames simply flows on: sapping its sources and playing out its regulated tidal courtship with the Channel sea waters, suffering indifferently and, latterly, manifesting a splendid capability for resurgence that is at once beautiful and always somewhat frightening. People – perhaps foolishly – once again fish its waters and thereby reaffirm its identity.

Such a capacity to rise, phoenix-like, from the impact of detrimental influences is sometimes seen as one of London's key characteristics. This is certainly how people must have felt when, after the great conflagration of 1666, an impatient populace immediately set about rebuilding a fabric that included London's most important building: the cathedral of St Paul, that 'minster in the east' serving as sisterly companion to St Peter's, 'the minster in the west' (i.e. Westminster Abbey). When Christopher Wren – whose radical replanning intentions the populace effectively ignored – attended a foundation ceremony for the former he is said to have called upon a worker to find any old stone from the ruins of the medieval cathedral. He was brought one that, coincidentally, had carved into it the word '*resurgam*'. By the time he attended the cathedral's formal inauguration, some thirty years later, London – in terms of another keynote that characterises the English as well as London — had rebuilt itself without most of the *grand projets* proposed by its architects. London, in other words, is a vital cultural product: the heaving work of generations of its inhabitants, of architects and builders who knowingly and unknowingly have slaved to serve and service the rapacious beast that is their master: to cultivate it, nurture it and, above all, constantly renew it while inhabiting it.

Within this life and in terms of constitutive architectural works, London's populace find all kinds of significances. In one sense, everyone and no one is necessary to its strange, on-going metabolism. And some individuals are more salient than others: erected as the heroes who figure within London's understanding of its own history.

And yet these individuals are frequently absorbed into a vital flow whose mainstream is prone to forget them and their works alarmingly quickly. A few architects – Christopher Wren in particular – somehow maintain their salience and continue to be at least noted and sometimes perceived as relevant figures by a contemporary generation. And a third set of heroes emerges from history to a contemporary prominence never enjoyed in their lifetime – architects like Patrick Gwynne (see page 332), whose time-capsule home in Esher lends him a status in death that he never enjoyed in real life. Works that were originally mediocre sometimes achieve significance over time – perhaps merely because they have survived as witness to a cultural history that we perceive to be increasingly important. Whatever truth and justice are, they apear to have a weak place in this dynamic of salience, reputation and perceived significance. Individuals stand forth as heroes for complex and obscure reasons.

To tackle multiple biographies – even briefly – is to be confronted by either too little information or too much. Too little is most common. But sometimes too much comes in the form of contradictory understandings and opinions, especially regarding character and talent, sometimes regarding authorship, dates and the like. And, of course, one is all too aware of those commonplace challenges concerning historical perspective and the relativity of values. It can then be a relief to turn to the substance of the architectural works these people have authored. One then enjoys the distinct advantage of relating historical issues to the built reality, as it now stands.

Of course, historical understanding can enrich experience, both before and after the fact, i.e. in bringing one to a work and helping to reveal its content by informing reflections upon reasons for being and disparate interpretative meanings. Nevertheless, at some point the thing in itself has to be engaged and appreciated directly, for what it is and how it is currently valued – at which point one is sometimes prompted to consider why a work is valued at all or insufficiently; or, how past generations have dealt with similar issues in striving to sustain a building's relevance to London's vitality. One is reminded that an elusive problem of legitimation always lies at the heart of all architectural practice.

However, even this more direct and non-academic approach can be fraught: always in danger of ignoring or neglecting those figures who were once significant but whose works have now disappeared or been transmogrified. On the other hand, there are notable architects who, curiously, appear to have had little effect on the course of architecture in general: those generously bestowed with honours in their lifetime, and then quickly forgotten in their absence. Lutyens, for example, may be one of the more notable figures of British architectural history, but his work seems to have been an historical dead-end apart from the practice example he established. And who now remembers the brilliance of Arthur Davis, one of the brightest of architectural stars who, still in his early twenties, was responsible for the design of the Ritz Hotel? Many architects once worthy of receiving the RIBA Royal Gold Medal now languish in old books perused only by PhD students hoping to add to their university's research ratings or give spurious content to ever-hungry media. Perhaps London needs a new monument: to the forgotten master builder?

Inevitably, one returns to a traditional perspective differentiating between the shifting nuances of what was once denominated as Customary or Arbitrary matters in relation to those contrasting and ostensibly more lasting values once described as eternal: what Wren referred to as the Natural or Positive causes of beauty. However, in lieu of Wren's fixed viewpoint on such matters we now enjoy a manner of understanding that constantly shifts and redefines these categories

living architecture, i.e. of experiencing the thing in itself; at worst, moribund architectural junk in some urban corner. This is how many historical works are frequently experienced, i.e. not as something in themselves, valued for what they are, but as relics serving an appetite for nostalgia. Such an appetite may be of value and provide much satisfaction, but the life referred to often lies within the narrative rather than the substance of the architecture. We then fail to appreciate it, in itself. However, even this simple point is problematic. For example, the manner of one's engagement with an architecture is crucially important. As Walter Benjamin pointed out, one does not stand contemplatively before architecture as before a painting in a gallery; one must provide a different kind of tactile attention – and upon that one word, 'attention' hangs a gaggle of issues. However, in fundamental terms, it is only by moving through an architectural work and, if only ever so briefly, by inhabiting it (even as a tourist or visitor), that one is able to bring its material and formal muteness to, as it were, 'life'. Cultural and social narratives can be of assistance, but only to the point where, paradoxically, one is able to throw them away and live with the thing in itself and for itself.

But what is 'brought alive'? What remains when narrative content is exhausted? Here, again, there are difficulties. An appreciated work is often said to 'lift' (or feed) one's spirit – in itself, a fascinating notion. Sometimes the architecture is attributed with a 'life', a character, an individuality; to acknowledge it is to 'meet' with it. Such a notion is, of course, absurd, but there is better basis upon which one might immediately connect with the artefact as it is in itself, upon which one might shift away from an intellectualised stance toward a more affective, magical-mythical one: to a state in which it is 'as if' the essentiality of the thing was personified. Then one might declare the building to be 'charged' in a manner that is surely projective, but nevertheless real. The alternative is a conceptual and intellectual relationship that adopts a stance of standing apart, rather than being inside the presence and nature of the phenomenon.

Of course, this 'meeting with' presumes the architectural work can sustain a content being attributed to it. Take a simple example: John Soane was a man in love with architecture. To visit his home in Lincoln's Inn (preferably on one of those now rare wintery days when hardly anyone is there) is to expose oneself to a

whilst still acknowledging a peculiar inter-relationship between continuities and discontinuities. Modernism focuses upon the latter, but it may be the former that is more interesting. For example, one of those necessitous 'eternals' is possibly the nature of the design challenge itself. Sir John Soane career epitomised the issue: engaging in projects as inescapably situated, and yet playing the game of architecture as if its challenges were an acknowledgement of the stirrings of some mythical Muse whose presence he sensed even within mere fragments of bygone works, even in the cast replication of their forms. William Butterfield is another such architect, one who appears to have engaged this same Muse, just as Lutyens did when he satisfyingly referred to Palladio as the 'big game'. One thinks of Stirling in the same terms. Or Charles Barry and Inigo Jones, Nicholas Hawksmoor, and Denys Lasdun. It is here that we discover greatness – perhaps not in the work, but in the manner the challenge has been undertaken and addressed.

This review of London's architects seeks to address such issues from a place where its feet are upon London's current pavements. From this perspective old and new must always endure a test of pertinence to current London life. Unless, for example, the place of Inigo Jones or Lord Burlington in architectural history and their extant works have the capability of being 'brought to life' they lapse into academic interest: at best inhabitants of a fascinating world of neo-mythic narrative that has a habit of getting in the way of the possible meeting with a character of place thoroughly imbued with a raw enthusiasm for architecture. Here is a place that is, at once, family home, gallery, office and architecture museum. It is much as Soane left it: a place rich with architectural fragments that drip with magical-mythical undertones, that embody a unified whole within the fractured part. Soane – vain, anxious, ambitious, insecure, embittered, but in love with architecture and architectural gamesmanship – accommodated the ghosts of whole architectures within his own architectural schema. A way of life is conjured out of, in and around, mute fragments of shaped stone: pieces of Westminster Abbey, for example, are given a ridiculous and joyous narrative that is at once mischievous, fun and yet deeply serious. Pieces of ancient achievement are elevated to the status of relic. No other building in London is so redolent with such qualities and to strive to appreciate them only intellectually and aesthetically is to somewhat miss the point. Soane gave the building a 'charge'.

Such discovery demands that we visit a place and engage it as sequence and rhythm of spaces, themes and characterisations of designed configurations and serendipitous relationships. The 'tectonic' of the thing is that conceptualised, formal relation of part and whole as an ordered and coherent unity. It rewards attention, but one has to appreciate this compositional content in very broad terms. However, it is the 'archi' component of a work — the peculiar manner in which the architectural author has, as it were, penetrated to the situated root of the challenges faced — that truly excites. And Soane penetrates to the root of the situation in an unexpected way: not only dealing with the demands of home, office, gallery and museum, but striving to play with the spirit of architecture itself and to give 'her' place within a work.

Most architectural works are without such depth. However, to say this raises another issue: how do we, now, deal with the situated nature of past challenges and seek to appreciate them? How do we appreciate the challenges and achievements of Soane some two hundred years

ago? Also, if architectural heroes had lives of practice in terms of three fundamental criteria – the pursuit of Survival, Success and Significance – then it is surely peculiar that so many formerly significant people can be so quickly forgotten and their works ignored. While St Paul's Cathedral was intended to be significant and remains so to this day, the Midland Hotel at St Pancras was an instrumental commercial railway venture that failed miserably and yet (only just) survived to become one of the capital's more loved edifices. And otherwise ordinary works – such as Bloomsbury's Georgian terraces, Kentish Town pubs and Soho offices – often bear a quiet value which, perhaps by accident, has survived and achieved a paradoxically ordinary kind of significance to those who lift up their eyes in order to attend to such things. What was once of insignificant value often, especially in the eyes of nostalgic conservationists, becomes of distorted significance to those fearful of realising that elusive 'quality' they value in the works of previous generations. And yet a contrary prejudice can blind us to the value of older works that sit uncomfortably with contemporary values (one thinks of classicism in general, but especially of works from the Victorian and Edwardian periods — many people have the greatest difficulty in appreciating these periods of architectural endeavour).

It is with such issues in my mind that I have tackled what is, at once, a simple and problematic topic as a kind of balancing act that has, on the one hand, salient names from historical records and, on the other, reference to the facts of extant works. The selections are the product of that dynamic. The work is not a gazeteer with regard to the subject it seeks to address - it would be three times as long to even begin to do justice

Opposite: St Magnus Martyr, Christopher Wren – a relatively unspoilt, converted or bombed and restored work of Wren, a church that is a simple accumulation of time and habituation.

to such an aspiration. Instead, this is the London I know and love: what I find on its streets, but with the knowledge that, in each instance, one needs to remind oneself that, 'someone once did this thing'. Here are the works of London's architectural heroes. With more space and time there might have been more of them and of noteworthy buildings (or parts of them), certainly more nuances and explorations of cross-themes, influences and inter-relations. There would also be references to individual works that have value but the author is otherwise forgotten or even unknown.

Finally, extensive reference has been made to a variety of dictionaries of architects, historical works and biographies, but no attempt has been made to provide extensive references and notes which would have significantly altered the tone of the book and its orientation toward what can be found on the streets of London.

On that note I should acknowledge an inspiration: Alastair Service's book on the same subject (1979). My first copy of that work fell apart from overuse and my second is already heavily marked. This was a work of erudition and quiet enthusiasm which it was my original intention to humbly add-to and re-issue. That was not to be, and this work is my own attempt to address the same topic. I do so on a somewhat different basis and with a somewhat different perspective, but always with one eye on Service's original. My hope is that he accepts the effort on these terms – perhaps one sound enough that someone, someday, will do the same: grasp a passed baton and enthusiastically celebrate an ongoing body of works. London: it's quite a city.

Above: George Street, sitting alone in the arched niche within the entrance hall of the Royal Courts of Justice, for which he was the architect (by H.H. Armstead, 1883-6; see page 174).
Below: Sir John Soane, a statue set into a niche on the northern perimeter wall of the Bank of England (by Reid Dick, 1937; this part of the wall was remodelled by Herbert Baker in the 1920s).

Experiencing London's architecture

What most people know and enjoy as architecture is actually urban design: a set of elements in configurational relationship that necessarily has much within the overall equation that is coincidental and accidental, dynamic rather than static. Nevertheless, the whole is held together in the form of an architectonic unity (or, in some instances, merely communicates the contrast: incoherence). Buildings are only one part of this overall phenomenon but, self-evidently they play a principal role, especially when a their façades are experienced as that kind of presentational 'masking' especially characteristic of the neo-Classical building whose compositional arrangement of Orders was once the most fundamental aspect of a building's architecture – a principal aspect, for example, of what Sir Edwin Lutyens once referred to as 'the big game' or 'grand manner'.

Below: SOM's tower at Broadgate receiving its sartorial attire, much in the manner Baker expressively employed the 'grand manner' to cloak his Bank of England building.

Above: Herbert Baker's Bank of England, standing above John Soane's defensive walling. (See page 246.)

To play such a game once almost defined what architecture was – a game Modernism rejected in favour of its own compositional and semiological orders. But one sees something parallel in many contemporary buildings. Take, for example, the manifest exhibition of ordering on the Bank of England by Lutyens' contemporary, Sir Herbert Baker, and compare it with the Broadgate Tower, also in the City, by the American firm Skidmore, Owing and Merrill (SOM). At the Bank, Baker's neo-Baroque 'Wrenaissance' façade poking above John Soane's screen wall lays claim to be a valid architecture in itself, almost irrespective of what lies behind. As well as being an expressive branding to the institution that is housed, it is also a kind of urban theatre, like that backcloth architecture Inigo Jones gave to his masques. Similarly, at Broadgate, the underlying structure has been similarly dealt with as the basis to a branding game imposing its own formal imperatives and criteria, and laying its own claim to creativity, legitimacy and respect. In both instances significance is given to a sartorial exercise which loosely 'follows' the structural reality in a distinctly expressive manner and finds its own ordering principles with which to address the public arena. Each of these façades lends attention to an 'architectural face' that takes its place as a part of the public realm.

In experiencing such aspects of a building we do so in a *tactile* manner, i.e. not contemplatively, as with a work of art in a gallery. This may be a 'thin' form of engagement, such as briefly passing by or walking through, but it is nevertheless an active and habitational engagement. And our appraisal of such experiences is itself interesting. In the case of a street architecture each individual part of the whole has a strong role in contributing to a perceived unity that is almost intangible and certainly elusive, except in those instances where, as in a traditional London square, the formalities of urban place are foregrounded. In other instances, we

play an important role in 'reading' an architectural coherence into the overall dynamic of street scenery and street life. The architecture is then composed of much more than just the buildings.

The interesting part of what is going on concerns our satisfactions or dissatisfactions: do we like what we are experiencing? In some peculiar manner, that appraisal is commonly made sub-consciously and immediately before it is dealt with rationally and critically. It seems we like or dislike in an instant, perhaps then modifying this initial reaction of reception or rejection on the basis of further engagement, e.g. by walking through and around, by examining it in detail, staying within the building and using it, and by learning more about its reasons for being. We work within the terms of our engagement in order to know its experiential content, to appreciate what is taking place and what is going on, to 'read' the architecture semiotically and consider what these signs reveal about its nature. We then find this attentive work either confirming or contradicting the initial appraisal (a critical approach that leaves one either indifferent, disappointed or strangely satisfied).

In addition, one has to work to understand one's own stance with regard to the experience. Sometimes a building will make a call upon an attentiveness that one may, for a variety of reasons, be unable to provide. For example, a criticism made by the neo-Palladians of Wren and, especially, Nicholas Hawksmoor's concerned the demands these architects placed upon one's capacity to appraise an architecture: one simply had to work too hard. And there is another fundamental difficulty: buildings are mute; they fail to declare their reasons for being, have them concealed from us, or perhaps embody a discernibly weak architectonic structure.

Experience appears to be as problematic as creativity. It may even include the demand that we 'wake up' from habituated frames of mind and ways of paying attention. Of course, at the heart of the issue of attentiveness and appreciation, there is an implicit issue of sound understanding and judgement. Here we step directly into a debate that was fundamental to the eighteenth century but which Modernism stealthily avoids: conventions of taste and fashion as important aspects of architectural appreciation. Much is at stake in all this, particularly that commonplace differentiation

between *culture* and *Culture* that refuses to wither and contrasts the satisfaction of what is merely appetitive with something ostensibly more significant. The former is creaturely and related to the biological nature of everyone's being; it can equally be this or that without significant social consequence. But Culture is a supposed body of significances embodied in works that successfully raise themselves to another level of meaning and significance. And here we are at the roots of the western architectural tradition: architecture as a function of the social order (and, in this guise, a cause of anxiety for writers such as George Bataille and architects such as Cedric Price).

However, contemporary culture continually upends the traditional paradigm of what is base and elevated, exhibiting appetites for those Dionysian powers that stir a culture (where belief, as T.S. Eliot noted, is a way of life) and disrupts the Apollonian refinements of Culture's pretensions. And coursing through this duad is Reyner Banham's differentiation between good architecture and good design: they are not necessarily the same thing. This is a point that turns us toward a recurring issue the eighteenth century neo-Palladians strove to rationalise is terms of 'moral sense' theory, Ruskin addressed in terms of 'flourishing', nineteenth century German philosophy dealt with as *Bildung, and* the French considered in terms of '*le bons sens*'. Even Vitruvius would have recognised the issue as a Roman concept of the *sensus communis* which refers itself to civic well-being – in turn, correlated with the Greek concept of *phronesis.* At the core of architectural works is an issue of appropriate intentions and civic well-being. To call it an art is perhaps to miss the point. Ruskin, for example, that hero of nineteenth century art theory, reformulated many of the eighteenth century's ideas about beauty, in particular by applying a moralistic overtone to the debate. But he was also unique if promoting the idea of a criterion of beauty concerned with civic vitality itself: "the appearance of felicitous fulfilment of function in living things, more especially of the joyful and right exertion of perfect life in man; and this kind of beauty I [...] call Vital Beauty." This was construed to be, in part, the product of a 'penetrative' imagination counterpointing an artist's capacity to exercise an 'associative' imagination that ranges from a supremely artful compositional skill to the entertaining exhibition of mere fancy. Here, we are at the heart of what Vitruvius dealt with as intent and the expression of that intention, and the conceptual basis of linkages between the consideration of what signifies and what is signified: a linkage that defines the essence of the challenge to an architectural author and lends an architecture its fundamental meaning.

Writing in 1914, Geoffrey Scott argued that architecture aimed toward "a pattern of the world as [man] would have it." An architecture is, in other words, by its nature symbolic and metaphorical. It is this which differentiates it from building (or, as Pevsner put it, marks the difference between a bicycle shed and Lincoln Cathedral). Some sixty years later, Pevsner's former pupil, Banham, was failing to resolve his discomforts regarding the art of architecture, and (now employing the technological references of another era) merely noted that it is rather like a black box and it may be better not to prise this open and peer inside: wherein lies a complex mix of instrumentalism and neo-Platonism, aesthetics and mythic charge, issues of attentiveness and social determinism, as well as those of *Bildung*, of penetrative and associative and vital beauties, of Culture and culture ... all of which makes the challenge of architectural appreciation and appraisal almost as problematic as architectural authorship.

One part of the black boxe's content includes forms of narrative offered by architects as causal explanation, historical association or literary substitute for experience of the thing itself (and, as such, sorely derided by Scott). However authentic narrative is not provided on a platter, but is self-made: a 'making sense' of one's lived experiences. The best narrative is the one you construct yourself: what is, in itself, an architecture of parts assembled together as an open-ended content of experiences, associations, and cross-references. One constructs this content as layers of significance constituted as a holding pattern of meaning that is always (one hopes) in a process of adaptation and modification. Here we turn to personal enthusiasms for a living game of playing at 'architective' by construing one's own historical 'movements', 'styles' and similar academic clichés that are nevertheless useful ways to give order to architectural experience. These personal constructs, as readings of a living city, tell us something about ourselves and the ways in which we live with our buildings. And they make reference – as their basis – to those sometimes heroic and sometimes strange, conflicted and ordinary figures who have improvisationally employed wit and inventiveness to give form to London's fabric – architectural authors such as Hawksmoor, who demanded of us that we wake up and deal with his designs as something challenging rather than merely convenient and pleasing.

Architecture, in these terms, is a part of the way we live and know the world in and about us. In the form of a Black Box, one likes to imagine it as well-travelled, scratched and dented, but always buzzing with a resilient vitality as well as intelligence And one imagines it bearing distressed stickers on its sides – perhaps something arcane reading: "Authentic building occurs so far as there are poets, such poets as take the measure for architecture, the structure of dwelling" (the philosopher, Martin Heidegger). Or simply saying "We rarely reflect how essential it is that all things should wear out and decay. We forget that it is not in our creations, the things we make, the order we establish, but in our functioning that life is fulfilled in us." (the psychologist, Esther Harding).

London is a good place in which to seek and find such endeavours. And the following pages present significant architects whose works can still be found on London's streets and still contributing to that civic 'flourishing' which establishes them as a valued part of a living metropolis, one in which cultural continuities are at least as interesting as the discontinuities of constant Modernist change.

A burgeoning beast: London's population growth

Almost one thousand years ago, in 1100, just after the Norman conquest, the population of London was approximately 15,000, growing to about 80,000 two hundred years later. By 1600 it was 200,000 and, by the time of the Great Fire in 1666, had expanded to 375,000 – already a European curiosity divided into three areas: the historic City; a suburban development that stretched along the Fleet Street/Strand axis to Westminster; and outlying areas of market gardens, including south of the Thames in Southwark (an area that the Commonwealth defences had enclosed between 1643 and 1647).

In his notable war-time work, Georgian London, John

Above: Staple's Inn, Chancery Lane: restoration of a medieval London building.

Summerson was prompted by the drama of aerial photography to describe an air-view of London at about 1615: "a tesselation of red roofs pricked with plots of green and the merlon-shadowed patches which are the lead roofs of churches. Within the blurred margin, the line of the ancient wall takes the eye ... Away to the west, clearly separate, is Westminster. The abbey church and the cloister are distinct ... Round them is a red-roofed colony, less compact, less imposing, and much smaller than London ... Between London and Westminster a line of buildings fringes the river – the palaces along the Strand ... like Oxford colleges ... whose great highway and approach is the river itself." Within a few years there were two new green rectangles north of the Strand: in Covent Garden and the fields of Lincoln's Inn. "And the houses around them are conspicuous by trim discipline – uniform, ungabled fronts." After the Great Fire of 1666 we see new squares in Gray's Inn Fields and Soho. Streets around these and Lincoln's Inn, Covent Garden and St James' pack close in upon them. In addition, new streets shoot northwards, eastwards and westwards. After 1720 the red brickwork of shabby gabled streets in the inner West End slowly yields to neatly parapeted rows of grey and brown brickwork. Nevertheless, Summerson notes, "someone at the top

of St Paul's Cathedral would still (on a clear day) have been able to see the entire city."

Between 1700 and 1750, the population rose from 674,500 to 676,750. London had become the largest city in Europe (with more than twice the population of Paris). By 1801 it was around a million, mostly living in multi-storey terrace housing, many in the fashionable 'Georgian' squares and town houses of west London. The city was now rich, powerful and sprawling. Change in the east was equally remarkable. "1801-3", noted Summerson, "coincides with the making of the first docks . . . [And] to the dock area come line upon line of brown cottage streets, each carrying the east-end invasion further towards the Essex fields." London was devouring its surroundings. Every road leading outward, was lined with terraces and villas and, in the wedges of country between, streets and squares were being filled in. Former satellite villages were engulfed. Hackney, Islington, Paddington, Fulham, and Chelsea had become suburbs. By 1831 the population had leapt to 1.66m and had a very low average age. By 1861, in the midst of the Victorian era, it was 3.323m, with the new railways playing a two-fold role: on the one hand extending the urban area ever outward; on the other, 'iron fingers' charging in toward the stuccoed terraces of Euston Square, the fields of Paddington, to Bishopsgate and Southwark.

By 1921 London's population was 7.5m, much of it in new suburbs of detached and semi-detached villas served by rail and road networks. In 1939, it peaked at 8.6m and by 1951 it was down to 8.2m, but by this time the definition of London's boundaries had become increasingly blurred and confused by politics and extensive suburbanisation. London was now an extensive south-east region in which outer residential areas were separated from the heartland ('Greater London') by a 'green belt' where development was not permitted. In 1965 administration of the central part was taken over from the London County Council (LCC)

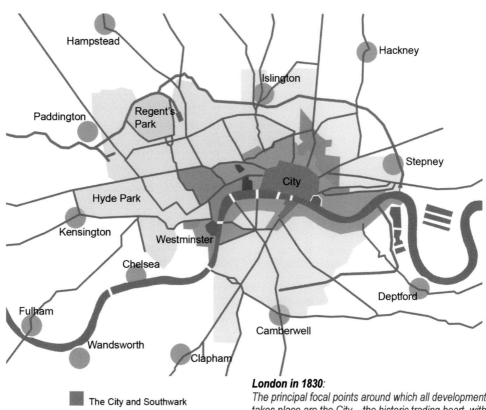

The City and Southwark

Westminster & the Tower

Irregular developments

Scattered suburban developments

Regular developments
in small units, mostly late
C17th and early C18th.

Regular developments in
large units (the West End
estates)

by the Greater London Council (the GLC removed by Thatcher's government in 1986. It was not until 2001 that so-called Greater London had its own Mayor.

Ironically, throughout this history the City itself attempted to benefit from economic controls, but had little or no interest in the spread of the metropolis or its civic government. From this arose a politics that embraced the City, the so-called Inner boroughs (leaning toward the left-wing), and the Outer boroughs (right wing).

London in 1830:

The principal focal points around which all development takes place are the City – the historic trading heart, with a royal outpost overlooking it from its south-east corner and St Paul's as its most important building – and, in the west, the Church, Crown and court at Westminster, around the Abbey. In the south, Southwark was a natural place of medieval development because of London Bridge. The second bridge was at Westminster (1739-48), thus reinforcing the two urban foci. The common denominator is the River Thames, which became the focal point of other kinds of development along its banks (with a difference between upstream and downstream of London Bridge, through which ships could not pass). Scattered suburban developments, market gardens and villages surrounded the city. 'Regular' developments began in the later C16th as a move westward out of the City, toward Westminster. This turned into the exploitation by the landed gentry of their large estates in the area – into what became the West End as we now know it.

After this date we enter an era of trains, the Underground, trams, buses and cars, prompting an entirely new pattern of suburban development. The current Circle Underground line encompasses much of the core, northern development. South of the Thames always adopted another pattern because of relative transport difficulties and much of the current communicative dynamic of London is concerned with improving transport networks within a city where it remains – as it always has – rather laborious to get around.

London is a city with much that is architecturally significant, but much more of the 'almost all right' that neglects to lend its authors the status given to heroes. It is best enjoyed on this basis, i.e. as a rich mixture of highlights and a mass of interplayed works inviting exploration and discovery. In the words of the architect Theo Crosby, "Much of the pleasure of cities comes from small scale, invention and complexity: a doorway, a bay window, a spire, an element suddenly seen and exploited in the context of the street. These are fragments, the result of intelligent intervention or forethought, that provides the markers by which one remembers and creates a mental structure of a city ... It is those fragments ... that remain memorable ... To recognise the [architectural] language and the players, to be able to see the jokes, is the richest pleasure of living in cities; to play the game is in itself a mode of establishing identity." (From 'The Necessary Monument', 1970.)

Midst it all, somewhere in the mix, one can occasionally identify the joy of architectural gamesmanship: what is playful, serious and rooted in the absurd joy of the game as an end in itself even as it gives service to a specific client and to society at large.

elusive individuals

The story of London's architecture begins with Inigo Jones and a Renaissance consciousness embodied in his works. Here begins a history of the architect as we now understand such a person, adopting a familiar vocational role. However, Jones was already more in tune with some of the architects ('master builders') of previous generations than the 'amateur architects' who characterised that subsequent era we label 'Georgian' (architecturally, a term that covers most of the eighteenth and the early nineteenth century, through to the Regency that preceded Queen Victoria's reign), during which an aristocratic 'Rule of Taste' ensured what is possibly a high point in architectural endeavour that is still celebrated as such. Later generations of architects were mostly professionals rather than amateurs – a novel role and status that was to be accompanied by a Victorian and Edwardian class consciousness of a kind that would possibly have been alien to Jones and perhaps prevented his patronage and rise to fame. Only in more recent, post-war, decades have architects once again come from all social classes.

This point is made in order to highlight the generality of social gating mechanisms that have sometimes been associated with the role of architect: someone who addresses vocational challenges demanding a capability bearing no essential relation to the facts of breeding. Nurture may provide advantage, but architects depend upon a high degree of natural competence and character that colours and particularises their creative commitments. However, the problematic issue of taste inevitably raises its head, underscoring an intriguing duality at the heart of architectural practice: knowing *what* to do as well as *how* it should be done. This issue is what the Roman architect Vitruvius referred to as a concern with the signified and signifier (with the implication of what the Stoics called a *lektón* as the crucial conceptual link between a referent and a given state of affairs). This challenge, combined with issues of circumstance and contingency, goes to the essential heart of architectural authorship.

It is with such considerations in mind that one turns to the lost and obscure people who – no doubt on the basis of a sound 'mechanical' skill and experience – found themselves to be the authors of architectures, i.e., to be placing the conceptual capacity of their imaginations and reasoning before that of what their hands, could achieve.

In drawing up an architectural schema, these men (for they invariably were men and, as these pages will demonstrate; salient names in the history of London's architecture are almost entirely male) were placed in a directional role addressing the two fundamental aspects of all architectures: the *arche* part of the created artefact as well as its *tectonic* aspects. Whereas the latter refers to a constructional and, it should not be forgotten, compositional set of issues, the former refers to the raison d'etre informing a strategic undertaking of building work: all that belongs to origins in the sense of the root causes, issues, criteria and the like at the heart of the situational-problematic at hand. Getting to the heart of the matter and being 'on target' with ones understanding and design proposals is a challenge that demands more than mere technical skills.

Whilst the 'speculative' (theoretical) Freemasons who sometimes served as the amateur architects of the eighteenth century might have enjoyed lending this notion the kind of meanings that could become at once esoteric, nostalgic and pragmatic (for example in references to Solomon's Temple, notions of the 'primitive hut' and the like, as a sound basis for the Orders of architecture), the issue of origins is a living one: a demand that the architect should have sufficient 'practical wisdom' that he or she can address their challenges as problems 'situated' in living cultural contexts of change and aspiration. In other words, the architect (or the master builder) is someone called upon to intelligently (perhaps perspicaciously) get to the root of what is at issue and, upon the basis of that understanding, erect a sound tectonic that expressively addresses and resolves (to advantage) such issues in the form of a resolved and coherent architectural work. As the French architect Le Corbusier noted, mankind does not work randomly and arbitrarily, but to a purpose – a point that was not made in order to advocate an instrumental attitude, but merely draw attention to the self-consciously intentional and high-minded basis of

Lambeth Palace

Lambeth Palace Road (at Lambeth Bridge), SE1.

This, the London residence of the Archbishop of Canterbury, has a long history but few parts that are genuinely old – among which the principal entrance, Morton Tower, of 1490, is the outstanding feature. Other parts of the Palace include the Great Hall (dating from the Restoration) and the Guard Room (originating in the C14th). Many of the buildings and much restoration work was the responsibility of Edward Blore, in the 1830s, just before Queen Victoria came onto the throne. The Chapel has a vaulted ceiling by Blore (1846), but the most impressive ceiling is possibly that below, in the crypt, dating from the C13th. The gardens, too, are an historic and important feature of the Palace. The adjacent bridge (first constructed 1871; tolled, as many of the early bridges, until 1877; reconstructed 1932, by George Humphreys and Sir Reginald Blomfield) was once the site of a famous river crossing.

an architecture.

However, this construction on the term only begins to lay hold upon all that is superfluous to basic needs – what are embellished in order to, simultaneously, satisfy appetites that are other than creaturely, or even merely agreeable. John Ruskin drew attention to such an essential redundancy and Nicholas Pevsner referred to the essential ingredient of aesthetic intent, which, he argued, differentiates between architecture in the guise of Lincoln cathedral and a bicycle shed that is merely a building. Such definitions and differentiations are, of course, nuanced and contentious. But we have every reason to believe this is how Vitruvius understood the concept when practising in Rome and no reason to believe that this was not the understanding of medieval cathedral builders and the many craftsmen who formed the secretive skilled guilds that sought to nurture and protect their vocational interests and, in the process, sometimes refer us to that strange extra that was to become the tradition of architecture as we know it.

It is upon this basis that we open the pages on London and its architects as the obscure authors of a few extant works that still have about them an elevated keynote reminding us that someone, intentionally and artfully, once did this thing, even though their names are lost and may never have enjoyed the kind of salience claimed by architectural authorship today.

St James Palace

The Mall/St James, SW1.

The palace was built in 1531-40 by Henry VIII, on the site of what had been a leper hospital of 1100; between the time of a fire at Westminster Palace in 1698 and when George III moved to Buckingham Palace in the 1760s, it became the monarch's principal residence. Most of the palace has been extensively remodelled since first constructed, but the north façade is essentially the Tudor original. The entrance through the emblematic gatehouse was heightened about 1750; the clock is 1832. The turret doors are 16th century. The Palace as a whole is a similar mix of overlaid building works, repairs and alterations. Jones' Queen's Chapel, of 1623-27, is adjacent. Two Norman Shaw buildings sit opposite. The Smithsons' Economist group is just up the road. A work by Denys Lasdun is nearby, as is work by Wren, Joass, Davis, Barry and others.

St Bartholomew, Smithfield, 1123 on

St Bartholomew The Great, located adjacent to London's Smithfield meat market, is one of London's finer architectural experiences. What you see at St Bart's is a wonderful amalgamation of architectural endeavours – both to create and destroy. The building was once part of a monastery and hospital, with a cloister, a building whose fabric goes back to the C12th and had been layered and layered, often with little respect to the work of previous generations (which is a remarkable comment upon architectural values in the Middle Ages).

In a perverse sense the real history of the church began when Henry VIII brought an already long history to a close in 1539, with the dissolution of the monasteries. The nave was demolished and an eastern stump left. That we still have something surviving – courtesy not only of Henry's demolition team, but also the restorers of the late nineteenth century – is remarkable enough. That history should contrive to present us with such architectural pleasures is extraordinary.

The photo opposite sums up the situation: the tomb of the church's founder, Prior Rahere (who died in 1143), was designed in 1405 and, although a careful work of art self-evidently respectful of the church and the importance of design, it nevertheless rudely crashes into the existing structure. The outcome has that 'romantic' – especially in this overall context – charm conservationists adore but would horrify them if one suggested doing something similar today. This keynote of work, interruptions and additions continues throughout the church. The equation might have been disastrous but, by some marvellous accident, it works – as an architecture of distress and disparity conjoined into an accidental but splendid coherence. History buffs love the place. However, in their blinkered appreciation, the church wardens now believe the church needs the addition of art – making the church a witness to how little architecture is appreciated for itself (as well as a question mark over what it is we now worship). One hesitates to deconstruct this sentiment but, thank God, this is still a living place and, if you pay attention, the architecture itself will speak to you.

Top: the restored medieval gatehouse that sits over the entrance. This was built by a parishioner who used timbers from the church and dates from 1595 and (restored 1916).
Middle: view from the former nave to the new frontage by Sir Aston Webb, 1880-1900, who gave the present church its roof .
Left: what remains of the cloister.
Opposite: the tomb of the founder, 1405, set within the Norman structure. The church was saved from demolition by Thomas Hardwick's repairs in 1790-1.

Tower of London, 1077 on

There is an architecture to the Tower, and it is not uninteresting. Within the complex as a whole, the 27 m tall White Tower is the central feature that remains substantially as it was in when completed, as the conquering sovereign's forbidding foothold in the eastern boundary of the City – a dominant place from which he could oversee the City's cowering and unfriendly inhabitants. The Tower remained an imposing place of imprisonment and executions until World War II although, officially, it was still a royal residence. Inside, residential conveniences included the St John's Chapel: a small Norman space of distinctly massive charm and it was not until the reign of Henry VIII (1509-47) that the sovereign moved to Westminster Palace and St James' Palace, in the west.

The entrance to the Tower is on the west side – at the Middle and Byward towers (adjacent to a Norman Foster building), along a stone causeway that replaces the original drawbridge. The Byward Tower acquired half-timbered parts during the reign of Richard II (1377-1399), but what you see now is the later restorations which paralleled rising tourist interest in the place.

The fortress was completed in stages, mostly between 1066 and 1307, beginning with the so-called White Tower, completed in 1080, which replaced a timber fort built by William the Conqueror; it was 'white' because it was constructed from creamy-coloured Caen stone brought over from France. However, the White Tower as we see it now is partly the product of restorative work by Wren, between 1663 and 1709 (he altered all the windows, for example). Not long after, certainly by 1750, the Tower was being opened to the public as an historical attraction. Anthony Salvin undertook further restoration work in 1851. And he was succeeded, in 1870, by the 'medievalising' John Taylor.

The outcome of it all is an overlay of architectures: a medieval one as a fortress; a more theatrical one of restoration, of mixed qualities; a tourist one of attractions that now includes Stanton Williams' fine approach work on the west side (2004; ticket office, cafes, etc.); and one of inhabitation (in the north-east corner, where yeoman warders and their families live). It is remarkable both to experience this set of overlays as one architectonic whole, and also to stand at the nearby vantage point of Tower Hill and look around: at nearly two thousand years of London history, from fragments of medieval walls on Roman foundations next to the Underground station, across to the Tower, beyond to the Mayor's City Hall (Foster again), Canary Wharf, and behind to the old Port of London Authority building, Lloyds, etc.

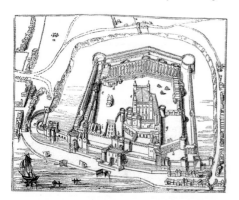

Above: the White Tower
Centre: nearby fragments of the City medieval wall built upon Roman foundations, near Tower Hill underground station.
Below: the Tower as it was in the early Middle Ages.

a. Lion's Tower. **b.** Bell Tower. **c.** Beauchamp Tower. **d.** The Chapel. **e.** White Tower. **f.** Jewel House. **g.** Queen's lodgings. **h.** Queen's gallery. **i.** Lieutenant's lodgings. **k.** Bloody Tower. **l.** St Thomas' Tower & Traitor's Gate. **m.** Place of executions.

Westminster Abbey, 1375 on

The abbey church devoted to St. Peter is a fine work of architecture whose unfortunate fate has been to end up as a secular tourist attraction and funeral vault celebrating significant past lives (beginning with the open tomb of Henry V's queen, Catherine of Valois, which sat here for three centuries, but now including all kinds of political, military and poetic figures). As at the Tower, one has to struggle to get to the architecture.

The origins of the church are obscure – claimed by its monks to be founded by King Serbert in 604 and then a legendary King Lucius of Roman days. The Abbey was certainly founded or refounded by Offa in the C8th and was the burial place of King Harold in 1040, having become a Benedictine monastery in the tenth century. About 1075 it was being written about as a building sat upon an island between the two mouths of the River Tyburn.

Later, Edward the Confessor (who reigned from1042 to 1066) turned the place into his mausoleum and a new structure in the Norman manner was started between 1045-1450. Simultaneously, alongside the church, Edward constructed a palace which included a hall rebuilt in 1394-1402 (the present Westminster Hall; photo below). It was about this time that the City of London began the rebuilding of St Paul's church (in 1087), no doubt to counter the rising status of Westminster, thereby establishing that pattern of twinned urban foci that has, to this day, remained fundamental to London's urban structure. However, a crucial phase of rebuilding was not to come until Hawksmoor designed the top halves of the two west towers (completed in 1734) – an intriguing exercise in 'baroque gothik'.

The principal part of the church is attributed to Henry Yevele (1320-1400). He is recorded as a London mason in 1356 and, by 1358, he was 'Disposer of the King's Works' at Westminster and at the Tower of London. In 1365 he was building Westminster Palace, where the Abbot's Hall and Residence are attributed to him (now a part of Westminster School). By 1375 he was in charge of rebuilding works at the Abbey that replaced Norman work by the Perpendicular style one sees today. Much of the stone came from Caen, in France, the Isle of Portland (Portland stone) and the Loire Valley region of France (Tuffeau limestone). The highlight of the Abbey – the Henry VII Chapel, of 1503-1512 – is the architectural gem of the complex. Later work was by Hawksmoor, as noted, and George Gilbert Scott, who made restorations during the nineteenth century.

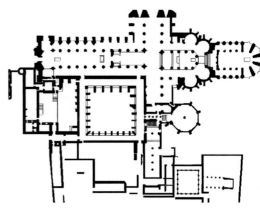

Above: Westminster Abbey – the West frontage and an overall plan.
Below: Westminster Hall.

Staple's Inn, 1586
(interiors 1937 and post-war)
Chancery Lane

Staple's Inn is another survivor from medieval days, although heavily restored in 1894 and again in 1936 when the frontage was entirely rebuilt. The old Hall behind was destroyed during World War II. All the windows are modern reconstructions and there is an element of romance in the reconstruction. Before the first restoration the building had sash windows and was rendered. The roof of the westernmost part was also made to conform to the eastern part. Nevertheless, the building is indicative of what much of London was once like.

Lawyers and temples

Inner Temple Gateway, 1610
Fleet Street

This building dates from 1610, was restored in 1748 and then again in 1905 (when it was actually moved back in order to widen Fleet Street) and it is an entrance way into the Inner Temple, one of four Inns of Court that have, since the Middle Ages, served as home to England's barristers. (Lincoln's Inn, Gray's Inn, Middle Temple and Inner Temple are Inns within the area of the City but, strangely, not under its jurisdiction.)

Top left: Staple's Inn.
Left: Temple church.
Below: Inner Temple Gateway.

That area inhabited by lawyers that sits between the historic cores of the City and Westminster comprises a web of fascinating courts: three (Inner, Outer and Middle Temples) of them to the south of Fleet Street and one (Lincoln's Inn) to the north. The old buildings here include the Temple church at Inner Temple (entrance, photo right). This was constructed by the powerful Knights Templar in the late C12th as part of a new monastic complex. The church comprises two parts: the Round Church and the Chancel (the latter built some fifty years later). Wren made internal changes, added to by Smirke and Burton in 1841. War damage resulted in some rebuilding and replacement of Wren features removed by the Victorians. The church now features as the church of Inner and Middle Temple – two former colleges of lawyers who acquired the buildings after the dissolution of the Knights in 1307.

backcloth
architecture

Inigo Jones 1573-1652
Sir Roger Pratt 1620-85
Hugh May 1621-1684

Inigo Jones 1573–1652

Above: *Staple's Inn, indicative of the general aesthetic of buildings in London during the life of Inigo Jones, prior to the Great Fire of 1666.*

Imagine the Tudorbethan London of the early seventeenth century: an inflated, dense place of narrow streets, alleys, courts and occasional grand buildings spreading away from an inhabited London Bridge and along the River Thames from around the Tower of London in the east, past wharves and the Gothic glories of old St Paul's, past the City's wrapping defensive wall that terminated near the mouth of the River Fleet (now beneath Farringdon Road), along past stately riverside mansions and intermittent water steps to the marshes around St Peter's – the suburban 'west minster' where Church, monarch and Court came together as a counterpoint to the enclave of the City and an intrusive Tower of London on its eastern edge. Here, in the one hundred years between 1540 and 1640, the population increased five-fold (much faster than, for example, Paris). London had become a great trading centre. Ships traded huge amounts of basic goods from Newcastle, Sweden, the Netherlands and elsewhere. And the River Thames, without its nineteenth-century embankments, was then described as "*a long, broad, slippery fellow*"; and an inhabited LondoCathedraln Bridge was "*worthily to be numbered among the miracles of the world.*" On its southern side was Southwark and the Globe Theatre. The streets were so thronged that visitors remarked they could scarcely pass.

Whereas, in the Middle Ages, capital had been expended on religious buildings, it was now allocated to buildings serving utility and commodity. But these buildings were often erected hastily and without regard for rule and regulation (in 1637 two hundred new dwellings in Wapping had to be torn down because they disregarded regulations). Nevertheless, London was on its way to becoming a place of brick buildings (obviating a shortage of timber), glass windows and coal-burning fireplaces, of bottles and to the novelty of new, cheaper iron wares and tools.

By the end of the 1600s London's population was 250,000 (in comparison, that of Norwich 30,000). It was the outstanding peculiarity of both England and Europe, now surrounded by coal-burning furnaces (processing glass, metals and bricks; coal production increased some seven-fold in this period) which populated the night scene like sparkling ornaments. The foundations of the Industrial Revolution were being laid and further technological change was about to solve remaining problems concerning the replacement of water by steam, the production and laying of rails, and the substitution of coal for wood. And London was already a strange

place to live: one whose inhabitants were described as living vertically like so many birds in cage houses that were narrow and five to six storeys high. Its buildings were romantically disorderly, but with a uniforming note of overhanging floors and pitched roofs topped by chimneys belching smoke from the coal fires serviced by new coastal fleets bringing coal from the north-east. French visitors were amazed at how Londoners lived among these fumes.

It is here that we find the birthplace of British architecture as a measured, regularised design discipline making reference to Italian and other European precedents. And the architect whose name is most closely associated with that birth was Inigo Jones – a figure whose influences resounded through architectural debate and enthusiasms for generations, who linked the architecture of England to contemporary advances in Europe, introducing London to what was then the novel idea of architectural regularity within its nascent public realm. Into all that was merely 'customary' was introduced a novel kind of higher cultural aspiration to 'regularise' the urban fabric of a thriving, changing city.

At the age of 33, Inigo Jones was described as 'a picture maker'. A few years later he was a royal masque designer of distinction and, by 1610, he was Surveyor to the heir to the throne, Henry, Prince of Wales. By 1615 he was Surveyor of the King's Works, having been granted the reversion of the post in 1613 ('surveyor' has the Latin equivalent of 'supervisor' – a role in construction foreshadowing that of the professional architect). He had become what John Summerson described as "*a great man: the pre-eminent authority at court on all matters of art and design.*"

Jones had done well, evidently making an impression that, to this day, has not been adequately explained, establishing himself as an architect, an innovator and a man of great influence exactly at the time as that other creative genius, William Shakespeare (1564-1616, also denigrated as an 'upstart'), was also making an impression upon English culture. The Globe Theatre – latterly reconstructed in Southwark by Sam Wanamaker, on a site adjacent to Tate Modern – was possibly a notable building whose thatched appearance disguised a Vitruvian and neo-Platonic content indicative of the pretensions and knowledge of 'mechanical' guild craftsmen rather than the 'speculative' Freemasons who, like Jones, were to be their replacement as architectural authors. But, unlike the Globe, which was constructed in

1599 and seriously damaged by fire in 1613, the year Jones was granted his reversion (and Shakespeare retired back to Stratford), Jones' architectural schema gave witness to a new era, new opportunities and new ambitions: in effect, the beginning of architecture as we have come to know it in England.

Our contemporary difficulty is that we take all this for granted. We find it difficult to appreciate Jones' work and have to imagine the Globe and the character of a half-timbered Jacobean London architecture that characterised the context in which he worked. (All that we have left is a Victorian restoration, Staple's Inn, in High Holborn: an architecture of gables and mullioned windows originating from 1586.) In essence, there was a continuity of concern and of world view throughout this period, but the expression Jones gave to these values introduced to London a northern Italian import that has come down to us as neo-Palladianism, i.e. a fashion of enthusiasms for the work of Andrea Palladio (1508-1580). However, it was all to come to an abrupt end with the Civil War that broke out in 1642. Only with the restoration of the monarchy in 1660 did fashion once again turn eyes toward Italy. It was then that the Grand Tour of the period began to rediscover what Jones had found on his trips to the Continent at the beginning of that century, and it was only then that architecture continued a development of a societal role with which we are now familiar. Jones was to be the great inspiration of men such as Wren and Hawksmoor, just as he was to serve the neo-Palladians of the early eighteenth century, such as Lord Burlington – by which time architectural practice was well into the age of the initiate and amateur.

Inigo Jones was born to a Welsh clothmaker somewhere in the Smithfield Market area and christened in St Bartholomew-the-Less – the official church of the hospital of that name, located in its grounds. According to Wren, Jones began his professional career apprenticed to a joiner in St Paul's churchyard – a not unusual path toward becoming a surveyor (one, as we have noted, that sometimes enjoyed architectural inclinations and intellectual pretensions). Here, Jones would have learned to draw and pick up Latin; in addition, it has been suggested, he would have been exposed to John Dee's celebrated *Preface to Euclid* (1659), in which Dee quotes Vitruvius and Alberti, encouraging readers to learn from these sources. He would have matured in a London whose artisans were then excited by Dee's Preface and its emphasis upon symbolic number and proportion and it is from this world, argues the historian Frances Yates, that Jones would later have been able to draw upon a skilled body of craftsmen able to implement his masque innovations. Similarly, she suggests, there are remarkable parallels between Jones' career at this time and that of Robert Fludd (1574-1637) – son of a high-ranking government official, but also a Rosicrucian, physicist, astrologer, occultist and mystic – and who may have accompanied Jones to the Continent.

Sometime before 1605, the year in which there is evidence of Jones producing masques at the court of James I, together with Ben Jonson, he was to be found accompanying (it is believed) the fifth Earl of Rutland on the first of two trips to Italy – then an arduous journey. Summerson suggests that much of his six-year sojourn was spent in Venice, where, coincidentally, Henry Wotton (1568-1639) – an aspirant diplomat, then a political refugee in Italy and the man who was later to publish the first English translation of Vitruvius – may also have been present.

Jones apparently studied painting and theatrical events, learning those skills that were to serve him as a masque designer to the court – what were, at that time, celebrated theatrical events presenting designers with major technical challenges in order to produce spectacular sleights-of-hand that might delight aristocratic audiences. (Incidentally, what Yates refers to as the first incidence of the large scale development by the state of machinery for peaceful purposes.) Magic – almost literally – was in the air.

The first drawings we have from Jones, made when he was thirty-two, are what Summerson describes as distinctly amateurish 'backcloth architecture'. However, a second trip to Italy was made in the train of Thomas, Earl of Arundel, in 1613-14, during which time Jones – now a significant figure at court – visited Florence and studied the *intermezzi* there, as well as studying Palladio's *Quattro libri dell'Architettura* in detail and visiting the buildings themselves. It was after this time that he began a committed and assured period of work as an architect. However, it is likely that Jones would not have drawn a distinction between his role as architect and that of masque designer. His famous spat with Ben Jonson illustrates two perspectives in conflict: that of the overall author of a complex architectonic undertaking, and an upstaged poet familiar with the classical primacy given to his art. In Jonson's satires Jones is portrayed as a 'Master-Cooke' who has all nature in a pot: "*he is an Architect, an inginer; A souldier, a Physitian, a Philosopher; A general Mathematician*" (*Neptune's Triumph*, 1620). Jones' stance is firmly Vitruvian: the architect is the supreme artist, and architecture is both a mathematical and a liberal art celebrating ideal values. Two of his masque figures illustrate his attitude: the twinned figures of *Theoria*, who looks up to heaven, and that of *Practica*, who draws with compasses in the ground.

Of Jones' forty-five recorded works, only seven survive. Four are in London – examples that, even as restored over the centuries, still bear the mark of his character and genius. Of these, the east façade of St Paul's at Covent Garden, the Queen's House at Greenwich, and the Banqueting House in Whitehall best illustrate what Jones achieved.

Left: the octagonal heart of St Bartholomew the Less, Smithfield, where Inigo Jones was christened. The church (founded 1184) as you see it now has the original tower (C15th.), but has otherwise been rebuilt (the central part of the church is by George Dance the Younger, 1973; extensive additional work was by Thomas Hardwick, 1823-25, who retained Dance's plan). It is within the grounds of the hospital and serves as its official church. St Bartholomew-the-Great is nearby.

Jones' extant London buildings include:

• **The Queen's House**, 1616-1635, Greenwich. Now a part of the National Maritime Museum, but originally (and bizarrely) located astride the Dover Road. Well worth a visit, particularly since it is adjacent to Wren's work at Greenwich. There is also a Hawksmoor church there (St Alfege, 1712-1718).

• **The Banqueting House**, 1619-1622, Whitehall. Now looking rather stately but designed as a party place for King Charles I – formal above ground and very informal below ground. It was originally part of a much larger scheme for the old Whitehall Palace here, but work was never completed. Ironically Charles was led to his beheading from the first floor window.

• **The Church of St Paul**, 1631-1633, Covent Garden ('the actors' church'). Actually significantly rebuilt (still to Jones' original design) but there is sufficient of the original architecture to impress. The recreations of the arcades and houses on the north side are from 1880. The Dixon Jones work on the Opera House arcade attempts to revive the arcades on the east side of the piazza.

• **Lindsey House**, 1638, at 59-60 Lincoln's Inn Fields. An elegant façade to a house in a square laid out by Jones.

• **The Queen Mary Chapel**, 1623-27. St James' Palace. Usually closed, except for services.

Left: the Queen Mary Chapel at St James' Palace is, like St Paul's at Covent Garden, a dignified and simple work, but without a west portico. The church has, we are told, the first 'Venetian' window in England. Such windows (an arrangement of three linked openings, the central one arched, and flanked by two rectangles) became a key motif in 'Palladianism'. It was apparently first employed by the Italian architect Donato Bramante (1444-1514) but has its origins in the triumphal arches of ancient Rome. Here, a large central and arched opening is usually flanked by two smaller passageways, usually also arched. As a Renaissance motif the dividing mass of the arch between the central and side openings was commonly eroded and replaced by a column or pilaster. Palladio notably used the motif in the arcades of the Basilica Palladiana in Vicenza, but it was to become peculiarly popular in C18th England.

merely a simple barn . . .

St Paul's, Covent Garden, 1631

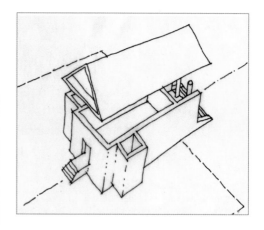

St Paul's, Covent Garden, is pure theatre. It was required to formally address the square to its east side and so has an entirely false frontage on that side, but its proper entrance is, of course, on the west side. This is the 'barn' foisted onto a land developer and features as part of a schematic whole that is indicative of West End developments for the next 150 years: a square, rows of grand houses, each speculatively developed, mews at the rear, perhaps a church and market. The context was one of London's first speculative developments in the West End – what, in turn, was set in the context of long-standing but rather hopeless attempts to prevent the City from expanding.

In 1631 the Earl of Bedford obtained permission from King Charles to develop his property where Covent Garden now stands. Bedford's ambitious conception was of a new quarter, complete with church, market and the rest – including a grand piazza. Simplicity was an appropriate keynote, not only on the basis of speculative criteria, but permission was only granted on the understanding that the works served as an ornament to London and were planned by the King's Surveyor. Bedford required, we are told, merely the development's chapel to be no more than a barn. "Then", said Jones, "you shall have the grandest barn in England."

Jones' witty conception of the church was an exercise in the vernacular and, as a Tuscan architecture, of the kind Vitruvius, Serlio and Palladio had all recommended as suited to country buildings. But he was returning to basic Vitruvian principle: to the roots of architecture in the form of the primitive hut:

an architectural exercise emphasising the 'archi' part of a tectonic undertaking. Universal Law – which meant order, and harmonic ratio – was to be manifest within a base configuration of sheltering construction. Law and what was merely creaturely and accommodative were to be married within the forms of Bedford's exercise in commercial speculation.

In essence, the building is remarkably simple: a two-square plan with internal galleries, but it has been significantly altered within the terms of the original conception. The sides were originally rendered, but the Victorians replaced this with brick; the ground level of the market has been raised, obliterating the steps that originally led up to the (false) east frontage (ditto at the west end); and the arches to the side of the east porch were added by the Victorians. Nevertheless, Jones' vital conception remains embodied – as if some imprisoned voice mutely crying out for one's attention.

Top: the drawing shows the church schematically, in its original form, with the steps that made it even more classical.
Right: the west frontage.
Far right: the east frontage onto the square. The building was re-cased in Portland stone in 1788-9, by Thomas Hardwick (adhering closely to Jones' design). Butterfield altered the interior in 1871-2. The side arches were added by Henry Clutton, 1878-82. The red brick facing is from 1887-8 (by A.J. Pilkington; originally, they were more narrow and low).

The Globe Theatre: a contextural note
1599–1613

The City of London during the early seventeenth century was a dense, growing and expanding trading centre, whose sovereign at Westminster was intent on containing growth within the old walls. It was a lost cause. The prosperous City pushed out in every direction, but particularly toward the west, the latter being developed as a suburb (which the City had no interest in governing). The land here was principally aristocratic and the King's permission was required for development to go ahead. In turn, Charles I was intent of any new development in the area should be an orderly ornament to London as a whole. This was the basis of Jones' involvement in Covent Garden. The speculator at Lincoln's Inn Fields was a William Newton, from Bedfordshire, who appears to have enjoyed the patronage of the Queen and developed the west side of the square. The extant Lindsey House is typical of the kind of town residence that went up here and along Great Queen Street, then reputed to be London's first 'regular' street, although there have been alterations, notably a lowering of window sills on the *piano nobile*. It is attributed to Jones and is indicative of a house typology that was to be widely adopted.

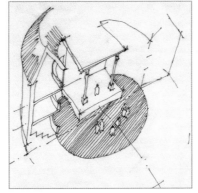

The latter-day recreation of the Globe Theatre, located adjacent to the Tate Modern, is often dismissed by architects as unworthy of their attention: a nostalgic folly and the product of misguided enthusiasms. However, although qualified by inherent inauthenticity the Globe is an important building. Yates, for example, argues that the Elizabethan public theatres were as novel, in their way, as Jones' neo-Palladian architecture. They were a new phenomenon – designs modelled on the Vitruvian text given to London's master builders who were organised and worked within the medieval tradition as practical masons, as opposed to hands-off 'speculative masons' who separated design from execution and were to appropriate the former's design role and status. She tells us that these building craftsmen of the later sixteenth century were greatly influenced by a copy of Euclid with a preface by John Dee extolling Vitruvian design virtues. Similar influences came from a man born one year after Jones: Robert Fludd. She also speculates that Fludd might have been with Jones on his visit to the Continent in 1605.

Right: late seventeenth century houses in Fournier Street, near to Hawksmoor's Christchuch in Spitalfields – early examples of 'regularised' Restoration terrace houses essentially similar to Lindsey but now stripped of an explicit order. The type was to become standard during the eighteenth century and enforced by the post-1666 building regulations imposed intended to control fire spread (1707, 1709, and 1774). These progressively reduced the amount of exposed timber on building façades and encouraged building in brick.

Top: the façade of Lindsey House. (see the references to Norman Shaw's New Zealand House and the sketch on page 187).
Centre: sketch of the Globe scheme – three storeys of heavy timber construction topped by a thatched roof. A standing pit is in the centre, into which an articulated stage housing projects.

a monument to the court of Charles I
The Banqueting House, 1619–22

Jones' Banqueting House in Whitehall takes the form of a large galleried room for formal dining and occasional elaborate masques set above a basement decorated with '*rock and shell worke*', where private drinking parties took place. It is also the last remaining fragment of the rambling, medieval Whitehall Palace, within which it stood as a strange, set-piece statement at odds with all around it: the initial commitment of what was intended to be a (never realised) grand palace.

The Banqueting House stands as evidence of how far Jones had come since the early days of masque design. Here is his backcloth architecture given a rich, three-dimensional substance and yet still, ironically, a theatrical set piece as well as the setting for other dramatic events. Theatricality is in its blood. It is a building stretching itself between the creaturely goings-on within its basement, the stupendous masque entertainments of the salon, and the profundity of its overall symbolic and proportional geometry: truly head in the clouds; feet on the ground. It is a virtuoso exercise and one imagines Jones giving it presentation, taking the applause, and sneering at Ben Jonson.

As a place of luxurious dinners, of singing, dancing, magical-mechanics and drunken parties, this was a building everyone knew to mimic that 'cosmic dance' and dimly echo its hierarchical and harmonic orderliness. It was here that an English 'sun-king' shone midst his court, formally feasted among them, partied to the early hours with them and, ultimately, walked out from an upper window to the platform where his royal head was separated from his body. The show was over. *Theoria* and *Practica* had their divorce.

The end niche (opposite the entrance) that once gave a distinct orientation to the double-cube of the principal salon was removed about 1625, for obscure reasons. Similarly, the exterior form is true to Jones in precise detail, but its materiality is quite different. As restored by John Soane, the Banqueting Hall is a Portland stone basilica. Originally, the basement was brown Oxfordshire stone, there was a dun-coloured Northamptonshire stone for the (entirely rusticated) upper walls and a white Portland only for the unfluted pilaster orders and balustrading – a subtle polychromy that is reminiscent of the shock to our imaginations when we are told the Greek temples were wildly painted. (Soane also replaced Jones' casement windows with sash ones.)

Some of the quiet sumptuousness that once characterised the exterior is still visible in the interior. Their relationship is tightly controlled, lending the building a rare architectural integrity. As on the outside, the lower order of the galleried salon is Ionic, the upper is Corinthian with a sub-frieze of masks and swags. In fact, the gallery and the sumptuous ceiling painted

Above: section (note the basement and tiny figures on the ground floor; see the photo on the opposite page) and ground floor plan of the Banqueting Hall. This is worth comparing with the great dining rooms at Greenwich Palace and Chelsea, by Wren.
Opposite page: the hall itself, and the Whitehall elevation, as renewed by Soane. It was here, ironically, that Charles I stepped out from the window onto the rude wooden platform where he was to meet his death.

by Rubens, together with the apparent absence of the basement, are the crucial differences. At the entrance are two sets of coupled Ionic pillars set around a tall doorway; at the opposite end was the '*neech*'.

Summerson describes this interior as having a 'forbidding immobility'; but this is nothing less than a nightclub out of hours, an empty theatre still awaiting its evening audience. It is a magnificent, symbolic framing that neo-Platonically references the order of the heavens and yet grounds the substance of the architectonic order

Left: interior of the Banqueting House.
Below left: external view of the Banqueting House.

high and dry
Watergate, 1626–27

The Watergate (below) that sits in Embankment Gardens, adjacent to Embankment station and Terry Farrell's Charing Cross office building, is contentiously attributed to Jones but was, in any case, executed by Nicholas Stone (1586-1647), a mason who (among other things) also worked on the Banqueting House. He was born near Exeter, spent time in Holland and returned to Southwark, where he set up a large practice, becoming the King's Mason to James I in 1619 and to Charles I in 1626. The gate sat on the water's edge before the Embankment was constructed and bears reference to the Fontaine de Medicis at the Luxemburg, in Paris. If he is the true author of the work, then it again underscores change going on in the tradition of masons and their adoption of a more cerebral posture.

in a fashionable and creaturely realm. We now take it all for granted and it is an effort to penetrate the formalities of Whitehall and open ourselves to the sheer showiness of this building strutting its authoritatively tasteful stuff midst an utterly disparate urban fabric in the courtly and marshy village of Westminster. It is no longer novel, just as it is no longer used as originally intended and now exists for more contemplative entertainment, denuded of that very vitality with which it was once imbued. Jones' design had promised a glorious architectural future and has ended its life as a conserved peculiarity enjoyed more for its ceiling art than the substance of its architectonic pretensions. But this is not bad for a work that is now nearly four hundred years old and arguably – despite attempts to emasculate it – sets itself as a landmark representative of the beginning of British architecture as we now know it.

location location location
The Queen's House, 1616–35

Why would anyone build a house for the Queen of England straddling a main public road to Dover? The answer lies in the disposition of royal land: to the north was the River Thames, London's life-blood and an eminently easy way to travel, where a principal royal palace was located next to the Thames: the rambling, red-bricked, gabled and chimneyed Palace of Placentia, begun in the mid-fifteenth century and later demolished for the Wren building that now stands there (the former Royal Naval Hospital). To the south was what is now Greenwich Park: an open area of palace grounds that grandly rises up to a hill to where Wren's Observatory is now located. Perhaps moving the public road was impossible or too expensive. Perhaps there was a certain wit to the design that both royal patron and architect enjoyed: Jones' design is both house and bridge, lining the approach road with tall brick privacy screen walls. Since life took place mostly upon the *piano nobile*, the road was simply ignored on the day to day basis of inhabitation.

It is all rather clever, but bizarre by later and contemporary standards. (The noise of carriages, for example, must surely have been intrusive? Robert Adams' late 17th century Kenwood House, in Highgate, is similarly witness to social relations between high and low that changed in the C19th and we now find rather opaque.) In other terms the Queen's House belongs to that architectural tradition of grand garden pavilions, from Palladio's La Rotonda to Le Corbusier's Villa Savoye (all of which have a similar neo-Platonic geometry as their basis). It is a set piece which, like the later Banqueting House in Whitehall, was designed to show its cultural standing and apparently makes reference to the Villa Medici, at Poggio a Caiano, designed for Lorenzo de Medici and completed by Giuliano da Sangallo in 1485. (In that instance the connection between the design's two halves – which, with Jones, is the bridge over the road – is a great hall.)

The house now makes a fine art gallery housing a notable naval collection, but it is rather forlorn and has a problematic restoration history. Paintings once on the ceiling of the great hall were long ago stripped out, later replaced by photographs (and why not?), and then again stripped out by the purists. Between 1708-11 the windows were replaced by sashes, then returned to casements; at the same time the northern steps were remodelled. The colonnades were added in 1807. The house became a part of the naval school in 1821 and a part of the hospital in 1892. In 1933 the house was restored and became a gallery. Further restoration (further altering earlier restoration work) was in the 1980s and more recent work has been by Allies & Morrison (the new visitor entrance under the steps). One awaits further stages in this contentious work, hopefully one that strives to acknowledge and celebrate the fundamental architectonic novelty of Jones' schema rather than an obsessive concern with history as such.

*The plan (**above**) is of the house before the sides were infilled by increased accommodation. Similarly, the photo of the arches (above) shows the house as one now approaches it from the west (the original arches are the central ones). Note the side walls on the model; these once lined the approaching road and gave privacy to the gardens (not quite up to the standards of security at Buckingham Palace and elsewhere today!).*

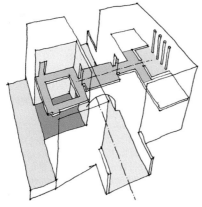

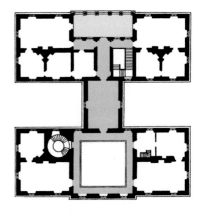

Above (clockwise): *the architectural schema of the house; a model, with screen walls and the additional wings; the original plan; and a current view along what was the main road to Dover, passing through the house.*

Initial work on the house was stopped when Queen Anne took ill in 1618 (she died a year later). The house was then thatched over at first floor level and work was not resumed (now for the queen of Charles I, Henrietta Maria) until 1630 – about the time that Jones was designing the Covent Garden 'piazza' and church. In fact, like Le Corbusier's white villa, the pristine Queen's House had a rather short life. Completed in 1635 there was a mere seven years before its courtly joys were rudely disrupted by the Civil War, just as the bourgeois life of Le Corbusier's villa, completed in 1931, was disrupted by World War II.

Overall, the house plan is a square with a galleried and cubic great hall serving as the central feature of the northern wing. The upper parts were neatly and economically organised for circulation, ceremony and service, essentially without corridors. However, they were closed by additional wings in 1661, adding to the accommodation and forming two east and west wings (in addition to the north and south wings) but somewhat detracting from the overall drama of an architecture on a north-south axis that enjoyed a formal sweeping stair to a terrace and entrance on the north, a loggia overlooking the gardens to the south and, in between, at its heart, provided the visitor with a carriage drop-off point on the Dover Road.

Internally, the most central and formal feature of the house is the double-height cube forming the great hall. However, one should perhaps imagine the house as transitional between the medieval house, centred around life in the great hall, and new standards of privacy that were to be eventually served by discrete movement passageways and the banishment of servants to concealed back stairs. On either side of the hall was a bedroom (at that time a rather less than private place) and a drawing room (or with-drawing room, used for private meetings and meals, etc.). There was also a 'closet', set more deeply within the plan, off the drawing room and probably the most private space in the house.

Perhaps this formed one 'apartment' (i.e., what in France was a sequence of antechambre/chambre/and cabinet off the hall as grand salon). The southern wing, at the level of the *piano nobile*, is dominated by the loggia (beneath which is the so-called Orangery). One presumes the room forming the bridge link over the road was a crucial common place whose view was originally east-west (along the road), and not into inner courts (now light wells). The additional wings were added for Charles II, by John Webb and the new form of house was used as Henrietta's official residence until her death in 1669 (she became, during the Restoration, the Queen Mother). After that, in 1690, the house became the residence of the Ranger of Greenwich Park and, in 1697-99, the road to Dover was moved to its present position (further north).

Sir Roger Pratt 1620–85

Hugh May 1621–84

Summerson remarked that Jones stands as an isolated historical figure and that it was Roger Pratt who later came to the foreground as a man who later picked up the Jonesian task of Italianising English architecture. Pratt – an architect who, in his day, was as eminent as Wren – was born in Norfolk and educated at Oxford and the Inner Temple. The Civil War prompted him to travel abroad and, from 1643 to 1649, he was in France, Holland, Italy (where he matriculated in Law at Padua; later, he resided in Rome) and Flanders (all of this largely on the basis of an inheritance after his father's death in 1640). He returned to London in the year of Charles I's execution and, now less interested in law than architecture, set about designing a house for his cousin (Coleshill, Berks; destroyed 1952), one of four significant residential works in a neo-Palladian manner. (Coleshill was considered so Jonesian that, for some time, historians attributed it to Jones.) But his most influential and copied house (demolished) was Clarendon House, in Piccadilly (1664-7). It was among the first classical houses in London and perhaps, as Summerson notes, the most striking.

Before the Great Fire, Pratt was appointed with Wren and May to review the condition of old St Paul's; after it, he was one of the three commissioners appointed to supervise the rebuilding of the City – resulting in a knighthood, in 1668.

Summerson notes that, upon Pratt's retirement, he had created "a type of house perfectly fitted to the noblemen and gentlemen of the later Stuart epoch – a type which, in spite of much indebtedness to the Continent, we may, without much exaggeration, call English." But the man himself appears to have been more than an amateur architect, writing in his notebooks that a prospective builder should *"get some ingenius gentleman who has seen much of that kind abroad and been somewhat versed in the best authors of Architecture: viz. Palladio, Scamozzi, Serlio, etc. to do it for you, and to give you a design on paper."* However, he appears to have later have built only for himself, designing Ryston Hall in Norfolk (later remodelled by Sir John Soane).

Extant London works include:
• **Eltham Lodge,** 1664
Of Dutch character; now Royal Blackheath Golf Club (reputed to be the oldest golf club in the world; note, this is not Eltham Palace).

Little is known of May's early life, but he appears to have worked for the Duke of Buckingham, travelling to the Continent and trading works of art for his client. He was born as son of a Sussex gentleman farmer and had Royalist loyalties, serving the court in Holland during the Civil War and returning to enjoy the King's favour after the Restoration. In 1660 he was appointed Paymaster of the Works; in 1666 he was temporarily Surveyor of the Works and had hoped for a permanent appointment, but was 'put by', as he phrased it, in favour of Wren. Nevertheless, he did well out of the King's patronage and, in 1673, was appointed Comptroller of the Works at Windsor Castle – among his more significant efforts at architecture, but swept away by the later works of Jeffry Wyatville. Previous to this, in 1664, May had assisted Wren, Pratt and Webb at old St Paul's. After the Fire, he was one of the three appointed surveyors supervising the rebuilding of the City (again with Wren and Pratt). After this time he was also involved in all kinds of architectural and interior work, none of which survives, but had the reputation of being 'a mature baroque style' which was on a par with anything Wren was doing.

May was responsible for completion work on Burlington House in 1667-8, after it had been purchased in an unfinished state by the 1st Earl of Burlington from John Denham. Richard Boyle's works in the early C18th completely remodelled the building (and it later became the Royal Academy; see page 83).

Lector, si monumentum
requiris, circumspice

Sir Christopher Wren 1632-1723
Robert Hooke 1635-1703

Improvisation, wit, inventiveness and
gamesmanship: the surviving Wren parish
and guild churches

The problem of attribution
Sir John Vanbrugh 1664-1726
Nicholas Hawksmoor 1661-1736
Thomas Archer 1668-1743
John James 1672-1746
James Gibbs 1682-1754

Vitruvius

Lector, si monumentum requiris, circumspice

"If you seek my monument, look around you."

Sir Christopher Wren 1632–1723

Wren's extant London buildings include:

• **The City and other parish and guild churches.** See page 54.

• **The Monument**, 1671-76, King William Street, the City. Wren and Hooke.

• **Royal Observatory**, 1675-1676, Greenwich Park. Now added to with work by Allies & Morrison (2008)

• **St Paul's Cathedral**, 1675-1711. Ludgate Hill, the City. Access during a service is free; otherwise there is a charge.

• **Chelsea Royal Hospital**, 1681-86. Royal Hospital Road. Also, some out-buildings by Soane, 1809-17.

• **Hampton Court Palace,** East and South Wings, 1689-1695.

• **Kensington Palace**, 1689-95 and 1702. Kensington Palace Gardens.

• **Morden College**, 1695-1700. Off St Germain's Place, Blackheath. This attribution is uncertain, but the building was built by Edward Strong, one of Wren's favourite masons.

• **Royal Naval Hospital for Seamen**, 1696-1702, Greenwich. This has a magnificent painted hall and chapel to visit, as well as the architecture as a whole (now, in part, Greenwich University and Trinity School of Music).

• **Marlborough House**, between the Mall and Pall Mall (opp. St James' Palace), 1709-11. Lower two storeys; third storey added by William Chambers, 1771-74; entrance 'hall' and some interior work by Pennethorne, 1860-62.

• **Chapter House**, St Paul's 1712-14. St Paul's Cathedral.

When, at the height of the Empire, national wealth and nationalist sentiments, high Edwardian architectural fashions sought to free themselves from the respective excesses of Ruskinian morality and the 'freestyle' in order to find inspirational sources that might serve national tastes and architectural predilections, they turned not to Inigo Jones, but to Sir Christopher Wren. From this inspiration was born 'Wrenaissance', a term alluding to a body of inclinations and preferences seeking to resolve the issue of a style suited to the age (i.e. a response to the *Zeitgeist*) by employing Wren's Baroque work as a suitably authentic bench-mark.

To this day, Wren remains the most famous of English architects. His initially privileged childhood was rudely interrupted by the Civil Wars (1642-51), depriving the family of income and, because of his father's role in the court of Charles I, threatening their lives. Nevertheless, Wren received a good education (apart from frequent interruptions) and, at fifteen years old, he was assisting in anatomical researches at Oxford. At eighteen he had formally entered Wadham College, where mentors admired his prodigious skills as an inventive assistant in mathematical and medical research. But his youth was not an easy time and Wren's experiences appear to have engendered a later preoccupation with survival, success and significance (which, as we shall repeatedly see, is hardly uncommon to architects). Small of stature and of slight build, this charming man was preoccupied with fame and permanent memorials and consistently determined to be an author who distinguished the enduring from the ephemeral in a manner that was as much personal as philosophical. (Just as, we are told, he was much concerned to turn his talents and industry into the security of capital assets – an ambition in which he was not entirely successful.)

In the following years Wren's research studies continued to call upon his intelligence and inventiveness through the years of the Commonwealth, under Cromwell – who was instrumental in securing Wren the position of chair of astronomy at Gresham College in

London (1657). His inventions during this period included devices for surveying, musical and acoustical instruments, developments in fishing, underwater construction and submarine navigation, and experiments in print-making. In his lectures he was conscious of what he referred to as the 'new philosophy' and opined that mathematics, *"being built upon the impregnable Foundations of Geometry and Arithmetick, are the only Truths, that can sink into the Mind of Man, void of all Uncertainty; and all other Discourses participate more or less of truth, according as their Subjects are more or less capable of Mathematical Demonstration."* And he condemned what he called *"the ungrounded Fancies of ... astrological Medicasters'*

Above: *The dome of Wren's Saint Paul's Cathedral: still London's most significant building, even after three hundred years. It's remarkable survival of World War II bombing, when all around was flattened, made the building even more famous and gave it an aura it still possesses.*

All buildings in the immediate vicinity are kept comparatively low (to about seven or eight stories) and a number of 'viewing corridors' are kept unobstructed from various high points around London to the dome. Thus the presence of the dome has a direct impact upon the politics of where tall buildings can be located and pragmatically underscores the Cathedral's symbolic status.

(pseudomedici and 'quack astrologers)." Such sentiments would not be out of place today.

Our prodigy later moved to a chair in astronomy at Oxford, in the year of the Restoration of Charles II, 1660 – at which the young Wren, largely as a consequence of his family's role in the court of Charles I, played a not insignificant ceremonial role. Charles at this time sought to bring together the grand figures of Gresham and Wadham as a reconciliatory grouping known as the Royal Society and Wren naturally figured significantly in unfolding developments. It was now – simply as exercises in applied mathematics – that he was drawn into challenges that stretched his inventiveness from science to defences and other building works. Her was also asked to design the Sheldonian Theatre (1663-9), as well as other works at Oxford and, at the request of the King, to propose a redesign of Whitehall Palace (1664) and a new dome for St Paul's Cathedral (upon which Inigo Jones had expended much effort).

Over the five-year period between 1661-66 Wren was to become thoroughly familiar with architectural issues and to challenges, drawing upon his belief that the practice of science called upon imagination as well as intuition and logic. This entailed, at the age of 33, a

visit to Paris – then a European centre for creativity that had overtaken Rome and Venice – for the purposes of studying its architecture. Here, Wren met with Mansart, le Vau and the great Italian architect, Bernini (1598-1680).

Having missed the Great Plague of 1665, Wren returned to London in time to witness the horrific Great Fire of 1666 that destroyed much of the City and, in particular, left old St Paul's as a burned-out shell. But Wren also returned to London with an English interpretation of then current French debate on beauty in design. For example, he now believed that, as he put it, *"There are two causes of Beauty: Natural and Customary. Natural is from Geometry, consisting in Uniformity (that is Equality) and Proportion. Customary Beauty is begotten by the Use of our Senses to those objects which are usually pleasing to us for other causes, as Familiarity or particular Inclination breeds Love to Things not always themselves lovely: Here lies the great occasion of Errors, but always true to the Test is Natural or Geometrical Beauty. Geometrical figures are naturally more beautiful than irregular ones; the square, the circle are the most beautiful, next the parallelogram and the oval. There are only two beautiful positions in straight lines, perpendicular and horizontal; this is from nature and consequently necessary, no other than upright being firm."*

There is, in other words, a crucial difference between significant matters rooted in what is orderly and immutable, and contrasting, customary habits of mind, i.e. between a rational consideration of eternal and lawful issues in relation to what is creaturely, modish and customary (or 'arbitrary'). Nevertheless, Wren was no pedant when it came to the precedents of the Ancients: drawing was a pragmatic research tool, geometry was important, but there was to be no subscription to arcane numerical theory; Vitruvius was important but every design had to be derived from first principles in the sense that it constituted the challenge of a situated idealism. He was, oddly, as much an empiricist as an idealist.

Turning to the Fire, Wren immediately engaged himself in the task of rebuilding and, in 1669, was appointed as the King's Surveyor and there began the fruitful years of an exceptionally long architectural career that lasted until fashions changed with the accession of George I to the throne in 1714, although Wren's Baroque tastes were, by then, quite out of fashion.

Between 1669-71 Wren designed a new customs house (a formal building representing the presence of the Crown with the City – a place that was still, in effect, a state within a state) and, a formal western entrance to the City at Temple Bar (1667-72). There followed the Monument to the Great Fire (with Hooke; 1671-6), the Greenwich Observatory (1675-6), Chelsea Hospital (1685-93), work at Hampton Court and Kensington Palace (1689 on), the Royal Naval Hospital at Greenwich (1696 on), St Paul's Cathedral and designs for some City churches replacing those destroyed by the Fire. Other works included St Clement Danes in the Strand, St James' in Piccadilly, and St Anne's in Soho.

These designs were disparate and inventive, invariably pragmatic and sometimes idealistic. Most were completed by 1690. Church steeples were added in the 20-30 years afterward, with Wren's own design of St Mary-le-Bow (1680) setting a fine example of what could be achieved. This work was, of course, undertaken by a team and Robert Hooke's name is significant, particularly during the 1670's and '80's. Nicholas Hawksmoor arrived in the office in 1684 and rapidly rose to an important position. Similarly, John Vanbrugh played a later role in the office, especially in the early 1700s up to the time when an ageing Wren was effectively dismissed from office. By 1711, when he suffered a serious illness, his style of work and dominance of the Crown's works was distinctly out of fashion.

Wren was dismissed in 1718 and died in 1723. Near his tomb in St Paul's crypt is a wall plaque reading: "*If you seek his monument, look around you*". However, by then, what was around the tomb was unsuited to the inclinations of a neo-Palladian 'Rule of Taste' that was to be the obsession of the eighteenth century. Ironically, this was to become the capriciousness of customary tastes (pretending to be anything but that) which vanquished 'natural order' in its Baroque guise and it was left to later generations to elevate Wren to his current high status as both scientist and architect.

During Wren's lifetime London was a small boom town. Between 1540-1650 its population grew five to sixfold and these inhabitants were increasingly reliant upon distant markets and nascent industrial enterprises. By 1700 the population had grown by another 50% and was approximately 600,000. That rate of growth was not sustained during the eighteenth century, despite London's expansion into the West End in the form of the architectural novelties of regular streets and squares of brick buildings. It is against this background Wren set about creating St Paul's Cathedral and the programme of parish churches.

Above: St Martin's, Ludgate Hill, a somewhat neglected but nevertheless interesting example of Wren's City churches, illustrating the architectural ingenuity with which liturgical demands were accommodated to difficult sites. See page 57. One sees this tradition masterfully continued in Butterfield's All Saints, Margaret Street (see page 167).

the minster in the east

St Paul's Cathedral

The two most important churches in London are St Paul's Cathedral – the minster in the east – and St Peter's, the abbey in the west, at Westminster. Both are key to London's urban topography and the politics of relations between the historic trading City in the east and the life of the English Crown and its court, Parliament and the civil service, and the Church located in what was once the low-lying, marshy lands at Westminster. Between these two locations is a ceremonial civic route from Buckingham Palace in the west, along the Strand and Fleet Street to St Paul's – a route used, for example, by Prince Charles for his marriage to Princess Diana. On such an occasion that route emerges from the urban fabric and then, afterward, in a characteristic English fashion, quietly sinks back into invisibility.

St Paul's is also important in another sense: its dome is central to a planning concept that has engendered a set of 'viewing corridors' from London's high points to the dome itself. Current intentions are that tall buildings should not intrude into these invisible corridors – a policy indicative of the significance given to St Paul's: the building is as important now (if for more mundane reasons) as it was in its Gothic form some four hundred years ago.

The present grandeur of the church is self-evident. It also has a long history that extends back to mythic origins as a Roman temple, then later as a wooden Saxon church, becoming a stone building in 632. After a fire of 1087, its fourth rebuilding was in the form of a Norman church. By the 1630s, the latter had become the distressed building Inigo Jones was called upon to repair – a work finally gutted by the Great Fire of 1666.

Wren came to the project of rebuilding in 1668 which, from an optimistic beginning, quickly became immured in controversy that had, at its heart, liturgical traditions and aesthetic preferences set against a baroque radicalism that aspired toward a bi-symmetrical and centralist design. Three different designs resulted in a so-called 'warrant' design and 'Great Model' finally being approved in 1675, but Wren cleverly obtained permission from the King to institute 'ornamental' changes. It was a ruse employed to disguise the works

Below: the architecture of St Paul's begins and ends in complex geometric ordering centred on the dome and the employment of modules that are at once geometric, spatial, perspective and structural. The plan has the dome as its central feature; to the east is the choir and apse; to the west is the nave and, as it were, the entry module that is the portico and steps; to the north and south of the dome are the transepts and their apsidal entrance doors that strive to equalise the overall symmetry of a plan that has been forced to elongate itself.

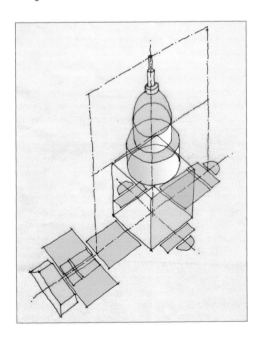

and actually make major changes over subsequent years up to the building's final completion in 1710. London then had an ornament to its fabric that could make a claim to European standing. It also had a dominant addition to its skyline that, ever since, has served a symbolic role only the most insensitive can fail to acknowledge and respect.

As realised, the building is not the centrally planned church Wren would have preferred and is, in fact, fundamentally a medieval plan suited to an established form of liturgy that the clerics did not want disrupted: 'custom' had been in conflict with Wren's notion of 'Positive' law and the architect did not have things entirely his own way. This is not only apparent in the long Latin cross of the plan, but also in the high outer screen walls that, from street level, conceal side buttressing to the nave. But, among all the design's features, it is the dome that is literally, metaphorically and symbolically prominent – an urban ornament modelled upon the ancient Roman Pantheon and deliberately intended to be symbolic of Protestant rivalry to the Catholic achievement of the dome of St Peter's, in Rome.

Overall, the architecture of St Paul's is a complex mix of liturgical, spatial, scenic and structural considerations that resolve themselves into a three-dimensional geometry not only striving to reconcile what Wren's Positive and Customary causes of beauty, but to do so with integrity and, importantly, without contradiction, i.e., as a resolved unity of composition and consideration. To the extent that liturgical politics allowed it, Wren gave the design a central emphasis married to the axial demands of the Latin cross. This is principally achieved by the drama given to the cathedral's vertical axis which clearly demonstrates Wren's concern with the pragmatics of those optical distortions which qualify the perceived ideality of abstract geometries. He sought to bring everything within his control, leaving nothing to accident and giving everything over to invention in that 'grand manner' which, to Edwin Lutyens, was to be the only kind of architectural gamesmanship worth playing. Here was a glorious symbol of civilised order: each part in its place within a harmonised and ordered whole. Here was architecture in all its lawful truthfulness, glorious and pretentious, arrogant and proud, product of a great nation and its Christian faith, the achievement of a heroic author and, above all, a counterpoint to the so-called arbitrary and customary life at its feet.

One should also note that the building is witness to the abstractions of power and money. It cost over £738,000 – an enormous sum in those days – and would never have been realised except for the established power of both church and monarch. Millennium Domes and Olympic stadia aren't quite of the same stuff simply because they lack such implicit philosophical content and intention: Wren's fundamental belief in the opposition of Natural Law (what is "Positive') to all that is merely Customary.

One of the most overlooked aspect of St Paul's is its most obvious: its scale (see, for example, the photo of the west façade, opposite). Few other London buildings manage to articulate the ordering of their fabric so grandly. It piles up, overwhelming the hubris of adjacent office buildings and bearing witness to Londoner's capacity to acknowledge the glory of their God. This orderly pile is crowned by the clever design of the dome: in itself, an architectural game of internal realities versus external perceptions informed by Wren's obsession with issues of 'optiks' mediating the difficult structural challenges presented by such a construction. The net result is a consummate tectonic that weights and prioritises the disparate parts of the whole in accord with the kinds of encounters experienced.

It is fundamental to such consummate gamesmanship that the architect is at once 'head in the clouds and feet on the ground'. While this may lend some people to read – rightly or wrongly – all kinds of arcane geometric and number symbolism into the architecture of St Paul's, such a viewpoint is always in danger of missing the key point: that Wren succeeded in *realising* profound significance in the ordering of space and structural form. Few buildings are similarly witness to such an achievement: at once an external perception (what stands within the public realm), an internal one (whose focus is beneath the dome), and a resolution of them both as three-dimensional form: of ideality and customary usage, of the symbolic and the mundane, structural integrity and the pragmatics of project management. The building stands there and says, "Someone once did this".

Perhaps all this is epitomised by the dome (see the sketch and photo overleaf). Its first reality is a clear differentiation between external and internal experiences – pragmatic, yes, but also exhibiting a design approach that is consistent with the scheme for the cathedral as a whole. The in-betweenness of these dualistic considerations is a clever structural exercise of domes within a dome that expertly addresses structural issues whilst delivering a geometric reconciliation of inside and outside form.

That the dome remains valued as perhaps the most significant feature of London's skyline can be attributed to many things, but so long as this remains true St Paul's will also stand witness to a long architectural tradition that instrumental values have threatened ever since the cathedral was completed. Mistakenly and irrationally or not, we demand such architectures – of whatever form and stylistic consideration. We thirst for their reassuring significance as motionless civilised works standing fast against all that is unknown and mutable. The alternative is an architecture of mere equipmentality, passing agreeableness and aesthetic entertainment. On the other hand, perhaps architecture can now only be that; perhaps we now find reassuring significances in other ways. Perhaps St Paul's was simultaneously the acme and swan-song of architectural endeavour? Three hundred years later we're still not quite sure.

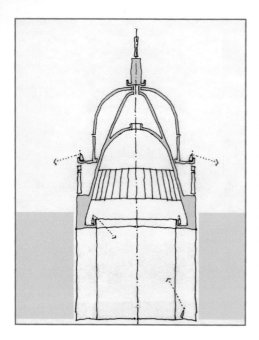

Robert Hooke 1635–1703

In 1665, Hooke, who had met Wren at Oxford, said of the latter: Hooke wrote that, *"Since the time of Archimedes, there scarce ever met in one man, in so great a perfection, such a Mechanical Hand, and so Philosophical a Mind."* But Hooke was hardly less and has a particularly high scientific reputation. The two became great friends and worked closely together.

Hooke was born on the Isle of Wight, but came to Westminster school as a young boy and then went on to Oxford. In 1663 he was awarded an MA, after spending time, like Wren, inventively serving scientific research. At this time he became employed by the Royal Society and at Gresham College. In 1666 he became one of the surveyors for the rebuilding work. From 1670 he was Wren's close collaborator and, effectively, his office manager inside the Surveyor's Office at Scotland Yard (a role taken over by Hawksmoor in 1693). They collaborated closely on many projects, including the City churches programme and the Monument – what is, in effect, a scientific experiment in disguise, intended to investigate gravity whilst also serving a civic role. Hooke, for example, would have been crucial to calculations for the roof of St Stephen Walbrook. Together, they also designed the Bethlem Hospital, the Monument, and the Royal College of Physicians building.

Right: the Monument – what Hooke referred to as 'the pillar at Fish Street' – was designed by Wren and Hooke as a memory to the Fire and also as a gigantic, 200 foot high scientific instrument. At the top of the 345 steps is a hatch to a ladder that leads up to a hinged lid at the top of the golden urn. At the very bottom of the column is a room used as a laboratory. In between is the void at the centre of the rising spiral stair – used for suspending a pendulum; and there are also a variety of other strategically positioned voids. Thus the construction could be used for measuring atmospheric pressure variations, gravitational, astronomical and similar experiments. However, what has been noted as an attempt to further scientific knowledge on a broad front – the kind of work Hooke and Wren undertook – was already over by the 1720s.

Top: diagram of the dome of St Paul's, indicating its complex double structure.
Opposite: St Paul's nave. If there is a disturbing fault to Wren's petrified achievement it surely lies in some obscure absence of emotional charge substituted by the imposing conceptualisations of great intellect effected over some thirty years. Here is a conception of Law that, in a quasi-scientific manner, is thoroughly and awesomely rational and still. There is the occasional resolved awkwardness, but no strangeness. Perhaps we no longer possess or can exhibit such certainties that stands fast in the face of mutability.

Improvisation, wit, inventiveness and gamesmanship: the surviving Wren parish and guild churches

The Great Fire destroyed some 87 churches and the 1670 City Churches Rebuilding Act resulted in fifty-one new or rebuilt works. These City parish and guild churches are rightly celebrated, but only half survive. Hobbyists will always find anything by Wren interesting, but the reality is that few of the City churches provide genuine architectural satisfaction – either because they weren't that special in the first place or, over time, have been significantly altered. Nevertheless some of them are very rewarding experiences and, strangely, some of the spires (many completed by Hawksmoor) are delightfully inventive. St Mary-le-Bow, for example, is one of the finest. Even the churches restored after wartime bombing are among the best, despite their intrinsic 'inauthenticity' (i.e. their relation to problematic issue of architectural recreation, which is not the same as Disneyland entertainments, although these two approaches to history sometimes enjoy a curiously blurred interweaving.

Above: the exemplary steeple of St Mary-le-Bow, Cheapside

The historian Kerry Downes summarises the churches in the following manner: *"Wren's churches well suited the liturgy and the society of their time; this is evidenced by their influence on English religious architecture of the eighteenth and nineteenth centuries. But by about 1840 many were in poor repair and increasingly unsuited to changes in taste and liturgy. Moreover, as the City of London became a place only of work, not of residence, churches became redundant and their sites more valuable than their fabrics. The ecclesiological movement led to refurbishment: high box pews were removed, stalls were introduced for robed choirs before the altar, and stained glass was inserted. The progressive damage of these changes was exceeded by the effects of the Second World War, after which only half the churches were left and almost half of those had to be virtually rebuilt, often with further liturgical and decorative changes. Thus St Bride's, Fleet Street, was reseated as a sumptuous collegiate chapel, and the least altered survivors have, like St Peter Cornhill, largely Victorian interiors. The concept of 'a Wren church' has changed profoundly since his time, but the remaining examples are among the best-known and most popular of his works."*

Popular, but with reservation: one feels that these churches are rather unfairly received by architects as production efforts – somewhat churned out in the pressurised manner of a set of franchised retail outlets today – and their value resides in an esteemed authorship rather than actual architectural virtue. That authorship is impossible to establish with any precision.

Edward Woodroofe, Robert Hooke, Nicholas Hawksmoor and others were involved in the Wren office, as well as many craftsmen on the actual works (who were often, like Wren, Freemasons). As today, the head of the office was the 'name' that took design responsibility, but all the churches appear to be collaborative efforts under Wren's strategic leadership and responsibility.

What makes these churches remarkable as a body of work is the inventiveness of the schematic conceptualisation. This always deals with the simplified liturgy of the period (no screened chancel and an emphasis upon the pulpit, etc.), and also with the need for an east-west orientation and a tower, often on old foundations or on a constrained site with a peculiar geometry (presenting a challenge to Wren's interest in optics).

To play at detective on these churches demands that one consciously brackets historical associations commonly attracting the unwary in order that one might directly engage the architectural gamesmanship as something of value in itself. In the main, history intrudes as layers of changes, particularly during the Victorian period and as a consequence of war damage, but it is worth attempting to get through all this to what Wren and his team were doing.

What one finds also has to be received critically, and the comments of one biographer are worth considering. In another historian's opinion (Sekler): *"Wren's architecture is characterised by one basic tendency which makes itself felt in two different ways: positively, it produces a feeling of order and clarity; negatively, it may breed monotony, dryness, and a feeling that elements are merely put together rather than integrated. The volumes of Wren's buildings are dominated by the simplest stereometric shapes, singly or in uncomplicated juxtapositions. The elevations are but little modelled or not at all, at most by the addition of such very simple elements as round niches or stepped-back bases. The treatment of façades, in fact, remains linear and two-*

dimensional and the articulating elements are put into the plane of the façade or in front of it without any plastic transitions. The resulting compositions are quiet and 'correct', with horizontals and verticals predominating over oblique or curved elements. In many cases simple geometrical figures coincide with the main lines of the building, and proportions can accordingly often be expressed in simple arithmetical units. ... Wren's designs rarely contradict the assumption that they originated in a process of a synthetic or additive nature. Although true integration is achieved in his finest creations." Whether Sekler is being complimentary or not is ambiguous, but he at least implies the need for a critical attitude to what is, in any case, this remarkable body of heritage.

The extant churches:

• **St Lawrence Jewry**, 1670-77
Gresham Street. Cheapside. The Guildhall church. Totally restored within the fire-damaged shell of World War II, but still a very good work to visit. Particular effort has gone into lending the asymmetrical plan an elevational treatment of being otherwise.
• **St Mary-at-Hill**, 1670-76, Love Lane, off Eastcheap. Burnt in 1988 fire; sad place, interesting location.
• **St Mary-le-Bow**, 1670-73, Cheapside. War damaged; restored. Pleasantly simple interior, but it is the tower that amazes. Originally designed to house an Ecclesiological Court of Appeal.
• **St Bride**, 1670-78. Steeple 1680. War damaged; restored.
• **St Dunstan-in-the-East**, 1670-71. Only the shell and tower of 1699 survives; war damaged. However, within and around the shell has been turned into a very pleasant garden.
• **St Edmund King and Martyr**, 1670-79, Lombard Street. Steeple 1707. Façade similar to St Martin, Ludgate; interior now a pleasant bookshop.
• **St Michael**, 1670-72, Cornhill. Tower by Hawksmoor 1718. Altered by George Gilbert Scott and worth visiting for that reason alone. Side aisles and vaulted nave.
• **St Olave**, 1670-76, Old Jewry. Only the tower remains.
• **St Vedast**, 1670-73, Foster Lane. Steeple 1709-12. War damaged; restored 1962. Pews arranged along the sides; worth visiting. Flat ceiling; single volume.
• **St Magnus the Martyr**, 1671-76, Lower Thames Street. Steeple 1705. Layers of restoration in the interior and worth visiting just for that experience. (See photo page 17.)
• **St Nicholas Cole Abbey**, 1671-77, Queen Victoria Street. War damaged; restored.
• **St Stephen Walbrook**, 1672-79, adjacent to Mansion House, Bank. Steeple 1717.
• **St James Garlickhythe**, 1676-83, Garlick Hill. Hawksmoor steeple 1713-17. Once described as 'Wren's lantern' because of the number of windows – now sadly reduced.
• **St Anne and St Agnus**, 1676-80, Gresham Street. War damaged; restored.

• **St Peter**, 1677-81, Cornhill. Restored 1872 by J.D. Wyatt.
• **St Martin-within-Ludgate**, 1677-84, Ludgate Hill.
• **All Hallows the Great**, 1677-83, Upper Thames Street.
• **St Benet**, 1677-83. Queen Victoria Street (west). Where Inigo Jones is buried. In a peculiar 'Dutch' style.
• **Christ Church**, 1677-87, Newgate Street. Only the tower and part of the shell remain.
• **St Clements Danes**, 1680-82, Strand. Steeple by Gibbs 1719.
• **St Anne**, 1680-86, Soho. Only tower (by S.P. Cockerell) remains.
• **St Augustine**, 1680-83, Watling Street. Only the tower remains.
• **St Mary Abchurch**, 1681-86, Abchurch Lane, off Cannon Street.
• **St James'**, 1682-84, Piccadilly. War damaged; restored.
• **St Alban**, 1682-85, Wood Street. Only the tower remains, now someone's offices.
• **St Clement**, 1683-87, Eastcheap. Flat ceiling type; single space.
• **St Andrew**, 1684-90, Holborn. Steeple 1703.
• **St Margaret Pattens**, 1684-87, Eastcheap. Steeple 1698.
• **St Andrews-by-the-Wardrobe**, 1685-92, Queen Victoria Street War damaged; restored.
• **St Margaret**, 1686-90, Lothbury. Typical plan (like St Lawrence Jewry) of main body plus side chapel. Interior is one simple volume.
• **St Mary Somerset**, 1686-95, Upper Thames Street. Only the tower remains.
• **St Michael Paternoster Royal**, 1686-94. College Hill. Restored 1966-8 by Elidar Davies.

All of the these churches are in the City except St James' and St Clement Danes.

St Stephen Walbrook

Among the finest of the surviving City churches is St Stephen Walbrook, at Bank (1672-87). Externally, it is unprepossessing: the exterior is not important apart from the tower which would once have raised itself above the surrounding roof tops (as Pugin later reminded us). At the ground, it is the entrance door and entrance sequence that is important – leading up steps into that part of the whole which is all important: the interior. Here, Wren strives to produce a centralised plan that, as at St Paul's, is rooted in the primacy of the square and cube, but neatly makes a transition to being a dome (of wood and plaster, thus lessening the structural loads as well as being more economic and sensible). Chancel, aisles and transepts are accommodated, but it is the centrality of the dome and the four vaults which run off in the four cardinal directions that hold the schema together. What at first appears to be a simple matter of nave and aisles turns out to be much more complex. Overall, the contrast between interior and exterior is striking (and one that would nowadays be unacceptable in a new building, especially a church).

Overall, this is a masterful exercise which recent liturgical changes have enhanced as a rather 'Scandinavian-blonde' approach replacing the old arrangement of pews and employing a central stone altar designed by Henry Moore. Site circumstance, customary issues and idealism have been brought together as a resolved, three-dimensional architectonic that manifests that all too rare and misunderstood capacity of inventiveness, wit, consideration and aspiration constituting the wonder of situated architectural gamesmanship.

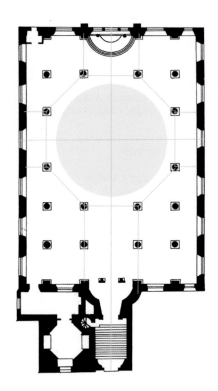

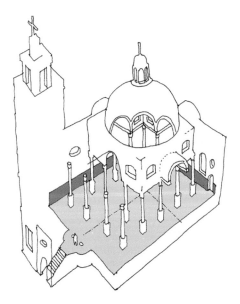

Despite its contemporary make-over (photo on the left), St Stephen Walbrook is one of the best of the Wren City churches. The plans given for these churches (as above) can be deceptive: the windows are usually high and a plan gives no indication of ceiling vaulting.

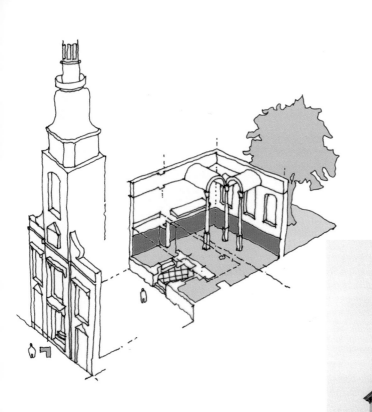

St Martin, Ludgate Hill

The richness of St Stephen Walbrook is worth comparing with St Martin, Ludgate Hill (1677-84) – the latter being more crude and significantly more neglected. Nevertheless, it has an inventive plan that handles a difficult site with adeptness. From an entry forced to be on the slope of Ludgate Hill the visitor is swung left and then right in order to enter from the west end, rising through two, short flights of steps. But in managing this exercise site space is given to a tower and vestry, and the main body of the church becomes more or less square, obtaining daylight from the only side possible (now a garden belonging to one of the City guilds). This schema also means that a gallery can be accommodated above the entry spaces. Unlike some other Wren churches, which have the tower as an adjunct to the composition, the tower at St Martin's forms a key part of the formality of the street façade. (See plan on page 61.) As this neglected church now stands its inherent gamesmanship is hardly acknowledged and somewhat countered and eroded by the indifferences of cumulative daily usage.

glory for old pensioners

Greenwich Royal Naval Hospital

The former naval hospital at Greenwich is a strange building: it doesn't look as if it could ever have served such a purpose. It was designed by Wren in 1695 as a way of completing schemes for Greenwich Palace (initiated by Charles II, to designs by John Webb; this is now the King Charles Block, 1664-9, on the north west side) and its central parts were constructed between 1696 and 1702 as a naval counterpoint to the army hospital at Chelsea. Vanbrugh, Hawksmoor and others all played a role in designing different parts, but the overall scheme is Wren's.

The French inspired layout (ref. the *Hôtel des Invalides*, in Paris) is breath takingly grand and faced the major difficulty of coping with Inigo Jones' Queen's House, allowing it a vista down to the River Thames. The latter is thus embraced, but rather incongruously since it is neo-Palladian while Wren's design is Baroque, and the two are separated by a major road (an integral part of the whole). The twinned domes on either side of the central axis are part of an attempt to cope with this conundrum, but the Queen's House remains a weak termination to an ensemble that is both wonderful and absurd, with the Observatory in the background, up the hill, in the park, and a once industrious river on the other side.

The hospital has two magnificent (and accessible) rooms: the Painted Hall and the Chapel – symmetrically located on either side of the central axis. The Chapel has an interior completed by James 'Athenian' Stuart (completed 1779-89), but it is the hall that most impresses. One enters through a high lobby under the dome which serves as a principal external feature. Ahead is a flight of steps into the main part of the hall and, at the far end, are more steps leading to a cubic space where the high table is located. The ceiling and wall paintings (celebrating British naval power and the triumph of Liberty and Peace over Tyranny, and taking nineteen years to complete; see page opposite) are by James Thornhill.

Nevertheless, no one has ever been sure what to do with the hall. It could not be used by the Pensioners when being worked on and was always too grand as a simple eating place. In 1834 it became an art gallery and remained that way until 1939, when it again became a dining room. In fact, this fundamental issue of purpose infects the whole complex and it is only recently that parts of the complex have been given a more meaningful role as Greenwich University.

Here, we have a fundamental issue, both at Greenwich and its equivalent at Chelsea: are they and were they ever fit for purpose as retirement homes? Their architectural grandeur is received as a celebration of the worthy lives and deeds, but these are singularly bizarre designs for aged pensioners on the last lap of their lives. This has always been a difficulty at

Top: view across the Thames from the Isle of Dogs.
Right: the Hall viewed from the entrance, beneath the dome. James Thornhill's paintings were completed between 1708-27.
Above: the similar dining room at Chelsea hospital. The first pensioners arrived in 1705; by 1815 there were 2,710 of them.

Greenwich and, while less so at Chelsea, both buildings bear an undertone of using old people as grist to the mill of architectural pretensions. This may be, in part, a contemporary perspective, but was probably self-evident when these buildings were designed. Certainly, the fundamental conception and the language of the designs are assertive and domineering rather than gentle and magnanimous.

the problem of attribution

*T*he City churches attributed to Wren are an example of the generality with which a sometimes titular office 'name' is attributed creative authorship despite the reality. Robert Hooke (from 1670, effectively Wren's office partner), John Oliver, Edward Woodroofe, and Nicholas Hawksmoor (and, later, William Dickinson), were particularly important assistants in his office, at times with considerable creative freedom. Also, the Coal Tax that paid for the works did not cover internal fittings, finishes, decorations, galleries and the like. These were left (with Wren's advice) to the parish and local craftsmen. Such nuances quickly complicate and cloud our need to identify design leaders and identify ostensible authoring heroes. For example, while the singularly important fact that Wren was personally responsible for the City churches is acknowledged, there is a tendency to ignore the realities of collaborative teamwork: what is not only iterative, but simultaneously and complexly interactive.

The kudos of heroic genius has always been an important underpinning of practice – particularly since the time 18th century men such as Gibbs, Adam and Chambers arrived fresh from their Grand Tour with a ready-at-hand experience of the 'real thing', able to spread out their drawings and show off drawing collections that gave evidence of their sound judgement and good taste. Such architects already enjoyed a status that not only blurred the medieval boundaries between design and execution, but consciously strove to underscore that differentiation. We have every indication that the spats between Inigo Jones and Ben Jonson reflected this issue in the early seventeenth century. However, one hundred years later, Richard Boyle (Lord Burlington) was able to stand apart from the executive dimensions of architecture in a privileged manner his cultured retinue at Burlington House could not enjoy.

While we have no reason to believe that things were ever different (i.e. conceptual architectural design, is by definition, cerebral and thus always somewhat apart from issues of execution) the rise of the 'speculative mason' in an era of 'aesthetic differentiation', as it has been termed, may have underscored the issue. That phenomenon of modernism (particularly during the eighteenth century) helped to engender the architect as a heroic person of sound taste as well as ability. The ambitious and aspiring young amateur of the early to mid-eighteenth century – making claim to experience, talent and perhaps hermeneutic knowledge – was a somewhat different creature to those architects who, some one hundred and fifty years later, belonged to a Victorian body of practitioners quite capable of tearing itself asunder on the basis of a discussion as to whether architecture was an art or a profession (in either case was thoroughly vocational).

Addressing this issue has, ever since, had subtle implications with regard to an architect's claim to legitimacy as well as taste, expertise and creative authorship. Survival and the success that aspires to significance – whether as artist or professional – has, since the time of Inigo Jones, required that the architect should pose as an especially talented individual: at once artful and expert, and always a person whose creativity is stamped upon the outputs from his studio. Clients demand such figureheads (the use of twentieth century acronyms not withstanding), clamouring for someone who can be credited with the penetrative insight, extraordinary compositional skills and a capacity to realise conceptual schema that raises architecture to an extraordinary status. Scholars, too, find diluted attribution to be inconvenient and, for historians, it complicates causal chains to the point that questions the validity of their discipline. We need and want the creative hero.

The counterpoint is a common sense understanding that it is teams and a practice culture that produces the work. There is not a contradiction that Wren may have used Hooke and Hawksmoor as collaborative creative authors and yet remained crucially important within a necessarily improvisational culture of production. This not only applied to Wren, Hooke and Hawksmoor but, more recently, has done to Yorke in his work with Rosenberg, Mardall, Alford and Henderson (see page 384), to Chamberlin in his work with Powell and Bon (page 352), to Stirling with regard to Gowan and Wilford (page 423), and to Foster in his relations with the likes of Spencer de Grey and Ken Shuttleworth (page 434). At the very least, the 'name' is a catalyst to situational potential as well as a convenient reference point within the recorded vicissitudes of endeavour and there is no simple way to disentangle such complex weaves (even when so many other factors are ignored from the equation).

Nikolaus Pevsner contentiously spent a great deal of effort in his pursuit of the 'heroes of the Modern Movement' as Hegelian individuals furthering the fulfilment of a modernist Zeitgeist. However, most of the time, architecture is not the work of a lone warrior, but an instance of improvisational team collaboration, leaving the hero as an ambiguous figure whose denomination tells us much about ourselves, our values and needs. Beneath the surface of such exercises is the need we suffer for heroes, as well as for unambiguous causal certainties. Nevertheless, when such concerns engender analyses of line thickness in order to attribute authorship to a drawing in Wren's office – thereby implying the true identification of creativity – then something has perhaps gone perversely wrong and is witness to a misunderstanding of the design process.

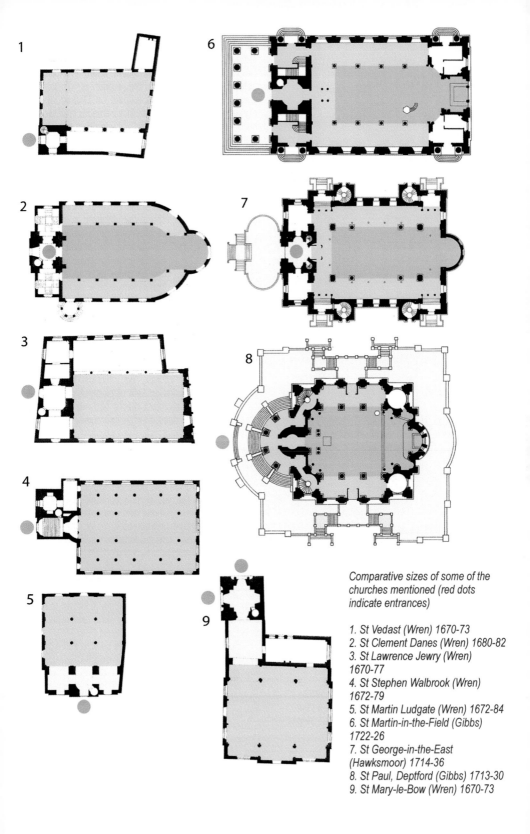

Comparative sizes of some of the churches mentioned (red dots indicate entrances)

1. St Vedast (Wren) 1670-73
2. St Clement Danes (Wren) 1680-82
3. St Lawrence Jewry (Wren) 1670-77
4. St Stephen Walbrook (Wren) 1672-79
5. St Martin Ludgate (Wren) 1672-84
6. St Martin-in-the-Field (Gibbs) 1722-26
7. St George-in-the-East (Hawksmoor) 1714-36
8. St Paul, Deptford (Gibbs) 1713-30
9. St Mary-le-Bow (Wren) 1670-73

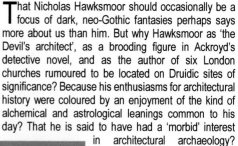

the Devil's architect

Nicholas Hawksmoor
1661–1736

Extant London works include:
• **Greenwich Palace**, work behind the colonnades, within the courts, and the west wing (1698-1704). Attribution is uncertain, but Hawksmoor is attributed with the (north east) Queen Anne Block and perhaps the west side of the King William Block. Now Greenwich University.
• the **Orangery**, Kensington Palace, begun 1704-5.
• **St Alfrege**, 1712-18, Church Street, Greenwich. Gutted in World War II and restored by Albert Richardson 1953. The upper parts of the tower are by John James (1730).
• **St Anne**. 1714-30, Commercial Road, Limehouse. Gutted by fire 1850; restored by Philip Hardwick, 1850-1; further restored by P.C. Hardwick, 1856-7, with A. Blomfield as assistant; by Sir Arthur Blomfield,1891; and by Julian Harrap, 1983-93.
• **St Mary Woolnoth**, Bank, 1714-27. The galleries have been removed, but character remains.
• **Christ Church**, 1714-29, Commercial Street, Spitalfields. In such a bad state that it was closed in 1957 as a dangerous structure. Recently totally restored, but now strangely devoid of character.
• **St George-in-the-East**, 1714-30, Cannon Street Road, off the Highway, Wapping. Only the shell remains, with a church of the 1960s.
• **St George's**, Bloomsbury, 1714-31. Restored.
• **Arcade Building** 1716-17, North side of the stable yard at St James' Palace, off the Mall. Jones' St Anne's sits opposite.
• **Westminster Abbey** west frontage, 1722-45 (the Gothic towers).
• **St Luke's**, Old Street (with John James), 1727-33. Roof removed 1859. Now used by the London Symphony Orchestra; conversion by Feilden Clegg.

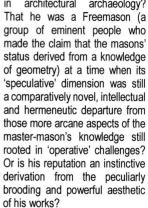

That Nicholas Hawksmoor should occasionally be a focus of dark, neo-Gothic fantasies perhaps says more about us than him. But why Hawksmoor as 'the Devil's architect', as a brooding figure in Ackroyd's detective novel, and as the author of six London churches rumoured to be located on Druidic sites of significance? Because his enthusiasms for architectural history were coloured by an enjoyment of the kind of alchemical and astrological leanings common to his day? That he is said to have had a 'morbid' interest in architectural archaeology? That he was a Freemason (a group of eminent people who made the claim that the masons' status derived from a knowledge of geometry) at a time when its 'speculative' dimension was still a comparatively novel, intellectual and hermeneutic departure from those more arcane aspects of the master-mason's knowledge still rooted in 'operative' challenges? Or is his reputation an instinctive derivation from the peculiarly brooding and powerful aesthetic of his works?

There is, of course, no obvious and simple explanation, but a distinct lack of biographical material on this illustrious architect marks him out as a blank screen awaiting to accept such projections.

Hawksmoor was born in Nottinghamshire, the son of a yeoman farmer. As a young man he was employed in Doncaster as a clerk of works. In this role he met the plasterer Edward Gouge, who, in 1680, brought him to London, where the young man became employed as Christopher Wren's 'scholar and domestic clerk'. It was in this role that Hawksmoor lived in the Wren household before taking over more responsible roles at the Office of Works, particularly between 1687-1701. He undertook all kinds of building accounting work and by 1691 (and for almost twenty years thereafter) was Wren's chief draughtsman on St Paul's Cathedral (taking over from Robert Hooke). However, by 1688 he is known to have been designing buildings as his skills and reputation developed while the noble Wren aged.

Between the later years of this service and a period when he was able to design in his own name, Hawksmoor was closely associated with a quite different character: Sir John Vanbrugh (1664-1726), the latter an apparently charming, gregarious man of Whig leanings (i.e. a man sympathetic toward the political grouping that was for a strong Parliament, a limited monarchy, resistance to France, and the Protestant succession to the throne), and who appears to have had the appropriate social connections engendering the kinds of commissions apparently denied to Hawksmoor. Hawksmoor entered into this arrangement with Vanbrugh as a forty year old, thoroughly experienced man of works whilst still continuing his role under Wren at the Board of Works.

Vanbrugh – a well respected dramatist, ex-military man and political radical is reported to have been, at that time, a novice at drawing and this, perhaps, already gives some indication of Hawksmoor's corresponding character, values and project role. They must have made quite a pair, embarking on schemes for enormous houses such as Castle Howard, in Yorkshire (1699-1712) and Blenheim Palace (1705-24). And, after Vanbrugh's death in 1726 (and after Hawksmoor had lost his job when Wren was dismissed), Hawksmoor returned to working on these two projects. Meanwhile, he also worked on schemes such as the Greenwich Hospital during a period in which he achieved a powerful role as comptroller to the Office of Works (in 1702) and as Wren approached his forced retirement (in 1718). Summerson records that, during this latter period, the Office was effectively a triple partnership of the ageing Wren, Vanbrugh and the young Hawksmoor, whilst also serving as an unofficial academy of architecture (Hawksmoor, it has to be remembered never went abroad to acquire the status that a Grand Tour gave to an architect).

There was also work in Cambridge and Oxford, but it was the 1711 Act for fifty new churches that produced the celebrated works still to be found in London: St Alfrege, Greenwich (1712, consecrated 1718); three Stepney churches, begun in 1714: St Anne's, Limehouse (consecrated 1730), St George-in-the-East, Wapping, Stepney (interior destroyed 1941), and Christ Church, Spitalfields (both consecrated 1729); and two others begun in 1716: St George's, Bloomsbury (consecrated 1731), and the rebuilding of St Mary Woolnoth, a City church patched up after the Great Fire (finished 1727). In addition, Hawksmoor also produced two churches with another commissioner for these fifty churches, John James (between 1727-33): St Luke's, Old Street, whose walls and fluted obelisk steeple remain, and St John Horselydown, Bermondsey (gutted 1940 and finally dismantled in 1948).

Hawksmoor, who had suffered from 'the vile distemper of the gout' all his life, finally died of 'gout of the stomach', at Millbank, in 1736. He is remembered as a man who gave to Vanbrugh the technical skills the latter man lacked, and was able to lend a 'charge' to his own designs that Wren – from whom everything had been brilliantly but academically learned – was never able to realise. Perhaps, somewhere within this ambiguous issue of 'charge', lies both the source of those darker attributions to the work of this man and an historical status that leaves Hawksmoor as a somewhat inaccessible architect's architect whose works often require a substantial effort before they can be appreciated.

Above: *St Anne. Limehouse*
Below: *Westminster Abbey's west towers*

Below: *St Luke, Old Street*

St George Bloomsbury, 1716–27

The fact that Hawksmoor has become the 'devil's architect' of novelists, historians and journalists anxious to excite their readers' fantasies gets between us and the architecture. St George's, Bloomsbury is a good example of the latter. The church exhibits the man's private concerns as well as his architectural inventiveness and idiosyncracities, but that damnable upper part to the tower overly excites interest. In fact, any architect-cum-speculative-mason of the day would place their work in the context of what the Ancients had achieved – and Hawksmoor was a keen historian of architectural precedent. In fact, Wren had similarly been fascinated by such things and many of the City church towers exhibit the peculiar role of these urban landmarks that it probably takes an old fashioned Post-Modernist like Venturi to appreciate.

The site of St George was a problematic site and numerous plans were proposed. That in itself is a rather ignored history, but the key point is our arrival at a design from Hawksmoor that obstinately strove to satisfy liturgical propriety in the face of the clergy's apparent readiness to accept a north-south axis which could accommodate more worshippers. In fact, to do so meant he could fulfil other demands of the site: stretching the plan between the two streets bounding it to north and south, each having a prominent façade, and enabling access from either side, i.e. from the old residential developments of Covent Garden and also from newer (and implicitly more prosperous) developments taking place to the north (where Bloomsbury Square had been laid out in 1661). But Hawksmoor's schema is at once brilliant, persistent, ambitious and flawed: perhaps an example of brilliant architecture and not so intelligent design.

The true façade of St George's sits on the west side and it is here that Hawksmoor provided equally balanced sets of access stairs leading under the tower and onto the central, east-west axis. Galleries were to either side. However, the Bloomsbury Way façade is clearly the presentational one of most importance and it is here that we are given a grand portico. This would only have been properly used once the parishioners – moved by the inconvenience of it all – switched to a north-south axis in 1781, removing the north gallery and adding new ones to east and west. Now that, ironically, the church has few parishioners and many more tourist visitors, all this has been changed back to the original schema in the recent restoration (which includes the reinstatement of the south gallery). But the character of the design begs one to forgive such fundamental faults – forgive, that is, if one enjoys what was once called a Gothic, irregular and heavy ('Greco-Gothic') manner – which the later neo-Palladians did not. This is not a quiet and still architecture. It is idiosyncratic, restless and robust, dramatic and assertive – until, that is, one penetrates to its heart. It is combinatory, allowing the parts considerable independent latitude before their

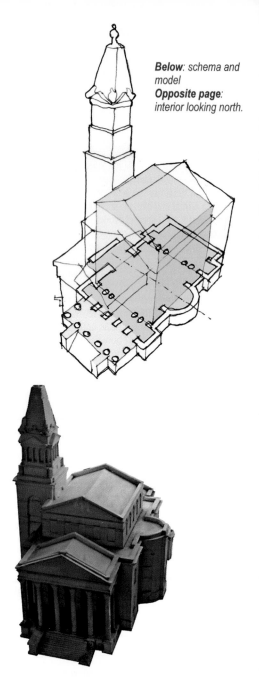

Below: schema and model
Opposite page: *interior looking north.*

conformance to an overall schema holds them in place. We appear to have a concern of moving from parts to the whole, rather than from the whole to parts. But the counterpoint is a still centre symbolised and effected by the cube.

It has been argued this approach – of an assertive, combinatory exterior and a still centre – is an interesting reflection of Restoration England that was already out

Above: St George, south front.
Top right: The 'beasts' at the feet of George Ist were removed in 1871 by G.E. Street and only recently restored (2007).

of accord with emerging tastes (as seen, for example, in Lord Shaftesbury's writing of the early years of the 1700s concerning good taste and a socially unifying 'common sense'). It is equally intriguing to find that this architectural character was deemed to be both ponderous and essentially 'Gothic'. It is an architecture of 'effect' in the sense that an impact is made upon the observer, who then must work to assemble individual effects into an architectonic whole – in the manner that Cicero had discussed the 'officium' and 'finis' of an orator, or Vitruvius had been concerned with 'intent' and the 'expression of the intent' with an implicit regard for effect on an audience. One's mind is meant to 'range' across the parts and seek out 'similitudes' and 'associations' (often historical). It is necessary to exert oneself in order to engage and grasp the architecture, rather than enjoy a comparatively passive – even inattentive – relationship.

Summerson saw Hawksmoor as a widely read man, fascinated by all things Roman: *"there is a streak of Gothic retrospection. Sometimes, it is evident, Hawksmoor is trying to work out Roman equivalents of Gothic compositions, to obtain medieval effects with components as nearly as possible antique. Naturally, it is in his turrets and steeples that this propensity is most evident."* And Kerry Downes remarks that Hawksmoor's art was *"essentially one of masses and spaces rather than of decorative detail. Architects have always worked from precedents; Hawksmoor sought them anywhere in the past or present, from the primitive to the increasingly fashionable neo-Palladianism of his maturity, extracting whatever could be used to move the beholder and eschewing the dogmatic and restrictive taste of Palladian orthodoxy which, for him, was 'but dress[ing] things in Masquerade."* In the end, Hawksmoor remains a 'difficult' architect, sometimes too difficult: one occasionally longs to touch upon that repose he clearly sought to realise but sometimes missed. His reputation has risen immensely in the last thirty or forty years, but then just about every architect one can think of has become grist to the mill of tourist content in that same period. Hawksmoor, however, will surely never be merely entertaining: his works demand a different sort of work from those who engage them.

St Mary Woolnoth, 1716-27

Historical change at St Mary of the Nativity began a long time ago – when William Butterfield arrived tin 1875 to remodel the interior by taking away the two galleries. However, as with many of the City churches, one is looking at a reincarnation that dates back to at least 1191. There was then a church of 1438 that burnt in the Great Fire, had Wren repair it in 1674, but was finally replaced by Hawksmoor's work. The reredos (the decorated screen behind an altar), pulpit and plasterwork are all Hawksmoor's – as are the incongruous pair of doors that float half-way up the west wall and once led onto the galleries. Butterfield stuck the fronts of the galleries to the walls, cut down the tall pews, added a platform and steps to the altar (thus requiring that the reredos be raised) and coloured tiles to Hawksmoor's black and white flooring.

In the original design, only the north and west façades were readily visible; the south side was not fully revealed until King William Street was constructed and the east side has always been relatively concealed. In other words the west front was not designed to be seen as we see it now and the tower would, of course, have been much higher than surrounding buildings. (This may be commonplace in Italy, but the nearest London parallel is perhaps Terry Farrell's Charing Cross Station contemporary façade on the narrow Villiers Street.)

However, one has to approach the historical dimension of the City churches with circumspection: it is useful, but as a *via negativa*, i.e. in an endeavour to strip away the layers of change and general entropic erosion that eat away at an original architectural schema which, only then, can achieve a proper appearance.

Apparently, the church was threatened with demolition five times between the 1840s and 1920 and is lucky to have survived. In fact, it is remarkable that St Mary Woolnoth has survived, even in the state it is in: complete with an Underground station and a Starbuck's housed in an 1897 'Wrenaissance' insinuation that has nestled up to Hawksmoor's edifice as witness to the skill of late-Victorian engineers. The church stands like some sad old man: alone, neglected, unnoticed – even here, at the heart of the City.

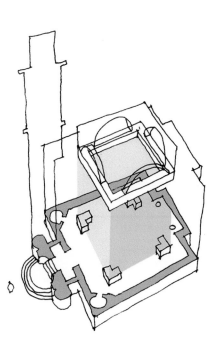

Top: the cruelly rusticated west front of St Mary Woolnoth – one of the marvels of London's architecture.
Left: the arrangement of the church, with a stable, geometric and spatialised cube at the heart of its schema.

67

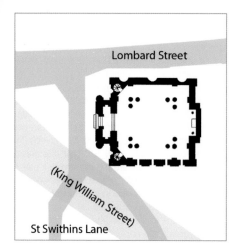

Above: the site plan of St Mary Woolnoth, indicating the original street alignments, before King William Street was constructed. This is now difficult to appreciate; the thunderous traffic along King William Street must be utterly different to the comparatively quiet side street off Lombard, in 1727, when the church was completed. One should attempt to look at the west façade in these terms.

Below: the interior of St Mary Woolnoth, looking east. The galleries were removed by William Butterfield in 1875.

St George-in-the-East, 1714-34

There is something quite wonderful in finding that, within the dramatic shell of St George, there nestles a 1964 church. It is not just the exhibition of different circumstances and religious concerns (or lack of them), but the shallow romance associated with the inhabitation of 'as-found' ruins (one thinks of how the Roman Colosseum once was). Hawksmoor is here nearer to those Roman references he enjoyed than he could ever have imagined. That intruding inhabitant is rather lacklustre: a simple, utilitarian post-war affair, but not one without its own ordinary charms which await the financing of a degree of harmonisation with Hawksmoor's work. It even manages to incorporate the Hawksmoor apse. And yet, of course, it is the 'mannerist' outside shell that impresses and is so essentially Hawksmoor. One has to imagine it as a populous suburban edifice welcoming its parishioners into the various openings that allowed them to crowd in to the nave and the galleries. The current difficulty is a disjunction between the contemporary lives of those parishioners and the cultural import lent to what remains of the building by the intelligentsia (what T.S. Eliot differentiated as culture and Culture, a concept paralleling Wren's belief in Positive and Arbitrary causes of beauty). The church was originally passed down from above by the Rulers of Taste to the unbelieving masses and this remains the essence of the predominating cultural equation. However, everyone now indulges in nostalgia, even the inhabitants of the local estates (the gentry of Wapping, across the road, surely go no where near the place) and St George as a shell possibly has, strangely enough, as much relevance as ever.

Above: the new church within the old shell of St George-in-the-East.
Opposite page: three views of Hawksmoor's St George-in-the-East

Sir John Vanbrugh 1664–1726

Extant London works include:
• **Vanbrugh Castle**, Blackheath, 1717-26. Westcombe Park Road.
• **Royal Arsenal**, Woolwich, 1719. Brass Gun Room; The Model Room; Gun Bore Factory (1717-1720's).

Vanbrugh was born in London, son of a merchant from Haarlem who had escaped Flanders as Protestant refugees. He appears to have lived in Chester and been educated there, but appears in 1681 as a London wine merchant. By 1686 he was in the army, resigned after six months and went to Paris (with a distant aristocratic relative), where he was imprisoned as a spy, being released in 1692 (after a total of four years). He briefly sojourned in Paris, returned to the army and began writing plays before, in 1698, meeting Hawksmoor and suddenly turning to architecture, winning two major commissions (Castle Howard and Blenheim Palace, as well as building his own theatre in 1702) and calling upon Hawksmoor to help him (while he continued to write plays and be involved in the intricate intrigue of the day). From 1702-13 he was Queen Anne's Comptroller of Her Majesty's Works. He was knighted in 1714, after a change of government, and continued working with Hawksmoor on a variety of projects, including the outer parts of the King William Block at Greenwich Hospital (1703-28).

With regard to the collaboration between Vanbrugh and Hawksmoor, Summerson argues that the dramatic novelties we see them introduce probably came from Vanbrugh, but Hawksmoor had control of the mode of expression. *"It was Hawksmoor, with his deep knowledge of the source books and of every sort of English architecture, his long experience of practical building, and, above all, his own discovery of those intrinsic [Baroque] architectural values ... who made the Vanbrugh manner possible."* Major works outside London include: Castle Howard, commissioned 1699; Blenheim Palace, commissioned 1704; and Seaton Delaval, begun 1718.

His epitaph read, *"Lie heavy upon him, Earth, for he laid a heavy burden on thee."*

Thomas Archer 1668–1743

Extant London works include:
• **Roehampton House**, 1710-12.
Ropehampton Lane, Roehampton. Now a part of
Queen Mary's Hospital.
• **St Paul**, Deptford, 1713-30.
• **St John**, 1713-28, Smith Square, Westminster. Burnt
out and rebuilt as a concert hall in 1965 (by Marshall
Sisson). The church was known as Queen Anne's
footstool because of its peculiar four corner features.
• **Russell House**, 1716-17, 43 King Street, Covent
Garden.

Archer was born in Warwickshire as the son of a country gentleman, former army colonel and MP. He went to Trinity College, Oxford and, from 1691, travelled on the Continent for four years where it is believed he travelled to Padua and Rome. From 1705 he held the sinecure position of groom-porter which, oddly, meant he was (profitably) responsible for the royal furniture and for gambling houses. At the same time he appears to have been practising as an architect (although not as his principal means of income). He applied himself to various country house works but it is St Paul, Deptford that is his greatest work. Appointed as a commissioner responsible for supervising surveyors such as Hawksmoor he secured two of the churches for himself: St Paul, Deptford, and St John, Westminster. Both these rather theatrical works are grandly Baroque and the latter (referencing Borromini's Sant' Agnese in Rome) has four idiosyncratic corner towers which earned the church the nickname of 'Queen Anne's footstool'.

St Paul, Deptford, would be one of London's more famous churches if sited anyway else but off Deptford High Street, one of the more impoverished parts of London. It is surely one of London's more enjoyable architectural 'ornaments'. Herzog & de Meuron used the church as a reference point in their design of the nearby Laban Centre (2003).

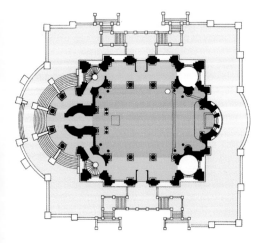

Above left: the west front of St Paul, Deptford
Left: the plan of St Paul's indicates surrounding steps that help to establish the church's presence and serve as a part of an unusual ritual of approach. Within, Archer appears to effortlessly establish the kind of centralised plan that others could merely aspire toward. Side galleries are to the north and south; and the east end once had private rooms serving local gentry who could afford them (church pews were sold in those days, providing income to the church). Transported to the West End, this church would be one of London's jewels.

Above: the interior of Thomas Archer's St Paul's, Deptford.

Below: John James' St George, Hanover Square – an interesting frontage that grabs the pavement into the portico.

John James 1672–1746

Extant London works include:
• **St Mary's Church**, Rotherhithe, 1714-15; steeple 1747-8' interior altered 1876.
• **St George's Church**, Hanover Square, 1721-5; redecorated 1875.
• **St Luke's Church**, Old Street, with Hawksmoor, 1727-33. Now converted into a concert and rehearsal venue.

As the son of a Hampshire parson, James' knowledge of building and architecture were acquired during his apprenticeship between 1690-97 with Matthew Banckes, the King's master carpenter, through which he also gained the freedom of the City of London. He rather immodestly claimed, *"perhaps no person pretending to Architecture among us, Sr. Chr: Wren excepted, has had the Advantage of a better Education in the Latin Italian and French Tongues, a competent share of Mathematicks and Ten Years Instruction in all the practical parts of Building."*

James is recorded as working at the Royal Naval Hospital, Greenwich (1699), as assistant to Hawksmoor; he became joint clerk of works in 1718, and clerk from 1735, when Hawksmoor resigned. At St Paul's Cathedral, James was recorded as a carpenter in 1707; he was then appointed master carpenter (1711), assistant surveyor (1716), and finally surveyor to the cathedral (1724) after Wren's death. In 1716 he was a Surveyor to the Commissioners for the 1711 Act for Building Fifty New Churches.

James also worked as surveyor to the dean and chapter of Westminster (from 1725) and was, after Hawksmoor's death in 1736, surveyor of repairs at Westminster Abbey from 1736 (completing the west towers). James also added the steeple to Hawksmoor's St Alfege, Greenwich (1730).

a man in vogue
James Gibbs 1682–1754

The man who is born into a Scottish Roman Catholic family, who lives for many years in Rome, who dies a Catholic and yet, somehow, manages to maintain a very successful career serving a Protestant aristocracy in a power structure deeply suspicious of anything Catholic is surely an interesting architect. John Summerson described Gibbs as, *"one of the most individual of English architects. Not a profound innovator [he] possessed an ability to select and combine the characteristics of other architects and fuse them into a style of his own."* That

Gibbs's extant London works include:
• **St Mary-le-Strand**, 1714-17; interior refitted 1871. This was not, originally to have had such a large tower. It was designed for a simple bell-turret and a nearby monumental column to Queen Anne. In the event, Gibbs was asked to enlarge the tower to what it is now.
• **St Clements Danes steeple**, 1719. Completing Wren's church and Gibbs's 1719 design for the steeple.
• **Octagon** 1720, Orleans House, Twickenham (the house itself was demolished,1927).
• **St Peter's Church**, 1721-24, Vere St., off Oxford Street.
• **St Martin-in-the-Fields**, 1722-26. Trafalgar Square. Perhaps Gibbs's most famous work. Interior altered by Sir A.W. Blomfield in 1887. Recent works to crypt etc. (2007-08) by John McAslan.
• **Sudbrook Park**, 1726-28, Petersham Road, Richmond. Now Richmond Golf Club.
• **St Bartholomew Hospital**, 1730-59. Smithfield. Now rather obscurely lost amid hospital life, but an interesting place to visit (see St Barts-the-Less and St Barts-the-Great).

'style' included the design of a church typology – St Martin-in-the-Fields, at Trafalgar Square – that has been widely copied, all over the English-speaking world.

Gibbs's influence also came, in part, from two published works: the very influential *Book of Architecture*, 1728, which mainly contains his own work; and *Rules for drawing the Several Parts of Architecture*, 1732. Wittkower suggested that such works are among the publications of the early C18th that are of equal importance to what was built: *"these works seal and break with the past."*

He points out two considerations. The first is a political context of inclinations that were, relatively speaking, democratic. This was architecturally manifest in the novel significance and import given to works that, once upon a time, have been so low in a hierarchy from churches to utilitarian buildings that they had been, until the C18th, 'without art' and of no concern to architects. *"English Neo-Palladianism"*, noted Wittkower (that period within which Gibbs' career features), *"opened the road to an almost functional approach to such buildings [as farms, for example] for modern need."* Architectural publications around the middle of the century onward now referred to farmhouses, cottages, and even labourers' dwellings.

Wittkower also noted that, *"From about the middle of the century one began to see classical antiquity with new eyes: the variable rather than the static quality of ancient architecture began to attract attention."* Gibbs' second book is interesting in this context. It picks up on a radical keynote in the work of Claude Perrault, published in France in 1683 and in England in 1708 and 1722. Here, Perrault offers the somewhat scandalous argument that, although there are two causes of beauty, the Natural or Positive and the Arbitrary or Customary, that pleasure is nevertheless largely derived from custom and habituation. This, combined with the observable inconsistencies of the Ancients, suggested a need to give reference to the Customary as well as to invite the simplification and better ordering of the classical Orders. The latter is what Gibbs picked upon and took a step further, further simplifying the Orders.

Gibbs was born in Aberdeen, son of a prosperous Catholic merchant. On his parents' deaths in 1700 he travelled to the Netherlands and then on to Rome. Less than a year later he turned to painting, for which he showed considerable talent. He remained in Rome until 1708, initially in order to train as a priest; however he was ejected from the Scots College there and later entered the architectural studio of Carlo Fontana (then the leading Roman architect), returning to London in 1709 where he immediately appears to have been well connected and have his unique training well received (for example, undertaking a courtyard with wings for Richard Boyle, at Burlington House, 1708-15).

By 1713 Gibbs had secured a co-surveyorship, together with Nicholas Hawksmoor, to the commissioners appointed for the building of fifty new churches that were to bring religion to the masses of burgeoning London. His first church, St Mary-le-Strand (1714), was a major contribution to the dominant Baroque of Hawksmoor and Vanbrugh (then effectively running Wren's office). However, it has been noted that Gibbs' Catholic faith, Tory sentiments and Baroque architecture were not entirely in tune with emerging fashions and political events: the Whigs in power, neo-Palladianism as the newly dominant taste, and a new King, George I, who, in 1714, not long after the union of England and Scotland in 1707, came to the throne midst all kinds of political complications between England, Scotland, the Protestants and Catholics, Tories and Whigs. St Mary's was deemed blatantly 'Roman' and Gibbs, suspected of being both Tory and a Catholic, lost his surveyorship in 1715 (an affair in which Colen Campbell - who had studiously omitted Gibbs from his edition of *Vitruvius Britanicus*, of that same year, appears to have played a role).

Nevertheless, Gibbs became the Tory country house architect of choice and even attracted patronage from Whigs, including that of Lord Burlington, for whom he created an entrance forecourt to Burlington House, in Piccadilly, 1715-16 (dem. 1858). By 1720 Horace Walpole could declare that Gibbs was the architect 'most in vogue'. It was in that year that he was appointed to design St Martin's, completed in 1726. In 1721-4 he completed a chapel-of-ease for the Earl of Oxford's estate around Cavendish Square – what is now St Peter's, Vere Street. However, by then the' Baroque inclinations of Gibbs were less fashionable than a more cool neo-Palladianism, which was, in any case, more of a Whig fashion, and Gibbs' style had to shift accordingly.

Perhaps it is this that prompted John Summerson to summarise the importance of Gibbs as follows: *"He belongs to no school, and although he was widely imitated his contribution to the further development of English architecture was slight. He is best described as the delayed fulfilment of Wren, as a brilliant continuator of a chapter closed about 1692, when the Vanbrugh-Hawksmoor episode began."* Nevertheless, works such as St Mary-le-Strand and St Martin-in-the-Fields remain among the more impressive of London's churches.

Above: St Mary-le-Strand, now islanded in the Strand, but still a well proportioned church with a fine interior (also a living church, where there are regular services). The two-storey schema of the west façade of St Mary-le-Strand. The interior of the church is a simple, single volume with an ornate, elliptical ceiling worth comparing with St Martins-in-the-Fields. In fact, St Martins, St Mary, and St Clements Danes make a fine trio to visit, especially in the context of seeking out the mediation of Gibbs' work between the baroque of Wren et al and the neo-Palladianism of Burlington's circle (and even of William Chambers, whose Somerset House stands opposite St Mary-le-Strand). See overleaf.

St Mary-le-Strand, 1714-17.
St Martin-in-the-Field, 1722-26.

Gibbs' most famous building in London stands in contrast to most of the City churches and their compromised inventiveness. The church is prominently sited, stand-alone and large, and attempts to unify all its parts into an orderly whole that has none of the agitated assertiveness of Hawksmoor. In particular, it marries portico, vestibule, the body of the church and a tower in a manner that suggests a refined Christianisation of the Classical temple and strikes a note of accord with new tastes that Wren and Hawksmoor *et al* could not satisfy.

Unlike St Mary-le-Strand – which Gibbs had lent a more intimate scale, avoiding the use of a giant order by stacking storey-height orders and lending the whole what Summerson refers to as 'rhythmical complexity' – St Martin's strides forward as a more grand and pretentious statement. But the church becomes all the more interesting in the context of St Mary-le-Strand (a church which, like St Paul's, has a two-storey scheme for the west façade) and also of the Wren church with a Gibbs steeple (of 1719) that sits just further east: St Clement Danes (1680-82; gutted in World War II and restored in 1958).

St Martin's takes elements from both these churches. For example, the roof of St Mary is an elliptical curve covered with decorative plaster work – which is what Gibbs provides at St Martin's. However, the latter church is aisled and the columnation and side galleries are taken from Wren's St Clement church (note the underside vaulting). The large portico serves as an external room and allows direct access through three doors to the nave and two galleries. Inside, there is a strong, enwrapping enclosure formed by the arched aisle columns and, importantly, by the ceiling. The overall impression is very successful, but the other two churches are possibly more rewarding. St Clement Danes is novel among the Wren parish churches, possessing fully-rounded arches sitting upon the pillars supporting the galleries. Light floods in from either side, both below and above the galleries. The restoration – absolutely accurate or not – is superb. Similarly, Gibbs' church has an exquisite combination of simplicity and well-proportioned detail. Perhaps St Martin, when restored (currently under way in 2008) will match these other two and justify its reputation.

Top: St Martin-in-the Fields (Gibbs). The church has recently had below ground modifications by John McAslan (2008).
Middle: interior of St Clement Danes (Wren)
Bottom: interior of St Mary-Le-Strand (Gibbs)

74

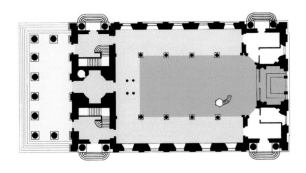

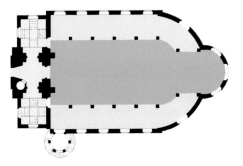

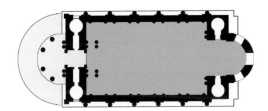

Left: comparative plans of (from the top): St Martin-in-the-Fields, St Clement Danes and St Mary-le-Strand. Note the compactness of St Mary and the architectonic clarity of St Martin, which now has a full temple frontage.

Below left: interior of St Martin-in-the-Fields. Note the elliptical ceiling (which approaches the vaulting Wren gave to St Clement Danes) and the full entablature on top of the columns – a curious Gibbs device.

Below: interior (beneath a gallery) of St Clement Danes (Wren; just east of St Mary). Gibbs does something similar at St Martin.

Bottom exterior of St Mary-le-Strand.

Vitruvius

Above: Piranesi's drawing of the Temple of Claudius, Rome, in 1757, drawn at a time when the voice of Vitruvius was the principal authority in all architectural matters.

Vitruvius (c. 80-70 BC; d. c. 15 BC) is hugely important within the history of European architecture: here, during the Renaissance, was the authoritative voice of an Ancient, bringing alive the moribund ruination still so apparent in Rome. That voice reverberated throughout the European cultural space, inspiring not only master-builders but any civilised and creative mind to bring a new vision of order and taste to accommodative acts of dwelling.

Ironically, Vitruvius had died prior to the great Augustian age of Roman architecture. However, it was not Vitruvius himself but his commentators and revisers who became important in treatises that, echoing his authoritative voice and providing examples of how his guidance was translated from principle to realisation, were commonly self-promotional. Palladio is an outstanding example. His treatise (apparently written before 25AD) was 'discovered' in a monastery in 1414. In fact, many people knew of it; what was novel was the interest now taken in ancient texts. The work, 'De Architectura' (also known as *The Ten Books of Architecture*) was grasped as an umbilical cord direct to the body of Roman civilisation. By 1486 the work had been republished. Translations followed, albeit rather freely, and travellers disseminated its contents.

Vitruvius' references to the origins of architecture and to the importance of the human body neatly fitted into a neo-Platonic tradition of philosophy that, in itself, was profoundly architectonic. Not only was God's creation hierarchical, with mankind in a privileged position, but it was the challenge of every architect to produce forms manifesting the immanence of the Absolute midst the creaturely, fallen stuff of a purposive but uncomfortably mutable Creation. Symbolic number, musical scales and geometry (all rooted in precedents set by the Ancients) were considered to be, self-evidently, the very stuff of creativity, just as they were to be the obvious basis of all arche-tectonic works.

In England, Henry Wotton's free interpretation, '*The Elements of Architecture*' (1624), was significant among a raft of works that were later published, especially in the eighteenth century. However, by then, interest in Palladio and the Ancients had become more sceptical and archaeological in orientation: Classical works were recognised as less consistent than originally supposed and, in the context of an acceptance of variability within the architectural tradition, attempts at defining a canon of architectural order suffered the influences of scientific rationality, novel instrumental attitudes, changes in the basis of patronage, and archaeological researches that paralleled an acceptance of the emerging power of a customary realm served by a scepticism and uncertainty that counterpointed former beliefs in revealed Authority. Toward the end of the C18th books such as Robert and James Adam's self-celebratory '*Works in Architecture*' (1773) and James Paine's '*Plans, Elevations and Sections of Noblemen and Gentlemen's Houses*' (1767) were sounding a note that was at once personal and nationalist. A transition to the nineteenth century's 'battle of styles' that set the neo-Gothic against the neo-Classical and infused both with conflicting notes of romanticism, instrumentality and calls for 'freedom' was soon under way.

Out of such muddied waters emerged a vision of Modernism as a new and more pure basis of architectural legitimation. By the period after World War I it was not so much any variety of Vitruvian fixity that was any longer important, but a spirit of change and adaptation upon the basis of rational principle. The so-called Art Deco movement was among the first indications that issues of stylistic form in architecture and the applied arts were now more subject to the vicissitudes of mass tastes and customary fashions than lawful architectural dictat.

And so it has gone on. But Vitruvius might have recognised much that is familiar in contemporary practice. There is a distinct, ingratiating note of self-legitimation and self-promotion in the work, but Vitruvius hit a more profound and philosophical note when he advised his readers that there are two principal aspects to all architectural matters: "that which is signified and that which signifies. What is signified is the matter set forth by what is said. What signifies this is a demonstration developed through the principles of learning." In other words, architects always deal with age old issues of what to do and how to do it; of intent and the expression of intent. For Vitruvius and architects of the Renaissance and long afterward, expression was a matter of learning in accord with principle, rule and precedent. The canonic Orders were all important. By the Machine Age of the late nineteenth and early twentieth centuries, this was no longer true. But, then as now, architects still found themselves – like Vitruvius – suffering a need to define and publicise the parameters of self-legitimation, and to worry about what to do and how to do it.

The rule of taste

The rule of taste

Taste is never an easy topic. In the early C18th it became bound to the notion of a *senus communis* (a sense of the community and an implicitly ethical relationship between people) and a person's sensibility with regard to its imperatives as if this were a sixth sense: one was simply meant to know what was right, proper, correct, tactful and appropriate. Such a sensibility was, of course, to be cultivated and carefully exercised in order that what was tactful, true, well-proportioned and thus beautiful could behaviourally result from such a frame of mind. As the philosophical Earl of Shaftesbury famously put it in 1709: *"the most natural Beauty in the World is Honesty, and moral Truth. For all Beauty is Truth. True Features make the Beauty of a face; and true Proportions the Beauty of Architecture; as true measures that of Harmony and Musick."* Taste was the proper mode of attunement to the dynamics of such a beauty. Taste was the clue to a correct mediation between Natural or Positive (i.e. lawful) causes of beauty and the Arbitrary, Customary (or creaturely and appetitive) ones. Taste would ensure 'good' form in all matters of creative work and public action. Such forms were appreciated in both their mundane aspect as simple appearance and propriety, as well as in a hermeneutic manner similar to the appreciation that Classical rhetoric was as much concerned with saying the right thing as with saying it well. Taste, in other words, was a rather serious matter in the eighteenth century.

What Shaftesbury and others maintained was, in essence, hardly new. But such an understanding became a fundamental feature of an epoch governed by what has been referred to as 'the Rule of Taste': a rule with roots in antiquity and now a dominant concept in England between the time of the Restoration of the Monarchy of Charles II (in 1661) and the Reform Bill of 1832, just prior to the reign of Victoria. As John Steegman phrased it: *"The governing class was small and closely preserved against intrusion from below, an oligarchy concentrating wealth and power together within its own circle and, though very conscious of the advantages to itself, conscious also of the responsibility such a system implied; they saw themselves as a class, independent both of the multitude and the Crown who, by reason of their birth, possessions, traditions and education were alone fitted to rule and in whose hands lay the remaking of England through the training and control of public opinion, without consulting or even pretending to consult the ordinary citizen."*

Taste was a bulwark opposed to excess – whether material (e.g., luxury and the pursuit of pleasure for its own sake), religious (e.g., Methodism), or architectural (e.g., the Baroque). Perhaps as never before, mere culture was set in confrontational opposition to that Culture which embodied taste. Those who had taste considered it their duty to exercise it for the well-being of society – membership of which had not yet entirely accommodated itself (as it eventually would) to eligibility founded upon wealth as opposed to property. And it was this wealth – as the new wealth of an expanding trading class at the heart of a burgeoning empire – that engendered a degree of anxiety coursing its way through the concept of taste.

In the eighteenth century taste came to bear within it the notion that you only really possessed it when born to it – everyone else was a pretender. On the other hand taste, by means of its expression, soon became the medium through which people sought to reinvent and reposition themselves in society, especially within the Empire.

Taste – what was to be cultivated and yet was intrinsically unteachable and dependent upon exposure to its rules – has always, in any era, been a situated capacity to judge and effect principle in particular circumstances and is, of course, fundamental to addressing the generality of issues that arise and take a simple form: *'what ought I to do and how ought I to do it?'* Taste addresses these questions in a spontaneous manner of knowing how one should behave toward others. As a mode of knowing-in-action (as some modern educationalists might refer to it) taste makes a claim to validity rooted in decisiveness and certainty, but not on the basis of reason. It can even like what its judgment rejects. Its opposite is not 'bad' taste but *no* taste.

In terms of its active nature, taste was (and remains), as Georg Gadamer has pointed out (in *Truth or Method*), not the ground of moral judgement, but — as productive supplementation – its supreme consumption. It is an active, situated and politic capacity to judge aright in particular circumstances, and in a manner that supplements law, principle and rule, thereby making reference to a larger societal whole. Properly, it is, in other words, a kind of innate *intelligence* that is considered to naturally penetrate to the root of what is at issue and, for that very reason, is very relevant to arche-tectonics. Certainly, taste is more than some fashionable quality that, by definition, enjoys a freedom to be equally this way or that – especially that much derided 'bourgeois taste' serving fashion's dumb corollary, but with pretensions to be otherwise.

Shaftesbury's notion of taste, (as an essential ingredient of 'a moral sense'), had within it a crucial ingredient of being intelligent and open-minded – what the French philosopher Henri Bergson was later to refer to as *le bon sens*: an open-minded *"intelligence which at each moment wins itself back to itself, eliminating ideas already formed to give place to those in the process of being formed."* Outside of the English context of class, German philosophy of the C19th understood the concept as *Bildung* – what emphasised the educated cultivation of an organically innate capacity within any individual's nature. Its contrast is a rigid and blinkered taste that is merely a habituated state of mind rather than a navigational aid to life. And when taste seeks to impose itself as rule – in the sense of imposition and a notion of correctness – that is exactly what it is in danger of becoming: paradoxically, the opposite of what is intended. Ironically, being 'taste-full' is, in itself, tasteless.

As 'moral sense theory' the notion of taste has quite reasonably, but rather unkindly, been derided as the notion that one could distinguish between right and wrong as easily as knowing someone is standing on one's foot. That is the implication of what Shaftesbury opined. But it was not what he intended. His reference was certainly not to taste in the sense of what is merely agreeable (a point that was to be of significant import in Kant's philosophical understanding of beauty), but to

Above: Hogarth's satire on taste in The Rake's Progress (1735). The prodigal young man spends his inherited wealth on a variety of matters that he hopes will exhibit good taste and adopted civility.

a 'Rule of Taste' exercised in a manner that no longer made explicit reference to principle and guideline, but to a vital (almost organic) notion of rule and correctness.

In the first few decades of the eighteenth century this conception of taste found its architectural expression in a rejection of the architecture of Wren, Hawksmoor, Vanbrugh, and Archer – which appeared to formulate an aggressive compound of parts that found difficult integration as a whole – replacing this by an approach that did the opposite: starting with a more subdued whole and, from it, deriving the accommodated parts.

Taste found its hero in Palladio rather than the Roman Baroque fashions that followed him, and in Jones – now reinvented as someone wholly English that the enthusiasts of the Baroque had misunderstood. In that period when an ageing Wren's influence was waning, together with the great man's life energies (in 1712 Shaftesbury refers to impatience with his long influence), and the Baroque of Vanbrugh and Hawksmoor was similarly losing its appeal, there stepped forward a notable aristocratic figure to lend architecture a new direction: Richard Boyle, the third earl Burlington. His neo-Palladian tastes – a formal proclivity notionally referenced back to a canon of practices and ideas gathered around the figure of Palladio – became the proper appearance of propriety, decorum and tact in a cultured society. And a well-ordered architecture was a natural bearer of such taste.

To discuss, as Rudolf Wittkower does, neo-Palladianism and similar Italian influences upon English architecture in terms of the nuances of rustication, 'Venetian' windows and quoins is to make no essential differentiation between that 'movement' and the generality of concerns common to Wren and Hawksmoor – except, perhaps, to draw our attentions to a different context in which available literary references and the establishment of the Grand Tour had made a considerable difference to the conditions of practice between the times of Jones and of Burlington. However, that crucial difference was the contextural dominance exercised by the Rule of Taste, as well as the rise of the so-called 'amateur architect'.

Of course, even within neo-Palladian taste, good design has, as its implicit basis, intelligence as well as formal preferences. But, within a cosseted neo-Palladian framework, it is now less readily observable – not because it is absent, but because it is now backgrounded. Vitruvian references to intent and the expression of that intent now *presumed*, as it were, an embodiment of the former and lent significance to forms of the latter. In fact, one might argue that the Rule of Taste saw no differentiation to be made – as if, absurdly, one might differentiate between lightning and its thunder.

For a brief period (it is always brief), men like Richard Boyle were at the heart of a confident culture that thought it knew what all this meant. Here was architecture as it was intended to be: a metaphor of harmoniously organised inter-relationships between parts that is implicitly on-target, that embodies – in the instance of a specific building and its formulation of commodiousness, firmness and delight – civility and a reassuring control that is at once responsive and anticipatory. Time, mutability and anxiety are, for a frozen moment, abolished. It is no wonder that the period stands as a benchmark of architectural achievement. We still live with memory of Taste's rule and of a kind of architecture that obstinately stands as a benchmark of what architecture reassuringly aspires toward.

To contrive a legitimate and convincing alternative became a keynote of the nineteenth century that continues, to this day, to engender an anxiety at the heart of an architect's pretences. And the neo-Palladianism of the eighteenth century continues to enjoy a strange, residual attraction whose informing certainties recurringly surface to disturb the contrasting formalities of the Modernist stance. Those former certainties haunt an era of architecture that has sawn off the neo-Platonic branch upon which it once comfortably sat. However, the core, underlying issue to Shaftesbury's concerns (to know what to do and to know how to do it, a capacity to formulate intent and its expression) remain the principal aspects of an art that neatly compounds twinned concepts: that of *arche* – an issue of situational origins accessible only to a perspicacious intelligence – and of tectonics – a tangible and composed putting together that must bear within itself its own, equally peculiar, 'charge'.

Inevitably, 'Rule', as an architectural canon, was to break down: its erosion manifest as a turning toward the picturesque and the sublime in a context of radical social, political and cultural change that included those archaeological researches acknowledging both science and art, and questioning a former authority given to the practices of the Ancients. As Georg Gadamer put it, a classical tradition of truth in the humanities was set against another modelled on scientific method. And architects came to know and address this as an instrumental rationale supplemented by a mode of artfulness that intrinsically knows of no reason for its being – its pointlessness is its point. Taste married to knowledge was to constitute the new rule. By the time of Soane and Nash, the era of the amateur-gentleman architect was drawing to its close and a nascent professional ideal was already being formulated and made manifest. By the time Victoria was on the throne (in 1836) society was a long way from Shaftesbury's neo-Platonic world and the idea of taste as the expression of a moral sense serving as the vehicle for addressing profoundly civic issues.

Ironically, taste has nowadays become a concept we find distasteful. It is considered to threaten a valued but enigmatic content of aesthetic awareness and art fulness even as it constrains a notional freedom to be this or that, especially to 'be oneself' as an ostensibly free-willed, unique person (or architect). Gilbert and George once quipped that they had no taste: they were artists. Taste has now become, in itself, inappropriate to a well-formed and independent mind – a conception that is perhaps the opposite of what Shaftesbury intended. However, in enjoying such an ostensible freedom, perhaps morality merely returns itself to taste in the guise of inclination – now without any context of cosmological, religious or political certainties, and often dismissive of such concerns.

a gentleman of taste

Richard Boyle, third Earl Burlington, 1694–1753

Burlington's extant London work include:
• **College residence**, Westminster School, Little Dean's Yard, 1722-30.
• **Chiswick House**, 1723-29 Chiswick.
• **Burlington House**
The house remains as the core of the Royal Academy, overlaid and supplemented by later Victorian work, and by the work of Norman Foster's office.

been replaced by the rectilinear, Late Victorian exercise of Barry & Banks). But Gibb's work was not to the taste of Campbell or, later, of William Kent – a man Boyle met with in Rome as someone enjoying a long stay in Italy and training to be a painter.

It was Kent that referred to that "Dam'd Gusto [that is, taste for the baroque] that has been [in England] for this sixty years past." Kent, or 'il Kentino' as he was sometimes known was brought back from Italy on Boyle's second tour, setting up with the other artist residents of Burlington House – which now had the reputation of being the most gay, artistic and fashionable house in town (Handel was already living there and, just as Kent was brought back as a rival to Campbell, a number of musicians were brought back to be set up alongside Handel). He had been born William Cant, son of an affluent Yorkshire joiner, who started an apprenticeship, broke it and came to enjoy local patronage before being funded on his own journey to Italy in 1709, where he stayed until returning with Boyle in 1719 (with whom he continued to stay until his death, thirty years later; he was then buried in the Boyle family vault, at Chiswick).

Wittkower is worth quoting at length on this couple: *The friendship which developed between the two unequal partners was an attraction of opposites. It was not only the difference of high and low birth, of careful education in one and a happy state of illiteracy in the other, but above all, a contrast of characters and talents. Burlington was a man of rigid principles, determined to follow a chosen path without compromise to the point of stubbornness – Pope called him a 'Positive man'; he was reserved, and unsparing of words and unbending even under his greatest trials. Kent was an artistic personality through and through. A man of happy temperament, often impulsive and capricious, warmhearted and impressionable, of frank but tactful bearing, fond of good things and good society. He was always full of ideas , always ready to work, but principles never swayed his easy amiability.*

And another historian, John Harris comments: *"The impulsive Kent was a perfect foil to the austere lord, who was a rigid theorist and learned scholar, the affection of each man for the other being based on the attraction of opposites. Kent's mistress, the fat Drury Lane actress Elizabeth Butler, and their two children, to whom he bequeathed his moneys, is not proof that Kent was only heterosexual. An agreeable companion to Lady Burlington when her lord was on his travels, he became her drawing master, inundating her with news from town when she was away in the country."*

Boyle, the third Earl Burlington, was born at Burlington House, in 1694, and succeeded his father in 1704. He enjoyed all kinds of privileges and high-status positions and spent his time between three houses and estates: in London, at Burlington House; at Chiswick; and at Londesborough, in Yorkshire. Two of these became the sites of notable works of London architecture.

Boyle – whom the historian Joseph Rykwert describes as supercilious, remote, and ambitious – steps forward in the first decades of the C18th as a passionate amateur architect – a man Horace Walpole called 'the Apollo of the arts' and someone determined to bring about what Lord Shaftesbury had called for: a national taste and national style nevertheless rooted in models to be found in Rome. In 1714 he set off on his Grand Tour to Italy, returning a year later, only to again set out on a return in 1719, this time resolved to learn more about Palladio at first-hand.

What had happened in the intervening period was a rise to ascendency of the liberal Whigs, after years of Tory rule, and the publication of Colen Campbell's *Vitruvius Britannicus*, in 1715. Boyle met with the author, a passion was awakened and Campbell became Boyle's mentor in all things architectural. In turn, Campbell set about addressing a variety of matters concerning Boyle's estates, e.g. modernising Burlington House, laying out the property to the north, and surveying the gardens at Chiswick. It was also at this time that James Gibbs provided Burlington House with a pair of sweeping wings – creating a forecourt that, in essence, still exists (those wings have since

Kent (*Il signor*) had returned to England as a talented painter and designer who then turned to architectural decoration and then to architecture itself. The architectural climate he stepped into had, as its context, a nationalistic note that had begun to sweep Europe and to become associated with a turning away from assertively Baroque and Mannerist tastes. However, while the Rococo emerged on the Continent, England invented neo-Palladianism: an orientation away from Wren et al to his predecessor Inigo Jones (and, in turn, Jones' references to Vitruvius). It was in such a climate that Burlington set about to foster a renaissance in painting, sculpture, music and architecture.

Between 1715 and 1724 Burlington set up the models upon which the whole of Palladianism in England was to depend. The energies of time, place and circumstance whirled around old Burlington House and Boyle set about creating his first architectural work: a bath-house pavilion in the garden at Chiswick (1717). Meanwhile, Campbell replaced Gibbs and modernised Burlington House into an exemplar of Palladianism (the façade work is still there, still visible, on the frontage and within the light wells to either side of the main stair, though overlaid by Victorian work and that of architects such as Norman Shaw and Norman Foster).

Kent was put to work painting ceilings at the house (also still extant) and was busy on all kinds of interior decorative work and on gardens for much of his career. Around 1725 he and Campbell worked with Burlington on designs for a new villa at Chiswick – another based on the Villa Rotonda – a set of state rooms linked to the family house. (The associated buildings have now gone.) In 1734 he was helping Kent design Holkham Hall in Norfolk but, following political disputes (and not long after his design of the York Assembly Rooms, of 1732), Burlington had already withdrawn from public life, closing Burlington House (but leaving his protégés there) and moving to Chiswick.

In the background to Burlington's endeavours was a mass of new publications aimed at amateurs and artisans – all of them seeking to promote rule and sound taste. By the middle of the century, however, there was a noticeable change: rule was being replaced by sensibility of the kind one sees in the rivalry between Chambers and Adam in a period when England became notable for country villas rather than the likes of Vanbrugh and Hawksmoor's efforts at Castle Howard, Blenheim and Seaton Delaval. And this new concern for sensibility often carried with it a personal note as well as a nationalistic one. Chambers own work, *Treatise on Civil Architecture*, of 1759, is described by Wittkower as *"elegant, eclectic, critical, encyclopaedic and, despite his strong classical bias, open to the voice of irrationalism"*. And Samuel Ware's *Complete Body of Architecture*, of 1756, was critical of Palladio and introduced the idea of a national English style now independent of Italian models; and Robert and John Adam's *Works in Architecture*, of 1773, was

Above: Burlington House as it is now and as remodelled, in the neo-Palladian manner, by Boyle.
Below: plan of Burlington House as illustrated in Campbell's Vitruvius Britannicus. The curved wings forming the courtyard are by Gibbs. These were later replaced by the current arrangement by Barry and Banks, now forming the courtyard entrance area to the Royal Academy.

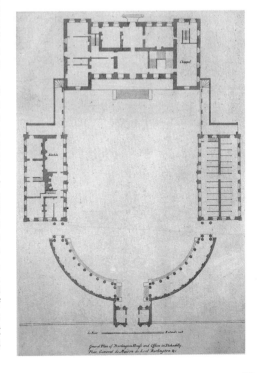

outspokenly personal and self-promotional.

These publications were associated with another change: a lessening of the traditional hierarchy in architecture from great significance to comparative insignificance, i.e. an acceptance that ordinary houses – even labourer's cottages – could be the legitimate subject of architectural design (as we see in John Wood the Younger's *Series of Plans for Cottages or Habitations of the Labourer*, of 1781). Under French influence that spread to England, the Vitruvian canon was also loosened: Gibbs offered simple arithmetic measures for the orders instead of the tradition of modules based on the diameter of the column, following Perrault, who had also simplified the orders in a publication of 1683.

In addition, a novel eclectic freedom began to arise within the framework of the Rule of Taste: Chambers was an example in his promotion of the Chinese style (*Designs of Chinese Buildings*, of 1757) for gardens and follies (e.g. his Pagoda at Kew Gardens). The 1740's and '50's are also give witness a celebration of neo-Gothic as well as Chinese motifs (e.g. Batty Langley's *Gothic Architecture Improved by Rules and Proportions*, 1742).

In the background to all this was Burlington's influence (especially designs such as the York Assembly Rooms, of 1732, a design referred back to Palladio and from him to the Egyptians).

Two years before his death, in 1753, Burlington was celebrated by an influential Continental writer at the Prussian Court of Frederick the Great as "*the restorer of true architecture*" and his influence was to continue for many years.

Chiswick Villa, 1726-29

There are all kinds of stories about Chiswick House, the home of Lord Burlington in London's western suburbs (then the countryside). What was it for? How did he use it? Among the more strange is that is an elaborate Freemason's temple. And yet one only has to approach the house – possibly astounded by the impression it gives of being five-eighths full size – and to then enter its interior in order to be immediately impressed by it's profound mix of high aspiration, considered domesticity and a strange privateness. Regardless of Freemasonry symbolism and an expected neo-Platonic content, this is self-evidently a gentleman's architectural hideaway: Burlington's country den, a place of intimacy, whether for himself or for entertaining friends and guests. Here the man could relish his enjoyment of architecture and the other arts it could house. Here was a garden pavilion, set apart — but, importantly, linked to — the old court-yarded house that his grandfather had purchased in 1682 (demolished in the 1920s, thus reinforcing the distorted perception some people have of Chiswick). It's all rather obvious when one looks toward the architecture itself and adds the link and missing old house to the plans that often exclude these necessary parts of the overall equation.

Even when just completed, the house aroused confused criticism. One commentator suggested it was "*more curious than convenient.*" Another revealingly remarked that it was too small to live in and too large to hang on a watch chain; and a third dismissed it as a "*small cupboard stuck with pictures.*" All missed the compound of architectural gamesmanship and deeply personal inhabitation which few other houses come near to (one thinks of the otherwise contrasting Soane Museum as a similar example). Certainly there is a degree of mystery – manifest, for example in the tiny room that sits above the elaborate 'Blue Velvet Room', accessed by a tiny spiral stair, the 'deepest' room in the house, and provided with a tiny window that looks down onto the (similarly idiosyncratic) entry area within the portico. But this, surely, merely underscores the point being made. Yes, it is, as it has been called, 'a temple of the arts', but such a description emphasises the wrong point: here one meets with the man himself.

Wittkower was in no doubt that Burlington was the sole author of the design, without significant assistance from Kent, although he employed an illiterate daughtsman called Samuel Savill and used Henry Flitcroft as a senior draughtsman on the project (apparently even most of the extensive garden features – which were then a part of the definition of 'villa' – were there before Kent made contributions). He describes the self-given brief as a garden pavilion attached to the main house, where 'ordinary' life continued. Thus, although the new 'villa' stands alone, as it were, it was designed to have a linking wing to the old house, i.e. it was conceived as one part of an architectural ensemble (or, perhaps, one should say 'habitational construct').

Above: *the front entrance (south east façade). Note (apart from the very elaborate and Baroque double stairs) the scale hinted at by the visitors at the entrance, then imaginatively remove them.*

This must have been especially true after 1733 when Burlington abruptly withdrew from politics and moved all his paintings, books, etc. to Chiswick, where he and his wife lived until their deaths.

Although the house is vigorously symmetrical in plan, this does not seem to apply to its usage. In fact, the plan divides between one side that is more private (and includes a bedchamber and the 'Green Velvet Room' that served as an antechamber), and an opposite wing that appears to be more public (for receptions, etc.). The latter is possibly, Burlington's own wing (it here that we have the ornate Blue Velvet Room that leads to the upper chamber). But whatever the scholarly truth of such matters they are secondary to the reality that this is, in fact, a commodious and considered plan that exhibits a real individuality and authentic architectural gamesmanship. It is the small moves that give this away: the link to the main house; the projecting side walls that create subsidiary external spaces; the chimneys; the manner in which the central part of a Venetian window is able to turn itself into a door; the strange entrance corridor from the portico; the ease of circulation that perhaps suggests one person rattling about. There is an artfulness and profound intimacy about the place that imbues such engaging architectural moves.

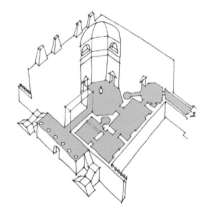

Above: *schematically, the house (rather like Stirling's Clore Gallery at Tate Britain) as a pavilion linked to an older building whose presence it almost denies. It is strongly presentational, and yet the entrance portico is almost as deceptive as Jones' east frontage to St Paul's, Covent Garden. One feels this is an architecture that turns in on itself whilst pretending to do the opposite, to secretly accept a linkage to the old house and indulge itself in the enjoyments of an enfilade of rooms set around the central hall. In other words, it hints at being very personal: a den at the bottom of the garden, now inflated into architectural grandeur.*

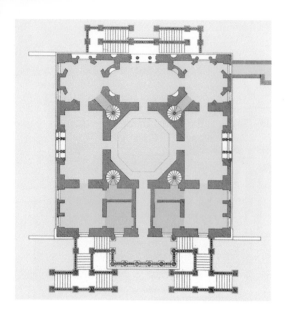

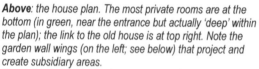

Above: the house plan. The most private rooms are at the bottom (in green, near the entrance but actually 'deep' within the plan); the link to the old house is at top right. Note the garden wall wings (on the left; see below) that project and create subsidiary areas.
Top right: the unusual entrance passage from the portico, as if a denial of that feature's actual role and significance.
Upper right: south west garden side. Note the projecting walls and chimneys.
Right: view to the link building on the garden (north west) side. (The original Jacobean house was demolished in 1788. Additions to the villa were made, in turn demolished, in 1956-7, when the dilapidated villa was restored.)
Bottom left: one of the smaller rooms (top right in the plan).
Bottom right: the octagonal central hall that serves as the heart of the work.

Colen Campbell
1676–1729

Extant London works include:
• **76 Brook Street**, 1725-26
Campbell's own home.

Campbell was born as son of a Scottish laird and possibly attended Edinburgh University, training as a lawyer before reinventing himself as an architect (possibly under James Smith, 1645-1731, one of Scotland's principal architects). He was already building by 1712 – the same year he designed a house outside London (Wanstead, now demolished). It was also in 1712 that Campbell designed a house in Essex called Wanstead, setting a new standard in classical design without the extravagances of Hawksmoor and Vanbrugh (since demolished). And it was around now that he was approached by a publisher to put his name to a work called *Vitruvius Britannicus* – a work on current British architecture, providing an introduction extolling Palladio and Jones, contributing to the selections and adding his own works (1715). The book was immediately successful and became quite influential (there was a second volume in 1717 and a third in 1725). In 1719 he was appointed as Architect to the Prince of Wales and met Lord Burlington, whom he encouraged to make another visit to Italy and for whom he undertook some remodelling at Burlington House. Upon Wren's death (in 1726), and midst some intrigue, Campbell became the surveyor at Greenwich, under the man who briefly replaced Wren, William Benson (1682-1754; later dismissed for ineptitude; Campbell had illustrated one of his designs in the *Britannicus*). Between 1720-25 Campbell designed and built Mereworth in Kent – a work referencing the Villa Rotonda and preceding Burlington's similar work at Chiswick. His reputation soon faded after his death in 1729, but he was buried at Westminster Abbey. Outside London Campbell worked with Burlington on Holkham Hall, a design exhibiting some of that very 'damn'd gusto' Burlington et al had criticised (compare with Kent's work at Horse Guards).

William Kent 1686–1748

Extant London works include:
• **44 Berkley Square** 1742-44.
• **22 Arlington Street**, 1741-50
• **Horse Guards**, 1751-3 (Kent's design, 1748, completed by John Vardy 1750-59; *see photo below*), including the **Old Treasury** building, 1733-37).
• Miscellaneous: the **Royal Barge** (at the National Maritime Museum, Greenwich, 1732); **Gothic gateway** in the Clock Court at Hampton Court, 1732.

a wild goth …

Kent was born in Bridlington, Yorkshire, son of a joiner. As a young man, he was able to find local patrons who recommended him to London people. Then, aged twenty five, he set out to Italy with John Talman (son of the architect William Talman) and Daniel Lock (probably on the basis of purchasing paintings for his patrons). They went to Florence and then walked to Rome via Sienna, where Kent started to learn to paint and socially establish himself with the English noblemen there. (The historian Joseph Rykwert describes Kent as

ingratiating, self-indulgent and unprincipled.) In 1713 his painting managed to win him the prize of a silver medal at the Accademia si San Luca (awarded by the Pope – something that was trumpeted in England). It was around now that he met with Burlington and also began to acquaint himself with architecture. The two set upon a strong friendship: the impulsive Kent and the austere, scholarly Burlington. Kent recollected a stay with Burlington in Genoa and how *"his lordship 'lik'd my designs so well both painting & Archetecture that he would make me promis at least to begin to paint for him the fierst when I come over."*

By 1720 Kent was established back in England and living in Burlington's house after some ten years in Italy. In this new, convivial household (which he was quickly calling 'our house') Kent was referred to as 'il Kentino', or 'the Little Rogue Kent', or 'the Honest Signior'. There now began a career as painter – for example, replacing Sir James Thornhill as painter at Kensington Palace, thus arousing the life-long enmity of Thornhill's son-in-law, William Hogarth, and later being appointed as Surveyor or Inspector of Paintings for the royal palaces – then as interior designer and furniture designer, and finally as an architect proper (as well as a garden designer, in which role Walpole noted that he *"leaped the fence, and saw that all Nature was a garden"*).

Kent's architectural status was achieved by 1730, no doubt in close collaboration with Burlington and his own endeavours to establish himself as a Palladian architect. (Holkham Hall, Norfolk, came in 1733.) But it had already begun in earnest when, in 1726, Burlington managed to establish Kent on the Board of Works as Master Mason (the basis of the Horse Guards building work). As a painter he appears to have been less than excellent. However, in correspondence between Kent, Burlington and Pope, we have the following comments: Kent to Burlington, 1738: *"[Pope is] … the greatest glutton I know … [he] told me of a soupe that must be seven hours a making"*; Pope to Burlington: *"[Come] and eat a mutton stake in the manner of that great Master, Signior Kent"*; Pope to Burlington, 1740: *"If he [Kent] proceeds in his carnality & carnivoracity, he must expect not to imitate Raphael in anything but his untimely end"*; and Pope to Burlington, 1734: *"[Kent is] a wild Goth … from a Country which has ever been held no part of christendome."* Kent was buried by Burlington in the family vault at Chiswick. He was unmarried, but kept a mistress at Covent Garden.

Sir Robert Taylor
1714–88

Extant London work include:
- **Asgill House**, 1760-65. Old Palace Lane, Richmond.
- **33 Upper Brook Street**, 1767-68.
- **Danson House,** 1766. Danson Park, Bexleyheath, Kent (An English Heritage property).
- **Ely House**, 1772. 37 Dover Street, Mayfair.
- **Stone Buildings**, 1774-80. In the collegiate Lincoln's Inn, east side of the Lincoln's Inn Square. (*See photo below.*)
- The **Lord Mayor's ceremonial coach**, 1758.

In 1750, there were two key figures dividing up London commissions: James Paine and Robert Taylor. Burlington, Cambell, Kent, and Leoni were dead or not practising; Adam and Chambers had yet to arrive on the scene. Taylor was the son of an Essex master mason who, at fourteen, was apprenticed to a sculptor. After the latter's completion, his father paid for what is described as a 'frugal' tour to Rome. He returned on news of his father's death to find the man had been bankrupt and there began a strenuous regime. His pupil George Byfield reported that *"Sir Robert Taylor had three rules for growing rich: rising early, keeping appointments and regular accounts"*; and Walpole commented that *"he never slept after four in the morning"*. But it seems he had friends, including a wealthy man who was one of the founders of the Bank of England. In 1744, as an unknown, Taylor was the sculptor for the reliefs to the pediment of the Mansion House (at Bank). By 1745 he seems to have been affluent enough to build himself a house and had started to practise as an architect, with commissions from the newly wealthy, principally bankers and directors of the East India Company, West Indian merchants and traders, lawyers and judges, and also soldiers and sailors who became wealthy through their exploits. He was involved in a dozen public buildings, possibly more than fifty country houses, and a large number of town houses (often speculative) in addition to groups or terraces of urban building. The high point of his career was work at the Bank of England (destroyed in Soane's work). Notably, he was the first architect to take pupils, as opposed to apprentices and Nash worked for him for eleven years.

George Dance, the Elder 1694–1768

George Dance, the Younger
1741–1825

The careers of Dance, father and son, cross that bridge between mechanical and speculative masonry, both becoming involved in Freemasonry. Dance the Elder was born as the son of Giles Dance, a City stonemason. As son of a freeman, George did not have to undergo an apprenticeship before being able to work in the City and he was admitted to the Merchant Taylor's Guild in 1725. Father and son worked closely together and were noted as Freemason's meeting at the Bell tavern in Nicholas Lane, where the former was master of the lodge. Together with his father, Dance was a part of a consortium of masons who constructed St Botolph, Bishopsgate (1725-8), to the design of his father-in-law, James Gould (surveyor to the South Sea Company).

Growing up when St Paul's was being completed together with other City churches, Dance the Elder was inevitably influenced by such work. His own parish church of St Luke's was designed by Hawksmoor and James, and completed between 1727-33 (where he is noted as having worked as a mason). This became important when, in 1735, he was appointed as Clerk of the City Works (an office purchased for £150, providing a virtual monopoly over architectural work in the City).

He appears to have done well and his son, Dance the Younger, was nominated to succeed his father in 1768. The Elder's most important commission was the Mansion House that now sits at Bank. Dance's other works were mainly in the City, and included: St Botolph's, Aldgate (1741-4); St Matthew's, Bethnal Green (1743-6); the nave of St Mary's, Faversham, Kent (1754-5); St Luke's Hospital, Old Street (1750-51);

Above: *Dance the Younger.*
Below: *the Mansion House portico, at Bank.*

and the corn market, Mark Lane (1747-50).

Dance the Younger was educated at St Paul's school in the City and, in 1758 was sent to study architecture in Rome. Here, he did well: as a pupil of Nicolo Giansimone Dance won the Gold Medal of the Accademia di Belle Arti, Parma, in 1763 and, in 1764, was admitted to the Accademia di San Luca; he was also elected a member of the Accademia dell'Arcadia, a select gathering of Roman literati. He returned to London in 1765 and before long won a commission to redesign All Hallows, London Wall. In 1768 he succeeded his father as Clerk to the City. At that time he became a founding member of the Royal Academy (together with his brother, the painter Nathanial Dance). It was also at this time that the young John Soane came into the office and even lived in Dance's home for some time. (Dance's father-in-law was a wealthy City merchant; he had done what many architects aspire to: to marry right and thus ensure success.)

Dance's other architectural works included the Piranesi-

Extant London work of Dance the elder includes:
• **Mansion House**, 1739-52. Changes to the Egyptian Hall were by Dance's son, 1795-96.
• **St Botolph-without-Aldgate**, 1741-44.
• **St Matthew**, Bethnal Green 1740-46.

Extant London work of Dance the younger includes:
• **All Hallows** 1765-7, London Wall. Dance the Younger's first building, at 24, replacing a medieval church and resting on Roman foundations. was apparently a great inspiration to Soane.
• **The Crescent**, 1765-70. The Minories (north of the Tower of London); a terrace of houses.
• **Guildhall** frontage 1788-89. Actually Indian Raj, and not neo-Gothic. (*See photo overleaf.*)
• **St Bartholomew-the-Less** church, Smithfield, 1789-90; in timber and rebuilt in stone to the original plan by Thomas Hardwick, 1823-5. (At the entrance to the hospital.)

inspired Newgate Prison (demolished; Dance had met Piranesi in Rome) and a frontage to the Guildhall in a mix of Gothic and 'Hindoo' idioms (1788-9). Among his urban planning work, Finsbury Circus remains; and there is also St George's Circus, with its obelisk, in Southwark.

There were many other grand urban projects, but none were realised. However, together with Robert Taylor, Dance was one of the architects of the 1774 landmark London Building Act which set the standard for later Georgian domestic architecture: houses divided into categories or 'rates', according to size, with regulations governing the width of walls, building heights, and elevational treatment. His designs for standard terrace house elevations, with blind arches of brick surrounding the first-floor windows, were built in their hundreds and became the norm for late Georgian London.

Bowdler tells us that Dance *"challenged the architectural orthodoxies of his day, and developed a singular approach to design, in which meaning and symbolism interacted with form, space, and precedent."* And, certainly, he had an interest in education, being appointed professor of architecture at the Royal Academy in 1798. Strangely, he failed to deliver any lectures and resigned the post in 1806, being replaced by John Soane, who took his duties far more seriously.

A mild stroke in 1815 ended his career but he was, in any case, now more interested in art and music than architecture (Haydn was apparently a close friend).

Above: Dance the Younger's frontage to the Guildhall forecourt (a unique, hard-paved London space that has the Roman amphitheatre outlined in its paving): all exotic 'Hindoo' rather than neo-Gothic.
Below: Dance the Elder's more orthodox exercise of St Botolph, on the eastern edge of the City (now rather isolated by highway engineers).

Andrea Palladio
1500-1580.

Palladio – whose work was a significant influence in Britain through the figures of architects such as Inigo Jones and Lord Burlington – was a celebrated Venetian architect representing a high point of achievement in an era (the Italian Renaissance) which, in turn, impressed itself as a benchmark of achievement upon the whole of Europe: Italy was again its acknowledged cultural home. His work was to be found in Venice itself and in the adjacent Veneto region of this once rich and powerful state. And it must have been a natural starting point for those travellers who, like Jones, Kent, Boyle and others had brought themselves on an arduous journey to northern Italy on their way south to the inspirational focal-point of the period: Rome itself.

The classical revival of Palladio's lifetime was, of course, more than the stylistic revivals of which we are familiar. Set against a now Christian background, it was a return to expressed standards of a civilisation whose physical remains lay scattered all over Italy and marked a hardly fractured tradition of continuity: here was manifest evidence of a benchmark of both civic and religious architecture that the Middle Ages of Northern Europe could only counter by the example of their cathedrals. Furthermore, the Roman employment of a complex and symbolic architectural language relating a unified whole to any of its particular parts proved to be thoroughly in accord with the intrinsically architectonic philosophical beliefs of an age that, in terms of its neo-Platonic worldview, construed Creation in terms of Euclidean geometry, Pythagorean musical ratios, number symbolism and a belief that beyond sensuous appearances was another reality (the Platonic Ideas) whose orderly dynamic constituted a 'music of the spheres' – a reality only cognisable by the eye of the mind rather than the body. The Gothic adhered to similar values, but Classicism appeared to give a more relevant and vital kind of legitimacy to architectural endeavours.

Palladio was born Andrea di Pietro della Gondola, in Padova, and was apprenticed as a stonecutter at 13. However, he broke his contract after a mere 18 months and fled to the nearby town of Vicenza where he became assistant in the workshop of notable stonecutters and masons. Here, his talents were recognised by Count Gian Giorgio Trissino, who also gave him the name Palladio, an allusion to the Greek goddess of wisdom Pallas Athene. In 1541 he moved to Rome to study classic architecture. Soon, he was practising as an architect and winning notable commissions and was significant among Italian architects proving that the classical language of architecture could be successfully adapted to the contemporary needs of civic society

Above: the figure of Palladio at Lord Burlington's Chiswick Villa.

and its modes of religion. Palaces, theatres, churches, and even the farm villa, now enjoyed a dignified unity of expression – and could enjoy publication as works of art equal to flourishing others such as sculpture and painting. His work exhibited a wit and inventiveness that was quite extraordinary and, in 1570, he published his works in a book that was to remain influential for some two hundred years or more – particularly in England, where the likes of Inigo Jones and the so-called neo-Palladians of the eighteenth century viewed his achievements as a comprehensive fulfilment of Vitruvian values.

But the context was all-important: the man and his works served as a reference point and benchmark of achievement thoroughly suited to the needs of English society during a period elevating notions of taste and order to the status of stabilising socio-political consideration. And yet, ironically, such classical architecture enjoyed its revival at exactly the time science was developing an alternative mathematical understanding soon to leave world views rooted in revelation and neo-Platonism as thoroughly anachronistic. The subsequent decline of neo-Palladianism was witness to a broad complex of societal changes. Modernism as an era of science, uncertainty, democracy and the instrumental pursuit of quantitative goals by quantitative means not only undermined architectural visions rooted in neo-Platonism, but arguably eroded the foundations of architecture itself, leaving it bereft of those traditional bases formerly sustaining its legitimacy.

competing ambitions:
Chambers and Adam

One wonders what the career of Foster would have been without Rogers; and vice versa. No doubt William Chambers and Robert Adam might have considered a similar question regarding their own, parallel, careers. Just as the post-World War II Grand Tour was to the USA, and both Rogers and Foster undertook travels together, Chambers and Adam were in Rome – the home of European architecture – at about same time on their respective Grand Tours, seeking education in the bench-marks of architectural excellence that might help to establish them as architects in their home country, and also establishing a rivalry that characterised their careers.

While the two Modernists sought to complete their education at Yale, Chambers and Adam undertook something similar in Rome: Adam arriving there in the year that the slightly older Chambers was leaving, in 1755, overlapping by a few months and prompting Adam great concern: *"All the English who have travelled for these five years ... imagine him [Chambers] a prodigy for genius, for sense and good taste ... he is in such great esteem; so intimate and in such friendship with most of the English that have been in Rome that they are determined to support him to the utmost of their power ... it will require very considerable interest to succeed against Chambers who has tolerable Friends & real merit."*

We have no record of what Chambers – the more mature, married, well-travelled, more architecturally educated and slightly older man had to say about Adam. But it is more to the point that both men had embarked upon their education at an auspicious time: what is rather misleadingly called neo-Classicism was in the air – which Summerson characterises with three considerations: an archaeological agenda; a distinctly modernist concern with a manner of architectural expression that was appropriate to its own time; and the mediation of eclectic tastes now more willing to choose between styles and elements. He deals with all three as varieties of romance, but they are also novel orientations toward history as well as a fracturing of the certainty of authority that had characterised the Rule of Taste at a time when enthusiasms and the notion of 'sensibility' was slowly emerging as a substitute for that of standards and rules.

Around the time both Chambers and Adam came to Italy and Rome we are witness to the new concern with antiquity having a distinctly French flavour to its enthusiasms. This, for example, is when the abbé Marc-Antoine Laugier (1713-69) published *Essai sur l'Architecture*, in 1753 – an exercise in rationality oriented toward fundamental issues of construction and the notion of the primitive hut as establishing a formal link between current neo-Classiciam and the beginnings of civilised life. The values expressed here epitomised much of the novelty characterising neo-Classicism: columns were to be free, avoiding the pilaster and never on pedestals; a pediment was always to express a roof behind and never to be broken, etc. The Orders, following Perrault, are approximations; Vitruvius is merely a guide; they are open to modification in accord with basic proportional theory.

In all, Laugier's voice was symptomatic of the degree to which much of Renaissance theory was being discarded. Truth was to be sought in first principles and a sound constructional logic. Eyes now began to wonder away from Italy toward Greek architecture as the precedent informing what the Romans had achieved. As a counterpoint, a key Italian figure within this scenario was Giambattista Piranesi (1720-78) – a remarkable man, the Antonio Sant'Elia of his day, who not only resisted this relative disenchantment with Rome but, in 1750, published the Carceri d'invenzione etchings, after an earlier publication covering Roman buildings in their contemporary, ruined condition (1748). By 1753, he was also publishing archaeological work striving to illustrate the supremacy of Roman architecture. And into this Roman scene of Italian and French debate stepped Chambers and Adam.

Interestingly, both men travelled in Italy as gentlemanly amateur scholars keen to disguise their ambitious intent and vocational commitments. However, Chambers possibly had the advantage: he had already spent a year studying in Paris (possibly with Blondel) and repeatedly returned to Paris during his five year stay in Italy. But it was Adam who was perhaps the more enterprising in the manner he entered upon serious archaeological undertakings which not only served his curiosity, but also his ambitions to return to England as what Summerson describes as *"the unquestioned and supreme authority in the little world of architecture."* Two years after arriving in Rome he set off to record the ruins of the palace of the emperor Diocletian, putting the work into book form on his return to London (in 1758) and publishing it in 1764.

These kinds of researches became fundamental to changes in architectural fashion as well as the parallel rivalries between Chambers and Adam. According to the latter, Chambers belonged to an older school (which included Burlington) that was a 'bastard Renaissance', neither of which was truly classical. In their stead he promoted a shift away from the 'masculine' flavour of work since Inigo Jones toward something distinctly more 'feminine', elegant and less concerned with 'rule': *"Architecture"*, he said, *"has already become elegant and more interesting. The parade, the convenience and social pleasures of life being better understood, are more strictly attended to in the arrangement and disposition of apartments. Greater variety of form, greater beauty in design, greater gaiety and elegance of ornament, are introduced into interior decoration: while the outside composition is more simple, more*

Respective ceiling treatments of Chambers (top), at Somerset House, and (bottom) Adam, at Osterley Park. To Adam, his rival's work was distinctly old-fashioned.

grand, more varied in its contour and imposes on the mind from the superior magnitude and movement of its parts." (From *The Works*, 1778.)

The 'Rule of Taste' was becoming relaxed in the sense that its standards (if not its authority) were being questioned. The new keynote was feminine grace. The corollary was a novel sentimentality manifest in paintings of rustic scenes and, in gardens, the replacement of vistas and prospects by landscapes and views. Ornament now had a new delicacy and less robust, three-dimensional quality. Fashion now deemed what had gone before as rather uncouth; fancy was in the air. (There is 1799 gravestone in Oxfordshire in memory of a woman who apparently died as a Martyr to Excessive Sensibility. As Stegmann notes, no doubt

quantities of other women married to brutal husbands possibly also died of 'excessive sensibility'.)

The Adam's intention (in their own words) was to produce 'movement' in a work which was meant to "*express a rise and fall, the advance and recess with other diversity of form, in the different parts of a building, so adding greatly to the picturesque of the composition.*" Chambers was not impressed by such 'affectations'. He, in turn, argued that he designed more in accord with the Ancients and other critics noted that he avoided the 'sweetness' and 'confectionery' of the Adams. Robert Adam retorted that the works of antiquity referred to were temples; he, alone, made reference to domestic works of that period. He declared: "I am no admirer of Palladio" and considered the latter's works to be ill-adjusted, meagre, and childish. And yet, oddly, he claimed that Vanbrugh understood better than either Inigo Jones or Wren the 'art of living among the Great': "*A commodious arrangement of apartments was therefore his peculiar merit, but his lively imagination scorned the restraint of any rule in composition; and his passion for what was fancifully magnificent prevented him from discovering what was truly simple, elegant and sublime.*" As John Stegmann pointed out, Vanbrugh neither attempted commodiousness, nor can one associate his interest in the sublime with what is 'simple' and 'elegant'. (One particularly sees the influence of Vanbrugh on Adam in the latter's later Scottish castles.)

Nevertheless, the Adam brothers did pursue such simplicity and restraint in their exteriors, unifying these with the interiors by means of similar decorative orders, frequently executed in the increasing viable and fashionable stucco (rather than stone or brick). But this was not always successful. Clients sometimes claimed that the final costs of achieving and maintaining the Adams' stucco details would have perhaps been cheaper in stone. However, to some degree, technology was coming to the rescue, particularly with Coade Stone, new stucco mixes and cast-iron. Products in these materials now found their way into product catalogues, offering novel choices and possible ornamental mixes to clients as well as architects.

Such choice already began to include Chambers' chinoiserie (as at Kew) and Batty Langley's neo-Gothic, but with little fashionable success – and what there was of such fancy merely underscored the authority of neo-Palladian tradition tastes that remained dominant until romanticism became more firmly established in the last years of the century. Still, the Adam brothers represented a dilution of that taste, providing an unorthodox twist to fashions with a content of 'confectionery' that was to give a lasting colouration to our perspective on what is 'Georgian'. A more purely decorative and sensuous detail emphasising line on surface was set as the complement to the architectonic ratios of space whilst eroding Baroque qualities the neo-Palladians had allowed mass to retain. The brick and stone of the latter were now replaced by the painted stucco that was self-evidently a theatrical conceit underscoring sensibilities substituting for the robust and solid strengths preferred by a previous generation. Nevertheless, for some twenty years between 1760 and 1780 Robert Adam was the most fashionable architect in Britain, before being overtaken by James Wyatt, who then banished the Adam success to Scotland, where Robert turned to a picturesque castle style which gave answer to Wyatt's neo-Gothic works.

Much of these changes in fashion were a prelude to the influences of the American and French revolutions, the period of the Regency, and those later changes instituted by the Reform Act of William IV's reign, in 1832. By then the concept of a Rule of Taste was moribund, the notion of a canon of correctness in architecture was merely a ghost haunting the discipline and even Classicism was losing a battle against the neo-Gothic as the high ground of architectural practice.

Chambers' advice to a young architect travelling to Italy: "Always see with your own eyes ... [you] must discover their true beauties, and the secrets by which they are produced". And, "work in the same quarry with M. Angelo, Vignola, Peruzzi and Palladio, use their materials, search for more, and endeavour to unite the grand manner of the two first with the elegance, simplicity, and purity of the last." (Letter given to Edward Stevens, who died in Rome in 1775. The same letter was given by Chambers to John Soane.) Chambers added that it was essential for a student to "make a better use of their time now than they formerly used to do, for unless they study hard and acquire superior talents, they will do little here; this country [is] swarming with artists of all kinds, that unless a man does much better than his neighbours, he will have but an indifferent chance of making his way." (Quoted by Soane's biographer, Gillian Darley.) While in Rome, Chambers himself had made the acquaintance of about a dozen aristocrats, nine of whom later became clients, so he was very aware of how important an industrious Grand Tour was.

mildness and affability

Sir William Chambers 1722–96

Extant London work include:
- **Somerset House**, 1776-1801, Aldwych. Chambers' most accessible work.
- **Pagaoda**, 1758-63, Kew Gardens.
- **Manressa House**, 1760-68, Roehampton Lane. Now a college.
- **Observatory**, 1768-69, Old Deer Park, Richmomd
- **Albany**, 1770-74, Piccadilly.

Chambers wrote of himself: *"I was born in Gothenburg, was educated in England, and returned to Sweden when I was 16 years old. I made three journeys to Bengal and China in the service of the Swedish East India Company."* And made a lot of money in the process.

Chambers was born the son of an English stockbroker and was educated in Ripon, where members of the family were well established. It was on his journeys east that he not only amassed a considerable fortune to add to that inherited (both parents now being dead), but made his acquaintance with architecture: *"I studied modern languages, mathematics and the liberal arts, but chiefly civil architecture."* He returned to Göteborg in October 1742, and left again in April 1743, bound for Canton (Guangzhou). His third voyage began in January 1748 and was again to China, from where he returned in July 1749 for the last time. Merchant adventuring was over; architecture beckoned.

As Swedish architects then tended to do, Chambers immediately set off for Paris. Here, he entered Jacques François Blondel's celebrated École des Beaux Arts in the rue de la Harpe. But before doing so he visited England, where he met his future wife and also made acquaintances that were to serve him well in the future.

At the École, he proved himself to be an exceptional draughtsman and met people who were to be the future leaders of French neo-Classical art and architecture of the 1760s and 1770s. A year after joining the school, he travelled to Rome and thereafter moved between the two cities, being married in Rome. It was also while in Rome that he met Robert Adam.

In 1757, the year Chambers published *Designs for Chinese Buildings* (in Sweden), he was appointed architect to the dowager princess of Wales at Kew (whom he had met in 1749), and architectural tutor to George, Prince of Wales (later George III). However, it is now that he is reported as *"drawing in a poor mean lodging up a long dark stair"*, and the inference can be drawn that his fortune was, by now, rather depleted. The year before, he had made a country house design that was rejected as too French and Chambers immediately set out to study the dominant neo-Palladian fashion that had, by now, been a key feature of the 'Rule of Taste' for some forty years. He was determined, as he wrote, to become *"Adapted to the Customs & Fashions of our Time, to the Climate and Manners of our Country, and to the wants & Feelings of its inhabitants."*

That opinion and its orientation toward all that is customary might well have been applauded by the Parisian architect Claude Perrault, some one hundred years earlier, but it was rather ironic in the context of rivalry with the Adam brothers. However, Chambers was also to wrap these reflections in a nascent professionalism that was then beginning to emerge. He not only called upon architects to be *"well versed in the customs, ceremonies, and modes of life of all men his contemporaries"* (so that he might effectively provide for their requirements), [but also to be] as well as skilled in accountancy, estimating, politics and the like."*

Such pragmatism had another aspect: an awareness that the ambitious architect of the day needed to promote himself through publications. In addition to the work on 'chinoiserie' – *Designs of Chinese Buildings, Furniture, Dresses, Machines and Utensils,* of 1757 – came *Proposals for Publishing by Subscription, Designs of Villas, Temples, Gates, Doors, and Chimney Pieces,* of the same year; an essay *Of the Art of Laying out Gardens,* again in 1757; a *Treatise on Civil Architecture,* 1759; and then a *Dissertation on Oriental Gardening,* of 1772.

When the Prince of Wales ascended to the throne in 1760, Chambers designed the coronation carriage and was appointed architect to the office of Works, but along with the also very fashionable Robert Adam, who was rather kept at arm's length by Chambers influence with the King.

It was this relation with the monarch that also ensured the foundation of the Royal Academy in 1769 – an institution, wrote Chambers, with two principal objects: *"the establishing of a well regulated School or Academy of Design ... and an Annual Exhibition."*

In 1770 Chambers became a Knight of the Order of the Polar Star, a Swedish award that King George allowed to be adopted as equivalent to an English knighthood. However, by 1774 – the year he set out for Paris to refresh his tastes – Chambers confessed that he was *"heartily tired of the profession."* This was just before he began on Somerset House, a work that took all of his time until his death in 1796 (a lengthy period that reminds one of St Paul's and of the more recent British Library project, one that can hardly have brought significant pleasure to Chambers). The project involved the demolition of the Tudor Somerset Palace that had especially fine additions by Inigo Jones and John Webb, and Georgian interiors by Henry Flitcroft (draughtsman to Burlington) and William Kent, but was in a sad state of disrepair. It was considered that everything had to go.

It was reported, that upon Chambers' death, a great procession attended the funeral: *"master workmen belonging to the Board of Works ... attended, unsolicited, to testify their regret for the loss, and their esteem for the memory of a man by whom their claims had ever been examined with attention, and decided with justice, and by whom themselves were always treated with mildness, courtesy, and affability."*

Right: the replica 18th century tall ship, "Götheborg. (Photo by Åke Fredriksson.) The ship ran aground at Göteborg in 1745, fully laden with goods such as tea, porcelain, silk and spices, and had almost reached dock after her third voyage to China, which had lasted a full 30 months. Chambers would have sailed in a ship like this to China.

Somerset House 1776-1801

It is one of the remarkable features of so-called Post-Modernism that it arrived in the U.K. at a time when a younger generation were starting to turn away from the attractions of the USA and back toward architectural works in Europe, particularly Paris, where the *grand projets* were the envy of Europe and the British team of Rogers and Piano were at the heart of it all designing the Pompidou Centre. In this context it is interesting to note that one of London's first and notable *grand projets* was the restoration work at Somerset House – a government building designed by an architect trained in Paris in the French tradition, and of the most significant *grand projet* of his day: Somerset House, intended to unite government offices in one great building and to also include three societies – the Royal Academy of Arts, the Royal Society, and the Society of Antiquaries – as well as provision for the King's Barge master, necessitating a direct link to the River Thames. In addition, the new building had to provide living accommodation for the heads of various departments housed there and also space for cooks, housekeepers, secretaries and many others.

Chamber's strategy was that, regardless of size, each department was to be given a vertical slice of the whole and its own entrance. Each of these slices comprised six storeys: cellar, basement, ground floor, first floor, attic and garret, with the lower two levels being accommodated within a forty foot drop across the site, from the Strand to the river, thus lessening apparent height within the central court.

Chambers solved this design conundrum by treating the offices as a series of grand town houses arranged in a quadrangular layout, extending across the whole site of the old palace and its gardens and out into the Thames. But, like many of London's open spaces, the central court eventually became a car park. By the 1970s, this merely underscored London's comparatively impoverished architectural ambition.

Characteristically, the project ended up costing three times the original estimate. Nevertheless, the design was considered in many ways to be modest. Only on the Strand side where a common vestibule leads into the central court was 'specimens of elegance' attempted. The other relative extravagance was the long winding stair (the Nelson Stair) serving the Royal Academy Exhibition Room situated at the top of the Strand Building. Here, Chambers included a series of decorated landings, or "stations of repose" from which spectators, *"might find entertainment, to compensate for the labour past, and be encouraged to proceed."*

While one commentator referred to Somerset Place as *"the work of an architect, who has manifested in its erection, a vast extent of intellect, as a mathematician, as an engineer, as an artist, and as a philosopher [...] an upright man"*, another wrote: *"In these damp, black and comfortless recesses, the clerks of the nation grope about like moles, immersed in Tartarean gloom, where*

Above: one of the doorways around the central court at Somerset House, each intended to lead to a separate department.

they stamp, sign, examine, indite, doze, and swear."

The building was never completed as Chambers intended but the opportunity was taken in the 1820's to complete the river façade with an eastern extension designed by Robert Smirke, appointed as the architect of new Kings College (finally completed in 1835).

In 1813 an access road to the newly completed Waterloo Bridge was opened, revealing the utilitarian rears of the western sides of the courtyard. This difficulty was resolved with a new wing for the Inland Revenue, designed by James Pennethorne, started in 1849 and completed in 1856. It was just after this, in 1864, that the river frontage was radically altered with the construction of Bazalgette's Embankment (housing massive sewers and a line for the Metropolitan and District Railway).

The work to change much of this was undertaken in stages during the 1980s and completed at the end of the '90's with a renewed court, a river terrace (linked to the Waterloo Bridge), together with an accommodation of the Courtauld Institute, the Gilbert Collection and Hermitage Rooms, and the usual set of cafes and museum shops. The central court of Somerset House has become a principal public space (complete with

playful fountains, winter ice-skating, etc.), from where one can access the river to the Southbank or go north through Covent Garden to the British Museum, through the Brunswick Centre and on to the British Library and St Pancras.

By then Somerset House was a sparkling feature of that strange Millennium phenomenon witness to London's rediscovery of the River Thames (what is, in part, reflected in Farrell's MI6 and Embankment Place buildings, as well as the London Eye, the Southbank refurbishment, the Tate Modern and Tate Britain refurbishments and extensions, City Hall, the extension of the embankment walkways, etc.).

Somerset House itself has an identity that lies calmly behind its foregrounded tourist attractions. It is a place to admire for its overall architectonic (which parallels the speculative urban square and Georgian terraces of the time), for the strength of its character and its quirky features.

Above: *view through the entry from the Strand*
Below: *inside the court since the building's conversion and the installation of a fountain. The latter has become a regular attraction for London families looking for somewhere to entertain their children in summer weeks. During the mid-winter weeks it frequently becomes an ice-skating rink.*
Note the separate front doors and chimneys to the block – it is treated as a set of London terrace houses.

Robert Adam 1728–92

Johnny, Bob, Jamie and Willy

Extant London works include:
- **Admiralty Screen**, 1759-61, Whitehall (north of Kent's Horse Guards).
- **Osterley Park**, 1761-80. Jersey Road, Isleworth (a National Trust property).
- **Syon House** 1762-68. Brentford.
- **Adelphi**, 1768-74, inc. the **Royal Society** 1772-74, John Street. A speculative development.
- **Kenwood House** 1767-69. Hampstead Heath (north side). Like Syon and Osterly, one of Adam's more accessible works. However, none of these exhibits some of that planning skill exhibited by the town houses.
- **Apsley House**, 1771-78, Hyde Park Corner (Wellington Museum).
- **Lansdowne House**, (now Club), 1762-68, on the south side of Grosvenor Square; house in **Portland Place**, 1776 (another speculative development); Nos 20 & 21 **Portman Square**, 1775-77; No. 20 **St James' Square**, 1772-74; **Chandos House**, 1770-71, Chandos Place (off Portland Place; now the Royal Society of Medicine); and nearby houses at 5-15, and 20-22. **Mansfield Street.**
- **Fitzroy Square**, 1790-1794, South side (again speculative).

Below: *the entrance front of Osterley Park*

Robert Adam was born at Kirkcaldy in Fife, the second son of the architect William Adam (1689-1748, the leading Scottish architect of his day). He was educated at the high school of Edinburgh before matriculating at Edinburgh University in 1743, which he left prematurely in 1745-6 to relieve pressures in the office of his father. This was, at this time, effectively run by Robert's brother, John Adam (1721-1792), who had gradually taken over Adam senior's affairs during the 1740s. Robert's younger brother, James Adam (1732-1794) was also educated at Edinburgh University, where he matriculated in the autumn of 1751, and, by 1754, was also a part of the firm (by when Adam Senior was dead).

Work undertaken after the elder Adam's death included the building and rebuilding of the highland forts after the conclusion of the Jacobite rising of 1745 (assisted by Paul and Thomas Sandby – draughtsmen who appear to have been important to the manner in which the Adams were taught to record and represent these forts in watercolour).

The firm was so successful that a significant amount of capital was amassed, enabling Robert to embark on an all-important Grand Tour. Robert and his brother James set off on respective tours in 1754–7 and 1760–63. In 1755 they were in Rome, accompanied by a talented draughtsman companion picked up along the way (Clérisseau). Robert pretended to be a talented dilettante, seeing the sights and taking drawing lessons. It was here that he made the friendship of Piranesi, and just overlapped his stay with that of William Chambers – his later rival. And, while in Italy, he set off to explore and measure the late Roman palace of Diocletian, at Split in Dalmatia (the recording of which was published in 1764).

A return to the British Isles in 1757-8 was to London, not to Edinburgh, where Robert now cut a cosmopolitan figure and surrounded himself with his drawings and collected items (which advertised his good taste) and set about attracting commissions. This was on his own, until brother James returned from Rome in 1763. Meanwhile brother William (1738-1822) added business acumen, and elder brother John Adam (1721-1792) supplied capital from the family estate and business interests in Scotland.

Robert was ambitious, and eager to overturn the dominance of Burlington's variety of neo-Palladianism. He boasted that he would build *"such a palace as Inigo [Jones] would stare at with amazement: make Palladio look blank, & make the Nation wonder."* Early work was post-Roman and rather Rococo, but was quickly superceded by something more antique, sometimes promoted by Italian draughtsmen such as Giuseppe Manocchi, who is credited with introducing the strong use of colour that became an established feature of the Adam style (accompanying a delicate use of mouldings that, used externally as well as internally, lent unity to a composition).

The first major commission was that of the Admiralty Screen Wall in Whitehall (1759). And, by 1761, Robert had been appointed as Architect of the King's Works (ironically, together with Chambers; James Adam succeeded his brother in this post in 1769). In 1767-69, when there were about twelve draughtsmen in the Adam office, came Kenwood House, but large commissions appeared to elude the two brothers (and the sisters who kept house for them).

In 1768 they decided to try their hand at speculative adventure (in part, in order to add a very large building to their portfolio) and purchased land on the Strand, facing onto the River Thames. This was to become the Adelphi, a scheme of twenty-four 'first-rate' residences constructed above a large set of vaulted warehouses that were served from the river. But it was disastrous: it is reported that they not only managed to build so low that the warehousing flooded at high tide, but the whole venture cost too much and was caught out by a credit crisis and the brothers were faced with dismissing some 3,000 workmen whom they employed. And so they came up with the idea of a lottery and this saved their fortunes. However, it didn't save their reputations at exactly the time there was a general downturn in commissions.

Undaunted, in 1773, the brothers started a large speculative development in Portland Place, but this was later caught out by the War of American Independence (all they finally designed were the façades, some of which still exist; the work beyond was by other builders). In order to cope the brothers published *The Works in Architecture of Robert and James Adam*, which appeared in sections between 1773 and 1778 and were reissued as two volumes in 1786 with a third, posthumous, volume in 1822.

Later in his career Robert (James apparently had little to do with the hugely successful practice during the 1780s and afterward) sought to link architecture to history and to settings (including one scheme for what was to look like an abandoned Roman camp). He also developed his practice in Scotland, being particularly successful in Edinburgh. However, speculative schemes were never far from his mind. After the Adelphi (1768-72) and Portland Place (1776-90), and Fitzroy Square (1790-94) – which was rather odd given Robert's admitted abhorrence of calculations and a reputation for being so poor in administrative and financial matters that this appears to have curtailed official patronage.

Ironically there was often a genuine wit and ingenuity applied to internal arrangements on difficult sites. Designs were often ingenious; however, they sometimes seemed labyrinth-like and were not always

appreciated by other architects. In 1821, C.R. Cockerell dismissed Robert Adam as *"not an artist of any force nor of very sound judgement."* It was deemed that *"he did not acknowledge the effect of the vista nor the good sense of it. In the obvious & palpable disposition of the house your way is never direct sometimes sideways like a crab, sometimes thro' alcove or corner you come into a magnificent room you know not how."*

Soane – who purchased some 9,000 Adam drawings – was more appreciative, but acknowledged a certain 'fancy and lightness' in the brothers' work. Nevertheless, there was certainly something about 'the Adam style' as a body of motifs that has produced endless numbers of 'Adam style' stairs, fireplaces, fanlights and decorative detail. This remains a popular if residual aspect of their work. On that point, in 1922, Arthur Bolton, curator of the Soane Museum, published a work on the Adam brothers and reflected that, *"Comparatively few people have ever seen a really first class Adam building inside and out, and their ideas of Adam work are too apt to be based on the exterior of the much altered Adelphi, the incomplete designs of Portland Place, Fitzroy Square, and possibly the Coffee Room of some hotel 'in the Adam style'. To such it is hoped that this work will be a revelation of the personality of a great architect, a stylist and decorative artist of the first order."* That difficulty remains and Kenwood House is possibly the most accessible of the Adams' London buildings.

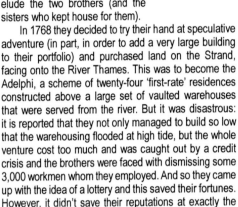

In his Home Sweet Homes of 1938, Osbert Lancaster the brothers Adam are marked down as distinctly better at interior design than architecture. Turning tastes for neo-Classicism to advantage, they "established it firmly on that smart and fashionable plane on which so many bright young men and shrewd old women so profitably operate." It was the brothers Adam who were to take the 'unpromising material' of neo-Classical pedantry and evolve it into "a style which remains one of the greatest glories of the applied arts in this country." They developed what Kent had started and established a new profession: the interior decorator (the scene of what Lancaster refers to as 'bright young men and shrewd old women').

Top: Adelphi view, showing one of the few remaining Adam frontages: strikingly refined and quite unlike Chamber's work (e.g. the nearby Somerset House).

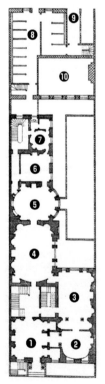

Left: the ground floor of the Adam-designed house for Lord Derby in Grosvenor Square, 1773-4 (now demolished).
1. Hall; 2. Ante Room; 3. Parlour; 4. Great Dining room; 5. Library; 6. Dressing room; 7. Closet, with wc and powder room (note the 'back stair' and another at the front of the house, adjacent to the 'grand Stairs'); 8. Stables; 9. Two coach bays; 10. Upper part of kitchen (below). The area on the right is a light well. Summerson describes such houses as "glamorous, gay, original, full of affectations which, nevertheless, are rarely tedious ... a harmony of spaces – a harmony in which many contrasts reside ... every room has been caressed in the architect's mind and persuaded into some delicate discipline mutually enhancing that of the rooms before and beyond it." (Georgian London).

Kenwood House, 1767-69

Hampstead Heath is an extensive swathe of ostensibly wild parkland that is, in fact, a carefully cultivated boundary zone between sometimes decrepit Victorian terraces on its inner, city, side and the often finer detached houses of early suburbia and the well-heeled historic villages of Hampstead and Highgate that lie on the outer fringes of central London. In the northern part of this recreational resource, stretched across the top of a hill, sits a fine and dignified villa whose gleaming white façade and twin side pavilions grandly face down upon an artfully worked landscape that scenically dips away into its own contrived picturesqueness: Kenwood House, designed and constructed in the eighteenth century for graceful aristocratic living, and now serving as a representative symbol of civilised life for the north London bourgeoisie.

As the London's masses who once thronged to the heath on holidays, people now come here to soak up a former generation's obsession with the poised and harmonic architectonics of place. They come in their thousands to listen to open air concerts on warm summer evenings, as couples enjoying Sunday morning breakfast, as the post-Sunday lunch gatherings of the chattering-classes strolling off their gluttony, and as individuals lost in private ruminations. They come here to enjoy the rhododendrons, to bemusedly observe cheeky grey squirrels, fight off pigeons and to simply sit, quietly, upon park benches carved with dedications to the memory of loved ones who once found solace here: *In memory of Olga, who loved this place – a kind and gentle wife.* Kenwood House, in other words, still palpably represents the proportioned and decorous architectonics of Culture as civilised living.

Formerly a Jacobean brick house dating from the early 1600s, the house was later purchased by a famous judge (William Murray, first Earl of Mansfield) who, in 1764, employed the equally judicious skills of the fashionable Robert Adam and his brother in order to reinvent this house as a country retreat away from the multitudinous discord of central London (the focus of his professional life). The final outcome – after another generation's supplementary work – was an impressive architectural ensemble: a collection of juxtaposed masses nudging up against one another and presenting themselves as a formal, coherent order: more public on the northern approach side and more private (and impressive) on the southern terrace, where a long, stark white façade dominates and overlooks this part of the Heath, providing views in the direction of central London and the ever-present dome of St Paul's. To one side, at a lower level but conveniently at hand (directly linked into the basement), a discrete late Georgian service wing maintains a dignified, background role that is nevertheless a significant aspect of the architectural whole, its London stock bricks self-consciously unpretentious in contrast to the principal blocks' splendid, painted stucco enlivened by Adam's idiosyncratic decorative detail.

Overall, it is all eminently 'readable': a mix of civility spanning a spectrum from commodious pragmatism to what verges on mannered frivolity; from the realities of chill wind and rain, mud on one's boots and horse dung being cleared in the yard, to polite and aesthetically self-conscious interplay and exchange in the Adam Library.

As a facilitating and celebratory architectural schema Kenwood was clearly designed to be mindful of this a to-and-fro that was the daily reality of its inhabitation: a civilised architectural stance that only comes alive when one acknowledges its pre-Victorian and neo-Palladian interweaving of Culture and culture. *Good God man: of course the servants see me pee into a pot – what on earth is the source of your prissy alarm?* This is a world more suited to Henry Fielding's Tom Jones – strutting his stuff among the squire's hired hands – rather than elevated characters belonging to the upstairs/downstairs stratifications characteristic of the Edwardian country home or even the inter-war years of nascent Modernism when Kenwood House had almost entirely lost any reason for being – except, that is, with regard to a latterday sentiment of nostalgia that was to save it from demolition. In the 1920s it was given over to the nation and is now a museum and art gallery complete, of course, with tea rooms and shop. A labouring staff and the bourgeoisie have taken over, turned the place into a

comforting spectacle, and it is the Judge who is now on display. The very stuff of his former home now mutely suffers the indecorous poking and prodding of curious tourists in search of entertainment, reassurance and a harmoniousness that contemporary architects often feel too embarrassed to provide.

Above: the Library at Kenwood, Hampstead Heath.
Below: Kenwood House, south façade, overlooking the Heath.
Although the Adam brothers were crucial to giving the house its current character, in 1793-6 George Saunders (1762-1839) added two prominent brick wings, the offices and kitchen buildings and brewery to the east side. This was a continuation of work started by Robert Nasmith (d.1793), who died at his home in Marylebone during the work he was doing at Kenwood.

Burlington: the Ionic temple inspired by the Pantheon in Rome, and an obelisk set into a pond, in the gardens at Burlington House, 1720s.

Greekish figures

Soane & Nash

After Adam and Chambers, two figures dominate the view of London's architecture during the later eighteenth and early nineteenth centuries: John Soane and John Nash. In contrast to their predecessors, these are recognisably modern figures: no longer amateurs, but quasi professional. However, they practised in a period when the vocational 'disinterest' that was supposed to characterise the twentieth century professional remained a blurred issue in which architecture, art and development were thoroughly intermixed (and to which, to some extent, we have returned). Soane, for example, died in the year the Institute of Architects (founded as a club in 1791) gained its Royal Charter and became the Royal Institute. However, winning this celebrated status at the end of a long history associated with the Rule of Taste and about the time young Queen Victoria came onto the throne was also the beginning of a problematic period in the history of Britain's architects.

In particular, the long period of Victoria's rule became witness to contentious moves building upon the Royal Charter and aspiring toward that form of market monopoly in exchange for service to the state and self-regulation that goes by the name of professionalism. Architects were still a crudely defined body during much of this transitional period. And most of them had become familiar with kinds of practice accepted as the norm by the Adam brothers but increasingly frowned upon by the likes of Chambers and Soane. The Rule if taste was, as it were, a coin whose flip side was the practice of architecture as a blatant form of self-service and conflict of interest of a kind we would, now deem to be distinctly sleazy. Professionalism (rooted in the notion of a 'professed' and disinterested vocation) was an ideal that cut right across dubious practices, applying the values inherent in an *noblesse oblige* to the world of commercial and mundane civil interactions.

But the notion of professionalism arose more or less in parallel with forms of aesthetic differentiation elevating the artist to a peculiar status of professed and idealised vocational commitment which, ironically, gave the professional ideal within an architectural tradition all the appearances of an expert and tradesmanlike attitude of mind at odds with the more elevated stance of the artist. From the latter's perspective architectural practice was associated with society's highest cultural endeavours, i.e. art, rather than contrasting entrepreneurial activities despoiling the land and people's values. But the reality was, and still is, that the practice of architecture is not an end in itself, but bound to the purposive ends it serves. While the professional ideal sought to address the issue of expert and disinterested service to society, the artistic ideal pulled away into a realm of deeply personalised ideality.

It was to take many years to resolve this struggle of opposed mind-sets, but a registration Bill finally did go through Parliament in 1934. However, societal trust went only so far and gave registrational and disciplinary controls over to a separate body from the RIBA – a body that, to this day, remains a club or, as the Times once described it midst Victoria's reign, the architect's trades union.

Nash was an architect who speculated in the manner of the Adam brothers. But Soane, his contemporary, is associated with this history of professionalism not only because he died in the year of the Charter (and when the first register of assistants seeking work was published, together with an evening lecture on 'dry rot'), two years after having being awarded the first of the Institute's Gold Medals, but because his name is closely associated with a nascent professional ideal.

Soane's reputation in this respect is possibly best illustrated by his attitude to training his young staff in their chosen vocation. Briggs (*The Architect in History*), tells us that Soane, *"gave his pupils plenty of practical work, including surveying, measuring, costing, and superintendence [he himself ran the Bank of England job, with a general contractor], as well as the making of working drawings ... He also established a brilliant academy of fine draftsmanship ... His very beautiful drawings made to illustrate lectures were prepared in his own office, and it is not too much to say that the production of these drawings formed a valuable part of the training provided for his pupils. It is interesting to note that during the 53 years of Soane's practice no less than 357 architectural studies were admitted to the Royal Academy exhibitions from Soane's office staff under their own names ... Probably, with about three possible exceptions, no architect since his time has ever provided in his own office – and that a busy office – such a complete or refined education for pupils."*

Professionalism in its colloquial sense of properly and honestly doing one's vocational job had, of course, a long history within the building trades. But the issue of professionalism arose with reference to speculative masons rather than mechanical ones. Jones, Wren, and Hawksmoor appear to have enjoyed a vocational commitment embracing a more or less 'professional' attitude. And Hooke, in particular, was noted for his scrupulous honesty and considered attention to commissioned responsibilities. But, from the late

Source of inspiration: a Doric temple in Sicily, nearly two and a half millennia old, its eroded and pock-marked face bearing a distressed pathos lending silent witness to an ineluctable and mute battle against nature's proverbial act of infinitely patient reclamation; ruins exhibiting an indomitable spirit of architectural aspiration and refinement – a quality that appears to live so long as any hint of the plasticity given to the limestone had not been entirely eradicated. Such architecture is simple, massive and powerful: the single-minded adherence to a constraining tectonic of trabeated stonework. One reads the words in the Guide: 'a potent cultural action set up alongside poetry, philosophy and the other Greek arts' and imagines the thrill of weary sailors arriving off-shore to the distant view of a shining symbol of civilisation sat upon the hilltop. The obvious parallel is Egyptian equivalents - here, interplayed with an utterly different and veritably astounding degree of intellectual and aesthetic aspiration embodied in the stones, as if some obdurate ghostly presence refusing to depart so long as there is the least chance that their fading echo might find acknowledgement.

eighteenth century on, associations of architects and surveyors slowly began to match concerns of legitimacy and style with core issues of professionalism in a modern state: education, expertise, codes of practice, an ethic of service and a capacity for self-regulation and self-discipline.

What was to become the battle of the styles which was to adopt neo-Hegelian undertones concerning a style appropriate to the age was shadowed by this other, professional, issue. From the end of the eighteenth century onward, for example, we see a novel formalisation creeping into training: a shift from apprenticeship to being articled, and then from lectures at the Academy schools to the first full-time schools of architecture. In the background (apart from issues of instrumental values, new technologies, needs and the like) was new emphasis given to disinterest when serving clients, as well as kinds of class change that slowly drew to an end that period when joiners, masons and the like could comparatively easily (with patronage, perhaps) make a transition from 'operative' to 'speculative status. Eventually, architects were to achieve the civic status accorded to clerics, doctors and lawyers, but which engineers realised long before them.

Among the landmarks of historic transition during Victoria's reign was the Great Exhibition of 1851. Architects subscribing to Pevsner's history of Modernism take that event as a notable beginning of its slow emergence, but it has been described by one historian of engineering as a creative sunset mistaken for a sunrise. It was in the decades before the Exhibition that British engineering made its greatest achievements. And it was also in those years that we see the emergence of the general contractor: men such as Thomas Cubitt. Architecture was to be assailed by change from many directions.

Later – by the time the RIBA had achieved Registration in 1934 and the so-called George VI style was in vogue as an inter-war period counterpoint to Continental Modernism – the Soane Museum in Lincoln's Inn was a quaint institution literally existing in the foggy shadows, awaiting rediscovery in latter years as grist to the mill of modern cultural tourism. In the City, what is reputed to have been Soane's masterpiece – the Bank of England – barely survived as a slightly modified but still remarkable screen wall that succeeded in backgrounding Herbert Baker's new work that towered above its parapet (see page 246).

Similarly, Nash's achievements in Regent Street – after years of neglect – had been recently demolished, prompting a fierce debate in a cultural climate still ambivalent toward long rows of Georgian terraces as well as the deplored achievements of Victoria's era. The period was conscious that something special had been lost and that the bombast of the imperialist architecture that replaced the Regent Street arcades was, on the whole, perhaps a less than satisfactory replacement. Nevertheless, his speculative artfulness in realising the 'Royal Mile' from the Mall to Regent's Park was, in itself, a monument to the architect and remains a unique example of London urbanism (and an inspiration to Terry Farrell's proposals for London). And, in the park itself, his remaining terraces were splendid (if then ignored) and rather dilapidated 'ornaments' to London's urban fabric.

If we make another historical leap forward, to the post-war period, we find Nash's terraces in Regent's Park being saved from demolition and restored to high-value status. And, in Dulwich, we find the mausoleum created there by Soane having survived ageing, war damage and indifference to enter an era of contemporary art galleries and be rediscovered by those who, merely a generation or more beforehand, would have rejected the place.

But it is Soane's comparatively small family house, museum, studio and gallery in Lincoln's Inn that sparkles with a rare quality of architectural gamesmanship and enthusiasm that is also, in another guise, evident at Chiswick House and is otherwise largely absent from publicly accessible works. Ironically, that enthusiasm has nothing to do with Royal Institutes and whether or not the practice of architecture is a profession or an art. It is simply a love of architecture itself – what is to be appreciated on its own terms.

the tall, thin tyrant . . .

Sir John Soane 1753–1837

Extant London works include:
• **Sir John Soane Museum**, 1800-34. Lincoln's Inn Fields.
• **Mausoleum and Dulwich Picture Gallery**, 1811-14. College Road, Dulwich.
• **Bank of England screen wall.** All of Soane's work behind the wall has gone, but this defensive screen wall is still splendid.
• **Holy Trinity Church**, 1824-28, Marylebone Road. Now used for other purposes.
• **St John's Church**, 1825-28, Cambridge Heath Road, Bethnal Green.
Interior burned out in 1870.
• **St Peter's Church**, 1823-25, Liverpool Grove, Walworth.
(Soane admitted he was not a church man and none of the above churches are particularly interesting.

John Soane was born near Reading, where his father was a bricklayer and, being self-conscious of his humble beginnings (something that followed him through all his life), he was to later (indicatively) change his name from Soan to Soane.

In 1768, at the age of fifteen, he entered the office of George Dance the younger after being introduced by a relative to one of Dance's assistants. He then lived in the Dance household, where he was described as *"handsome, quick, enthusiastic, and possessed of considerable charm of manner, as well as unlimited power of work."* The latter trait appears to have stuck: his own office ran from 7-7 in summer, and 8-8 in winter. And at one period of his life he made a daily walk from Ealing to his office in Lincoln's Inn, and back again. And he also retained great respect for Dance, in later years acting as his emergency draughtsman, called upon when necessary. At seventeen he moved into the office of Henry Holland. Here – where he remained until 1778 as a valued, well-paid member of staff – he made a special study of estimating, surveying and builders' pricing and learned the business side of architectural practice (Holland's father was a rich master builder with extensive City contacts). But it was here that Soane also developed a deep suspicion of confused roles and blurred boundaries between architect, specifier and builder.

Holland at this time was working with Lancelot 'Capability' Brown on a variety of country house schemes and Soane now lived in the Holland household. Meanwhile, Soane entered the Royal Academy schools and, in that same year, won a coveted drawing prize. By 1777 he had joined in the self-promotion-through-publication game, preparing a work on garden seats, temples, etc. and, in that same year, he won the RA's Gold Medal prize – an occasion when he was congratulated by both William Chambers and the man who presented the prize, Sir Joshua Reynolds, who counselled the students: *"choose some particular walk in which you may exercise all your powers; in order that each of you may become first in his way"*. There followed an interview with the King, a trip to Italy (between 1778-80, while the book was published) and, upon his return, commencement in practice (which, in fact, he had started in 1777, whilst still employed by Holland).

In 1778 Soane set off (via Paris) on his tour abroad with Reynold's advice in mind and letters of introduction from George Dance and William Chambers in his pocket. In Italy he was able to meet with the celebrated Piranesi and other foreigners, generally seeking out those with strong reputations and ridding himself of national prejudice. His immediate *poste restante* address was the famous meeting-place for British visitors in the Piazza di Spagna, the Caffè degli Inglesi, decorated with murals in the Egyptian manner by Piranesi. All kinds of measured drawings were made, of what was recent as well as ancient. In Rome, this included drawings of the Villa Albani (1762), home for Cardinal Alessandro Albani's collection of antiquities that were displayed architecturally throughout the house, loggias, and gardens, often embedded into the walls or set in front of mirrors. This was to have a profound influence on the young architect. Of equally profound influence was to be a meeting with William Pitt and a resulting friendship that was to lead to one patron after another (as well as to appointment as architect to the Bank of England).

Ironically, Soane's first commission upon his return was an essay in the rustic or primitive hut manner, based on arc-Antoine Laugier's influential *Essai sur l'architecture* (1753). At this time he was also an avid reader of Goethe and Rousseau. This interest in 'origins' as the source of sound architecture was never to leave him, leading to all kinds of studies that influenced his later lectures, e.g. studies of the origins of language, architecture, ornament, religious and sexual symbolism, primitive customs, laws, and religion. It was along these lines that, in 1813, he became an active Freemason.

In 1784 Soane married the niece of George Wyatt, who died in 1790 and left his daughter an inheritance that helped to purchase property in Lincoln's Inn. In 1792

Soane purchased no. 12; in 1813 he acquired the no. 13; and in 1823 he purchased no. 14. This reworked set of three Georgian town houses was bequeathed to the nation and managed to survive as a unique glimpse into the mind of Soane. But the house's failure to please even his son, George, is indicative of both the criticism Soane was occasionally suffering and relations with his children: "*The exterior*", wrote George, in 1815, "*from its exceeding heaviness and monumental gloom, seems as if it were intended to convey a satire upon himself; it looks like a record of the departed, and can only mean that considering himself as deficient in that better part of humanity – the mind and its affections – he has reared this mausoleum for the enshrinement of his body.*" This deeply personal attack was merely another aspect of criticism that first emerged in 1796 when an anonymous critic published a poem claiming that Sir Christopher Wren would have been pained to see "*pilasters scor'd like loin of pork [...] the Order in confusion move, Scroles fixed below and Pedestals above [... and] defiance hurled at Greece and Rome.*" Similarly, in 1801, he purchased Pitzhanger Manor, in Ealing – rebuilt, apparently, as a design vehicle for teaching his sons architecture (he was, so it seems, an autocratic father) – for which neither of cared much, to Soane's bitter disappointment. By 1810 this was clear, and the house was sold.

In 1788 Soane won the position of architect to the Bank of England (succeeding Sir Robert Taylor). Work soon began that lasted until 1833. However, only the perimeter screen wall now remains. In 1806 he succeeded George Dance as professor of architecture at the Royal Academy – something Soane saw as the climax of his career. There followed an exhaustively detailed set of lectures on the history of architecture culminating in criticisms of contemporary work that resulted in the lectures being suspended until 1813 – the resumption of which was handled so erratically that it led some people to consider Soane to be going mad. That speculation might, in fact, have had some basis: his sons continued to give him immense trouble and he blamed one of them for the death of his wife, in 1815.

It was around this time that Soane designed a mausoleum at Dulwich (1811-14), for his friend Sir Francis Bourgeois (now the Dulwich Picture Gallery) and a work strongly influencing Robert Venturi when working on the Sainsbury Wing of the National Gallery project (see page 412).

In 1831 he was knighted and later was awarded the Institute of Architecture's first Gold Medal. But all the while he continued to be an enthusiastic self-publicist (a preoccupation that remains, to this day, a constant feature of many an architect's practice). He was buried at St Pancras Parish Church, north of the St Pancras station, in a mausoleum of his own design (in which his wife is also buried).

Above: the Soane Museum's breakfast room.

There is delight and regret in Soane, a man of raw ambition and probity, of humour and bitterness, and what he had to say and what he did in Lincoln's Inn are, perhaps, the content of an architectural psychologist's dream. As a self-confessed lover of architecture he surrounded himself with the subject as a fluidity of historicity and values firmly rooted in the epochal sensibilities of his day and vicissitudes of his own fate. Soane held antiquity in high esteem, but was convinced that the proper resort of such sentiments in England was in the Gothic of the Middle Ages. At a time when fashions enjoying ruins as romantic garden follies was transmogrifying into something less enchanted and more morally qualified, Soane insinuated into the strange place that was his home, office, gallery and museum elements that, possibly, were as much stabilisers of his emotional metabolism as they were expressions of his delight in all architecture and its profoundly historical contents. This is no more evident than in a basement suite constructed at no.14: the Monk's Yard, Cell and Parlour, constructed from bits and pieces salvaged from works at Westminster Palace and from Soane's own fantasies. Here was the refuge of one Padre Giovanni: a hermit – a curious fellow much given to comfortable teas with friends and the consumption of sufficient wine that it could provide bottle ends set into the paving of the yard.

Above: the Soane family vault at St Pancras old Church.

Here is a man who played seriously, wrestling with his entangled inner reflections as much as with the complex issues of realising fantasies within the confines of his residence. We witness much of this in a peculiar document – at once irreverent, humorous and bitingly satirical – in his *Crude Hints Towards A History of My House*, of 1812, written some twelve years before the Monk's Parlour was created. Here, he mocks archaeologists and their speculations, looking forward to a future time when their spades would reveal ruined parts of his house that would variously suggest a Roman temple, a chapel, a place of burial and a prison.

We are told that the Bank of England was Sir John Soane's masterpiece, but we have no way, apart from historical hearsay, of knowing whether or not this is true. Direct experience is absent from the appraisal, although the remaining expanse of external walling gives clues to this architects capabilities: defensive, almost windowless and doorless, yet grand and urbane despite its function to exclude and defend. However, there is an easier way to reassure oneself about the capability of this architect: a visit to the home he left to the nation, now the Soane Museum. It is a marvellously vital place: at once family home, architects office, gallery, and a display cabinet of architectural bits and pieces that manifests exhibits Soane's appreciation of architecture's potent nature. However, apart from the dense mix of disparate uses, spaces, features, fittings, and objects, the Soane house is a marvellous architectonic exercise: a veritable cabinet of curiosities.

Anticipating Semper's later work, and taking his cue from studies in Rome and earlier Laugier's work on the primitive hut, Soane soaked himself in ruminations upon the archaic, primitive underpinnings of architecture. Here was a subject he was in love with and celebrated on a daily basis. Architecture was alive. And Soane was in constant dialogue with it, just as it spoke to him. He related to its fragments as if they bore within themselves that strange mythic quality of the whole of which they were once an integral part. The topic of origins was, at once, crucial to an archi-tectural fabrication and the creation of a charged commodiousness, just as it was the vehicle of a school-boyish enthusiasm for collecting and showing off. Like a Wittgenstein that would go from awesomely obsessing over construction details to the front-row stimulations of a Hollywood flick, Soane went from equally serious aspects of his architectural work to the enormous fun of candle-lit parties at which his collection was displayed to friends and colleagues.

Above: *rooms in the Soane Museum (reception room; double picture wall; first floor drawing room).*
Opposite page: *beneath the rear dome, looking east, with a bust of Soane in the centre.*

The scene of these events is a story of three adjacent terrace houses acquired, stripped of key rear parts and partly sold off, and of an on-going cobbling together that was a lifetime's project with obscure beginnings and no particular end except that which old age and experience drew to a close.

The story begins with marriage to the daughter of a wealthy builder, inheritance and the design and construction of no. 12, in 1792. He was already collecting from this period and, in 1808, he purchased the freehold of the adjacent house, no.13, acquiring its rear yard (where the Dome is) for an office extended off from the main house. Access to the office was from the rear entrance. By 1812 he was rebuilding no. 13 but, sadly, his wife died two years later; however, he had been able to move out of no. 12. In 1823 he purchased no,14 and again used its rear yard (where the Monk's Parlour and current Picture Room are), walling off what is now the western Picture Room, later acquired by the Trustees after Soane's death. This room had been used as a part of the office ('E' and 'N' in the plan).

By now the house was famous and John Britton published a book called *The Union of Architecture, Sculpture and Painting* in 1827, with Soane himself publishing *Description of the Residence of John Soane, Architect* in 1830. In 1834 the open loggias at the front of the house on the ground, first and second floors were enclosed and incorporated into the rooms behind them. All the time, acquisitions continued until Soane's death in 1837.

The outstanding place in the domestic parts is the Breakfast Room on the ground floor, but the entire floor is interesting and one can only speculate regarding the arrival of clients and guests into the Library and Dining Room, withdrawing to the upper private spaces on the First Floor (above which were bedrooms). In the rear parts we enter into an architecture that not only delights in itself but admits to elements of pure fantasy. On occasion – as with the Monk's Parlour – such fantasy is at once playful and deeply serious, perhaps as if Soane was living out his interest in the 'archi' part of architecture as an exploration of myths of origin. Here, architecture is something at once living and profoundly historical, reaching back to the ancients but also, unlike many of his contemporaries, adopting a serious attitude to the Gothic. It was all grist to the mill, all to be embraced, engaged and enjoyed – as were the arts (sculpture and painting) which adorned architecture and used it as housing and setting.

To visit Soane's house in Lincoln's Inn is to meander among cobwebs layered upon of a man's loving courtship of Architecture itself, as if this were a tangible spirit to be embraced and brought to appearance. But the man himself, like his house, remains a cabinet of curiosities and enigmas. In particular, Soane the collector and maker of his own house stands as a magician weaving a spell of affect from disparate ingredient parts whose intermix and intercourse defies

conventional rules of association. The implicit order is at once manifest and yet opaque, strangely affective even as it arouses rational inquiry and simple wonder. Here is that 'pataphysics' of the proto-Dadist Alfred Jarry: the impossible science of singular occurrences, of things that happen only once: eruptions into cultural space that are, in themselves, a kind of magic – almost mythical happenstances possessing an expressive fluidity of appearance and form. The informing voice is Architecture herself, as if manifesting in multiple physiognomic guises. To encounter this spirit in one of her poised stances and to be caught unawares – awakened – by her shifting potency can be especially stimulating.

Soane has insinuated the spirit of Architecture herself into the tectonics of place as a rare and possibly dangerous compound of Apollonian and Dionysian characteristics that is as threatening as any other god who, freed by the mind that construes and conjures it, turns around to consume the author in the fulfilment of some Faustian bargain. Soane conjures up his muse and courts a devil – one whose spirit, as Mephisto declares, *"penetrates the marrow of the earth."* Indicatively, in Gandy's drawings of Mr and Mrs Soane in the loggia of their house as palace their figures are diminutive and the architecture aggrandised. The playful, situated love of the game is envisaged as an enraptured climax in which the player is implicitly without choice in the moves made and affects engendered: Architecture now vaunts herself through the vehicle of the architect's creative genius. Perhaps as a counterpoint Gandy and Soane repeatedly fantasised upon the theme of Piranesian ruination as architecture's moment of exhausted fulfilment and collapse. The ruin offers us Architecture as a benign sublimity: a prostrate somnambulant goddess, exhausted of Olympian creativity. Now, we can creep forward and safely indulge our curiosity.

And so the Soane Museum rewards study – but only to a degree: analysis makes one exhausted, in danger of missing the point, of seeing overlaid sentences and words but not sensing meanings or poetic affects.

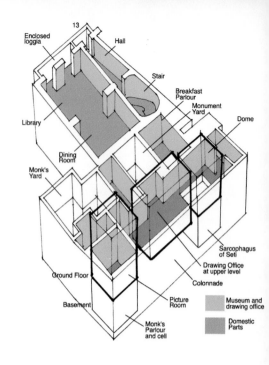

Above: the general schema of the Museum from the north, where a condensed architectural content is located in what was the rear yards of three houses.

Below: in the Monk's Parlour, one of the more intriguing features of Soane's Museum in the manner it more directly touches upon the architect's psychology.

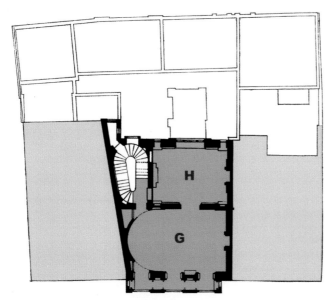

First floor, ground floor, and basement (rear parts only) plans of the Soane Museum.

A. Library
B. Dining Room
C. Breakfast Room (see page 108)
D. Ante Room (see page 110)
E. New Picture Room, added by the Trustees
F. Picture Room (see page 111)
G. South Drawing Room (see page 110)
H. North drawing Room
J. The Monk's Parlour, with the Cell to the north and the Monk's Yard to the south (see page 112)
K. The Crypt
L. Ante Room
M. Sepulchral Chamber and Dome
N. West Chamber

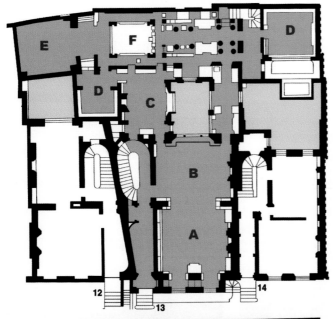

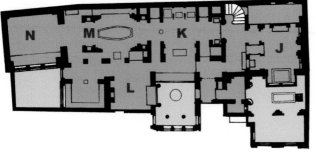

Dulwich Picture Gallery 1811-17
Bombed in World War II and rebuilt.

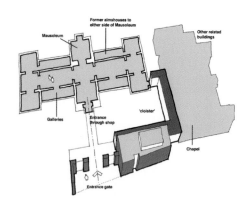

The DPG was London's first purpose-built art gallery – a peculiar commission for a building that was to be at once gallery, mausoleum and a place where alms women (six 'Poor Sisters') were housed (in some ways, not so different from the curious mix Soane housed at Lincoln's Inn). Its principal purpose was to house a collection supplementing those already owned by the Dulwich College – a collection bequeathed by Sir Francis Bourgeois (1757-1811). The work was to be adjacent to an old Jacobean quadrangle and Soane started off being contextual and offering his clients five designs (all with a quadrangle) to suit a very low budget. It was the beginning of a problematic project at a difficult time in Soane's life. For example, engineering and dry rot problems prompted John Rennie, the engineer, to suggest that Soane bring in Robert Smirke – a former pupil Soane detested. And the low budget (to which Soane contributed by foregoing fees) forced all detailing to be utterly simple – something for which the building is now praised.

By 1815 three allotted bodies were in the mausoleum and, by 1817, the building was open to the public: only to be criticised for its character: merely indicative Orders and brick instead of stone or render, lack of classical detail and poor lighting (the last point being ironic, given its reference by Robert Venturi at the Sainsbury Wing of the National Gallery). The plan was straight forward: a long gallery of five rooms set in one

row (a scheme deriving from the tradition of the long gallery in English country houses, each room being a cube or double-cube to the picture-rail, linked by plain round arches, as George Dance had once used), with the almshouses along one side and the mausoleum itself located at a central point on the façade. As has been noted, the plan is vaguely like that of the gallery at Castle Howard (by Vanbrugh).

Summerson makes the point that Soane's simplified brick construction artfully introduces slight breaks and recessions to separate out the various elements, a device he attributes to the influences of Vanbrugh (a hero to Soane). And the mausoleum also shows the influence of Robert Adam (at Mistley church, Essex), another Soane hero. It is in the mausoleum that we also see Soane's use of urns to provide a quaint picturesqueness to the architecture. Certainly, the end result is quite remarkable and in contrast with anything else of the period.

As we find the Gallery now – remodelled, extended and rebuilt after serious war damage (1953) and, more latterly, with additions by Rick Mather – the almshouses have gone, replaced by additional gallery space, and the ivy that once covered the building has been removed. The current (1952) exit on the east façade derives from a suggestion by John Summerson for an entrance here – which it was until the Mather scheme was realised. That latter scheme cleverly goes back to the quadrangle concept and attempts to further its formation (although underscoring the need to somehow achieve completion).

This page: views of the Dulwich Gallery.
Top right: the Museum today, with Rick Mather's entry pavilion and access route defining one side of a possible quadrangle, leading to the new side entrance. In the background is Dulwich College.

Opposite page
Top: diagram of the present arrangements, with additions by Rick Mather (2000).
Centre: view to the new access route, alongside the old College building.
Bottom left: the Mausoleum.
Bottom right: the gallery interior.

Henry Holland 1745–1806

Extant London works include:
• **Brooks Club**, St James' 1776-78. Now in the context of the Smithson's Economist complex. Portico removed 1778; further alterations 1890, 1938 and 1951.
• **Dover House**, 1787-8, Whitehall screen.
• **Albany**, Piccadilly, 1803-4. Side wings in the forecourt; the covered way to Vigo Street, Nos 10 and 12 Burlington Gardens, at the Vigo Street entrance; Piccadilly frontage by Chambers.
• Sloane Street, Cadogan Place, and Hans Place: area laid out and developed by Holland.

Henry Holland was a rare architect of the eighteenth century whose success was not founded upon a Grand Tour. He was the eldest son of a successful master builder who executed much of Lancelot ('Capability') Brown's landscape work and, after a short period training in his father's building yard, Holland entered into an informal partnership with Brown (in 1771), undertaking the man's architectural work – meeting not only Brown's influential clientele, but his daughter, whom he was to marry.

Various country house commissions were undertaken, but Holland's first independent work of significance was Brooks's Club, St James's Street, (1776–8; this was toward the end of the period that Soane was in the office). It helped that he not only owned the land on which the club was built, but his father had built the club's then current premises. The club was a fashionable place with the Whig (liberal) aristocrats who were to become his principal patrons; through them Holland met the Prince of Wales who, in 1783, joined the club and appointed him as his architect (resulting in Carlton House, now demolished, and work on a house in Brighton that Nash was to later convert into the now famous Brighton Pavilion).

It was on the basis of the Carlton House commission that Holland visited Paris in 1785 and employed French draughtsmen in London. The basis of this was the land speculation that Holland had entered into in 1771 (a common thing for architects to do at that time), borrowing money from his father. This was partly used to take a lease on some 89 acres of land in Chelsea. Here, between a twenty year period from 1777 to 1797, he built what was known as Hans Town, consisting of Sloane Street, Cadogan Place, and Hans Place – now largely demolished, but then very fashionable. It was here that Holland built what is now Sloane Place as his own, show-piece residence.

In 1787-8 came the rebuilding of what is now Dover House, in Whitehall, for the younger brother of the Prince of Wales. He filled in the courtyard of the existing house, built in the 1750s, with a circular, forty foot galleried vestibule inspired by French plans with which he was now familiar. The entrance portico in Whitehall features Greek Ionic columns designed on the basis of a temple in Athens and set into a rusticated screen wall inspired by the library of Hadrian in Athens (both taken from a contemporary book recording these works: The Antiquities of Athens (1762)).

In 1803 Holland remodelled William Chambers' Melbourne House (1771-4) in Piccadilly as residential chambers, adding two ranges of apartments in the garden on the north, named the Albany, flanking a covered way known as the Ropewalk, which has a tent-shaped roof of narrow boarding with a distinctly Chinese flavour. (Chambers, as the replaced Tory architect, was still in practice at the time.)

Finally it is worth noting that Holland followed in the footsteps of Robert Adam as a considerable collector of antiquities that might exhibit his good taste, thus influencing Soane, who was to later purchase casts and the like that Holland had collected (Holland employed a young draughtsman named Charles Heathcote Tatham, whom he sent to Italy to undertake this work; Tatham later published influential books based upon his researches). But Soane, who started his career as an assistant in Holland's office, sourly dismissed Holland as 'a bricklayer architect'. Nevertheless, Holland was a founding member of the Architects' Club in 1791 (with George Dance, S.P. Cockerell, and James Wyatt) and appears to have enjoyed keen practical interest in new materials and methods of construction, such as mathematical tiles, fireproofing, Hartley's 'fire-plate', and pisé (a French technique of rammed earth construction on brick or rubble foundations). In 1793 he published papers on the problems of fire prevention, and in 1797 on agricultural cottages and on pisé.

Below: Dover House, the Whitehall screen.

an ambitious visionary
John Nash 1752–1835

Extant London works include:
• **Sundridge Park**, off Plaistow Lane, Bromley, 1796-9. Now a hotel.
• **Southborough House**, Ashcombe Avenue, Surbiton, 1808.
• **Houses**, 66-71 Great Russell Street 1778.
• **Carlton House Terrace**, 1827-33.
• **Regent's Park and terraces**, 1812-25. Particularly Cumberland and Chester Terraces; also Park Crescent.
• **Royal Opera House Arcade**, 1816, Pall Mall
• **Haymarket Theatre**, 1820-21, Haymarket, on a formal axis to St James' Square. Only the frontage is his.
• **All Souls**, 1822-25, Regent Street / Portland Place. Part of the Regent Street development. All his work, apart from the street aligment, is now gone.
• **West Strand Improvement**, 1830.
• **United Services Club**, 1827, Pall Mall
• **Marble Arch**, 1828. This was the entry arch to Buckingham Palace, later moved to its present location.

Below: the Regent's Park, 1830 (until 1811 Marylebone Park).

Although the career of John Nash – who attracts epithets such as unihibited, irrepressible, irresistible, amiable, and amusing – parallels that of Soane, the latter considered Nash to be an architectural charlatan. However, Alastair Service reports a letter from Nash to Soane in which it is suggested that Soane is architect to the Lords, Nash himself is architect to the King, and Smirke – a man both apparently disliked – was architect to the commons. That King was George IV, who had become Nash's great patron when he was Regent – a patronage that lasted until George's death in 1830, when Nash's career came to an abrupt end. He then retired, suffered a stroke and was dead five years later, just before Victoria ascended to the throne, and leaving the Regent Street and Regent's Park development as his monument. But although there was rivalry between Nash and Soane and the latter did express disdain, the two appear to have been reasonably good friends. It seems that Nash – described as by the historian Gillian Darley as a man of *"enormous personal charm, wit and a quickspark of theatrical brilliance as a designer of grand urban projects, which Soane could not fail to appreciate"* – teased Soane about his freemasonry even whilst the latter provided Nash with a sumptuous dinner. Nash even tolerated a severe Soane design midst his own, more opulent elevations in Regent Street.

If Nash's later career was a brilliant success, his earlier years were not, being marred by speculative disasters and a first wife who, bizzarely, seems to have dissipated much of his income on milliners. He was born the son of a millwright and, from the age of fifteen to twenty-three, worked in the office of Sir Robert Taylor (the sculptor-turned-architect). By 1775 he had left there and set up on his own as architect and speculative builder. But by 1783 he was a bankrupt and withdrew to Wales, where he established a new practice. And, by 1897 he was attempting to divorce his first wife.

By 1796 the irrepressible Nash had bounced back (assisted by the employment of a talented French refugee and draughtsman called Augustus Charles Pugin (1769-1832), father of Welby Pugin). He had a flourishing practice, had developed an interest in the picturesque (mixing classicism with an Italianate vernacular), had become a skilled designer of picturesque country houses and cottages and, in order to bolster this approach, enjoyed relationships with the landscape designers Thomas Johnes, Uvedale Price, Payne Knight and Humphrey Repton. A partnership with Repton lasted from about 1795 until 1802, at which time Nash was designing a conservatory for the Prince of Wales, at Brighton, where Repton was working on the landscaping.

It was upon this basis of this success that Nash returned to London in order to try again. By 1798 he was newly married to Mary Ann Bradley, and enjoying affluence and royal patronage. Summerson once argued this to have been based upon marriage to the mistress of the Prince of Wales, but this remains disputed.

In 1806 Nash was appointed architect to the Department of Woods and Forests. It was in the latter role that he laid out the park north of the Marylebone Road as a radical scheme approved by his patron for a fashionable residential area of villas and terraces in a park setting: the Regent's Park. So as to connect the development in the new park (where the Regent was to have a new villa) with the heart of the monarchy around the Mall area, Nash designed a remarkable linkage between it these two locations that remains without precedent in the history of London.

Nash's role was consolidated when James Wyatt died in 1813 and he was appointed Surveyor-General of the Works, where he was joined by Smirke and Soane in a general reorganisation of responsibilities in that office. Each had different roles (see the reference to a letter in the first paragraph), with Nash looking after Carlton House, Kensington Palace, St James and the royal lodges at Windsor Park. Nash also attended to work at the Brighton Pavilion (1815-22) and, when the Regent became King in 1820, he was given orders to attend to a reconstruction of Buckingham House (despite the fact that Soane was supposedly responsible for that building). It was a poisoned chalice: the King (as George IV) became unpopular for his extravagances and Nash earned criticism for his services.

It was also in this context that Nash was accused of fraudulent activities in the Regent Street scheme and prompted an 1828 Select Committee to comment that, *"it was undesirable for official architects to acquire a financial interest in property for which they might be called upon to give a valuation."* Nash was, of course, declared to be honest, but a member of the Committee also noted that, *from what he had heard of Mr Nash, he should be inclined to think that he was incapable of dishonesty [...] he must say that, as a manager of public money and as an exhibitor of taste, he was sorry the public ever had anything to do with him."* It was a point that was fundamental to debate coursing its way through C19th practice: disinterest as a required aspect of professionalism. Nash was, of course, exonerated on every charge, but he and the King were outraged by this investigation and George proposed a peerage for his architect. However, he was dissuaded from doing this until Buckingham Palace should be completed – which the King, dying in 1830, never lived to see. And on that occasion Nash's patronage came to an abrupt end. He was removed from the works at Buckingham Palace and dismissed from his post at the Office of Works. Attempts to nail the architect continued, his designs were criticised and, upon his death in 1835, his reputation was at its lowest point – one from which the Victorians did not wish to rescue it.

Nash and his patron had given London a remarkable urban development that strove to unite grand frontages and landscaping in a manner to be found nowhere else in the metropolis. It remains a great source of inspiration to the contemporary architect Terry Farrell. But such admiration selectively divorces urban and architectural merits from the odour of sleaze surrounding Nash's reputation in a manner that only another architect deeply involved in the realities of property development could manage to achieve. Certainly, the development's socio-economic patterning tells a rather familiar story. For example, Soho, on the eastern side of Regent Street, is a rich mix of housing, the sex trade, low-end clubs, some high-end restaurants, theatres, offices (especially for people in the movies and the media world), specialist shops, and some remains of tailoring and similar crafts activities that once flourished here. Mayfair, on the western side, has the highest office rents in London, is the location of some of its more expensive residential properties, of the tailors of Saville Row, many art galleries and the boutiques of Bond Street, embassies and five star hotels. An indicative aspect of the divide between these two subtly divided communities is taste – the difference between Saville Row together with the Burlington Arcade, and Carnaby Street together with Berwick Street market and Old Compton Street.

Regent Street intentionally separates the two into its west and east aspects. However, its other, north-south axis, strives to unify the grand Nash terraces of the Park's perimeter with the gentlemen's clubs of Pall Mall and the royal palaces of the Mall. It all adds up to a fascinating juxtaposition of Culture and culture, together with characteristically English class underpinnings of that differentiation.

Nash designed the Regent Street Quadrant himself (see page 255), the park terrace façades, siting of the villas, etc. The quadrants were removed in 1848 and the whole was rebuilt by Norman Shaw and Sir Reginald Blomfield, 1906-23. Nos.14-16 were for Nash himself (dem.). The façades of Cornwall and Clarence Terrace were by Decimus Burton. Nash did Ulster Terrace, York Terrace, York Gate, Susses Place, Hanover Terrace, Kent Terrace, St Andrews Terrace, Chester Terrace, Cambridge Terrace, and Park Square. These were all built 1821-30. Executant architects did what was behind the façades and sometimes attempted changes. Park Crescent was rebuilt to the original design in 1963-5 (as offices). The Park Villages, to the north, were designed by James Pennethorne (1801-71) who, from 1820 was an assistant in Nash's office.

Chester Terrace, Regent's Park

an architecture of urbanity

The Regent Street scheme stretching itself between the Mall and the Regent's Park not only betrays almost many aspects of English society, but is also a fine example of the English playing at *grand projets*: it invariably goes wrong, but gets there in the end. Nash's 'Royal Mile' (to which, it must be said, there is a long history that involves two other architects, John White and James Wyatt, who drew up preceding schemes that were clearly influential upon Nash) was intended to create a linkage between the Prince Regent's opulent Carlton House in the Mall (sited where Waterloo Place now is) and the royal park to the north (which, then, lay on the suburban boundaries of a rapidly changing and expanding city, just beyond the Marylebone/Euston Road that was constructed to get cattle into London from the west). But underlying a what we might now term a 'life-style' aspiration was a raw world of property and project management.

Below: Nash's scheme overlaid upon an 1852 map of central London (by when New Oxford Street had been created by James Pennethorne, Nash's former assistant). Note the proposed route from Trafalgar Square to the British Museum, a proposition notionally resurrected and elaborated by Foster when working on the Great Court (see page 437).

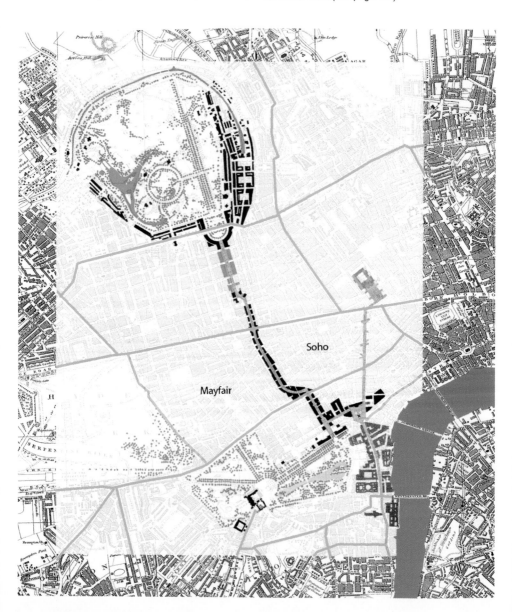

Soho

Mayfair

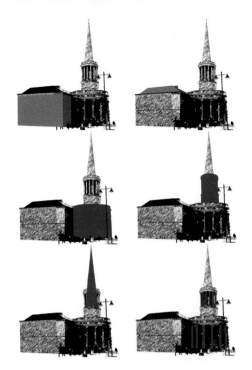

The interior of All Souls, Langham Place (1822-5) is less than special (and has been altered), but the manner in which Nash has dealt with a simply readable architectonic as an urban set-piece serving a role within the greater architecture of the Regent Street scheme is quite remarkable and has withstood the assaults of the buildings around it to maintain its dignified stature on a north-south axis terminating here before swinging around into Portland Place and up to Park Crescent (now offices) and the Regent's Park. His use of a Gothic spire on a classical motif of a tempietto is quite unusual.

The generality of the scheme given the assent of Parliament with a Bill of 1813, was realised, although not without those difficulties which included Nash's own questionable investments. As noted earlier (page 118), its success depended, in part, upon an enforced divide between the artisans of Soho and the gentry of Mayfair, consolidating the latter as an extension of gentrified and aristocratic inhabitation near to the royal palaces. But it was not to be. The Regent did not come to the Park and, ironically, he wilfully demolished Carlton House in the Mall, a house on which he had already lavished large sums of money. Instead, Nash had to accommodate the celebratory Duke of York column at Waterloo Place, terminating this part of the route with the Carlton House terraces that run east-west along the Mall. Here, the scheme ran west to what was then Buckingham House and east to (the new) Trafalgar Square. Nash proposed a new street run from here up to the new British Museum (a scheme occasionally resurrected in various guises; Lethaby, for example, had a scheme of 1891 for 'Sacred Way' between the Museum and Waterloo Bridge; Foster hoped for a route from the new British Library, through the Museum and down to the River Thames).

Nash's planning difficulties included the fact that significant parts of the planned route between his A-Z intention had recently been completed. For example, he had to align Regent Street further east than he wanted (to clear the rears of houses at Cavendish Square), and negotiate Langham House at the bottom of the already existing Adam Brothers developments in Portland Place. In particular, a kink at Langham was forced upon him, which he handled with the marvellously simple device of the rounded portico of All Souls church (an otherwise ordinary work). Similar ad hoc adjustments were made elsewhere – in cutting a linkage through from the Park to the Thomas Hardwick's new Marylebone church, for example (which had its frontage enlarged so as to play a role in Nash's grander scheme). Another difficulty came in designing Regent Street itself. First, Nash created something special at the junction with Oxford Street in order to slip the character of the development over this cross axis. And, at the southern end, he created an arcaded quadrant where the road swung around to the present Piccadilly Circus – a northern termination to a short axis from Carlton House.

Today, similar issues to those addressed by Nash's planning continue to prompt schemes from Terry Farrell for Buckingham Palace, the three royal parks (St James', Hyde Park and Regent's Park), and the length of the road between Paddington and Kings Cross, with particular attention to its junction with Nash's arcade at the top of Portland Place., where an entry point to the Park has never been satisfactorily resolved. The Nash scheme remains, in other words, an important aspect of London's vitality and, in some ways, a continuing project, continuing to prompt further developments in a city that, being polycentric, is averse to *grand projets*.

Sir James Pennethorne 1800–71

Extant London works include:
• Contributions to the Regent Street scheme, **Park Village**, etc., under Nash.
• **Christs Church** 1836-7, Albany Street, St Pancras.
• **West Wing**, Somerset House, 1856 (see page 96).
• **Public Record Office** 1851-6, Fetter Lane (added to by Sir John Taylor, 1891-6).
• **Rear of the Royal Academy** (see Lord Burlington, page 83; former Museum of Mankind; before that, offices for London University) 1866-70.

Pennethorne may or may not have been fathered to Nash's wife by the Prince Regent, or he may, on the other hand, have been the son of some of her relatives – no one knows. Certainly, Nash showed him great favour. Pennethorne entered his office in 1820 and his employee had the young man trained in drawing by Augustus Charles Pugin (1821-3), and assisting Pugin in putting together his *Specimens of Gothic Architecture* (1823).

Born in Worcester, he later lived with Nash in his new house in Regent Street and, in 1823, set out on two years of travel (financed by Nash). He spent much time in Rome and in southern Italy (1824-6) before returning via Paris, where he briefly worked for Augustus Pugin's brother-in-law Louis Lafitte. Pennethorne was clearly intended to take over from Nash, whom he served as chief assistant from 1828, working on all the projects in the office, principally the Regent Street works and the interiors of Buckingham Palace. But with the death of the King, a new government and Nash's effective dismissal, Pennethorne found he was working in an office that was rapidly winding down. In this period he completed the Park Village scheme as a Nash speculation, finished just before Nash's death in 1835.

Obtaining work after this period was not easy, but in 1838 Pennethorne was appointed one of the Joint Architects to the Commissioners of Woods (later becoming the sole holder of the office) and, in 1840, he was made Joint Surveyor to the Land Revenue Department. He assisted with new roads cutting through older parts of London: New Oxford Street and Commercial Road (the latter in the Docklands). He also laid out Kennington Park (1841-51), Victoria Park (1842-5) and Battersea Park (1858). By 1845 all his work was coming from the government (on buildings for which no competition was required and he became a salaried employee). In this (quite well remunerated) capacity he designed the neo-Gothic Public Record Office in Chancery Lane (1851–70; the west wing was built to the designs of Sir John Taylor in 1891-6);. In 1852-6 he designed a new west wing at Somerset House for the Inland Revenue, externally echoing the main building by Sir William Chambers (facing onto Waterloo Bridge).

For this work the RIBA awarded Pennethorne a special Gold Medal (1865) and knighted him in 1870. A host of other government projects followed, many abortive, some including works to Buckingham Palace (on all of which he got a fee as well as a salary). He died a well respected architect, but without broader influence.

Opposite: *a Pennethorne villa at Park Village, on the north eastern corner of the Regent's Park (1820s). This is a particularly fine set of houses that manage a curious combination of architectural, neo-Classical pretension, and 'village' aspirations. The resulting character has served as a model ever since (see overleaf).*

Pennethorne's Park Village

Park Village is a curious idyll on the north-east corner of Regent's Park that survived steam trains charging into Euston Station by a hair's breadth and now stands as a rather up-market fantasy of congenial living. Designed by Pennethorne whilst with Nash (responsibilities are ambiguous), and a part of the latter's Regent's Park scheme, the 'village' is mostly one small road, a disparate mix of villas and a small terrace: Greek, Italianate, Gothik. Nowadays, the Crown insists on uniformity of a different kind and everything is painted the same off-white – something that would probably have shocked Pennethorne and Nash, for whom the falsity of render was to be painted to actually look like stone. But this leaning toward being almost too-sanitised does not detract from the inventiveness of Pennethorne's work.

Thomas Hardwick 1752–1829

Extant London works include:
• **St Mary**, 1787-90, Overton Drive, Wanstead.
• **St Mary**, 1813-17, Marylebone Road, Apse added 1883-4.
• **St John's Wood Chapel**, 1813, Park Road.

Hardwick was born in New Brentford (son of Thomas, a master mason, 1725-98) and became a pupil of William Chambers from 1767. He attended lectures at the RA, winning medals and set off on a Grand Tour in 1776 (to 1779; it was at this time that he met Soane). On his return, he won a competition for a prison and was the architect for the penitentiary that was on the site of the current Tate Britain building, at Millbank (1812). He later resigned this post in 1813 on the basis of the poor remuneration, was replaced by John Harvey and then by the always practical Robert Smirke, who found his foundation work inadequate. From 1809 Hardwick worked on St Bartholmew's, saving it from demolition and reinventing Dance's octagonal parts of St Bartholomew-the-Less (also worked on by P.C. Hardwick). Being an architect who worked on churches, prisons, workhouses and the like rather than country houses, Hardwick failed to be elected to the Royal Academy, but he was a founding member of the exclusive Architects' Club (1791).

Philip Charles Hardwick 1822–92

Extant London works include:
• **Hotel**, Paddington terminus 1851-3. Central pediment sculpture by John Thomas; altered internally.
• **Australia and New Zealand Bank**, 1854, Threadneedle Street.
• **St John**, 1855, Lewisham Way, Deptford.

Philip Hardwick's son, Philip Charles Hardwick (1822-1892), was also an architect of repute taking over many of his father's surveyorships (including those of St Bartholomew's Hospital (1856-71), Greenwich Hospital, and the Charterhouse) and seamlessly continuing the family practice when his father became ill in 1847. But the son was firmly of the newer, neo-Gothic persuasion although he did switch between styles. In this guise he designed a number of churches and country houses. He also designed a number of grandiose City bank buildings, some schools and the terminus hotel at Paddington (1851-3. He had begun practice in Edward Blore's office, then with his father; in turn, Arthur William Blomfield was his pupil, 1852-5. Upon his death The Builder blandly reported him as 'an able architect and an honest man'; and the Athenaeum complimented him on and his 'sound common sense, combined with his artistic and literary attainments'.

Arthur Blomfield was a pupil of Hardwick.

Right: Philip Hardwick.

Philip Hardwick 1792–1870

Extant London works include:
• **Goldsmiths Hall**, 1829-35, Foster Lane, City. Interiors altered after WWII damage.
• **City Club of London Club**, 1833-4, No.19 Old Broad Street, City. Top storey by Louis de Soissons Partnership, 1979.
• **Lincoln's Inn**: Completion of Robert Taylor's Stone Buildings, 1842-5; also, the New Hall and Library, 1842 (completed by P.C. Hardwick).

Born and educated in Soho, Hardwick entered his father's office in 1808. He combined the skills of architect and engineer and is best known for dock warehouses (especially at St Katherine's Dock, 1826-7, (demolished; only the Doric columns remain) and the Euston Arch (also demolished). In 1815 he travelled to Paris and, in 1819-19, to Italy. He took ill in 1847 and his son, P.C. Hardwick, continued the practice. He was elected R.A. in 1841 and awarded the RIBA Gold Medal in 1854.

Sir Robert Smirke 1780–1867

Extant London works include:
- **Royal Mint, Tower Hill** 1809-15.
- **St Ann's church**, 1820-22, St Anne's Crescent, Wandsworth.
- **St Mary's church**, 1821-24, Wyndham Place, Bryanston Square, Marylebone (the peristylar portico around a circular steeple is copied from St Ann's).
- **Kings College**, and **Somerset House**, Strand 1830-35: the east wing to Chamber's work.
- **British Museum**, 1823-46.
- **Inner Temple works**: nos 9-13 Kings Bench Walk; Paper Buildings 1838-39 (south front rebuilt by Sydney Smirke 1847-8).
- **Royal College of Physicians**, 1824-7, Trafalgar Square. Now Canada House.
- **Customs House frontage**, 1825. Lower Thames Street. Frontage to D. Laing's building of 1813-17 (after failure of the foundations).
- **Earl Brownloe's House**, 1836, No.12 Belgrave Square (Portuguese Embassy).
- **Paper Buildings**, 1838 and 1848, Kings Bench Walk, Temple, with Sydney Smirke
- **Oxford & Cambridge Club** 1838 and 1848, Pall Mall, with Sydney Smirke.

Above: the British Museum frontage and principal entrance.

Robert Smirke, son of an artist (also named Robert), had a privileged upbringing in London and his architectural career began when his father influenced George Dance the Younger to help find a place for his son, then aged fifteen, in the office of Dance's former pupil, John Soane. The relationship between the young employee and employer (Smirke was not a fee-paying apprentice) lasted only a few months but Soane did give him a copy of Laugier's *Essai sur l'architecture* (of 1755) and this was to influence Smirke all his life. After leaving Soane he returned to Dance and beagn to attend the lectures at the Royal Academy, where he was soon winning medals for his drawings. Clearly, Soane had lost a worthy employee.

Travel at this time was sorely disrupted by the Napoleonic Wars, but Soane and his elder brother Richard managed to set off in 1802 and spend two years in France, the Southern Netherlands, Germany, Austria, Italy, Sicily, and Greece (witnessing Lord Elgin take the statues from the Parthenon, something Smirke found rather disturbing). Upon his return to London in 1805 the young man started a practice that was soon (with the assistance of his father, Dance and other Royal Academicians) to become the largest in the country – to a large degree based upon his reliability and reputation for technical skill, particularly with regard to rectifying the defects of other architect's work, rather than design brilliance. One of his first and influential commissions was the Theatre Royal in Covent Garden (1809; dem. 1856), criticised by Soane and thus initiating a public controversy and a new rule at the RA forbidding the criticism of living British artists. Much of the debate revolved around the use of antique precedent and, in particular, Smirke's foregrounding of a portico against a background of simple massing – of which Soane was severely critical. Matters continued in this vein when the rising young star was appointed, in 1815, as one of three architects overseeing for royal and government works at the Board of Works: the thirty-three year old Smirke, a sixty-three year old Nash, and a sixty-two year old

Soane. Smirke was at the top of his profession, largely serving Tory clients who included Robert Peel and prompting the press to refer to 'the Prime Minister and his pet'. The pet was, by now, engaging upon a series of significant Greek Revival projects: Kings College, in the Strand; a building for the Royal College of Physicians, the British Museum and many miscellaneous works.

In 1853 Smirke received the RIBA's Gold Medal, after having retired in 1845.

Below: the British Museum Reading Room in the midst of reconstruction work and the formation of the Great Court by Norman Foster. (Note the portico in the background, one of four in the Court.)
Bottom: the Reading Room as it is, after the formation of the Great Court surrounding the building. On the upper floor, behind the windows, is a restaurant.

Sydney Smirke 1798–1877

Extant London works include:
• **BM Reading Room**, 1852-7.
• **Royal Academy Galleries**, 1866-70.
• **Imperial War Museum**, 1838-40,
Lambeth Road, Southwark. Portico and dome.
(Current interiors by Arup Associates).
• **Conservative Club**, 1843-4, No.74 St James's Street (with George Basevi).
• **Dr Johnson Buildings**, 1857-8, Inner Temple.

Sydney Smirke's most famous work is the domed Reading Room of what was the British Library, 1854-7 (and the Museum itself was completed under Sydney's direction). He was born in London, became a pupil of his brother and travelled to Italy and Sicily in 1820, remaining there for a few years before returning to become the clerk to the King's works at St James' Palace and marrying in 1828. His career blossomed and continually interacted with that of his brother, for example taking over the work at the B.M. when his brother retired in 1846. The design of the Reading Room in the Museum's central quadrangle made significant use of cast iron (as well as having a *papier mâché* ceiling some 150 mm thick) and it made Sydney's reputation.

In 1860 he was awarded the RIBA's Gold Medal. His final work was the range of galleries at the Royal Academy that sit behind Burlington's house (1866-70).

Charles Robert Cockerell
1788–1863

Second son of S.P. Cockerell, born in London, educated at Westminster School and, when sixteen, began training as an architect in his father's office. In 1809 he went to Robert Smirke and, in 1810, set off on a Grand Tour lasting until 1817. What retained the young man was the exploration of Greek ruins. Since this was during the Napoleonic Wars, making France and Italy inaccessible, Cockerell set off to Constantinople and from there to Greece. Here he met Byron, other ex-patriots, artists, and archaeologists, travelled the islands with others who made the then radical discovery that some of the ancient Greek temples had been strongly painted. The revelations continued: not of

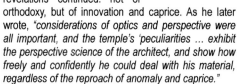

orthodoxy, but of innovation and caprice. As he later wrote, *"considerations of optics and perspective were all important, and the temple's 'peculiarities ... exhibit the perspective science of the architect, and show how freely and confidently he could deal with his material, regardless of the reproach of anomaly and caprice."*

Cockerell ended up in Sicily, where he measured the Greek temple of Jupiter Olympius at Agrigento. By 1814 he was able to visit Italy and travel to Rome, Florence and the usual sites. He returned to London in 1817: to architectural practice and later, in 1828, to marriage. But his travels were still strongly in his mind and he became a founder member of the Traveller's Club (now in Pall Mall, in an Italianate building by Charles Barry, 1829-32).

He succeeded his father as surveyor of St Paul's Cathedral, in 1819, and was architect to the Bank of England, in succession to John Soane in 1833. He was elected ARA in 1829, RA in 1836, and made professor of architecture in 1840. Described as the 'prince of neo-Classicists', Cockerell's work is, as one might expect, characterised by an exacting fastidiousness. Nevertheless, Watkins comments that he was *"concerned with self-improvement, both architectural and moral. Full of self-criticism, he was vigorously opposed to the dry manner of the Greek revival in which he had been trained by Smirke."* His works include the University Library, Cambridge, the Ashmolean Museum (his most significant work) and Taylor Institution, Oxford, and St George's Hall, Liverpool (1851-6). Little of his work survives in London.

Celebrated by Goodhart-Rendel, who claimed that *"Never has there been a more accomplished English architect than he, nor one more originally creative"*, Cockerell was a scholarly Victorian architect with as strong a reputation in France as England. His honours are a measure of his status in Europe: in France, he was one of the eight *associés étrangers* of the Académie des Beaux-Arts, an associate member of the Institut de France, and a chevalier of the Légion d'honneur. He was one of the ten members of merit of the Accademia di San Luca in Rome, and a member of the royal academies of Bavaria, Belgium, and Denmark. He was also a member of the academies of Geneva and Genoa, of the Archaeological Society of Athens, and of the American Institute of Architects.

Cockerell was the first architect to be awarded the RIBA's Gold Medal, in 1848, and was also its first professional President, in 1860, around the time Butterfield had just completed a work utterly contrary to everything Cockerell believed in: All Saints, Margaret Street. On the other hand, he appears to have held distinctly Ruskinian moral views characteristic of that period. Although his leanings were toward the Greek, they were coloured by Italian experiences, hence producing a Graeco-Roman approach. In a lecture of 1843 Cockerell declaimed his Vitruvian values: *"The universality of certain primordial forms in all styles favours the notion of innate ideas, the cube, the sphere, the ellipsoid ... common to the art of all time and people."*

It is perhaps difficult for us to now appreciate what Cockerell's research findings implied, how these fractured a perspective on the Ancient culture as resolved, internally harmonious and consistent: there weren't a few simple rules; ancient architecture was inventive; it was as intrinsically 'wayward' as contemporary architectural work. And it could be exquisitely refined: Cockerell was the first to measure the entasis on the Parthenon. Thus his books became a great influence and helped to promote Greek Revival studies as an exotic variation to Roman ones. He was buried in the crypt of St Paul's Cathedral.

Cockerell's second son, Frederick Pepys Cockerell (1833-78), was also an architect, travelling abroad and setting up in 1858. He designed no. 25 Old Bond Street (1865), and Highgate School (1865-8). He was Secretary to the Royal Institute of Architects in 1871 and a Trustee of the Soane Museum.

His father was Samuel Pepys Cockerell (1753-1827), author of St Anne's church tower, Soho (1802-6) and the architect who laid out Brunswick and Mecklenburgh Squares. 1790-1807, also residential parts of Bayswater between Edgeware and Bayswater Roads. Born in Hull, Somerset, the elder Cockerell began his career in the office of Sir Robert Taylor, for whom Cockerell retained affection all his life. In 1774 he was a District Surveyor for the parish of St George's, Hanover Square and later was employed in the Office of Works as Clerk for the Tower of London. Other such appointments followed, including a role developing the Foundling Hospital's Bloomsbury Estate

William Wilkins 1778–1839

Extant London works:
- **University College**, 1827-8, Gower Street.
- **National Gallery**, 1834-8, Trafalgar Square.
Sainsbury Wing extension by Vebnturi Scott Brown.
- **Former St George's Hospital**, (1828-59), now Lanesborough Hotel (1966-91), Hyde Park Corner.

Wilkins was born in Norwich, educated at Cambridge University, graduating in 1800 and setting off to the Continent for four years (to Greece, Asia Minor and Italy). But his father had brought him up to be an architect and he was already exhibiting at the RA in 1799.

Wilkins set up in practice in Cambridge in 1804, and then in London in 1809, working in the fashionable neo-Greek style, in which he was greatly respected – although his scholarship is considered to have hampered his creative inventiveness (better liked for his detailing than his massing, for example). How Wilkins obtained the National Gallery commission is a mystery. He made a proposal that the Prime Minister approved in 1833 and won against competition from Nash and Cockerell (the whole affair was denounced as a 'job' by the newspapers). Unfortunately, the building opened to a storm of abuse which sorely troubled Wilkins and he retired the following year. This may, in part, have resulted from having to use the columns from King George's recently demolished residence,. Carlton House – which determined many of the proportions and lent the Gallery a weak portico to set against the mass of its body. (The rear parts of the Gallery were added by E.M. Barry in 1867-78. The vestibule was also altered by Sir John Taylor in the 1880s. Recent works are by the architects of the National Portrait Gallery and the Royal Opera House, Dixon Jones (2000).) He is described as showing more scholarship than Nash or Burton and more sensibility than Smirke (but, like most other architects, was disliked by Soane). He posed as a scholar and a man in love with the theatre (running and maintaining six of them in East Anglia), but appears to have been a controversial critic and letter writer criticising the works of other architects.

Below: The National Gallery frontage, now directly linked to Trafalgar Square, work designed and executed by Norman Foster as a modification to former work by Charles Barry and Edwin Lutyens.

the curious case of the Wyatt dynasty

When Smirke, Nash and Soane took over the overseeing of the Board of Works in 1815 they were a triumvirate replacing one man: James Wyatt (1746-1813), father of Benjamin Dean Wyatt who, in turn was the son of a successful builder called Benjamin Wyatt (1709-1772). Whilst a dynasty is unusual, it was once commonplace for family members to occupy the same trade area (for example, surveying, architecture, building, other crafts or arts disciplines related to architecture and design). Other examples will be found scattered throughout this text. This complex mix of familial inter-relations, of building and architecture, says much about a transition between the elder Benjaman Wyatt born in 1709, the largely Victorian interlude culminating in the career of Sir Matthew Digby Wyatt, and the weak continuation of such traditions today. Benjamin could be a builder and architect in that age of amateurs and initiates; Matthew lived in a world of nascent professionalism. Their disparate worlds are at once familiar and yet quite different from today's teaching regime and modes of practice.

• **Benjamin Wyatt** (1709-1772); farmer, timber merchant, building contractor and sometime architect. He was best known as an inventor of spinning machines. His son William became an architect and builder (1734-80), as did Joseph (1739-85); Samuel was an architect (1737-1807); as was James (1746-1813). James had two architect sons and two architect grandsons. Another son called Banjamin was a land agent who had a son, Lewis William (1777-1853) who was an architect.

• **Samuel Wyatt** (1737-1807), third son of Benjamin. Master carpenter to Robert Adam, nicknamed 'The Chip', timber merchant and building contractor, and assistant to his brother, James. He designed Trinity House at Tower Hill, London (1793-6). In connection with this he was a lighthouse designer who also experimented with cast iron, made extensive use of Coade stone and also of slate (from quarries managed by his brother (another Benjamin, d. 1818), for cladding and other purposes. He was the inventor of a 'sympathetic hinge' by which both leaves of a double door opened simultaneously and, in 1787, he devised a prefabricated 'movable hospital' for use in the colonies. In 1800 he submitted a proposal for a cast-iron replacement for London Bridge.
Extant London works of SW include:
• **Trinity house**, 1792-4 (rebuilt after war damage).

• **James Wyatt** (1746-1813), younger brother of Samuel and sixth son of Benjamin; President of the Royal Academy, nick-named 'The Destroyer' for his work on cathedrals. In 1762 he found a patron who took him to Rome and he studied in Venice, returning in 1768. James was fond of Palladio, but not the Roman Baroque. But while in Rome he met the Royal Librarian, who brought James to the attention of King George III. Until 1774 James was in practice with his brother Samuel and, together, they designed and built a now famous but lost building: the Pantheon, in Oxford Street – a grand, winter meeting place that had a huge impact. Horace Walpole called it 'the most beautiful edifice in England'. Success followed, much of it as country houses (with Wyatt travelling in a coach equipped with a small drawing board), but he soon had the reputation of being a poor administrator and businessman. However, Wyatt had a knack of getting around this. He had, reported the sculptor John Bacon (1777-1859) 'such a peculiar talent in making everyone feel that he was so entirely absorbed in the wishes of his employer that his want of respect in not coming was soon forgotten'. No doubt this is why Wyatt obtained many public appointments. But, upon his death in 1813, the office of works was in financial chaos. The prime minister, Lord Liverpool, apparently remarked that Wyatt as "*certainly one of the worst public servants I recollect in any office.*" Nevertheless, in the 1790s, the King thought him the foremost architect in the nation.

Later in life Wyatt discovered an enthusiasm for the Gothic, serving as a bridge between the Gothik as Rococo and the more serious Gothic revival of the C19th. For example, in 1796 he designed the infamous Fonthill Abbey. But it all came to a sad end: he died penniless and in huge debt. He had four sons: **Benjamin Dean** (architect), **Matthew Cotes** (painter and sculptor), **Charles Burton**, **Philip William**; and also one daughter, **Jane**.

Below: James Wyatt

Extant London works of JW include:
• The **staircase** on the end of the Banqueting House (1808-9) is by James Wyatt.
• **Royal Military Academy**, Woolwich, 1805

• **Joseph Wyatt** (1739-1785), fourth son of Benjamin,

practised as a mason and architect in Burton-on-Trent, but without distinction.

• **Charles Wyatt** (1758–1813), nephew of James and Samuel Wyatt; an architect working in India.

• **Sir Jeffrey Wyattville** (1766-1840), eldest son of Joseph Wyatt and grandson of Benjamin Wyatt (1709-1772), articled for seven years to his uncles Samuel. He then entered the office of his other uncle, James, by then a fashionable London architect. In 1796 he was appointed surveyor-general and comptroller of the office of works. In 1798 he entered into partnership with a prosperous carpenter and building contractor – a move that apparently set back an ambition to be elected to the Royal Academy (not achieved until 1824, long after John Soane had publicly criticised those architects who chose to "lose that high distinction and degrade themselves and the Profession by becoming contractors"). The age of professionalism was arriving. Meanwhile, Wyatt took pride in his client list. Half-way through his career he apparently arrived at a total of four Dukes, one Marquess, seven Earls, one Baron, three Baronets, one General, and several distinguished but untitled gentlemen; these included great landowners, collectors, and significant men of taste. By the time he died he claimed to have worked for four sovereigns, seven Dukes, three Marquesses, seventeen Earls, three Barons, five Baronets, four Knights, a foreign Duke, and a Count, and well over thirty other distinguished gentlemen. Much of this work was alterations so as to add convenience and this he did on that note of professionalism that characterised the better architects of the day: Linstrum tells us that his work was well administered and every drawing was personally signed-off. In 1824 Wyatt's name was changed to Wyattville and, in 1828, the King knighted him for work at Windsor Castle (won against the competition of Soane, Nash and Robert Smirke). When the Institute of Architects was formed Wyattville was immediately made an honorary fellow; in 1835 he presented Soane with the first Gold Medal. The Institute was given its royal charter in 1837.

• **Benjamin Dean Wyatt** (1775-1850), eldest son and pupil of James Wyatt. In 1797 he went to India, returning six years later to train as an architect in his father's office. He designed the Drury Lane Theatre of 1812 (against his father's wishes that he should enter the competition). He remodelled Aspley House, exceeding the budget by three times. His last important commission was the granite column in memory of the Duke of York at the bottom end of Waterloo Place (1831-4). He died insolvent.

Extant London works of BDW include:
• **Drury Lane Theatre** ,1810-12

Drury Lane and Catherine Street, Covent Garden.
• **Lancaster House** 1825. Corner of The Mall and Green Park. Wyatt replaced Smirke as architect after the foundations had been constructed.
• **The Devonshire Club**, 1827, No.50 St James's Street.
• **Aspley House** ,1828-29. Hyde Park Corner (No.1 London) – an Adam house refronted etc. by Wyatt (see the Waterloo Gallery).
• **The Duke of York Column**, 1831-34. Waterloo Place and The Mall – the beginning of Nash's triumphal 'royal mile' to Regent's Park.

• **Matthew Cotes Wyatt** (1777–1862), painter and Benjamin's brother. Three of his four two sons – **George Wyatt** (d. 1880), **Henry Wyatt** (d. 1899) ad Sir Matthew Wyatt (1805-1886) – were architects and builders.

• **Lewis William Wyatt** (bap.1777-1853), son of Benjamin Wyatt (1745-1818) and architect nephew of James Wyatt. Apprenticed to Samuel, his uncle, from 1795-1800, when he then went to work for James.

Extant London works of LWW include:
• **Nos 12-17 Suffolk Street**, 1822-3.

• **Philip Wyatt**, (d.1835), youngest son of the James Wyatt nephew of Samuel Wyatt, cousin to Sir Jeffrey Wyattville.

• **Thomas Henry Wyatt**, (1807-1880), architect son of the barrister Matthew Wyatt (1773-1831) and cousin of Samuel, Benjamin, and James Wyatt; educated in Brussels; articled to Philip Hardwick; set up on his own in 1838 (the practice became very large). President of the Royal Institute of British Architects 1870-73, and awarded the Royal Gold Medal for Architecture in 1873. By 1838 he had acquired substantial patronage from the duke of Beaufort, the Earl of Denbeigh, and Sidney Herbert and David Brandon joined him as partner. This partnership lasted until 1851. His son Matthew (1840-1892) became his father's partner in 1860.

Extant London works of THW include:
• **St Andrew**, Bethnal Green, 1841, with Brandon.
• **Garrison Church of St George**, Woolwich, 1863.
• **Knightsbridge Barracks**, 1878-9.
• southern part of **Brompton Hospital**, Fulham Road, 1879-82.

• **Sir (Matthew) Digby Wyatt** (1820-1877), architect and art historian, trained by his elder brother; travelled on the Continent 1844-6. He was later Secretary of the Great Exhibition of 1851, Surveyor of the East India Company and the first Slade Professor of Fine Art at the University of Cambridge. He assisted Isambard Kingdom Brunel on the London terminus of the Great Western Railway at Paddington Station (1854) and later designed a considerable expansion to the Bristol station, Bristol Temple Meads (1871-8). He also enlarged and rebuilt Addenbrooke's Hospital in Cambridge (now the Judge Institute of Management; 1866). Wyatt published many works, designed carpets, tiles and wallpaper. He enjoyed a national reputation and had a large practice. He was the Vice-president of the RIBA and received the RIBA Gold Medal in 1866.

Extant London works of MDW include:
• **Paddington Station**, with I.K. Brunel and Owen Jones, 1854-5.
• **Jewish Cemetery**, West Ham, 1867.
• **courtyard** of the former India office, Government Offices, Whitehall, 1867.

William Inwood 1771–1843
Henry William Inwood 1794–1843

Extant London works include:
• **St Pancras New Church**, 1819-22, Euston Road. A Greek St Martin-in-the-field.
• **All Saints**, 1822-24, Pratt Street, Camden. Now the Greek orthodox church. Previously St Stephens.
• **St Peter**, 1824-6, Regent Square, Holborn.
• **St Mary**, 1824-7, Somers Town, St Pancras.

William, the elder Inwood, was the son of a bailiff to Lord Mansfield, who owned Kenwood, in Highgate (built by the Adam brothers). He designed numerous houses, but his better known works were all carried out with the assistance of his son, who joined his father's practice around 1809. Together they entered a competition for the St Pancras New Church in 1818. The younger Inwood was immediately sent out to Greece to research detail and character (resulting in an 1827 publication on the Erechtheion, in contrast to his father's much respected work on purchasing estates and renewing leases). Henry returned via Rome and began the detailing on what ended up as the most expensive church of its day and a Greek version of Gibbs' St Martin's. The famous caryatids stand as guardians over the entrance to the vaults beneath the church. But it criticised as hastening the onslaught of the neo-Gothic. In a diary entry in July 1821, C.R. Cockerell, dismissed it as "*simple Greek – radiates bad taste thro' the whole*".

William and Henry also collaborated on other churches, including All Saints, Camden Town, and Henry experimented with neo-Gothic (receiving the barbed criticisms of Pugin). The elder Inwood also worked with another of his sons, Charles Frederick (1799-1840). A third son (born 1802) was also an architect but next to nothing is known of him.

The elder architect died in penury. His son Henry William was lost at sea whilst travelling to Spain (after having sold items taken from the Acropolis to the British Museum to fund the journey). William Butterfield was briefly in the Inwood office.

Left: *St Pancras New Church.*

George Basevi 1794–1845

Extant London works include:
• **The Conservative Club**, 1843-5, 74 St James' Street. The elevation was with Sydney Smirke.
• **Terrace Houses** in Belgrave Square 1825-40, but not the corner villas. Also, the Thurloe Estate, South Kensington, 1827-30; Pelham Place and Thurloe Sq., 1839-45.
• **Holy Trinity**, 1839-41, Twickenham.
• **St Saviour**, 1840, Walton Place, Chelsea.

Born in London as son of a City merchant who was brother-in-law to D'Isaeli, Basevi became a pupil of Sir John Soane in 1810, entering the RA schools in 1813. In 1816 he set off to Italy and Greece for three years, returning to set up in practice. He obtained various surveyorships, building private houses and, among other things, laying out the Thurloe Estate (Thurloe Sq., etc). Rather like Ibsen\'s master builder, he died in 1845 while inspecting the western tower of Ely Cathedral. He had the reputation of being 'cold and haughty', but very professional (he named his son Palladio). Basevi was a founding member of the Institute of Architects.

Thomas Cundy 1790–1867

Extant London works:
• **St Paul**, 1840-3, Wilton Place, Knightsbridge.
• **St Michael**, 1844-46, Chester Square, Pimlico.
• **St Barnabas**, 1846-50, Pimlico, with Butterfield.
• **St Mark**, 1847, Hamilton Terrace, Marylebone
• **St Saviour's**, 1864, Plimlico.

Son of another architect, also Thomas Cundy (1765-1825). The younger Cundy trained with his father and succeeded him as surveyor to the Grosvenor Estate (1825-66), in which role he was responsible for the layout of Grosvenor Gardens and Grosvenor Place, including an early block of apartments (Belgrave Mansions, in Grosvenor Gardens).

James Burton 1761–1837

Mention must be made of this builder in the context of the role of his son, Decimus, and the enormous impact of James Burton's relationship with Nash,.

Burton was the son of a Scottish builder living in London (William Haliburton), and was articled to a surveyor named James Dalton in 1776. By 1785 he was undertaking speculative building (as many surveyors and architects did). By 1823 he had been responsible for the erection of 2,366 houses in London, as well as numerous other developments. His construction methods were subsequently criticized, and he was sometimes regarded (fairly or not) as the epitome of the Georgian jerry-builder. Early developments are characterised by a uniformity and austerity of elevation, allied to spacious formal layouts consisting of terraces, squares, and crescents.

Burton played a crucial role in the major projects undertaken by Nash. In 1815, for example, he began building part of Waterloo Place, and in 1816 he allied himself firmly with Nash by taking many of the leases for the proposed terraces around Regent's Park, and for a number of the villas within it (including The Holme, 1818, designed by his youngest son, Decimus, for the elder Burton's own occupation). The alliance was further strengthened when, in 1817, Burton took the leases of five of the largest blocks on Regent Street – a financial involvement that effectively guaranteed the success of the project.

Burton also constructed the grand terraces built around Regent's Park, 1823-6, the last of these being Chester Terrace. However, Nash (as the architectural overseer responsible for elevations) was apparently highly critical of Burton's interpretation of his designs, and in vain sought the complete rebuilding of the terrace. After all this, Burton moved on the designing (with the assistance of his son, Decimus) and developing the coastal town of St Leonard's, where he was later buried.

Right: Basevi's terraces in Belgrave Square, Knightsbridge, 1826-37.

Extant London works include:
- **Regents Park**: **Cornwall** and **Clarence Terraces**, 1823. Also, **Grove House**, north-western corner (now Nuffield Lodge), 1822-4; **The Holme**, 1818, Inner Circle (wings were added in 1911 by Bertie Crewe; more alterations were carried out in 1935,when a dome was replaced by a balustrade); **South Villa**, 1819, Inner Circle; the **Marquess of Hertford's villa**, 1825 (north-west corner, Outer Circle; rebuilt in the 1930s as the American Ambassador's residence); **Hanover Lodge**, 1827, remodelled by Lutyens in 1911 and restored as a student hostel 1961-4; **St John's Lodge**, 1829, Inner Circle (Barry made later changes); and a large house for James Holford, 1832-3.
In addition, the layout of the Gardens for the Zoological Society, 1826-41, and for the Botanical Society, 1840-59. Also the Camel House (1830-1), Giraffe House (1836-37), and the Ravens' Aviary (1827).
- **Athenaeum Club** 1827-30, Waterloo Place. Attic storey added 1899-1900.Ann attic storey has been added later.
- **Royal Naval Club**, 1828-31, 160 Bond Street
- **United Services Club** 1858-9, Waterloo Place. East side enlargement and alterations to the principal elevations, inc. the frieze.
- **The Union Club**, 1841-50, Trafalgar Square
- **Hyde Park Corner** was an urban space dedicated to the celebration of the Hanoverian dynasty, national pride, and the nation's heroes and was laid out by Burton. Here we have **Constitution Hill (Wellington) Arch**, 1827-8 (based on the Arch of Titus); originally for Buckingham Palace, now at Hyde Park Corner. Eighteen years after completion it was given, much to Burton's annoyance, a large memorial to the Duke of Wellington. This was later removed, but then replaced by the current angel-driven chariot of 1883. Also, the **Ionic Screen**, 1824-5, and the **Lodge** at Prince of Wales Gate, 1846 (also Cumberland, Grosvenor and Stanhope Gates, 1825-6). Burton also laid out the adjacent St James'. Green, and Hyde Parks. In 1851 he was responsible for the removal of Nash's arch to what is now Marble Arch.
- **Palm House**, 1845-8, Royal Botanic Gardens, Kew (in cast iron, with the engineer Richard Turner). This is one of the most imposing survivors of the type. Also, the **Museum of Economic Botony,** 1855-7, the **Temperate House**, 1859-62, the entrance gates on Kew Green, the water tower and chimney, 1845-8.

Decimus Burton 1800–80

The tenth son of James Burton – the very successful builder, who did much of Nash's work and built Bedford Square, Russell Square, etc. Decimus was educated as an architect in his father's office, from 1816, where he was allowed to design Cornwall and Clarence Terraces and some of the villas in the Park (of which his father was the builder). But he was never formally articled to anyone, nor did he undertake any foreign study visits – he simply stepped high up the social ladder of building opportunity and got on with it. However, he did take drawing lessons from a George Maddox and did attend the Royal Academy lectures of John Soane, who appears to have influenced Burton's enthusiasms for populating his home with antique sculptures; like Soane, Burton also had an extensive architectural library.

By the age of twenty-three the younger Burton was a successful architect. His work was almost always neo-Classical rather than Gothic; after the work with Nash at Regent's Park, he had a strong leaning toward the picturesque. In later life he travelled extensively in Europe and North America.

Below: the Holme, Regent's Park

It has been commented by one biographer that, "*The qualities of efficiency, professionalism, and an educated sensitivity to the wider implications of design for the creation of distinct urban environments rather than any kind of 'genius' are the hallmarks of Decimus Burton's architecture*", but this may reflect a prejudice against builders which, from Burton's attendance at Parliamentary Committees and the like, does not seem to have hurt his esteemed standing. He was, in fact, a founder member and later vice-president of the Institute of British Architects (1834).

Below: Wellington Arch, Hyde Park Corner. This was once parallel to Burton's screen wall, just to the north, and moved in 1883. Soane once proposed a royal processional route from a gigantic new palace at Hyde Park corner to Windsor, but it was superceded by Nash's work at Buckingham House (altering it to Buckingham Palace).
Bottom: the Athenaeum Club.
Bottom left: the Palm House, Kew, 1845-8.
In this context it is worth mentioning the cast iron and glass pavilion of the 1851 Exhibition in Hyde Park. The sub-committee appointed to deal with competition entries comprised Charles Barry, Cockerell and Owen Jones, with the engineers Robert Stephenson, William Cubitt and Isambard Brunel. Joseph Paxton took a chance and submitted late – but it was a design that could be built in time, a factor that was increasingly worrying to the committee. His flat-roofed glass house shocked everyone and Barry threatened to resign if its nave was not covered by a vault – rationalised as a way of saving trees already in the park. Seven weeks later the detail drawings were complete. That toward the end of July; by late September the first columns were going up. When completed the so-called Crystal Palace – 1848 ft x 408 ft – had consumed 3,800 tons of cast iron, 700 tons of wrought iron, 900,000 sq. ft. of glass and 600,000 sq. ft. of wood. In accord with the latest chromatic theory, the whole structure was dramatically painted to a scheme by Owen Jones in bright colours (which the High-Tech school of the 1970s onward continued to reinvent). The structure was rebuilt at Sydenham in south London and burned down in 1936.

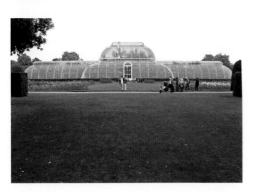

Lewis Cubitt 1799–1883

Extant London works of Cubitt include:
• **Kings Cross Station frontage**, 1851-2.
Undergoing extensive work in 2008, in conjunction with St Pancras Station (now the Eurostar station) and a general renewal of the area.

Lewis was the youngest of three Cubitt brothers: Lewis, Thomas and William, and was known as the brightest but laziest of them. He was apprenticed to his brother Thomas in 1815 and later at the offices of H.E. Kendall, then in partnership with the other brothers until this was dissolved in 1827 (Thomas going off on his own, but being re-joined by Lewis in 1831). He designed many of the houses built by the brothers Cubitt in Bloomsbury and Belgravia during the 1820s (e.g. Eaton Square and Lowndes Square). The Kings Cross Station frontage demonstrates what he was capable of.

Below: Kings Cross Station, the simple original plan (the ticket office is at the top) and the splendid frontage.
The Victorian London rail termini placed architects in a direct confrontation with engineers who, on the whole, made merely awkward formal junctions between disparate sets of concerns and values. Kings Cross remains one of the better examples. The 30 m arched spans to the rear sit upon brick arcades. The clock tower roof is typically 'Tuscan villa' style. As described in the The Builder magazine of 1851, Cubitt had depended upon "the largeness of some of the features, the fitness of the structure for its purpose, and a characteristic expression of that purpose."

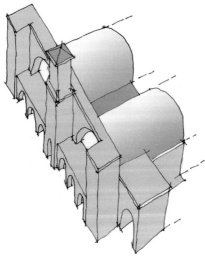

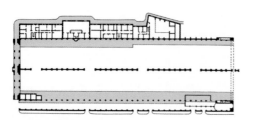

the general contractor as architect . . .

Thomas Cubitt 1788–1855

Extant London works include:
• **Various estates** (see below).

Cubitt began his career as a journeyman carpenter and sailed to India as a ship's carpenter. Returning in 1809, he set up as a master carpenter and was joined by his brother William. In 1815, he made the step of setting up as a general contractor who directly employed other trades. Having a permanent waged workforce to feed with work (and disliking working with architects), Cubitt began to speculate: the Calthorpe Estate, Gray's Inn; Highbury Park; Stoke Newington (Albion Road); Islington (Barnsbury Square); Bloomsbury (south side of Tavistock Square, west side of Tavistock Square, Woburn Place, Endsleigh Street, most of Gordon Square, the south side of Euston Square; Eaton Square in Belgravia (nos. 103-118); Albert Gate (mansions on the east and west sides), buildings in Pimlico ('Mr Cubitt's district') and Clapham Park (where he had his own home).

Cubitt had his own legal and letting department and the architectural work was done in his own office, through a staff of architects and surveyors. The man himself was often addressed as 'architect', but preferred 'builder'. William left the firm in 1827, Lewis in 1832, and Thomas occasionally acted as architect himself. Among his many other exploits and interests (including sewage disposal, smoke control and public works) Thomas played a part in creating the London Building Act of 1855 and was a guarantor of the Great Exhibition of 1851.

In 1827 the partnership between the three brothers was dissolved. William and Lewis both concentrated on speculative work, and Lewis re-joined William in 1831. After working on a royal mansion on the Isle of Wight, Cubitt managed to become close to Victoria and Albert (as 'our Cubitt'). At royal insistence, he was given the government contract to build extensions to Buckingham Palace designed by Edward Blore in 1845-50 and by James Pennethorne in 1852-6. His eldest son, George, became MP for Surrey, and was raised to the peerage as Baron Ashcombe. He had come a long way up the social ladder and, on his death, his estate was worth over £1m.

The the well-judged, the
imaginative
and the fancifull . . .

Sir Charles Barry 1795-1860

Charles Barry (Jnr) 1823-1900

Edward Middleton Barry 1830-80

Sir John Wolfe-Barry 1836-1918

A.W.N. Pugin 1812-50

Sir William Tite 1798-1873

The Gilbert Scotts
Sir George Gilbert Scott 1811-78

William Butterfield 1814-1900

Owen Jones 1809-74

George Edmund Street 1824-81

Other figures:
Lewis Vulliam 1791-1871
J.J. Scoles 1798-1863
Anthony Salvin 1799-1881
Benjamin Ferrey 1810-80.
John Shaw (the elder) 1776-1832
John Raphael Brandon 1817-77
John Loughborough Pearson 1817-97.
Samuel Saunders Teulon 1812-73
James Brooks 1825-1901
George Frederick Bodley 1827-1907
William Burgess 1827-81
George Goldie 1828-87
Sir Ninian Comper 1864-1960.

The changing Victorian townhouse

The well-judged, the imaginative and the fanciful...

Terms such as taste, fancy, memory, imagination and judgement were once key to the philosophical tradition of the later seventeenth and the eighteenth centuries at a time when new sciences were setting the pace and architectural ideology was making its gradual transition from a neo-Platonic stance to something more doubting and unsure but still firmly rooted in reason. In 1729 the poet and critic John Dennis (1657-1734) followed Hobbes (1588-1679) in noting that: *"For Memory may be justly compar'd to the Dog that beats the Field, or the Wood, and that starts after the Game; Imagination to the Falcon that clips upon its Pinions after the Game; and Judgement to the Falconer, who directs the Flight, and governs the Whole."* But reason in the form of a discerning and discriminating function of judgement had its contrast: that 'fancy' Sir Henry Wotton (1568-1639) had noted (in his *Elements of Architecture*, of 1624) as being "wilde and irregular." However, reasoned judgement and fancy were acknowledged to be close partners in all the arts. Fancy could be at once celebrated and denigrated, depending upon its relation to judgement. When conjoined with sound judgement, for example, fancy might be saved from its inherently capricious status: to be, for example, what Hawksmoor referred to as 'good fancy'.

However, Hobbes considered that 'extravagant fancy', no matter how admirable, could not save a work where there was a *discretionary* fault. Here was a philosophy that found architectonic order and system within an admirable work, and it was here that fancy found its substance within an ordering function leaning toward a scientific and philosophical nature set in contrast to the mere poetry of fancy. Philosophy was to provide a mechanics of order to the passions and affections. In Hobbesian philosophy, fancy and judgement range across the parts of a building, noting differences and similitudes, thus enabling the productive function of imagination to find unity among what is always in movement. Hawksmoor's Baroque church work, for example, frequently exemplifies a Hobbesian architectonic that juxtaposes assertive parts into a unified whole that has, at its heart, a still centre (for instance, a geometrical cube). However, where a reasoned philosophical content was weak or even absent, then fancy – now implicitly indispensable – must, somehow, do both the ordering and arranging: *"So far forth as the*

Fancy of man has traced the ways of true philosophy, so far hath it produced very marvellous effects to the benefit of mankind. But where these precepts [of philosophy] fail ... there the Architect, Fancy, must take the philosopher's part upon herself [...] not only to be the Poet to place and connect, but also the Philosopher, to furnish and square her matter."

This sounds distinctly problematic, if not self-contradictory. But what Hobbes had in mind was what Ruskin (1819-1900) later referred to as a skilled 'associative imagination': a positive capacity, elevating uncouth or 'mere fancy', and one that all artists should possess. Nevertheless, the artist was to aspire to take such an elevation to an altogether higher plane by means of what Ruskin referred to as a 'penetrative imagination', i.e. a curious kind of judgemental intelligence informing artistic endeavour, and placing it 'on target' in the Aristotlean sense that creativity had the task of marrying principle and the particulars of any situated challenge.

By the time Ruskin was providing such subtly nuanced philosophical instruction similar notions interlinking art, reason, judgement and morality had long been at the root of European artistic endeavour. Toward the end of the seventeenth century the French poet Rapin had written: *"Among the particulars of this Art, the Subject and Design ought to have the first place, because it is, as it were, the first Production of the Wit; and the Design in a Poem is what they call the Ordannance in a Picture."* However, *"The great painters only are capable of a great Design in their Draughts [...] and only great Poets are capable of a great subject in their Poetry."* With regard to the latter it was believed that the peerless neo-Classic poet (or architect), considerate of how his poetry might fashion manners and morals, must not only be a virtuous person but, in his undertaking, exercise a reverence for antiquity. And this implied a second rule: the poet should inventively base his work upon reference to a suitable myth or thesis, i.e. a congenial source rooted in works of the Ancients, to be imaginatively and inventively adapted and ordered in accord with what was read as the particularity of the moment. The challenge was to marry an appropriately edifying theme together with the nature of the creative situation in all its situated particularity.

Such reasoning gave art an underpinning of formal legitimacy and thoroughly imbued architectural endeavours, as well as those in other arts. The expression of fancy was to be founded upon something more sound, just as the architect's imaginings were to find some basis that would lift a work from being mere building to the idealist significance of architecture. Such sentiments and beliefs that were to be echoed in England by Lord Shaftesbury – a principal author of moral sense theory at the beginning of the eighteenth century – and served as 'the Rule of Taste' between the Restoration and the Regency, a period that has been celebrated as a high point in British architecture at exactly the time its essentially neo-Platonic basis was being undermined by that post-Copernician world view which, as Hannah Arendt (1906-75) noted, was beginning to mature into the post-Euclidean mathematics, doubt and uncertainty characterising modernity. Against such a background, one sees Ruskin's philosophy as a striving to lend artistic endeavour a new foundation of legitimacy and to lend the marriage of principle and particularity a new basis in radically altered circumstances.

Underscoring the Christian basis of art, Ruskin referred to the authors of such works as those who exhibit a capacity to create work evidencing *"in all its relations the weight, prevalence, and universal dominion of an awful, inexplicable Power; a chastening, animating, and disposing Mind."*

The truth that had concerned earlier poets and artists – the truth that was fundamental to works that took Nature and, as Pope put it, 'methodised' it – was now less formally idealised to the extent it sought to cut through Rule and access a more ambiguous truthfulness. The age-old Vitruvian concerns of intent and expression of that intent now aspired to a novel kind of vitality. Echoing previous concerns regarding an informing soundness to art, Ruskin referred his readers to a note of hollowness within an otherwise worthy work when there was an absence of a design intelligence constituted as the acuity of what 'penetrative imagination', i.e. those considerations which, when married to the daring of a skilled 'associative imagination' (which elevates mere fancy) have the capacity to establish the work as a flourishing kind of 'Vital Beauty', i.e. that "felicitous fulfilment of function in living things, more especially of the joyful and right exertion of perfect life in man." When we have the presence of both an associative and penetrative imagination, then we perhaps have life and fire. The authoring poet's tastefully thematic nobility was now a perspicacious intelligence whose moral content grasped at what was 'vital' and fundamental

to mankind's flourishing – exactly what an architect is meant to do when formulating a marriage of tectonic expertise with all that refers to what is, at any given moment in time or place, fundamental, original and thoroughly disambiguated (the 'arche' of the term).

Ruskin's concern with the intelligence of a 'penetrative' content within a work stood as a substitute for those once commonplace thematic concerns rooted in the guiding wisdoms of myth but commonly degenerating into vacuous erudite posturing. By implication, it was now no longer sufficient to make reference to the Ancients and, as an architect, to their canon of architectural Orders as a content that implicitly defined what architecture was and what it embodied. No amount of archaeological endeavour could ever be more than a metaphorical substitute for what was, at any moment in time, original, i.e. the truth of that moment in the sense of its particularised manifestation as those problems, aspirations and similar causes that prompted action and the address of a creative challenge. Architecture was to be 'vital': a concern that stood as a profoundly Modern expression given to an age-old issue, one similar to Louis Sullivan's neo-Darwinian dictat that architectural form, as he put it, should 'follow' function.

Ruskin's mid-nineteenth century philosophy stood in contrast to developments which, one hundred years earlier, had fancy leaning toward kinds of

Above and opposite: *George Street's All Saints, Margaret Street – a radical urban church seeking to simultaneously root itself in modernity and a religiosity that located its heart in the lost rituals of the Middle Ages. To a good member of the Church of England in the 1830s any suggestion of symbolism was suggestive of popery. Picinae and sediliae were regarded as superstitious features; altars were hardly used; chancels fell into disuse; pews were sold to the rich while the poor were banished to galleries. Reason and not emotion was dominant. The Tractarian movement and the so-called Ecclesiologists sought to change all this, promoting a 'pointed architecture' (as Pugin referred to it) that embodied, in its arches, all-pervading verticality and similar features (symbol of the resurrection), old forms of worship.*

'romanticism' that caused notions of a canon of correctness in architectural matters to lose ground to Taste's now fashionable references to 'sensibility' as opposed to reasoned standards. The Gothic now lost its barbarous undertones as the 'Other' of classicism. Soane, for example, considered the Gothic to be the natural 'antique' reference in British architecture. Nevertheless, Taste remained under the domination of the monarch, the court, and the aristocracy. Power and Culture (as opposed to culture) remained tightly interwoven as a pattern of patronage that held until the changes of the 1832 Reform Bill gave cognisance to the Industrial Revolution and a new bourgeois class: when Whigs and Tories were no longer euphemisms for the City and the Landed, as they had been in the early eighteenth century. Foregrounded debate to change in the arts – concerning Neoclassicism, the neo-

Gothic, antiquarianism, romanticism in general, and changes witnessed in genre painting (such as works from Constable) replacing the Historic, Heroic and Grand – were surface to a deeper kind of turbulence. With Democracy at the door (still a term of abuse in the early nineteenth century), the Noble and the Tragic now became the everyday of the Humble and Domestic. Taste – as a canonic rule – went out of fashion and architects began to elevate the intrinsic (and inherently mundane) tectonic content of their art.

But, at the heart of a new-found restlessness, there was an anxious endeavour to find legitimacy of stance; British architecture was in turmoil and a so-called 'battle of the styles' was to characterise most of the nineteenth century.

Against this background the voices of Pugin and Ruskin stood out as attempts to root the expression of British architecture into an organic relation with sound intent (whether one was to consider this in terms of religion, morality, tectonics, or a penetrative understanding). But they gave no acknowledgement to the forces of instrumentalism and professionalisation that were lending architectural practice a novel socio-economic basis. (Ironically, some of the criticism against what was fanciful was not, in essence, different to Vitruvius' ravings against those fanciful fresco wall paintings depicting an unrealistic architecture of strange, spindly and unlikely elements.)

By the 1830s Soane's idiosyncratic neo-Grecianism was quite out of fashion, even though he remained leader of his profession until his death in 1837. The young Pugin, for example, derided his work. But other kinds of change were also going on. A body of architects that had happily intermixed trades people with amateurs had become fragmented into architects, surveyors, builders and engineers. Mixed project interests were strongly criticised, as was the lack of knowledge among poorly educated architects. One, writing in 1835, claimed that there was no more than one in five architects that properly understood their profession: *"They can only be called artists ... Measuring, valuing and estimating for builders, is as much a part of the architect's profession as the making of designs; and if members of the Institute [which sought to exclude the trades people] still persist in [excluding surveyors, etc.] I should recommend them to alter the name of the Institute, and call it the Institute of Architectural Artists."* Which, of course, is what Pugin and Ruskin wished them to be – a sentiment that, toward the end of the century, was to divide the body

Above and opposite: Barry's Reform Club of 1841, and the adjacent Traveller's of 1832, exhibit a novel form of an Italianate style: no portico; no columns, or pilasters; an implicit rather than explicit presence of an Order; the strong cornice that tops the building – no balustrade and no attic storey (the roof accommodation is cleverly lit from the atrium). It is not neo-Palladian, neither is it Greek Revival. The underlying issue was, in part, that being true to ancient Greek precedent implied columns, portico, no pilasters, a single storey, no basement and no attic – being archaeologically correct placed architects in a corner. This stand-alone palazzo demonstrated a new set of possibilities.

of architects.

The Institute (what was soon to receive a royal charter and become the Royal Institute of British Architects) was formed in 1834 in a climate of uncertainty and insecurity among architects that underpinned a surface of confidence. If tradesmen were derided and excluded, so were builders and engineers. But the latter had been more quick to associate together and professionalise themselves. That, in part, was also the aim of the Institute, among whose membership were architects thoroughly in empathy with sentiments expressed many years earlier: "*The claims of the untaught, ignorant and presumptuous, must not only be disallowed, but repelled with indignation and contempt, till at length they are consigned to that obscurity whence they ought never to have suffered to emerge*" (a comment made in 1810), and "*The indiscriminating mixture of the artist and the artisan is one of the principal causes of the decadence of true taste, which should be removed as a deadly fungus from the incumbered stem of the fine arts*" (1814).

It was all a long way from Lord Burlington, et al. Even Sir John Soane lectured at the Royal Academy in the 1830s saying, "*We have long had too much reason to complain of mechanics of every description, from the bricklayers to the paperhanger, being identified with Architects; and, of what is equally fatal to the advancement of the Art, that architects, who ought always to be the intermediate persons between the employer and the employed. Lose that high distinction and degrade themselves and the Profession, sometimes by becoming Contractors [and speculators]*

... prostituting the credit of their Profession, sometimes by taking large tracts of Ground and parcelling it out to Tradesmen employed by them, and at other times by taking Ground and becoming builders themselves."

No doubt he had the likes of John Nash in mind, as well as the Adam brothers, Holland, etc. Sentiment had changed very quickly from those days in the later eighteenth century when architecture, building, surveying, and speculating were all one. Such was the change in attitude that Sir Jeffrey Wyattville (see page 131) was excluded from the RA for some twenty years because of a previous association with a tradesman.

The principal issue in the background was the system of architectural education – or lack of it. There were two aspects to consider: articled pupillage, followed by a Grand Tour by those who could afford it; and lectures at the Royal Academy (set up in 1768). The former was subject to a cult of personality (as it still is), and subjective treatment, as well as disparate standards. Lectures at the Academy were so inadequate and oriented toward the general body of fine artists and sculptors that it was to produce that movement which, dissatisfied with the Academy and also with the failure of the Institute to live up to its educational promises, formed the Architectural Association in 1847. Architects were catching up with society in general (and engineers in particular) by discovering the professional ideal. Around this time (in 1838) the architect John Blyth (1806-78), complained that the RA gave the student no guide and that his works were not uncommonly "*judged of, not by the real standard of excellence, purity, propriety, and practicability of execution, but by their power of pleasing the fancy. It is thus that young architects, knowing that their designs will for the most part be judged by artists, not infrequently aim at producing pictorial and picturesque effects.*" (A criticism not entirely out of place today.)

When set up, the Institute had the firm aim of countering competition and the erosion of status, principally by formulating a code of ethics. At its opening address it was stated that the aim was to "uphold in ourselves the character of Architects, as men of taste, men of science, men of honour" (the first woman was not admitted until 1898). However, in effect, it turned itself into an upper-class club. This, in turn, merely reflected what was happening to 'the profession' as a whole. It is estimated that at the beginning of the period 1790-1819 that recruitment from the upper class was about 6%, and from the working class 27%. At the end

of that period the upper class comprised some 16% of all architects and the working class membership had fallen to 6%. In a similar manner, the number of architects who had been apprenticed to builders during 1790-1819 fell from 12% to 5% during the period 1820-49; those articled to an architect rose from 63% to 76%. Even in 1837 it was being noted that entry to the profession required a considerable private income.

Meanwhile, the period between the end of the reign of George IV (the former Prince Regent) and the Great Exhibition of 1851 was witness to a massive change in taste against the generality of Georgian architecture and its informing values. The idea that building regulations should enforce architectural taste – as the categories of the Building Act of 1774, drafted by Sir Robert Taylor and Dance, had effectively done – was now anathema. The resulting 'Baker Street' style was deemed to be monotonous and boring, particularly with regard to a lack of ornamentation at exactly that time new stucco mixes, Coade Stone, and varieties of mass-produced metal ornaments were offering architectural tastes novel choices. But some looked upon the loss of the Rule of Taste with a tinge of regret.

In 1835 C.R. Cockerell summed up what he saw as a decline in taste by saying, *"the absence of taste proceeds ... not from a deficiency of talent if properly cultivated; but ... rather the absence of taste and encouragement in employers; who have not had the means of forming a good taste, and who have not had the wealth, during the last half century of taxation, war and dear living, to encourage those secondary arts which are expensive in this country."* Aristocratic patronage – if now on a more plutocratic basis with regard to its sources of wealth – continued, but the period of the Regency and late Georgian was, as John Summerson put it, *"an aristocratic society with bourgeois leanings' which had become a bourgeois society with aristocratic leanings."* Patronage from the upper class continued, of course, but it had already been noted that *"The time for building palaces, castles and cathedrals is gone by, or nearly so, and that for town halls, schools, museums, libraries, theatres and laying out public gardens in all towns and villages, with comfortable and elegant mansions,* is approaching." (J.C. Loudon, 1835).

One of the major vehicles of change was to be distinctly less than fanciful: that most potent of cultural forces, religion. Here, fashionable concerns with 'sensibility' were paralleled by reactions against Enlightenment values reflected in a post-revolutionary generation's emphasis upon emotional values and forms of the liturgy. Neo-Classical 'preaching houses' (as Nash had created in the 1820s at All Souls) became unsuited to a religiosity attuned to its Catholic roots. In France, the Abbé Fournier of Nantes wrote, in 1833, something that might well have been said in England by the likes of Pugin: *"The cathedral of Vannes is worth a hundred of these Greek temples of modern architects which have no kinship with our Christian ideas, no shadow, no meditation, no mystery."* And, of course, he was right. Temples belonged to a culture that saw no difference, in its *religio*, between politics and belief. Christianity, its personal beliefs and rejection of the public arena as a realm of salvation and significant action were abhorrent to the Romans; it was seen as perverse.

Pugin's liturgical rationality called for surrounding graveyards (*"nothing can better awake earnest feelings of devotion than passing through the place where the faithful sleep"*); choirs separated from naves (externally in terms of form; internally in terms of decoration); a tower with a steeple – deemed to be the most characteristic feature of a church; and a porch suited to baptisms, on the south side. To label an enthusiasm for the neo-Gothic as a mere extension of the C18th picturesque in gardening, follies, and the like is to miss the point of the power of aesthetics and issues of 'charge', or what Peter Zumthor calls 'atmosphere', in the context of the Industrial Revolution with its associated socio-economic and political issues. Pugin, for example, emphasised the sound constructional basis of the picturesque, rather than gratuitous irregularity – form must derive from the logic of the plan and the appropriate articulation of parts (nave, choir, presbytery, etc., all expressed clearly in the roofing), and not from arbitrariness. In a telling phrase, he commented that a building arranged to look picturesque *"is sure to look like an artificial waterfall."*

With Pugin, this was militant Catholicism; but the Anglicans soon took up a similar cause. The two trends converged. (Catholic emancipation began in 1778, but did not become significant until the 1829 Act.)

By the time of the Great Exhibition in Hyde Park, of 1851, the neo-Gothic had begun to follow the same path as the neo-Classical: toward an archaeological correctness. Debate over polychromy in both Gothic and classical works became heated; but even classical architects began to look at architectural works as built structures and not just formal arrangements of the Orders. But not all sentiment was so dour. While Pugin ranted, fancy had turned to 'Merry England', tournaments of the like held at Eglinton Castle in Scotland, and preferences inclining toward 'Elizabethan' country houses. People called Wilkin became De Winton, Mullins became Moleyne and the architect Jeffrey Wyatt was to become Sir Jeffrey Wyattville.

This sentiment had not only been made proudly, nationalistically and unusually manifest at Westminster, but also in the dozen or so books published between 1830 and 1840 on that vaguely Elizabethan style of strong silhouettes and large glazed windows that was to flourish in the hands of Anthony Salvin. By the 1830s this had become the preferred style for country houses, even if, in town, a rendered Italianate style still prevailed (new leases sometimes insisted upon a rendering of brick façades). The plans and sections of the former reflected a deeper attitude to the picturesque in which the villa and the castle sometimes became merged types and bi-symmetry is artfully counterpointed. Meanwhile, in town, the neo-Classical moved on from the Greek Revival (or 'survival', as Betjeman refers to it) with Barry's Italianate style of *palazzo* for the Travellers and Reform clubs.

Midst the replacement of what had been a normative idealist aesthetic by a body of relativist and eclectic historical-aesthetic concerns, it began to be suggested that the real issue was the revival of ideas, not styles. People were looking for those elusive qualities we refer to as authenticity and integrity. But it was to be a long struggle (one that hasn't ended). Paxton's Crystal Palace of the 1851 Exhibition was, within the frame of these developments, rather less influential than one would suppose from its size, its popularity and the role it has been given within Modernist ideology. Although it is quoted as the sunrise of a new era of engineering ingenuity, at least one historian of engineering has pointed out that it is more of a sunset on a remarkable period.

Above: *a page from Owen Jones' book on ornament, The Grammar of Ornament.*

Rather than Paxton, perhaps it was Owen Jones who was the more important figure of the event. He received the RIBA Gold Medal in 1857 but remains largely unknown in architectural circles although his 1856 book, *The Grammar of Ornament*, remains to this day a best seller, perhaps again because of that tempering of his fancy reflected in his comment that, *"If we would return to a more healthy condition, we must even be as little children or as savages; we must get rid of the acquired and artificial, and return to and develop natural instincts."* The ornament of 'primitive' was superior because, *"being the result of natural instinct is necessarily always true to its purpose; whilst in much of the ornament of civilised nations the ornament is oftentimes misapplied ... by superadding ornament to ill contrived form."*

Neo-Gothic and neo-Classical were to enjoy a brief reconciliation of sorts after this period,. While Street was struggling with his glorious Gothic edifice, the Royal Courts of Justice, in the Strand, Norman Shaw was to offer an admixture of the Elizabethan and Inigo Jones in the City, introducing what was labelled (labels, always labels!) the 'Queen Anne' style. More particularly, in this style, high culture and low culture also found a meeting ground of sorts that was to flower in the great burst of country house building that was epitomised by the work of a young Lutyens, and to die as 'Wrenaissance' in the same hands. Shaw was to be the new hero, a man encouraging his pupils to fight that other form of momentous change in architecture we have already referred to: the professional ideal as a form of regulated control of the body of architects. This was a struggle that was not, in Britain, to be resolved until the mid-1930s – to be followed, within some thirty years by severe criticisms laid at the door of a monopolistic and, it was claimed, instrumentally inept profession. The theme of fancy and forms of orderly and intelligent contrast – of, in other words, Dionysian and Apollonian forces – continues. In essence, it is an issue of intent and expression of that intent, what Vitruvius referred to as 'that which is signified and that which signifies'.

A final word from Goodhart-Rendel: *"In the days of true neo-Grecianism the highest praise a work of architecture could receive was conveyed by the epithet chaste. ... Let us say that in due time the neo-Grecian style became matronly, and that what in the succeeding style might be mistaken for voluptuousness was in reality nothing but the chubbiness of new born innocence. For chubby seems to be the exact adjective that will describe the character of neo-Classical architecture in its Early Victorian phase. Possibly this chubbiness was not necessarily infantile, but was the desired antipole of the aristocratic, the academic, the esoteric. It may thus be explained as a cherished characteristic of that style that was deliberately, proudly, middle-class."* Choice specimens were named, by their producers, 'Fancy Style'.

Opposite page: Brookfield Village, Highgate, 1865: romantic Gothic applied to a set of villas, perhaps fitting with a sentiment of Albion indulging its self-satisfied capacity to be nostalgic as an aspect of defining the national character.

The roots of this style are in late 18th century romanticism and the irregular picturesque style of 'cottage ornés' that developed at the beginning of the 19th century: in brick, with steep roof, large windows, fretwork, crestings and the like, perhaps with a tower, and façades designed as aggregated wholes (of still regular parts rather than the subdivided and bilateral and symmetrical unities of neo-Classicism). We also see the generality of this compositional approach to the design applied to the popular neo-Classical 'Tuscan villa' house type.

burned out by architecture

Sir Charles Barry 1795-1860

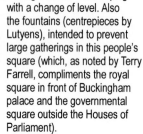

Extant London works include:
• **Palace of Westminster and Houses of Parliament**, 1840-60. Completed by E.M. Barry 1860-70
• **The Travellers' Club**, 1830-2, Pall Mall.
• **The Reform Club**, 1838-41,. Pall Mall.
• **Dulwich Grammar School** 1841-2.
• Nos **12,18-19** and **20 Kensington Palace Gardens** 1845-7.
• **Trafalgar Square**, 1840.
Layout of the square, terracing and side walls coping with a change of level. Also the fountains (centrepieces by Lutyens), intended to prevent large gatherings in this people's square (which, as noted by Terry Farrell, compliments the royal square in front of Buckingham palace and the governmental square outside the Houses of Parliament).
• **Bridgewater House**, 1847-9, Cleveland Row, north side. Built as a *palazzo* for the first Earl of Ellesmere.

Charles Barry was born in Westminster as the son of a successful government stationer and book-binder. He apparently had little formal education and set his bedroom up as a studio, constantly drawing on the walls and re-papering them. In 1810 he was articled to Middleton and Bailey, of Paradise Row, Lambeth, surveyors to the parish. He stayed there six years, became the manager of the practice and thoroughly educated in all matters of practice and building. He was immediately exhibiting paintings at the Royal Academy.

In 1816 Barry inherited money left in trust to him by his father and set off to France and Italy, then Greece and Constantinople, then travelling on much further than most people on a Grand Tour, to Egypt and Syria (virtually unknown places to English architects), getting to Aswan and Philae, and to Jerusalem, Baalbeck and Damascus, finally travelling to Smyrna, Cyprus and Malta. He then went to Rome and Florence via Sicily, returning to England in 1820 via Venice, Milan and, once again, France. By anyone's standards it had been quite a tour, confirming in Barry that Italian architecture was superior to anything else. Barry now set up in practice and was successful in receiving both patronage (including being recommended by John Soane) and winning competitions. Much of this work was in Manchester and some in a Gothic style, with which he was never entirely comfortable. While colleagues benefited from the new church building in that idiom, Banks was happier doing Italianate country homes and the like.

From 1829 Barry's career was marked by a series of brilliant competition successes: the Travellers' Club, Pall Mall (1829), the Birmingham Grammar School (1833), the new Houses of Parliament (1836), and the Reform Club, Pall Mall (1837). In the latter, his covering of the central court by a glazed roof was particularly successful. It was at this time that the association with Pugin began and Barry used his excellent drafting capacity on the drawings submitted for the Palace of Westminster competition. But the fundamental design – mixing experience of designing schools requiring substantial circulation with what he knew of gentlemen's clubs – was distinctly Barry.

Despite the burdens of the Houses of Parliament project, Barry continued with many country house commissions (largely extensions and the like) and further public works commissions, such as laying out Trafalgar Square (1840). We are told that he "*often rose at four, before working until breakfast at eight o'clock. After the day's business he dined at six or seven, had a brief nap, conversed or read until eight, drank tea, and worked until midnight.*" He neither lectured or wrote. And he disliked publicity and public office, declining to take up an offer of RIBA Presidency in 1859 (serving as vice-President instead; Charles Cockerell became President in 1860). He was elected RA in 1844, but from that time on he suffered bouts of illness that, after 1858 were more serious.

Barry married in 1822, after returning from his Grand Tour. He had five sons and two daughters. **Alfred Barry**, a priest, (1826-1910), turned out to be his father's biographer. **Edward Middleton Barry** (1830-80) entered the office of T.H. Wyatt before joining his father, for whom he completed work at Westminster. **John Wolfe-Barry** (1836-1918) became a famous engineer. **Charles Barry**, the eldest son, was also an architect.Barry was awarded an RIBA Gold Medal in 1877.

a riverside club...
The Houses of Parliament

Right: aerial view of the Palace of Westminster. Credits: aerial photo © Parliamentary copyright 2007. Photograph by Deryc Sands.
Below: detail of the west façade.

Whether the Houses of Parliament should be attributed to Barry or to Pugin, as the latter's son, claimed, is a mute point. The commission was Barry's, won on the basis of a competition; the character of what one experiences is very much Pugin – something which, perhaps, already says something about the way in which we experience architecture.

The two came together when Barry brought in Pugin to assist with work at Dulwich College, but more of a partnership was established when Barry decided to enter the competition to replace the Houses of Parliament that were burned down in 1833. The terms of the competition called for a Gothic or Elizabethan style, and also for the drawings to be in pen and ink. Barry was a pencil man no one was better than Pugin – trained in his father's office – at a neo-Gothic style. The result was a design that Pugin was to refer to as a classical body in Tudor dress. But the two were clearly in harmony, with Barry turning to the enormous technical problems the project engendered whilst Pugin handled the detailing. (They worked together on the project from 1935-7 and 1844-52, but Pugin's son was to later claim, in 1867 and after Barry's death, that it was his father that was the true author of all the detailing.)

What was intended to be a six year undertaking was to be a much longer project. The problems of the bad ground, alone, were enormous, calling upon engineering ingenuity (which included one of the first concrete rafts to deal with the soft ground and quicksands) and novel skills for building out into the river. (a wall was started in 1837). And then it all had to be fireproofed, prompting Barry to turn to iron for the roofs. The site was also covered in working buildings and the client was a multi-headed beast that was to sap Barry's energies. But he already had very useful skills developed on previous projects: in circulation and handling the requirements of a gentleman's club, for example. The Builder magazine referred to it all as *"the greatest combination of contrivance in planning, skill in construction, business management, and true art, that the world has seen."* It was exhausting. Only half-way through the project, in 1849, Barry declared: 'No less than between 8,000 and 9,000 original drawings and models have been prepared for it, a large portion of which have emanated from my own hand, while the

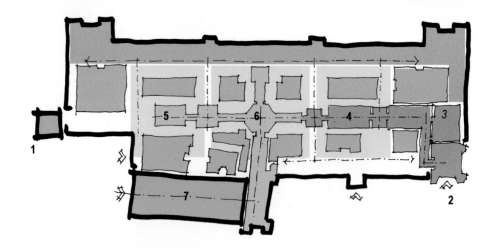

Above: *on the west side is the old Westminster Hall (C14th; walls 1097).*

whole of the remainder have been made under my own immediate direction and supervision.' The heating and ventilation system – a huge technical demand at that time – was handled separately and was merely one of numerous complications and interferences Barry had to suffer.

Controversy plagued the job. Barry's diary shoes that, even on his daughter's wedding day, he was drawing details. When he died in 1860 – worn out by the job, it is said – the interiors had still not been completed and Barry was still in bitter dispute with the Government over fees. What had been estimated to cost approximately £700,000 had, by then, already cost £2m and Barry's relationship with those who paid his fees was constantly suffering disputes over remuneration – issues finally resolved but, declared The Builder in 1860, the outcome was *"the greatest injustice that has ever been the lot of architect employed for ... a government."*

While the exterior of the building was being sculpted as the history of Britain, the interior suffered complicated heating and ventilation design problems hardly alleviated by the tall tower that acted as a chimney. There was a dispute over the clock, over paintings, and acoustics in the completed halls, all of it prompting inquiries that sapped Barry's time and energies, as well as his political wit. From 1844 to his death in 1851 Pugin was again back on the project, now collecting thousands of casts from medieval models and thereafter as salaried superintendent of wood-carving – the role that was the prompt Pugin's son to make the claims he later did (but, as it has been pointed out, Barry had already proven his ability to design in the Perpendicular manner before winning the competition).

The Houses are still much as Barry and Pugin left the complex (plus a host of security additions, including tank traps), but the Commons was bombed during World War II, in 1941) and rebuilt by Giles Gilbert Scott (reopening in 1950).

The architectural schema of the complex enjoys fundamental set of considerations: the concept of a riverside palace; 'fixes', such as Westminster Bridge, the Abbey and, in particular, Westminster Hall; the elaboration of the complex as essentially a one storey building with a subsidiary upper level (the plan covers a large area and mostly comprises courts and high-ceilinged features); the deliberate punctuation of the horizontal spread of the building by taller features that emulate Gothic spires; a regular plan, closely considered plan of courts, halls, axial corridors and side-rooms, formal routes and informal places; and an overall decorative programmme exhibiting a relentless verticality to offset the horizontality of the massing.

Fundamentally, the building is diagrammatically symmetrical about a central east-west axis, with the Central Hall at the heart of the arrangement and the two debating chambers to either side (the Commons organisationally related to the old Westminster Hall, and the Peers linked to a royal suite and the royal entry point on the south side, at the Victoria Tower). One long corridor runs along the river side (with a terrace, unifying the whole both internally and externally, and a series of internal courts punctuate the whole. But what

Opposite page: The Clock Tower (Big Ben, 1) is on the far left of the diagram and the Victoria Tower (the sovereign's entry point, 2) is on the right, leading into a royal suite (3) to one side of the Peer's chamber (4). The House of Commons (5) is on the other side of a central hall (6). The river frontage is a principal ordering feature that unites the disparate parts behind the façade. Towers punctuate the manner in which Barry establishes an occupation of the site as a court-yarded private world and, overall, the plan is punctuated by courts (the green areas). The old Westminster Hall (7) is on the Parliament Square side, opposite Westminster Abbey.

***Below**: Barry's body decorated by Pugin is remarkably regular rather than picturesque – striving to add verticality to the broad, horizontal mass of the complex.*

is so difficult to communicate in drawings, diagrams and photographs is Barry's success in creating a setting for a layered and interwoven set of rituals and conventions which together constitute the life of the Commons and the Peers, their relations to the monarch and to service staff, etc. This is a complex culture of privilege and power that Barry attuned himself to in terms of a club – which is rather how the place functions.

Charles Barry Jnr. 1823–1900

Extant London works include:
• **Holy Trinity**, 1856, Tulse Hill.
• **St Stephen**, 1868–82 , College Road, Dulwich
• **St Peter**, 1873. Dulwich (and the public library)
• **Burlington House forecourt buildings**, 1869-73 (As Banks & Barry.)
• **Dulwich College**, 1866–70.
• **Great Eastern Hotel**, at Liverpool Street, 1880-4.
• roof of the **Royal Exchange** atrium, 1884.

Charles Barry Jnr. entered his father's office in 1840. He was of frail health, decided to travel and, upon his return entered into partnership with his father's chief assistant, Robert Richardson Banks (1813-72), as Banks and Barry. When Banks died in 1872, Barry took his son **Charles Edward Barry** (1855-1937) into partnership. Aston Webb was a pupil in the office. He was President of the Institute from 1876-9 and the Royal Gold Medallist of 1877.

Edward Middleton Barry 1830–1880
Extant London works include:
• **St Saviour**, 1856, Hampstead.
• **Floral Market and Opera House**, 1859, Covent Garden (see page 428).
• **Charing Cross Station hotel**, 1863-4.
• **Temple Gardens Building**, 1878, Middle Temple Lane.

The third son of Charles Barry, E.M. Barry took over his father's practice in 1860 and completed work at Westminster, 1866-8. He was Professor of Architecture at Kings College, London, 1873-80, and completed a number of works in his own name.

Sir John Wolfe-Barry 1836–1918

Mention should also be made of John Wolfe-Barry, the distinguished engineer. He was the youngest of the elder Charles Barry's sons. He worked on many railway projects, including the Circle Line, bridges over the Thames east of Westminster, Tower Bridge after Horace Jones' death, etc. He played a strong role in the Institute of Engineers (at one time their President) and was a keen advocate of standardisation in engineering practices.

the genius as medievalist
Augustus Welby Northmore Pugin 1812–52

Extant London works include:

• **Houses of Parliament**, 1835 on. With Barry.
• **St Peter's Woolwich Presbytery**, 1842, Woolwich New Road. Extended by E.W. Pugin.
• **St Thomas of Canterbury**, 1847-48, 60 Rylston Road, Fulham.

Pugin haunts English architecture. But it is not many architects that supplement their income by running a wrecker chasing after booty from ships grounded on the Goodwin Sands. Or have been shipwrecked themselves. And it says something about the frustrations of getting to this man that one has to introduce him in this way. By rights, he should have a large place in this work; in fact, apart from the Palace of Westminster, there is very little of him in London. St Thomas' stands out, but is possibly not his best work. The Houses of Parliament was undertaken with Barry and undoubtedly stands as his greatest achievement, although marred by contentious claims to authorship.

His figure has all the romance and danger of that man who ran the wrecking business and sailed choppy seas. He is said to have remarked, *"I have lived an hundred years in forty"*, and his life was to end, ironically, in the year the Houses of Parliament opened, having been released from Bethlehem Hospital (Bedlam) three days before dying at his home in Ramsgate. Another irony is that this is the man who wrote so forcefully and persuasively about 'good' art and morality, advocating a return to medieval Christian sources as a radical new basis for art and its tastes when his most significant work is his contribution to Barry's work at Westminster. One is reminded that, in Roman times, religion and politics were not divisible and that the early Christians – with their private salvation and concern to divorce the state and their religion – were deemed to be perverted, superstitious and a threat to public order and imperial aspirations.

Pugin's father (Augustus Charles Pugin, 1762-1832; a long-term drafting assistant to Nash) was already a great advocate of the arts of the middle ages and it is in his service that the young man learned to draw and acquire a taste for all things pointed, growing up among many students also learning from the elder Pugin. He was 'discovered' by a member of the firm of royal goldsmiths in the print room of the British Museum, where he was copying the prints of Dürer. This began the start of a glamorous career, but Pugin was keen on boats and the stage as well as medieval design. It was from acting friends that he said, *"I first imbibed the taste for stage machinery and scenic representation to which I afterwards applied myself so closely."*

At seventeen he was a stage carpenter. There followed a period to the mid-1830's when Pugin started a furniture firm (that failed; he was even imprisoned for non-payment of rent, in 1831, the year he first married), was twice married and became engaged in architectural works. He was quickly publishing books on imaginary medieval themes and, between 1835-6 (still in his early twenties) he published three books of his designs for furniture and metalwork. It was also in 1835 that Pugin converted to catholicism, designed himself a home in Salisbury, and began architectural work for the firms of James Gillespie Graham and for Charles Barry – in fact, he assisted both men in submitting competition entries for the new Houses of Parliament. And, in 1836, he published his most famous book, Contrasts, or, *A parallel between the noble edifices of the fourteenth and fifteenth centuries, and similar buildings of the present day; shewing the present decay of taste: accompanied by appropriate text.*

Pugin's rules:
• *There should be no features about a building which are not necessary for convenience, construction or propriety.*
• *All ornament should consist of enrichment of the essential construction of the building.*
When George Gilbert Scott read these lines he felt *"awakened as if from a dream."*

Opposite: *detail of the Palace of Westminster (the Victoria Tower is in the background).*

By 1837 an independent career as an architect was under way. Designs for country houses, catholic churches, metalwork and stained glass filled his time. Clearly, he was a remarkable and prodigious man, manifest in part by the fact that he never had an office but worked by himself, relying on a close group of colleagues who understood his swiftly drawn designs.

In 1841, Pugin published *The True Principles of Pointed or Christian Architecture*, in which his message was directed at the architect with a work modelled on the values of Laugier's work, *Essai sur l'architecture*, of 1753, but now in reference to a Gothic rather than Classical approach. Here he states his two great principles for design: *"1st, that there should be no features about a building which are not necessary for convenience, construction or propriety; 2nd, that all ornament should consist of enrichment of the essential construction of the building."*

In 1843 he built a house overlooking the sea, at Ramsgate. However, his second wife died in 1844 – the same year Barry asked him to return to the Houses of Parliament project, on which he worked until his death (with Barry protecting the work of his assistant and enabling Pugin to work with his preferred fabricators). But it was also now that his career began to decline, his designs were criticised (including by Ruskin, who was opposed to and offended by his Catholicism) and he received fewer commissions. However, designs shown in the medieval Court of the 1851 exhibition were well received.

Two further attempts at re-marriage failed, but a third effort was rewarded in 1848. Together they had two children and Pugin now did most of his work from home. Tired by constant overwork and the application of mercury, Pugin's health finally broke down in February 1852 and he was certified insane (although the theory is that he suffered from mercury poisoning). He died in 1852 and Edward Welby Pugin, his son, took over his practice.

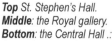

Top *St. Stephen's Hall.*
Middle: *the Royal gallery.*
Bottom: *the Central Hall .:*
Opposite page: *the House of Lords, perhaps the most ornate room in the Palace.*

Credits: photos this page and opposite © Parliamentary copyright 2007. Photography by Deryc Sands..

survival, success & significance
Sir William Tite 1798–1873

Extant London works include:
• **The Royal Exchange** 1841-4
Bank. External attic storey added and courtyard heightened by addition of a Corinthian order in 1988.
• **Scottish Presbyterian Church** 1824-7
Regent Square, St Pancras (described as ' a reduced verision of York Minster).
• **Nine Elms Station** 1838
Vauxhall.

Tite was born in the City, son of a successful Russian merchant and it is fitting that his best work is the Royal Exchange, perhaps the grandest façade in the City and one its more successful buildings.

Tite was educated in the area and became articled to David Laing, 1812. He attended the Soane lectures at the Royal Academy (1818), setting up in practice in 1824, but only travelling later and for one year, in 1851 (following a serious illness). City connections continue in his role as Director of two banks. And was also an MP for Bath. He was President of the Architectural Society which later (in 1842) merged with the Institute, and later became twice President of the RIBA. As an architect he was awarded the Institute's Gold Medal in 1856. He was also (among many other positions) a Trustee of the Soane Museum, and so on, being knighted in 1859 and, in 1870, being honoured as a Companion of the Bath.

Most of Tite's work came from railway companies =, for whom he was involved in valuations, purchases and sales, new stations, etc. (Nine Elms is typical, but most are outside London). He did well, remarking that, 'I inherited a fortune, I married a fortune, and I have made a fortune'. But historians don't like him or respect his work (one refers to Tite as 'venal'; others aren't much kinder).

Ironically, Tite was not among the 38 competitors for the Royal Exchange, but none could be built within the allocated budget and he was brought in as advisor, then putting forward his own design against that of Cockerell and winning out by 13 votes to 7. It appears to have been an unseemly affair, with everyone but members of the Committee favouring Cockerell's design. However, the Royal Exchange remains a remarkable ornament of the City that somehow manages to continually reinvent itself.

The first Exchange was a copy of something similar in Antwerp and was built in 1566 as a place of commercial exchange by Sir Thomas Gresham. Its typology was relatively simple: a central courtyard surrounded by an arcade, and shops on the first floor. It burned down in the Great Fire of 1666 and was rebuilt looking somewhat different but having the same typology, having a plan labelled 'Clothiers, Jews, Jewellers, Hamburg, Italian, Scots, etc. This must have been very similar to the first building, which is described as being arcaded and having a stair to the north and to the south up to about one hundred shops (a bazaar). Above the southern gate was a tower. However, like the first building, it appears not to have been very substantial and was repaired and then much rebuilt in 1820, only to be burned down in 1838. It was now that Tite's building was constructed: a more substantial work, now oriented east-west, but otherwise with the same typology. It was only now that a roof was provided (by the younger Barry, in 1888).

Trading ceased at the Royal Exchange during World War II and afterward, it became office space with, rather appropriately, the Mermaid Theatre group starting up in the courtyard. Significant change came in 1988 when Fitzroy Robinson designed an entire new attic storey (hardly visible externally) together with

Above: the west façade, one of the City's more grand frontages.
Below: the second Royal Exchange, built after the Great Fire.
Opposite page: the Royal Exchange today (the central area is now a cafe).

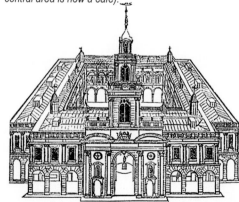

new classical features on the interior matching those designed by Tite. And it all works rather well, the new height satisfying the neoclassical advice to add to the height of rooms something like one and a half times their width.

Around the court are a set of up-market shops which, in a sense, continue the tradition of such things on this site. However, it is externally that one sees Tite's design providing a model that developers have long neglected in their pursuit of maximising internal office space: a set of small perimeter retail units which greatly enliven the street, taking up an edge zone and leaving a rational and regular heart much in the manner that the Richard Rogers office has been handling sites ever since the design of the Lloyds '86 building. It is surprising the City is without more buildings of this type (just as it is surprising that it has always neglected its backland of alleys that provide an alternative to the principal streets, and certainly to that ill-fated 1950s policy of a 'pedway' system, which still lingers about). Only recently has it decided to promote more retail content in new developments (having seen the success of this at Canary Wharf).

Top left: one of the perimeter shop units, with a mezzanine.
Top right: the first Royal Exchange, 1566.
Middle: plan indicating the retail units. Those on the interior are at a higher level than the external units. Note the north and south entrances which continue the original pattern, but now as secondary entry points.
Bottom: view of the south-east corner. The new attic storey is hardly visible behind a parapet.

'why am I here?'

George Gilbert Scott
1811–78

The Midland Hotel at St Pancras Station, recently refurbished and converted back into a hotel and luxury apartments, is remarkably popular. Its author, Gorge Gilbert Scott, was one of the most famous, successful and prolific architects of the C19th. With 29 architects he had the largest practice in Europe (which, in itself, is an interesting comment on working methods and relations with builders, etc., as well as a comment on size). He was so busy he had little idea what he was doing at any one time, famously telegraphing his office from a northern town to ask what he was doing there.

The former Midland Hotel sits adjacent to the British Library, Colin St John Wilson's impressive but less than perfect work that has the merit of employing the same bricks used by Scott. What makes the hotel so popular? We're told it is because of its Germanic, fairy tale castle associations; that we're all children at heart. But then why are such features attractive? The argument is regressive, taking us no where. The contrast with the building is Scott's equally ignorable Foreign Office building, in Whitehall: a government building with a sad history of inception, victim of style wars and political interferences, but nevertheless a worthy work that has some very impressive interiors. It is those interiors which attract people and not the building's exterior architecture.

Scott, son of a clergyman and grandson of a well-known biblical commentator, was born in Gawcott, a village in Buckinghamshire. He appears to have enjoyed drawing old churches and his father – somewhat of an experienced amateur architect himself – placed him with a local architect, James Edmeston (1791-1867), another son of a clergyman as well as a prolific hymn writer who had started up in 1816. (Edmeston is described as a dissenting architect recommended to his father by a travelling agent to the Bible Society. He complained that Scott wasted his time sketching medieval buildings.) He completed his pupillage in 1831 and went to the builders Grissell and Peto, where he gained valuable practical experience (in particular, by superintending the construction of Charles Fowler's Hungerford Market, in London).

Extant London works include:

• **Broad Sanctuary**,v 1853. Block of houses ion front of Westminster Cathedral, with entrance to Westminster School / Dean's Yard. Scott also did the monument in the middle of Broad Sanctuary (1859-61).

• **Harrow School Chapel**, 1854-57, also the **Vaughan Library**, 1861-3. North west London.

• **St Barnabas**, 1857 Woolwich.

• **St Matthias**, 1858, Richmond.

• **St Mary**, 1858. Stoke Newington Church Street

• **Kings College Chapel**, 1861-2. Strand.

• **Foreign & Commonwealth Office**, 1861-68. A fine building that is, nevertheless, better for its interiors than exteriors.

• **Albert Memorial**, 1862-72. Impressive but still as problematic an experience as it ever was. This was the work that won him a knighthood.

• **St Pancras Station / Midland Hotel**, 1868-74. Now the terminus for Eurostar. The hotel has been restored, extended, and the parts of the old building converted to apartments. Barlow was the engineer on the railway shed behind.

• **St Mary Abbots Church**, 1869-72. Crnr of Kensigton Hight St./Kensington Church St.

• **St Michael-at-Bowes**, 1874, Southgate.

• **Westminster Abbey** – like many other architects who have contributed work to the Abbey, Scott did the front of the Heny VII chapel, the Rose Window and the North transept (up to the level of the porches), all on the Parliament Square side, and the Chapter House.

Above: visitors enjoying the staircase in Scott's Midland Hotel (before refurbishment).

Between 1832-34, as the fashion for the neo-Gothic was rising to its height, Scott was to be found working for Henry Roberts (1803-76), an architect who had set up on his own in 1830 after working Scott completed his pupillage in 1831 and went to the builders Grissell and Peto. Here, as an unpaid assistant, he gained valuable practical experience (in particular, by superintending the construction of Charles Fowler's Hungerford Market, in London). Between 1832-34, as the fashion for the neo-Gothic was rising to its height, Scott was to be found working for Henry Roberts (1803-76), an architect who had set up on his own in 1830 after working for Robert Smirke. In 1832 Roberts had won a competition to design the Fishmonger's Hall, in London and he took Scott on as his assistant. (It was around this time, just before his father's death, that Scott went with his father to see a dilapidated church and, being too busy himself, recommended a Mr Annesley Voysey (1794-1839, a man with the reputation for designing the first London office building, in the City), who was the grandfather of C.F. Voysey.)

In 1835 Scott was invited by his friend Sampson Kempthorne (1809-73, someone who emigrated to New Zealand in 1842) to work on designing new workhouses (554 of which were constructed throughout England and Wales). Kempthorne, a former pupil of Annesley Voysey, had a father whose friendship with one of the Poor Law Commissioners led to the son being appointed architect to the new body, providing model designs in its 1835 report, and employing the young Scott. Two months later Scott's father died, throwing the young man and the family on their own resources. Scott now grabbed the reins and set up on his own. Literally. He wrote to all his father's friends, soliciting patronage, then rode the countryside to meet with them and offer his expertise. "*For weeks*", he wrote, "*I lived on horse-back.*" Scott would then crash into a design and travel at night from Union to Union (he designed four in Northamptonshire, adapting Kempthorne's model, and forty-four in total).

These appear to be hard measures forced upon a poor parson's son by difficult circumstances. However, Scott, in his own autobiography, was at pains to reveal that his mother had been well born and well connected. In fact, the large family Scott came from, together with its extended position within the clergy, were to stand him in good stead. And he was clearly ambitious although, upon marrying his cousin, he reflected that she helped to draw him away from *"hard, unsentimental pursuits"*. Kenneth Clark notes that, whilst he liked to offer an image of modesty, it was firmness and audacity that brought him success. And hard work.

But success was not immediate, despite the workhouse opportunities. To assist with the winning jobs Scott entered into a partnership with William Bonython Moffat (1812-87), a former joiner from Cornwall with whom he had been a pupil at Edmeston's office. It was Moffat who won the first job they drew up together and so they decided to collaborate in partnership. Between 1838 and 1845, they designed mansions, lunatic asylums, and churches in addition to workhouses.

The first of the churches was completed in 1838 – a design with defects that had been repeated in no less than six other churches before Scott had time to notice them. By his own admission, he had fallen into "*an abyss of shams.*" But success went to the heads of the partners, particularly (says Scott) to the head of Moffatt, who not only became extravagant, but adopted that arrogance for which architects are famous and upset the firm's clients. Interestingly, it was Mrs Scott who turned up one day to announce to Moffatt that the partnership was at an end. Afterward, Moffat rampaged on from one speculative development to another and, by 1860, was arrested for debt. Scott, at 35, considered that he had escaped a speculative mania (however, it appears that he spent the rest of his life being a friend to Moffat).

Meanwhile, Scott came across the works of Pugin: writings that excited him to enthusiastic fury – helped, no doubt, by coming across the radically conservative Cambridge Camden Society as ecclesiastical clients (High Church Anglicans) of a more demanding flavour.

This page: visitors on the principal staircase in the Foreign Office. Scott had intended the building to be neo-Gothic but the Prime Minister, Lord Palmerston, famously objected that it must be neo-Classical. He put the competition entries aside and was about to appoint Pennethorne when Scott engaged in battle – one he lost. 'French Gothic' turned to 'Italian Gothic' and Venetian Byzantine – what Palmerston called "neither one thing nor t'other – a regular mongrel affair." Scott was then forced to purchase costly books on Italian neo-Classical architecture in order to stay on the job. It was the kind of struggle Street was also to experience on the Law Courts.

Above: Scott's Foreign & Commonwealth Office (St James' Park side).

look at our work. I have seen three or four men with drawings awaiting correction or approval grouped around his door. The door flew open and out he came. "No time today!"; the cab was at the door and he was whirled away to some cathedral where he would spend a couple of hours and then fly off to some other great work at the other end of the kingdom." On one of his journeys Lethaby claimed that Scott noticed a church he admired and inquired as to the architect was: "Sir Gilbert Scott", was the reply.

In 1857 Scott published Remarks on Secular and Domestic Architecture, Present and Future, a reworking of Pugin and arguing for the Gothic and against the Classical as an appropriate English style in all matters. The Building News reported upon his work that it had 'the merit of being a thoroughly national revival of the Gothic style. In sentiment and in detail it neither offended by its violence nor sacrificed English to modern sympathies. If not remarkable for its originality, or its energy, it was always pleasing, moderate, and sensible. Indeed it had, in common with its author, a geniality that was eminently impressed upon everything he did." It was an auspicious time for him: in 1859 he was awarded the RIBA Gold Medal (an award which Professor Donaldson attempt to reverse' see page 226).

But trouble was in the air. In 1858 Scott won a prestigious commission for new government buildings in Whitehall, but it was to prove a poisoned chalice. The architect was very pleased with himself and later said: 'my details were excellent, and precisely suited to the purpose. I do not think the entire design so good in its elementary parts. It as rather set and formal. With all its faults, however, it would have been a noble structure; and the set of drawings was, perhaps, the best ever sent into a competition, or nearly so'. In fact, he was third in the competition for one building and unplaced for another. But a change of government presented an opportunity and Scott was off, somehow ending up with the appointment. Not everyone was pleased, including another new Prime Minister (together with the likes of Charles Barry Jnr, and the architect and MP for Bath Sir William Tite, who was among Scott's opponents).

In brief, Scott proposed Gothic for the buildings, but the new premier (Palmerston) wanted Neoclassical and not what he referred to as "French and Italian with a dash of Flemish." A compromise Italian-Byzantine solution was proposed and rejected by Palmerston: "neither one thing nor t'other – a regular mongrel affair." Scott gave in, bought books and went to study in Paris, finally coming up with a design that was approved in 1861. The Foreign Office was completed in 1874 and actually included some very fine interiors. But the sad exercise was not entirely a loss: Scott was able to reinvent his original design as the winning entry for the Midland Grand Hotel competition of 1865 – what is undoubtedly his most popular building (what Clark describes as the west end of a German cathedral with several Flemish town halls'). Even Scott thought the design was too good for its purpose.

But there was something real here: Scott even set out to meet Pugin and quickly became a disciple. "I was", he said, "a new man". His practical, instrumental mind had become intoxicated.

It was at this time, in 1838, that Scott entered a competition for a Tractarian memorial to the protestant martyrs – a design whose success, he admitted in his autobiography, was owed to the influence of his friends (although, he noted, it was a design that only Pugin could better). And then, in 1845, came success in an international competition to design a church in Hamburg, where he considered that he electrified the Germans and introduced them to the Gothic. In the process he also introduced himself to the idea of being a talented global phenomenon. A dizzy career was off. He had joined, as we would now say, The Club. As Clark notes, an incomplete list published in 1878 gave the names of over 730 churches with which he was concerned after 1847, 39 cathedrals and minsters, 476 churches, 25 schools, 23 parsonages, 41 mansions, 26 public buildings, 58 monumental works and 25 colleges or college chapels. (Gavin Stamp reports a more recent historian estimating at least 879 works.)

Around 1858, when T.G. Jackson was in the office, Scott had the largest practice in Europe, numbering twenty-seven staff (which, in itself, is interesting and says much about the nature of design responsibility and the relations with contractors and craftsmen.) Jackson recalled that, "He was up to the eyes in engagements and it was hard to get him to

Scott failed to win the competition for the Royal Courts of Justice, a commission that went to his former pupil, George Street (who had entered the office in 1844), but at the time he was undertaking the design of the Albert Memorial (completed 1872), the building that was to result in his knighthood. (He also completed the adjacent Albert Hall at this time.)

The work for which Scott has been most criticised – restoration on cathedrals and other church buildings – is also the most difficult to disentangle with fairness. Upon his death one of his former pupils, J.T. Micklethwaithe, said of him that, *"he could restore a design from a few remains with a skill that ensured a very close resemblance to the original work, and that faculty may have tempted him to carry out the work of restoration to a greater degree than modern criticism approves of. On the other hand there are two or three things to be considered. In the first place, the custodians of a building on which Sir Gilbert was employed would not have allowed him to do anything else than restore it in the manner he did, and those restorations he treated as he did would, in all probability, have been done much worse if he had not done them, or if they had been done by men who did not possess his skill."*

By 1870 Scott was taken ill, contracting his practice and handing control over to his two sons, George and John. He finally died of a heart attack in 1878. The obituarist of The Builder wrote that, *"If he had not the great gift [of genius] he however possessed others which in these days are perhaps even more conducive to success. He was indefatigable in business and a fervent worker. No chance was ever missed, no opportunity neglected, and thus he obtained a somewhat unenviable notoriety among less energetic or less industrious architects, of being over anxious to obtain commissions."*

More latterly, Scott's Midland Hotel has enjoyed considerable popularity and now fronts the refurbished St Pancras Station, destination for the cross-Channel Eurostar trains since late 2007.

Below: the east side of Scott's Midland Hotel / St Pancras Station as reinvented for Eurostar, 2007. Behind the former hotel sits W.H. Barlow's iron train shed, spanning 243 ft (74 m) – then and for twenty-five years, the largest in Europe (1864; bottom photo).

Keeping it in the family:
the Gilbert Scotts

- George Gilbert Scott, 1811-78.
- George Gilbert Scott (Jnr.),

1839-97, (son of Sir George elder).
- John Oldrid Scott, 1814-1913, (son of Sir George elder).
- Charles Marriot Oldrid Scot 1880-1952, (son of Oldrid).
- Sir Giles Gilbert Scott, 1880-1960, (son of Sir George, Jnr.).
- Adrian Gilbert Scott, 1882-1963, (son of Sir George, Jnr.).
- Richard Gilbert Scott, (son of Sir Giles).

Below: *the staircase at the Midland Hotel, St Pancras (George Gilbert Scott) prior to restoration and the hotel's conversion.*

Scott was the beginning of a rather talented line of architects. His son, also named **George**, appears to have been rather undecided as to whether he was an architect or scholar. He went to Eton, then entered his father's office as an articled pupil and later as an assistant, but was persuaded to attend Cambridge University. He seems to have been significant in shifting neo-Gothic tastes away from early English and Continental models to late English Gothic (e.g. St Agnes, Kennington, in brick but also in the 'debased' Perpendicular style; bombed). Gavin Stamp quotes Alexander Thompson describing Scott's appearance as follows: *"he made his appearance in black knee breeks black silk stockings high heeled shoes with large buckles, blue coat, yellow vest white neck cloth with stiffener and frilled shirt – he is one of the Queen Ann folks."* But his later years – after inheriting significant wealth from his father – were marred by mental instability and he died as a permanent resident of his father's Midlands Grand Hotel, suffering from acute cirrhosis of the liver and heart disease.

And there was another architect-son: **John Oldrid Scott,** of we know relatively little except that he continued his father's practice. Again, his work was mostly ecclesiastical. He was admitted to the RIBA in 1878 (his proposers being Charles Barry Junior, George Edmund Street and Benjamin Ferrey) and is described as having started in practice in 1864. He completed his father's Scottish projects, modifying the design of the spire at the University of Glasgow and acting as consultant for new buildings at the university until 1901.

In his later years John Oldrid was assisted by his son **Charles Marriot Oldrid Scott**, articled to Reginald Theodore Blomfield 1898-1902. He returned to his father's practice in 1902-3, but briefly obtained a place with George Frederick Bodley to widen his experience in 1903 before returning to his father's office as partner in 1904. He either did not attempt, or did not pass, the qualifying exam and was admitted LRIBA in the mass intake of 20 July 1911 (his proposers being George Luard Alexander, a colleague at Bodley's, Richard John Tyndall (both of whom had recently passed the qualifying exam and had been admitted ARIBA) and an elderly former assistant of his grandfather's, Charles Robert Baker King). John Oldrid and Charles Marriot appear to have won few commissions of their own.

But the most famous Scott was **Giles**, the architect who gave his name to Waterloo Bridge (what the tourist boats romantically like to tell visitors is called The Ladies Bridge), the K series of telephone boxes, and the power

station shell at Bankside that is used as the basis of the Tate Modern. Apart from being an RIBA Gold Medal winner, he worked on the Guildhall and, immediately after his death, his office took the opportunity to provide something different to what the old man would have given to the Guildhall as a west library and administration wing. (See page 312.)

In turn, his son, **Richard Gilbert Scott**, more recently gave the Guildhall its Art Gallery - a curious Post-Modern cum Olde English cum neo-Beaux-Arts design adjacent to Dance's frontage and drifting around in a land of its own, post a dramatic shift in fashions in the early 1990s recession.

Generations of the Gilbert Scotts at the City Guildhall.
Top: *Giles Gilbert Scott north side offices, (1955-7; the design is worth comparing with the Bankside Power Station – the current Tate Modern – completed about the same time.*
Middle: *office and library, 1966-9, completed after the death of Giles by Richard Gilbert Scott, as if to say: 'the old man is dead; let's get on with some moderne stuff!' The design exhibits some curious neo-medieval 'jettying' and is now in precast concrete, but is rather well executed and helps to form the courtyard in front of Dance's façade that now has the foundation line of the old Roman arena marked in its paving.*
Bottom: *the recent Guildhall Art Gallery (1999) by Richard Gilbert Scott – again, well built but, as a design, idiosyncratic and almost original in its curiously mix of sources. The building also houses the City's Marketing Suite.*

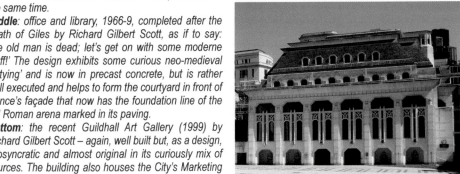

a coarse-grained genius
William Butterfield 1814–1900

Kenneth Clark described Butterfield as a better architect than Gilbert Scott, but a man with a discordant, sadistic hatred of beauty who offered us indigestible detail – which is one way of describing All Saints, Margaret Street, but one that begs questions about taste, beauty, aesthetic satisfaction, good design and the like. But it is true: it takes most people some time to become accustomed to All Saints and to be surprised as they (perhaps) slowly came under its spell. It is a masterly work, exhibiting an exhilarating intermixture of what Ruskin referred to as penetrative and associative imagination. Oddly, the work reminds one of Lutyens, who once remarked about his love of Classicism: *"In architecture, Palladio is the game. It is so big – few appreciate it now and it required training to value and realize it. The way Wren handled it is marvellous. ... Under the hand of a Wren it glows and the stiff materials become as plastic clay. I feel sure that if Ruskin had seen that point of view he would have raved as beautifully as he raved for Gothic. ... it is a game that never deceives, dodges, never disguises."*

Perhaps Ruskin might have asked why Lutyens could not play that game in terms of the Gothic? The point is not the style of game but gaming as such. That gaming is 'correct' by being on target and not for those stylistic reasons taste proffers. In fact, it sometimes invites one's taste almost against inclination. To that extent All Saints demands participation and a contribution to its experience, much in the manner that Hawksmoor's architecture does. It has the potential to come alive, but it asks that you join in the work of realising an elusive, momentary vitality. It exhibits gamesmanship as a sound value – and one devoid of the negative associations commonly lent to that term.

Having said all that, one is aware that many people will share Clark's opinion. There can be discomfort. The enormous tower, for example, is less relevant to the experience in Margaret Street than justifies its overbearing massiveness. But then it has, to a large extent, lost the low-rise context that would have made it a feature of the skyline in the area. Its imposing message is one of might and brute, dominating presence, around which the other parts are gathered in quiet repose. It is robust in the sense of an extraordinary strength of character that stands freely and independently, on its

own, addressing you as its very determined self, and without sentiment. It is artful, but is 'gritty' in the urbanistic sense of some 1950s sensibility. And yet, walk into its south-facing forecourt on a sunny London day and you will be architecturally welcomed and embraced in an unusually considerate manner.

Nevertheless, it must be admitted that Butterfield's design is almost confrontational. It can only be experienced directly for what it is, unfettered by all associations. Only on that basis can one 'meet' with it. Perhaps no other architect could have created it. But is it 'sadistic' and exhibiting 'a hatred of beauty', as Clark (a man who detested the neo-Gothic and leaned toward Apollonian Classicism) suggested?

Butterfield was born, in 1814, into a Nonconformist family of nine children whose father ran a chemist's shop in the Strand. At seventeen he was apprenticed to a builder, Thomas Arbor. However, the business soon collapsed and, two years later, the young man had entered into architectural training, initially as a pupil of E.L. Blackburne, later with William and Henry Inwood, the architects of St Pancras Church, and afterward spending time working in Worcester.

Extant London works include:

• **St. Matthias**, Stoke Newington (1851-53) Bombed and poorly restored, 1854.
• **All Saints**, Margaret Street, London (1859) Butterfield's outstanding London work.
• **St Alban's**, Holborn, 1859-63
• **St Mary Brookfield**, Dartmouth Park, London (1869-75) Chancel by G.E. Street, 1881. A pleasant, simple barn.
• **St. Augustine's**, (1870-76), Queen's Gate.
• **St John**, 1864. Glenthorne Road, Hammersmith.
• **Vicarage**, 1859-60, 14 Burleigh St., Covent Garden
• **Chapel**, Bishop of London's Fulham Palace, 1864-66, Fulham Palace Road.
• **St Augustine**, 1870-77, Queen's Gate, KensingtonSt Mary Magdalene 1881-83. Windmill Hill, Enfield.
• **Holy Innocents Church** 1883-4. Kingsbury Road, Kingsbury (west of Golders Green).
• **St Michael** (1870-76) 1887-90, Bogard Road, Woolwich.

The Margaret Street frontage of All Saints. As for most churches, the bell tower is an address to people at large and has little ofrnothing to do with the interior of what lies below it. This is also true of Butterfield's building. However, the lower level of the tower has a distinctly observable impact within the interior, forming the south-west corner bay, where the font is located. The south-east corner of the forecourt also displays a remarkably contrived clash of architectural parts whose cramming together epitomises the overall design challenge facing Butterfield on this small site. Note the recurring gable motif and the scale of the entrance gate/screen, with its lamps and pavement bridging (especially against the brute mass of the tower).

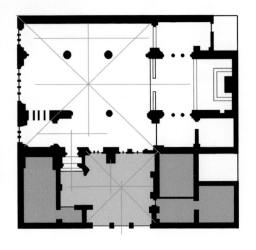

All the time, he was studying Gothic architecture and absorbing Pugin. By 1840, at twenty-six, Butterfield was opening the doors of an office in Lincoln's Inn and putting himself about as an architect. His first job was a chapel for his uncle, completed in 1843, in Bristol. A year later he was elected to the Camden Society.

Why Butterfield moved away from his family's religious predilections toward the faith of his sister's husband and family – High Church Anglicanism – and to have become interested in the work of the Cambridge Camden Society, founded in 1839, is unclear. But from now on Butterfield was at the heart of the religious revival in Victorian society: a man whose life revolved around his family, his work, and a faith that called upon him to apply his skill as designer to every aspect of liturgy (and, in this role, he had articles appearing in the hugely influential Ecclesiologist, published by the Cambridge Camden Society).

Initially, Butterfield's work was firmly with the framework of rule laid down by Pugin and the Society: C14th English Gothic. But something more idiosyncratic began to quickly emerge, particularly at All Saints – a design which turned him into a national figure

Above: the plan of All Saints is a masterful exploitation of the constrained and small site, of controlled access, axial controls, orientational devices, and overlapping spaces that are profoundly considerate of the various ways in which the site needs to be inhabited. A strong geometrical underpinning to the overall picturesque composition no doubts helps to achieve the design's effects (only suggested in the above diagram).

The forecourt is, in itself, a special space that serves for arrival, exist, common access point to each of the three component parts of the scheme, and as a place of surprising calmness set behind the entrance gate and screen that helps to shelter this space from the street.

By the time one enters the church itself one has already made a short but effective journey of architectural choreography that draws one toward the deepest part of the plan: the altar. Here, again, the inner body of the church is designed as the kind of cube that Hawksmoor employed as a still centre in his Baroque church designs. In fact, there is an underlying note of similarity between Hawksmoor's work and Butterfield's robust and picturesque massing of interplayed parts, despite the utterly different styles.

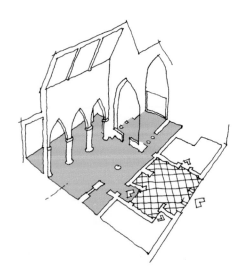

of importance. When it was completed, Butterfield was known as the author of the most discussed and characterful neo-Gothic building in England. Published as a design drawing in 1853 it was already the talk of the nation's architects. *"And in All Saints, right in the heart of joyless London, he is able, at 34, to deal his most tremendous blow"*, was one comment. It was his principal work, even in his own mind.

It was also at this time that Butterfield made a brief foray abroad, returning to comment, *"you will think me odd of course but I am more than ever persuaded that an Architect gets but little by travel. I am only glad that I had made up my own mind about a hundred things in art before seeing Italy."* He was, indeed, an odd fellow. To Norman Shaw it seemed that, *"we are all in much the same boat, except Butterfield, who is in a boat of his own all by himself."* But to Philip Webb, Butterfield was a significant influence.

In terms of his own character, he was a man who sounds, on the one hand, daunting: a cold, possibly humourless and inhospitable figure, later with bare office rooms in the Adam's terraces at the Adelphi, sloping off to the Athenaeum club and having little or no contact with contemporaries. But he is otherwise described as a warm, loving family man delighting in his sister's family. Like many other talented architects he was described as the be-whiskered figure of a tyrant who habitually wore steel-rimmed spectacles and a black frock-coat with grey trousers. In the context of a London largely made up of architectural witnesses to good taste he was a significant figure midst of radical upheaval.

But historians not only see his later work is an exhausted spirit, but he himself became somewhat bitter about the basis of belief and society's turn in a secular direction. To Coleridge, he wrote: *"The faith & the tradition which made strong men of our fathers are going. There will shortly [...] be nothing left for us to believe in but ourselves, and that faith [...] is comfortless"* (letter of 1883). By the 1890s he was an anachronism. And to a later generation he epitomised all that was tasteless and ugly about the Victorians.

Summerson tells us that Butterfield possessed neither T-square nor drawing board. All he employed was a pair of folding compasses and a two foot (60 cm) rule. He apparently made rather nasty little drawings that were then sent to the office for development. They would then be returned and an interactive process of development would ensue. His assistants, says Summerson (who, it has to be admitted, was hardly a fan), were all 'bread and butter' men who arrived dot on 9.45am and vanished at six. Apparently, he sat in a separate office and his clerks would bring their drawings to him, which he annoyingly corrected in ink (they drew in pencil). Summerson also remarks that Butterfield died, in 1900, after a period of senility – which may have something to do with this man who, always shrank from publicity of any kind and sent an envoy to receive his RIBA Gold medal.

Churches *"and his secular works were confined to certain collegiate works at Oxford, two large houses, a hospital, and a few other things of small importance"*, wrote Summerson. But in his lifetime, this abstemious bachelor had designed nearly one hundred buildings (including Merton College, 1864; Keble College, 1876; and Balliol College Chapel, 1857, all in Oxford). As always, most of this work appears to have been absorbed or vanished. There is little of it in London that draws especial attention – except the outstanding work of All Saints, begun in 1849 and structurally completed it 1855.

Above: the interior, of All Saints looking east from the entrance, and the street frontage.
Right: schematic diagram of the central part of Butterfield's design.

a new religion of design
Owen Jones
1809–1874

Above: a typical Jones design.

Jones is an unknown in the contemporary architectural world, but he received the Gold Medal in 1857, largely on the basis of work on the Crystal Palace, his publications, colour research and interior designs. Being a pattern-maker (as William Morris) was a major design role in the C19th. One biographer says of him: *"Jones was to become one of the most influential, prolific, and well-known designers of mid-nineteenth-century Britain. A man of his time, he made a major contribution to the development of design theory and education at a point when design was considered to reach beyond the aesthetic sphere and into the realms of economics and morals. And his spectacular architectural schemes and designs for consumer goods catered to the needs and desires of a growing and increasingly affluent and leisured middle class."*

In 1825 Jones was articled to Lewis Vulliamy and, 1930, set off on a Grand Tour travelling to Egypt, Turkey, and Spain, following an interest in polychromy and taking it into the new areas of Egyptian and Islamic architecture and decoration. The journey included six months of study at the Alhambra. Returning to England in 1834, Jones prepared the publication of his work, issuing the first three volumes in 1836 (but not completed until 1845): magnificent colour illustrations that contributed to the growing use of polychromatic detailing and decoration in nineteenth-century British architecture. The printing was so demanding that Jones became an expert and ran a publishing business selling illustrated books. From 1840 he was designing tiles, textiles, carpets, wallpapers and furniture. As a man in the right place at the right time, in 1856, he published the influential Grammar of Ornament.

Jones designed buildings with ordinary exteriors and spectacular interiors. Much of this was said to derive from his experience as a supervisor on the 1851 Great Exhibition. For example, he designed pioneering structures that boldly declared their use of cast iron, including the Manchester Art Treasures Exhibition of 1857; drawings and a model for a People's Palace at Muswell Hill, Middlesex (1858-9); and a series of drawings of about 1860-62 for the *Palais de Cristal* at St Cloud near Paris. However, none of the projects was realised. What was realised was St James's Hall, between Regent Street and Piccadilly which was, for almost fifty years, London's premier concert hall (1858). He also designed the Crystal Palace Bazaar in London's

West End: a great emporium, situated between Lower Regent Street, Oxford Street, and John Street, also 1858. In 1859 he designed the West End showroom of Osler's glassware. Their glittering interiors, dedicated to leisure and consumption, were said to be extraordinary. The barrel-vaulted ceiling of the main hall at St James, for example, was painted red, blue, and gold and was lit from below by star-shaped gas burners, causing the whole surface to glow like stained glass. The ceilings of the other two buildings used real stained glass. In Osler's showroom Jones used large mirrors to enhance the brilliance of the space. The Furniture Gazette of 1874 claimed the effect to be fairy-like: 'one of the sights of the metropolis'.

In addition, Jones completed many other exhibitions and interiors and won many prizes. This work was rooted in the radical colouring Jones gave to the structure of the 1851 Crystal Palace. Lecturing to the Architectural Society in 1835, he argued that cast iron should be widely and frankly used and that new architectural forms appropriate to it should be developed. He radically suggested that Christianity – the principal informant of architectural design – had been superseded by science, commerce, and industry; architecture needed to accept this state of affairs and should use materials and forms relevant to the new 'religion'.

When the Crystal Palace was shifted to Sydenham, Jones continued to play a major role in designing for the annual visitation of 2m visitors, in the process making major contributions to colour theory and its application in practice. In 1836 he joined the RIBA and became its vice-president in 1867. He died in 1874 and swiftly disappeared into an obscurity in which, so far as most architects are concerned, he still rests. He received the RIBA Gold Medal in 1857.

gothic as a living language
George Edmund Street
1824–81

Extant London works include:
- **St Paul's**, 1858, Herne Hill, Camberwell
- **St-James-the-Less** 1860-61. Thorndike Street, off Vauxhall Bridge Road (midst the Darbourne & Darke Lillington housing scheme). Street's first London church. See page 363.
- **St Mary Magdalene**, 1868-78, Delamare Terrace, Paddington.
- **St John the Divine** 1870-74. Vassal Street, Lambeth. Bombed and restored.
- **The Royal Courts of Justice**, Strand, 1871-82.
- **No 4 Cadogan Square**, 1879. A corner town house.

There are arguably only two neo-Gothic buildings in London to match Barry and Pugin's work at the Palace of Westminster and Scott's Midland Hotel: a grand complex filling an entire urban block and dominating the street its sits upon. The first is Waterhouse's Natural History Museum. The second is the Royal Courts of Justice in the Strand, designed by George Street.

Street was born as the son of a London solicitor who attended schools in Mitcham and Camberwell until the age of fifteen, when his father retired and moved the family to Devon. At that time he wanted to become a clergyman but found his first employment back in the family law office in London. However, his father died a year later and George took painting lessons and explored the local architectural antiquities with his brother Thomas. By the age of seventeen he was articled to Owen Carter of Winchester, an enthusiastic antiquarian architect who produced both classical and Gothic designs. Here, Street was Carter's pupil for two years and his assistant for a third, before moving to London in 1844, when he found a place in the office of George Gilbert Scott. It was in Scott's office, working on projects such as the church competition in Hamburg that Scott won, that Street and his colleagues turned their backs on the English Decorated Gothic still preferred by Gothic revival purists such as Pugin. Here, a more confident eclecticism and a powerful language of High Victorian architecture were born.

In 1849, at twenty-five, Street started up on his own, now being a highly gifted draughtsman with good experience. But he had already been doing work on his own in Cornwall, where he exhibited an independent interpretation of the neo-Gothic that was later to 'develop' (as he termed it) into something rejecting the confines of Pugin's historical and geographical boundaries to architecture – he preferred a more eclectic approach. Throughout, the mainstay of his work was churches. The first was St Paul's, in Herne Hill (1858). Then came St. James-the-Less, with its mixed French, German and Italian themes. In fact, Street gave many lectures and wrote a number of books on Gothic design in Europe.

Street's major project came in 1867, with the competition for the Royal Courts of Justice, a project that was to last until his death (with overtones of Barry at Westminster and, more recently, Colin St John Wilson at the British library) – a magnificent, difficult and compromised design, incongruously completed when the Queen Anne was in the ascendent.

Betjeman describes Street as the most active, genial and influential of the 'hard' neo-Gothic architects and tells us that Street's office (which became large) was a jolly place. There was one assistant who stuttered and could sing better than he could speak, so Seddon, Shaw (who appears to have learned much from Street's drawing style), and William Morris, who were then in the office, chanted to him in Gregorian plainsong through rolled-up foolscap. Street, on one Ascension day, gave them all the day off, remarking, "I know some of you can sing." But at a more personal level, it was during the Courts project, in 1876, that his wife of twenty-two years died; he married again and, eight weeks later the second wife died.

This was also during a period that honours came his way: in 1871 he became a full RA; in 1874 he received the RIBA Gold Medal (after Ruskin had turned it down on the basis that he no longer wrote about architecture, his efforts had been in vain, and the profession was engaged on works he could not approve of). In 1881 he was professor of architecture at the RA and President of the RIBA (when the Royal Courts of Justice were being completed). When he died, he was buried in Westminster Abbey next to his old colleague George Gilbert Scott. His son (d.1938) carried on the practice.

urban theatre
The Royal Courts of Justice 1867-82

In 1867 Street and a number of other distinguished architects entered a competition for new law courts in the Strand – one of a series (as for the Palace of Westminster, the Foreign Office, Royal Exchange, Kensington museums, etc.) that defined a new status for the profession. It was a mismanaged project and the judges could not pick a winner satisfying their criteria (a design by Burgess stands out). Edward M. Barry and Street were appointed to come up with a joint design: Street on elevations and Barry on the plan); Scott called in lawyers; in 1868 Street was appointed to complete the design on his own and, when it was published in 1871 there was more controversy over a new design that was much altered and clearly owed something to Burgess

(he ended up completing seven plans, all owing much to Burgess and Waterhouse). The stone Strand frontage is impressive, as with the brick rear parts, but the building was not completed until 1882 and, by then, fashions had moved on and the judges were no longer satisfied with a building in accord with old criteria.

Street's original design had all the hallmarks of Barry's court-yarded classical body (in plan) and Gothic dress. But the planning was distinctly flawed and such issues of convenience and picturesqueness were to dog the history of the project (dubbed 'an Acropolis of the law').

The site changed, the government frequently interfered on the basis of financial and aesthetic criteria, the site changed back. Eventually, a design was agreed. Street must have been exhausted.

However, the final plan is deceptively simple: boldly organised around a central hall, with the courts

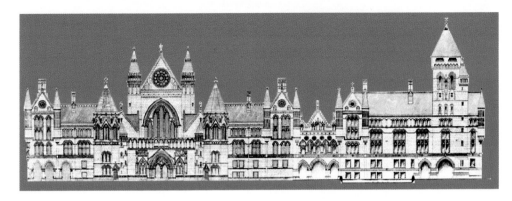

*Street's work at the Law Courts bears distinct parallels with the generality of what Barry did at Westminster: 'rational' plan, picturesque massing and detail, government interference, etc. **Above and left**: the Strand façade.*

ranged down two sides, with private access, surrounding offices and other facilities. Offset against this is the picturesqueness Street battled to lend to the play of masses – even if the clock tower on the south-east corner (criticised as utterly redundant to the programme) was less prominent than he had hoped for. Even when bids for the construction came in, in 1873, opposition continued and Street had to appeal to the Prime Minister, Gladstone. Ironically, fashions were already changing: 1871 was the year Norman Shaw introduced that idiom to be referred to as 'Queen Anne' at the Royal Academy (Shaw had served in Street's office for four years from 1848). In any case, the picturesque for country houses was one thing; for a major public building, it was quite another matter.

One year after Street died, Queen Victoria formally opened the courts, in 1882.

Below: despite its picturesque street frontage, the Royal Courts are planned simply and boldly. 'H' is the central entry hall; 'C' are runs of court rooms to either side. (See Barry's Houses of Parliament for something similar, but this time as a classical body in Tudorbethan dress.)

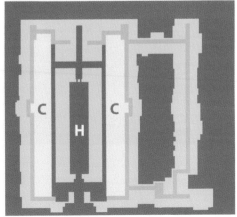

Street's law courts betray battles with bureaucrats and budgets that parallel Wilson's later experiences on the British Library and, to some extent, those of Barry on the Houses of Parliament and Scott at the Foreign Office. Here, there is a spareness to an architecture one expects to be more ornate, and yet there is just sufficient richness for it to work (Street had intended the upper floors to have mosaics). But strip stylistic issues out of the equation and one sees an architect whose work might be contemporary (the stone perhaps now concrete, the hardwood Finnish birch ply, the marble floors in terrazzo).

As Wilson's British Library building or Stirling at No.1 Poultry, here we have a building already out of period when completed (1882), at a time when the 'Queen Anne' had become fashionable.

The man himself is given a place in a work arranged by Blomfield and created by H.H. Armstead (1886). The architectural schema – including the vaulted hall he had to fight so dearly for – clings on to its overall coherence, vitality and vibrancy like some Hollywood hero on a cliff edge.

Opposite top: the central hall.
Opposite bottom: one of the long corridors giving access to the courts (below).

some other figures ...

While contemporary urban transport is principally an issue of roads, airports, and the viability of an aged railway system, for the Victorians it was shipping and the brute novelty of steam trains noisily slicing through a mostly new urban fabric, engendering speculative booms that peaked around the mid-1840s.

With regard to shipping, the scale of the East End docks (completed by the time Nash also completed Regent Street and the Regent's Park) draws attention to what was associated them with: warehouses, secondary industries (many of them very polluting) and rows of tightly packed and coal-fuelled terrace houses for the working classes. London had become a boom town that engendered a programme of Regency 'preaching houses' and early Victorian church building, underscored by religious and liturgical issues informing church design (epitomised, for example, by Butterfield's All Saints).

In an urbanising, industrialising society that, in many places, was becoming incredibly ugly in the broadest cultural sense of the word, a moralistic version of the picturesque rose in salience and attraction within a general context of uncertainty as to what architecture was now all about – an anxiety that had hardly begun to resolve itself until the end of the century, in a more confident (if still class-ridden) late Victoria and Edwardian era before World War I. The fundamental significance of architecture may have remained the same, but its programme of works and the nuances associated with their detailed consideration had, in one hundred years, altered radically, as had issues of commissioning and patronage.

While huge parts of London were being rapidly laid-out and developed, architects were orienting themselves toward the novelty of professionalism whilst designing buildings such as the Pall Mall clubs that are as indicative of structural social change as Scott's work houses, churches for the masses and new kinds of public buildings such as the town halls and museums beginning to spring forth (what Betjeman referred to as 'the architecture of the people').

In terms of taste, the Greek revival style of men such as Smirke and Wilkins at last withered, to be supplanted by Barry's Italianate work and, of course, the neo-Gothic

'Medievalist' style preferred by Pugin (Middle Pointed or Decorated, as opposed to Early Pointed or Early English, as Betjeman terms medieval variations).

Meanwhile, the design approach of the Regency period (to begin with a simple and regular exterior, capable of almost being anywhere, complete with portico and simplified external features, then sub-dividing the interior) hardly matched the complications of what was going inside. Calls for 'greater convenience' were being married to technical change, new tastes, and the kinds of social restructuring that were to result in the backstair arrangements of the stereotypical Edwardian house.

Architects had to find a manner of handling such changes. Intent and expression of intent were still divorced in the minds of many architects; however, many were actively seeking the substance of integrity that turned away from neo-Classicism as alien and unacclimatised to Britain and its culture. A national style was required and Gothic was increasingly salient as the naturally indigenous candidate. In an age of Progress, the challenge, as Goodhart-Rendel puts it, was seen to be a combination of the 'polish' of a contemporary attitude to architectural design, combined with "the romantic forms of more savage times." As ever, practitioners were divided. Lethaby, for example, differentiated the medievalists into the 'hards' and the 'softs': "One group turns to imitation, style, 'effects', paper designs and exhibition; the other founds on building, on materials and ways of workmanship and proceeds by experiment. ... the former were primarily sketchers and exhibitors of 'designs', the others thinkers and constructors."

The 'hards' including the likes of Butterfield who, Betjeman said, "worked on the principle that, since he was building in an age when workmen knew how to use brick and cast iron, he would build in brick and cast iron where those materials were most easily come by"; in other places, such as the West Country, he employed stone on the same basis as Street. He, like Street, adopted the Gothic as a living language – an attitude that was to grow and develop, flowering as a unique body of varied works belonging to the 1880s and '90's, when Britain was a most curious place: a wealthy, industrialised global power ridden by class consciousness and

Above: Gustave Doré's depiction of London ('Over London by Rail, 1870).
Opposite: the George Street house at No. 4 Cadogon Square.

political strife and yet self-consciously defining many of the characteristics and public rituals that have, ever since, defined what it means to be British.

Above: *Salvin.*

• **Lewis Vulliamy** 1791-1871.
Son of a celebrated clock maker who became articled to Sir Robert Smirke and started attending lectures at the RA in 1809, winning medals. In 1818 he set off on a four year Grand Tour, mostly in Italy. He was an eclectic designer: Gothic churches and Greek for buildings such as the Law Society. He had a reputation for being idiosyncratic, but with also of being thoroughly professional.
• The Law Society Hall, Chancery Lane, 1828-32. Library extension to the north by William Holden.
• St Barnabas, Addison Road, Kensington, 1828-9.
• St John's church, Richmond, 1830-1.
• St Michael's church, Highgate, 1830-2.
• Hickey's Almshouses, Sheen Road, Richmond, 1834.
• Congregational Church, Vineyard, Richmond, 1831.
• Christs Church, Woburn Square, 1831-3
• The Royal Institution, frontage, Albermarle Street, 1838.
• Christ Church, Jamaica Road, Rotherhithe, 1838-9.
• St Peter's church, Bethnal Green, 1841.

• **J.J. Scoles** 1798-1863.
Born in London; pupil of Joseph Ireland; travelled 1822-6; in practice collaborating with Nash , planning much of Gloucester Terrace and Gloucester Gate, 1827-8. His later work was mostly Roman Catholic churches.
• Our Lady, Lisson Grove, 1836.
• St John the Evangelist, Islington, 1842.
• Roman Catholic Church of the Immaculate Conception, Farm Street, Mayfair, 1844-49.
• Oratorians' House, Brompton Oratory, 1853.

• **Anthony Salvin** 1799-1881.
Born in Durham. Worked for Nash; set up on his own in 1828; had a large practice for whom Norman Shaw worked before going to Street (who must have been influenced by Salvin's picturesque neo-Elizabethan style, e.g., at Harlaxton Manor, when creating his 'Queen Anne' style). As the designer of country houses, described as the aristocratic architect *par excellence.*
• St Stephen, Hammersmith, 1850.

• **Benjamin Ferrey** 1810-80.
Born Christchurch, Hants. Started under the elder Pugin; toured on the Continent; went to William Wilkins; started up in 1834; had very large practice. RIBA Gold Medallist 1870.
• St Stephen, 1845-7, Rochester Row, Vincent Square, Westminster.
• All Saints, Blackheath, 1857-67.

• **John Shaw** (the elder) 1776-1832.
• Born Bexley, Kent; articled to George Gwilt the elder; began in practice in 1798.
• St Dunstan-in-the-West, Fleet Street, 1829-33.

• **John Shaw** (the younger) 1803-70.
Born in London; pupil of his father.
• 191 Fleet Street, 1834.
• Goldsmiths College, Deptford, 1843-4.

• **Samuel Saunders Teulon** 1812-73.
Born in Greenwich; articled to George Legg; worked for George Porter; set up on his own about 1840.
• Christchurch, Croydon, 1851-2.
• St Mark, Silvertown, Woolwich, 1861-2.
• St Mary, Ealing, 1866-73.
• St Stephen, Rosslyn Hill, Hampstead, 1876.

• **John Raphael Brandon** 1817-77. Articled to W. Parkinson, 1836.
• Catholic Apostolic Church (Church of Christ the King), 1855 (with brother Joshua Arthur), Gordon Square. There is also the Holy Trinity Church, Townsend Road, Richmond, by these two brothers. Betjeman remarks the former is one of the finest pure medievalist churches in the Pugin tradition anywhere in England.

• **John Loughborough Pearson** 1817-97.
With Ignatius Bonomi, at Durham, 1831-41. He then briefly worked for a George Pickering before coming to London. He spent five months with his friend Anthony Salvin, before became Philip Hardwick's principal assistant. He then set up on his own. Most of his work

Above: Bodley. **Below:** Burgess

• **George Frederick Bodley** 1827-1907. First pupil of G.G. Scott (1845-50) and close friend of the younger Scott. In partnership with Thomas Garner from 1868-97. In 1903 he was an assessor on the Liverpool cathedral competition won by the twenty-one year old Giles Gilbert Scott, whom Bodley was appointed to assist. RIBA Gold Medalist 1899; RA in 1903.
• St Michael, 1876-81, Camden Road, Camden. (Admired by Betjeman)
• Holdy Trinity, 1902-04, Prince Consort Road (As Service notes, the exterior does not prepare one for the interior; it was also admired by Betjeman.) (Near the Albert Hall, which is by Captain Francis Fowkes, 1823-65, and Major-General H.G.D. Scott.
• Eton Mission Church at Hackney Wick, begun 1889.
• Holy Trinity, Prince Consort Road, 1901–6.

• **William Burgess** 1827-81.
Articled to Edward Blore in 1844; assistant to Matthew Digby Wyatt, 1849; travelling on the Continent 1849-54. Another 'hard'. Articled to Edward Blore in 1844; assistant to Matthew Digby Wyatt 1849.
• St Anne's Court (working class dwellings), c1875, Wardour Street, Soho.
• No.29 (the 'Tower House'; formerly no. 9) Melbury Road, Kensington, 1875-80; his own home (with a remarkable interior; last known occupant Jimmy Page).

• **George Goldie** 1828-87.
Born in York.Came to London and set up Goldie, Child and Goldie. Undertook mostly Roman Catholic work.
• Church of the Assumption, Kensington Square, 1875.
• St James, Spanish Place, Marylebone, 1885-90.
    • Church of the Holy Redeemer, Cheyne Walk, Chelsea, 1895.

• **Sir Ninian Comper** 1864-1960.
Born in Scotland. In 1883 he was articled to G. F. Bodley, in London, later entering partnership with William Bucknall (until 1905). A late advocate of all things Gothic, especially Perpendicular, with a strong historical and liturgical basis to his work; had a large practice.
• Gothic altar with riddle posts and a hanging pyx for the chapel of St Matthew's clergy house, Westminster, 1892.
• St Cyprian's, 1903, Clarence Gate, Marylebone (near Baker Street). As Service notes, the exterior does not prepare one for the interior; it was also admired by Betjeman.
• Eton Mission Church at Hackney Wick, begun in 1889.
• Holy Trinity, Prince Consort Road, 1901–6. (Near the Albert Hall, which is by Captain Francis Fowkes, 1823-65, and Major-General H.G.D. Scott.)

was on churches; later in his career he fell foul of SPAB and was branded a destroyer.
• St Peter's, 1863-5, Kennington Lane (also a parsonage, an orphanage, and schools within one group).
• St Augustine, Kilburn Park Road, Kilburn, 1870-81. (Claimed as Pearson's best work).
• St Dunstan-in-the-West, Fleet Street, 1831-3. Neo-Gothic; strange octagonal space. Impressive, dominating tower.

• **James Brooks** 1825-1901
Born Hatfield, son of a farmer; articled to Lewis Stride; set up in practice 1852. RIBA Gold Medalist 1895. Also one of the Lethaby / Betjeman 'hards'.
• All Hallows, Shirlock Street, St Pancras, 1889
• Church of the Ascension, Lavender Hill, Battersea (completed by J.T. Mickelwaite), 1973-83.
• St Andrew, High Road, Willesden, 1886-7.
• St Mary, Church Lane, Hornsey, 1888 on
Other churches have been altered or are no longer in use.

the changing Victorian townhouse

Above: three parts of a late C18th Georgian façade, the central part showing Regency modifications and, especially a rendered ground floor and the addition of a portico with Doric columns (all in Eaton Place). **Centre**: a house from the 1830s, showing a similar typology, but now more thoroughly Italianate – and completely rendered. **Right**: the final stage in this evolution; the implicit order of base, giant order and attic has now been replaced by the formula Barry favoured: a cornice that replaces the attic storey and Italianate rather than Grecian features.

The next stage was the 'Queen Anne,' (**bottom left**) in which we see brick replacing render, gables been introduced, and bay windows added as a cousin of those 'Elizabethan' influences enjoyed in the 1830s (Hans Place). Vernacular variations on these themes (with vestigial features) populate and delineate hundreds of London's Victorian streets. (**Bottom right**; Kentish Town).

The sister house type of the terrace houses in the centre of town was the neo-Classical suburban villa of a type one sees in, for example, Park Village (by Pennethorne) and St John's Wood.

freedoms, sweetness and light . . .

The Architects of London

So what was the Queen Anne?

Richard Norman Shaw 1831-1912
W.E Nesfield 1835-88

J. J. Stevenson 1831-1908

John Dando Sedding 1838-91
Henry Wilson 1864-1934

E. W. Godwin 1833-86

Philip Speakman Webb 1831–1915

William Morris 1834-96

Sir Ernest George 1839-1922

C.R. Ashbee 1863-1942

Ernest Newton 1856-1922

A 'free style': is there any such thing?

C.F.A. Voysey 1857-1941

Arnold Dunbar Smith 1871-1918
Cecil Claude Brewer 1866-1933

Alfred Waterhouse 1830-1905

John Francis Bentley 1839-1902

C. H. Townsend 1851-1928

the LCC Architects

Sir Horace Jones 1819-87

Sir Joseph Bazalgette 1819-91

Thomas Leverton Donaldson 1795–1885

In 1869 Arnold summarised Britain's social equation in the following terms: *"So we have among us the spectacle of a middle-class brought up in a way unexampled anywhere else; of a professional class brought up on the first plane, with fine and governing qualities, but without the idea of science; while that immense business class which is becoming so important a power in all countries, on which the future so much depends and which in the leading schools is, in England, brought up on the second plane, cut off from the aristocracy and the professions, and without governing qualities."*

Those architects who aspired to be 'professional' were seeking to occupy, as Anthony Trollope put it, *"a calling by which a gentleman, not born to the inheritance of a gentleman's allowance of good things, might ingeniously obtain the same by some exercise of his abilities."* But the degree to which this was also (as a registered and regulated, monopolistic profession) a business-like calling was at the heart of that contention dividing the body of architects and surveyors between registrationists and 'art-architects'. The traditional patrons of the latter were the rich and powerful. But with the coming of an industrial society professionals proliferated and their clients multiplied. These clients now, in the later part of the C19th, included natural allies who were 'progressive' members of a newly liberated middle-class patronising the young men expressing their architectural values in the Queen Anne mode.

One of the principal fathers of that style was Norman Shaw. However, the popularity of the Queen Anne style ran parallel to a thoroughly politicised issue with the general body of architects that deeply concerned and defined their status in society and which Arnold had referred to: professionalism.

In 1891, Shaw – a man described by Edwin Lutyens as the greatest architect since Wren (and who, in turn, has been acknowledged to be one of the greatest of British architects) – joined with others in writing a letter to the Times that concerned an issue still at the heart of architectural practice: *is architecture an art or a profession*? And by the latter Shaw meant a discipline to be promoted in schools, gated by the award of a diploma, and both a trade and business, as well as a profession.

At that time (sometimes characterised as 'the naughty nineties') many 'architects' were what we would now call surveyors. The proper way to enter the profession was as an articled pupil, perhaps after studying at an art college or attending occasional classes such as those of the Royal Academy schools and the Architectural Association. One worked and learned at the same time. The idea that one's principal mode of education was in the full-time isolation of a school and then an examined entry to a codified profession – now the most common way to enter the profession – was anathema to those who declared architecture to be an art (and, incidentally, would remain anathema to architects such as Donald McMorran, well into the post World War II period).

But the sceptics were swimming against the tide. Leanings toward professionalism had been evident since the late eighteenth century, in the manner in which men such as Soane and Chambers had practised. An industrialised society was everywhere professionalising its expertise and the state was providing the protection of close practice (as in law and medicine) in return for the monopolisation of honourable and expert, self-disciplined professions characterised by vocational commitment and service.

It was a debate with a long history and one that reached a crucial point around 1891 when a bill was proposed to Parliament – incidentally, opposed by the RIBA, who had their own ambitions regarding professionalisation, with themselves as its controlling body – a stance they have never since abandoned. One provincial architect referred to the contention among architects as 'the Practical Architects versus Fancy Men and Faddists'. And Shaw had no time for the RIBA, which he, as well as the Times newspaper, dismissed as a trades union.

In the letter sent to the Times by Shaw, A.W. Bloomfield, John Sedding, T.G. Jackson, L. Alma-Tadema, and E. Burne-Jones, it was protested that, whilst matters of sanitation and the like could be subject to examination the *"artistic qualifications, which really make an architect, cannot be brought to the test of examination ... No legislation can protect the public against bad design."* The point was once indisputable and then merely contentious. It has now been carefully laid aside, not just in architectural practice but in fine art. Society's attitude to the issue is highly ambiguous. However, at that time, Shaw et al had no reservations: professionalisation would be a disaster for architecture, and they quite rightly opposed the rather bizarre contention of the RIBA President, Alfred Waterhouse, that architecture was two-thirds business or profession, and one-third art.

In the background to all this was Arnold's "*middle-class brought up in a way unexampled anywhere else.*"

If an aggressive, sober and religious middle-class were 'surviving' in early Victorian Britain, they had achieved 'success' by the 1870s and '80s. Whether they were to realise 'significance' is a moot point concerning the substance of modern Britain's cultural scenario, but that period of success was also one during which – at the height of class consciousness and when a veritable army of people were in domestic service – this newly affluent class turned to the 'Queen Anne' with enthusiasms mixed with a degree of affluence and relaxation their parents and grandparents had not experienced.

During this period, when class consciousness was at a zenith and those confessing to be architects rose in numbers by 60% in twenty years (from under seven thousand to over eleven thousand, still half the number of barristers and one quarter the number of clergy), one in six of the labour force was in domestic service (1891). In the Victorian middle-class home, with its coal fires, kitchen ranges, heavy laundry work and over-furnished rooms, comfort depended upon service.

That form of comfort, which was to last up to the First World War, had been won in the early Victorian period by a middle class that struggled for a place in society with determination, sobriety, energy, concentration and self-control. Matthew Arnold saw them as philistine. He urged upon them Hellenistic virtues of 'sweetness and light' – the former referring to an enthusiasm for beauty as an end in itself ('art for art's sake'); the latter referring to the light of intellectual enquiry. Sweetness, as Mark Girouard, has noted, would dissolve ugliness; light would smooth away intolerance and bigotry. It is a broad prejudice regarding the Victorian period that still lingers.

If those philistine qualities were ones to be associated with neo-Gothic enthusiasms, then their opposite of sweetness and light became associated with a celebration of the child's innocence, a charitable concern for the welfare of the poor, for health, temperance, laughter, new galleries and museums, swimming baths and free libraries and, as Girouard puts

it, *"pubs without beer, Churches without dogma, and clothes without corsets."* As a counter to industrial realities tempered by the power and wealth of the nation, the middle classes – divided between business people and a professional class – sought after unsullied rural idylls underscored by snobbish anxieties with regard to both blue-collar workers and the 'county set'.

Here, as Girouard puts it, were the 'nice' people *"living pleasantly on pleasantly adequate incomes in a pleasant world of tennis parties and dances and summers at the seaside. Within this world was an equally distinctive inner world of people who were artistic and progressive as well as nice, who felt a little superior to the Philistines, who travelled to Italy, went to the Grosvenor Gallery, and varied their agreeable tennis parties and dances with equally agreeable sessions with their decorator or committee meetings to improve this or to preserve that."*

Above: the graphic art of Kate Greenaway (1846–1901), Walter Crane (1845-1915), and Arthur Rackham (1867–1939) characterise a sentiment in British tastes up to the 1914-18 war and lingered beyond that until the next war in 1939, when Rackham died. Greenaway had a long friendship with Ruskin and Shaw designed a house for her in Hampstead. (Thackham, whose period of success was really after Greenaway's death and up to about 1920, lived in a Hampstead house designed by Voysey.) Crane was a friend of Morris and, in the 1880s, joined him in socialist causes, in fact becoming the illustrator for the movement. In 1884 he was a founder member of the Art Workers Guild and, from 1888-93, was president of the Arts & Crafts Exhibition Society. The work of these artists on childrens' fairy stories and the like was a perfect complement to the raw social realities surrounding a privileged middle class of artistically and progressively minded 'nice' people.

New attitudes even came through as a new politics. For example, the Progressive Party of New Liberals and Fabians dominated the London County Council in the 1890s and demanded a programme of education and similar welfare measures (as manifest, for example, in the 'Board Schools' programme of Queen Anne style school buildings). And just as the progressives considered that everything could be reconciled with its opposite, so the Queen Anne architect married Palladianism with the Elizabethan: what Goodhart-Rendel referred to as *"a Gothic game played with neo-Classical counters."*

Shaw – the man identified as the father of the Queen Anne style – was one of the leading architects of his day. Lutyens, for example, wanted to go to his office but the queue was so long he went to Ernest George instead. He was, as it were, the Jim Stirling of his day, although he posed as a man who promoted architecture as a Ruskinian affair of inspired building rather than formal design *"I'm a house man, and soil pipes are my speciality"*, he quipped. As Pevsner noted, he was also an artful improvisor and *"was never afraid of mixing styles and he relished unexpected solecisms."*

Shaw's reputation was founded upon work that avoided the neo-Gothic whilst elevating a British vernacular to architectural status (or, if you prefer, lending it architectural pretensions). *But perhaps it* was Phillip Webb – another hero of the day and someone nearer to the heart of Arts & Crafts sentiment – who more properly adopted the stance of master builder. Like other Arts & Crafts architects of the day, the work of both architects was characterised by 'honest building', a concern with sound craftsmanship and by and the introduction of good design into every aspect of life.

Style, argued Betjeman, was an afterthought to Shaw, an architect whom he considered to be *"the founder of modern English architecture as we know it"* (he was writing in 1952). Certainly, his 'free' works set a new benchmark. However, as Shaw aged his work turned in a more formal and classical direction – notable, for example, in the former Piccadilly Hotel and, especially, the Alliance assurance building in St James' – and did so in that very period, around the turn of the century, when Lutyens and many others also returned to the disciplined formalities of the neo-Baroque as 'Wrenaissance' after a period of experimentation in a variety of 'free' styles.

The Arts & Crafts values within which 'freestyle' was to particularly flourish were to find an established place in British culture. As a sentiment turning toward the vernacular and the unpolished, the hand-crafted and the 'as-found' – as well as enjoying a residual longing for an ambiguous art status counter to academic pretention – these still find expression to this day. Here was architecture that was about art expressively rooted in craftsmanship, professional expertise and building, and set against notions of the discipline as what bears a refined and pretentious academic status. Here was a notion of architecture that bluntly confronted the challenges of architectural improvisation that Shaw's Viennese contemporary, Otto Wagner, advised students to be as 'a path of troubles and thorns'. As 'freestyle' – whether leaning toward neo-Classicism or the Picturesque – practice in this manner enjoyed a creative freedom especially coursed by that familiar issue of 'ought' which is, paradoxically, as profoundly 'situated' as it is ostensibly 'free' (one thinks of Frank Gehry referring to standing before a blank sheet of paper as a dangerous place to be).

But however more or less free, architectural practice might be, the art issue at its heart had, by the time Shaw was practicing, become a particularly difficult issue. *"The architect"*, Frank Jenkins once wrote *(in Architect and Patron)*, *"must be primarily an artist, but an artist of a rather special type, for no other art is expressed through a medium as complex as a building"*, and the Arts & Crafts movement addressed such matters by inventing terms such as 'art architect' and 'art worker', failing to find terms that celebrated design and craft as essentially different to that body of concerns rooted within an 'aesthetic differentiation' defining the status of art to this day and leaving architecture in a problematic condition with regard to its terms of legitimacy.

Of course, to ask whether architecture is 'profession or art?' is rather pointless. It is architecture: a specific kind of situated and symbolic response to habitational challenges concerning what belongs to 'arche' as well as issues of tectonics, but hardly to those issues of 'art' whose abstracted pointlessness, as Kant had pointed out at the end of the eighteenth century, is its essential point (thus, in one philosophical sweep, undermining a purposeful architecture's confused pretensions in this regard).

So what was the Queen Anne?

By the 1850s the notion of correctness in the neo-Gothic began to wane and be replaced by more free and robust references and mixes of English and Continental styles, but always with contention when it came to issues of suitability. Public buildings still enjoyed the favour of ostensibly less fanciful neo-Classical tastes, despite many successful attempts to apply medievalism to these types (e.g. Street's Law Courts and Waterhouse's Natural History Museum, but especially the Palace of Westminster). However, toward the end of the century a baroque form of neo-Classicism was to return within the framework of the same developing nationalistic sentiments that had fed the neo-Gothic. (Interestingly, Cockerell had celebrated Wren as early as the 1820s, in his lectures at the Royal Academy.)

To some extent such developments also manifest themselves as early as the 1850s as a robust variety of classicism with its own picturesque content, for example Cuthbert Brodrick's Leeds Town Hall (1853-8), as compared with Waterhouse's Manchester Town Hall (1868-77). But the major, intermediary stylistic development was to be dramatically introduced into the architectural scene by Norman Shaw's New Zealand House, of 1872, a comparatively small office building in the City (now destroyed), but one that came to be seen as one of the key works marking the introduction of the 'Queen Anne style'.

It has been suggested that, with New Zealand House, we are looking at a free adaptation of historic elements and not an attempt at revival. Perhaps, therein lay its comparative freshness. Certainly, its tone clearly hit a keynote of informality and (as one London newspaper suggested) comfort that, in the context of the City, and other neo-Gothic and neo-Classical alternatives, inspired many young men.

Pevsner was to reflect upon the style as simple and reasonable: an undated and rational solution to nineteenth century needs (but having little or nothing to do with styles deriving from the reign of Queen Anne, 1702-14). Mark Girouard describes the style as friendly, capricious, and artistic, and ostensibly aspiring to Matthew Arnold's virtues of sweetness (the creation of enjoyment and beauty) and light (the result of intellectual curiosity). But he also defines it as an eclectic 'architectural cocktail' dominated by elements derived mainly from seventeenth and eighteenth-century England: red brick, small-paned sash and bay windows, steep roofs, and gables (straight, curved, and stepped).

In fact, New Zealand House was a soundly neo-Classical façade of four symmetrical giant-order pilasters engendering three double-storey bays infilled with neo-Elizabethan windows, all of this set upon a base (with characteristically and informally off-set entry door), capped by a cornice Jim Stirling would have enjoyed with, above it, a set-back attic storey of dormers. It was an enlarged townhouse, of a traditional variety, complete with half-basement, borrowing from vernacular features, adapted to the City as an office building and given a distinctly mannerist broken pediment as well as neo-Elizabethan decoration off-set against the plain brick pilasters. In fact the façade is, as a type, veritably neo-Palladian in essence and formally similar to Jones' exercises in Lincoln's Inn, in the 1640s (see page opposite). Freedom still needs navigational orientation.

Girouard suggests that the Queen Anne style was developed in three interlocking architectural circles: one centred around J.D. Sedding, Philip Webb and William Morris (from Street's office); the 'Old English' manner of Norman Shaw and W.E. Nesfield, and their pupils Edward Prior and W.R. Lethaby; and a group of architects trained in the office of Gilbert Scott. However, there is (as always) a background out of which such a movement emerges. Goodhart-Rendel looks to William Nesfield, and also to earlier architects such as the relatively unknown John Shaw. He also argues that the style should, perhaps, be named the 'Board School' style because of the number of schools built in this style (following the Education Act of 1870 and the School Board it set up) by the architects J.J. Stevenson (1831-1908) and E.R. Robson (1836-1917).

Chief among the style's standard features were white-painted and subdivided sash windows. In addition, there was, white painted cornices, door cases, and balconies, segmental arches with brick keyblocks over windows taller than they are wide; upper parts of doors filled with leaded glass; curved and shaped gables; tall chimneys with ornamental ribs and capped by over-sailing brick courses; brickwork that is fine and rubbed, with very fine joints; large, thin stone corbels supporting balconies; and tops of roofs and balustrades in white-painted wood. Bedford Park, in west London, exhibits many such features. The Queen Anne became a central part of the Arts & Crafts movement, suiting its essential values and temperament of cultivated domesticity. There is something quite informal about it which is absent in Georgian and Regency Italianate houses.

Above: expansive Queen Anne terraced townhouses, in Cadogan Square, Chelsea, from the 1880s. These were family houses complete with ample servant quarters in basement and attic storeys. Note both the similarities and differences to the typical Georgian terraced townhouse.

As Goodhart-Rendel noted (writing in 1934): *"in these easy-going gabled homes the front doors call for no red carpet across the pavement, there are no balconies needing awnings, and it would be perfectly possible to come to dinner otherwise than in a carriage and pair. [...] Into Regency terraces not many people will be rich enough to go; into standardised flats many will continue to be unwillingly herded. The ideal expressed in [many Queen Anne style houses], even if it appealed to us as it did to our fathers, would be no longer within our reach. It should not, however, be allowed to fade without a sigh."*

However, for reasons that remain somewhat obscure, Shaw (and, after him, Lutyens, Davis and many others) used their creative freedom to determine that neo-Classicism remained a valid and rewarding framework for addressing issues of intelligently getting to the true root of a situational problematic and holding that at the centre of design and project endeavours. Its framework of rule was its own kind of freedom.

But neo-Classicism remained a heavy and tainted burden for many architects. And, out of their notion of freedom and anxiety concerning a Modernist mode of expression, something new was to eventually emerge that sought to embrace both professionalism and art as a non-contradictory package of values and one that had no place for the stylistic canons of Classicism. However, as we know, the ghost of Classicism still haunts contemporary tastes, predilections and practices and occasionally erupts into presence on the architectural scene.

In the 'Queen Anne style' we have what Goodhart-Rendel referred to as "a Gothic game played with neo-Classical counters." Actually, with New Zealand House, the game was perhaps the opposite (the scheme is fundamentally regular, like the Jones building in Lincoln's Inn (below)) although most residential examples carefully interplay compositional elements in exactly the manner Goodhart-Rendel suggests: mildly irregular and with a careful choice of details that proved hugely attractive to artistically-minded elements of the middle-classes, both its 'aesthetes' and 'progressives'.

At (the now lost) New Zealand House (sketch **above**), such freedoms and irregularities were counterpoints to an underlying 'structural' regularity that bears parallels with Jones' mid-seventeenth century work in Lincoln's Inn. Expressively, however, Shaw introduced features from a Tudorbethan period in a manner that nowadays bears similarities to Jim Stirling's introduction of disparate historic themes.

Extant London works of Shaw include:

• **Lowther Lodge**, Kensington, London 1873-1875. Now Royal Georgaphic Society with 2006 extension by Craig Downie.

• **196 Queens Gate**, 1874-6.

• **6 Ellerdale Road**, Hampstead, London, built for himself. The house for **Kate Greenaway**, Frognal, London, 1885, is around the corner, as is NO. 61 Fitzjohn Avenue, 1876-7.

● **Old Swan House**, 17 Chelsea Embankment, London, 1875-77. Also, **Cheyne House**, 1876 (on the south corner of the block); **Nos. 15** and **9-11** Chelsea Embankment and **the Clock House**, at No. 8 Chelsea Embankment. These all foliowed the newly completed Embankment, 1870.

• **Bedford Park**, London, the first "garden city" suburban development: housing, including St Michael and All Angels Church, 1879-82 Laid out and partly designed by Shaw (before handing works over to other architects). Houses include Nos. 19-22 The Avenue; Nos. 3 and 5 Queen Anne's Gardens; Nos 23-4 Woodstock Road; Nos. 5 and 7 Blenheim Road; No 6 Bedford Road; No. 3 Newton Grove and other semi-detached houses in that road. There is the gabled terrace in Priory Gardens, 1881. There is also the Tabard Inn and shops, in Bush Road, 1879-80.

• **Other houses** include: No. 8 Melbury Road, Holland Park; Nos. 60A, 62, 68 and 72 Cadogan Square, and No. 170 Queen's Gate, 1888-90.

• **St Mark's Church**, 1877-84, Coburg Road, Camberwell.

• **Albert Hall Mansions**, at Kensington Gore, London, England, 1879 to 1886. Also **Nos. 200-222 Cromwell Road.**

• **Savoy Theatre**, London, 1881..

• **Alliance Assurance**, St James', 1881.

• **New Scotland Yard**, on the Thames Embankment, London, 1887 – 1900 (North and South buildings; now known as the Norman Shaw Buildings and used as Parliamentary offices; also see Hopkins' Portcullis House). There are also police stations at Holmes Road, Kentish Town (1891-6) and Walton Street, Chelsea (1894-95).

• **Royal Academy restaurant**, 1881-5, Piccadilly.

• **Holy Trinity church** 1885-9. For the Harrow Mission, Latimer Road, Paddington.

• **Bishop's House**, NO.5 Kennington Park Place, Southwark, 1894-96.

• **Alliance Assurance**, 1902-5, No. 78 St James' Street, facing along Pall Mall, opposite the earlier

'I'm a house man, and soil pipes are my speciality'

Richard Norman Shaw
1831–1912

Shaw – one of the most famous architects of the late 1900s – was born in Edinburgh, into a family that was impoverished, his father dying two years after he was born. In 1846 his mother moved south to London, following her eldest son, who had moved there and become successful as a shipping agent (later to found the Shaw Savill Line). It was here that Shaw entered an unknown architect's office before working with a fellow Scot, William Burn, between 1849-54. He not only acquired a sound training within Burn's successful country house practice but also met William Eden Nesfield there. The two became firm friends, sketching Gothic detail together and even attending Pugin's funeral.

At this time Shaw was also attending the Royal Academy schools (then under the direction of the classicist C.R. Cockerell, whom he later revered) and winning prizes – sometimes used for Continental travel to Italy and also to France and Germany, now among the newer northern destinations where Gothic inspirations could be found. (He remained loyal to the RA all his life, giving lectures there and becoming a Royal Academician in 1877.)

Between 1856-8 he was working in the office of Nesfield's famous uncle, Anthony Salvin, but he then leapt fully into neo-Gothic work at the office of George Street, where he took over from Philip Webb as chief assistant. Also working here at that time were the brothers J.D. Sedding (1838-91) and Edmund Sedding (1836-68). However, Street's office was not untypical in not allowing assistants much opportunity to design (Shaw recalled that Street, a rapid designer, would never even let his staff design a keyhole) and Shaw left in 1860 to set up in practice together with Nesfield, formally being partners from 1866-9.

The two worked separately but evolved similar

Opposite page: *Shaw in Hans Town, Knightsbridge, an estate first developed by Henry Holland, after 1874 extensively redeveloped in the Flemish 'Queen Anne' style of red brick and irregularity that redefined the area's value.*

building for the same client.
• Former **Piccadilly Hotel**, Piccadilly Circus, London, England, 1905 to 1908; his last work.

Above: *Swan House, Chelsea Embankment (1876), about which Pevsner remarked: "The oversailing upper floors ... are in the tradition of timber-framed building. The oriel windows on the ground floor are a favourite English motif of about 1675, the excessively slender windows above are Queen Anne – but the delicate, even piquant ensemble is Shaw and no one else and had a great deal of influence in England and America."*

tastes in designing neo-vernacular details – what Shaw referred to as 'Old Sussex' mannerisms and what everyone else called 'Old English'. Planning reflected what had been learned from Burn, but the 'Sussex' detailing (tile-hanging, half-timbering, tall chimneys and the like) also referred to what George Devey (1820-86; an exceptional draughtsman and able artist designing country houses) was doing at that time, whilst being informed by the design discipline one could see in the work of Butterfield and Street. Alongside the 'Old English' style country and suburban houses, Nesfield and Shaw were also following the example of such architects as Philip Webb, J.J. Stevenson, and E.R. Robson in exploring a new 'Queen Anne' vocabulary of red-brick walls, tiled roofs, and informally disposed white sash-barred windows.

Shaw quickly established a notable reputation. His first major commission came in 1870 for Lord Armstrong, for whom he built the grand neo-Tudor mansion called Cragside, in Northumberland – the hi-tech house of its day, complete with hydraulically powered machines and a lift. In 1870 it was generating hydroelectric power and in 1878 had a form of electric lighting. (The client, Lord Armstrong, was an engineer, manufacturer and inventor keen on all things hydraulic.)

It was now that the 'Queen Anne' aesthetic was extended to the design of the New Zealand Chambers office building (1872), in the City – a work that surprised the profession and brought Shaw to everyone's attention (bombed in World War II). In 1874-6 Shaw designed and a home for his family at 6 Ellerdale Road, Hampstead and, by 1877, he had been elected to the R.A. This was also the time (1876) that a parting of ways came with Nesfield. Shaw went off on his own and commissions kept coming in. At this time came the commissions for, among other work, the Albert Hall Mansions and the Bedford Park estate (an 'artistic suburb', occupied almost entirely by artists, who appear to have eagerly taken to the style). His assistants at this time included Ernest Newton, E.S. Prior, Mervyn Macartney, Gerald Horsley, and R.W. Schultz, all of whom were increasingly allowed (largely because of Shaw's health problems) to do some elevations and other detail work, but never the planning.

In 1879 he had William Lethaby as his principal assistant, replacing Ernest Newton. Shaw's assistants used to meet to discuss architecture and called themselves (with an emphasis upon an English orientation) the St George's Art Society, later to be the Art Workers' Guild (founded in 1884).

It was at this time that Shaw's distaste for the RIBA (an institution he viewed as no more than a trades union) surfaced over registration proposals that were then haunting and dividing the body of architectural practitioners. Shaw had no doubt: it was an art. In 1884 his had pupils in the office had started the Art Workers Guild, but Shaw himself remained distant from the politics of the arts and crafts movement and especially from Morris' socialism. However, in 1891, together with

T.G. Jackson, he co-edited *Architecture: a Profession or an Art* as an opposition to the idea of registration and monopoly control of the profession.

At this time – during the 1880s – the character of Shaw's work began to change, moving toward more sober and pragmatic considerations and even toward outright classicism, turning back to Wren and the man who was a revered teacher at the Academy schools, C.R. Cockerell. His work was now more tempered and conservative, and interests turned to new technicalities such as foundations, concrete, boilers, drains, and plumbing, and took a conservative view of interior design, in which he favoured a simple richness. (Saint comments that, "An able and solid constructor, he was at perfect ease with modern materials such as iron beams and mass or reinforced concrete. But he saw them as devices on which he could play the tunes he wanted, not instruments with a destiny of their own. Puritanical critics at the time and since have found Shaw's pragmatic indifference to structural 'truth' shocking.") And he could be shocking with work we now take for granted. New Scotland Yard (1888), for example, is one that caused outrage in the newspapers.

By 1896 (at, incidentally, the time Lutyens was coming to the fore) he was officially in retirement but acting as a consultant on a broad range of projects, including Regent's Street redevelopment and a façade for the former Piccadilly Hotel (Piccadilly through to Regent Street), 1904-8). It was all now high Baroque, not Queen Anne.

Shaw died, in 1912, midst all kinds of frustrations and was given a tomb designed by Ernest Newton (at Hampstead Church). He, in fact, designed sixteen new churches, but is reported as writing; *"You know I am not a Church man, I am a house man, and soil pipes are my speciality."*

Above: *New Scotland Yard (North building). In the 1970 reprinting of John Betjeman's 'Ghastly Good Taste', of 1933, Betjeman took the sentence, "Influenced by Voysey, and reacting from the sham classicism of Norman Shaw, came the Art Nouveau movement of 1900 ... Its greatest exponent was ... a Scotsman, Charles Rennie Mackintosh, who died almost forgotten in 1924'. But he then adds a note (written in 1970) regarding Shaw: "Who, I now realise, was our greatest architect since Wren, if not greater." And he is probably right. The Alliance Assurance of 1902 is masterful in a way that its neighbour, the building he designed for the same client in 1881, is not.*

Above: Shaw's Alliance Assurance building of 1901-5, which Goodhart-Rendel describes as a design "that seemed to set all the traditions of its neighbourhood at defiance." And it certainly is a superbly assured composition, one that shows just how different Shaw's later work was to the style that had established his reputation as a young man. Far more Baroque than Lutyens would probably have approved of at that time, the design nevertheless shows Lutyens how an old man can play the classical game the younger architect was just beginning to enjoy. Ernest Newton was Shaw's chief assistant on the design.

Below: the south and west elevations.

Right: the earlier, Queen Anne style, Alliance Assurance is opposite the 1905 building.

William Eden Nesfield 1835–88

Extant London works include:
• The lodge at the Royal Botanic Gardens, Kew, 1866 (next to the Marianne North Gallery). The elder Nesfield designed the Avenue Gardens and a lodge, 1864.

Nesfield, five years younger than Shaw and possibly showing more promise as a young man, was the son of a successful landscape gardener (William Andrews Nesfield; 1793-1881). Educated at Eton, he became a pupil of William Burn, 1851-3, then to his uncle, Anthony Salvin, 1853 to 1856. In 1862 he published *Specimens of Mediaeval Architecture* based on his sketching studies in Europe (sometimes with Shaw). It was at Burn's that he met Norman Shaw, with whom he shared offices and perhaps work from 1863-76 (no one is sure of the exact relationship).

No significant independent work of his exists in London; however, Goodhart-Rendel makes him a significant figure in the development of the so-called Queen Anne style of architecture (e.g. a cottage at Kew and Kimmel Park, 1866-8, in Denbighshire). He patterned unorthodox business practices after his father, developing a parity between himself and his patrons, was inordinately selective in his commissions and clients, favoured freedom of design over prestigious commissions, eschewing that self-promotion favoured by the likes, for example, of Voysey. Nesfield renounced his associate membership of the Royal Institute of British Architects, yet actively participated in the Foreign Architectural Books Society. A heavy drinker with the reputation of being a womaniser, (which may have contributed to his break with Shaw) he was the occasional sparring partner of J.M. Whistler. He retired – still a bachelor – in his mid-forties (about the time he split with Shaw), married at fifty and was dead at fifty-three (of scirrhoma of the liver).

Below: Shaw's hotel (now the Meridien) in Piccadilly – his last work. The western-most bay was not built as intended (someone else had the lease), but the frontage is very grand (unfortunately the Tea Terrace has a 1986 glazed addition). In response to the loss of the last bay, Shaw filled in the last bay of the colonnade (a device which enabled him to build higher further back).

John James Stevenson
1831–1908

Extant London works include:

• **Board School,** Anglers Gardens, St Pancras, 1874 (with Robson). This was part of a programme under E.R. Robson (1835-1917) that resulted in 289 new schools (for some 350,000 children), mostly in the Queen Anne style and, later, a typical Edwardian neo-Georgian style.

• **Lowther Gardens**, Kensington, 1877-8. Shaw has nearby buildings.

• **Nos 63-79 Cadogan Square**, Kensington. 1881-3.

• **Nos 63-73 Cadogan Square**, 1885-6.

• **No. 1 Fitzsjohn Avenue**, Hampstead, 1883.

• **42-58 Pont Street**, Kensington, 1876-8.

Stevenson's life and work parallels that of Shaw, but on a more quiet note. He was born in Glasgow, was a pupil of David Bryce in 1856, went to London and to Gilbert Scott's office in 1858, travelled in France and returned to Glasgow and a partnership with Campbell Douglas (1860). This ended in 1868 when Stevenson moved spent two years writing and travelling before moving to London and partnership, in 1871, with E.R. Robson (formerly Chief Architect at Liverpool), whom he had met at Scott's and who was now the Architect to the new London School Board. This partnership lasted until 1876, but it was during this period that Stevenson and Robson developed the mannerisms of the Queen Anne style. This was particularly evident at the Red House of 1871 (demolished) – intended to be a demonstration urban version of Webb's Red House and paid for by Stevenson (his family firm had a chemical works in Jarrow, on Tyneside). He termed the style 'Free Classic' and it was to be widely imitated. (It was contemporary with Shaw's New Zealand House.) At Cadogan Square, Stevenson attempts to provide standard house plans with façade variations.

Below: Lowther Gardens.

John Dando Sedding 1838–91
Henry Wilson 1864–1934

Extant London works include:
• **St Augustine's**, Highgate, 1885-8. (Tower by Harold Gibbons, 1925.)
• **Holy Trinity**, Chelsea, 1888–90. Many Arts and Crafts features. Completed by H. Wilson, Sedding's partner, 1892-5. West frontage similar to Kings Chapel, Cambridge. Ceiling of wood replaced by plaster after World War II damage, 1959.
• **Holy Redeemer**, Exmouth Market, Clerkenwell, 1887-95. (Adjacent to Tecton's Finsbury Health Centre).
• **St Peter**, Mount Park Road, Ealing, 1889; executed 1892-3 by his partner Henry Wilson.

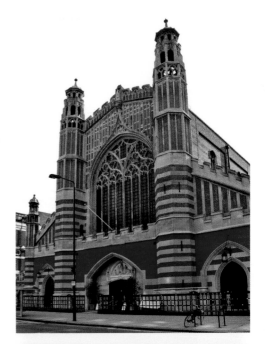

Above: Holy Trinity, 1888-90. Note the 'New Scotland Yard' stripes. In form, the building somewhat turns away from Pugin and Ruskin and back toward a barn-like, 'preaching house' style now dressed in Perpendicular garb.

Sedding was articled to G.E. Street from 1858-65, then joined his brother in practice (d.1868). Sedding then moved from Cornwall to London to practise architecture and design furniture, ornaments, etc. His London work includes the Church of the Holy Redeemer, 1887-8, Clerkenwell; Holy Trinity, 1888-90, Sloane Square; and St Peter, 1892, Ealing; with Henry Wilson, his assistant). Sedding is celebrated by Pevsner as a man who embraced machinery, who in 1892 declared that, *"Let us not suppose that machinery will be discontinued. Manufacture cannot be organised upon any other basis. We had better clearly recognise this ... rather than rebel against the actual and the inevitable"* – a sentiment of belief that was still radical at that time but, as Pevsner noted, did not fit with the history of the arts in Britain and with its educational values, class structure and social contrasts.

Wilson was born in Liverpool and worked for J. Oldrid Scott before going to Belcher and then Sedding.

After Sedding's death in 1891 he carried on the practice together with Charles Nicholson. He designed the altar rails, grilles and street railings of Holy Trinity. He became the first editor of the Architectural Review (1896-1901) and taught metalwork at the RCA and at the Central School of Arts and Crafts.

There is an architect called Edmund Harold Sedding (d.1921) who was John Sedding's nephew; his father, an architect and musician, was also called Edmund (1836-68).

Edward William Godwin
1833–86

Extant London works include:
- **Nos 1 and 2, The Avenue**, Becford Park, 1876.
- **4,5,6 Chelsea Embankment** (Chelsea Physick Garden), for Gillow & Co, 1877-8.
- **44 Tite Street**, for Frank Miles (1878)
- **Tower House**, 46 Tite Street, a block of four studio flats, 1881-3.
- **Fine Art Society**, 148 New Bond Street, London, new lower parts, 1881-2.

Above: *44 Tite Street, 1878.*
Opposite page: *46 Tite Street (1883), a stack of four studio flats.*

Described as a charming dandy, Edward Godwin appears to have been a remarkable character. Born in Bristol, son of a prosperous currier and leather cutter, he was educated in London but returned to Bristol where he became articled to a William Armstrong, City Surveyor, Architect and Civil Engineer (1848-53). By 1854 he had set up on his own and built up a successful practice with Henry Crisp (1825-1896). This culminated in winning the competition for Northampton Town Hall (in 1861). He moved to London in 1862; however his wife died in 1865. Success continued with work outside London until Godwin 'ran off' with the actress Ellen Terry in 1868. They lived in the country and there began a new phase of Godwin's creative life: costume and theatre design, furniture, carpets, tiles, textiles, interiors (e.g. for Oscar Wilde, in Tite Street), and studios, including the first two house types at Bedford Park. There were also articles in architectural magazines, theatre criticism, scenery and production. In particular, he championed modular furniture and mass production at affordable rates.

The affair with Terry ended six years after it had started and, in 1876, Godwin married a young

Tite Street was a remarkable colony of creative types on a par with Bedford Park but, as Girouard notes, "Late Victorian society made fun of Bedford Park, but had no difficulty digesting it. Tite Street was more than it could stomach." The names that populated the residences and studios here included: Wilde, Whistler, Dicey, Miles, Sickert, Stuart-Wortley, Pellegrini, etc. Godwin started off in the street with a large house for Whistler and ended up with a whole series of designs, only two of which survive (nos. 44, for Frank Miles, and a set of four studios at 46). Tite now includes a work from Tony Fretton (2002, which continues the tradition of the street).

designer in his office. He died in 1886 and, perhaps not uncharacteristically, his widow then married J.M. Whistler (the *enfant terrible* of the street), in 1888, as Bohemians apparently did. (Godwin had designed a studio called The White House for Whistler in Tite street, now demolished.)

Godwin's best work is outside London (e.g. the Northampton Guildhall, 1861-4).

Philip Speakman Webb 1831–1915

Extant London works include:
- **The Red House**, 1859-70. Upton, nr Bexleyheath, south east London. With Morris.
- **Studio**, 14 Holland Park Road, 1864-5.
- **Studio**, 1 Palace Green, Kensington,1868–74.
- **Studio**, 35 Glebe Place, Kensington, 1869.
- **Studios**, 91–101 Worship Street, London, City (EC2), 1861–3.
- **No 19 Lincoln's Inn**, Holborn, 1868.

The house was designed in the so-called neo-vernacular 'parsonage' style developed by Pugin, Street, and Butterfield for their small vicarages, cottages, and schools: picturesque, free of academic convention and based on good building and simplicity. The house (1859-70) became an 'arts & crafts' showcase for its garden, furniture and internal decor as well as the house design itself.

Meanwhile, in 1861, after leaving Street in 1859, Web became a founder member of Morris, Marshall, Faulkner & Co. – Morris' design firm. As an architect, worked flowed in, including three London studio-houses for painter friends, including V.C. Prinsep (1 Holland Park Road, 1865), G.P. Boyce (West House, Glebe Place, 1869), and George Howard (1 Palace Green, 1868-74). Through his membership of the Hogarth Club from January 1859 until its dissolution in December 1861 Webb received several commissions from non-painter members, including a terrace of combined dwellings, workshops, and shops, for craftsmen (91-101

Webb was born in Oxford, son of a physician with drawing skills and a mother equally talented. Both taught him to draw. He intended to be a painter but changed his mind when, at seventeen, his father died. In 1849 he was articled to John Billing in Reading, worked as his assistant until 1854, then moved to Bidlake and Lovatt in Wolverhampton – an experience that appears to have exposed him to the horrors of the Industrial Revolution. Two months later he had moved to Oxford to work for G.E. Street at half the salary. Here, as Street's chief assistant, he met William Morris. In 1856 the office moved to London and Webb, together with Morris became members of the Pre-Raphaelite Brotherhood. In 1858 Morris, about to marry, asked Webb to design him a house in south-east London: what was to become the famous Red House (named after its red bricks and tiles).

Worship Street, London, 1861-3). In the spring of 1864, he took chambers at Gray's Inn, where he spent the rest of his working life. In 1877 Webb and Morris formed the Society for the Protection of Ancient Buildings (SPAB).

Webb declined election to the RIBA or the RA, believing them to be too much concerned with the professional and social status of members, although (as if the Cedric Price figure of his day) he did join the Sanitary Institute in order to become an expert on drainage.

Below: the Red House – a famous house for a famous client who actually only lived there five years. The house is quite remarkable but self-evidently a young architect's first major work, with odd internal arrangements and details, and less-than-satisfying interiors (perhaps because they are now mostly without the original decorative schema).
Right: a painted window on the first floor.

Red House plans. Top: ground; **Bottom**: first floor. The external picturesqueness engenders some internal awkwardness obviated by the decorative schema, but the overall planning is less impressive than the house's picturesque qualities would suggest..

Below: Webb's studio house at 35 Glebe Place was completed in 1868-9 for the artist G.P. Boyce. The house was extended one bay more in 1876 – and the original drawings show it just as we see it now: a rather strange (as well as 'free') assemblage of features (note, for example, the doors, associated areas, and cute cottage gables). See page 207 for the house that sits opposite.

On Webb's Gothic:

Goodhart-Rendel remarked that with Webb, "the elevation exactly expresses the plan, the architectural features indicate the construction, the nature of materials dictate the forms they are made to assume, any irregular necessity is emphasised and as it were dramatised; and if all that is not Gothic, what is? ... Any sensitive architect must feel the awkward charm and the singularity of his work, but his ultimate importance in history is likely to derive less from what he built himself than from the example that he set to others in his care for minute detail in design and in the process of workmanship. [...] There is no real evidence that Wyatt, Salvin, Burn, or any but a very few of their predecessors or contemporaries, ever drew a bedroom chimney-piece of the back stair banisters in their lives. All matters of process, too, of the pointing of brickwork, or the tooling of stone, had customarily been controlled by a clerk of the works interpreting a conventional specification, until Webb, and, of course, William Morris, awoke their age to full consciousness of craftsmanship. [...] The tenet, however, that the mark of the worker's tool can add positive value to the finished work, a tenet that is probably based less upon aesthetics than upon sociological sentimentality, was left for Webb to propagate, and was the foundation of the whole movement known as Arts and Crafts."

Rendel continues in this manner to open up an issue that is quite contemporary: sentimentality supplants the difficulty of an aesthetic judgement. It is easier to say, 'I like the brickwork', than to comment on the window proportions. However, he also hints at another kind of sentiment: the linkages being formed between the works of Webb, Morris et al and a notion of the status and skills of the medieval master builder. While this may, in itself seem romantic (and had such a content), anyone with hands-on familiarity with building work will have realised that the ostensible divide between the cerebral and theoretic orientation of the architect and the executive or mechanical skills of craftsmen (which the early Freemasons celebrated as the difference between speculative and practical Masonry) may touch upon the essence of what it means to be an architectural author, but somewhat misses the point: there is considerable 'cerebral' content to much building work, to the planning, anticipation and coordination that stands as common ground between the building architect and the hands-on master builder. The building architect stands on ambiguously defined ground mid-way between art, on the one hand, and craftsmen on the other. The Arts & Crafts Movement grasped at this essential point and (in Morris' case especially) linked its sentiments to political radicalism. Here are some important roots of Modernism. As in the quip concerning the definition of a consultant, most contemporary architects, in forgetting this point, are a long way from home.

Real art must be "made by the people and for the people, as a happiness for the user and the maker."

William Morris 1834–96

It is surely deeply ironic that Morris should represent all that is High Victorian, old-fashioned and conservative to Modernists tastes when he was none of these things. He was a hugely influential designer, poet and thinker whose disciples included W.R. Lethaby, C.F.A. Voysey, Ernest Gimson, and Edward Prior as the chief protagonists of what came to be known as English 'free style'. If there are any heroes in the history of architecture and design, then Morris is high up on the list. He was not an architect, but can hardly be ignored.

Morris was the son of a City financier and his wife, a teacher of music. He had an upbringing probably understated as, *"the ordinary bourgeois style of comfort."* He was a medievalist and romantic by natural sentiment, having started to read Walter Scott and four years old and completing it by the time he was seven. His schooling, however, was unhappy, resulting in opinion leaning against the classics and the belief that children should acquire practical skills as well as intellectual knowledge, and that education should be lifelong. Nevertheless, we are told that he was also discovering talents as a storyteller, transfixing his schoolfellows with rambling Gothic stories and establishing the persona of the oddball or outcast that clung to him in later life.

In 1852, five years after his father had died and the family had to move to a more economic home in Walthamstow, he entered Oxford University, where new friendships and new enthusiasms changed his life. His intention had been to enter the church, but he and Edward Burne-Jones both decided to be radicalists, reformers and artists. And, in 1856, Morris entered the Oxford office of G.E. Street. Here, as one biographer (Fiona MacCarthy) tells us, *"Morris never practised as an architect, his two years in Street's office were crucial in terms of the experience he gained in techniques and materials as well as in his growing awareness of the psychological importance of buildings as orientation points within society, repositories of history, and keepers of the soul."* And it was here that Morris met another man who was to be so important in his life: Phillip Webb.

It was now that Morris became committed to that belief in the inseparability of mind, hands and heart, using natural artistic and craft abilities to experiment with stone carving, clay modelling, wood carving, and the first of his illuminated manuscripts. To 'know' how to work with the hands and to employ a handcraft technique was to be fundamental to the rest of his life and to his Ruskinian ideas of the dignity of work.

Street's office now moved to London and Morris took up rooms with Burne-Jones. He ordered furniture and the pair painted it in a rich, medieval style. McCarthy interestingly notes that he had entered a conventionally female domain and was soon to extend his play within it by turning to cooking. And he now became a painter, leaving Street's office in 1856.

Soon, he was painting walls, loving the labour of the work and falling in love with the woman that was to be his wife – from our point of view an important event because it resulted in him asking Webb to design a house: the so-called Red House. They occupied the house in 1860 and friends were invited to come and decorate it: *"Have nothing in your houses that you do not know to be useful or believe to be beautiful"*, as he said. It was a remark later amplified in lectures: *"What business have we with art at all unless all can share it?"* (what turned out to be a rather sore point in his life); *"I don't want art for a few, any more than education for a few, or freedom for a few"* (a value that was to later flower as revolutionary socialism); and, as a kind of Adolf Loos criticism of Establishment aesthetic values, he remarked that artists are out of touch with everyday life, that they *"wrap themselves up in dreams of Greece and Italy ... which only a very few people even pretend to understand or be moved by."* (a remark he apparently considered did not apply to his excursions in pursuit of Icelandic myths).

Here, at the Red House, was the beginning of what was to become the influential Morris & Company – originally known as Morris, Marshall, Faulkner & Co., unofficially known as 'the Firm' and having seven partners: Morris, Peter Paul Marshall, Charles Faulkner, Dante Gabriel Rossetti, Edward Burne-Jones, Philip Webb, and the painter Ford Maddox Brown. Pevsner, characteristically conscious of neo-Hegelian, epochal events, refers to the establishment of the Firm as marking *"the beginning of a new era in Western art."* And, although he exaggerates the point, there is some truth in his remark that, *"We owe it to him [Morris] that an ordinary man's dwelling-house has once more become a worthy object of the architect's thought, and a chair, a wallpaper, or a vase a worthy object of the critic's imagination."* However, at a more mundane level, the arrangement of commuting from the Red House to studios in central London didn't last and, in 1865, the Red House had to be sold, Morris and family moving into town to live above the studio and workshop in Bloomsbury. By now he was back into writing poems (including The Earthly Paradise, 1968-70) and these became hugely popular, In fact, Morris was offered the poet laureateship, which he disdainfully rejected. He now turned, in addition, to illuminated manuscripts, to Norse legends and to his personal equivalent of the 'Grand Tour' in the form of two journeys to Iceland (in 1871 and 1873).

His life was unconventional: his wife was having an affair with his close friend Rossetti and the three lived together in Oxfordshire (Kelmscott Manor) as well as London (at Kelmscott House, in Turnham Green) in an unusual ménage à trois.

In 1875, after much financial mismanagement and argument, the Firm was reconstituted under William Morris' sole ownership. From this time the company was officially Morris & Co. and it now entered a new period of consolidation just as the aesthetic movement of the 1870s and 1880s got under way, both creating the style of the time and accruing profits from it. Now came the wallpapers, natural dyes, tapestry, rugs, carpets, printing, etc. for which his firm was to be famous.

But it was now, during his success in catering for 'the swinish rich', as he called them, and in despair at class divisions and his failure to influence anything at the working class level that Morris turned to action, forming the Society for the Protection of Ancient Buildings (SPAB, or Anti-Scrape), becoming involved in anti-war movements, and making lectures in which aesthetic standards (or lack of them) was corresponded to social conditions and moral standards. Even while working on royal palaces he was joining in Marxist protest groups.

MacCarthy tells us that, *"At the age of almost fifty, at a time when the Firm was prospering and Morris' literary reputation was secure, it was an act of almost insane courage, and he wrote of it in terms of a homecoming, a final recognition of inevitable destiny. His 'conversion', as he called it, came as an all-suffusing joy."* But it was a path of troubles and thorns. By 1885 he was in court for attacking a policeman. Asked who he was, he retorted: *"I am an artist, and a literary man, pretty well known, I think, throughout Europe."* But the ironies and contradictions were too obvious to a man so dedicated to a cause of revolution whilst celebrated as an aesthete – a role and predicament that surely remains of huge relevance today. Bizarrely, his originality as a political thinker continued to derive from his belief in the supremacy of art.

Oddly, it was only in the late 1880s that Morris began to positively associate with the Arts & Crafts movement, although he was never against industrialisation as such. It was now that he also set up the Kelmscott Press, saying its purpose was *"to produce books which it would be a pleasure to look upon as pieces of printing and arrangement of type."*

By early 1896 it was evident he was ill. He died later that year in a coffin moved, MacCarthy informs us, *"by a traditional farmers' wagon, painted yellow and red and festooned with vine leaves, for the final few miles' journey to Kelmscott church, where Morris was buried on a stormy day. Philip Webb later designed his tomb."* Henry van de Velde, commenting on Modernism on the Continent, remarked in 1901 that, *"The seeds that fertilised our spirit, evoked our activities, and originated the complete renewal of ornamentation and form in the decorative arts, were undoubtedly the work and the influence of John Ruskin and William Morris."* A few years later, the Futurist Marinetti was to come to lecture in London and disagree rather strongly: Ruskin was 'deplorable'. No doubt he considered Morris in the same terms.

Left: the upper access gallery to the principal bedrooms at the Red House. The house is remarkable for its so-called 'free style' and the narratives associated with Morris and his friends. However, as a work of architecture, it is, in terms of the familiar Vitruvian values of firmness, commodiousness and delight, rather weak, despite its thematic daring and its iconic role in the history of British housing.

Sir Ernest George 1839–1922

Extant London works include:

- 1870s: **terraces**, Harrington Gardens and Collingham Gardens, Kensington (1881), also Nos 5. 105-6, 110-113 Mount Street (1885-90), and 18-20 South Audley Street, Mayfair.
- **No. 8 Stratton Street**, 1871. Also Nos 18-20 South Audley Street and Nos. 5, 105-6, and 110-113 Mount Street. (All Mayfair).
- **Nos. 6-7 St Mary-at-Hill**, City,1873.
- **Beehive Coffee Tavern** and **Hambly Houses** on Streatham Common, 1877-79.
- **Nos. 50 and 52 Cadogan Square**, 1885-7.
- **St Andrew**, 1886, Guildersfield Road, Wandsworth.
- **Claridge's Hotel**, 1894-7, Brook Street, Mayfair (since enlarged).
- **Royal Exchange Buildings,** 1907-10, Cornhill, City.
- **Royal Academy of Music**, 1910, Marylebone Road (recent addition of 2002 by John McAslan).
- **Golders Green Crematorium**, 1905.
- **Southwark Bridge**, 1915-1921, with the engineer Basil Mott.

Below: a detail on one of George's Harrington buildings.

The more one sees of George's work the more one realise that this was a remarkable architect. His housing in Harrington and Collingham Gardens is Queen Anne on steroids: outstandingly and daringly original. He was born as the son of a prosperous ironmonger, just off the New Kent Road. At school, as a fine draughtsman and watercolourist, he developed an interest in architecture and became articled to the (short-lived) architect Samuel Hewitt, winning the Royal Academy Gold Medal in his final year, 1859. He was then briefly in the office of Allen Boulnois (1823-1893) before setting off to Europe on a study trip. On his return, in 1861 he went into partnership with Thomas Vaughan (1839-1875).

After Vaughan's death, George entered into partnership with Harold Peto, and they began one of the most successful architectural practices of the day (almost as successful as Shaw's). With Vaughan on the office management side and George designing, the office had, by the early 1870s, become established as a sound practice, designing commercial, domestic, and some ecclesiastical work, principally in London and Kent. Over a thirty-year period the office employed a continuous flow of talented architects, including Edwin Lutyens, Herbert Baker, E. Guy Dawber, Arnold Mitchell, and J. J. Joass. Even the first two women members of the RIBA, the sisters Ethel Mary Charles (1871-1962) and Bessie Ada Charles (1869/70-1931), were trained by 'E.G.', as George was known in the office.

In 1876, exactly a year after the early death of Vaughan, George entered into partnership with Harold Ainsworth Peto (1854-1933), fifth son of a celebrated public works contractor Sir Samuel Morton Peto (1809-1889). The practice immediately sprang into another successful phase throughout the later '70s and '80s, practising in the Queen Anne style and making particularly good use of terra-cotta. This is evident in the work for the Peto Brothers speculation at Harrington and Collingham Gardens (1880-88), which established George and Peto's reputation as outstanding domestic architects.

Most of George's work was domestic, the public buildings being inconsiderable in number, and the church work confined to a few small works. Added to a short list of country houses were many town residences with which the firm almost formed new quarters of

London, such as those in Mount Street and parts of Chelsea. Before George ceased to take an active part in work his last designs even included the Shiapur Palace for the Maharajah Holkar of Indore, 1914-15. Peto suffered ill health and retired in 1892 to concentrate on landscape gardening and interior design. George now entered into a partnership, with Alfred Bowman Yeates (1867-1944).

George had married in 1866 he moved to Crown Hill, Croydon, and in 1888, after his wife's death at the age of 34, he built 'Redroofs' in Ryecroft Road, overlooking Streatham Common, where he lived until 1903. He was a diligent painter and water-colour artist, and the influence of his sketching work not only in England but especially in Belgium, Holland and France makes itself evident in his picturesque design. He published volumes of his etchings on the Loire, and on the Mosel and in Belgium, Venice, etc., and was a constant exhibitor of his water-colour drawings at various galleries.

In 1896 George was awarded the RIBA Gold Medal. In 1910 he was elected an associate of the Royal Academy, and full member in 1917. He was President of the RIBA between 1908 to 1910, and received a knighthood in 1911. He retired in 1920, at the age of 81, and died in 1922. However, political changes had severely impacted the work flow of the practice well before World War I.

Above and *below*: Harrington Gardens has an almost aggressive street frontage – except that it isn't the front: that is around the corner, where the houses are accessed from a private garden. Similarly, the adjacent Collingwood Gardens scheme shows the same kind of striving after individuality.
Below right: Audley Street, Mayfair. Mount Street is around the corner.

Opposite page: 52 Cadogan Square, by Ernest George and Peto, 1885. The area was first developed from about 1770, with a second phase from the late 1870s. (No. 50 is also by George.)

Charles Robert Ashbee 1863–1942

Extant London works include:
• **Nos 38 and 39 Cheyne Walk**, Chelsea, 1896-1913.

Ashbee was the son of a wealthy merchant and, ironically, a fastidious and well respected book collector, Henry Spencer Ashbee (1827-1900), now famous as a publisher of erotic works (left to the British Museum), world traveller, supposed womaniser and a man embarrassed by his son's homosexuality. Against that unusual background Charles Ashbee attended Cambridge University and, in 1886, entered the world as a socialist: determined to both do good and be an architect. In 1887, the year the elder Ashbee's wife walked off with the children (to be rudely disinherited), Ashbee began work with the established church architects Bodley and Garner (Bodley, 1827-1907, a former pupil of Scott; Garner, 1869-97).

Ashbee took up residence at Toynbee Hall in Whitechapel, a newly established institution graduates from Oxford and Cambridge, set up in response to a shocked public outcry following reports of poverty, disease, overcrowding, and crime in east London, and particularly in Whitechapel. The graduates were meant to undertake part-time educational or social work in the area and Ashbee ran a Ruskin reading class.

It was out of this situation and work that, in 1888, Ashbee established the Guild and School of Handicraft, in accord with Ruskinian values and making furniture, metalwork, and painted decorations on a similar basis to Morris. By 1900, forty men were working there. As his biographer notes (Crawford), the Guild was an attempt to serve the men who worked there: *"It was a co-operative workshop, with important decisions made by the guild in committee and profits (when there were any) shared among the members. Although Ashbee designed most of the guild products, he worked hard to nurture the craftsmen's own creativity. In a sense it was not this table or that decanter that was the object of his creativity, but the human story of the guild. And just as his workshops stood far to the east of other arts and crafts workshops in London, so Ashbee stood apart in the arts and crafts movement because he was mainly interested not in design or technique or the reform of public taste, but in the workshop experience of the men – and at this stage they were all men – whom he employed."*

Between 1896 and 1913 he designed a series of houses in Cheyne Walk, Chelsea (only two survive). It was also in the mid-'90's that, shocked at East End demolitions of historically valuable works, he initiated what became the famous Survey of London. In 1898 he married and, in 1902, moved the Guild and 150 men, women and children out to the Cotswolds (where, incidentally, he made a friendship with Ananda Coomaraswamy). However, by 1907 the Guild was liquidated and only a few craftsmen stayed at Chipping Campden. In 1911 Ashbee and his wife had the first of four children, just as the First World War was about to interrupt everything. He then ended up in Cairo, later reinventing his career as an architect and town planner in Jerusalem. He retired from this role in 1922 (partly because of lack of control, partly because of his discomfort with Zionists) and spent the next twenty years in retirement with his wife. In 1935 he was surprised to find himself celebrated as one of Pevsner's 'pioneers of modern design' and spent the last few years of his life basking in that glory. So far as Pevsner was concerned, Ashbee was notable as a man who turned his back on the 'Ludditism' of the Arts & Crafts movement, and of Ruskin and Morris.

Left: entrance to the Cheyne Walk house.
Opposite page: *Neo-Voysey in Glebe Place, by James Gorst, 1996, opposite Webb's studio house (in the background of the photo).*

Ernest Newton 1856–1922

Newton was born into a family of a property agent and, at seventeen, was lucky enough to enter the office of Norman Shaw – then a sought after practice. He stayed here three years and then set up on his own, completing country house designs that addressed a vernacular of constructional parts rather than this or that style – mostly small works in Kent. Serenity, simplicity and dignity are the adjectives given to his work: an architecture of the 'everyday'. In conjunction with colleagues from Shaw's, he was a founder of the Art Workers' Guild, and for some years edited the Architectural Review. He was President of the RIBA in 1914 and he was awarded the Gold Medal in 1918. In 1919 he was elected as Royal Academician, and created CBE in 1920. His only extant London work is the County Fire Office, which dominates Piccadilly Circus (1924).

a free style: is there any such thing?

No term sums up the architectural struggles of the late nineteenth century more than 'freestyle': meaning to be free of the conventions applying to this or that style, particularly the neo-Gothic or neo-Classical, in all their varieties of imposition and constraint. Yet nothing could be more fraught and paradoxical. Architecture has to be addressed in terms of intentions and their expression, and 'freestyle' actually refers to a form of choice that, nevertheless, demands an orientation and commitment bearing rules within itself.

A contemporary instance of this issue is a house designed by James Gorst in Glebe Place (opposite a Webb house) where, in 1996, this architect adopted the mannerisms of two masters of the game (Voysey and Mackintosh) so as to inform the freedom exercised with expressive order (and, one supposes, coherence and integrity). Ironically, his counterfeit house is possibly as good or better than the real thing, but without claims to novelty or formal originality. It confronts us with an issue of architectural quality that is at once rooted in style and yet independent of it, which employs freedom in order to enslave itself, and which finds its originality within the framework of what already exists, although in a new context of playful endeavour. The work flies in the face of a fundamental tenet of progressive modernism and its historical awareness: that a work must be organically true to its time and place. For example, it was on a neo-Hegelian note that Mies van der Rohe told us, "Architecture is the will of the epoch translated into space. Until this simple truth is clearly recognised, the new architecture will be uncertain and tentative. [...] It must be understood that all architecture is bound up with its own time, that it can only be manifested in living tasks and in the medium of its epoch. In no age has it been otherwise." That sentiment was the basis of Nicholas Pevsner's search for heroic 'pioneers' manifesting the spirit of the Zeitgeist and realising it as the substance of built form. In other words, modernism's 'freedom' is deeply bound to notions of integrity and authenticity. With more subtlety than Mies or Pevsner, Ruskin addressed architectural challenge in terms of a 'penetrative imagination' and a 'vital beauty' that was indicative of a natural societal 'flourishing'. Take away the conventions of style, and integrity (expressive of what a design 'wants to be', as it is sometimes phrased) is then supposed to shine through unhindered as an architecture of flourishing vitality, with all the 'honesty' of nature and thereby all her rights to subsist in the world. Perhaps it is in that spirit that Gorst engages the heresy that Freestyle - now interpreted as a set of established architectural values and mannerisms – is capable of being summarised as a contemporary style of substantial qualitative value and without irony. The contemporary concern with a supposed authenticity of signature and character is substituted by a contrived posture that, paradoxically, epitomises freestyle, both literally and metaphorically, and yet still seeks integrity. In contrast, Modernism seeks a Hegelian architectural mode of action in which intent and its expression – like lightning and thunder – cannot be divorced. Whom is more 'free'?

"the International Style, Pevsner, pioneers: all nonsense"

C.F.A. Voysey 1857–1941

Extant London works include:

• **Veranda, entrance and hall** to No. 71 South End Road, Hampstead, 1890.
• **Forster studio**, No.17 St Dunstan's Road, Bedford Park,1891.
• **Britten Studio**, 17 St Dunstans Road,1892 (now the Hungarian Reformed Church).
• **14 South Parade**, Bedford Park, 1881-9.
• **Nos.14-16 Hans Road**, Kensington, 1891-4 (opp. Harrods).
• **Annesley Lodge**, No. 8 Platt's Lane, Hampstead, 1895 (for Voysey's father)
• **Dixcote**, North Drive, Totting Bec, 1897.
• **16 Chalcot Gardens**, off England's Lane, Hampstead, 1898.
• **Gordan Dene**, Princes Way, Wimbledon, 1899 (partly altered).
• **The Orchard**, Shire Lane, Chorley Wood, 1900-01. Also **Hollybank**, Shire Lane, 1903-4.
• **Sanderson's Factory**, Barley Mow Passage, Turnham Green, 1902.
• **War Memorial**, corner Hatfield Road and The Causeway, Potter's Bar, 1920.

To be admired and named by the likes of Charles Rennie MacIntosh, J.J.P. Oud and W.M. Dudock as mentor is surely cause enough to lend attention to this architect who has the reputation of being one of the leading architects of the Arts & Crafts movement and was published in Germany by Herman Muthesius between 1901-5. In the 1890s Voysey was a leading architect; however, his work was almost all domestic and commercial, never public and, at one time, his name was said to be as closely associated with 'wallpaper' in the manner that Wellington was with 'boot' (many designs are still available). His work is scattered all over the country (he designed some 150 buildings and had some 247 major clients), but his name is as much associated with details of door furniture and the like as with commodious architectural design that lends grandeur to the ostensibly simple country cottage. In 1940, the year before he died, Voysey received the RIBA Gold Medal.

Right: Nos.14-14 Hans Road, west side of Harrods – Voysey being urbane rather than rustic.
Opposite page: The corner house at Platt Lane, now divided into flats.

London has little by Voysey, although he started up in practice here in 1881. He was born in Yorkshire as the son of a clergyman who became something of a martyr, moving with the family to London in 1871 and attending Dulwich College for two years before leaving in order to be taught privately. His father Charles (1828-1912) appears to have been quite an influence: a controversial figure who spent eighteen months in Jamaica, then came to London as curate to churches in the East End before moving to Tadcaster, scene of his expulsion from the Church of England in 1871. He then founded the Theistic Church and moved to London, with a chapel in Piccadilly. His son – who was to practice somewhat in the manner his father preached, believing in directness, simplicity and uncompromising clarity of statement – thought of himself as the dunce of the family, and decided the only profession he could turn to was his grandfather's, i.e. architecture (the grandfather was Annesley Voysey, 1794-1839, a man who, like Voysey, delighted in tracing his ancestry back to Wesley).

In 1873 C.F.A. became an articled pupil of John Pollard Seddon (1827-1906; see page 195), an interesting architect belonging to a family of successful London furniture-makers who opined: "We want neither a new nor a universal style, we should know nothing about styles; the very name is a hindrance to architects, however useful to antiquary [...] Let us leave to posterity our productions and be sure that if we work simply, neither copying nor striving for singularity."

Seddon had been a founder member of the Architectural Association, served as Secretary to the RIBA and was particularly known as a Gothic revival designer of churches who no doubt had quite an influence upon Voysey. However, after five years Voysey moved on, in 1879, to a brief period with Saxon Snell (1830-1904); Snell had been apprenticed in the office of Sir James Pennethorne, afterwards becoming assistant to Sir Joseph Paxton and then to Sir William Tite; he specialised in hospital work.

No doubt work with Snell and his two sons was not to Voysey's satisfaction: he quickly moved on to spend time working for George Devey (1820-86), an architect of country houses with distinct 'Queen Anne' leanings; he was also a member of Voysey's father's church. Devey's first works of 1848 were notable for their attention to the local Kentish vernacular. By the time Voysey was working in his office, Devey enjoyed a stable practice with clients such as Liberal politicians and the Rothschilds (for one of whom he created what was described as a 'a palace-like cottage'). Voysey said of Devey: "When asked by his client to join a house-party, Devey would make the most fascinating catch-penny sketches while dressing for dinner and present them during dessert, charming everyone but getting them worked out by his clerks who had to make all the details on the traditional lines of a bastard Jacobean period." Although a solitary figure who avoided publicity, his work was studied by the likes of W.E. Nesfield and Richard Norman Shaw, probably

leaving things out:

Goodhart-Rendel noted that, "[Voysey] had put his theory into a nutshell when he said that he wrote specifications chiefly in order to tell builders what to leave out; and his meticulous elimination of unnecessaries produced quite agreeable results as often as not. For the brick or tile facing then most usual in small houses, he substituted rough-cast plaster, propping up extremely thin walls, which he thus could weather-proof, by long sloping buttresses – sometimes necessary and sometimes perhaps less so. Walls and rooms alike he made as low as bye-laws would allow, and the usual complication of small roofs he replaced by large simple roofs springing almost from the ground. Windows he made long ranges of very small leaded casements, varied by small round apertures in unexpected places. His chimneys would be high and large, surmounted by tall, thin chimney-pots. At the eaves, gutters would be projected on prominent iron brackets, the water from them being conducted into prominent wooden water-butts. At the front door the function of a porch was likely to be served by a large flat projecting shelter ... if there were any ornamental detail inside or out, it would present combinations of hearts, of straight stemmed flowers rather like toasting forks, and of birds either perched or in flight. All external woodwork, including the water-butt, would be painted a vivid green." He could have added continuous drip moulds, plain gables and roofs of green slate.

Above: the Sanderson Factory

influencing their own, more well-known 'Old English' style of work.

In 1881 Voysey set up on his own and married the following year, largely surviving as a wallpaper and textile pattern designer until his first architectural commission came along in 1888. The great influence upon him was Arthur Heygate Mackmurdo (1851-1942), who showed Voysey how to do this work and introduced him to several manufacturers. Mackmurdo had attended lectures by John Ruskin (1819-1900) whilst studying at the Ruskin School of Drawing and, in 1874, he toured Italy with Ruskin himself, before setting up his own architectural practice in London. He then met William Morris (in 1877 (then in his most fecund period as a pattern designer rather than a social activist) and, in 1882, the stimulation of an interest in the applied arts resulted in the founding of the Century Guild of Artists which aimed to produce decorative work in every branch of interior design and *"to render all branches of art the sphere no longer of the tradesman but of the artist."*

From setting up in practice until the 1914 war Voysey enjoyed a successful practice and an international reputation. Muthesius noted *"the sign of primitiveness"* in his work and Baillie-Scott wrote that his drawings applied *"the most careful and conscientious forethought"* in order to eliminate all possible error. But not everyone was a fan. One American writer referred to Voysey's favourite motif – a heart in the following way: *"Nothing could be easier than to attack the type of small house which has grown up in England in the past decade or two, which consists principally of a vast roof with numerous chimneys resting upon walls not much higher than the curb of a cyclone cellar, in which appear rows of little windows, reminding one of the side of a tram car, and elaborated with the sort of detail so much approved of by the school of 'new art'."* He then proceeded to satirise the cuteness of *"[...] little green shutters with heart-shaped holes cut in them and the oversized green barrel to catch the rain water."* Even Goodhart-Rendel found the leap, as he termed it, from fairy tale book to reality, in poor taste.

Voysey's 'style' was, in fact, well worked out and established itself early, tending toward numerous variations upon long and thin plans, buttresses, large roofs and chimneys topped with black pots, rough pebble-dash rendering, simple volumetrics, carefully considered surface patterning, and so on – all of which Voysey saw as a tradition that he respected and remained faithful to, but was not its slave (overall, the mixing of a Nash cottage orné and an English vernacular).

He used similar constructional motifs over and again and in a letter to John Betjeman he wrote: *"[...] I have only applied old tradition to new conditions [...] there is nothing new in my architecture, but new thought and feeling."* However, perhaps that significant new content included an architectural arrogance eliminating the client from a work – an attitude Voysey tended to justify as an architectural form of integrity bearing thoroughly Ruskinian moral undertones (as with Sullivan, Wright and others). Certainly, he had no time for stylistic recreations: *"Eschew all imitations"*, he advised; *"Strive to produce an effect of repose and simplicity"*, an admirable quality he otherwise summarised as: *"Simplicity, sincerity, repose, directness and frankness."* These were all Ruskinian virtues, but realised in terms of a radical simplicity. Revealingly, he wrote: *"Try the effect of a well-proportioned room, with white-washed walls, plain carpet and simple oak furniture, and nothing in it but necessary articles of use, and one pure ornament in the form of a simple vase of flowers, not a cosmopolitan crowd of all sorts, but one or two sprays of one kind, and you will find reflection begin to dance in your brain."*

Voysey was, as biographers and critics have noted, a Ruskinian moralist, a purist and authoritarian, a man in favour of pain and against all luxury. In 1927 he was described as *"a rock among successive seas: inveterate in his likes and dislikes, unyielding to any fashion of thought or of sentiment, unmoved by changing vogues, a man whose artistic convictions are at one with his spiritual ideas and identified with his whole attitude toward life and work."* In other words a Victorian who was rather out of place in inter-war Britain. However, such sentiments were not entirely out of place in inter-war Britain.

Although the 1914-18 war effectively ended Voysey's career (it had been declining since about 1906), he maintained a strong reputation. He also maintained a role in the Art Workers Guild and stuck to his opposition to the RIBA's policy of professionalism and architectural education. Ironically, the RIBA was to award him its Gold Medal one year before he died, in 1941.

Cecil Claude Brewer 1871–1918
Arnold Dunbar Smith 1866–1933

Extant London works include:
• **Mary Ward House**, Tavistock Place, Bloomsbury, 1896-7.
• **Heals**, Tottenham Court Road (first part), 1914-16.

Below: *Voysey's Britten Studio, Kensington: a model artists home, some two-thirds of the plan being given over to a readily accessible studio. The Britten Studio is an interesting attempt at the typology of an artist's residence: mostly studio, including discrete living accommodation, with the bedroom on the first floor, in the roof space.*

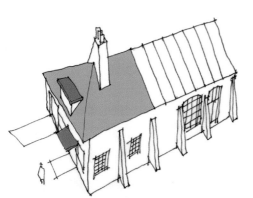

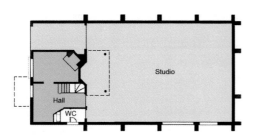

The claim to fame of this couple lies with the Mary Ward building, which they won in competition in 1895. In the early 1890s Brewer was living at University Hall in Gordon Square, Bloomsbury, a settlement devoted to work among the poor. Smith was also there. They became friends and entered the competition together, won and on that basis set in in partnership.

Previous to that, between 1890-3, Brewer had been articled to F. T. Baggallay. While there, he studied at the Architectural Association and at the Royal Academy schools. In 1894 he joined the office of Robert Weir Schultz in Gray's Inn and entered a circle of people associated with Lethaby – a lasting influence on his work. The practice was successful (mostly with domestic work) but, by about 1910, when another major competition (the National Museum of Wales) was won, the flavour of their larger work was distinctly Baroque rather than Freestyle. Brewer now had health problems and retired from the practice. After his death, Smith continued, notably designing the first phase of the Heals building (extended by Sir Edward Maufe in 1937). His practice then continued until 1933, but without other notable work in London.

Above: *Brwer & Smith's Mary Ward House.*

Alfred Waterhouse 1830–1905

Extant London works include:
• **Natural History Museum**, 1866 and 1870-80, South Kensington.
• **Nos 17-18 Lincoln's Inn**, 1871-2.
• **Nos 11-12 Park Lane**, 1878.
• **No 1 Old Bond Street**, Mayfair
• **King's Weigh-house Chapel**, Mayfair, 1889-93.
• **Congregational Chapel**, 1883-7, Lyndhurst Road.
• **National Liberal Club**, 1885-7, Whitehall Place (staircase rebuilt after war damage; now partly a hotel).
• **National Provincial Bank**, at 207-9 Piccadilly, 1892-4 (now NatWest bank).
• **Prudential Assurance HQ**, 1879 and 1899-1906, Holborn Bars (with his son Paul).
• **Royal Institute of Chartered Surveyors**, 1896-8, Great George Street (additions by Paul Waterhouse).
• **University College Hospital**, 1896-1906, Gower Street.

awkward triangular site. Though distinctly conventional in its Italianate classical decoration, this building was extremely up to date in its steel and concrete fireproof structure, and in its servicing and electric lighting. There was also the Grove House School of Tottenham, St Paul's School, Hammersmith, 1881-7, and the City and Guilds of London Institute, 1881-6.

Waterhouse was known for the practicality of his designs which included the National Provincial Bank in Piccadilly, a set of chambers as a commercial venture with his brothers in Carey Street (1872 and 1879-95), and the Prudential Assurance Company, for whom he designed some twenty-seven buildings in the years between 1877 and 1904, establishing what is probably the first example of an architectural house style (including their HQ in High Holborn).

Waterhouse's work had a thoroughly Victoria consistency in its use of high-quality materials, attention to practical details, and a general solidity whose underlying concern was

Waterhouse's finest design – the Manchester Town Hall – is not in London. But we do have a few others by this notable architect and fan of terra-cotta, particularly the Natural History Museum.

Waterhouse belonged to a strongly Quaker Liverpool family and, in 1848, began his life in architecture articled to P.B. Alley and R. Lane, in Manchester. Upon the completion of his articles in 1853 he set off travelling in France, Italy and Germany after which he set up in practice with commissions coming from relatives and other Quakers. He was immediately successful and, by 1865, had a London office – which was equally successful. By the end of his career he had completed some 650 works and his son, Paul Waterhouse (1861-1924), had joined him in practice in 1891. National fame came with the Manchester assize courts, 1859, and with the remarkable Manchester Town Hall of 1868, and the iron-framed Natural History Museum (1866 and 1870-80) – the latter being completely clad in terracotta with designs completed by Waterhouse.

He designed many country houses and churches. In London, the latter includes the King's Weigh-house Chapel in Mayfair, 1889-93, and the Lyndhurst Road Congregational Chapel, London, 1883-7. Institutional work included the National Liberal Club in London (1884-7), where three floors of large public rooms and four of bedrooms and service rooms were combined on an

good planning, suitability of scale and sound structure. He was particularly famous for his use of terracotta on all occasions. But, by the time he suffered a stroke, in 1901, tastes had already turned against his work. He was awarded the RIBA Gold Medal in 1878 and was President of the RIBA 1888-91. The son, Paul Waterhouse, was President of the RIBA 1921-3. He completed the design of the University College Hospital. His grandson and great-grandson also continued the practice.

Below: view to the central hall of the Natural History Museum.
Right: the Prudential, in Holborn.

John Francis Bentley 1839–1902

Extant London works include:
• **Convent of the Sacred Heart**, Hammersmith Road, 1868-82.
• **St Mary's**, Cadogan Street, Chelsea, 1877-82.
• **Our Lady of the Holy Souls**, Bosworth Road, Paddington, 1882.
• **Westminster Cathedral**, 1894. Also, the Archbishop's House, the Clergy School, the Diocesan Hall, and the Choir School, all in the Cathedral precinct.
• Miscellaneous:
house at **No 235 Lancaster Road**, Paddington, 1863; presbytery and two altars, **St. Peter and St Edward**, Palace Street, Westminster, 1863-67; Lady Chapel and Baptistry, **St Francis of Assisi**, Pottery Lane, Paddington, 1863; Lady

Chapel and aisles, **St Mary of the Angels**, Moorhouse Road, Paddington, 1869-87; east end, **Our lady of the Assumption**, Warwick Street, Pimlico, 1874; **Corpus Christi**, Brixton Hill, 1885-7. Bentley also redecorated St Botolph, in the City (1889); Redemptionist Monastery, Clapham, 1891-93; furnishings for St James', Spanish Place, Marylebone (1890 on); altar at St Gabriel, Warwick Square, Pimlico, 1890. There is also a church of Bentley's just outside London, at Watford (Holy Rood).

Bentley into partnership but he appears to have had an ambitious eye on independent practice and set up on his own in 1862. (While, we are told he was waiting for commissions!), Bentley took on all kinds of work, particularly detailed designs for other architects.

By 1868 Bentley was building his own commissions, mostly for the Catholic church (including the seminary of St Thomas at Hammersmith, 1876–88; since 1893 the Convent and High School of the Sacred Heart). In all, he designed five churches: the church and presbytery of St Mary at Cadogan Street, Chelsea (1877-9); the church of Our Lady of the Holy Souls at Bosworth Road, Kensal New Town (1881-2); the unfinished portion of Corpus Christi Church, Brixton Hill, 1886-7, in Early Decorated style; the church of the Holy Rood at Watford, 1889 to 1900; and the Church of St Luke's, Chiddingstone Causeway, Kent, 1897-8, (this time for the Church of England). Various other additions, repairs, new decorations were provided for a number of London churches, but Bentley's great career

Below: Westminster Cathedral front.
Opposite page: view down the nave. The upper parts remain mostly in brick, although Bentley saw these surfaces in mosaic.

London has two hugely important buildings, both churches: Westminster Abbey and St Paul's Cathedral. What non-Catholics often forget is the other minster in the west: Westminster Cathedral, designed by J.F. Bentley.

Bentley was born son of a wine merchant, privately educated and, as a youth, expressed an interest in architecture, even volunteering on church restoration work. But his father was opposed to such a career choice and placed the young man with some Manchester mechanical engineers. Within months the young man was indentured to a firm of builders in London, Winslow and Holland. However, the father died a year later and Holland placed the young Bentley in the office of Henry Clutton (1819-1893), presumably because Clutton could offer the sort of professional education he himself could not provide, although there appears to be a religious connection: Clutton was catholic and Bentley was now baptised into that faith and adopted the name Francis (1862). Prior to that, in 1860, Clutton invited

opportunity came in 1894, when he was commissioned to design a new Catholic Cathedral. Its conditions were that the new building should not compete with Westminster Abbey; should have a vast nave giving an uninterrupted view of the high altar; and should be capable of being erected comparatively quickly, with the decoration added later. On that basis, Bentley set of on an Italian tour to seek precedents and ideas.

The cathedral is not only bold in its usage of brick and stone, but the design is marked by its scale, simplicity, and avoidance of superficial ornament to three vast nave bays, each measuring some twenty metres square and surmounted by a concrete dome. A fourth bay nearest the nominal east forms the sanctuary, and beyond it is an apse; the nave itself is flanked on each side by an aisle, outside of which are a series of chapels. "I have broken', Bentley declared, *"the backbone of that terrible superstition, that iron is necessary to large spans."* In his review in the Architectural Review, Shaw remarked that the new cathedral was *"beyond all doubt the finest church that has been built for centuries."*

At the time of Bentley's death in 1902 the whole fabric of the building was complete, except for the final 50 feet of the campanile, but only a part of the marble revetment of one chapel had been installed. It was consecrated in 1910, but the first great ceremony held in the cathedral was Vaughan's requiem, in 1903. By then, the marble decoration was largely complete, but comparatively little of the mosaic decoration had been carried out.

It seems that an RIBA committee met the day after Bentley's death to approve the award of its Gold Medal. However, after consulting the King, it was considered that the award could not be made posthumously. (No doubt there is an interesting story behind that outcome.)

Above: *internal light fitting in Westminster Cathedral. The interior decoration has continued since Bentley's death. Much of the nave work is 1956-64 (by Dom Aelred Bartlett, following Bentley's drawings); elsewhere, J.A. Marshall of Bentley, Son & Marshall worked up the designs.*
Below: *view to the 86.5 m high Cathedral campanile, from the 2006 EPR office and retail development opposite, and across the EPR-designed piazza in front of the Cathedral (1975).*

Charles Harrison Townsend
1851–1928

Extant London works include:
• **All Saints Church**, Ennismore Gardens, Knightsbridge, 1892.
• **Bishopsgate Institute**, 1892-94, Bishopsgate, City.
• **Whitechapel Art Gallery**, 1899-1901. Whitechapel High Street. Since extended by Colquhoun and Miller, 1988.
• **Horniman Museum Library & Lecture Rooms**, 1896-1901, and 1910-11 (library addition). 100 London Road, SE23. Since extended: Allies & Morrison, 2002; Archetype, 1994.
• **United Free Church**, Links Road, Woodford Green, 1904.
• **House**, No 2 Temple Fortune Lane, Hampstead Garden Suburb, 1912. Also, houses at Nos.135-141 Hampstead Way.

Below: the frontage of the Bishopsgate Institute.

Townsend was born in Birkenhead, the son of a solicitor and his wife, a Polish pianist. At sixteen, he was articled to the Liverpool architect Walter Scott (to 1872) and, from 1873-75, was with Charles Barry before joining Edward Robert Robson's office at the recently formed London school board. It was about this time that he also started to travel, particularly to northern Italy. In 1877 he set up his own office and, between 1884 and 1886 was in partnership with Thomas Lewis Banks. He joined the RIBA in 1888, but was also a member of the Art Workers Guild (one institute being pro-registration and the other anti-registration).

Townsend's practice handled mostly small domestic and ecclesiastical works; however, in 1892, he won the competition for the Bishopsgate Institute (described as an H.H. Richardson influenced design: a cultural centre for local inhabitants and City workers, but located well away from the centre of the City and adjacent to Liverpool Street Station). Then, in 1897, came the Whitechapel Gallery (also on the edge of the City, in the East End) and, in 1901, the commission for the Horniman Museum – a museum for the anthropological collection of a wealthy tea-merchant, deep in south London's suburbs.

In Muthesius' *Die Englische Baukunst der Gegenwart*, of 1900, Townsend was celebrated along with Voysey as exponents of a new 'modern' approach to design: *"the prophets of the new style."* Similarly, Service places him on a par with Mackintosh in his capacity to apply 'free style' to larger public buildings. In 1894 Townsend wrote, *"What does much of the work of the present day for which the artist claims originality show us? [...] The man of fashion [...] calls the result 'the simplicity of originality'. It is not. It is, instead [...] a negation that is a poor substitute for invention."*

Unfortunately, Townsend's later work failed to match the promise of the Bishopsgate, Whitechapel and Horniman commissions. This may, in part have had to do with the new fashions for revival of Baroque and French Renaissance architecture; it may also, as one biographer notes, have been the outcome of what is described as Townsend's own equivocal and confused attitude towards the value of architectural traditions. After WWI, his practice withered in a design-climate that had now moved on from the Freestyle he favoured.

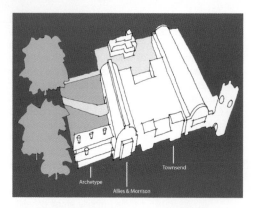

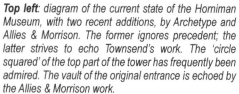

Top left: diagram of the current state of the Horniman Museum, with two recent additions, by Archetype and Allies & Morrison. The former ignores precedent; the latter strives to echo Townsend's work. The 'circle squared' of the top part of the tower has frequently been admired. The vault of the original entrance is echoed by the Allies & Morrison work.

Below middle: view across all three phases, with the Archetype's contrasting building ('Centre for Understanding the Environment') in the foreground and the A&M building after that, with Townsend's tower in the background. (Two works that appear respectively rustic and hard-edged in comparison with the softness of Townsend's design.)

Bottom left: view to the street façade of Townsend's building. The large mosaic panel is by Robert Anning Bell.

Bottom right: the street façade and ;gable; of the Allies & Morrison extension.

Opposite page: the softened tones and forms of the street frontage of the Horniman.

The LCC architects

That we should list the architect department of the London County Council says something important about the history of London architecture: its public programme of works for the mass of the people inhabiting the capital.

London used to be the City; however, by 1851 the affluent historic core accounted for only one twentieth of the metropolitan population – and it wanted no part of a London-wide system of governance. Furthermore, at that time, the Church of England had been the principal organ of local government. London, according to one historian, was a hotchpotch of archaic administrative arrangement of varying levels of democracy and efficiency. Life in London was regulated by more than 250 local Acts of Parliament and more than 10,000 commissioners were entrusted with various tasks in the metropolis. The challenge – to reconcile local and metropolitan differences – remains with us to this day, but change began in 1855 when the Church lost its role in local governance and a unitary body was set up called the Metropolitan Board of Works (whose work included construction of the Thames Embankment and a drainage system in new streets such as Shaftesbury Avenue, Northumberland Avenue and Charing Cross Road).

Despite – perhaps because of – its successes, the Board developed a culture resulting in maladministration and serious corruption. The situation became so bad that a Royal Commission was set up to investigate it: finding that improper speculation had taken place in land bought to make street improvements. The outcome was that, in 1888, the Board was superceded by the London County Council – although its boundaries fell far short of the actual urban area and this was to quickly become a long, politicised debate resulting in the later formation of the Greater London Council (realised in 1965 as the Conservative government's attempt to control London). In the meantime, the LCC built in the Inner Boroughs whilst the Outer Boroughs became the refuges of a gardening middle class served by the expanding transport network: electrically-driven transport from 1900, and the first oil-fuelled motor buses running from 1905, serving a total London population of some 6.6m in 1901 (the London built-up area almost doubled in size between 1900 and 1914; this growth was especially in an area beyond an eight mile radius from Charing Cross, e.g. Morden, Mitcham, Hendon, Golders Green).

From the beginning (and despite a strong aristocratic presence) the LCC was a local authority distinguished by its political radicalism and a taste for innovation. And, among other great social issues, slum clearance and deprivation were high on its agenda. A reformer of 1907 noted that the census had revealed at least 3,000 Londoners were living eight or more to a room, 9,000 were living seven or more to a room and some 26,000 were six or more. By that time the Peabody Donation

Above: a block at the Boundary Estate, 1897-1900: the redevelopment of a slum area called 'The Nichol'. (Architect of the southern blocks: Charles Winmill.)
Below: the Euston Road Fire Station (1901-2, from the Fire Section of the LCC, then `under Charles Winmill). *Opposite page*: the admirable Millbank Estate, 1897-1902, on the site of the demolished Millbank Prison. The style of many estates – the taller, five to six storey blocks criticised in 1907 as 'skyscrapers' and 'vertical slums' – was Philip Webb mixed with the influences of visits by Fleming and his colleagues to housing estates in Vienna and elsewhere.

Fund (now the Peabody Housing Trust) had, between 1862 and 1907, provided some 11,000 'hygienic living rooms'.

In order to address these conditions of overcrowding and deprivation an Architect's Department was formed at the LCC in 1890, with Thomas Blashill as Architect to the Council (ex MBW; replaced upon his retirement in 1899 by W.E. Riley) and Owen Fleming (socialist and a former AA student) as Head Architect of the Housing Division. By 1900 the larger LCC housing estates had come into being among a programme of works that was to include schools, libraries, fire stations and swimming baths – all promoted by Acts such as the Housing of the Working Classes Act (1900), the Education Act (1902), and the Town Planning Act (1909). Some 10,000 houses and flats for some 17,000 people, on twelve major estates, were constructed by WWI, although this was merely a fraction of what was needed.

• The Shoreditch Boundary Estate was the first and typical of the LCC's programme: demolition, followed by new blocks with open courts between them. The designs bear a German influence: high roof spaces that, in medieval Germany were used for storing the harvest, were now employed for drying clothes.

Other early LCC developments:

• **Shelton Street**, off Drury Lane, for 284 people, 1891-94, architect Rowland Plumbe.
• **Cable Street**, Shadwell, 1893-6 and 1896-1901.
• **Hughes Fields**, Deptford, cottages for 666 people, 1893-95.
• **Trafalgar Road**, Greenwich, 51 cottages, 1901.
• **Green Street** and **Boyfield Street**, Southwark, four housing blocks for 418 people, 1897-1900.
The programme after this time was enlarged and included:
• **Churchway**, St Pancras, 1900-2.
• Leather Lane to Gray's Inn, Poplar, 1900-2.
• **Millbank Estate**, behind the Tate Gallery, Millbank, 1897-1902. On the site of the penitentiary there; the outlines of which are reflected in the angled flanks to the site plan; for 4,430 people. Perhaps the finest and best preserved of this type of work. Hogarth House, the earliest block, was designed by R. Minton Taylor (similar to his Cookham House on the Boundary Estate). Taylor did all the other blocks except Gainsborogh House (by Winmill). The two nearby schools are by the London School Board, dating from 1901.

• **Bruce House**, near old Clare Market, Kemble Street, 1904-6. Architect to the LCC, J.R. Stark. A lodging for 699 men, part of the Kingsway/Aldwych works and improvements. (reconstructed as flats, 1992-4). Compare with the nearby **Wild Street Peabody Estate** of 1880-1 (by H.A. Darbishire).
• **Baltic Street**, near St Luke's Church, Old Street, 1899-1905.
• **Webber Row**, off Waterloo Road, Southwark, 1902-7.
• Bruce House, for single working men, Drury Lane, 1907.
• **Totterdown Fields Estate**, 1229 two-storey cottages for 8788 people, off Church Lane, Tooting, 1903-11. An attempt to create suburban houses rather than flats.
• **White Hart Lane Estate**, Tottenham, 1911 onward. By 1912 some 781 two-storey cottages had been constructed on a large site.
• **Becontree Estate**, Dagenham, started 1922. 167,000 people by 1937. Perhaps exemplifying how not to do it.
• **Bellingham Estate**, Lewisham, 1921 on: cottage estate with interesting layout (2,674 dwellings), but similar problems to Becontree.

the City's architect
Sir Horace Jones 1819–87

Extant London works include:
• **Smithfield Market**, in three sections: meat market, 1866-7; poultry and provision market, 1879-83; and the fruit and vegetable market, 1873-5 (burnt in 1958 and replaced).
• **Billingsgate**, Lower Thames Street, 1874-8; converted into offices, 1985-9 (by Richard Rogers). A building still looking for a role in life.
• former **Police station**, 1 College Hill, City, 1885-6.
• **St Andrew's House**, off Charterhouse Street, 1874. Working class flats similar to the first municipal flats, also by Jones, of 1865 (the latter demolished).
• **Guildhall Free Library and Museum**, 1870-72
• the **Griffin** memorial, to mark the site of Temple Bar, 1880.
• **Leadenhall Market**, City, 1881.
• former **Guildhall School of Music**, John Carpenter Street (west side), Victoria Embankment, 1885-7. Perhaps the outstanding extant work from Jones.
• **Tower Bridge**, with Sir John Wolfe-Barry. (Erected mostly after Jones' death), 1886-94. Wolfe-Barry's office apparently did most of the detailing.

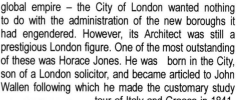

During the period of explosive growth during the nineteenth century – and despite being the historic core of Britain's capital and the heart of its global empire – the City of London wanted nothing to do with the administration of the new boroughs it had engendered. However, its Architect was still a prestigious London figure. One of the most outstanding of these was Horace Jones. He was born in the City, son of a London solicitor, and became articled to John Wallen following which he made the customary study tour of Italy and Greece in 1841-2. He then set up in practice with Arthur Ebden Johnson in 1846. Fame came with his appointment as architect and surveyor to the City of London, in 1864, in which role he was also president of the RIBA (1882-4) and was knighted in 1886. He was, of course, an enthusiastic Freemason. He is said to have had a large and prosperous practice.

Right: the dragon or so-called griffin on the site of Wren's Temple Bar, marking the western entry point to the City of London.
Opposite page: *Tower Bridge – the gateway to London from the sea before the Thames Barrier was constructed – is actually an interesting design. One surely has to be tired of architecture not to enjoy its theatricality, whose character was prompted by the presence of the Tower of London. It forms a splendid river gateway, tourist symbol, division between City and Docklands and link of north to south London. Its design and location has a long history complicated by different land levels between north and south, and by the need to allow the passage of shipping. Jones' role in the design is strategic rather than executive, most of the architectural detail actually being handled by the engineers.*

Above: Leadenhall Market – on the site of a medieval poultry market – was rebuilt under Jones in 1881 and now serves as a backlands lunch-time resort – bars, restaurants, and shops and a fine example of a mode of provision sadly lacking in the City which, in the 1950s sought to leave the streets to cars and get pedestrians up on a 'pedway' network (still evident all over the City). Apart from such issues Leadenhall is also a fine piece of architectural gamesmanship – also a neglected aspect of City architecture. The geometry of the complex subtly and deceptively intrudes itself into the backlands employing the dominance of its central crossing. But the gamesmanship is also evident in the way Jones extends the reach of the Market to perimeter streets, stretching the façades to locations they don't belong. For example (**top right**), the upper windows have progressively smaller spaces behind as they run into a neighbouring property – to the point where there is nothing behind and Jones simply carries on a screen wall with windows now filled with metal grille-work. Architects would now execute such a thing with acute self-consciousness; Jones is totally matter-of-fact about the gesture.

Sir Joseph Bazalgette
1819-91

Architecture, urban form and engineering were often entwined in Victorian London and there is a need to mention a man who was important to the London we experience today, a man who worked closely with architects and gave many of them significant design opportunities on the streets he created: Joseph Bazalgette. He kept a large private practice and his biographer notes that Bazalgette's role "was to monitor the progress of private bills passing through parliament of works which would have an impact on the public amenities of London. These would include railways, tramways, docks, water supply, and the energy utilities – gas, electricity, and hydraulic power. He produced a detailed annual report to the board on these schemes and he was a well-known and influential figure in the committee rooms of the houses of parliament." In addition: "Unlike many civil engineers, Bazalgette assumed a continuing responsibility for the works he designed and constructed and was responsible for maintenance, staff changes, development of operational techniques, and renewable contracts for the supply of materials."

When Joseph Bazalgette was elected president of the Institution of Civil Engineers in 1884, he appropriately made a presidential address which discussed "*those engineering works which promote the health and comfort of the inhabitants of large cities, and by which human life may be preserved and prolonged*". Nothing could have been a more important issue in Victorian London, at that time and, in his role at the Metropolitan Board of Works (replaced by the London County Council which, in turn, became the Greater London Council and, finally, the Greater London Assembly), Bazalgette played a very important role in giving Londoners a (relatively) decent and healthy place to live. The coincidences with Horace Jones are the date of birth, Jones' appointment (just at the time Bazalgette was completing the famous sewage works along the Victoria Embankment), as Surveyor to the City of London, and the fact that his last work, the Guildhall School of Music, is located on Bazalgette's Victoria Embankment.

Bazalgette was born in Enfield, son of a naval officer, grandson of a Frenchman. In 1836 he became an articled pupil of John Benjamin Macneill, the eminent Irish civil engineer, in Londonderry. In 1842 he set up in private practice as a consulting engineer in London – at a time when railway mania gave him lots of work (too much, in fact, prompting illness). He returned in 1848 to a new role: assistant surveyor to the second metropolitan commission of sewers for London. In 1852 he was appointed engineer, and remained in that role until the commissioners were replaced by the Metropolitan Board of Works (MBW), in 1856 – to whom he was again appointed engineer (until 1889, when the Board was replaced by the LCC).

The great task facing the MBW concerned sewage and the realisation of a scheme conceived around 1850. The principal task was the embanking of the Thames. This involved three major works: the Albert (1868), Victoria (1870), and Chelsea (1874) embankments – a total length of 312 miles, for which 52 acres of riverside land was reclaimed.

The Thames River, Prevention of Floods Act of 1879 also imposed the duty of implementing requirements for 40 miles of river frontage, an undertaking Bazalgette described as "*one of the most difficult and intricate things the Board have had to do.*" In addition, an act of 1877 empowered the MBW to purchase twelve Thames

bridges from the private companies owning them and free them from tolls. One outcome was that Bazalgette replaced three of the bridges with new structures to his own design: Putney (1886); the steel-link suspension bridge at Hammersmith (1887); and the iron arch structure at Battersea (1890). The removal of tolls led to demands for new river crossings below London Bridge and Bazalgette was involved in three major design schemes: Tower Bridge (designed under Horace Jones); Blackwall Tunnel; and Woolwich free ferry.

In addition to these river concerns, Bazalgette was attempted to ease horse-drawn traffic congestion in the capital by initiating a programme of new thoroughfares, principally: Southwark Street (1864); Queen Victoria Street (1871); Northumberland Avenue (1876); Shaftesbury Avenue (1886); and Charing Cross Road (1887). He was made a companion of the Bath in 1871, and knighted in 1874.

Below: the Embankment at Waterloo bridge, looking east to the City and Canary Wharf.

"father of the Institute of the profession"

Thomas Leverton Donaldson
1795-1885

Thomas Donaldson has the credit of being a principal creator of the Institute of Architects, founded in 1833 and quickly establishing royal patronage in 1837. The other authors included Philip Hardwick, Thomas Allom, William Donthorne, and John Buonarotti Papworth.

When awarded its royal charter in 1837 the Institute became the Royal Institute of British Architects in London, eventually dropping the reference to London in 1892. The context was a variety of attempts to form exclusive clubs in the later eighteenth century and the pressures for architects and surveyors to professionalise themselves during the nineteenth century. If the latter constituted themselves as external imperatives, there was an internal one to establish control over the body of persons calling themselves 'architect' and, in fact, the RIBA remains to this day a club of those who are entitled to name themselves 'architect'.

That restriction was not established until 1938, as the last of three Acts of parliament (1931, 1934 and 1938) which formulated the terms of professional status – in effect, a contract between architects and the state, the latter receiving monopolistic controls in return for self-regulation and expert service to society. In the meantime, between the Institute's founding and the Acts, the RIBA sought to be perceived as the guardian of architecture rather than the interest of architects. However, it was not long before the Times was referring to it as the architects' trade union and that reality was to form the basis of bitter struggles during the last few decades of the nineteenth century: was, as Shaw and others asked, architecture a profession or an art?

Donaldson himself was the son of a London architect and District Surveyor. In 1815 (after adventures in the military) he entered the Royal Academy schools under John Soane, won medals, became a founder of the Architectural Students' Society, did the usual grand tour for four years, and set up in practice in 1823 having obtained honorary election to four Italian academies.

In 1834 Donaldson was instrumental in establishing the Institute of Architects and acted as Treasurer of an ad hoc committee. He was then instrumental in forging connections with architects in foreign academies.

His London buildings include the library at University College, 1848-9; University Hall (now Dr Williams Library), Gordon Square, 1848-9; and the German Hospital, Hackney, 1865.

In 1838 he won the competition for the new Royal exchange, but Tite took the job from him. Apart from devising the Institute's motto, 'Usui civium, decori urbium', and designing the Mycenean lions medal of the Institute, he was also the first professor of architecture to be elected to the newly founded chair at University College, London, in 1842. In this role he divided his subject into architecture as a fine art – which he treated from a historical point of view – and architecture as a science. Like many other architects, he is described as a man who always dressed in black. He was awarded the RIBA Gold Medal in 1851.

gifted and departed

gifted and departed . . .

By the time Edwin 'Ned' Lutyens was moving on from his precociously brilliant series of 'freestyle' country houses in London's Surrey commuter belt to designing his first central London building – the 1904 'Wrenaissance' exercise for Country Life magazine, in Tavistock Street, Covent Garden – the Queen Anne style was a moribund cause among architects (although it had, by then, been warmly absorbed into the vernacular). Lutyens had thoroughly explored his own version of a free, neo-vernacular approach to architectural gamesmanship and now saw himself drawn to the 'high game' that was also the seductively 'big game' of neo-Classicism.

At that time, at the turn of the century, all the principal figures of the Gothic revival were dead and, apart from a handful of residual Gothicists – such as Comper, who was one of those taking the Gothic revival into its third, post-Black Death (of 1348) phase of Late Decorated or Early Perpendicular – most architects were divided between two principal streams of architectural value (admittedly not without some intermixture).

One of these streams was to enter a dead-end that hardly survived the trauma of the First World War and was pretty effectively terminated off by the second, although it still occasionally erupts into vitality and was arguably at the emotional core of much so-called Post-Modernism. The other stream enjoys the hindsight that sees in it some of the significant roots of Modernism. And Lutyens, like Shaw, arguably had a place within both of these streams.

As a common denominator to architectural practice at the end of the nineteenth century, freedom in terms of classicism, in the Gothic or this or that period or national style, or the non-style of mere building technique (the novelties of Tudor, Flemish, Elizabethan, the vernacular and the rest) was followed by a more quiet and disciplined approach to any manner of architectural signification and expression. There was now, as Goodhart-Rendel put it, *"a demand for the cup that might cheer but could not inebriate – in other words, for an invigorating but essentially negative simplicity."* Apollo was in the ascendent, not Dionysonic stirrings.

Ironically, no one in Britain was anticipating the high-octane mix of culture and art to revolutionary sentiment being concocted by the likes of the Futurist Marinetti who, in 1909, was to declare: *"We will glorify war - the only way to cleanse the world – militarism, patriotism, the destructive gesture of freedom bringers, beautiful ideas worth dying for, and scorn for woman."*

Below: the figure of Justice on the corner of John Belcher's Chartered Accountant's Hall, City.

Here was one aspect of a truly free and frightening Modernism; few appreciated how real his words would become within merely a few years, especially not those at the heart of the world's largest global empire.

The first of these two streams of inclination comprised a group who had seen the Queen Anne taken into the realm of public buildings as a splendid if somewhat indigestible variety of what Goodhart-Rendel picturesquely described (not without enthusiasm and respect) as the inventions of a 'bric-à-brac' architecture. Finding themselves in 'the morning after' of such bric-a-brac exuberance, many members of this stream reacted with a call for more discipline, scholarship and correct grammar – particularly with regard to what had been termed 'free classic'. The notion of being 'free' was still highly valued, but not to the extent it exhibited lack of discipline and order. (An essentially ideological sentiment that was, perhaps, unconsciously tinged by the rise of labour, unions and class conflict.)

Norman Shaw had first taken the Queen Anne into the sphere of public buildings with his New Scotland Yard building of 1886, a design literally founded upon granite hewn by the convicts of Dartmoor. And while Ernest George was romping around west Kensington formulating novel mixes in residential design, John Belcher, in 1890, offered the City his neo-Baroque Chartered Accountants' Hall – a work most people now take for granted, but one that shocked and delighted observers at the time. During the 1890s this direction of architectural design erupted into all kinds of expressed bravura applied to town halls, public libraries, art galleries, stations, hotels, banks, swimming pools, and even public houses (buildings still surviving all over London, sometimes witness to the tax-gathering wealth local authorities once enjoyed). In the end, in its more attenuated forms, this body of work bore within it that Edwardian conservatism and those imperialistic values which, after the First World War, informed numerous war monuments as well as the works of Lutyens and Baker in South Africa and India.

In this group were architects such as Aston Webb, John Belcher, Ernest Newton, Reginald Blomfield, the later Shaw, and one of the smartest kids on the block: the unapologetically Francophile Arthur Davis – a man representing the novel dominance of French tastes in architecture.

French influences were quite strong at this time. While the nationalistically driven 'Wrennaissance' sentiment within this grouping looked back to the

Above: the figures of an architect and a rather sceptical workman on the frieze of the Chartered Accountant's Hall, City.

frontage of St Paul's and copied its turrets and cupolas wherever they could (such as on William Young's New War office, in Whitehall, adjacent to Jones' Banqueting House), the alternative of Beaux-Arts influences enjoyed a resurgence and an aspiring young architect could, on the one hand, enjoy an established form of pupillage in Britain (preferably with an architect who was a Royal Academician) or, for those who could afford it, seek a superior form of training in Paris. Frank Verity (d.1937), who joined his father Thomas in a practice designing theatres and then cinemas, was an example who followed experience at the Royal College of Art, at University College and the Architectural Association with studies in Paris.

With or without Beaux-Arts or 'Wrenaisssance' content, this stream of sentiment was, by the 1930s, in the inter-war period, to evolve into the so-called 'George VI' style: aesthetic values then leaning toward a stripped neo-Georgian whose advocates were as equally shocked by a nascent Continental Modernism as by the parallel and populist 'Jazz Moderne' of an age that now had radio and 'talkies'. The Arthur Davis who, for example, strutted his stuff at the Ritz in 1905 was, by the early 1930s, the traumatised architect whose clients insisted upon work being executed in the Jazz Moderne manner.

The contrast to this troubled leaning in all its varieties of form was the alternative 'free' school of sentiment that continued the traditions of Pugin, Morris et al, resurrected Webb as its hero, leant toward socialism, and would have heartily agreed with the comment that: *"Amongst these cheap splendours of false taste and false luxury we are delighted when we find a seat really well made, a good oak table thoroughly strong on its legs, woollen curtains that really look like wool, a comfortable and solid chair, a cupboard which opens and shuts well showing us inside and outside the wood it is made of and the object for which it is intended; let us hope that a return of those healthy ideas in the making of furniture as in everything else, that we may come to understand that true taste consists in appearing as one is and not as one would wish to be ..."* That was written in France, by Viollet le Duc, but it could have come from a number of Continental sources (Loos comes to mind) or, in Britain, from the likes of Lethaby, Morris, Voysey or many others in the Arts & Crafts who were attuned to a radical shifts in the social equations of taste, fashion and consumer power. This second stream had sought to move on from the Queen Anne toward something more free and pure in the sense of being without historical references and free of a scholarly and intellectual capriciousness. Ironically, that capriciousness had, in Wren's day, been deemed to be the curse of creaturely and appetitive masses rather than the educated and attuned; now – as Loos, in Vienna, so strongly stated – it was the other way around.

In this other stream were the likes of Mackmurdo, Voysey, Ashbee, Stokes, Harrison, Townsend, Lethaby, Mackintosh and others whom we have learned to link with foreign names such as Horta, Olbrich, Behrens, Sullivan, Wright, Loos, Neutra and Schindler in an (always loose) trans-Atlantic movement that, at times, had a lost purity of mind and body as its deepest concern. It is here that we find the selected heroes of Modernism: links in a chain extending back to Morris, Ruskin, Pugin and French voices such as le Duc. Their common denominator was a sentiment of sympathy toward some vague, inherent knowledge attributed to the vernacular (and thence to crafts). The age of the *Volk* was upon us. Sentiments such as this were to flower in the post-war period as an English version of the Modernism celebrating so-called rationalism and functionalism as a neo-Hegelian manifestation of the 'spirit of the age'. And its European reference was to swing entirely away from generations of attention

Above: sign at the Blackfriar pub, Queen Victoria Street, City, exhibiting those Arts & Crafts kinds of sweeps and curves that, on the Continent especially, were to flourish as Art Nouveau.

Opposite page: the same pub. It was built in 1875 but the art work was begun in 1904-6, by the sculptors Nathaniel Hitch, Frederick T. Callcott, with Henry Poole and the architect H. Fuller Clark making contributions. Poole attended the Royal Academy schools from 1892. His father had been an architectural carver, and much of Poole's work was architectural sculpture, particularly for Lanchester and Rickards. Among his works for them include sculpture for Deptford Town Hall, the porcelain work for 144-146 New Bond Street, and the high relief spandrel figures of angels for Methodist Central Hall, Westminster. Fuller Clark also did an idiosyncratic building in Riding House Street, W1 (1908).

given to southern Europe and turn, instead, toward Scandinavia.

But this stream of sentiment was by no means unified. For example, while its anti-machine aspect was widely spread across western Europe and, in Britain, focused around the Art Workers Guild and its Exhibition Society spin-off, the British tended to be unfavourable toward the Continental fashion of Art Nouveau and its exotically swirling shapes that were intrinsically difficult for the machine to cope with. Nevertheless, such was the success of this latter stream of design and its ideological rationale (as offered by historians such as Pevsner in the form of 'pioneers' constituting a coherent movement) that we suffer profound difficulty in seeing and appreciating what the other group achieved. There is now very little interest in Lutyens' classicism, Blomfield's sweeping 'grand manner' façades of Regent

Street, Shaw's Piccadilly hotel, Aston Webb's work along the Mall, or even the works of William Holden before his Underground stations (in fact, little genuine interest in them beyond a fringe of architectural academics and anoraks), little in Joass or Arthur Davis, et al, to say nothing of that 'free', mixed body of public works of the 1880s and '90s that remains mildly shocking if only we could only open our eyes to the games being played out.

Passing time devours past saliences like some indifferent wave washing the shore clean, but the extent to which many formerly salient architects have been largely forgotten, even within the profession, is itself interesting. If, for example, we examine the list of Gold Medallists over a fifty year period, from 1892 to 1942 (overleaf), it is noticeable that only a few are names most architects will now recognise. Near the top of that list we obscurely have Lord Leighton, the famous and wealthy artist who commissioned George Aitchison (the Gold Medallist of four years later) to design the remarkable Leighton House for him, and was awarded the Gold Medal in 1894. Fifty years later, in 1942, we have Curtis Green who, as a young man, in 1904, author of a large west London electric generating station serving the radically influential new underground railways. He is now an obscure name. The same might be said of James Brooks (1895), Ernest George (1896), George Bodley (1899), Thomas Collcutt (1902), Aston Webb (1905), John Belcher (1907), Arthur Evans (1909), T.G. Jackson (1910), and so on. These people may have been influential in their day, but most of these men (never women, although note the presence of a woman in the photo on page 235) are as elusively obscure as any medieval master-builder. Few practising architects either know or care about their works.

And, if this is the fate of Gold Medallists, then what chance have the likes of Treadwell and Martin, C.H. Worley, and Frank Elgood of being acknowledged? These were architects who could ill-afford to posture and, instead, vigorously sought to be opportunistically and characteristically Edwardian in the manner they handled smaller jobs. All, it would seem, were grist to the mill that serves London's voracious appetite.

Perhaps Edwin Lutyens – the Frank Lloyd Wright of British architecture (who, paired with Herbert Baker, form the Rogers and Foster of their day) – epitomises this issue. To examine the work of this genius is to be astounded. Perhaps no architect since Burlington and Wren have offered so much as this thoroughly affable

Fifty years of RIBA Gold
Medallists, 1892 to 1942:

1892 César Daly, France
1893 Richard Morris Hunt, USA
1894 Lord Leighton, RA
1895 James Brooks
1896 Ernest George, RA
1897 Dr P.J.H Cuypers, Holland
1898 George Aitchison, RA
1899 George Frederick Bodley, RA
1900 Professor Rodolfo Amadeo Lanciani, Italy
1901 (Not awarded; death of Queen Victoria)
1902 Thomas Edward Collcutt
1903 Charles F. McKim, USA
1904 Auguste Choisy, France
1905 Sir Aston Webb, PPRA
1906 Sir L. Alma-Tadema, RA
1907 John Belcher, RA
1908 Honoré Daumet, France
1909 Sir Arthur John Evans, FRS, FSA
1910 Sir Thomas Graham Jackson
1911 Wilhelm Dorpfeld, Germany
1912 Basil Champneys
1913 Reginald Blomfield, RA, FSA
1914 Jean Louis Pascal, France
1915 Frank Darling, Canada
1916 Sir Robert Rowand Anderson, FRIAS
1917 Henri Paul Nenot, Membre de L'Institut, France
1918 Ernest Newton, RA
1919 Leonard Stokes
1920 Charles Louis Girault, France
1921 Sir Edwin Landseer Lutyens, OM, KCIE, RA, FSA
1922 Thomas Hastings, USA
1923 Sir John James Burnet, FRIAS, RA, RSA
1924 Not awarded
1925 Sir Giles Gilbert Scott, OM, DCL, RA
1926 Professor Ragnar Ostberg, Sweden
1927 Sir Herbert Baker, KCIE, RA
1928 Sir Guy Dawber, RA, FSA
1929 Victor Alexandre Frederic Laloux, France
1930 Percy Scott Worthington, FSA
1931 Sir Edwin Cooper, RA
1932 Dr Hendrik Petrus Berlage, Holland
1933 Sir Charles Reed Peers, CBE, PPSA
1934 Henry Vaughan Lanchester, PPTPI
1935 Willem Marinus Dudok, Holland
1936 Charles Henry Holden, MTPI
1937 Sir Raymond Unwin
1938 Professor Ivar Tengbom, Sweden
1939 Sir Percy Thomas, OBE, JP, MTPI
1940 Charles Francis Annesley Voysey
1941 Frank Lloyd Wright, USA
1942 William Curtis Green, RA

man (with, in fact, a rather sad private life riddled with anxiety). Ironically, we have little of his prodigious output in London that sparkles with genuine originality. But we do have the Cenotaph: that strange, enigmatic stone edifice in Whitehall that speaks to us in strangely mythic terms regarding its references to the pivotal trauma of World War One. So much and so many careers were disrupted by that latter event. And yet, the period afterward – up to World War II – was a interlude in which, despite the myths of social revolution, nothing much really changed at the deep core of British values, as even a cursory examination of the history of the City of London quickly reveals. As always, we need to remember the continuities as well as the changes. And with the hindsight that doesn't know where we are but considers itself conscious of where we have been, it is now possible to see a complex continuity to the years before, between and immediately after the two World Wars. To adopt such a perspective is to underscore strands of continuity that stretch back from the post-war period through to the early years of Victoria's reign.

What possibly unified many of the architects of this period was a resurgence of interest in a marriage of architecture and sculpture – what was, in origin, another French influenced development. Belcher, for example, marvellously mixed sculpture and architecture at his house for accountants. Young's New War Office was said by one critic to have been 'saved' by Alfred Drury's sculpture. And the enormous 'Peace Quadriga' that was put together by Captain Adrian Jones for the top of the Wellington Arch, at Hyde Park Corner, epitomises a fulsome enthusiasm that managed to serve everyone's tastes.

However, the World War I – which resulted in a two-and-a-half times inflation rate in building costs between 1914-20 – ended sculptural programmes as well as the fulsomeness of Baroque neo-Classicism in general. The Empire may have been larger than ever, (and still providing work for many British architects), but it was now, in its heart, profoundly troubled.

On a less philosophical note we have to remember that the above changes in style, taste and value took place at a time when suburban London had (like the Empire it ruled) been rapidly expanding. While the better off middle-classes could enjoy the likes of the houses built on the Eton College Estate, to the north of Primrose Hill, on the edge of the central area, many

James Brooks (1825-1901), a typically forgotten RIBA Gold Medal winner, 1895. He set up in practice in 1852 and most of his work was ecclesiastical. His London works include: St Columbia, Kingsland Road, 1871; St Chad, Nicholas Square, Shoreditch, 1868; Ascension Church, Lavender Hill, Battersea,1873.

of the older areas of Inner London (then the LCC area) were being described as a desert of deprived humanity. Those who could – and there were increasingly many of them in the Edwardian area – used new transport systems to escape Inner London: the electrically-driven Central Line in 1900, electric trams from 1900 onward, motorbuses of 1906 onward and, after 1910, extensions of the underground system.

Between 1902 and 1906, Acton's population increased by 52%, Chingford's by 86%, Hendon by 73%, Barnes by 71%, and Merton and Morden by 156%. Golders Green's acres of semi-detatched houses vaguely inspired by Voysey, Baillie-Scott and Ashbee are an example of land speculation associated with the approvals for a new Underground line opened in 1907. Here was privacy, a garden, a proper kitchen and bathroom, gas and electricity – all designed by mostly anonymous architects. The Hampstead Garden Suburb development of 1906 on, laid out by Raymond Unwin, epitomised the better possibilities of such schemes, although it failed to fulfil its social ambitions and remains an odd place of real and aspirational privilege mixed with a quiet inwardness and cultural isolation.

Class values in this mixed equation were evident in the lack of pubs and music halls in these new suburbs. But the cinema was to change all that. The first opened in 1906 and, by 1912, there were 500 of them in London and its suburbs – a flowering that was to reach its zenith with the remarkable movie palaces of the 1930s. (Now, like the equally remarkable Californian coffee houses of the 1950s, largely an extinct species of architecture. Service to the culture and tastes of the masses appears to be, in historical terms, significantly less robust than service to the Culture and tastes of the upper classes.)

Class values married to land scarcity also engendered that most unlikely and un-English fashion for blocks of apartments located within convenient reach of central London. As a type, they never enjoyed the status of the individual house, but some later examples – notably by Tecton, at Highgate, in the 1930s – offered a promise that the social housing programmes of the 1950s and '60's failed to fulfil, but which still serve as an example to contemporary efforts that have again brought the apartment block to the forefront of housing provision in London. In them – even the smaller, less grand, lower middle-class blocks on turn-of-the-century suburban streets leading away from the disorder of central London – still had a room for the maid. But, within a few years, many of the bedrooms given over to youthful sons were to become empty and desolate, and architects such as Lutyens were to design an enormous number of memorials.

Educating heroes and francophile sentiments

In 1884, Richard Phené Spiers, Master of the Royal Academy School of Architecture, had unfavourably contrasted articled pupillage with Continental practice: *"The first great failing in England is that the student coming straight from school is not prepared to make that use of the practical training to be had in the office which is universally assumed. He has little or no knowledge of either freehand or geometrical drawing, of physics, mechanics, or of any of the elements of architectural style; he flounders about, therefore, in the sometimes styleless design of the architect in whose office he may be placed, and acquires by the longest possible process a certain knowledge of a mixture of style and no style, second-hand; his powers of reasoning in design, as a rule, are not brought into play until his articles are terminated, and then want of time and absolute lack of training at once curtail his ideas and cramp his imagination. He has picked up an idea here and there in the office, and numerous details, but he finds himself unable to grasp the composition of a building of any size. In many cases he has never had an opportunity of visiting or studying any one of the buildings the drawings of which he has been continually at work on [...] He has, in fact, taken from three to five years to learn imperfectly what might have been learned in one or two if his mind had been previously trained to receive it."*

The answer was to copy the French competitive system and the first schools of architecture – at Birmingham, Liverpool, University College and the Architectural Association – that enjoyed three to four year courses moved in this direction (enabling students to avoid the RIBA Intermediate examination for association membership and, from 1920, its Final examination).

Reginald Blomfield was among those promoting such new courses. And, in 1913, Arthur Davis set up the First London Atelier. From 1912, courses aimed at a Rome Scholarship, as in France and a Faculty of Architecture was set up to administer the system. Until 1942 this was chaired by Blomfield and members were taken from the principal schools: the RA, the RIBA, etc.

In contrast, in 1912, the Italian radical Marinetti attacked the English attachment to Rome, Venice and Florence *"which we consider running sores on the face of the peninsula."* And, in 1913, the philosopher T.E. Hulme also undermined the rationale of the Rome scholarship by attacking the humanistic tradition – which he unfavourably compared with modern, mechanical and geometric art – and suggested that it

was *"the business of every honest man at the present moment to clean the world of these sloppy dregs of the Renaissance."*

Within a decade of being set up the Rome School was seen as a bulwark against such Modernist tendencies, thus revealing other aspects of educational change that began to occur around 1890, at a time of an economic depression and at a time when the RIBA was striving to realise a profession closed to unqualified outsiders. Like Shaw, Blomfield – who certainly considered the Rome Prize to be an anti-professional strategem – was firmly opposed to registration. Similar calls for a more disciplined approach to architectural education and the promotion of art occurred around 1930, in similar economic conditions of recession and, again, the underlying motivation was protectionist as well as reactionary.

Ironically, the radically Modernist 'High and Over' house, 1929, was commissioned from Amyas Connell, Rome scholar of 1926, by Bernard Ashmole, Director of the British School from 1925 to 1928. Even Faculty members lobbied in the house's favour. Blomfield was not happy. In his 1932 memoirs he complained, *"Fifty years ago it was the fashion to say that the only way to become an architect was to work with one's own hands; now it is the fashion to say, leave it all to the engineer."* However, young architects, especially, saw the Prize system as providing welcome disciplines but promoting thoroughly reactionary values. *Just as the registrationists and anti-registrationsists were bitter opponents,* Classicism and Modernism became soundly polarised.

Whilst noting such sentiments it is again worth referring to the figure of Goodhart-Rendel and his erudite comments on this subject – a man who became president of the RIBA in 1937-9, and in 1936 accepted the directorship of the Architectural Association School of Architecture.

He was born in 1887 (and died in 1959). Between 1902 and 1905 he spent much time in France (where his grandfather, Lord Rendel, had a villa), becoming an enduring Francophile. In 1902, at Lord Rendel's insistence, he added the name of Rendel to his own. In 1905 he studied music at Cambridge but, by 1911, he was practising architectural design rather than musical composition. He found himself happily soldiering during WWI but, because of health issues, was not at the front and was reluctantly demobbed to return to architecture.

Above: students of the Architectural Association, 1920. The presence of a woman is interesting.

Summerson tells us that Rendel, *"in the course of the next twenty years became one of the most prominent and interesting figures in the profession. This was due ... to his vivid personality, keen wit, and willingness to devote himself assiduously to professional affairs."* It was said that, *"In society and in the committee room he was distinguished by a patrician elegance, by an ironic and slightly plaintive manner of speech, and by the sparkle of a wit issuing from a combination of logical thought and a profound love of paradox."*

In his work *English Architecture Since the Regency* (1953, Goodhart-Rendel noted that, *"We must remember that in that country [France] the Roman lamp of Vitruvian architecture lit at the Renaissance had since then been carefully tended and never extinguished. At the Ecole des Beaux Arts the accumulated experience of generations concerning [...] difficulties in design [...] was handed down from teacher to pupil, so that, if the pupil chose to experiment, he experimented with his feet on solid ground. Even more important in the curriculum of the École des Beaux Arts, always has been, and still is, the study of order, rhythm, and logic, in planning, and the cultivation of sound sense and reasoning in construction. To say that all this in England had been lost at the time we are considering would not be true, because something of it survived Victorian emotionalism, and much of the rest of it we never had."* (A point that possibly hints at his unpopularity with young architects when at the AA.) He went on to note that, *"Training in the less severe schools of Gothic and of Bric-à-brac had accustomed them [British architects] to look at architectural form rather with the eye of the scene-painter than with that of the scholar."* Commenting positively on the Beaux Art work of Arthur Davis, our critic suggested that, *"Designing like this could only be learned at school, where most English architects at that time had been – shall we call it privately educated? – by the uncertain method of pupillage."*

Understandably, Rendel as Head of the AA failed to attract the loyalty of the young Modernists of the 1930s and so resigned in 1938. After World War II, the school was to become a London centre of radical attitudes to architectural design even less sympathetic to Goodhart-Rendel's inclinations and values. Real change had finally arrived. But it had taken a long time.

Lutyens' extant London works include:

• **16 Little College Street**, SW1, for the Hon. Alfred Lyttelton, 1895.

• **St John's Institute**, (now The Church Union Faith House), Tufton Street, SW1, 1898.

• **Street Clock**, Tower House, Southampton Street, WC2, for Sir George Newnes, 1903.

• **Country Life building** (now Citibank), Tavistock Street, WC2, 1904.

• **Offices for The Garden**, (now Pitcher & Piano), Redland House, 42 Kingsway, WC2, 1906.

• **St Jude's**, and **Free Church**, Hampstead Garden Suburb; also two parsonages, 1908.

• **The Institute**, and houses in North Square and Erskine Hill, Hampstead Garden Suburb, 1908.

• **36 Smith Square**, SW1, for the Rt. Hon. Reginald McKenna, 1911.

• **7, St. James's Square**, SW1, for Henry Farrer, 1911.

• **Roehampton House**, Wandsworth, SW15, (additions and garden) for A. M. Grenfell, 1911

• **Theosophical Society's Headquarters** (now British Medical Association), 1911-24.

• **The Corner House**, Cowley Street and No. 8 Little College Street, Westminster, SW1 for Lady Norman and the Hon. F. Maclaren, 1912.

• **Pedestal** for Equestrian statue of King Edward in Waterloo Place, 1912.

• **Mausoleum**, Golder's Green Crematorium, London for the Philipson family, 1914.

• **Cenotaph**, Whitehall, SW1, 1919.

• **Britannic House**, Finsbury Circus EC2, for the Anglo-Iranian Oil Co. Ltd., 1920.

• University College School War **Memorial**, Hampstead, NW3, 1921.

• **Tomb** of Sir Cecil Harmsworth, Hampstead Garden Suburb, London, 1921

• former **Midland Bank**, 196 Piccadilly, W1, 1922 (now an art gallery).

• Civil Service Rifles War **Memorial**, Somerset House, Strand, WC2, 1923.

• Royal Naval Division Memorial **fountain**, Admiralty, 1924.

• former **Midland Bank HQ**, Poultry, 1924, EC2 (extensions 1935-1939); with Gotch and Saunders.

• **Grosvenor House**, Park Lane, W1 (elevations only), 1926.

• **Memorial** to Dame Louisa Blake, Tavistock Square, WC2, 1926.

• **Mercantile Marine War Memorial**, Tower Hill, EC3, 1926.

• **Terminal House**, Grosvenor Gardens, SW1 (elevations only), 1927.

• **Monument** to Lord Cheylesmore, Embankment Gardens, WC2, 1927.

• **Flats** in Page Street and Vincent Street, SW1, for the LCC, 1928 (Lutyens is said to had no interest in housing, even though he controversially won the job from another architect).

• **68 Pall Mall**, SW1 (elevations only) for Victor Behar, 1928.

• **Central Club – YWCA** (now Jurys Hotel Great Russell Street), 16-22 Great Russell Street, London WC1, 1928.

•**120 Pall Mall**, SW1 for Messrs Crane Bennett Ltd (now Banco Sabadell), 1929.

• **British Industries House and Hereford House**, Oxford Street, W1 for Gamage's (elevations only, latterly C&A), 1929.

• **Midland Bank branch**, Leadenhall (adjacent to the proposed Rogers 'cheese-grater'), 1929.

• **Aldford House**, Park Lane, W1 (consultant for elevations), 1930.

• **66 Lincoln's Inn Fields**, WC2 (restoration of façade) for Messrs Farrer and Co. 1930.

• **Brook House**, Park Lane, W1 (façades only), 1932.

• **Lamp standards**, West front, St Paul's Cathedral, WC2, 1933.

• **North House**, (now Linden Lodge School), Wimbledon, Surrey (also lodge) for R. Wilson Black, 1934.

• **Reuter's and Press Association**, Fleet Street, WC2, (inc. The Codgers public house), 1935.

• **Elliptical Room**, Greenwich Maritime Museum, London for Sir James Caird. 1936.

• Admiral Beatty and Admiral Jellicoe **memorial fountains**, Trafalgar Square, SW1, 1937-1939.

Numerous pedestals, memorials and statues bases, and the like have been omitted. Most of Lutyens' work in London after 1920 is exteriors and not interiors. Much of his work has been altered, adapted or otherwise compromised. Examples such as Lindisfarne Castle and Castle Drogo, outside London, are owned by the National Trust and readily accessible. For listings see http://www.lutyenstrust.org.uk. Work abroad includes buildings in South Africa, India and Rome.

architecture's joker
Sir Edwin Landseer Lutyens
1869–1944

In the decade leading up to World War One Lutyens, still in his thirties, was already famous for a series of remarkable country houses (in 1897 he was working on twenty-five commissions). When he died, in 1944, he was acknowledged as the greatest twentieth century British architect. He had been knighted in 1918, awarded the RIBA Gold medal in 1921, elected to the Royal Academy on 1921 and made its President in 1938. In 1913, when Country Life published a book of his houses, he had London's aristocracy at his feet and the rest of the profession green with envy. However, by the time of his death, Lutyens was an old man whose style of architecture was long past its sell-by date and not at all in accord with those passing fashions which, since WWI, had brought varieties of Art Deco (or the Jazz Moderne as it was once called) and Modernism to the foreground.

To Nicholas Pevsner, Lutyens was, *"the paradox of the revivalist in whose work geometry is more insistent than in that of any living architect bar Corbusier, the crowning paradox of the twentieth century architect of prodigious gifts who contributed nothing to the mainstream of development in twentieth century architecture."*

In contrast, when Country Life published the architect's biography in 1950, the author celebrated Lutyens as, *"our greatest architect since Wren if not, as many maintained, his superior."* Nevertheless, Lutyens was to remain in obscurity until rediscovered by the American Post-Modern Movement, who reintroduced the British to his merits and prompted a major, celebratory exhibition of his work in 1981-2, at the Hayward Gallery – the latter a Brutalist exercise Lutyens would have thoroughly detested.

In truth, at his death, he was considered to be the representative of an irrelevant architectural agenda, celebrated only by the likes of his contemporary, Frank Lloyd Wright, who, in 1951, was to pay homage to Lutyens' stature as an architect. But Wright possibly saw in Lutyens a similar figure to himself: celebrated as genius and yet strangely of little influence upon the mainstream of practice. Subsequent to his death he was mostly ignored by a post-war Britain with other concerns and values. The 1951 Festival of Britain brought a long period of neoclassical inclinations in British tastes to a firm closure; the 'George VI style', as it has been called, was abruptly replaced by Modernist values with Scandinavian leanings.

The Post-Modernist period of his rediscovery bore ghostly undertones of that nostalgia and the values

characterising anti-Modernist tastes of the 1920s through to the 1951 Festival – a form of sentiment that still lingers in some quarters. On this point it is worth noting the extent to which Lutyens became a thoroughly traditional, humanist architect. In 1931 he remarked that, *"These adventurous young men thrill me tremendously and all my sympathies are with them. But good architecture needs more than bright ideas, and by my traditional standards most modern buildings seem to me to lack style and cohesion, besides being unfriendly and crude."* He explained: *"My generation is – perhaps I ought to say was – a humanist generation. We believed that the measure of man's architecture was man, and that the rhythm of a building should correspond to the*

Below: 36 Smith Square, typical of Lutyens' 'Wrennaisance' work around 1911.

Above: The rear of the British Medial Association building, 1911-24.
Opposite: the 'Garden' magazine building (1906), in Kingsway. (The 1904 'Country Life' building is nearby, in Covent Garden.)

rhythms familiar in human life. All architecture must have rhythms that affect the eye as music does the ear, producing vibrations in the brain." Perhaps if he had studied Le Corbusier or Lubetkin he might have found similar concerns to his own, but 'crudity and unfriendliness' would still have been keynotes that have always haunted Modernism.

Despite his standing between the wars, Lutyens' best work in Britain had been completed during a twenty year period before WWI, work that was mostly domestic and generally within the Arts & Crafts tradition. After that war, during a period when Modernism gained its definition and aroused the enthusiasms of young men and women in British schools of architecture, Lutyens was more notable as an architect who had been soundly buried within his own rediscoveries: that of classical formalities and the 'grand manner' inspirations of Palladio and Wren which had begun to characterise his corporate work in the decade or more before the war and continued in the 1920s. He famously wrote to Herbert Baker (in 1905): "In architecture Palladio is the game!! It is so big – few appreciate it now, and it requires training to value and to realise it."

The best of Lutyens' work was to be abroad: for example, the immense war memorials in France and the ill-fated colonial work in Delhi. However, the substance of his' fame was undermined at its height, with the arrival a war that had so little glory, was to fracture the socio-economic cohesion of the nation and to sour the rest of his life. The period afterward was spent serving pre-war clients, undertaking dozens of memorials, tombs and cemeteries (he undertook 126 for the War Graves Commission), doing corporate work on what we would now acknowledge as a 'shell and core' basis, working on

doomed projects such as that for Liverpool Cathedral, worrying about spending so much time abroad on imperialist projects in India (an engagement initiated in 1912), his wife's eccentric obsession with Theosophy and her infatuation with Krishnamurti, during the 1920s, and about bank overdrafts (not helped by the search, in 1919, for a house needing less than seven servants which resulted in the purchase of one requiring ten).

The award of an RIBA Gold Medal in 1921 was arguably celebrating an architect who was not past his prime but already irrelevant to the patterns of change then taking place. Later, a younger generation emerging from World War II perhaps hardly noticed the passing of a man whose work was so associated with an era of class divisions, colonialism and a world view seriously shaken and then fractured by two devastating world conflicts. A self-satisfied Edwardian world of what Mary Lutyens has described as innocent places of fastidious wealth, enjoying the finest craftsmanship in oak, stone and brick, where one would hear the clink of teacups and the crack of ball on mallet, was, by then, rather distant (although many of its values lingered on as core aspects of English culture). However, Goodhart-Rendel's obituary pointedly noted that, "He seems to leave behind him a grey world, full of grim architectural Puritans on the one hand and gentleman-like architects who do the done thing on the other. He took Shaw's place, but who is to take his?"

But then, some thirty years later, Lutyens' work was rediscovered and celebrated once again: largely as the conscripted champion of an alternative to Modernist values. Since then his memory and works have not been forgotten, but kept alive as grist to the mill of cultural nostalgia in general and architectural tourism in particular: his work reduced to being as superficially entertaining as his jokes. It is an ironic fate for work that often exhibits a rare humanity and stature, as well as the spirit of a man for whom architecture was a profoundly significant game and for who the term 'game' was anything but less than deeply serious.

As a character, Lutyens was apparently charming and ingratiating, having a love of wit and puns. Life and the practice of architecture was to be – or appear to be – fun. Described as bubbling with friendliness, he became well connected and keenly supported by family friends and early clients.

Small, balding, pipe-smoking and genial, we are told that he easily won clients and persuaded them to his intentions. For example, having angered, Lady Hardinge, wife of the Indian viceroy, over some detail of the work undertaken in New Delhi, he wrote to her: "I will wash your feet with my tears and dry them with my hair. True, I have very little hair; but you have very little feet." Of course, he won her favour.

Oswald P. Milne commented that, "He had a wonderful way with clients. He was marvellous not only in dealing with materials but in dealing with human beings. He always got them to spend what he wanted

Lutyens is reported to have poorly paid his assistants, but to have treated them kindly with respect. It says much for his talents and character that even historians can congratulate the great man on this point. His office assistants included, at one time or another, E. Baynes Badcock (with whom he is described as being in an 'informal partnership' for three years, to 1901); A.J. Thomas, who subsequently ran the office during Lutyens's absences abroad until 1935; Edward Hall and George Stewart were – both long-serving assistants; J.J. Joass, J.D. Coleridge, Milne, H.L. North, J. Murray Easton, Sir Hubert Worthington, and Sir Basil Spence; and Lutyens' son Robert.

Oswald P. Milne, who worked in the Bloomsbury Square office (actually Lutyens' home) from 1902-5, described the office as follows: "Lutyens occupied the front room, and the large back room was the drawing office, with perhaps three pupils and three or four draughtsmen. There was also a little office by the stairs where the secretary worked. I believe that the telephone had just been introduced … He was a great worker. If not visiting a job, he stood working at his drawing-board in the front office – I do not remember him ever sitting down – legs apart and usually smoking a pipe. He spoke somewhat incoherently; he never explained himself; his wonderful fund of ideas and invention were expressed not in speech but at the end of his pencil. If we were in difficulties we would invite him to come over and help us out. He would put a piece of tracing-paper over the drawing, and in a minute or two he had sketched half-a-dozen solutions to the problem. He then put a ring round the one he preferred and left us to carry it out. He never gave explanations or talked about the work, but somehow we managed to pick up what he wanted."

Lutyens apparently remarked (as many architects do) that, "everything should have an air of inevitability", but he was a humanist rather than a religious man, resisting Baker's advocation of a Christian cross on the war memorials in France. But it says something of his neo-Platonic architectural beliefs that, when a student asked 'What is proportion?', Lutyens replied, "God." This time he probably wasn't joking.

them to spend." In fact, he seldom worked for the landed aristocracy, and most of his clients were self-made or second-generation rich: bankers, solicitors, shipowners, publishers, stockbrokers (some of them dubious characters, like Willie James, the half-American crony of Edward VII, or Julius Drew, the founder of Home and Colonial Stores, who would add an 'e' to his name and ask Lutyens to build him an ancestral castle in Devon. Lutyens claimed that he attempted to make his clients purr with his blandishments while bringing them around difficult corners.

The irony is that much of what Lutyens left the profession concerns what may be deemed to be trivial. In a lecture given to the AA, he remarked: *"There is wit and may be humour in the use of material. The unexpected, where it is logical, is fun"* and his sketches exhibited a schoolboyish wit, e.g., a drawing of Gandhi on a camel, captioned, *"You should see Mysore."* Dying of lung cancer, he joked that, if given a peerage, he should be known as Lord Cough of Cough. As an apprentice architect, articled to Sir Ernest Newton, he picked up a preference for drawings and photos taken from low down – what he called a 'worm's eye view', a rustic term still familiar in architectural circles, particularly with regard to those bottom-up axonometrics enjoyed by Jim Stirling. Like many architects today, Lutyens always took a pen and small note pad around with him, so that he could illustrate his jovial banter with sketches. Similarly, he may have influenced another custom: the

Above: *sculpture (a fat boy with a goose) on a corner of the building (by Sir William Reid Dick).*
Opposite page: *the former Midland Bank HQ, in Poultry (Stirling and Wilford's No1 Poultry appropriately sits opposite). The building is steel-framed.*

From 1876 the family spent half of each year living near Goldalming, in Surrey, and Lutyens learned to roam the local countryside looking at cottages and new constructions. He famously drew the outline of cottages and barns on a sheet of glass with pieces of soap, and visited local building sites and a carpenter's shop and was quickly noted as a child with a remarkable imagination, memory, observational and drawing skills. In 1885 – the year he was introduced to Norman Shaw and suggested amendments to the great man's drawings – Lutyens enrolled in the National Art Training School in South Kensington, but left two years later, before completing the course, and, in 1887, began work as a paying apprentice at the offices of Sir Ernest George & Peto (where the entry queue was much shorter than at Shaw's more fashionable office). It was here that he met his colleague and later collaborator, Herbert Baker, who remarked upon Lutyens' remarkable intuitional capacity regarding the skills of the profession. But the office was not a place he enjoyed; he only stayed one year, leaving with additional drafting skills and practical knowledge, but now eager to set up on his own and forge his own path.

Lutyens began his own practice on the familiar basis of a house commission for a family friend, undertaking work founded on what was being done by Philip Webb and Norman Shaw. It was at this time (in 1889) that he was introduced to a formidable and pertinacious woman, Gertrude Jekyll (1843-1932), for whom Lutyens designed a house, Munstead Woods. He found her a huge advocate of his skills and teamed up with 'Aunt Bumps' to carry out a whole series of commissions upon which she acted as advisor and landscape designer. For example, it was Jekyll who introduced Lutyens to Edward Hudson (1854-1936), a man who was to commission three houses from him and was also the editor of a venturesome lifestyle magazine of the period called Country Life. This, from its later founding in1897, was to strongly promote Lutyens' work as well as commissioning him as the architect for the magazine's offices in Tavistock Place (1904).

In the year that magazine was founded Lutyens married Lady Emily Bulwer-Lytton, the daughter of a viceroy of India (against her family's opposition and forced to heavily insure his life). By then he was already doing rather well and the couple moved into Bloomsbury Square where they have been described as being 'over-housed, under-furnished and under-staffed'. Lutyens' studio was on the ground floor.

But while Lutyens' fame grew as a domestic architect of note, his interests swung in the direction of Wren, Palladio, geometry and such other familiar neoclassical themes, first exhibiting them in his design for the Country Life offices – described as 'a slice of Hampton Court Palace' – and exemplified by two City buildings: his former Midland Bank headquarters building in Poultry (opposite Stirling's No1 Poutry) and Brittanic House, in Moorgate. And yet it is interesting that this aspect of his work – something claimed to be

drawing on table cloths which might also have come from Lutyens' sojourns in Delhi, where he had a circular blackboard made up as a table top and supplied each dinner guest with a chalk. By then he was a long way from his Surrey childhood, roaming the English countryside and absorbing vernacular traditions.

L utyens was born in London as the son of a soldier turned successful painter. Suffering from rheumatic fever as a child, he was prevented from attending boarding school and gained, in his own mind, the advantage of staying at home (by then in the country south-west of London): *"Any talent I may have had ... was due to a long illness as a boy, which afforded me time to think, and to subsequent ill-health, because I was not allowed to play games, and so had to teach myself, for my enjoyment, to use my eyes instead of my feet. My brothers hadn't the same advantage."* Frailty also meant that he became close to his mother – the first of many women who were to be so important to his career (his wife Emily; Barbara Webb, wife of the local squire where he grew up; Gertrude Jekyll, a formidable artist and craftswoman turned gardener, with whom Lutyens completed over one hundred garden projects; Lady Sackville, mother of Vita Sackville-West, and so on).

rooted in youthful enthusiasms for the Wren-manner house of one of his patrons near his home in Surrey, and eminently more suited to urban contexts than the freestyle of his much admired country houses – now tarnishes his reputation.

The many extant examples (from the brilliant to the bland) of this urbane architectural style so epitomising the tastes of the era, make little impression upon contemporary sensibilities. In fact, around the time the Country Life offices were completed, such work was already tired and old-fashioned by the Continental standards of Loos, Behrens et al, and especially to the likes of Filippo Tommaso Marinetti who, in 1912, came to lecture and shock the radicalist lady members of the recently formed Lyceum Club with his misogynist Futurism, talk of fast cars, the sanitising effects of war, political protest, and the glories of the machine. It was to take some fifty years before one could begin to talk of any significant influence of Futurism upon British architectural thinking. In the meantime, the reputation of Lutyens' work ironically seemed to rest as much upon the man's character as his architectural talents. With regard to the latter, it is his early domestic work and his work in France and India that sustains his reputation. Arguably, only one (very simple) London work – among many – touches upon his originality

within a Neo-Platonic architectural framework of belief that Lutyens employed to sustain his revivalist gaming: the Whitehall Cenotaph.

Besides the RIBA Gold Medal Lutyens was awarded in 1921, he became the first architect on whom the Order of Merit was conferred (1924). Among his other many honours, he was elected an academician in 1920, knighted in 1918, and he was created KCIE in 1930.

The Cenotaph, 1919

It is perhaps fitting, but nevertheless ironic, that London's finest example of Lutyens' work is arguably the Cenotaph: a comparatively small civic monument to the dead of WWI; witness to a significant change point in his career, devoid of domesticity, religiosity or commerciality. That it remains a significant memorial, now embedded in annual civic rituals, says much about the success of the design as well as the depth of pain caused by war.

The basis of the design for a cenotaph (meaning an empty tomb) was Lutyens' 'Great Stone' that was used in the many memorials he designed for France and erected as part of the temporary Great War Shrine in Hyde Park, in August 1918 – a forgotten and much criticised attempt to address the grieving of the nation which, nevertheless, confirmed the need for a permanent memorial. In 1919 (and despite the lack of success of the temporary shrine) the architect was approached by the Prime Minister and asked to design a 'catafalque' for a site in Whitehall. The challenge became what has been described as 'a mathematical pilgrimage in search of the sublime', a continuation of Lutyens' fascination with subtle geometries, with entasis and the like.

The design came quickly and was temporarily constructed in timber and plaster in readiness for an Allied Peace Day march past, and the permanent work was completed in 1920.

What is remarkable about the Cenotaph is the degree to which it – as an abstract symbol – struck an instant note of appropriateness: an unadorned, austere and simple work that is making a deep and worthy impression, as the Times newspaper put it at the time. Such was the clamour (contrasting with the temporary Hyde Park monument) that the design was made permanent. *"The new Cenotaph erected in Whitehall to the memory of 'the glorious dead"*, wrote the Times, *"was the centre of what was perhaps the most moving portion of Saturday's triumphal ceremony. The Cenotaph is only a temporary structure made to look like stone; but Sir Edwin Lutyens' design is so grave, severe and beautiful that one might well wish it were indeed of stone and permanent."*

Lutyens now submitted drawings for a permanent Cenotaph, writing, *"I have made slight alterations to meet the conditions demanded by the setting out of its lines on subtle curvatures, the difference is almost imperceptible, yet sufficient to give it a sculpturesque quality and a life, that cannot pertain to rectangular blocks of stone."* He was referring to the entasis he had introduced to the horizontal and vertical lines – subtleties given to the Stone of Remembrance first designed in 1917 and placed in the many cemeteries designed by him.

All the horizontals of the Cenotaph are, in fact, slightly curved, as are the verticals. Each conforms to a curve that is 1801 feet and 8 inches in diameter and the horizontals are made up from parallel spheres to that diameter; the verticals also meet at that height above the ground. In fact, numbers strangely fascinate those who describe the Cenotaph, just as they obsessed Lutyens. The overall height is given as 35 feet, the base is 15' x 8'6", the top is 11'6 x 6'6." The laurel wreaths at the ends are 5 feet in diameter, the one at the top 3'6." All letters and Roman numerals are approximately 5" square.

However, this fascination with the monument's geometry and measure may be a classic instance of the chicken and the egg: which came first? Much comment is given to these refinements but, in fact, the temporary Cenotaph – which established the work's appeal and popularity – came before the stone edifice with its refined entasis. To the extent one might argue the work embodies some strange mythic quality, this is clearly independent of the props of rational geometries and the more arcane aspects of architectural pretensions that Lutyens indulged in.

Here, we are firmly in that dark territory described by Adolf Loos (1910): *"When walking through a wood, you find a rise in the ground, six foot long and three foot wide, heaped up in a rough pyramid shape, then you turn serious, and something inside you says: someone is buried here. That is architecture."* (The tumulus, of course, was without entasis!) Some vague element of that appreciative sentiment of the sublime – of what embraces pain and terror as well as beauty – must somehow echo within Lutyens' design for the Cenotaph. Otherwise it could never have become the civic symbol it is (nor had such a status reinforced over many years).

To link these disparate architects is, in itself peculiar. However, it is not unreasonable to look upon the Cenotaph as a work thoroughly and somewhat bizarrely within the spirit of Loos' sentiment that there can only be an architecture of death, that all else was merely 'dumb building' within a vernacular tradition (a point that touches upon the nature of Lutyens' early work and with which he might not have been unsympathetic). There, of course, the parallels end. In other terms, a mature Lutyens would have represented to Loos all of those intellectualised and Establishment values alien to his appreciation of the *Zeitgeist*. And while debate on that point is always a turbulent and unresolved current, Lutyens own architecture of death mutely stands in Whitehall as a dignified and brooding form whose significance is independent of it all, perhaps including the ritualised pomp and circumstance that attends to the ceremonies that take place on its steps.

The Cenotaph, with George Gilbert-Scott's Foreign Office in the background.

St Judes, Hampstead Garden Suburb 1908

Hampstead Garden Suburb is a place you either love or find curiously disturbed by its subscription to an abstracted urbanistic idealism far removed from the realities of Inner London, whether it be the latter's ubiquitous terraced housing or its West End mansions or mansion blocks (and especially from the mass of disorderly, often deprived and decrepit London). But in the Suburb – midst its mix of neo-Georgian and Arts & Crafts influences – is one of London's most impressive churches: St Jude's, by Edwin 'Ned' Lutyens (1909-11). Externally, the church is memorable for its restraint and an elemental, abstracted classicism. The detail is relatively minimal. The overall forms are mildly picturesque, but in accord with a demanding classical symmetry. This is, in fact, a grand barn at the heart of the community (now mostly Jewish, so that the potential congregation

functional elements: nave, aisles, crossing and side chapels. Internally, the architecture possibly outdoes Bentley at Westminster Cathedral with its simple and powerful vaulting that is richly but softly painted (none of the glitter of the mosaics of Westminster and St Paul's). Here, the classicism is self-evident, but reductive, as if merely constructional necessities to the mass of brickwork: a kind of mere underscoring and outlining. But then Lutyens arbitrarily introduces a most curious mannerist (wonderful and impure) interaction of heavily timbered aisle roofing and brick vaulting, without which it all might have been *too* simple. It has charm and yet strength, mixed with quirkiness that does not obtrude – expressive, perhaps, of the architect's own character?

is severely restricted), much in the spirit of Jones' exercise in Covent Garden. The Pevsner Buildings of England guide calls it eclectic, but it is Lutyens at his most masterful and in full control (he referred to the design as 'Romantic-Byzantine-cum-Nedi'). Here, he has no need of the language of the 'high game' of classicism. He knows it and can apparently go beyond it. To refer to this as eclecticism is perhaps to miss the point. The architect seems to have been seeking a power of simple form and texture: of brickwork, the occasional stone detail, large and low sheltering roof and a form simply expressive of the fundamental

Right: the clay-tiled roofs of St Jude's sweep down across the side aisles and project forward of the west front to provide a welcoming forecourt. The heavy bell tower (of 1915) dominates the ensemble but has no presence on the interior. Their principal interruption is a series of dormers that light the aisles. It is a building that longs for a busy life all around it – exactly what is entirely absent.

Below: looking east, toward the crossing and the altar. Like many churches, St Jude's exuberant scale is out of proportion to the current vitality of its congregation, its somewhat distressed interior witness to a former vibrancy and aspiration that the architecture nevertheless strives to maintain.

Opposite page: one of the side aisles.

in the shadow of Lutyens
Sir Herbert Baker 1862–1946

Extant London works include:
- **Royal Empire Society**, 1938.
- **Bank of England**, 1921-42.
- **India House,** Aldwych, 1928-30 (with A.T. Scott.)
- **14 & 15 Langham Place**, 1930.
- **South Africa House**, Trafalgar Square, 1930-5.
- **London House**, Guilford Street, 1936-8, a Commonwealth students' hostel for the University of London.

Poor old Baker: best known as a man villified for replacing Soane's work at the Bank of England – scooping out what was behind the defensive screen wall and piling up a 'grand manner' work that belongs to an era when top-lighting for clerks could be replaced by electric switches. To Simon Bradley (*The Buildings of England* series) he was a talented professional and no match for Soane's imaginative genius.

It was at Ernest George's office that Baker met Lutyens and recalled that Lutyens, "though joking through his short pupillage, quickly absorbed all that was best worth learning: he puzzled us at first, but we soon found that he seemed to know by intuition some great truths of our art which were not to be learned there." It was Lutyens that brought Baker to work on some of the government buildings in Delhi, but it was also here that the two fell out and Lutyens met, as he called it, his 'Bakerloo'. Lutyens had acceded to Baker's idea of the location of the principal buildings on a site whose gradient, he was unaware, would obscure the view of the portico of the grand Viceroy's House from a crucial axial place. This became a cause of bitter dissension between the two architects, Lutyens lost the argument and never forgave his former friend for what he deemed to be a surrender to expediency (which perhaps says something about their respective characters).

Baker was born in Cobham, Kent, son of a gentleman farmer, and became articled to a cousin, Arthur Baker (1841-1896), in London for three years, from 1880. He then went to Ernest George and Peto, where he met Lutyens. In 1891 he set up on his own and set out for South Africa in 1892, meeting Cecil Rhodes (who apparently, and ambiguously, said of him: "I like the look of that young man. He doesn't talk too much"). He subsequently designed the prime minister's Cape Town residence, Groote Schuur (1896). Altogether he designed some many public buildings and some 300 houses, the latter in his so-called Cape Dutch simple massings of whitewashed walls and random-laid stone, generous verandas, broad tiled roofs, high gables and

The Bank of England, rising above Soane's screen wall. The Royal Exchange portico is to the right. The monument in the foreground is by Aston Webb (1920).

chimneys, and wood-beam interior ceilings. Lutyens visited in 1908 and they informally discussed forming a partnership and, in 1912. Lutyens invited Baker to collaborate with him in New Delhi. Instead, of a partnership with Lutyens, Baker established a London partnership with Alexander T. Scott (1887-1962), and designed a number of buildings that included the Bank of England. He also served as one of the architects for the Imperial War Graves Commission, 1917-28, and designed some 100 cemeteries. At the Bank of England, Baker designed a steel-framed, stone-clad office building, seven storeys at its highest, with a ring of vaulted, top-lit, Soanian bank halls along the lower perimeter base. Attentive to symbolism, he attempted to embody what he claimed was the Bank of England's "tradition of the private house" and "that invisible thing, Trust." At the core of the complex was a domiciliary executive core. Everywhere, the building was lavishly embellished with allegorical sculptures, marble mosaics of historic coins, Greek inscriptions, and wall paintings depicting contemporary bank staff at work. (He claimed that, *"Content in art, national and human sentiment, and their expression in architecture, seem to me to be of the greatest importance."*) His artistic collaborators included the sculptor Charles Wheeler and the artist D.Y. Cameron.

Among his many honours, Baker was elected RA in 1932, knighted in 1926, and created KCIE in 1930. He was awarded the RIBA Gold Medal for architecture in 1927.The Baker family home was Owlett, in Kent, built in 1683 and residence of the Bakers since 1796. He always returned here when in England and donated the house to the National Trust in 1937.

Extant London works include:
- **Warehouse**, Great Eastern Street, Shoreditch, 1881.
- **St-Bartholomew-the-Great**, Smithfield (placing the ruin into order), 1886-8.
- **No. 20 Queen Street**, Mayfair, 1880s.
- **No. 23 Austin Friars**, City, 1888.
- **1 The Grange**, Merton, 1889. (Detached house.)
- **Nos 13-15 Moorgate**, former Metropolitan Life Assurance, 1890-3. (With Ingress Bell.)
- **Victoria & Albert Museum**, 1891-1909. Parts beyond Webb's wing are older.
- **French Protestant Church**, No. 9 Soho Square, 1893 (it has a school in nearby Noel Street).
- **Royal United Services Institute**, 1893-95. Genuflecting to the adjacent Banqueting House.
- **St Alban's Church**, Margravine Road, Fulham, 1894-6.
- **Houses**: Nr 2 (Windemere) and No. 4 (The Gables), Blackheath Park, 1895-6.
- **1 Lansdwone Road**, W11, 1900. House of 1845 significantly extended by Webb for himself.
- **115-121 Tooley Street**, Southwark, 1900-1. Now a block of flats.
- **Thames Warehouse**, Stamford Street, 1901.
- **Mumford's Flour Mills**, High Road, Greenwich, 1897 (facing Deptford Creek).
- **Imperial College of Science & Technology**, off Exhibition Road, 1900-6.
- **Canadian National Railways**, Cockspur Street, (now altered at the lower level (between Pall Mall and Trafalgar Sq.), 1908. See page 374.
- **17-19 Cockspur Street**, 1909.
- **Admiralty Arch**, The Mall, 1908-9 (with sculpture by Thomas Brooks).
- **Royal School of Mines**, Prince Consort Road, 1909-13.
- **Buckingham Palace**, 1912-13 (a re-facing of the existing façade by Blore fronting Nash's inner courtyard was achieved in under thirteen weeks!) .
- **War memorial**, in front of Tite's Royal Exchange, City, 1920.
- **Artillery House**, Westminster, 1925.
- **36-44 Moorgate**, City, 1928 (former Ocean Accident).
- **Royal Air Force Club**, Piccadilly, 1925. (Post-war work is probably by Webb's son, Maurice Webb).
- **Camberwell New Cemetery** chapel and lodge, 1928-9.

Sir Aston Webb 1849–1930

Webb is another of those talented, successful and significant architects: RIBA President, 1902-4; RA in 1903; knighted in 1904; CB in 1909, KCVO in 1914 and GCVO in 1925; RIBA Gold Medal winner, 1905, etc. He was born in Clapham, son of an engraver and water-colourist, educated privately and later articled to Banks and Barry, before spending a year travelling abroad and then commencing practice on his own in 1873, together with Edward Ingress Bell (1837-1914; Bell had worked for George Gilbert-Scott from about 1852-60).

Webb and Bell's breakthrough was winning the 1891 competition for what became the Victoria & Albert Museum, a work consolidated by others for the government. H. Buckley Creswell (articled to Webb in 1890; he is principally remembered for *The Honeywood*

Above: Royal School of Mines, 1913.
Left: Buckingham Palace, 1913, a design of considerable more elegance and presence than many neo-Classical and 'grand manner' buildings, but one we have difficulty in appreciating. Its façade reconstruction was remarkably completed in thirteen weeks. The work (together with the Admiralty Arch etc.) was the result of a 1901 competition won by Webb. Also see the gate lodge, memorial and fountain (with Sir Thomas Brock as sculptor).

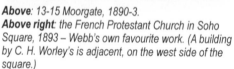

Above: 13-15 Moorgate, 1890-3.
Above right: the French Protestant Church in Soho
Square, 1893 – Webb's own favourite work. (A building
by C. H. Worley's is adjacent, on the west side of the
square.)
Opposite: Admiralty Arch.

File) rather sarcastically said of the architect that,
"Webb was essentially a happy little man; he gloried
in his powers and nothing seemed to bother him or to
obstruct the fecundity of his ideas. A little man he was,
alike in bodily make-up and in his conventional outlook
on life [...] It was beyond thinking that he cared a sniff for
the work of Morris, Philip Webb (who was no relation),
Nesfield and so forth. His contentment was sumptuous,
his demeanour modest to admiration; he was widely
esteemed both personally and professionally, and he
was truly an artist from his toes to the tips of his fragile
lightly boned fingers, characteristically blackened with
the soft H.B. lead with which he slapped his designings
down on cartridge paper 'because it bites so nicely',
hissing through his teeth meanwhile like an ostler curry-
combing a horse, in exultation" (from Service).

Perhaps Web was the Foster of his day. Like that
latterday hero, he at one time had the largest practice in
the UK. In later life he was assisted by his son Maurice
Webb (1880-1939).

250

Concealed considerations

Webb's Admiralty Arch is not only an isolated set-piece on its own, or even in relation to the Mall (in Edwardian times known as 'processional Way' by the LCC and the Press) but is part of a ceremonial route submerged within the urban fabric of London until those state occasions arise (such as the wedding of Charles and Diana) when Westminster and the City – or rather, the minster in the west and the minster in the east – are linked together. Then, a route emerges: from Buckingham Palace, through the Admiralty Arch and Trafalgar Square (beneath Nelson), along the Strand and Fleet Street (past the Royal Courts of Justice and the Griffin marking the boundary of the City), up Ludgate Hill to St Paul's. And then after the event, everything returns to normal. Webb's design (1905-7; constructed 1908-11) suffered severe criticism when completed simply because it mixed the typology of the triumphal arch with that of offices to either side and residential accommodation above, turning the whole into a screen. The origins of the scheme lay in a competition he won that proposed a 'rond point' and colonnade in front of Buckingham Palace, all as part of a scheme celebrating the life of Queen Victoria (who died in 1901). The rond was constructed (with Sir Thomas Brock's sculpture at its centre), but not the colonnade. Meanwhile, the Mall was widened into a boulevard and Webb given the opportunity to design a termination to the processional way before it reached Trafalgar Square. (The central gates, incidentally, were the largest in the country at the time.) It was after this, in 1912, that Webb replaced (and transformed) Edward Blore's rather dreary frontage to Buckingham Palace.

Sir Edwin Cooper 1874–1942

Cooper was a Scarborough man who was articled to Hall and Tugwell in that town between 1885-89. He then went into a firm in York before moving south to London and the firm of Goldie, Child, and Goldie before returning to Scarbough to enter into a partnership with an older, established architect as Hall, Cooper, and Davis. However, by 1903 he was in partnership with Samuel Bridgeman Russell, until 1910, before then setting up on his own. He entered and won competitions, but his big opportunity came with a 1912 competition for Port of London Authority's new headquarters on Tower Hill – on which basis he was knighted, in 1923. This rather neo-American design led to other commissions with the same client, including the port facilities at Tilbury.

On a similar river and sea-oriented note Cooper won the commission to design a new building for Lloyds of London (their first custom-designed headquarters and one important to the story of the Rogers building of 1986), completed in 1928 and demolished in 1976; only the Leadenhall portico remains, now as a feature of the Rogers scheme. Cooper's assistant, Terence Heysham, continued the practice and completed the '56 building for Lloyds – demolished in 2007 to make way

for a Foster-designed building). The Lloyds commission was followed by Cooper's last major City building: the National and Provincial Bank, Princes Street, a Renaissance-style palazzo building with a grand Corinthian order (adjacent to Lutyens former Midland Bank building, opposite Stirling's No. 1 Poultry).

After this, Cooper became a specialist in schools, medical and hospital buildings. He was elected RA in 1937, and was treasurer of the Academy. He also succeeded Sir Edwin Lutyens as president of the Incorporated Association of Architects and Surveyors, a rival body to the RIBA, in 1937, and interestingly refused to pay the standard fee to the Architects' Registration Council, on its establishment in 1933, and was therefore technically not legally entitled to the designation of architect. Nevertheless, he was awarded the Gold Medal in 1931.

Extant London works include:
- former **National Provincial Bank**, at Bank, 1929-32.
- **Port of London Authority**, Tower Hill, 1912-22.
- **Marylebone Town Hall**, Marylebone Road, 1911.
- **Star and Garter Home** (for war veterans), Richmond Hill, 1921-5.
- **Devonport House**, Romney Road, Greenwich, 1926-9. Nurse's home.
- **No. 20 Cavendish Square**, 1930.
- **Crematorium** and chapel, St Marylebone cemetery, 1937.
- **Marylebone Town Hall,** 1914-20, and adjacent **public library/health centre**, 1937-39.
- **40 St Mary Axe**, 1942. Next to the Gherkin.

Left: Cooper's Port of London Authority building, proudly and boastfully looking east over the docks it purportedly managed. The reality (which paralleled Whitehall's overview of its global Empire) was that there was an unruly reality out there. The upper part of the building has a huge statue of Neptune overlooking the scene – soon to be overlooking Lutyens' war memorial sitting at his feet. There was to follow another fifty years before the London Docks were to close to traffic and prompt the regeneration of the Docklands area that has been going on ever since and probably has another generation before its completion. The interior was converted by Michael Hopkins for Willis Faber.

Professor Sir Reginald Theodore Blomfield 1856–1942

Two quite different architects are considered to be largely responsible for the acceptance of Beaux-Arts influences after decades of contrary sentiment (in academic as well as fashionable circles sensitive to the social smartness of all things French, especially after the 1903 visit to Paris of King Edward): Arthur Davis (who started on the Ritz in Piccadilly the year Edward went to Paris; see page 290) and Reginald Blomfield (pronounced Blomfeld), who wrote a significant book on French architecture, published in 1911.

Blomfield was the son of the Reverend G.J. Blomfield (a curate in Exeter) and the nephew (by his mother, daughter of Charles J. Blomfield, 1786–1857, the Bishop of London) of **Sir Arthur William Blomfield** (1829–1899), who established a successful ecclesiastical practice, restored Southwark Cathedral, and designed the Royal College of Music in Kensington (1883); Sion College, Victoria Embankment, City (1886); and Denton Hall at 87 Chancery Lane (1863).

As a man noted for both intellectual and sporting prowess, Blomfield left Oxford University to train with his uncle, attend the Royal Academy Schools and then set up on his own in 1884. He was to be awarded the RIBA Royal Gold Medal (in 1913), become a President of the RIBA (the uncle had been vice-President as well as president of the AA), awarded a variety of other honours including being elected RA in 1914 and, like his uncle, he was to be knighted (1919). He was also a prolific and erudite author as well as having a large and prosperous practice and serving as Professor of Architecture at the Royal Academy (1907-11). After a year on the Continent, Blomfield became an articled pupil (taught free of charge) while studying at the Academy schools (from 1881). However, the training with his uncle did not, apparently, suit the young man and he left after two years and set up on his own. He is said to have found his uncle's office (where Street's work on the Royal Courts of Justice was being completed) typical of most others of the day (and probably today): *"run by a managing clerk, two or three assistants and half-a dozen cheerful young pupils whose usual remark every morning was; 'any spice in the papers?'."*

His own office was in the same building as E.S Prior and he was soon in with a new crowd and as enthusiastic as them regarding Shaw's work. His first jobs came from family connections (mostly in the church), but in order to survive he also wrote and undertook commercial sketching (Prior and Newton named him 'the commercial sketcher'). With some of these same architects Blomfield was a founder of the Art Workers Guild, was made its secretary, did a poor job and, upon hearing complaints, resigned in a huff. It was around now that he joined with others in setting up a short-lived furniture company and also wrote a history of Renaissance architecture in England, defining the term for future generations.

Blomfield's publication of architectural books in the 1890's helped to shift fashions away from the 'bric à brac' style of the previous years toward the more ordered and consistent 'Wrenaissance' style of the Edwardian period. Later, his tastes emphatically shifted toward French architecture. After WWI he lost country house clients and undertook memorial work as well as work on Regent Street. However, it as an historian that the erudite Blomfield remains eminently readable.

Note: Sir Arthur Blomfield had two sons, Charles J. Blomfield, and Arthur Conran Blomfield (d.1935), who were also architects.

Extant London works include:
- **Nos 49 & 51 Frognal**, Hampstead (the latter for himself), 1886.
- **No. 20 Buckingham Palace Gate**, 1895.
- former **United Universities Club**, Pall Mall East, 1906-7.
- **Nos 18-19 Fleet Street**, 1898-9.
- **Goldsmith's College**, 1907-8.
- **NatWest Bank**, 224 King's Road, Chelsea, 1909.
- **St Paul's Cross**, St Paul's Churchyard, 1910, with Sir B. Mackennal.
- **John Barker store**, Kensington High Street, 1912-14.
- **32 Threadneedle**, City, 1919-20.
- **RAF memorial**, Victoria Embankment; eagle by Sir W. Reid Dick. 1921-3.
- the **Quadrant**, Regent Street/Piccadilly Circus, 1914-30 (see Norman Shaw section).
- **Lambeth Bridge**, with the engineer G. Topham Forrest, 1932.
- **No. 4 Carlton Gardens**, 1934.

Regent Street

Regent Street has a certain grandeur – until one looks more closely and sees that most of the buildings – apart from the County Fire Offices (**bottom left**; Ernest Newton, 1924-7) – have little dignity and presence apart from their pretence). However, Blomfield's design is by far the most vigorous and impressive part of the Quadrant of the street (**below**). It is based on Shaw's original design that was altered contrary to the old man's intentions, prompting Shaw's resignation some six months before he died. Other objections came from the shopkeepers (mostly regarding issues of day-lighting) and Ernest Newton, Sir Aston Webb and Sir Reginald Blomfield were asked to modify the master's design – which appears to have come down to Blomfield. What we now see is his modifications (1923-8).

Above: Air Street, between Piccadilly and Regent Street, with Shaw's transitional arch and superstructure.
Below: Ernest Newton's County Fire Office. The lion and Britannia on top are sculpted by Herman Cawthra.

North of the Quadrant, the best Regent Street buildings are possibly those by Burnet and Tait (the New Gallery range, on the west side), 1920-5. Most of the buildings elsewhere in Regent Street (including around Oxford Circus, 1911-23, and Dickens & Jones, 1919-21) are by Henry Tanner Jnr (1876-1947), assisted by his brother E.J. Tanner (1887-1939), his father, Sir Henry Tanner Snr (after 1913) and another brother, W.H. Tanner, a surveyor (from 1920). Liberty's is by E.T and E.S. Hall (1914), (who also did the half-timbered section of Liberty). At the time, the loss of Nash's buildings was (for some obscure reason concerning nostalgia for all things Georgian, then very fashionable) a prominent and popular source of outrage (after the event; in 1905 the Times had voiced prevailing sentiment in referring to Regent Street as 'beneath contempt').

Above: the east side of the Quadrant.
Below: the west side of the Quadrant.

John Belcher 1841–1913
Arthur Beresford Pite 1861–1934
John James Joass 1868–1952

An inquiring mind

John Belcher was born in Trinity Square, London, son to the architect also called John Belcher. He was privately educated in London and Luxembourg, later spending time in Paris (1862-3) as an architectural student before entering his father's practice as partner, in 1865. After his father retired in 1875, Belcher was joined by James W. James, and then, in 1885, by Beresford Pite, (later a partner, to 1896).

During this time Belcher became significant within the Art & Crafts movement, chairing the first meeting of the Art Workers' Guild. Whilst resistant to too much homage given to vernacular traditions, he was keen that the sculptor should work with the architect from the early days of a commission as 'the most perfect achievement can be attained by their joint action'. The work that brought fame was the Institute of Chartered Accountants, off Moorgate, in the City (1890-93) and it admirably exhibits this ambition.

In the later work of the office, as illness restricted Belcher's contribution, the hand of Joass became more dominant. Mappin House, the former Royal Insurance building at the corner of St James and Piccadilly, Whiteley's stores, and Holy Trinity Church, Kingsway, all indicate the bolder touch of Joass. In 1915 Joass wrote that Belcher *"was endowed with a most receptive and inquiring type of mind', and that 'new ideas appealed to him irresistibly."*

From 1904-6 Belcher was president of the Royal Institute of British Architects, performed publicly as a solo bass singer, and even lectured at the Institute on church organs. Ironically, it seems he was better known to the public as a musician than an architect. He was a founding member of the Art Workers' Guild, was elected RA in 1909 and received the Gold Medal in 1907.

Extant London works of Belcher and Pite include:
• **Catholic Apostolic Church**, Camberwell New Road, 1876-77 (now a Greek Orthodox church).
• **No. 2b Melbury Road**, Holland Park, 1877.
• **Chartered Accountants' Hall**, Great Swan Alley, EC2, 1888-93.
• **Redholm**, 2 Champion Hill, Camberwell, 1887. Belcher's house for himself.

Below: the side street elevation, extended by Joass, looking east, with Joass' work in the centre (where the doorway is). The end bays to the east are by Whitfield (changes are detectable, and the character of the sculpted frieze is distinctly more coarse). So characteristic was Belcher's style that one Edwardian advertisement once offered 'instruction in the Gothic, Renaissance, Classic and Belcher styles'.

Above: the principal frontage of the Chartered Accountants' Hall, City (actually on a side street).
Below: Whitfield turning the corner in the manner of Belcher and Joass, thus completing the block as a natural unity before becoming a thoroughly 1960s stylist.

The Chartered Accountants' Hall is both interesting in itself – as Belcher and Pite's original – and as an example of architectural gamesmanship in its later stages, by other architects.

Some thirty five years after its completion in 1893 Joass was asked to extend the building to the east. This he did in exactly the same manner that Belcher and Pite had created the original, west part (and principal frontage). And then, another thirty or so years later, during the '60's, William Whitfield was asked to make another significant extension. As an exercise in architectural gamesmanship that is surprisingly rare, Whitfield acted in the manner of Joass, rounding the corner with another rather grand entrance statement on the south-east corner – as if to say, 'let me show you how I can do it too' (with a doorway that is a standard 210 cm high, and seems surprisingly mannered and diminutive). And then he moves straight into '60's Modernism: an exercise that mixes a neo-Louis Kahn divide of 'served from serviced', complete with characteristic bush-hammered concrete.

Above: former Mappin House, 1906 – another Mannerist exercise from Joass. *Below*: 31 Weymouth, 1910 – Joass producing work that almost had a 1930s feel.
Opposite page, top: : 37 Harley Street.
Opposite page bottom: Burlington Arcade; south end by Pite, 1911, north end by Bates & Sinning, 1937.

In search of the golden city

Belcher's first principal assistant, Beresford Pite, was born in Walworth as the son of the architect Alfred Pite. His education began in London at King's College School, and the National Art Training School in South Kensington. From 1876 to 1881 he, like Joass, was articled to his father in the Cardiff office of what was then Habershon, Pite, and Fawckner, his father leaving the partnership in 1878. Meanwhile, Pite's architectural studies continued at University College and the Architectural Association in London. He won a drawing prize in 1882 on the basis of a 'humorous travesty' for a West End club, after which he declared, "I have found the Golden City" – which he felt it should be the ambition of every architect to help bring into being. He then spent a year travelling in Germany and France with his brother, also an architect (William Pite). Returning in 1884, he worked briefly as a draughtsman for The Builder magazine, responsible for a series of brilliant illustrations.

From 1882 (the year Pite was admitted as a student to the Royal Academy) to 1897 he was first improver, and then managing clerk, in the office of Belcher, making a particular contribution to the design of the Institute of Chartered Accountants building in the City (1888–93). While with Belcher he became involved with the Art Workers' Guild (founded in 1884), later becoming its master. Although playing a significant role in the Belcher office, he never became a partner (probably by agreement: he carried out private work for his father and brother). He left the practice in 1897 (and was succeeded by Joass). After 1900 much of Pite's time was spent teaching. Following an invitation from his friend and founder of the Art Workers' Guild, W. R. Lethaby, he became the first professor of architecture at the newly formed Royal College of Art (a post held until 1923; *"Reject dullness,"* he pleaded with his students) and also architectural director of an educational project bringing together architects, artists, and builders, at the LCC's School of Building in Brixton (where, incidentally, Ron Herron later attended).

Pite selected his projects carefully and, being deeply religious, was attracted to churches and sacred symbolism. The finest of Pite's churches is Christ Church, Brixton Road, London (1896-1902). Outside England, he was involved in work which included missionary buildings in Palestine, and a notable cathedral in Kampala, Uganda (1911-13). He appears to have attracted many respectful admirers. Near the end of his life, A.E. Richardson compared him to the Roman twin-faced god 'Janus bifrons', for his ability to look with equal passion into the past and the future. (He had a since destroyed building in Great Portland Street – actually three old town houses converted into one – covered in ceramic tiles and swirling patterns. With a distinctive neo-Michelangelo flavour to his later work, Pite was, said Alastair Service, *"the least classifiable, least predictable architect of his age."* To Goodhart-Rendel he was an *"arch rogue, a gifted and beloved rebel [...] with a continuous cannonade of surprises".*

Extant London works of Pite include:
• **77 Welbeck Street**, (Marylebone Dispensary) 1892.
• **82 Mortimer Street**, 1893-6, (the sculpture – a parody of Michelangelo's New Sacristy – was modelled by J. Attwood Slater, carved by Thomas Tyrell).
• **37 Harley Street**, 1899-1900 (sculpture by F.E.E. Schenk).
• **126 Great Portland Street**, 1898.
• **31 Old Bond Street**, 1898-1900.
• **42-44 Mortimer Street,** Marylebone, 1904.
• **73-77 Great Titchfield Street**, Marylebone, 1905.
• Former **Amalgamated Approved Societies building**, Euston Square, 1908 (now in a Greek revival style).
• **Christ Church**, Brixton Road, 1901-7, (a mix of Greek, Byzantine and Mannerist styles).
• **All Souls School**, Foley Street, 1906-8.
• **St Anne's House**, Mortimer Street and Great Titchfield Street, 1905.
• **30 Euston Square**, 1906-8.
• **Library**, Bridgeman Road, Islington, 1906-08.
• **Library**, Thornhill Square, Islington, 1909.
• **Burlington Arcade**, Piccadilly entrance frontage (to Samuel Ware's design of 1818), 1911 (upper part), and again early 1930s (lower part), Piccadilly. (The north end is 1937, by E. Bates & W.G. Sinning.)

The silent sailing architect

John James Joass was born in Dingwall, Rosshire as the son of an architect for whom he later worked before becoming articled to John Burnett while studying part-time at Glasgow School of Art. He then worked for R. Rowand Anderson, in Edinburgh, won a student prize in 1892, and travelled to Italy. Returning in 1893, he worked first for Ernest George and then, in 1897 (just as Pite was leaving), John Belcher, then two of the best known architects in London. Encouraged by Belcher, he had lots of opportunities to make a contribution and, in 1905, became a partner in the practice. After 1909, he effectively ran the firm himself.

His biographer notes that Joass was elected to the RIBA Council where he failed to utter a single word; however, when Joass retired, it was to indulge his passion for sailing his cruiser and occasional racer Macnab, which he partly designed and which was anchored at Poole Harbour, in Dorset. Only a year before his death Joass won first prize in a Cowes to Dinard race. Despite this enthusiasm, during his final illness he appears still to have been finishing drawings for his office. The mannered nature of his architecture bears comparison with that of early Holden (see page 309).

Extant London works of Belcher and Joass include:
• **88 Fleet Street**, 1900-02 (formerly Birmingham Daily Post).
• former **Electra House**, 76-92 Moorgate, City, 1900-03 (for the Eastern Telegraph Company; now London Metropolitan University). Much more crude than the Chartered Accountants' Hall.
• **Royal London House**, Finsbury Sq., 1904-5. Now Triton Court.
• **Mappin House**, 156-162 (east) Oxford Street, 1906-8. The fourth bay is by Joass from 1929.
• former **Royal Insurance**, Piccadilly/St James', 1907-8.
• former **Mowbray's Bookshop**, 28 Margaret St, Marylebone, 1907-8.

Extant London works of Joass (after Belcher's effective retirement in 1909 and death in 1913):
• **Whiteley's Dept. Store**, Queensway, Bayswater, 1909-12) At this time the firm changed its name to Belcher and Joass.
• **Holy Trinity Church**, Kingsway, 1910-12 (never completed; now ironically serves as a rather fine entrance to the adjacent offcie building).
• **Royal Zoological Society**, Outer Circle, Regent's Park, 1910-12.
• **Royal Society of Medicine**, Henrietta Place, Marylebone, 1910-12.
• **No 31 Weymouth Street** (house), 1910-13.
• **Mappin Terraces**, London Zoo, 1913. (Now rather forlorn.)
• **Lex Garage**, Brewer Street, 1927. (Now offices.)
• **Royal London House**, Finsbury Sq., 1926-30 (to the east of the first Royal London House).
• **Clarendon House, No.17-18 New Bond Street** (Louis Vuitton), 1932.
• **No.9-10 Saville Row**, 1927-8.
• **Abbey House**, Baker Street, 1928-32 (dubbed 'the tomb of the unknown borrower').

Opposite page: the Royal Insurance building, Piccadilly, 1908.
Left: Royal London House, 1929. The building immediately to the west was also Royal London House, by Belcher, 1904-5 (now Triton Court, altered by Sheppard Robson, 1980-5, with a large new archway).

sculptural adornments

Below: Neptune, atop Cooper's Port of London Authority building, 1912-22.
Bottom: sculpture at the entrance of the Royal School of Mines, by P.R. Mountford, 1916-20.

One of the notable features of London architecture from the last decade of the 1800s through to WWI was an exuberant sculptural adornment of architecture, particularly in the 'free' classical works. But there was here a common denominator with the Arts & Crafts stream of architectural values: a marriage of sculpture and architecture that briefly flowered and has been since forgotten. Philip Johnson's 'turds in the plaza' has hardly been an adequate substitute and a more recent marriage is often witness to a shot-gun union prompted by cynical developers, the opportunism of artists enjoying a peculiar contemporary status, or the egocentric self-congratulation of architects flattered by a partnership that is often an underscoring of dissatisfaction with their aesthetic attunement.

The sources of this neo-Renaissance enthusiasm (as Stuart Gray reminds us) is again French, at a time when Paris was beginning to replace Rome as the centre of European art studies. One outcome of the political disturbances of 1870, e.g. the self-exile of Aimé-Jules Dalou (1838-1902), who taught at Lambeth School of Art and then at the South Kensington schools before returning to Paris in 1879. He was succeeded at the latter by another émigré: Edouard Lantéri.

Meanwhile, another Frenchman, Alphonse Légros (1837-1911) began teaching sculpture at the Slade. Students who came from Lambeth to South Kensington and the Royal Academy schools, as listed by Gray, included: C.J. Allen, W.A. Colton, Henry Poole, John Tweed, F. Brook-Hitch, Wenlock Rollins, F. Lynn-Jenkins, Abraham Brodbent and Charles Hartwell. One of the prompts linking such people with architects was the Art Workers' Guild, of 1884 (which started off as the St. George Society, after the name of the pub where its founders met). Its first master was a sculptor, George Blackwell.

Whilst one aspect of the works realised by these artists sought simplicity, modesty of scale, a richness of materials and autonomy for the artist, much of it reflected the monumental nature and colossal scale of much High Victorian and Edwardian architecture. (One thinks of the Albert Memorial, and especially to the Peace Quadriga atop the Wellington Arch, at Hyde Park Corner.) Notable sculptural works of the period included Alfred Gilbert's (ill-treated and ill-located) Eros statue, George Frampton's Peter Pan (dumped in Kensington Gardens) and, of course, Captain Adrian Jones' Peace Quadriga (now the ignored feature of a traffic roundabout), as well as the 'pieces' noted in these pages for individual buildings. Contemporary architects (and clients) interested in art and architecture could do worse than refer themselves to the Edwardians – who, at least, sought (and found) a true integration.

This page: a charming figure on Joass' 1930 extension to Belcher's Chartered Surveryors' Hall building of 1895. Note the utterly different tone to works of fifteen years earlier (and that of thirty years later).

Left: the Chartered Accountants' Hall, by Belcher: where does the architecture end and the sculpture begin? The work sings the enjoyment of an 'enlivened' architecture in which sculpture and architecture exist in a true marriage quite distinct from art being merely stuck on the building (or juxtaposed to it, as 'turds in the plaza', to use Philip Johnson's memorable phrase).

Right top: figures on Beresford Pite's 82 Mortimer Street, modelled by J. Attwood Slater, carved by Thomas Tyrell.

Below: 'puti' on Joass' former Royal Insurance building, by Bertram Mackennal. The sculpture at the entrance is by Alfred Drury.

Centre right: sculpture on Burnet & Tait's current LSE building, 99 Aldwych.

Bottom: allegorical figures (Britannia between two other figures personifying higher and lower mathematics) at Bank, on top of Edwin Cooper's bank building, by Ernest Gillick.

The grave danger within this enthusiasm for sculpture and architecture was a spurious allegorical content. Stuart Fray tells us, for example, that, on William Young's War Office building in Whitehall, the sculpted

figures were called upon to represent 'The Fatherless Widow', 'The Winged Messenger of Peace', 'The Horrors of War', 'The Dignity of War', 'Truth', 'Justice', 'Victory' and 'Fame'. On the other hand, the few people who look up and notice the work are unlikely to know or care about these specific references: the sculpture surely works at a more primitive level, sentimental or not. The allegorical content works in an ambiguous manner and has a degree of meaning that comes from mere allegory as such – as many a contemporary client knows when given a legitimating narrative for an architectural proposal (e.g. Daniel Libeskind excited and satisfied his clients at a London university by telling them the pattern of lights in his design for a lecture hall ceiling was the constellation of Orion – which he had coincidentally noticed on a site visit). On the other hand, there is arguably something elementally attractive about the fundamental reality of stone being formed into a figurative shape and adorning a building that now eludes us.

Thomas Edward Collcut 1840–1924

Collcutt was the Royal Gold medallist of 1902 and the Institute's president from 1906-8. He was born in Oxford, became articled to R.W. Armstrong, worked in the offices of Miles and Murgatroyd, and then became assistant to George Street. He also served some time in the office of P.C. Lockwood, at Brighton. He then travelled extensively on the Continent before setting up in practice, briefly, with H. Woodzell before practising on his own (from 1872).

First experiences in competition winning taught him that the Gothic was no longer modish (Town Hall, Wakefield, 1877) and he changed to a 'free Tudor' style with French elements. But he was also a designer to the P&O Line and undertook the interior design of music halls for many vessels (interior design and furniture became an important aspect of his practice). From 1908 he was in partnership with Stanley Hinge Hamp, whom Gray credits with introducing "a quite extrordinary exuberance into the firm's work."

The RIBA Journal reported that Collcutt – 'Always the most practical of constructors' – employed an instructor two or three times a week to expound construction to his staff, which included Leonard Stokes and J.S. Gibson. Beresford Pite said of him (in 1907), that he had the capacity to design charming buildings "which displayed extraordinary vigour and grip, and that peculiar power to design Gothic works as they really were supposed to be." He has been described as a man of innate modesty, but of strong opinions: 'a model of integrity.'

Right: 181 Oxford Street (now painted white, as if to disguise the real architecture).

Extant London works include:
- **181 Oxford Street,** 1886.
- **Wigmore Hall**, Wigmore Street, 1890 (originally Bechstein Hall; frontage extended by Walter Cave, to Nos. 36 and 38, 1909). The celebrated hall began life as the Bechstein Hall, an adjunct to its showrooms.
- **Palace Theatre of Varieties**, Cambridge Circus, 1889-93.
- **Nos. 45-47 Ludgate Hill**, 1890 (Bank branch).
- **Imperial Institute**, Kensington, 1893; only the large tower remains.
- **The Croft**, Totteridge Green, Barnet, 1898; his own house.
- Additional storey to the **Athenaeum Club**, Waterloo Place, 1899.
- **Lloyds Register of Shipping**, Fenchurch Street, 1900. Sculpture by Sir George Frampton and Frank Lynn Jenkins. (Now a part of the complex by Richard Rogers).
- **Gloucester House**, Piccadilly and Park Lane, 1904.
- **Savoy Hotel**, Strand: alterations, 1896, extensions, and Savoy Court, 1903-4.
- extensions to **Mill Hill School**, NW7, 1907. Library, the Murray Scriptorium, tuck shop. Adjacent to a chapel by Basil Champneys.
- **Thames House**, Queen Street, 1912.
- former **University Hotel**, Endsleigh Gardens, now residence of University College, 1912.

Above: the Lloyds Register building.
Below: the Savoy Hotel. Savoy Court (on the east) was first offices, then residential suites and later a part of the hotel; to the west we have the West Block offices. Between them and the original Embankment block of 1888 (probably by Arthur Heygate Mackmurdo; no one is quite sure) were the entrance hall, lounge and foyer. (The stainless steel cladding to what was a terracotta arch was added in the 1930s, but still supports a gilded figure by Lynn-Jenkins of Count Peter Savoy.)

Above: the Wigmore Hall frontage was extended (to the west) in 1909 by Walter Cave (to provide additional showroom spaces). The hall itself has always been notable for its comforts, convenience, and, of course, acoustics. It is basically a 'shoe box' design, but Collcutt modified the conventional design to provide a curved rather than flat ceiling, and removed most decorative finishes (which had an acoustic function). The decorative pieces are by Gerald Moira.

T.E. Collcutt's splendid Palace Theatre, Cambridge Circus, 1888-91. The materials are red Elliston brick and Doulton pink terracotta. It was originally designed and built as an opera house for D'Oyly Carte with an interior to suit.

the mansion block

Given that the dominant typology for a London house is the independent, tiered and terraced town house derived from medieval sources – the kind that Jones elevated to neo-Palladian status in Lincoln's Inn Fields and the Georgians and Victorians used to define the peculiarity of London's character – it is strange that Londoners adapted their style of dwelling to that French peculiarity, the apartment: one of many within a larger urban block with a unique architectural character. That they did so reflects the difficult choices available to the middle classes in the later nineteenth century: either move out to an Outer London suburb, or find a place within the dense and expensive Inner London boroughs that were riddled with poverty and deprivation as well as ostentatious wealth.

The answer to this dilemma was the oddly named 'mansion block': actually an apartment building (with each dwelling interestingly called a 'flat' (an even more odd term) because it comprised accommodation on one floor, complete with servants, instead of the usual stacked arrangement), and invariably offered a unity of architectural pretension that an individual dwelling rarely achieved. In particular, the public spaces of a block frequently aspired toward a degree of grandeur and opulence (which many of the more suburban blocks do not share).

Mansion blocks were first constructed in the 1870', but it was not until the period between the mid-1890s and about 1905 (when there was a building slump) that one saw dozens of this building type constructed all over Inner London. Shaw and R.J. Worley's mansion blocks near the Albert Hall is a fine example, but others are included in the list below. Perhaps the finest Modernist set of blocks is High Point, in Highgate.

• **Harewood House** and **No. 15 Hanover Square**, 1900, by Paul Hoffman.
• **St George's Terrace**, Gloucester Road, @ 1900, by Paul Hoffman.
• **Alexander Court**, Queens Gate, about 1900, by Paul Hoffman.
• **Marlborough Chambers**, 70 Jermyn Street, 1902-3, by Reginald Morphew.
• **Manor House**, corner of Marylebone Road and Lisson Grove, 1903, by Gordon and Gunton. Unusual Arts & Crafts inspired composition.
• **North Gate**, corner of Albert Road and St John's Wood High Street, 1901-3, by Frank Elgood.
• **No. 112 Jermyn Street**, 1900, and **Nos. 70-72 Jermyn Street**, 1902-3, by Reginald Morphew.
• **Hanover House**, Regents Park Road, 1902-3, by E.P. Warren.
• **Blomfield Court**, Maida Vale, 1904. Boehmer & Gibbs. Maida Vale has many blocks along its length, becoming typical of arterial ribbon development around the turn of the century. The History of the County of Middlesex gives the following description:
"The first flats were planned in 1890, when Nos 1 and 3 Maida Vale, at the corner of Blomfield Road, were to be replaced by one or two buildings before the end of 1891. As Maida Vale Mansions (later Cunningham Court) the block had 22 flat-holders in 1902, when it was the only one on that side of the road. The adjoining site of Nos 5 to 35 (odd), however, had been leased for rebuilding in 1895 and was filled with Aberdeen and Blomfield courts in 1903. with Clarendon Court between them. Clarendon Court was claimed in 1917 as the first and most up-to-date of its kind in London, with flats, single chambers, a restaurant, and a booking office for theatres. Farther north, beyond Clifton Avenue, nos. 63-73 Maida Vale in 1900 and nos. 95-103 in 1902 were to make way for flats, built as Alexandra Court by 1906 and Sandringham Court by 1908. Much of the open land south-west of the main road had likewise been filled with blocks: Carlton Mansions, for 90 flat-holders, at the north-west end of Portsdown Road, and Elgin Mansions, for 80, and Ashworth Mansions along the north side of Elgin Avenue, all by 1902, and the nearby Biddulph Mansions in 1907 and Delaware Mansions in 1908."
• **No.12 Hyde Park Place**, Bayswater Road, near Marble Arch, 1903, by Frank Verity, an architect who argued that no mansion block should have corridors and that the main staircase and entry hall should be central architectural features.
• **25 Berkeley Square**, 1903-4, by Frank Verity.
• **Harley House**, Marylebone Road, 1903-4. by Boehmer & Gibbs. Typical 'free' in being vaguely Mannerist, French, Gothic and Baroque all at the same time. Also, **Sandringham Court**, Maida Vale, 1908, by Boehmer & Gibbs.
• **The Chambers**, corner of Piccadilly and Bond Street, 1905, by Read and McDonald.
• **Waterloo Court**, Hampstead Garden Suburb, off Hampstead Way, 1908-09, by Bailiee-Scott. Freestyle, built for 'working ladies', originally with communal dining room and similar shared facilities. See page 276.

Above: flats near the Albert Hall. On the left is Shaw's Albert Hall Mansions of 1879. On the right is the adjacent Albert Court, R.J. Worley's work of 1894-1900, in Prince Consort Road.
Below: flats in Bury Street, St James, opposite the Economist group, by G. Thrale Jell, 1909.

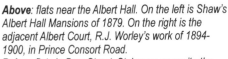

Above: the transformation that had taken place by the 1930s. Here, Modernism arrives in London as the two Highpoint blocks of flats by Tecton (see page 320).

Henry John Treadwell 1861–1910
Leonard Martin 1869–1935

Extant London works include:
• **No. 31 Maddox Street**, 1894-5.
• **Rising Sun pub**, Tottenham Court Road, 1897, (also, **Old Shades pub** (1898), Charing Cross, 1898; **Old Dover Castle**, Westminster Bridge Road; Edinburgh House, Kilburn; **Shelley's Hotel**, Albermarle Street; **the Black Swan**, Carter Lane, City).
• **Nos 18-20 Coventry Street**, 1892-4 (corner building, adjacent to the Trocodero development)
• **Presbyterian Church**, West Norwood, 1897.
• **Nos 41-43 Whitehall**, 1904.
• **Holy Trinity Mission Church**, Tulse Hill, 1904.
• **St John's Hospital**, Lisle Street, off Leicester Square, 1904.
• **No. 5 Dering Street**, 1904.
• **Nos 5-7 Westbourne Grove.**
• **No. 23 Woodstock Street.**
• **No. 74 New Bond Street**, 1906.
• **No. 7 Dering Street,** 1906.
• **No. 124 New Bond Street**, 1908.
• **No. 20 and No. 55 Conduit Street,** 1906.
• **No. 78 Wigmore Street**, 1906-7.
• **No. 1 St James' Market**, 1907 (the street commemorates the market for St James' Sq. once here, rebuilt by Nash).
• **No. 3 Woodstock Street**, 1907.
• **No. 7 Hanover Street,** 1907.
• **No. 106 Jermyn Street**, 1906-7.
• **St John's Church**, Herne Hill, 1910.
• **No. 60 St James Street**, 1910.
• **Nos 78-81 Fetter Lane**, City.

Both Treadwell and Martin were pupils of John Giles (Giles, Gough and Trollope), setting up in practice together in 1890. First works were 'fever hospitals' for the metropolitan Asylums Board (not the most socially prestigious client). Like other young architects, they entered many competitions, won places but never the big job (and thereby fame and 'significance'). Instead, they left behind them a string of small works that epitomise the period, particularly around New Bond Street, Jermyn Street, and nearby (mostly for developers and, as Alastair Service notes, *"far removed from the restrained Georgian tradition*

Opposite page top: The Old Shades pub, 1898, and Nos.41-43 Whitehall, 1904.
Opposite page bottom: 124 New Bond Street.

Left: No. 7 Dering Street, Mayfair, 1906. (The Buildings of England gives T & M's No. 5 this as No.4 and totally ignores No. 7 – which is by far the most exciting building.) This work is typical of such much during this period that worked within the framework of the Georgian town house site parameters, but strove to establish a commercial reality without the aid of flashing neon and similar devices (which, no doubt, these architects would have used if it had been available). The contemporary parallel is Tokyo sites: narrow and desperate for attention.
Below: 74 New Bond Street, 1906. Note the residual Art Nouveau influences.

and perhaps only comparable with the gaiety of the gabled houses of Amsterdam built around 1650"). Martin attended Lambeth School of Art. After Treadwell died in 1910 he continued alone until 1929, undertaking suburban housing and buildings in Africa. He then went into partnership with E.C. Davies. Further work included Nos 7-9 Buckingham Palace Road; two-storey neo-Georgian work at Ilchester Place, Kensington, 1929; and flats in Palace Gate. A busy little office of arguably more importance than many more famous architects as contributors to London's character.

ferreting away 2

C.H. Worley d.1906

The Worleys (C.H. and R.J.) are frequently mentioned in books and guides on the period, but not in biographies. Perhaps this is, in part, because they get mixed up. The most interesting seems to be Charles H. Worley and a small group of West End buildings by him between about 1890-1910. The other Worley – Robert James (1850-1930, of Worley & Saunders – appears to have been an altogether more cavalier character involved in all kinds of speculative developments. However, his obituary in The Builder of April 1930 tells us nothing about the man. Time and space prevent further investigation, but my guess is that C.H. is a son who died young (both names are given by The Buildings of England as the authors of 41 Harley Street). C.H.'s most dramatic works are 3 Soho Square – a design whose contrast with an adjacent eighteenth century terrace house sums up so much of that assertiveness which characterises the architecture of the late Victorian and Edwardian period – and the remarkable (and rather mutilated) Nos. 1-3 Old Compton Street. Like Treadwell and Martin, Worley represents the large body of architects who ferret away, give London its character, and are forgotten.

Extant London works include:
• **28-30 Wigmore Street**, 1890-2.
• **42 Harley Street**, 1892.
• **Nos. 51, 55-56 Welbeck Street**, 1893-4.
• **84 Wimpole Street**, about 1895.
• former **De Walden Rooms**, Charlebert Street, St Johns Wood, 1898-9.
• **No. 37 New Bond Street**, 1901.
• **Nos.6-7, St George Street**, 1904-5.
• **Nos. 1-3 Old Compton Street**, 1904-07.
• **No. 99A Charing Cross Road**, 1904-7.
• **No. 3 Soho Square**, 1903.
• **No. 12 Moor Street**, 1904-10.

Above: 37 New Bond Street, 1901
Left: Worley's exuberant corner building at Old Compton Street and Charing Cross Road (1907) is a remarkable virtuoso exercise – which the bookshop owners appeared not to have noticed.
Opposite page: 3 Soho Square, 1905. This is by far the most refined of Worley's designs.

Halsey Ricardo 1854–1928

Extant London works include:
- **8 Great George Street**, Westminster, 1888.
- **Nos 55** (for his father-in-law) and **57 Melbury Road**, 1902.
- **8 Addison Road** (Debenham House), W8, 1905.
- **117 Old Church Street**, Kensington, 1914.

Ricardo has only one London building of significance: the remarkable Debenham House, at 8 Addison Road – faced from bottom to top in glazed bricks, with lavish faience dressings.

He was born in Bath to a father who had trained as an architect and then turned to business, just as his father, in turn, had been a famous Dutch-Jewish economist. The young Ricardo attended Rugby and became articled to a Cheltenham architect, John Middleton; he then moved on to Basil Champney's office. He spent a year in Italy and then, in 1878, set up his own London practice. And he married the daughter of Sir Alexander Meadows Rendel, whose firm continues as Rendel, Palmer and Tritton, civil engineers. Father-in-law helped with railway work in India; having private means he never extended his practice or employed anyone.

Ricardo was thoroughly into the Arts and Crafts movement, his niece remarking that the entire Rendel family had to have homes fitted with De Morgan tiles and pottery, Morris wallpaper and chairs, etc. All of this (and much more) was evident in Debenham House, whose exterior was one of the inspirations behind the glazed tiling of the new Underground stations.

Above: *two of the many interesting plot rebuildings of the type designed by Treadwell & Martin et al are in Maddox Street, off New Bond Street. Here, No. 47 enjoys a Flemish flavour to its detailing in a rich, dark-coloured tiling (by Walter Williams, 1892, for a firm of tailors). The adjacent No.4 5 is from 1907 (architect unknown). No. 49 on the other (west) side is the sole remaining survivor from the eighteenth century, although the other buildings retain its fundamental typology. This area has a wealth of interesting buildings from this period.*

Below: *the villa at 8 Addison Road. The street porch leads through a covered passage to the house.*

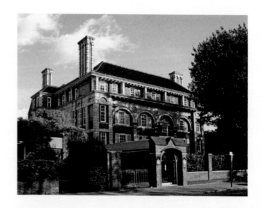

Mackay Hugh Baillie Scott
1865-1945

Extant London works include:
• **Waterlow Court**. The Court sits at the end of Heath Close, off Hampstead Way, in Hampstead Garden Suburb. It was designed as a quad of 51 self-contained apartments for 'working ladies', 1907-9.

Scott was born into a wealthy family in Ramsgate and his father intended him to be an Australian sheep farmer, but he ended up articled to the City Architect of Bath. He then went to the office of Fred Sanderson on the Isle of Man. In 1901 he and his wife moved to Bedford, where Scott was undertaking furniture design and promoting himself as an architect of the so-called 'domestic revival'. In 1896 he won a commission to design rooms for Queen Victoria's grandson in Germany (where Scott's work had been published). Like others in the Arts & Crafts movement he now began to adopt more historical tones to the style of his work and became a well-known name for domestic work (rather like Lutyens and Voysey). In 1909 A.E. Beresford became his partner.

Waterlow Court has a quadrangular plan, with apartments on the ground floor accessed from a perimeter open corridor with arched openings out onto the garden of the court, from where stairs lead up to maisonettes on the upper levels. Externally, the façades are given a medieval half-timbered treatment; inside the quadrangle is a more Voyseyesque grouping of windows and use of pebble-dash render.

the death of the picturesque

The Edwardian period was witness to a distinct lessening of the influence of the picturesque and a return to formality and bilateral symmetry. Although the term suggests an arbitrariness to architectural arrangements that feigns necessity where the prompt is actually a compositional concern derived from a way of seeing – as if the design were in a picture, with other considerations as secondary – the picturesque broke the formalities of neo-classicism by allowing other criteria to inform architectural design.

The picturesque – which also concerns colour and texture as well as an interplay of three-dimensional forms – sometimes engendered a wilfulness which, in the early 1930s, Goodhart-Rendel characterised as an abnormal necessity feigned in order to justify a preferred aesthetic outcome (it sat for its portrait). The reintroduction of a fashion for bilateral symmetry and the tempering of picturesque inclinations was indicative of a new sentiment which viewed the picturesque as all "that flouts reason, that entertains caprice, that hastily and half-heartedly makes terms with necessity and then abandons itself to unregulated fancy" (Goodhart-Rendel). Interestingly, that definition – which deemed the picturesque to be intrinsically illogical and non-architectural – characterises all kinds of architectural practice, of whatever stylistic, moral and aesthetic inclination. The picturesque is, in fact, far from dead.

The Late Victorian version of the picturesque was ostensibly 'free', but had to establish some form of navigational purpose and concern. This was provided by Pugin, Ruskin, le Duc, Morris, Lethaby et al. Their agenda of morality, truthfulness, honest expression, craftsmanship, social value and the like became legitimating informants of a search for new ideological bases to practice that bore within them a polarity of Culture opposed to culture, of a supposedly grounded authenticity opposed to scholarly caprice. It is within the generality of this context that Lutyens 'Wrenaissance' could stand itself upon some middle ground and address issues of scale and monumentality whilst avoiding the turn to an alien Beaux Arts tradition (see, for example, page 290). As an intended marriage of Gothic and the English tradition of classicism, St Jude at Hampstead Garden Suburb makes an interesting London counterpoint to the glitz of The Ritz. Their emerging common denominator was to be a sentiment of temperance as shocked by the Jazz Moderne as it was wary of the tradesmanlike undertones of the continuing professional ambition and the rude baldness of an emerging 'utilitarianism' which was perceived as the hallmark of a nascent Modernism.

Above: picturesque Waterlow Court, 1909.
The street entrance leads through a covered way to the arcade that runs around the inner court.
Previous page: looking back to the street entrance within the covered passage; the perimeter ground floor covered access route (leading onto stairs giving access to the upper apartments), and the actual inner court itself. (Osbert Lancaster would have referred to the Voysey character of the inner court as 'Art Nouveau'.)
Perhaps the most 'picturesque' element that strikes a modern eye is the mock-Tudor half-timbering. Overall, however, the architecture is composed so as to avoid the nineteenth century's notion of the picturesque à la Philip Webb et al.

The Hampstead Garden Suburb

Hampstead Garden Suburb is a peculiarity in London: a residential development that takes up a large swathe of urban land just north of Hampstead Heath and a place one either loves or finds curiously disturbing. Its origins were in the ambitions of the reformist Dame Henrietta Barnett (1851-1936; married to the vicar of an East End church and founder of the Whitechapel Art Gallery) who sought to both protect the Heath from speculative development that was following the march of the Northern Line out from central London (the couple had a weekend home there called St Jude's Cottage), and also to provide cooperative housing for the lower classes.

A Trust was formed in 1906 which was to own and administer 243 acres of land whilst promoting actual building through co-partnership companies in which each tenant had a share. The planner Barnett brought in was Raymond Unwin, who had designed Letchworth (1904), now moved to the new suburb area and set about implementing her ideas. Unwin was instrumental in realising a new Act, of 1906, that enabled him to plan in a picturesque manner the unamended building regulations would have prevented (e.g. residential 'closes' and roofs without fire breaks between dwellings).

A browse through The Buildings of England offers a host of architects whose work can be found in the Suburb: M.H. Baillie Scott, Courtenay Crickner, J.B.F. Cowper, Geoffrey Lucas, Michael Bunney, E. Guy Dawber, W. Curtis Green, Edwin Lutyens, A.J. Penty, Edwin Pulser, Fred Rowntree, J.C.S. Souter, G.L. Sutcliffe, Charles Wade, Herbert A. Welch, and T.M. Wilson, and others.

Styles range from a full neo-vernacular to a formal neo-Georgian, with some houses successfully mixing the idioms. The original scheme (groups of cottages, a village green, playgrounds, allotments, mixed classes in close proximity, etc.) was very informal, but Lutyens arrived to design the central buildings and sometimes introduced a distinct formality that Unwin managed to avoid in other parts (see page 244). The overall coherence they achieved between them is not really evident until one leaves and enters surrounding urban areas.

A Hampstead Garden Extension was laid out by Unwin in 1911-12. To this day the Suburb remains very pleasant but retains a peculiar air of being withdrawn from London as a whole: ironically inorganic in its extended unsustainability; a post-war, Jewish-dominated setting in the guise of a quaint late nineteenth century English village; a place for the affluent middle-classes rather than Barnett's rehoused lower classes, where the forlorn, centrally located church of St Jude sits disconsolately, without much purpose any more.

Above: neo-Georgian house by Lutyens, Erskine Hill, .
Below: flats by Parker & Unwin, Heath Close, 1911-12.
Bottom: houses in South Square, opp. St Jude's

getting about

Akey part of the dynamics of London's historical development – as fundamental as the Westminster/City split and the political divide between Inner and Outer boroughs – has been the systems and patterns of transport that supplemented and then replaced those

Below: Covent Garden tube station, as modernised and with some period features (such as signage) removed. Many of the railway station architects took up Halsey Ricardo's ideas on building within London in glazed tiles and bricks (of which Debenham House, in Holland park, 1905-7, is a fine example) and their ox-blood red forms still populate London's streets. Typically, they have a classical body and vaguely Arts & Crafts detailing.

traditional means of getting about London: by foot, by horse, carriage and water-boat. Dramatic change came with the mid and later-nineteenth century linkages between London and other rapidly expanding cities facilitated by the steam trains that came charging into the urban fabric to new termini at places such as Kings Cross, Waterloo, London Bridge, Victoria, Paddington, etc. These rail lines also established the framework of an outer suburban development (Service tells us that, by 1880, there were 350 railway stations in central and suburban London), but a different grain of transport change within the core of the urban fabric itself came with the horse-drawn omnibus (first used in 1829) and its railed equivalent – the former becoming the motorbus and the latter the electric tram. And, of course, horse-drawn cabs. By 1900 there were some 3,000 horse-drawn buses and trams, carrying an estimated 500 million passengers a year.

Major change came with the introduction of electrically-driven vehicles in 1901, at first operating only in the western suburbs (trams were kept out of central London as a strange aspect of late nineteenth century borough politics and class values). By 1903

these were providing an estimated 394 million journeys whilst the horse-drawn buses provided for 287 million journeys; but, by 1910, the electric trams were providing 764 million journeys against 287 million on the horse-buses. And then, from 1905, both means of transport were faced with competition from the petrol-driven omnibus – which, during the 1950s – eventually won the battle.

In the meantime, electricity revolutionised yet another means of getting about the capital: the underground system that had been introduced with the Metropolitan District Line's underground steam trains in 1863. What was a very uncomfortable and polluted means of transport was to be transformed by both electricity and new ways of tunnelling (the first tunnels had been 'cut and fill'; the new method employed what was called the 'Greathead Shield'). Initially, the application of electricity was not a success – the first stretch of electric tube, the City and South London (1890), paid all the penalties of the pioneer. But in the early 1890s one Act of Parliament after another allowed for new lines to be constructed underground. The first, in 1891, was for the Central Line (opening in 1900); then came Acts for the Northern Line, of 1892-3 (opening in 1901), the Waterloo, Bakerloo, etc. Interestingly, the first of these lines aimed to connect the City with the outer suburbs. For example, the Central Line was from Bank to Shepherds Bush, where the suburban trams started. And the Northern Line started between Angel-Bank-Clapham. Then came the linking of the major rail termini. For example, Waterloo to Baker Street (approved in 1893), opened in 1906; Kensington to Piccadilly to Kings Cross, also opened in 1906; the Northern Line between Charing Cross, Euston and the new suburbs of Golders Green, in 1907.

A key figure in all this was Charles T. Yerkes (1837-1905) an American whose Underground Electric Railways started the Northern Line and developed others as well. He arrived in London the same year that the new Central Line proved such an instant success (1900) and immediately applied all his American financial speculative experience to London. Together with a banker and a solicitor this shrewd trio set about bringing to life stalled proposals, electrifying the Metropolitan District, cleverly using franchises and building the first phases of the Northern Line. Most of the investments came from abroad and benefited Londoners more than the investors. Even Yerkes died in debt, just as his schemes were coming to fruition. (We are told his motto was, *"It's the strap-hangers who pay the dividends"*; he also described his business methods in terms that sound rather contemporary: *"Buy up old junk, fix it up a little and unload it on the other fellow."* Not much changes.

The various stations for the new lines were designed by architects including:

• **Delissa Josephs**, 1895-1927; son of Solomon, an architect of synagogues and industrial buildings; he designed a number of London synagogues himself, and also became an expert in superstructures over the booking and lift halls of London underground stations (often hotels, mostly now altered in one way or another). He also did a number of blocks of flats (e.g. Rutland Court, Rutland Gardens, and Fitz James Avenues, North End Road, all in Kensington, 1902); West End works such as 37-39 and 299 Oxford Street, 43-44 Albermarle Street, 169, 170, 219 and 225 Tottenham Court Road, etc.; in the City he did West India House, Leadenhall, and others).

• **Leslie William Green** 1875-1908; died aged thirty-three after having designed no less than fifty stations in five years as an architect to the Underground Electric Railways Co. (stations, tunnels, platforms for the Baker Street and Waterloo Railway, the Great Northern, Piccadilly and Brompton Railway, and the Charing Cross, Euston and Hampstead Railway.

Below: Russell Square station – a fine example of an original station, with relatively few alterations and additions.

Curtis Green 1875–1960

Extant London works include:

• House, **No.2 2 Hill Brow**, Bromley, 1899.
• **Chiswick Power station**, 1899-1901 (now The Powerhouse, 1985). This includes Powell-Tuck Conner & Orefelt's very fine and rather neo-LA studios of 1989.
• **No. 20 Meadway**, Hampstead Garden Suburb, c.1906.
• **106 Lombard Street**, City, while at Dunn & Watson, 1906 and 1915.
• **Cemetery, chapel and lodge**, Beaverwood Road, Chislehurst, 1910.
• House, **No. 6 Duke Street**, 1921-2.
• **Wolseley House**, 157-160 Piccadilly, 1920–1 (adjacent to the Joass building and opposite the Westminster Bank by Green).
• **157-160 Piccadilly**, 1921. Bank and offices.
• **63-65 Piccadilly**,1922-3. Bank and offices.
• **Stratton House**, next to Devonshire House. 79-80 Piccadilly, 1929.
• **London Life Association building**, 81-82 King William Street, City, 1925-27.
• **Scottish Widows,** 28-30 Cornhill, 1934-5.
• Police station, **Scotland Yard**, the Embankment, 1937–40. Adjacent to Shaw's building.
• **20-23 Lincoln's Inn Fields**, 1936–7 (with Wimperis, Simpson & Guthrie).
• **Dorchester Hotel**, in Park Lane, 1930-1 (replacing Owen Williams).
• **St George**, Waddon, Croydon, 1932.
• **200 Euston Road**, Bentley House,1937.
• **Fortress House**, 23 Saville Row, 1949-50 (by Curtis Green, Son & Lloyd).

Green became RA in 1933 and was awarded the RIBA Gold Medal in 1942 after a career that got under way with the power station of 1899 serving the new electric underground trains. Green was born in Alton, Hampshire, son to a barrister who died when Curtis was young (and, apparently in a state of ill-health that kept him away from school and on sailing dinghies). He initially studied engineering at West Bromwich Technical School before moving on to architecture at Birmingham School of Art on the basis of his skilled draughtsmanship. He then moved to London and worked for G.T. Hine and was then articled

to John Belcher while he attended the RA schools. In 1897 he joined the staff of The Builder, as a rather gifted illustrator travelling Europe and sketching new buildings for publication (which, no doubt, taught him an enormous amount).

Meanwhile, Green started his practice in 1898, designing many smaller houses. When Lutyens first went to New Delhi, he asked Green to take charge of his office while he was away – an undertaking that possibly enlarged his understanding of monumental work in the grand manner. In 1910 he was taken into partnership by Dunn and Watson, with the idea that Dunn would retire and Green take his place. However, Watson died, the war came and Curtis served with the Red Cross and then in the Artillery. After the war he was left as the sole inheritor of the practice. He was on his own until 1927, when his son Christopher and his son-in-law Anthony Lloyd joined the practice (which they continued after his death as Green, Lloyd, and Adams).

Below: the former bank building at 63-65 Piccadilly, 1923, located opposite The Ritz (by Arthur Davis).

Basil Champneys 1842–1935

Extant London works:
- **Bedford College**, NW Wing, Inner Circle, Regent's Park, 1910-13.
- **St Luke's,** Kentish Town, 1867–70.
- **Oak Tree House**, Redington Gardens, 1873.
- **Hall Oak**, in Frognal, Hampstead, 1881, his own home.
- **Chapel** at Mill Hill School, 1898. The school is by Tite (1825-7); there is also the Big School, by Colcutt (1905).

Above and below: Green's Scottish Widows building in Cornhill (1935) includes a masterful and indicative, if minor, touch: an arched entrance to an alley that demonstrates an easy accommodation between the symmetry of the façade and the alignment of the alley. There is a comfortable ease with which this is accomplished that is now a lost art.

 Champneys was awarded the RIBA Royal Gold Medal in 1912 but, ironically, never became a member of that institute because – in the tradition of the Arts and Crafts movement – he regarded architecture as an art allied to painting and sculpture rather than a profession.

He was born in Whitechapel, son of a local rector, studied at Cambridge and then became a pupil of John Pritchard, diocesan surveyor of Llandaff. He began private practice in 1867, midst the heights of the Gothic Revival. However, he was among the first to design in the Queen Anne mode and he also 'freely' worked in the late Gothic, neo-Jacobean, and early English Renaissance styles. He has a long list of buildings in Oxford and his best building is in Manchester; his London buildings are given above. In London he was apparently a familiar face at the billiard table at the Athenaeum club.

Aldwych and Kingsway

American influences in London around the turn of the century implied Beaux-Arts influences, the best example of which is the presence of Bush House, sitting on the north side of Aldwych, facing up Kingsway. It was designed by Harvey W. Corbett of the New York firm Helme & Corbett (1920-3). The entablature has symbolic figures of America and England, in that special relationship we have come to know so well.

Aldwych and Kingsway were created as one of the few and extraordinary exercises in London town-planning by the LCC. Clearances started in 1820 and the intention was one grand, coherent and harmonious set of Imperial-classical buildings. It did not, as usual, happen, but there is still an international flavour to the architecture.

A French influence is evident at the Waldorf Hotel, by A.M & A.G.R. Mackenzie (1906-8). Colonial presences once included India House (Herbert Baker & Scott, 1928-30), adjacent to a Foster-designed hotel (on the west corner), and Australia House (on the east end), the latter designed by Mackenzie again (1913-18, again in a French flavour). Its huge sculptures are by Harold Parker and Sir B. Mackennal (both Australian). John Burnett has a presence at No. 99 (former General Accident building), 1909-11 (now a part of the London School of Economics).

Above: Mewés & Davis's Morning Post building of 1906-7, now a hotel conversion by Jestico &Whiles (1998). The two top stories (which surely add to the building aesthetically) are 1928.
Below: Australia House, A.M. & A.G.R. Mackenzie, 1913-18.

The two theatres (Strand and Aldwych), either side of the Waldorf, are by W.G.R. Sprague (1905). French influences are again present in the Mewes & Davis former Morning Post building of 1906-7, on the westerns side of Aldwych (additional two top storeys and dome by G & T.S. Vickery, 1927-8; converted to a hotel by Jestico & Whiles in 1997-8).

Kingsway connects Strand/Aldwych to Holborn, clearing slums in the area. Its formal opening took place in 1905, but the buildings came over a period from then to 1922. Most of the buildings were by Trehearne & Norman: Imperial House, 1912-13; York House, 1913-14; Alexandra House, 1915-16; Prince's House, 1920-1. The southern end blocks at the meeting with the Aldwych were designed when Thomas Tait was

T & N's designer: the east block (redesigned behind the façade by Rolf Judd, 2000), 1913-14; the west side 1919-22 (which includes the 1996 restaurant with the glass ceiling designed by Julyan Whickham). The most notable buildings at the north end are also by Burnet and Tait (e.g. Kodak House).

Henry Vaughan Lanchester
1863–1953
with
James S. Stewart, 1866–1904
Edwin Alfred Rickards, 1872–1920

Extant London works include:
• **Deptford Town Hall**, 1903-5.
• **Methodist Central Hall**, Westminster, 1905–11. (After the death of Stewart.)
• **Third Church of Christ Scientist**, Curzon Street, Mayfair, 1910-12.
• **Nos 144-6** New Bond Street, and **No. 11** Bond Street, 1911-12.
• **Beckenham Town Hall**, completed 1932.
• **Hackney Town Hall**. Also, wall and toilets, Wilton Way, 1934-7.

Above: Westminster Central Hall, 1911.
One of Lanchester's more famous works is the former Umaid Palace, in India (347 rooms; now a hotel).

Lanchester's life spans an interesting period and his career reflected this: a bright young competition winner, together with Rickards; a man with a career on the side in India (mostly in town planning, from about 1912) that aroused the professional jealousies of Lutyens; a town-planner; writer, academic, editor (of the Builder, from 1910-12); RIBA vice-president (twice); and RIBA Gold Medal winner, in 1934. He was born in London, son of the architect H.J. Lanchester, to whom he became a pupil, then an assistant in the office of Frederick James Eedle, Thomas William Cutler and George Campbell Sherrin, then working for other architects before setting up a practice in 1894, and then with Edwin Rickards and James Stewart in 1899 on the basis of winning a competition for Cardiff Town Hall. Rikards (described as a lively, London-bred artist, a brilliant ornamentalist, cleverest of draughtsmen, and incessant talker) and Stewart (who came from the office of Leonard Stokes, had also been in Sherrin's office, and is described a former R.A. Gold Medallist and 'shrewd Scotch critic') died rather young – Stewart 'tragically' and Rickard after service during the war, after a long illness. Lanchester was then joined by G. Lucas in 1920 and T.A. Lodge, in 1923, and did even more town halls, also winning a competition for Leeds University.

Right: Deptford Town Hall, 1906 (now a part of the Goldsmith's College campus). The difference between the two town halls is remarkable. The sculpture on the Deptford building is quite outstanding in its references to the seafaring basis of the town's economy (at that time). The Hackney Town Hall is very near to Matcham's Hackney Empire.

trans-Atlantic influences
Sir John Burnet 1857–1938
Thomas Smith Tait 1882–1964

Burnet and Tait are a true cross-over: twenty-five years difference between them is the difference between an Edwardian and a post-war almost Modernist practice, but they were colleagues and partners. Burnet came to London in 1904 as a celebrated Scottish architect. It was here, in Edinburgh, that he met Tait and became his assistant, in 1903. Tait then entered the Glasgow School of Art, won prizes and, on Burnett's advice, made a continental tour before returning to join Burnet's new London office.

Burnet was born in Glasgow, son of a successful architect and, in 1874, he joined the atelier of Jean-Louis Pascal in Paris and in 1875 was the first of several Glasgow architects to enrol at the École des Beaux-Arts. (He studied under Jean-Louis Pascal and worked in the Paris office of François Rolland) Successfully in practice in Glasgow he had, by the 1890s, begun to inform his work with American influences – something that Tait was to reinforce. In 1896 he made the first of several visits to the USA, the impact of which was immediately evident in his work.

As a successful architect, Burnet was invited to design the Edward VII galleries at the British Museum, in 1904 (the basis of establishing a London office). Following its completion in 1914 there was a host of honours: a knighthood and the bronze medal of the Paris Salon, followed by the gold in 1922; the RIBA Royal Gold Medal, in 1923; election to the Royal Scottish Academy in 1914, and the Royal Academy in 1925. However, WWI was a very difficult period and it was immediately after the war that Tait was made a partner. However, their relationship was hardly an easy one. Tait had been induced to assist the rival practice of Trehearne and Norman outside office hours, designing for them the elevations of a number of large commercial blocks connected with the Kingsway and Aldwych improvements.

This arrangement came to Burnet's notice in 1913, causing serious differences, compounding an earlier disagreement over a premiated but unauthorised entry in an unofficial design competition for Regent Street. Tait left for New York, where he set about joining a firm designing banks and even met Frank Lloyd Wright. Burnet meanwhile regretted what had happened.

Tait returned and designed Shell Corner (designed

Extant London works include:
- **King Edward VII Galleries**, British Museum, 1904-14.
- former **General Accident Buildings**, No. 99 Aldwych, 1909-11.
- **Kodak Building,** Kingsway, 1910-11. One of the first buildings to positively expressits steel frame. Tait is apparently responsible for the American quality and lack of detail.
- **Royal Institute of Chemistry**, Russell Sq., 1914-15.
- **Second Church of Christ Scientist**, Palace Gardens Terrace, Notting Hill, 1921.
- **Westmoreland** and **Vigo House**, Regent Street, 1920-25 (west side).
- **Selfridges**, its completion in conjunction with the American firm of Graham, Anderson, Probst, and White, 1919–24.
- **Adelaide House,** London Bridge, 1921-25 (then the largest and most American office building in London, with its mullioned façades and deep Egyptian cornice, a by-product of Tait's voyage to Egypt for the war memorial at Port Taufiq).
- former **Lloyds Bank HQ**, 15-22 Cornhill, with Campbell-Jones and Smithers, 1925-7.
- **15-22 Lombard**, City. 1927-30.
- **Unilever House**, Embankment, with J. Lomax-Simpson (with sculptures by William Reid Dick),1929-32. As of 2007, just a façade.
- former **Daily Telegraph building**, Fleet Street, 1928-31 (with Elcock & Sutcliffe). Now frontage to offices behind (Goldman Sachs, by EPR Partnership 1988-91).
- former **Bechstein** showroom, 28 Brook Street, London, 1929–30.
- **Mount Royal**, Oxford Street, 1932.
- **Chelsea House**, Lowndes Street, 1934-5.
- **Burlington School**, Hammersmith, 1932.
- **Curzon Cinema**, Mayfair, (1933.
- **Burlington Girls School**, Wood Lane, Hammersmith, 1936.
- **Steel House**, Tothill Street, 1936-7.
- **German Hospital**, East Wing, Fasset Sq., Dalston (1935-8).

1914-15, completed 1919-20), and Adastral House on Kingsway, about1915 (see the notes on Aldwych and Kingsway).

Then, in 1918, Burnet made an offer of partnership and a new phase of their relationship began, but Burnett's role rapidly diminished during the 1920s. Finally, he retired in 1930. Francis Lorne (1889-1963) now became Tait's partner – a man who had worked for Bertram Goodhue in New York and who brought with him several refugees from the Wall Street crash of 1929, most importantly his brother-in-law Gordon Farquhar.

Work abroad followed and, in 1938, Tait was offered a knighthood, but a breach of confidentiality that found its way from a bridge party to the gossip columns, and for which Tait was not responsible, resulted in its being withdrawn. In effect, World War II ended Tait's career. But any study of trans-Atlantic influences – so important, in recent decades in office design especially, must refer to Burnett and Tait.

Above: Adelaide House (1921-5), at London Bridge, City. There is an elemental, un-English quality about the design which is more than neo-Egyptian features and manifests a distinct neo-American robustness that recurs in British architecture to frighten most of the native practitioners – the 1980s was the last instance, when phenomena such as Canary Wharf gave a similar fright to the London profession.

The building is, of course, steel framed. Other innovations included the building's internal mail system, its central ventilation and a miniature golf course on the roof. Even the wharf was rubber floored (as was Lombard Street about the same time) in order to reduce noise.

Right: Kodak House (1911) in Kingsway was one of the first London buildings to abandon the classical rules regarding façade composition. Here, Burnet clearly indicates the steel framing behind.

In Stuart Gray's book on Edwardian architecture he notes that Burnet "made important contributions in this field [of working drawings] until the standard ... in this country approached that of America." This was an intriguing aspect of professionalisation well before the Acts of the 1930s established a state-approved market monopoly on the basis of service, expertise and self-discipline – in turn, a mere thirty years before the severe criticisms of the 1960s resulted, some twenty years later, in reform of the profession and later attempts to sustain professional standards (by means of compulsory Continued Professional Development, etc), especially in the face of the rise of the project manager (at a time, during the 1980s, when American practices were arriving in London in significant numbers on the back of banking deregulation in the City).

Ironically, in the meantime, British architects first dropped any aspect of their profession with a numerate basis, and then any tectonic aspect which did not serve pure formalism. The net outcome is an art bias in schools of architecture that returns the profession to the 'art or profession' arguments of more than one hundred years ago even while the profession as a whole poses as ever more professionally expert and competent.

Left and Opposite page: Selfridges, in Oxford Street, perhaps one of the strongest façades in London and one of those 'grand manner' buildings that (like the Port of London Authority building, for example) looks as if transported from the USA.

Selfridge had made money in retailing, in Chicago, and came to London in 1906. The general scheme came from Albert Millar, of the Daniel Burnham practice, but the key elevations are from Francis S. Swales, a Canadian architect trained at the École des Beaux Arts in Paris. R. Frank Atkinson also played a role, dealing with the LCC's building and fire regulations; and the engineering came from a Swede practising in New York (Sven Bylander). As with the Ritz, the LCC's regulations demanded that the masonry enclosure to the steel frame should take no cognisance of the frame's structural role.

Millar remained the architect on a second phase of construction (1920-4; after the first nine, eastern bays) led by Graham, Anderson, Probst & White, with Sir John Burnett as the London consultant (they designed the entrance and its canopy).

Arthur Joseph Davis 1878–1951

Imagine: you are a young Englishman trained at the École des Beaux-Arts, demonstrating yourself to be a brilliant student in one of the premier ateliers (that of Jean-Louis Pascal) and you are employed by a famous French architect. At twenty years old you are made his associate on the design and construction of the prestigious Carlton and Ritz hotels in London; at twenty-two you are the London partner. Noted for your flair and masterly planning, you are later elected as an associate of the Royal Academy and then, thirty

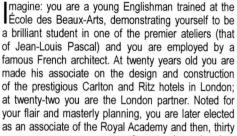

years after returning to London, have a 'nervous breakdown' because the Cunard Line insist your designs for the interiors of Queen Mary are in the (by then) fashionable *Jazz Moderne* style (or Art Deco as it is now called). In a context notable for the celebration of Le Corbusier's work in Paris, Pevsner's designation of Gropius as the genius of Modernism, flapper girls, advertising, radio, the likes of the Chrysler Building and the dreaded tastelessness of *Jazz Moderne*, you must (like many

Extant London works include:

• **Ritz Hotel**, Piccadilly, 1903-6.

• former **Steam Packet Company,** Nos 29-34 Cockspur Street, 1906. Extended three bays in 1914 (further extended to the corner in 1925. Façade later incorporated in to a hotel (2001).

• **Inveresk House**, (346 Strand), 1906-7. Former Morning Post; now a hotel. Attic storey added in the 1920s.

• **Cavalry Club**, 127 Piccadilly (1908-11). First five bays are 1888; porch and corresponding bays by Davis.

• **Royal Automobile Club**, Pall Mall, 1908-11 (with E. Keynes Purchase). Pediment sculpture by Ferdinand Faivre; otheer carvings by Rajon and G.H. Mabey.

• former NatWest Bank, **41 Lothbury**, 1921-31; also **51-53 Threadneedle**, 1922-36. This was the London County and Westminster Bank for whom the firm also designed buildings in Antwerp, Brussels, Nantes and Valancia.

• **St Sarkis Armenian Church**, Iverna Court, Kensington, 1922-3. Baptistery 1937; sacristy 1950. The vicarage of 1922 is also by Davis.

• **No. 6 Chesterfield Hill** (Mayfair House), 1923.

• **Nos 25-29 Golden Square** (for Dormeuil Frères), 1924.

• Shop front: **corner Regent Street and Conduit**, 1924.

• former Hudson Bay House **52-68 Bishopsgate**, 1928-29. The adjacent end façade in St Helen's Place is also Mewes & Davis, 1929.

• former **Morgan Grenfell Building**, 23 Great Winchester Street, 1925.

• former **Cunard Building**, 88 Leadenhall, 1930. This commiisiion was related to others for ship interiors.

• former **Allied Assurance**, Nos.1-4 Bartholomew Lane, 1932-3.

There is also **Polesden Lacey** (a remodelled Georgian house, 1906). Now a National Trust property, 30 km from central London.

Below: former Bank, 41 Lothbury..
Opposite: the Royal Automobile Club in Pall Mall. The building in the background is by Donald McMorran (see page 335).

other people) have wondered what was happening to your treasured Beaux-Arts values, as well as your promising career. You then spend your last years watching Modernism emerge and take over, rejecting all the architectural values you stood for and celebrated. Such was the life of Arthur Davis.

Davis was born in Leinster Gardens but educated privately in Brussels before entering into an architectural education at sixteen. He was trained by a famous tutor, Jean-Louis Pascal, and then entered the practice of Charles Mewès (1858-1914) in 1898. He was soon back in London, having worked with Mewès on the Carlton Hotel (1901) and then the Ritz design – a building of Beaux Arts character (designed down to the cutlery by the architects), but with an innovative steel frame made in Germany to a design by a Swedish engineer who had worked in Chicago. The building then had the largest steel frame in Europe (although the building regulations prevented its expression by thin walling) and was also innovative in its use of piles. With its mansard roof and crusty details, elaborate Louis XVI interiors and street arcade the Ritz, with its 112 rooms and 24 suites, brought Parisian fashions in architecture back into the heart of London and played a significant role in countering anti-French prejudices. Cesar Ritz is quoted as remarking that the Ritz (with its double glazing, bathrooms to every room, brass instead of wooden beds, etc.) was *"a small house to which I am pleased to see my name attached."*

There followed a string of admirable commissions for the practice, including Inveresk House (for the Morning Sun, 1906-7), the splendours of the Royal Automobile Club, Pall Mall (1908–11), City banks and designs for the Amerika and Kaiserin Auguste Victoria liners. Such was the success of these designs that Cunard asked Davis to design interiors for Cunard's Aquitania, in 1913.

Life was good for this short but dapper, good looking young man who apparently enjoyed the company of elegant women and resisted marriage until he was forty-five and could enjoy meals in his own-designed restaurant at the Hyde Park Hotel. Friends included other architects such as Edwin Lutyens, A. E. Richardson, Charles Reilly, Oliver Hill, and Herbert Austen Hall. But it appears that he was a (manic depressive).

Suddenly Mewès died, in 1914, (aged fifty-four) and Britain was at war with some of the firm's former clients. In 1916 Davis entered the army and served in France, doing hospital service, but had a nervous breakdown in 1917. He later entered practice again under the Mewès and Davis umbrella in partnership with Charles H. Gage

and post-war work included the Armenian church of St Sarkis, Iverna Gardens, Kensington (1928). Davis was now heaped with various honours (for example, he became Chevalier de la Légion d'honneur and was awarded the Belgian Ordre de la Couronne) before a further collapse in 1933 and further troubles.

Distressed by the insistence of the directors of the Cunard Line that his interiors for the Queen Mary should be in the *Jazz Moderne* style of which he disapproved, Davis suffered a nervous breakdown on their completion in 1935 – at the same time what has been described as a 'troubled' marriage ended (he had been married in 1923).

Davis died in 1951, the year of the Festival of Britain – whose architecture, no doubt, would have horrified him. A biographer suggests that his last years were overshadowed by the Modern Movement's rejection of what Davis deemed to be the civilised values inherent in traditional classical architecture – something he regarded as wholly unnecessary, since he and Mewès had shown how the classical language was entirely compatible with new building types such as modern hotels and ocean liners. Nevertheless, a photograph of 1947 shows Davis as dapper and confident-looking as ever.

Above: the dining rooms of the RAC and the Ritz, looking like scenes from the trans-Atlantic liners for which Davis designed interiors.
Photos courtesy of The Ritz and the RAC.
Opposite page*: the Ritz arcade on Piccadilly and the pool at the RAC (photo courtesy of the RAC)*

Emanuel Vincent Harris 1876–1971

Extant London works include:
- **Upper Street Underground Station** (for the LCC), Islington. Apparently a homage to Dance's Newgate Prison.
- **Nos 2 and 3 Duke Street**, St James', 1910-12; unusual 'Roman' front. (With Thomas A. Moodie.)
- **Board of Trade bldgs.** 1915-59, between Whitehall and the Victoria Embankment (worked stopped in 1941). Now Ministry of Defence.
- **13 Carlos Place**, off Grosvenor Sq., 1924.
- **24 Old Bond Street**, former Atkinson's. 1925-6.
- **10 Fitzroy Park**, Highgate, 1932. Harris' own home.
- **Kensington Central Library** (1955-60).

Harris – who became RA in 1942 and was awarded an RIBA Gold medal in 1951 – once wrote (to Donald McMorran, once his assistant), *"'we both know there is only one thing that really matters and that is 'the work'. All the rest is vanity though it does sweeten labour."* The reference to 'the work' is a strangely esoteric expression, but whether this indicates something of obscure interest about this pair or whether it was an appropriation expressive of Harris' dedication to all things classical remains opaque.

He was born in Devon and became a pupil of James Harvey, architect, of Plymouth, before moving to London to study at the Royal Academy schools while working in the offices of E. Keynes Purchase, then Leonard Stokes, and finally with Sir William Emerson for three years before joining the architects' department of the London County Council (1901) before setting up in practice in 1904.

Above: the Ministry of Defence (designed as Board of Trade and Air Ministry) is Harris' most prominent London work. Built in phases, from 1939. Over that time some original features were dropped (1934-6) in favour of elements taken from Holden's design for the same competition. Pevsner referred to the building, when completed, as "a monument to tiredness." (Actually quite a fine building, perhaps similar to the British Library and the Paternoster project, with the monumentality of Holden's Senate House.) The entrance sculptures are by Charles Wheeler (representing Earth and Water; 1949-52).The interiors were designed to accommodate fragments of earlier buildings.

Harris tackled endless numbers of the competitions that were abundant in those days and became an especially successful architect of public buildings. In particular, he won a competition for Glamorgan County Hall (with T.A. Moodie, who later left to live and work in South Africa, the practice lasting 1910-12), which was seen to introduce French and American flavour contrasting with, for example, what Lanchester was doing on a similar building type.

Sir Albert Edward Richardson
1880–1964

Extant London works include:

For Verity:
• **flats**, Cleveland Row, St James's, and in Bayswater Road (both 1906).
• the middle section of 169-201 **Regent Street** (1908-9).

With Gill:
• former **Regent Street Polytechnic**, Upper Regent Street.
• flats, **Nos. 10 and 19 Berkeley Street**, 1910-1916
• Sir Arthur **Sanderson** & Sons in Wells Street, 1930–32,.

With his son:
• the **Chancery Lane safe deposit**, 1945-9.
• 1, 3, 5 **Stone House Court**, rear of 65-66 Houndsditch, City, 1928-31.
• the former **Financial Times** building (now Bracken House), Cannon Street, 1955-8.
• the **AEI** building, Grosvenor Place, 1958.
• the **chapel and library**, St Mary's College, Twickenham, 1961.
• **St James'** church (Wren), repair of war damage, 1968.

*Ironically, Richardson is possibly now best known as the author of the original Financial Times building that was altered by Michael Hopkins (**above**). The latter clearly thought there was sufficient merit in the brick north and south wings of the old FT building to retain them as counterpoints to his new replacement of the central printing hall. Hopkins picks up the basic features of Richardson's architecture and carries them through to the new work, particularly the neo-Classical order of base, middle and upper storey, as well as the bay-window motif and the character of the attic storey.*

Born in Hackney, son of a printer, Richardson was articled to an architect named Thomas Page, in Gray's Inn Road, in 1895, and he subsequently served in the offices of Evelyn Hellicar (1898-1902), Leonard Stokes (1902-3), and Frank T. Verity (1903-6). He then set up in practice with another of Verity's assistants, Charles Lovett Gill. He wrote two notable books on British classical architecture before war service, after which, in 1919, he had the chair of architecture at the Bartlett school of architecture, University College, London- and stayed there for twenty seven years (ensuring Modernism was spurned and only the classical tradition was taught in what is now one of the most notable schools of architecture).

Richardson was elected RA in 1944 (then becoming its President), received the RIBA Gold Medal in 1947, and was appointed KCVO in 1956 – by which time he was thoroughly out of touch with young architects and seen as a reactionary.

The London Zoo Penguin Pool designed by Tecton with Ove Arup (1934) is a memorably controversial work of design: loved by critics and hated by its occupants – the penguins. It now lies forlornly at the Zoo, without purpose. In the background of the photo is the top of Casson Conder's elephant and rhino pavilion of 1965.

the refined, the modern, and
the vulgar . . .

Charles Henry Holden 1875-1960

Sir Giles Gilbert Scott 1880-1960

George Grey Wornum 1888-1957

Sir Evan Owen Williams 1890-1969

Wells Wintemute Coates 1895–1958

Amyas Douglas Connell 1901-80
Basil Ward 1902-1976
Colin Lucas 1906-88

Berthold Romanovich 'Tolek' Lubetkin 1901-90

Erno Goldfinger 1902-87

Joseph Emberton 1889-1956

David du Aberdeen 1913-87

Patrick Gwynne 1913-2003

Edwin Maxwell Fry 1899-1987

Donald Hank McMorran 1904-65
George Frederick Whitby 1917-73

the refined, the modern, and the vulgar . . .

Below: the building Maxwell Fry, as a young voice of Modernism, deemed to be "vulgar and childish, displaying all the worst sentimentalities of uncultured commercialism."

The Hoover sits up a main road west out of London, typical of strip roadside developments at that time. The architects were Wallis, Gilbert and Partners who first produced plans dated 20th May 1931. With incredible speed, the drawings were developed and signed off in September 1931. Hoover moved into their new building in January 1932 although the inauguration luncheon was delayed until May 1933. The building is now – some might say appropriately – a Tesco supermarket, but listed and celebrated by academics, conservationists and the middle classes generally. Note the 'frame' in relation to Osbert Lancaster's satirical drawing of the 'Modernistic' style, page 301.

The definitive history that lends a satisfying narrative and rationale to those changes in British architecture marking the period between the Late Victorian, the Edwardian, and the inter-war years up to the 1951 Festival of Britain has yet to be written. The usual emphasis is upon cultural fractures rather than insidious continuities and, with the hindsight we now enjoy, it is perhaps those continuities that mock the constant references to Modernistic change. Certainly there *was* remarkable and radical change, but the Post-Modern movement of the late 1970s and 1980s, for example, manifest an indignant outburst of residual sentiment that mixed a contemporary dynamic with what many saw as some unpleasant body prompted to emerge from a submarine condition. And that sentiment continues to occasionally re-emerge. A building built in Piccadilly, adjacent to Emberton's Simpson building of 1935 and opposite Shaw's strident hotel frontage of 1905, was erected in 2007 as strangulated witness to the fact that PoMo and the body of sentiment informing it lives on, but with little semblance of the wit and inventiveness of Shaw, Joass, Belcher, Lutyens, Burnet, Green et al.

From a broadened perspective this latter example perhaps stands together with other contemporary works that seek to apply a love of narrative – here as the weak distillation of a residual allegorical content more fulsomely found as the literary informants of late Victorian and Edwardian architectural sculpture. Contemporary culture is in love with narrative. Similarly, the fashion for treating façades as if they were large works of pattern-making is a novel version of the painterly viewpoint that has always been the essence of the picturesque tradition (now suitably flattened and abstracted). And dice-throwing and similar devices of pseudo-complexity theory insinuated into design stand as a residual version of what was once the strength of neo-Platonic belief and sentiment coloured by superstition and the pretence that architecture can both subscribe to and declare some otherwise hidden truth.

As Modernists, we continually focus on change and differences in architecture, but it is such implicit continuities that can be more fascinating. It is interesting to note, for example, that Vitruvius voiced a protest against implausibility in architectural expression. Truthful tectonic expression, it seems, is hardly an idea novel to either Modernism or the neo-Gothic. Their intermixture of moral content with the pragmatics of instrumentality which once attuned architectural ideology with Darwinism as well as prevailing socio-economic values underscores a familiar justificatory stance that architects feel forced to adopt.

There are also socio-economic continuities that belie stories of radical change. For example, the traders of the City of London – arguably the most architecturally dense and dynamic part of London, certainly in recent decades – have been, in social terms, notoriously conservative throughout the City's history, despite the fact that capitalism, as has been noted is, by its nature, phenomenally radical. Physically, the place has traditionally been inward looking, even turning its back on the river activities underlying its wealth and, instead, centring itself around Bank, relative to which it was once considered important to have an address within ten minutes walk of the Bank of England – coincidentally to about where the old Roman wall ran. That social conservatism was meant to have broken down after World War II but, as David Kynaston's history of the City points out, such traditions weren't seriously eroded until the 1980s. Before that, particularly in the twenty years after World War II, life in the City was recognisably similar to what it had been fifty or even one hundred

Above: the Odeon, Leicester Square: mutilated in 1967, somewhat recently restored, but still robustly suggesting something of what it was in 1937, when completed by Andrew Mather & Harry Weedon. The founder of the Odeon chain was Oscar Deutsch (1893-1941), a scrap merchant who opened his first cinema in 1928. By 1933 he had 26; by 1937 he had 250. Weedon, an architect from Birmingham and a former WWI pilot, designed some 300 cinemas.

Such forms of populist architecture indicatively have a short life span. The California coffee shop syndrome of the USA in the 1940s and '50's is another example of a vigorous and original style that has virtually evaporated, despite contributions from the likes of Lloyd Wright and John Lautner. These counterpointing idioms of culture ill-fit the hegemonic conventions of Cultured taste, architectural ideology and professional self-understanding, manifesting a curious dualistic aspect of architecture that is sometimes (and inappropriately) denoted as 'architecture versus building'. It isn't that simple and one is reminded of recurring subversive eruptions (Punk is an extreme example) that occasionally emerge as bottom-up phenomena to disrupt Cultural sleep-walkers. There is a power-politics of culture at issue, from which architecture is not immune.

years before. Only in the mid-1980s, coincident with banking deregulation and an influx of foreign banks (and their architects) did the City forcefully burst traditional boundaries and expand both outward (including across the river) and, more latterly, upward.

On the other hand, there are notable and restless keynotes characterising the emergence and establishment of modernism in the sense of its correspondence to the novel socio-economic values which first emerged in seventeenth century England as a concern with quantified goals to be achieved by quantifiable methods, and with the abstractions of power and money (as managers tell us, if you can't measure it you can't manage it). One manifests anxieties with legitimation (what, ostensibly, pertains to the likes of truth and authenticity). Another, in contrast, concerns the caprices of fashion (what, paradoxically, can equally be this or that). While acting on different planes, both inform the vital heart of society in the same a manner a neo-Hegelian element within modernism obsessively refers us to attunement with the spirit of the *Zeitgeist*. Similarly, the Rule of Taste effected in the early eighteenth century – and adumbrated to either side of that era – can be seen as counterpointing a parallel, implicit concern with instrumentality that coursed its way through the Industrial Revolution and became particularly evident in the nineteenth century.

By the 1920s and early 1930s, however, the consumerist post-war reality of the so-called First Machine Age was enjoying forms of expression slicing through the architectural streams we earlier noted as characterising Edwardian sentiments and its dialectic of freedom and discipline. The gifted Arthur Davis, for example, was to suffer working in the *Jazz Moderne* idiom (dramatically introduced at a Parisian fair in 1925 and later known as *Art Deco*) induce such stress that it prompted a nervous breakdown. Similarly, if less dramatically, Roger Fry – then emerging as a notable name in British Modernism – dismissed road-side buildings such as the Hoover factory in west London (a style of architecture that was to particularly flower in the USA) as beneath contempt. It is now a treasure of the conservation movement. (The might have been said of the now celebrated frontage and entrance lobby of Williams' Daily Express building.)

Despite such ambivalence, Modernist architectural ideology was to establish a firm grip upon architectural sentiment and the accepted conventions of form in the after-years of yet another World War. Nevertheless, this

Above: a 1929 Bakelite telephone (also see Giles Gilbert Scott's K series telephone boxes, page 313).

status of acceptance was frequently considered to be infected, as it were, by those same strains of English conservatism inclining both away from the inter-war influences of French, German and Russian radicalism and toward a less corrosive, Scandinavian brand of Modernism. By the late 1950s this was considered to be distinctly effete and scepticism soured the tastes of an architectural version of the gritty-minded 'angry young man' brigade of the 1950s, erupting in the early-1960s as a hedonistic joy in all things consumerist and materialistic among a youthful sector of the body of architects, especially as Archigram's polemics facilitated by cheap photocopying technology.

This was quickly followed by a counter-period in which the two fundamental streams in architectural sentiment fought a battle in the guise of High Tech versus Post-Modernism - adherents of the former bizarrely leaning toward socialism mixed with militaristic imagery (grey being its favourite colour), and the latter leaning toward its own variety of hedonistic nostalgia, occasionally tempered by a more disciplined and critical fringe (one thinks of Quinlan Terry and John Outram).

This dualistic struggle was to die overnight during the recession that hung over architectural endeavours from about 1990 to 1994. It evaporated. This has never been properly explained, but architects awoke from those dark years into a period when the British public finally embraced Modernist values (in housing, for example, everyone suddenly wanted an open-plan loft penthouse at the top of a tower, overlooking the river from large sliding windows and broad terraces). In a privatising world shorn of the chains of socialism and about to elect Tony Blair, even some council blocks were refurbished and sold off as desirable high-rise living. This would have been unthinkable a decade earlier (one thinks of CZWG's Cascades building of 1988 as a

precursor of such tastes and the first of post-1960s tall residential buildings).

But architects had been witness to a significant change in the pre-recession decades: their focus of attention and ideological reference shifted from where it had been throughout the post-war years – across the Atlantic, in America – back to Europe. It was no longer New York, which had succeeded Chicago, or even its successor, Los Angeles, which had dominated sentiments in the '60's through to the '80's. Instead, it was first Paris, then Berlin, then Barcelona (followed by London itself) as European cities took turns to be in the architectural and urbanistic spotlight.

Previous to this in 1951, the focus had been upon the Scandinavian countries – an attention given to northern Europe as counterpoint to France and, especially, Italy, that again has its roots in the 1920s and '30's. Established taste at that time had been firmly within the framework of a neo-Georgian taste that had come to favour in the Edwardian period and, by the 1930s, provided a defensive position against the incursions of a nascent Modernism which, imported from the Continent, enthused young architects such as Roger Fry and Denys Lasdun. In 1932 the former was designing refined neo-Georgian houses; by the mid-1930s he was a committed Modernist with work such as the Sun House in Hampstead (1937). On the other hand, Lasdun was designing his first house of 1934 in an Arts & Crafts manner; but, by 1937, he was designing a neo-Corbusian exercise in Newton Road, in west London.

In 1924 the architect Trystan Edwards had written that, *"The period of domestic architecture from which of all others we have most to learn is the Georgian."* In contrast, he pointed toward 'the materialists' who had Morris as their hero and who held a doctrine of design that *"has been a prolific source of bad manners in architecture."* It is a telling (bourgeois) comment. The Ruskinian notion of 'constructional candour' was similarly dismissed and the new buildings of Regent Street were considered a poor substitute for Nash's 'charming' terraces (which, ironically, had been decried a mere twenty years before). Nevertheless, by 1934, the intellectually as well as physically towering Reginald Blomfield was despairing. In a book of his lectures of that year he sadly remarked that his keynote was humanistic, but that *"It is perhaps too much to hope that these critical studies will induce the younger generation*

to study the master-pieces of a bygone art [...] The danger nowadays is that [...] we are suffering from the aftermath of war, the break-up of tradition and the loss of all standards of value. The fashion flits from one sensation to another, restless, sterile, and impatient, and for the moment it is the cult of ugliness that holds the field in Literature, Music and the Arts."

Alan Powers has attempted to cast an organisational net upon the period's sentiments of taste by associating them with the name of George VI, who came to the throne in 1937. Power's thesis is that *"a national style more stylistically inclusive than modern, or even Art Deco, ... achieved its peak in the years between 1936 and 1952."* And its characteristics were: *"It is orderly and restrained, linear, two dimensional, and uses clear colours. It is a selective form of classicism, with the majority of its references taken from the period of about 1770-1840. It relies on composition, using largely unornamented surfaces, with small incidents of ornament, or at times a small-scale over-all pattern. Stars and stripes are favoured, as are flower patterns. It seems to be centred on the graphic rather than the plastic arts."* (See Reynold's passport insignia, above.) In a series of BBC talks at that time one commentator gave a lecture summarising the characteristics of British art as *"common sense, honesty and soberness"*; those of contemporary architecture included *"orderly restraint."* It was within such a cultural framework that the Georgian Group was founded in 1937 and, in 1938, Evelyn Waugh was writing in Country Life magazine that Modernism was to be rejected in favour of *"that superb succession of masterpieces from Vanbrugh to Soane which are grouped, far too vaguely, under the absurdly insular title of 'Georgian'."*

Whatever their stylistic leaning – allied in differing degrees to the generalities of the George VI style, the residual vitalities of the 'grand manner', a nascent Modernist sentiment, or the thrills of Jazz Moderne – London's architects shared life as inhabitants of what has been called the 'First Machine Age' and were struggling to formally adapt. At the conservative heart of the George VI style, for example, was a continuing predicament concerning taste and form that had British architects trapped within a stream of innovation and socio-economic change that not only affected their profession, but quietly lent it navigational orientation, whatever the pilots on board thought was going on.

Above: stamp issued in 1930 commemorating the transatlantic flights of the Graf Zeppelin – the Machine Age in action.

The first advertising agency had been founded as long ago as 1881, in Philadelphia. The early years of the century had seen the introduction of electric vacuum cleaners and, later, valve radios (with the first British broadcasts in the early 1920s); in 1910 Henry Ford had introduced cars to the mass production line. By 1930 the Graf Zeppelin had been around the world and sumptuous transatlantic ocean liners (some fitted out by the likes of Arthur Davis) were enjoying their heyday; by 1937 aluminium airplanes were making the first commercial flights across the Atlantic. In 1927, the first 'talkie' was introduced to set the movie industry off into a booming marriage with Jazz Moderne. And jazz itself had the upper classes jigging about as never before (perhaps even at Davis' Ritz).

The Francophile sentiments that saw Lanchester and Rickard's Westminster Central Hall, Mewés and Davis' Ritz, and Burnet's northern wing of the British Museum all erected about the same time were witness to a 'reticence of the Anglo-Saxons' (as an Architectural Review article called it) that was considered to be British architecture's saving grace. But to a later critic, Reyner Banham, they manifest a squeamish failure of nerve to embrace the machine and, especially, the Glasgow School of Mackintosh et al that was being welcomed across Continental Europe: the generality of English 'free' stylists had become opposed to the machine, despite British works and proclamations that inspired others on the Continent (especially Germany). 'Free' meant, on the one hand, a romance of handicraft; on the other it meant a tempered sensibility often acting within the framework of neo-Classicist inclination that, after World War I, struggled to maintain its position, in spite of altered socio-economic circumstances.

What it did not embrace was that radical contrast to Banahm's 'squeamishness', the misogynist Marinetti who, in 1921, had summed up the Futurism he had first proclaimed in Paris, in 1909, as *"the defence of youth against all senility, the glorification of illogical and mad innovative genius, the artistic sensibility of mechanisation, of speed, of the music hall, and of the simultaneous interpenetration of modern life, words in freedom, plastic dynamism, noise-intoners, synthetic theatre."* The rude obtrusion of the Machine Age into the British cultural scene not only adopted the form of an offensive Marinetti glorifying machine guns, warplanes and the subjection of women, or a Jazz Moderne that shocked Maxwell Fry into remarking upon factories such as the new Hoover set down beside the suburban Great West Road were *"vulgar and childish, displaying all the worst sentimentalities of uncultured commercialism."*

However, it seemed that everyone, but especially the Modernists, inclined toward kinds of purification (a keynote that was to be associated with alarming political consequences). In California, Schindler and Neutra fruitfully and positively expressed this early twentieth century concern as an architectural agenda of open spaces, balconies and the enjoyment of fresh air and exercise. In France, a similar keynote found expression as Le Corbusier's call for a sanitising coat of white Ripolin paint, as well as his remarkable Villa Savoye (1928): an idealist, terraced weekend play-pavilion in the landscape ironically informed by Neo-Platonic proportional and geometric concerns. And Berthold Lubetkin was to import such sentiments to London's architecture in the guise of the crisp lines of the High Point flats and, especially, a children's delousing facility built beneath Tecton's otherwise remarkably innovatory Finsbury Health Centre. Besides Lubetkin, there was an influx of Continental émigrés – such as Erno Goldfinger – who settled, practiced in London and demonstrated what could be achieved. And there was Emberton, the Canadian Wells Coates, and the civil engineer Owen Williams. And in the slipstream of it all came home grown young architects such as Denys Lasdun, who quickly graduated from a discreet neo-Georgian to full-blown neo-Corbusier style (but one that was not to flower until the post-war years).

However, on the whole, even this nascent English Modernism also became tempered. Holden's radical station designs turned toward brick, as did some of Maxwell Fry's work. And, after World War II, it was the more gentle Scandinavian Modernism (exemplified by Alvar Aalto's Villa Mairea, of 1939) that was at first fashionable, not the literally more brutal approach of Le Corbusier (who, in the aftermath of World War II was discovering the rude joys of the 'primitive hut').

Against this background the RIBA's new headquarters in Portland Place, of 1934 – intended to serve as a symbol of the architectural profession, its contemporary relevance and legitimacy, as well as provide more mundane accommodational services

– was arguably a profoundly appropriate symbol of inter-war architectural sentiments that evidenced Edwardian roots and continued to influence immediate post-war tastes.

Modernism, as something formally radical, often shocking and occasionally innovatory, may have tempered neo-Classicist taste and enjoyed the patronage of a certain intellectual class that could engender the likes of Wells Coates' Lawn Road apartments (also 1934), but the real spirit of Modernism – as a Pevsnerian *Zeitgeist* – was in the popularism of the Jazz Moderne which stretched across classes and continents, and popped up in the local High Street as flashy cinemas, as well as works such as the comparatively restrained Hoover building.

Above: *Wren, on the facade of the RIBA headquarters building designed by Grey Wornum. (See page 314.)*

It was this spirit that was to continue after World War II as the fantasies of Archigram: informed by Machine Age comics and by post-war American consumerism, condemning neo-Scandinavian tastes in architecture as effete and inadequate. The counterpoint – cousin to the sentiments informing the George VI style – emerged once again in the '70's and '80's as Post-Modernism, but it was alive and well even as machines churned out issues of Archigram in the form of McMorran and Whitby's Wood Street City Police Station (1965; see page 335).

But it is perhaps figures such as Patrick Gwynne – an otherwise lesser architectural talent – and not David du Aberdeen or Connell, Ward and Lucas, who epitomise how the 1930s became the 1960s. His Homewood house is a wonderful exhibition of Le Corbusier's Five Points, later blended together with James Bond enthusiasms of the kind that were to discomfort Erno Goldfinger. (See pages 304 and 332.)

Meanwhile, in the inter-war period, architecture in the City and for City institutions such as banks, held to the 'grand manner'. While New York erected the Chrysler building, the Empire State and the Rockefeller Centre, Lutyens gave London Britannic House, the Midland Bank HQ, and the likes of the 120 Pall Mall building, and Curtis Green was providing fine works in Piccadilly as well as the City.

These were frequently fine works (such as Lutyens 120 Pall Mall), but expressed a culture bound to its past – both glorious and traumatic, presenting a brave face and a stiff upper lip on its present (in India, for example, as in the City, life after World War I went on as before, as if utterly unaware of what was to come in the immediate

future). These architects failed to acknowledge and adapt to a *Zeitgeist* that, meanwhile, in Continental Europe, had prompted Nicholas Pevsner to enthuse about the 'harsh' realities of Modernism and was busy marrying the dynamic of a Machine Age architecture to the fascist dreams of Mussolini and the Third Reich. Lutyens' humanism stood little chance against the Machine Age's strange varieties of puritanism.

From another perspective one looks back on the inter-war period as yet another stage in a history of modernism – from Inigo Jones onward – as the struggle of Architecture to catch up and adapt. Perhaps that has been its intrinsic nature and challenge: to heroically respond to what is going on and be as one with it, never able to either manifest pretended hidden truths concealed by Shakespeare's 'muddy vestures of decay', or quite take the lead in a inexorably constant and fearful process of mutation that perhaps runs counter to its intrinsic purpose of reassurance. Perhaps Architecture and architects always needs to be one step behind. Whatever the truth of such matters, this inter-war period was nevertheless witness to some significant architectural talents at work and London still presents some fascinating works.

Opposite page: one of Lutyens better late-career, 'grand manner' façades (120 Pall Mall, SW1 for Messrs Crane Bennett Ltd (1929, now Banco Sabadell)), sitting quietly in Cockspur Street, opposite New Zealand House (1957-63, by Robert Matthew, Johnson-Marshall & Partners).

It employs his 'Delhi Order' (complete with bells, see **above**) and has a dignity and yet lightness that is Lutyens at his best (possibly better than his much-lauded façades in the City). This is architectural gamesmanship at its best: not only penetrative, where appropriate and allowed to be so, but compositionally inventive, artful and witty.

Notice the listed and black-painted K2 (Giles Gilbert Scott) telephone box – what it symbolises is equally powerful as all of Lutyens' neoclassicism.

Above: meanwhile, in New York – an entrance in the Rockefeller Centre, 1930-39 (lead architect, Raymond Hood, who has a building called Palladium House on the Marlborough Street and Argyll Street corner, 1928).
.

Above: the building that was exciting many young English architects and disturbing many others – Le Corbusier's Villa Savoy, of 1928.

Holden's extant London works include:
- **Belgrave Hospital for Children**, Clapham Road, 1899-1901.
- **Law Society Library extension**, Chancery Lane, 1902-4 (next to Vulliamy's building of 1831).
- former Norwich House, **127-129 High Holborn**, 1904.
- former British Medical Headquarters (BMA), **429 Strand**, 1907-8 (later Rhodesia House and then Zwimbawe House). Sadly, the controversial Epstein sculptures were mutilated in 1937.
- **Evelyn House**, 54-62 Oxford Street, 1908-10.
- former Kings College for Women (now **Queen Elizabeth College**), Campden Hill, Kensington, 1914-16 (St James' Palace style; later additions 1959-70, by others).
- **Senate House**, University of London, 1932. Also, **SOAS**, in Thornhaugh Street, 1939. Holden was appointed in 1931 after a lengthy submission and interview process that ended up with an interview over dinner at the Athenaeum Club. His final design (always including the 65m high tower) was pleasing to him because it was without "any tricks of the 'Grand Manner'." The entrance hall has a stripped Greek character that has made it an attractive scene for movie-makers. Holden's designs were intended to cover a large part of Georgian Holborn with a single, giant scheme. The tower had a steel frame, but the other buildings are traditional masonry, which Holden felt would last longer. The scheme was never completed as intended because the University could not afford it; they also denied Holden's intention to adorn the tower and blower buildings with sculpture (they perhaps recalled the fuss over the Epsteins at the BMA). Parts of the scheme to the north – buildings for Birkbeck College, the students' union, the School of Oriental and African Studies, and the Warburg Institute – were completed after the World War II.

Charles Henry Holden
1875–1960

John Summerson said of Charles Holden that he was "*the last of the Edwardians and the first of the English Moderns*." His early works – such as the Law Library (1902), the Sanatorium at Midhurst in Sussex (1904-6), and the Bristol Central Library (1902) – have a considerable power to their presence without resorting to that English Baroque 'Wrenaissance' that became so fashionable, or leaning toward that vaguely Adamesque, stripped classicism that later informed the so-called George VI style of the later 1930s. The Law Library, for example, is a delightful exercise in space, mass and line.

Holden was born in Bolton, Lancashire, the son of a textile engineer. On leaving school he was a railways clerk and an apprentice in a chemical laboratory before starting a mechanical drawing class at a local YMCA. He then became articled to the Bolton firm of D.F. Greene and then F.W. Leeson, in Manchester (1892), where he attended the local technical College and School of Art and repeatedly won prizes for his work. For example, AaBuilding magazine competition set nine design problems and Holden won five first places, three seconds, and one third. And it was here that he met L.G. Pearson, who was later to be his partner; together with other students, they called themselves the Walt Whitman Society, after a love of that man's poems.

Holden had completed his studentship by 1896 and entered the office of Jonathon Simpson, in Bolton. He then came to London in 1897 as an assistant to C.R. Ashbee's , whose wife Janet visited Holden and

- Holden **London Underground stations**, 1923 to 1938:

Acton Town, 1932-3; Arnos Grove, 1932 (possibly the best-known station); Bounds Green; Balham, 1926; Boston Manor, 1934; Chiswick Park, 1932-3; Clapham Common, 1923-4; Cockfosters; Gants Hill, 1937-8, built 1947 (Moscow underground influences; refurbished by Richard Rogers Partnership 1994); Clapham South, 1926; Colliers Wood, 1926; Ealing Common, 1931; East Finchley (refurbished by Avanti, 1996); Hounslow West, 1931; Merton, 1926; Morden, 1926 (office block added 1960); Northfields, 1932-3; Oakwood (with C.H. James); Osterley Park, 1934; Piccadilly Circus, 1925-8 (with S.A. Heaps); Redbridge, Eastern Avenue, 1937-8;

Ruislip Manor, 1938; South Wimbledon, 1926; Sudbury Town – the prototype for Alperton and Sudbury Hill, 1930-1; Southgate; South Harrow, 1935 (with C.A. Heaps); Tooting Bec, 1926; Tooting Broadway, 1926; Turnpike Lane (restored 1996); Wood Green; Wanstead, 1937-8. There are also two termini, at Uxbridge and Cockfosters, in reinforced concrete and glass.
- 55 Broadway (London Transport HQ), 1927-9.

Above: the Law Society Library extension, 1914. Holden's approach is primarily concerned with massing of a kind that was to become his trademark. The interior is less interesting.
Left: detail of the façade – which has parallels with Joass' Mannerism (see Joass' Royal Insurance building, 1908, on page 261).

Two years after entering Ashbee's office Holden went to Percy Adams (1865-1930), a hospital specialist, and started to attend the RA Schools. By 1907 he was a partner and, in 1913, Lionel G. Pearson joined and the firm became Adams, Holden and Pearson.

Early works in this role had a definite Mannerist undertone (e.g. the Strand building for the BMA, the Law Courts extension, and the Kings College building in Kensington; one brings to mind parallels with Joass).

Then came World War I and Holden served as a lieutenant in France (with the London ambulance column) and left with the rank of major. After this he joined the War Graves Commission and undertook a number of works in France and Belgium (alongside Reginald Blomfield, Herbert Baker, and Edwin Lutyens). Together with his assistants, notably W.C. von Berg and W.H. Cowlishaw, he designed sixty-seven cemeteries.

It was also during these years that the office had Frank Pick as a patron and Holden designed many London Underground stations. This included a branded prototype for seven stations completing the southern part of the Northern Line, using Clapham South as a model (1925; later stations, such as Arnos Grove, Boston Manor and Osterley significantly shifted from Portland stone to brick). Suddenly, as Stuart Gray has pointed out, the public were being exposed to a decidedly 'modern' architecture.

On the basis of this success came the commission for the 55 Broadway HQ building (1925-29), which is

his partner in 1906, at their home in Hertfordshire, and found "*bananas and brown bread on the table; no hot water; plain living and high thinking and strenuous activity for the betterment of the world.*" Ashbee later said of him: "*I know most of the men in my profession in one way or another, and I know that the real architects can be numbered on the fingers of one's two hands. Old Bodley is one, and Philip Webb, and Lethaby, and Harry Wilson, and unknown by his own name, 'ghosting' in the offices of another man, Charles Holden of whom perhaps I may have something to say some day.*"

similar in feeling to Holden's other great work of this period: Senate House, for the University of London. With both these major commissions Holden designed austerely detailed, geometrical masses, in a style which (in the Arts & Crafts 'free' design tradition) aimed not to be a style.

In 1936 Holden was awarded the RIBA Gold Medal and after World War II he turned down ('declined to accept') a knighthood (it would, he argued, *"alienate me from ordinary people"*). His final years were dominated by World War II and the planning challenges of reconstruction in the City and at the Southbank. His role in the City included the insistence that William Holford also be appointed – the man who ended up as architect for the buildings near to St Paul's. Whilst he and Holford were making their plans, he commented: *"There is ... much to be said for retaining the lines of the Roman and some of the medieval roadways, but this retention must contribute to, and not interfere with the development of any part of the City ..."* The radical as a young man was, as an old man, a dangerous beast. Most of their proposals – including the demolition of the Mansion House in order to provide a roundabout, together with schemes for double-decker roads and car-parking at roundabouts – were thankfully never carried out.

In 1942 Holden wrote a reply of protest to a friend's remarks about industrialisation: *"It comes simply to this: that I was born in an industrial age; that I was urged by a passion for building and for service; and that I have an invincible belief in the power of the human soul, the God in man, to rise above and master ugliness and desolating conditions. I had to exercise this passion even in the industrial age into which I was born."*

Above: *Senate House, 1932, for the University of London – all that was constructed of a massive scheme.*
Bottom: *the entry lobby of Senate House.*

310

This page: Holden's BMA building in the Strand (now Zimbabwe House), 1908. The building and the author's selection of the New York sculptor, Jacob Epstein, for in-situ-carved works, were equally shocking to their audiences. Controversy erupted over the naked figures and they were later mutilated. The design has the distinctly mannered undertones one also finds in the work of John Joass.

Extant London works include:

• **War Memorial Chapel,** Church of St Michael Chester Square, Belgravia (1920-21). Similar work includes: Chapel on London Road, Harrow, London (1905 – 06); chancel of All Hallows' Church, Gospel Oak (1913-15); alterations to south chancel chapel, Church of St Mary Abbot, Kensington (1920-1921).

• **K series telephone box.** K2 1924; K3 1930; K6 1935, designed for mass production. (It is still attractive and still around in tourist areas.) The cast-iron design with its neo-Regency feel was undertaken at the time Scott became a Trustee of the Soane Museum and manifests a Soanean influence.

• **Chester House**, Clarendon Place, W2, 1925-6. Scott's own house.

• **Church of St Alban**, North End Road, Golders Green (1925, built 1932 – 33).

• **Chester House** (his own home), Clarendon Place, Paddington, London (1925-26).

• **St Francis of Assisi Church**, High Wycombe (1929-30).

• **Whitelands Teacher Training College**, Wandsworth (1929-31).

• **North East Tower,** Our Lady of Grace and St Edward Church (RC), Chiswick (1930).

• **Phoenix Theatre façade**, Charing Cross Road, London (1930 with Bertie Crewe).

• **Cropthorne Court** (private residences), Maida Vale (1930-1937).

• **Whitelands College chapel**, West Hill, Putney, South London (1928-30).

• **William Booth Memorial Training College**, Denmark Hill, Camberwell, south London (1932).

• **Vincent House**, Vincent Square, Westminster (1932; consultant).

• **Fountains House**, Park Lane, London (1935-38; consultant).

• Private house, **22 Weymouth Street**, Marylebone (1936).

• **Waterloo Bridge**, 1937-2, with Rendel, Palmer & Tritton (the engineers). The structure is cantilevering box girders and not truly arched, as it appears.

• **Battersea Power Station**, 1929-35 (some exterior details only; with S.L Pearce, H.N. Allot as engineers, and J. Theor Halliday, architect).

• **Bankside power station**, 1954-60 (with Mott Hay & Andersen, engs.); now the Tate Modern (compare with the Guildhall offices).

Sir Giles Gilbert Scott
1880–1960 (son of Sir George, Jnr.)

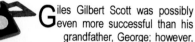

Giles Gilbert Scott was possibly even more successful than his grandfather, George; however, there is little of his work that is remarkable and influential in London (apart, ironically, from aged and Listed K-series telephone boxes), although he has latterly come to fame for being the author of what is now the Tate Modern building.

As a young man, Scott was schooled in Windsor at Beaumont, because his father liked the J.F. Bentley buildings there. He was later articled for three years to Temple Moore and started his own practice in 1902. It was in 1903, aged twenty-three (and much to his own surprise, as well as that of the Anglican competition committee), that Scott, a catholic, won the commission for a new Liverpool Cathedral.

Encouraged by Temple Moore, he undertook the design for a 'cathedral for the twentieth century' at home, in his spare time. The submission of Moore, his employer, got nowhere, but Scott's own career was

• **Guildhall municipal offices**, City, 1955-7
Scott repaired the Guildhall roof after World War II bombing with hidden steel trusses. The Guildhall to the top of its windows is original (although restored); above that is by Horace Jones). The offices along the west side are by Richard Gilbert Scott, 1969-75, the son of Giles. It is as if the old man was still warm in his grave and a younger generation eagerly comes forward to grab the reigns and now strut their stuff with a fashionable, early '60's work. This finally constructed work still, nevertheless, bears hints of historicism in its neo-medieval overhangs (what, perhaps, would now be addressed in terms of historical contexturalism and 'memory traces' that lend the design a narrative content).

• **North and South Blocks, County Hall**, London (1939 and 1950-58).

• **St Mark**, Biggin Hill, Bromley, 1957-9.

• **Chamber of the House of Commons**, Palace of Westminster (1945-50); restoration.

• **Our Lady of Mount Carmel Church**, (RC), Kensington Church Street, 1954-59.

launched on the basis of his winning design. Initially, it was decided that one of the assessors, G.F. Bodley (the other assessor was Shaw) should join with Scott. It wasn't a happy arrangement and Scott felt severely hampered until Bodley died in 1907, just before Scott had determined to give up and resign. He was to work on the cathedral (his most famous work) for most of the rest of his life, simplifying the original neo-Gothic design, lending it a more classical flavour and designing every detail that craftsmen and artists had to execute. (In fact, the first bay of the nave was not completed until 1961, a year after Scott had died.)

After the cathedral win there began a series of church commissions which, in Gavin Stamp's words, established Scott *"as one of the most accomplished and sophisticated inter-war ecclesiastic designers in Britain in the several churches he designed for both Anglican and Roman Catholic parishes."*

Scott's later life was filled with controversy. First, over proposals for a new bridge at Waterloo; over the post-World War II rebuilding of Coventry Cathedral, a commission from which he resigned, leaving the opportunity for an open competition, which Basil Spence won; and then over Bankside Power Station, argued to detract from St Paul's and promote the corrosion of London's fabric. During this period Scott was firmly a part of that rather disoriented classical spirit labelled the 'George VI style': a broad body of taste neither Modern nor Art Deco nor properly classicist or anything else and which, during the mid-thirties, Country Life was promoting as a middle path between robust Neoclassicism and Modernism.

Like many other architects of that period, the inter-war work of Giles Gilbert Scott has to be seen within this framework (lent an intriguing undertone by his love of fast cars and the Buick he idiosyncratically drove; one thinks of the young Smithsons driving a Willys Jeep in the early 1950s).

Ironically, he is now noted for designs such as the K6 telephone box, with its John Soane inspired roof, and for having been the author of the building that was the basis of Herzog and de Meuron's Tate Modern (which is worth comparing with the north block of the Guildhall, designed at the same time). But the other work that bears examination is Scott's rebuilding of the war-damaged House of Commons, with regard to which he noted: *"bearing in mind that the Chamber forms only a small portion of an existing large building, we are strongly of the opinion that the style adopted should be in sympathy with the rest of the structure, even if it has to differ in some degree in order to achieve a better quality of design."* The new work was opened in 1950 but few people, at that time had a good word to say for what was described as 'Neon Gothic'.

An American assistant in Scott's 1920s office commented that, *"it was a small office, not more than 8 to 10 altogether, very informal and apparently unbusinesslike, but it was our pride never to have delayed a job from lack of drawings. Sir Giles designed everything himself, down to the smallest detail, but did not do a lot of visiting"* (surely a novel attitude to project management). Scott was elected RA in 1922, and knighted in 1924, awarded the Royal Gold Medal in 1925 and the even more prestigious Order of Merit in 1944. From 1933-35 he was President of the RIBA.

Above: the two K telephone box designs.
Left: the Guildhall offices (the Bankside Power Station without the chimney and with a few windows). In the foreground is a 1960s Barbican 'gateway', designed by Giles' son, Richard.

George Grey Wornum
1888–1957

Extant London works include:
- **RIBA**, Portland Place, 1932-34.
- **Kensal House**, 1-68 Ladbroke Grove, 1936-38; (inc. day nursery) with Maxwell Fry.
- **No.3 9 Weymouth Street**, 1936.
- replanning of **Parliament Square**, 1952.

a symbol to the nation (without foreign accents)

Grey Wornum was born in London as the son of a doctor and grandson of a keeper of the National Gallery. He attended the Slade from 1905-6 but then became articled to his uncle, Ralph Selden Wornum, his uncle, before working for Simpson & Ayrton. He attended classes at the AA, did well and set on his own in 1910.

He had a first job as a studio for a cousin but work was scarce and he worked freelance for Herbert Batsford and as book illustrator and editor. During WWI he was badly wounded and lost an eye, but he again took up practice in 1919 in partnership with Philip D. Hepworth. Louis de Soisson also joined them and, in 1921, Hepworth left. Soisson and Wornum practised together and apart and, during this period, Wornum travelled to Sweden and even became a friend of Eric Mendelsohn. He was on the AA Council and, from 1930-31, served as the AA's President. After this time Wornum practised on his own (although he was later in practice with Edward Playne from 1950, when he was the RIBA Vice-President) and, in 1932 came the RIBA competition. It was an auspicious time for RIBA (see opposite).

Wornum's wife, Miriam, was an American artist and she had a significant influence on colour design and textiles used in the RIBA building. Further decorative work followed, including the interiors of RMS Queen Elizabeth (1938-45) and designing the Coronation route (1938), but there was not other architectural work of significance.

Wornum was awarded the RIBA Gold Medal in 1952 and was awarded a CBE, announced merely two days after his death in 1957. His last years were largely spent in the USA and the Bahamas.

The RIBA headquarters building in Portland Place is a celebratory erection, as well as being indicative of a set of architectural values striving to maintain balance between Classical traditions and contemporary inclinations toward discretion in matters of expression. Perhaps Burlington would have approved.

The building is celebratory in that it follows upon the 1925 union of the warring parts of the body of architects fighting to realise registration (notably the Society of Architects and the RIBA) and control of a new closed profession – an ambition realised by a series of Acts of Parliament between 1931-8. (The 1931 Act merely restricted the use of 'Registered Architect'; the 1938 Bill remedied this so that 'architect' itself was now a protected entitlement for those whose education, as defined by a Board of Education, was acceptable to a Registration Council.)

In effect, a body of experts had, in return for protection and monopolistic controls, promised a high educational standard and a form of self-regulation intended to be to the general benefit of society. True, the RIBA did not get what it wanted – full control of the profession – and it remains a club promoting architects in the guise of a charity promoting architecture, but the achievement of a close status and a monopoly over the title 'architect' was a significant step. The 'memorialist' lobby of around 1891, as Norman Shaw had named it, had at last been defeated: architecture was indeed a profession and not, as Shaw et al had protested and advocated, an unexaminable art. To this day and from this building, the RIBA continues its battle for hegemonic control over the profession, doing so from what increasingly looks like a pleasant but expensive, pretentious and unsuitable building: Grey Wornum's elegant design.

It is against this background that the immediate outcome of the 1931 Act was a building competition attracting 284 entries. It was overseen by Robert Atkinson as a former Principal of the Architectural

Association and Director of Education at the RIBA (and designer of the Daily Express lobby), together with Charles Holden, Sir Giles Gilbert Scott, H.V. Lanchester, and Percy Worthington. The site was the outcome of what had been a lengthy process of search and negotiation which had concluded during the severe years of recession with a lease of the Portland Place corner site. (The background reality of the Depression is an interesting comment upon cultural power and wealth at that time. Clearly, architects had it.)

The brief called for a design that would express the '*dignity and significance to the national life of the profession of architecture*'. Voysey wrote to the Times and called for elevations that reflected "*the spiritual and unseen character of a nation.*" This was, "*the unseen quality we wish to see expressed, freely and sincerely without any foreign accents.*" London was, after all, the home of the British Empire.

Above: figure above the main door, by B. Copnall.
Below: the two upper floors were added in 1957-8 by Wornum.
Bottom: the bronze doors (by James Woodford; the two side pillars are also by Woodford).

The submissions were, of course, controversial. Goodhart-Rendel wrote that there was little of first-rate skill but, thankfully, little of second-rate slickness. There were, he noted with some wit, "*several designs for an Institute of Swedish Architects, a clever design for an Institute of Genoese Architects, some interesting designs for warehouses and a large sprinkling of designs for American luxury hotels.*" The 'grand manner' was notable by its absence except, perhaps, as a ghost secretly haunting Wornum's design.

That design was primarily selected for its plan and section, and the manner it placed a grand staircase so as to move hundreds of people to the principal halls. However, inevitably, costs were drastically cut and the scheme was amended (with the assistance of Giles Gilbert Scott). Nevertheless, its best features remain the grand staircase and also the library, together with impressive cast front doors. The building is surely a remarkable period piece that one can't imagine being designed at any other time or place. Whether it is suited to a contemporary profession is a moot point, but it surely plays a positive role in maintaining the social pretensions of the profession.

Sir Evan Owen Williams

1890–1969

Extant London works include:

• former **Daily Express frontage**, 120 Fleet Street, 1930-33. This is the first true curtain-walled building in Britain. The printing works behind were by Ellis & Clarke (dem.). Owens was also consulting engineer on the adjacent Telegraph building.

• Former **Peckham Pioneer Health Centre**, Peckham, 1933-5. St Mary's Road, SE15. Converted to flats about 2000.

• **flats**, Valencia Road, two blocks, 1937, since altered by tile hanging.

• **Synagogue**, Gladstone Park, 1937-8.

• former BOAC maintenance **hangers**, Heathrow, 1950-5.

In 1907, when Edwin Lutyens was already quite famous for his Arts & Crafts country houses and was well into exploring 'Wrenaissance' architecture, Owen Williams was starting an engineering apprenticeship.

*Whilst the structure and the Vitrolite cladding of the Daily Express (**above and opposite page**) is by Owens, the interior of the lobby was designed by Robert Atkinson, with plater reliefs by Eric Aumonier.*

He was born in Tottenham, was educated locally and, in 1907, he took an apprenticeship with the Metropolitan Electric Tramways Company whilst simultaneously attending evening classes at the Northern Polytechnic Institute, from which, in 1911, he graduated with first-class honours in engineering. Now, at about the time Country Life was publishing Lutyens' works, Williams started work in the field of prefabricated concrete engineering. He then worked briefly for the Indented Bar and Concrete Engineering Company and, in 1912-16 for the American-owned, Trussed Concrete Steel Company, first as senior designer and afterwards as chief estimator. In the former capacity he designed his first building, a six-storey cabinet factory for the Gramophone Company (later EMI) at Hayes, Middlesex. But most of his responsibilities concerned bridges, docks, reservoirs, and industrial plant. In 1916-17 he worked for the Wells Aviation Company, designing a flying boat; then in 1917-18 he was chief engineer at the Admiralty shipyard at Poole, where he built reinforced concrete lighters and tugs.

After World War I Williams started up as a consultant engineer. His first break came

with the 1924 British Empire Exhibition at Wembley, where the forms of the stadium and other structures had far more to do with the engineer than the architect, Maxwell Ayrton. Suddenly, and ironically unrecognised by his contemporaries, Williams was knighted at the age of thirty-four.

In 1929 the contractor on the Empire event, McAlpine, invited Williams to step forward as architect as well as concrete engineer, in order to design the Dorchester Hotel. The structural candour of the work was too much; he was sacked, taking the opportunity to send all the drawings around to the newly appointed architect, Curtis Green. But then followed the Daily Express buildings in Manchester and Fleet Street, with their dramatic use of curtain walling, and the Boots factories in Nottingham; the Peckham Pioneer Health Centre (1935); the Dollis Hill synagogue; and the Wembley Pool. (It was in 1938 that Tecton completed the Finsbury Health Centre; see page 322.)

After World War II, William's work switched to highways and bridges rather than buildings, although he still completed the structure of the Daily Mirror building (1955-61) in Holborn (now demolished and replaced by a Foster design for Sainsbury). His attitude to architects as 'decoration merchants' hardly helped endear him. There was also a bluntness about his architectural work devoid of those humanist and socialist concerns informing the work of Tecton on their Finsbury Health Centre. Nevertheless, some of his work is remarkable and it is worth looking at the Daily Express building in Fleet Street to gain an idea of how shocking his work was in that era. (What you see is basically an office frontage to a production shed – a traditional factory *parti*.)

Amyas Douglas Connell 1901–80
Basil Ward 1902–76
Colin Lucas 1906–88

Extant London works include:
• **66 Frognal, Hampstead**, 1936-8. The client had to go to the High Court before the house could be constructed. An MP described it as "one of the greatest acts of vandalism ever perpetrated in London."

Connell and Ward worked their way from New Zealand in 1924, studying at the Bartlett (1924-6) and later establishing a partnership with Lucas (1933), who had studied at Cambridge and married Connell's sister. Their key work is High & Over, Amersham, Berkshire (1929). The partnership was dissolved in 1939.

Wells Wintemute Coates 1895–1958

Extant London works include:
• **Lawn Road** flats, 1934. Since 'restored'.
• **10 Palace Gate** flats , Kensington. 1937-9.
• **Hampden Nursery School** in Holland Park, 1936.

It is reasonable to presume that the fact Coates was born and raised in Japan was significant in his later career as a designer. He lived in Tokyo until he was eighteen, when he set out on a cruise that took him to China, Egypt, England, and finally New York (where he apparently went up the Woolworth Building). He then enrolled at McGill University College in Vancouver, reading mechanical and structural engineering, but these studies were interrupted by the war, in which he fought in the trenches in France and Belgium with the 2nd division of Canadian gunners before applying to train as a pilot with the Royal Naval Air Service. He made his maiden flight over Orléans and Blois on 18 July 1918, shortly before the armistice.

Coates then returned to Canada, graduated in 1922 and came to England for postgraduate studies, completing a PhD in 1924. He then started work as a journalist for Lord Beaverbrook, on the Daily Express. (Beaverbrook was a rich Canadian who had come to England, given money to the Conservatives, immediately created a baron and nicknamed Been-a-Crook. But he liked to have other Canadians working for him.) Coates became the paper's Science Correspondent, in which role he went to Paris and met Le Corbusier, as well as making friends with Maxwell Fry in London. Some form of obscure opportunism now led him into retail design before he picked up a commission for a block of apartments in Belsize Park: what was to be the Lawn Road flats, designed for Jack Pritchard. A development company called Isokon was formed and each Isokon flat was equipped by Coates with purpose-designed minimal furniture and fittings (with meals and laundry provided centrally).

The reinforced concrete apartments, completed in 1934, were self-consciously experimental. The flats then became a gathering point for the Hampstead avant-garde, with the Bauhaus émigrés Marcel Breuer, Walter Gropius, and László Moholy-Nagy as early residents. To Pevsner, the Lawn Road flats were the "giant's work of the 1930s."

After this Coates stood as a natural leader of British Modernism. He was a founding member of Unit One – a group of architects and artists – and of the MARS Group of architects (Modern Architectural Research Group). Product design followed (notably for Ecko Radios), as well as studios for the BBC. But he was particularly interested in the idea of mass-produced housing and, during the war, designed the AIROH aluminium house. However, his dreams and other schemes were not realised; he had entered a difficult period of his life. His marriage had ended in divorce in 1937 and his emotional life is reported by his biographer as being in perpetual disarray; he was bad at managing finance, and his arrogance and tactlessness antagonised all but the most forgiving of his clients.

In 1955 Coates departed UK shores for Harvard University, dying of a heart attack over there in 1957.

Above and **below**: the Lawn Road flats – as famous for its early inhabitants as for the purist and vaguely maritime lines of its architecture (it sits like a docked ocean liner). The block was designed as a standard set of flats with shared facilities, so that young professionals could move in with the minimum of belongings. As Coates commented, ""We cannot burden ourselves with permanent tangible possessions as well as our real new possessions of freedom, travel, new experience- in short, what we call 'life'." And he wrote to prichard: ""My scheme provides a place which every actor in this drama can call his own place, and further than that my idea of property does not go. This is the room where I sleep, this is where I work, and this is where I eat. This is the roof garden where everyone can turn out ...This is the garden where everyone goes. It's like a park."

Extant London works include:
- **Nos. 85-91 Genesta Road**, Woolwich, 1933-34. Lubetkin's first completed building in this country, before Tecton.

As Tecton:
- **Highpoint I**, 1933-5, and **Highpoint II**, Highgate, 1936-38.
- former **Gorilla House**, 1932-3; **Penguin Pool**, 1934; **North Gate Kiosk**, 1936-7 (altered), London Zoo.
- **Six Pillars House**, Crescentwood Road, Dulwich, 1934-5.
- **Finsbury Health Centre**, 1938.
- flats: **Sadler House, Wells House, Tunbridge House**, Roseberry Avenue, all 1938-49, Open egg crate structure by Ove Arup used for the first time.

Skinner & Lubetkin, and **Skinner, Bailey and Lubetkin:**
(Note: it was first Skinner and Lubetkin, and then Skinner, Bailey and Lubetkin, suggesting Lubetkin's background role in these later partnerships.)
- three estates for Finsbury: **Priory Green** 1937-51; **Spa Green**, Rosebury Avenue, 1938-46 (now listed; the aerofoil roof design, by Arup, was intended to channel air over drying clothes); **Priory Green**, Collier Street, 1943-52 (the largest of the Finsbury estates). Also, **Priory Green extension** (Priory Heights), Wynford Road, 1946-57.
- **Hallfield Estate**, Bishops Bridge Road, Paddington, 1946-54 (Designed by Tecton, but executed by Denys Lasdun after the practice split up.)
- **Lakeview**, Old Ford Road, 1953-56.
- **Bevin Court**, Cruikshank Street, Islington, 1946-54 (now listed).
- **Dorset Estate**, Diss Street/Ravenscroft Street, 1951-57 (Daunting, but with a splendid central stair.)
- **Sivill House**, Columbia Road, 1960-2.
- **Cranbrook**, Roman Road, 1955-65.
- **Tabard Garden Estate**, Tabard Road, 1962-65.

Berthold Romanovich 'Tolek' Lubetkin 1901–1990

Hidden Tecton: members included: Douglas Bailey, Anthony Chitty, Lindsay Drake, Michael Dugdale, Valentine Harding, Denys Lasdun, Godfrey Samuel, Francis Skinner.

One can't be entirely sure of anything where Lubetkin is concerned, but it seems he was born in Georgia, son of a relatively wealthy Jewish engineer and spent most of his life denying this Jewish identity, even claiming to have been the son of a famous Russian admiral. It appears that he was educated in St Petersburg and Moscow and, by 1914, was already well travelled in France, Germany, England, and Scandinavia. Aged fifteen, he enrolled at the Stroganov Art School in Moscow and, after the Revolution, he attended the SVOMAS (free art) studios in St Petersburg and Moscow, and the VUTEMAS (advanced state workshops of art and industrial art) in Moscow. It was now that he is said to have come into contact with Rodchenko, Tatlin, Malevich, Mayakovsky, Vesnin, Popova, and Gabo – a celebrated grouping later to be added to by Klee, Grosz, Picasso, Braque, Léger, Gris, Soutine, Cocteau, Ernst May, Bruno Taut, and others. Our man was clearly fated for stardom.

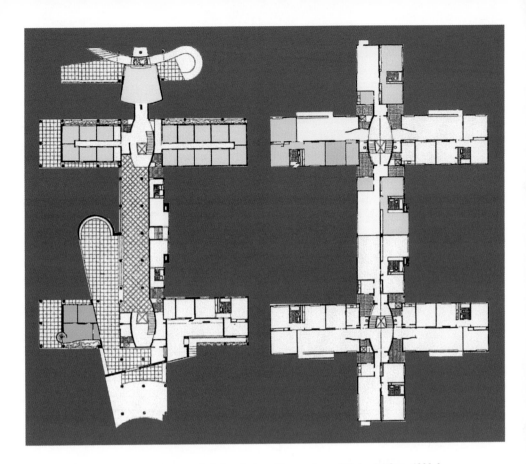

At twenty-one Lubetkin accompanied the first Exhibition of Russian Art to Berlin, in 1922, and afterward attended the Bauschule at the Technische Hochschule, at Charlottenburg, and the Höhere Fachschule für Textil und Bekleidungsindustrie (1922–3).

There was then a short study scholarship in Vienna, before a move to Poland where he took his diploma in architecture at the Warsaw Polytechnic (1923–5). It was here, he later claimed, that the name Lubetkin - the name of a dead Jewish person – was adopted in order to enter the university. Lubetkin then moved on to Paris, assisted in the construction of the Soviet pavilion at the Exposition des Arts Décoratifs (where he first met Le Corbusier) and attended the École Spéciale d'Architecture, the Institut d'Urbanisme, the École Supérieure de Béton Armé, and the École des Beaux-Arts. He also participated in the independent atelier of Auguste Perret, to whom Lubetkin later acknowledged an enduring creative debt.

Lubetkin's first independent architectural work was a block of apartments with Jean Ginsberg, completed in 1931. However he saw little prospect of further work and cast his eyes toward a place yet untainted by Modernism and Modernists: London.

Lubetkin made several exploratory trips and, in 1931, was even offered the commission for a private

Above: plans of Highpoint One, 1933-6.
Below: Highpoint One entry lobby.
Opposite page: garden view (the gardens and the facilities they provide are quite extensive).

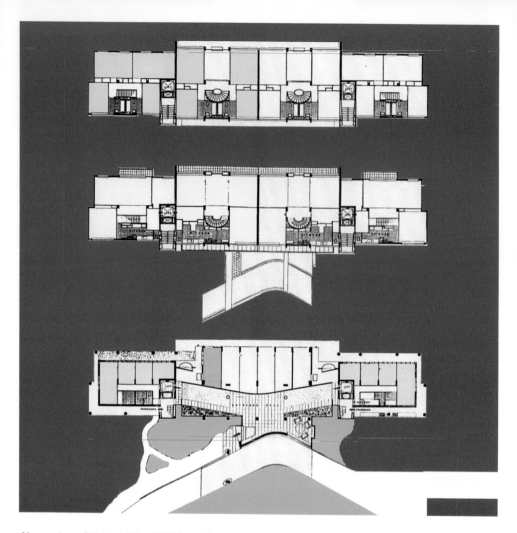

Above: plans of Highpoint Two, 1936-8, which remains one of London's more impressive apartment blocks.
Below left: Finsbury Health Centre – still a remarkable building.
Below right: the infamous entry canopy caryatids which upset so many purists. Lubetkin had a penthouse at the top of this block.

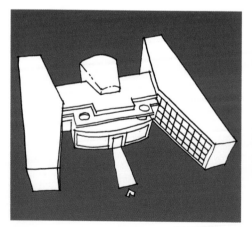

This page: The Bevin Court building in Islington (130 dwellings), near to Kings Cross, is far less strident than the later Skinner, Bailey & Lubetkin buildings. The central stair is especially impressive and the façade is indicative of Lubetkin's compositional concerns. The four-storey Holford House is a part of the same scheme; the two-storey Amwell House was added by the same practice 1956-8.

house in Hampstead (which proved abortive). However, in 1932 – together with six harvested graduates of the Architectural Association – he formed the Tecton partnership. He was, of course, the dominant partner.

John Allan, Lubetkin's principal biographer, tells us: *"His belief in building design as an instrument of social progress was underlaid by a profound appreciation of architecture's rational disciplines and emotive power. His Marxist convictions and his experience of the Russian Revolution implanted high expectations of architecture's role in transforming society, both through the provision of new and relevant building types – 'social condensers' [a distinctly Cedric Price concept] – and through its aesthetic capacity to project the image of an oncoming better world. Lubetkin's buildings were characterised by clear geometric figures, technical ingenuity, and intensive functional resolution. He dissociated himself, however, from the contemporary doctrine of functionalism, and sought a deeper synthesis of human, architectural, and philosophical values. Formal composition and a lyrical playfulness differentiate his designs from much* of the work associated with the international style; also unusual was Tecton's method of presentation whereby the rationale of a scheme was depicted in didactic analyses, witty cartoons, and slogans."

Fittingly, many first commissions came from the left-wing London borough of Finsbury (for example, the thoroughly impressive and now neglected Health Centre). However, the outbreak of World War II stopped progress on the designs of housing for the borough and, in 1939 Lubetkin was married (to an assistant in Tecton), naturalised, and abruptly moved with his new wife to a remote part of Gloucestershire, where he managed a pig farm. This move has never been satisfactorily explained, but being alien, Marxist, Jewish and (claims his younger daughter) a child witness to Russian *programs,* was probably sufficient prompt.

Allan insists Lubetkin was applying for registration as an architect and still using his Highpoint penthouse throughout the war and, by 1943, Lubetkin and Tecton were back designing for Finsbury and Lubetkin's design concerns were shifting to include stronger architectural expression in the form of façade pattern-making (arcanely making reference to kilim rugs, etc.). Spa Green and Bevin Court probably stand out, but later works from Tecton become progressively less interesting.

By 1948 Tecton had broken up. In part, this was prompted by Lubetkin taking an ill-fated appointment as Architect Planner to the Peterlee New Town, in 1947, but he resumed practice together with Francis Skinner (formerly of Tecton) and Douglas Bailey, producing several housing schemes in Bethnal Green. From the mid-1950s, however, he again withdrew from professional attention and in 1957 even considered emigrating to China. But he didn't, and Margaret Lubetkin's deteriorating health later caused them to give up the farm and move to Clifton, Bristol, in 1969. (She died in 1978.)

It was not until 1982 that Lubetkin emerged from the twilight to receive an RIBA Gold Medal and bask in the glory of being an old Modernist hero of some repute. Perhaps, however, that reputation as a talented architect will for ever be coloured by the ambiguities of his character and personal history.

Erno Goldfinger

1902–87

Extant London works include:
• **2 Willow Road**, 1939 (A National Trust property – by far the most interesting of the Goldfinger designs, although not the most dramatic or fashionable – that being the Trellick Tower).
• **Greenside School**, Westville Road, Hammersmith, 1950-3.
• **Brandlehow Primary School**, Brandlehow Road, 1951 (now extended).
• **10 Regents Park Road**, 1954-56.
• **45-46 Albermarle St**, 1955-7.
• French Tourist office, Piccadilly, 1956.
• **Alexander Fleming House**, Elephant & Castle, 1959-67.
• **Haggerston School**, Weymouth Terrace, 1962-7.
• **Balfron Tower** (part of the Brownfield Estate), nr. St Leonard's Road, 1965-7.
• Metro Central Heights (formerly Alexander Fleming House), Elephant & Castle, 1959-67 (to be dem.).
• **Trellick Tower**, North Kensington, 1966-72.

Below: Tecton's Hallfield Estate, at Paddington.

Below: Goldfinger's Trellick Tower, a remarkable expression of a complex section a la Le Corbusier.

"Mr Bond, it was a most evil day for you when you first crossed my path. If you had then found an oracle to consult, the oracle would have said to you "Mr Bond keep away from Mr Auric Goldfinger. He is a most powerful man. If Mr Goldfinger wished to crush you, he would only have to turn over in his sleep to do so." From the novel Goldfinger, Ian Fleming (1959).

"There are good and bad architects. I am a good architect." Erno Goldfinger.

The Chairman of the residents association at Trellick Tower was Lee Boland. Ms Boland once told reporters: "I met Mr Goldfinger in the lift once. I didn't know who he was but he kept asking me about the faults and what I liked and didn't like. I said I liked everything, except the designer hadn't put a broom cupboard in the kitchen. 'Bloody women,' he said. 'Never satisfied'."

The story is clichéd, but it does tell us something about the man: the tale of a minor encounter in the lift at the RIBA building in Portland Place. Here, a tall model of testosterone and good looks entered into a contretemps with a female member of staff half his bulk in getting into the building's diminutive elevator. "Do you know who I am?", the building's visitor contemptuously muttered: *"I am Erno Goldfinger!"* To which the retort was: *"I don't care if you're bloody James Bond."* This indignant underling's remark no doubt hurt her adversary more than she appreciated. He had already been in another contretemps with the author of the 007 novels, his former Hampstead neighbour Ian Fleming, who had mischievously used the name 'Auric Goldfinger' for the evil, gold-loving figure in the 1959 novel of the same name. Even Goldfinger's wife had been transmogrified into a heroin addict. Goldfinger had been alarmed, especially since the Jewish, foreign, gold-loving Marxist characterisation was not the kind of thing that would endear any architect to clients during the Cold War climate of that period (especially since Goldfinger had designed the offices of the Daily Worker and Communist Party in London).

Goldfinger's biographer, Lycett, tells us that *"Both Erno and his fictional counterpart Auric were Jews who had come to Britain during the 1930s. Both had overwhelming egos"*. And [...] both had *"an almost maniacal attachment to their own vision of the world which had its symbolism in a substance – gold in the case of Auric, reinforced concrete in the case of Erno."* Lawyers were called in. Asked for an opinion of the manuscript, an office colleague of Goldfinger mischievously remarked that the only difference was that *"You're called Erno and he's called Auric."* The outcome of it all was that the publishers agreed to make it public that all characters were fictitious, pay Goldfinger's costs, and do other minor things – including the delivery of six copies of the work to the Goldfinger household! Fleming was livid and asked the publishers to issue an erratum changing the character's name to 'Goldprick'. (A request that was not effected.)

The story is revealing. Goldfinger certainly had the reputation of being an overbearing, arrogant and bullying egotist (*"Everyone always seems to have known me"*). And it is perhaps not unfitting that his most famous extant work, Trellick Tower (completed 1972), should have been seen not only as the last gasp of a moribund mode of housing provision, but also of Brutalist sentiments. On the other hand, overbearing arrogance is hardly unusual among a talented fraternity of architects who have a reputation for such behaviour toward people seeming to be lesser creative mortals (or lower down the food chain, such as an employee) and Goldfinger does appear to have had a sense of humour.

A similar figure, for example, was Le Corbusier, whom Goldfinger met during his fourteen years in Paris (where his youth included time spent working for Auguste Perret, where Lubetkin had also worked). But there may have also been a distinctly English element in it all. Fleming himself was hardly without a similar reputation (enhanced by dissolution) and near the same age as Goldfinger.

Erno Goldfinger was born in Budapest, son of a wealthy lawyer, landowner, and industrialist. Early years were spent among the mountains of Transylvania, and later at school at the Budapest Gymnasium, but the family left Hungary following the communist putsch in 1919 and Goldfinger spent a year at Le Rosay School, in Switzerland, before moving to Paris in 1920 to prepare for admission to the École des Beaux-Arts. Paris, of course, was then the only place any young man of real artistic ambitions could be.

Initially, Goldfinger had been drawn to engineering (the family business had been in forestry and sawmills), but he discovered Hermann Muthesius's *Das Englische Haus* (1904-05: English domestic architecture within the Arts & Crafts tradition as observed by the German

Willow Road 1939

Goldfinger initially practised architecture in London from accommodation in Bedford Square, one of the city's best preserved and impressive squares of 18th century terrace houses, of which the architect was a confessed admirer. This enthusiasm was used against public indignation at his scheme at Willow Road, citing conformity with surroundings and the tradition of Georgian building. He entitled an Architectural Review article of the time 'The Decline of the Street – and an Attempt to Restore it'. The design, in other words, self-consciously strives to reconcile tradition and modernity.

The first scheme for apartments was rejected by the LCC. In 1936 Goldfinger amended the design to a terrace of four houses, further changing the design in 1937 so that the central pair were amalgamated into one (to be his own home, No. 2 Willow Road). House No. 3 was for Richard Wilson, a civil servant; No. 1 was a speculative development. However, he retained the vestige of a four-bay design.

The section has much in common with the traditional London town house and its mode of 'vertical living' as opposed to a horizontal Continental style. However, the small scale of the block reveals a contrary intention to suggest horizontality and that the building is one large villa (again, a traditional device, as used by Nash). This is principally achieved with the central window of the street façade, unifying the block with one long, horizontal element emphasised by a framing concrete surround. Similarly, the upper windows give no indication of the different living units behind them. In this way the three terrace houses pretend they are one pavilion (with classical 'ends', etc.). Again, the ground floor – entrances, garages, maids' rooms, kitchen (later moved to the first floor), wine store (and, originally, a tradesman's entrance) – is developed in such a way that the reality of separate entrance recesses and garages are disguised and unified. The window feature also plays a clever structural role. Goldfinger was anxious to remove the concrete columns and use thinner steel columns (like the window mullions) to free the window of structural intrusions and give a fee, 'look-no-hands' appearance. He does not do this on the rear façade. In addition, the street window is horizontally divided by a subsidiary feature: a light-shelf, used to reflect light onto the ceiling. This also serves to disguise the fact that there are thin steel stanchions beyond the glazing, holding up the upper floor.

Because the design employs a concrete frame and columns (following Le Corbusier's famous Five Points), Goldfinger is able to employ a comparatively free plan. He emphasises this in the way he locates the supporting columns free of walls and façades (particularly at the rear; at the front, this game is subverted by his wish to remove visible supports and offer a wide, unobstructed view out to the Heath). However, the party walls are his primary constraint and the 'freedom' that is possible lies mainly in an ability to locate lightweight partitions and sliding screens in the area around the central spatial fixes made by the spiral staircase, rising services and the fireplace. His intention was that the L-shaped space around the central spiral stair should be dynamically divisible by the screens. However, this freedom was again deliberately constrained by a split in level in order to differentiate front from back (similar to the manner that Adolf Loos split levels in his house designs). Thus the inherent freedoms provided by the construction are carefully orchestrated so that the idea of flexibility and openness is constantly offset against the constraint of particular commitments. Other floors were more conventional in arrangement, although the rear part of the upper floor was given over to three rooms with moveable walls in between: two rooms for the children and the third for a nanny. All walls were brightly coloured and two were left as bare plaster so that the children could draw and scribble upon them. The children's beds were fitted into recesses and the nanny had a foldaway bed. Other bedrooms also had built-in cupboards acting as room dividers. The flat roof enabled the internal bathrooms and the top landing to be top-lit. Interestingly, the design is thoroughly informed by Neo-Platonic geometries adapted to this small, suburban villa.

Although the home – although small – was that of a comparatively affluent and left-wing professional couple it nevertheless had two garages, rooms for two live-in servants, another room for a nurse, a wine cellar and (originally) even a separate tradesman's entrance (such were the social demands upon the respectable middle-classes of the later 1930s). The kitchen (alongside the maids' bedrooms) was on the lowest floor and a dumb waiter ferried meals to a servery on the piano nobile above. Another spiral stair, smaller than the main one, led from the servants area up to the ground floor entrance (a kind of upstairs/downstairs equation enforced at ground level and symbolised by the design of two stairs rather than one going from top to bottom). Around 1961 a small kitchen was created on the first floor (within the former servery area) and the original lower floor was converted into a family apartment, including a one metre extension toward the garden. This enclosed the piloti that had formerly stood free – idealism was giving way to pragmatism.

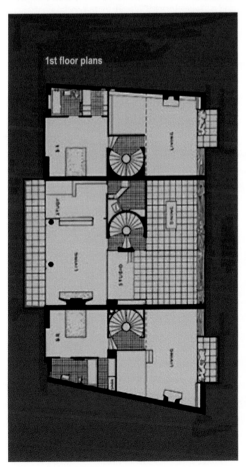

1st floor plans

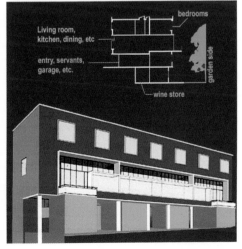

Living room, kitchen, dining, etc

entry, servants, garage, etc.

bedrooms

garden side

wine store

cultural attaché in London). The work, as we shall see, appears to have had a seminal influence upon the young man.

He later enrolled at the Ecole des Beaux-Arts but then became exposed to another influential work: Le Corbusier's Vers Une Architecture. It was another awakening: "So there I was in the Beaux-Arts, I'd finished my second class and had two valeurs in premier class. And here came out this absolutely staggering book, unreadable, but fabulous: Vers une Architecture. So all these things we were doing wasn't really architecture. So said Corbusier. We are going towards an architecture [...] Not a new architecture, not an old architecture, just towards architecture."

Corbusier was approached, but Goldfinger was passed on to Auguste Perret – who became another influential figure in his life. A new phase had opened in his life and his social activities (as with Lubetkin) now became associated with a host of notables: Loos, Mies, Man Ray, Lee Miller, Bill Brandt and others – including Lubetkin – frequenting the Parisian café scene (among whom Goldfinger, characteristically, recalled himself as being a central figure).

Then into this scene stepped an English woman of distinction: Ursula Blackwell, who had been a student of Amédée Ozenfant (of the Corbusier association) when teaching at Chelsea School of Art, and who was now in Paris continuing her studies. There was a meeting and romance blossomed. Two years later they were married and the couple moved from a French scenario having emerging political troubles on its Germanic door-step to London, where Ursula had a place as heiress to her part of the Crosse & Blackwell foodstuffs empire, founded in 1850.

Their immediate home was, appropriately, the new block of flats designed by Lubetkin and Tecton, Highpoint 1.

Goldfinger hardly had a thriving practice during these years, but he and Ursula managed to acquire a property in Hampstead, adjacent to the Heath itself, and set about making proposals for a speculative residential development (the one that was to apparently upset Fleming) which would include suitable accommodation for themselves.

What is interesting about this remarkable scheme – and makes the design so much more interesting than Trellick, for example – is its attempt to recreate the Georgian terrace vernacular in Modernist guise, complete with characteristic neo-Platonic measures underscoring the elemental and pure nature of the architecture. As with his marriage, Modernism was to be married to English tradition. Appropriately, the scheme was complete in another sense: the design was put together at a time when no self-respecting middle-class family would be without quarters for a maid (or two), no matter how small. Therefore what we can now visit as a National Trust property is keenly pivoted upon a unique historical moment in time that was soon to be cruelly interrupted by World War II. Of course, afterward, live-in servants and maids were to be an historical memory for the middle-classes and Ursula had to become an architect's housewife.

Fleming was, no doubt, entirely familiar with the fierce controversy over the Goldfinger terrace in Willow Road and one imagines that he was hardly sympathetic. The architect had to battle, despite the fact that this design is by far the most sensitive of all those he devised and still stands as an admirable work. In the meantime, while maids may have been dismissed and Ursula had to do the washing up herself (while the telephone rang in the middle of the night with those spoof calls regarding Mr Bond), there were social housing programmes demanding keen architectural talent.

Goldfinger's biographer tells us that, "The force of his personality, charming at times, explosive at others, was at the root of his achievement, and during his lifetime was almost better known than his architecture. His late work can now be seen, however, as the only major expression in Britain of the mature modern architecture of the 1950s and 1960s, deriving directly from the radical architectural thought of continental Europe in the period of the First World War." In fact, as an old man, Goldfinger was largely forgotten, described by himself as demonised, and by others as embittered and a 'Gucci Socialist' hungry for the social significance of a knighthood. If he had lived but a few years longer he would have found himself celebrated in an era hungry for architectural heroes and eager to give awards. On the other hand, it is quite likely that, ironically, the media would only have dealt with him as the unfortunate source for the figure in the Bond novel and movie.

His must famous work, Trellick Tower, remains iconic and loved by many architects but characteristically tainted by its nature as social housing and its Brutalist aesthetic, no matter how good the flats and views are and how many young architects want to live there. On the other hand, Willow Road – where the traditionalist hidden deeply within Goldfinger's character is revealed – arguably remains a far more relevant design to London's unique urbanism. In these terms Goldfinger perhaps epitomises the cultural predicaments of the inter-war period more than this radicalist poseur might have ever admitted.

Joseph Emberton 1889–1956

Extant London works include:
- **Summit House**, Red Lion Square, 1925.
- façade to the **Olympia** Exhibition Hall, 1929-30. At the rear, in Sinclair Road, is another Emberton block, 1936. Also, a large garage in Malaise Road, 1936.
- **Simpson's** department store, 1935-6 (for DAKS Simpson, then a pioneer in mass-produced clothing; now a Waterstone's bookstore); uses welded plate girders designed by Felix Samuely (the first in London); the façade – with its novel ground floor windows intended to obviate reflections – is enlivened at night by thin coloured neon lights and the interior had elegant shop-fittings and modern furnishings (elements of which remain).
- **No. 73 Great Portland Street**, 1937.
- **HMV**, 363-367 Oxford Street, 1938-39.
- **Stuart Mill House** flats, Pentonville Road, 1951.
- **Stafford Cripps Estate** buildings, Old Street, 1953-6. Three twelve-storey Y-plan blocks.

Above: the former Simpson's, in Piccadilly.
Below: Summit House, Red Lion Square.

Emberton was born in Staffordshire and became articled to Chapman & Snape, Newcastle under Lyme. He then won a scholarship to the Royal College of Art in 1911 and worked for the London architects Trehearne and Norman from 1913 to 1914. During WWI Emberton served in the Honourable Artillery Company, first as a gunner in Egypt and later as a trajectory officer in France, and was badly wounded in October 1918 (suffering nightmares about this for the rest of his life).

In 1918 he entered the office of Sir John Burnet and T.S. Tait, until he established a practice with P.J. Westwood, from 1922 to 1926. They designed exhibition pavilions and established a name for retail design as well as a reputation as Modernists, particularly after the Olympia façade design.

It was now that Emberton established an international reputation, particularly for the Royal Corinthian Yacht Club (Burnham-on-Crouch, 1931), and was selected to represent Great Britain's entry in the 1932 New York exhibition that produced the "The International Style" book by Hitchcock and Johnson.

During the Second World War Emberton was housing officer to the Ministry of Aircraft Production, architectural adviser on hostels to the Ministry of Works, and consultant to the Ministry of Supply on the design of steel houses. The Simpson building remains his finest work.

sunshine midst the gloom

David du Aberdeen 1913–87

Extant London works include:
• **TUC Congress House,** 1948-57.
• **Swiss Centre,** Leicester Square, 1961-6.

Aberdeen's claim to fame is the TUC's Congress House, won in competition in 1948 in a post-war period when the TUC's seventy staff represented nine million unionists. It was a grim period in London's history, with the Depression tears still fresh in people's memories. But, especially among architects, it was also one of optimism and hope for the future of post-war Britain.

One has to imagine this work of bright, transparent Modernism arriving in a tightly urban street of terraced, Georgian central London: a place prone to the dense fogs partly caused by air pollution. By the time the building was completed in 1957, the country was well on the road to recovery, the Clean Air Act was two years old and Aberdeen's building was a significant social symbol. Rock'n'roll was at the door, a service economy was developing and an 'angry young man' syndrome had arrived on the arts scene.

However, the opening also coincided with the beginning of a long period of union battles with governments of all political persuasion, reaching its finale with Margaret Thatcher's (employer and MI5-assisted) victory against the miners in the early 1980s. And Aberdeen was not to design another significant building.

In addition to the planning requirement that the building be no more than 80 feet high, tightly constrained by light angles, and that at least 10 per cent of the ground floor area of the site be kept open, the brief called for a conference hall, a training college, libraries, and a dining hall, together with a council suite, administration offices and supporting facilities. Aberdeen's scheme organises these disparate requirements within the overall framework of a three-sided courtyard building which latches itself onto the end of what was then a YWCA (designed by Lutyens; the building is now a hotel). This court was designed to bring daylight deeply into the block, even down into the basement conference hall, but it is also a pivotal, organising void to which everything else relates.

Aberdeen developed the overall architecture as a set of compositional elements within an underlying organisational formality, as if the overall scheme was a body laid on the ground, with a more significant head and two less significant side parts. At the lowest levels – the axial rear, in the deepest basement – Aberdeen filled the available space of the site with the boiler plant, stationery stores, a 'recreation room' and a 50 vehicle car park. He then added a floor accommodating the conference hall, large foyer, cloakrooms, kitchens and related facilities serving delegates and staff.

The ground floor sits between the conference hall and the upper parts of the building set around the central court. Here are the recessed entrances and major lobby spaces, the reception and stairs to the conference hall below, and lifts to the offices and committee rooms above. This is where everyone comes and goes, where cars enter ramps down to the lowest basement, where the General Secretary enters a lift to the top floor council chamber, and committee members head up to the committee rooms.

Although there are two entrances (one at each side, for the TUC at the front and tenants at the rear) the orientation of traffic is firmly toward the principal street façade on Great Russell Street. This is where Aberdeen locates a large figural sculpture called *The Spirit of Brotherhood*, designed by Bernard Meadows. But even here, he provides two entrances: a dominant one beneath the Meadows sculpture leads past the reception into the Memorial Hall lobby and, from here, a 'horse-shoe' stair leads downstairs to the conference room lobby. An adjacent entrance served by a vehicle drop-off point leads into a public 'street foyer' that offers a broad, direct view into the court and another stair down to the conference hall lobby. (The court was not designed for use; it is filled with upstanding rooflights to the conference hall below.) The entire first floor was given over to the training college and the rear top floor provided a caretaker's penthouse. Above, tenants were located one wing and the TUC administrative offices and committee rooms were opposite, on the Great Russell Street side.

Throughout, there is a clear differentiation of 'served spaces' (e.g. the offices) from 'serving spaces' such as plant area, kitchens, etc. For example, four cores, not clear on the ground floor, 'pin' the layered parts together. The formal axis supporting this divide

A foggy day, in London town:
it had me low, and it had me down.
I viewed the morning,
with much alarm,
The British Museum, had lost its charm.
How long I wondered, could this thing last,
but the age of miracles, it hadn't past.
And suddenly, I saw you standing right there.
And in foggy London town,
The sun was shining everywhere.

(George and Ira Gershwin, 1937.)

situates the head of the building on the side street. This is where the most important spaces are stacked, including the General Secretary and, right at the top, the council chamber. At the opposite end – toward the end wall of the court – is the most important part of the building toward which everything else relates: the end wall upon which the Epstein memorial sculpture hangs. The whole scheme is entirely inwardly oriented and a tour de force of planning.

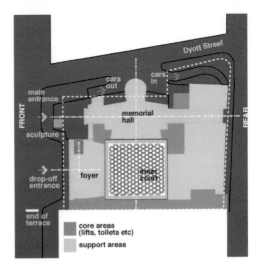

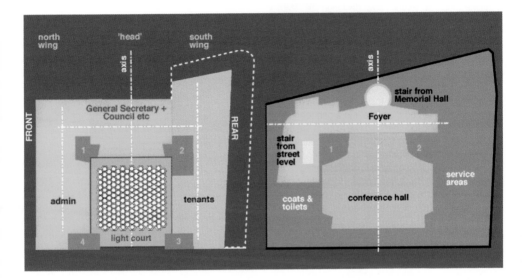

Right: TUC Congress House when opened, at a time when London has very few Modernist buildings. One thinks of the Royal Festival Hall as an obvious parallel: two very symbolic public buildings addressing the masses of post-war Britain.

Top: the site plan. This was carefully arranged so as to cope with different visitors (including for congresses) as well as people working in the building. Note the central light well. There is a distinctive body reference within the planning (left/right/head/feet).

Centre: the general scheme for the internal floors. On the left, the upper floors; on the right, the ground and basement floor (the hall is beneath the light well and has a glass ceiling).

Patrick Gwynne
1913–2003

Extant London works include:
• The **Homewood**, Esher, 1937-8 (The Gwynne family home, where the architect lived all his life.).
• **Four houses**, Coombe Hill Road, Kingston, 1959.
• **4, Beechworth Close**, Barnet, 1961.
• **The Firs**, 24 Spaniards End, Finchley, 1959.
• **115 Blackheath Park**, Blackheath, 1968. (An utterly kitsch design striving to be good?)
• **Nos 3 and 4 Beeworth Close**, Hampstead 1916-3.
• **The Dell Restaurant**, Hyde Park, 1964-5. The wonderful Serpentine Restaurant of the same date was demolished.
• **No.10 Blackheath Park**, 1968. A surprisingly bad design.

Homewood, in Esher, was designed by Patrick Gwynne as a young and promising architect then working with Denys Lasdun at the office of Wells Coates. At 24, Gwynne had persuaded his father to allow him to design a new family home on their property (the existing family house was, apparently, too near an increasingly noisy road). Daddy agreed, the home was built and Patrick lived there ever after. When his parents died he turned the place into a pad for himself and boyfriend, who together held (we're informed by the guides) rather entertaining dinner parties featuring, for example, a central table lamp that flashed when Gywnne considered a speaking guest was getting boring.

Completed in 1938, the house is clearly inspired by a mix of Corbusier (the Five Points, Villa Savoye, etc.), and Aalto (the Villa Maira) and is as good as it gets as an example of English Modernism of the period. It's an elegant and large but simple enough house, with spacious principal rooms on the first floor – separated into a living wing (with a long kitchen off it) and a sleeping wing – plus servants and study, garaging, etc. on the ground. The arrangements are very 1930s upper middle class and the house strikes a traditional note with its clear division between owners and servants, service rear and formal garden frontage. The surrounding gardens are very pleasant and the whole makes quite a contrast with London's East End that underscores the capital's historic westward orientation. Overall, it is not on a par with the European masters and has none of their originality, but it's good stuff and worth a visit, most especially for the 1950s and '60's modifications in Gwynne's study that are wonderfully 1960s James Bond and perhaps draw attention to the link between the '30's and the '60's that is more often denied rather than underscored.

Born in Porchester, son of a naval officer, Gwynne attended Harrow School and discovered the nascent English Modernism on family day-trips to the country. He entered the office of Coleridge & Jennings on what has been described as 'sub-Lutyens houses'. Then, in 1934 he found a job with Wells Coates (where he met Lasdun, who was to provide the bizarrely Baroque fountain on the house's terrace) and left to set up on his own in 1937, on the basis of the new family home. Both parents died during World War II and Gwynne took Homewood over, converting and refining its features.

It was also at this time that Gwynne won a competition to design a large restaurant for the Festival of Britain. Another restaurant built near to the Serpentine in Hyde Park was recently demolished (one remains). Meanwhile, his practice flourished and included many new houses, residential conversions and the like for actors and celebrities.

Below: the Homewood garden frontage. The living wing is on the left; the opposite wing is bedrooms above and studio below. In the diagram, the living wing has a service wing, top left, and a garden balcony adjacent to it, with a stair down to the terrace. The large windows of the living room overlook the garden; behind it is the kitchen (with direct access from the service wing). In between the living and bedroom wings is a lobby and large spiral stair. The design is, of course, thoroughly rooted in geometry and proportion, in the neo-Platonic manner, but now as a gesture of purity rather than cosmological belief.

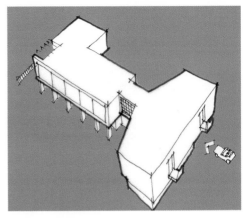

Edwin Maxwell Fry 1899–1987

Extant London works include:

• **Sassoon House**, Peckham, 1932-4, a block of working-class flats, with the engineer Kirkwood Dodds.
• **Miromonte** (private house), Fitzgeorge Avenue/ Warren Rise, Kingston, 1936-7.
• **Kensal House**, Ladbroke Grove, 1936. Rehousing for slum-dwellers, financed by the Gas Light and Coke Company (to prove gas was safe). Fry's most significant work in the UK. (With the housing consultant Elizabeth Denby.)
• **Sun House**, Frognal Close, Hampstead,1936.
With Jane Drew:
• **Passfields**. Lewisham, 1949-50.

Fry was born in Cheshire, son of commercial traveller from Canada, later a chemical manufacturer. During served in WWI and, in 1920, entered Liverpool University School of Architecture, under Professor Charles Reilly. Upon graduating Fry worked in New York before joining the office of Thomas Adams and F. Longstreth Thompson. His interest in planning, an important component of the Liverpool course, was to remain with him. As a partner in Adams, Thompson, and Fry, he designed in the refined neo-Georgian style typical of the 1920s. It was in 1924 that Fry met Wells Coates, who attempted a conversion to neo-Corbusian Modernism. That approach to architecture arrived in the guide of Gropius (1883–1969), the former director of the Bauhaus at Weimar and Dessau, who came to England in 1934 (at the time Sassoon House was completed). Fry set up a partnership which enabled Gropius to practise in England until his emigration to the USA in March 1937.

From 1939-44 Fry served in the Royal Engineers and ended the Second World War as town-planning adviser to the resident minister in west Africa. In the immediate post-war period, he gathered a group of talented young assistants, and worked in partnership with his second wife, the architect Jane Drew (1911-96; Fry had married in 1926, and was divorced and remarried in 1942). It was now the firm designed the Passfield Flats, Lewisham (1949), and a Riverside restaurant for the South Bank exhibition (1951).

Work in Africa began to figure strongly in the firm's commissions. However, Fry and Drew also spent three years in India, influencing the decision to invite Le Corbusier and Pierre Jeanneret as architects for the secretariat and law courts at Chandigarh (while the couple designed much of the housing). There was little further British work. Between 1952 and 1959 Denys Lasdun and Lindsey Drake assumed charge of the Fry and Drew office, running their projects in Britain while the latter worked on the Indian projects. Fry was awarded a CBE in 1953; in 1964 he was awarded the RIBA Royal Gold Medal, and elected ARA in 1966.

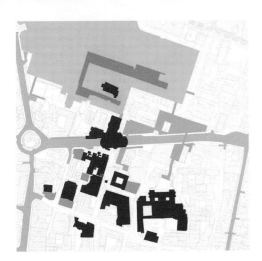

Donald Hank McMorran 1904–65
George Frederick Whitby 1917–73

Extant London works include:
- **Phoenix School**, 49 Bow Road, 1951-2.
- **Lammas Green** estate, Lewisham, 1955-7.
- **100 Pall Mall**, 1955-58.
- **Police station**, Wood Street, City, 1965.
- Central Criminal Court (**Old Bailey**) extension, 1973.

Some people simply don't fit any category, and that applies to McMorran and Whitby. Their two most significant works – the City police station in Wood Street and the Old Bailey extension, respectively completed in 1965 and 1973 – seem to belong to a world thirty years earlier. And yet they have a masterful, idiosyncratic strangeness that still gives them presence.

McMorran was educated at Harrow County School and served his articles with Horace Farquharson, then went to Vincent Harris for eight years. He returned to enter a partnership with Farquharson in 1935. He appears to have been active within the RIBA and well respected, being elected to the RA in 1962 and serving as one of the competition assessors who selected Chamberlin Powell & Bon for the Golden Lane estate. He died months after the completion of the Wood Street police station.

Whitby attended Ealing Grammar School, then the Regent Street Polytechnic – a study interrupted by the Second World War, during which he was in the Dunkirk evacuation, then in Africa (where he was wounded) with the Royal Engineers, before ending his service in England designing Bailey bridges. He returned to Civvy Street in the practice of Walters & Kerr-Bate, qualified in 1947 and set upon his own before later joining McMorran in 1958. He made a major contribution to the practice but also died months after the completion of his major work, the Old Bailey extension.

The Wood Street police station (on a site that was heavily bombed in World War II), is a particularly fascinating building: at once an Italian palazzo complete with pitched roof, large chimneys and central courtyard (where police horses and dogs are kept), together with a campanile, now as contemporary conjoined tower-and-podium typology (the tower being sleeping quarters for bachelor police offices – now, of course, largely taken over for offices and senior staff). The podium or palazzo block has peculiarly abstracted rustication and the walls of the reception lobby are lined with Roman stones found when the foundations were being dug.

Top: the Wood Street area, where the Roman fort was once located adjacent to London Wall, with the current Wood Street forming the fort's north-south axis. This is a rich architectural area mixing history and modernity, with buildings from Rogers, Foster, Sheppard Robson, Farrell, Giles Gilbert Scott, Chamberlin Powell & Bon, Wren, Dance and others. McMorran's police station is located centrally within this grouping (the rectangle with a central court in the plan).

Above: the station now. The church tower is the remains of a Wren church that was bombed in World War II. The former accommodation tower (once very prominent) is now surrounded by other towers and is used by senior staff.

Opposite page: Sun House, 1936 (Maxwell Fry)

Right: Ronald Ward in Oxford Street (1951; celebrating the Festival of Britain; latterly incorporated into a Zara shop designed by John McAslan). The design is distinctly pre-war and, in those terms, accords well with many other buildings of the later 1930s, and with coffee shops, exhibition stands, cinemas and the like. Within a few years Ward's architecture would be learning from the American post-war tradition of SOM (Lever House, New York) and providing London with one of its better and earliest office towers at Millbank. (For Ward, see page 380.)

Modernism: tainted and untainted

Sir Leslie Martin 1908-2000

Peter Meinhard Moro 1911-98

Sir Colin St John Wilson 1922-2007

Patrick Hodgkinson 1930

Neave Brown b1929

Peter Chamberlin 1919–78
Geoffry Powell 1920–99
Christoph Bon 1921–99

Peter Denham Smithson 1923-2003
Alison Margaret Smithson 1928-199

Eric Alfred Lyons 1912-80

Michael Neylan b1931
William Ungless b1934

John William Charles Darbourne 1935-91
Geoffrey James Darke b1929

Gordon Benson b1944
Alan Forsyth b1944

Sir Denys Lasdun 1914-2001

Sir Basil Urwin Spence 1907 -76

Edward Cullinan b1931

Sir Philip Powell 1921-2003
John Hidalgo Moya 1920-94

Sir Robert Hogg Matthew 1906-75
Sir Stirrat Johnson-Marshall 1912-81

Ronald Ward 1909-73

GMW
Fran Gollins 1910-99
James Melvin b1912
Edmund Ward 1912-98

YRM
Francis Reginald Stevens Yorke
1906-1962
Eugene Rosenberg 1907-90
Cyril Mardall (Sjöström)
1909-94
David Allford 1927-97
Brian Henderson b.1920

Richard Rubin Seifert 1910-2001

Archigram
Ronald Herron 1930-94
Peter Cook b1936
Warren Chalk 1927-87
Denis Crompton b1927
David Green b1937
Mike Webb b1937

Cedric Price 1934-2003

Modernism ... tainted and untainted

Andrew Derbyshire, once a well known post-war English architect, reminisced that, *"When I left the AA [the prestigious Architectural Association School of Architecture] in 1951, fired with enthusiasm to build the welfare state, I sought, like most graduates, to join the public service. We thought of private practice as money-grubbing, unfitted to pursue the ideal of social architecture."* Similarly, Ron Herron, a member of the Archigram group, another well-known and respected architect of the '60's and '70's, went to meet his maker proudly knowing that he had never worked for a speculative developer. And one of the more prestigious figures of those years, Leslie Martin, appears to have built upon his success at the Festival of Britain in 1951 by taking on large planning consultancy projects and handing on their development and execution to young architects he worked with in his studio and at

Above: *the bar at the Royal Festival Hall, from the official record, 1951. Regrettably, the recent refurbishment by Allies & Morrison filled-in this dropped area around the bar which had a peculiarly strong impact upon surrounding areas (health, safety and disabled access is quoted).*

Cambridge University (one thinks of Colin St John Wilson, undertaking the problematic British Library, and Patrick Hodgkinson designing the Brunswick Centre as a block of luxury flats). On a similar note, Peter Foggo, once the lead designer at Arup Associates during its most prestigious period of practice, did not suffer the ignominy of speculative work until he undertook the City's No. 1 Finsbury Avenue (1984; now a part of Broadgate, which he also master-planned and partly designed).

Post-war London architectural activity divided itself into three principal sectors: an extensive public building programme (including schools, university and hospital projects, but especially housing); cultural projects such as the South Bank (which introduced Modernism to the British public) and the later National Theatre; and what was frowned upon as 'commercial' architecture, of the kind undertaken by Colonel Seifert, GMW, Ronald Ward and others.

In other words, the period was not dissimilar to the programmatic conditions of the post recession years after 1995. Its hero, Sir Denys Lasdun, famously undertook two of these three categories of project: notably, the Hallfield School in Paddington and the so-called 'cluster' group of social-housing tower blocks in east London. Without approbation he also designed an up-market block of luxury apartments on the edge of Green Park (the first of the post-war period) and a less prestigious custom-designed office building for IBM, adjacent to his National Theatre. However, he stopped short at speculative building developments existing simply as a means to the end of making money and it was not until the late 1980s that his practice (by then Sir Denys Lasdun, Peter Softley and Partners) joined in the property boom and designed the speculative Milton Gate, in the City. By that time the heroes of the post-war period were older men overtaken by new events, values and tastes.

Like the young Derbyshire, a large number of post-war architects were engaged on urban renewal, slum clearance and the design of extensive new housing estates. Besides the work of Tecton, one thinks of projects undertaken by the Corporation of London (the City), the LCC and its successor the GLC, together with the Architects' Department of Camden Council. For example, the megastructural Barbican in the City, by Chamberlin Powell & Bon; the equally megastructural Brunswick Centre, in Holborn, and the Alexandra Road project designed by Neave Brown (the last and

The logo on the cover of the 'official record' of the Royal Festival Hall, designed by F.H.K. Henrion, illustrated by Gordon Cullen, David Dewar Mills, Henrion and Joseph Mayo, written by Cough Williams-Ellis, 1951 – soundly in keeping with the graphic tradition of the so-called George VI style of the 1930s. Ellis introduced the book by saying, "In a world darkened by doubt and danger a great work dedicated to the arts of peace has valiantly arisen. It shines to us and all men as an uplifting symbol of grace ...."

impressive, but perhaps least pleasant of such concrete beasts); and the large, brick-faced World's End Estate in Chelsea, where Eric Lyons demonstrated his skill in undertaking public housing that stood in salient and significant contrast with his cosy and contemporaneous work on the private Span estates in south London.

In turn, such works were to be contrasted with the low-rise/high-density housing work of architects such as Darbourne & Darke, undertaken toward the tail end of this era, especially in the early to late 1970s. In fact, London's housing of this period remains a fascinating and somewhat neglected topic that, by the mid-1970s, was fading into housing society projects undertaken by firms such as Farrell & Grimshaw (e.g. 125 Park Avenue) and Neylan & Ungless – often deliberately suburban in character, even when centrally located. However, within a few years Margaret Thatcher was to end a sometimes fine era of social provision and a national asset was to be handed over to free-market appetites (she also ended the post-war programme of new towns, many of which were aimed at depopulating London and as a means of coping with its heritage of slum properties and war damage). Even one of the great achievements of that housing programme – the Parker Morris space standards – were to lapse.

While such a broad programme of works was going on, London's historic core – the City – offered little of architectural value and interest besides the Golden Lane estate and the Barbican. New buildings had started to go up in the mid '50s, but Nicholas Pevsner, among many others, condemned much of the new work as worthless. The mean, early '60s neo-Miesian towers along London Wall (a part of what was then, in trans-Atlantic language, optimistically and indicatively called Route Eleven) epitomised the spirit of commercial office building during these years – a type waiting to be reinvented during the 1980s, together with the arrival of computers, American tenants, their architects, more trans-Atlantic tastes, and the novelty of speculative buildings specifically designed with the cultural needs of City money-spinners in mind. It was now (as the former London Docks closed and the economy as a whole moved more soundly toward a service economy) that the City sought to invert its historical traditions of conservatism and introversion by expanding outward and upward.

In 1959, the City initiated its futuristic Pedway network, aimed (bizarrely) at taking people up onto walkways, leaving the streets to cars whilst neglecting the rich potential of an age-old network of back alleys, away from traffic, that still (but only just) exists to this day (Leadenhall Market is one of the best examples). Nevertheless, Lombard street was, in the immediate post-war period, still paved in rubber (to quieten the sound of wheeled traffic so as not to disturb the bankers) and, in 1966, Ian Nairn could write about the City as "still as insular as if it were walled and gated." But times were slowly changing: the 'old' City was about to become the 'new' City and, as its biographer, David Kynaston, phrased it, a club no longer.

The very 'commercial' Colonel Richard Seifert first made an impact in the City with Drapers' Gardens (1962-5; dem. 2007), soon followed by GMW's rather elegant Commercial Union Tower (1963-9) – the latter a piazza-and-tower equation that was an updated version of the podium-and-tower typology characterising many office buildings in the post-war period and reflecting an enthusiasm of the Holden and Holford's otherwise conservative report of 1946 advocating the placing of buildings at the centre of a site, so as to increase the amount of daylight entering offices.

Seifert's work frequently had a tectonic expression that has now evaporated from the agenda of most British architects; however, much of his practice's work (spread all over London) is notable for being so forgettable. His reputation was somewhat resurrected in the post-recession era of the 1990s, by when every architect had

Opposite page: the literally gritty reality of 1950s and '60's 'New Brutalism' at the Hayward Gallery, on the South Bank, the product of the LCC and employees such as Ron Herron, Denis Crompton and Warren Chalk (admittedly, they had a rather more exotic original concept modelled on the Mappin Terraces at London Zoo, by Belcher & Joass, 1913-14). Many architects are now very nostalgic about such works.

been forced to admit they were either in business or out of practice but, apart from Drapers' Garden (1962-7) and Cutlers' Gardens (1978-82), his firm's best work was in the West End, not the City. In particular, there is London's towering landmark of Centre Point (1959-66): marvellous above ground and banal at street level (a recurring difficulty with Seifert's work), where highway engineering intruded its voice (they 'intervened', as architects horribly like to say).

Stylistically, the post-war period had the Festival of Britain as its great landmark: to this day represented and ghosted by the Royal Festival Hall's mix of Scandinavian values wrapped by a later generation's tougher neo-Corbusian concerns, followed by even more coarse ambitions that surrounded and islanded the building with the deck of the South Bank Centre (similar to the Barbican deck and with an historical pedigree that goes back to the likes of the Adams brothers' work at the Adelphi). Here, 'Brutalism' found its heroic but rude and intentionally gritty voice.

Two of the celebrated heroes of that 'Brutalist' era were Alison and Peter Smithson, whose Robin Hood Gardens Estate on the Isle of Dogs (a rather late example of such ambitions) strove to modify the underlying typological agenda of Le Corbusier's towers in green spaces to 'streets in the air', but was equally fated to become another unloved concrete monstrosity bearing a sad composure and a variety of strapped-on security measures manifesting the oft quoted and painful cliché learned during this era of provision: what is owned by everyone ends up being owned by no-one, especially when the landlord is a largely absent local municipality.

These two prickly heroes of the period also gave London one of its outstanding private developments, near to the Lasdun apartments overlooking Green Park, and still a rare ornament to London's fabric: the Economist complex in St James. Here, the gritty toughness that coloured Brutalism's values was lent an elegant sartorial presentation that has never been equalled by similar speculative developments all across London. It remains surprisingly refreshing.

It was the Smithson's who were the heroes of a still younger generation immediately following them, the latter giving voice to a mix of Machine Age Futurist values, nineteen-thirties comic-book graphics, and an appetite to emulate the consumerism of post-war American 'pop' culture in the guise of a grouping called Archigram. Its members were fronted by a sparkling

Collecting ads . . .

The mid-1950s witnessed an art world that invented 'Pop', the term construed by Lawrence Alloway to describe a set of values and a body of debate that ran counter to British architecture's post-war marriage of art and science, and an orientation toward all things Scandinavian. The art scene was witness to the 'Kitchen Sink School', the 'Social Realists', etc., and enjoyed an acute sensitivity directed against the neo-Platonic, high-cultural values of previous generations. Its debates centred around an informal and short-lived gathering called the Independent Group, who purportedly shared a serious curiosity in the vulgar customs of popular culture as a source of vitality, interest and value – what Alloway described as "an acceptance of science and the city, not on a utopian basis, but in terms of fact condensed in vivid imagery." He also remarked that the Group's agenda was "something both more simple and more intimate, more common and more fantastic ... a serious taste for popular culture, a belief in multi-evocative imagery, and a sense of the interplay of technology and man [...] an extension of aesthetics into the man-made environment and a consequent shift of both in the iconography and space of art. Space became defined as intimate, occupied by known objects or images, a world in close-up, with aesthetic distance drastically reduced."

And it was Alloway who famously declared, 'But Today We Collect Ads' – an enthusiasm expressed in the 1956 exhibition 'This is Tomorrow', about which Alloway noted: "The feeling is not an easy one to set down, but it was a kind of subjective sense of the city, as a known place, defined by games, by crowds, by fashion."

As architects associated with members of the Independent Group, Peter and Alison Smithson represented sentiments opposed to Futurist-inspired calls to renew European cities and expressed more interest in an existentially-inspired sentiment embracing the grittiness of urban life and its social issues: what, as an approach to architectural design, Reyner Banham was to label 'New Brutalism', a term first employed in the Architectural Review of December 1955.

In an era far removed from the eighteenth century Rule of Taste, the artists Gilbert and George could, when asked "What's your favourite colour?, declare: "We don't have taste. We're artists."

"Let us be frank about it: most of our people have never had it so good. Go around the country, go to the industrial towns, go to the farms, and you will see a state of prosperity such as we have never had in my lifetime – nor indeed ever in the history of this country." Harold Macmillan, Prime Minister, 1957.

critic and teacher who was strangely anti-academic, distinctly apolitical, and even anti-intellectual (Peter Cook), and perhaps had their grounded pillar of strength in an East End boy who made good: Ron Herron, a man whose charismatic personal stature and graphic talents were witness to the regrettable fact that rather more is needed for success in an architectural career.

In an era when 'what it does for you' was said to be more important than 'what it looks like', there was a certain irony to Archigram's graphic polemics which perhaps underscored the argument that architecture enjoys a true substantive value as a built thing. Its heroism lies in the situated nature of acts of conception and realisation, and the concept of graphic action as an intermediate stage in practice is plausible but unconvincing (whether it is Piranesi, Sant'Elia, Tschumi or Herron at issue).

Herron's built contribution to London's fabric – at the South Bank, whilst working at the GLC with Denis Crompton and Warren Chalk, also of Archigram – stands in marked contrast to his principal built work: the conversion of an Edwardian building for Imagination; a gem hidden behind an Edwardian façade (recently and perhaps appropriately, threatened by its own client's expanding and changing needs). Nevertheless, as polemicists, Archigram dared to frontally attack Architecture's traditional ideological stance as a coherent unity resistant to all that is mutable, inconsistent and part of the threatening flux of time. The daunting unpredictability of change was positively embraced by propositions substituting 'features' and an aim to 'extend the available range of choice' for a tradition of reassurance in formal fixities (nevertheless, perhaps with the same end-intention). Change, when it came, was to leave the group high and dry. Forty years later, however, the young subversives were old establishment members whose grouping included a knight of the realm and who were collectively RIBA Gold Medal winners. Oddly, Significance had been realised, even without particular Success.

The post-war period of London architecture was manifestly at an end when, during the later 1970s and particularly during the 1980s, its architects came to divide themselves into two camps: between so-called Post-Modernists and High-Tech enthusiasts who, between themselves, engendered a debate largely devoid of that social, ethical or moral content taken for granted by an earlier generation. It was a debate

Above: Patrick Gwynne's neo-James Bond studio desk at Homewood. (In/out/pending trays at one end, an intermediate writing space, and a drawing board complete with an American Mayline drafting machine.

drawn to an abrupt close by the economic recession which arrived in late 1989 and lasted until about 1994. During that period approximately one third of the profession was unemployed, one third had a name-plate up at the door and nothing to do on the drawing board (architectural computing was still comparatively primitive, and expensive; most architects had not yet discovered the joys of the desk-top computer) and only one third had work.

When dawn broke the struggles of the '80's were quietly and quickly forgotten in a manner that remains without explanation. Post-Modernism was dead and, with it, died its contrasting posture, Hi-Tech.

Architects emerged into a reality that was arguably post-modern in a more profound sense. The low-cost desktop computer had become a reality; the Internet had arrived; a new era of constructional techniques, tolerances and practices was emerging; the *Zeitgeist* was now characterised by the dynamics of algorithms and complexity theory; decoration and ornamentation were making a comeback; and even former Hi-Tech heroes such as Foster began to churn out works rich in historical reference as an architectural garb – but now referencing Modernist precedent rather than a neo-Classical one. (Interestingly, there is only one neo-Gothic PoMo building in London: GMW's Minster Court, in the City.) Everyone was now more genuinely 'post-modern'. Certainly, Modernism's ideological alliance with left-wing sentiment was now a vague memory, as was an era of architect's departments in local authorities. Kynaston's booming City of well-rewarded financiers may have been 'a club no longer', but the RIBA was once again a club of private practitioners.

ARCHIGRAM EIGHT

Above: *Archigram Eight, 1968: 'Popular Pak Issue', including description of an Archigram exhibition installation in Milan (a 'Milanogram') on the theme of "personal choice that one can have over one's environment and the ways in which new combinations of parts can catalyse that choice." The ostensibly satisfying reassurances of neo-Platonism had at last been superceded by hedonistic consumerism. The issue's editorial claimed that, in the future, "we can take advantage of techniques like market research, high-stress technology, consumer-assembly but make sure that the context for them breaks out of the limited barriers of taste, town-planning and the various mystiques invented by so-called 'experts' – the latter being of point of populism that was almost a throw-back to an Arts & Crafts anti-academic sentiment bearing echoes of Adolf Loos' scathing voice. However, Loos would hardly have shared an enthusiasm for the sentiment that the future was to be bottom-up, not top-down. Anything resembling Shaftesbury's (dreary) notion of taste was utterly rejected; all that Wren had deemed to be (hedonistically) creaturely, arbitrary, material and mutable was to enjoy a Futurist embrace. Architecture and architects had to dump their baggage and adapt to the circumstance of Pop.*

Changing times ...

Peter Davey, Peter Smithson and Peter Cook in conversation, 1984:

PD: What is culture?

PS: Progress – survival and progress.

PD: Do you accept the political dimension?

PC: No. It gets in the way.

PS: Particularly as you get older, you get like that: if you have gifts, you're obliged to offer them somehow to the community.

PC: I don't rate the community that highly. ...

PS: But isn't the morality inescapable?

PC: It may or it may not be – I want to go forward hoping that it can be escaped. ...

PD: (to SPS) So, your architecture is a potential statement?

PS: That's right ...

PC: I've always found the whole thing [socialism] like doing PT at school!

PS: I disagree with Peter Cook's position. In the 50's, we decided that we had to make artefacts that brought the benefits of the Modern Movement to working people ... This commitment was implicit in our artefacts; it was implicit that there was to be more equity in society. That was the tradition which we inherited from the [Philip] Webb time – but it was fractured at home. We had to get it back from the Continent.

Ted Cullinan (2008 Gold Medal winner) on an 'English architecture' and the notion of architecture as being liberating (1984):

"The period of the nineteen hundreds seem to me a fairly certain time for this tradition [an architecture of liberation] to run out of steam. It was a period of quite shattering invention and consequent ideas, of electricity, radio, movies, motor cars and flight; of Einstein's proposal of the First Theory of Relativity and most powerfully our own art, the idea of cubism and the idea of the machine allied to the existing idea of art as liberator. And it is at this time that England ... falters and loses its domestic architectural traditions in the developing and inventive sense and starts to see it only nostalgically. ... The period ends in the 1950s when England, through the Smithsons and others, becomes connected to an international tradition, to an architecture of hopeful invention ... England is now part of a large scene; and though one can trace a number of peculiarly local reactions in the design of buildings, none could be said to constitute a live and particularly English tradition ... for the strange thing about a living tradition in architecture is that it needs to be inventive and energetic, to be liberating, to respond to the present, to create futures, the opposite to the debased use of the word traditional to mean nostalgia. In a way its like Gertrude Stein saying that America is the oldest country in the world since it's lived in the present for the longest."

Sir Leslie Martin 1908–2000

Extant London works include:
• **The Royal Festival Hall**, Southbank, 1951.

Martin stands as a peculiar figure in post-war British architecture: an achiever himself, as designer and teacher, knighted at a relatively young age, and someone who was crucial to the career of many other architects.

He was born in Manchester, son of a church architect, and studied architecture at Manchester University. He graduated with an MA in 1932 and a PhD in 1936, and began teaching at Manchester in 1930. In 1934 he was appointed head of the school of architecture in the Hull College of Art and had four students, but managed to attract Serge Chermayeff, Maxwell Fry, and Marcel Breuer, the mathematician Jacob Bronowski, the artist Laszlo Moholy-Nagy, and the critics Herbert Read and Morton Shand (among others) to lecture both to his students and audiences.

At this time he acquainted himself with artists and critics such as Morton Shand, Barbara Hepworth, Ben Nicholson and Naum Gabo. With the latter two he edited Circle: International Survey of Constructive Art, first published in 1937. Together with his wife, Sadie Speight, he had started in practice in 1933, and between 1935 and 1939 completed several conversions and small houses in the north of England. This work was within the modern movement, but largely built of brick with some local stone. He also did some furniture design.

However, work must have been sparse: in 1939 Martin moved on from Hull to London, working for the London, Midland and Scottish (LMS) railway as principal assistant architect for a modernisation and development programme. The war shifted the nature of this railway work and, in 1948, nationalisation brought the firm's programme to a halt. Martin now grasped an opportunity to join the team appointed to set up a festival of Britain, in London, under Robert Matthew, the LCC's architect.

He was placed in charge of the project and built up a team including Peter Moro and Edwin Williams as his principal assistants. Their major challenge was the design of a large concert hall for 3,000 together with all the necessary foyer and ancillary accommodation on a small site (the Royal Festival Hall).

Later, in 1953, Martin succeeded Matthew as architect to the council during a period when the LCC architects department was involved in a large programme of building projects. However, by 1956 he was back in education: appointed the first professor of architecture at the University of Cambridge and head of the department of architecture, where he established a research Centre for Land Use and Built Form Studies (renamed the Martin Centre in 1973, after Martin had been at Cambridge for sixteen years), particularly noted for the work by Martin and Lionel March on planning geometries in housing.

Between then and 1986 Martin and his wife established a private practice in Cambridge, undertaking many major consultancy projects, including one for a new British Library, and the housing project in Holborn called the Brunswick Centre, but encouraging others to take over executive work. He designed Harvey Court, a Cambridge residential court composed with stepped terraces for Gonville and Caius College in Cambridge, designed with Patrick Hodgkinson and Colin St John Wilson and completed in 1962. Hodgkinson later executed the Brunswick project and Wilson undertook the execution of the British Library – both projects dominating their respective careers.

In addition to teaching and practising, Martin played an important role as a competition assessor – notably, one of three who selected Jørn Utzon's design as the winning entry in the Sydney Opera House competition. His advice was also instrumental in the appointment of Stirling and Gowan at Leicester; Chamberlin, Powell, and Bon at Leeds; and Denys Lasdun at East Anglia (all university projects). He even recommended Alison and Peter Smithson for the Economist commission. Richard MacCormac, one of his more distinguished students, wrote after his death: *"No architect of his generation sustained a more consistent intention to relate theory to the procedure and outcome of design."*

Martin was knighted in 1957 and was awarded the RIBA Gold Medal in 1973. He was also the Institute's vice-president (1955-7).

Despite its early 1960s refronting, the addition of a surrounding concrete deck and a certain degree of sanitising during the RFH's recent refurbishment, it remains one of London's most important architectural works. **Above**: the river frontage. **Below**: the south façade. **Left**: Cullen image and section through the auditorium, from the Official record. **Bottom**: the refurbished interior, beneath the auditorium.

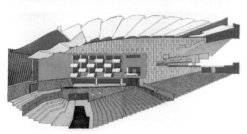

*A*fter the 1951 Festival the fate of the R.F.H. became entangled in a number of proposals for the area. To some extent these always included addressing earlier cutbacks to the R.F.H. programme, particularly the loss of a second chamber or 'small hall' as it became known. By 1953 a master plan from Leslie Martin was in place envisaging a science area of learned societies and various government departments; by 1956 a proposal for a tall tower within that master plan had become the Shell building that still sits opposite Waterloo Station (designed by Howard Robertson). The latter entailed demolishing the last remaining part of the festival other than the R.F.H.: the 'Telekinema'. As a replacement, a low budget home was found beneath the arches of Waterloo Bridge for what was to become the National Film Theatre.

Martin left the LCC in 1956, but both he and subsequent LCC architects considered the debate concerning a second chamber was also an opportunity to amend the building. The new ICA (Institute of Contemporary Arts, now in the Mall) was also looking for a home, and, together, these needs prompted the idea of a chamber and gallery on the Southbank. This is what became the Southbank cultural centre comprising the Queen Elizabeth Hall, the Purcell Room and Hayward Gallery.

There was even a feeling that the neo-Scandinavian sentiments of the 1951 design of the Hall were, as Warren Chalk characteristically remarked, an example of 'nautical whimsy'. Reyner Banham agreed. In 1967 he wrote that the amended R.F.H. was "restrainedly academic in its planning, ingenious in its sectional organisation, technically complex, eruditely modern, and unmistakably continental in its choice of style. And it has been extraordinarily fortunate in its later alterations: largely the work of Robert Maxwell and Allan Forrest, these broad and generalising simplifications of the exterior, paring away fidgety elements of the lamentable 1951 style, have revealed even more clearly its debt to the work of Le Corbusier in the nineteen-thirties. Here, thanks to sympathetic scholarship, the most derivative phase of English modernism was laid to rest with a flourish of erudition as apt as a Latin epigram."

The new generation undertaking this 'laying to rest' developed the Southbank on a more gritty keynote: what Banham was to label 'the New Brutalism". This novel aesthetic preference informed the evolving proposals for the area and involved three architects in the 'Special Works Group' who were to form one half of the famous Archigram team: Warren Chalk, Ron Herron and Denis Crompton. These three worked under Noran Engleback, John Attenborough and later Geoffrey Horsfall in a climate that partly embraced the Brutalist aesthetic on the basis on protecting the proposed chamber from external noises such as a proposed helicopter service that was to run along the length of the river. Herron was to undertake work on the cladding of the new buildings (modified from in-situ to precast because of opposition from Hubert Bennett, who had succeeded Leslie Martin)

Above: photos by Leslie Collier, 1951, of the riverside and south frontages of the RFH.

and Chalk was involved with the new walkways that were to prove so unloved and controversial. But it was apparently W.J. Appleton and Jimmy Blyth who were largely responsible for the implementation of building work, in 1964.

Bob Maxwell had spent time on the design of the R.F.H. façades and works were started in 1963-64 (by which time Maxwell was no longer at the LCC; consequently there is controversy about responsibility for the actual work). In any case, the 'nautical whimsy' was removed without sentimentality and changes implemented that included removing all of Robin Day's 1951 furniture, replacing transparent terrace balustrading and removing a decorative pattern of small windows in the cladding. The south side (having a temporary façade designed by Trevor Dannat) became a rear end and the front car park was excavated to provide a new entrance lobby and cafe, entirely altering the flows into the principal lobby area (which now had entrances on the river side). Vehicles were now brought around to the river frontage, under a new pedestrian deck at first floor level. Interestingly, these changes are things that are have been partly reversed by Allies & Morrison's refurbishment work (completed 2007).

Peter Meinhard Moro 1911–1998

Extant London works include:
- **Fairlawn School,** Forest Hill, 1958.
- **No. 20 Blackheath Park**, 1958 (Moro's own home).
- **St John's Estate**, of Tooley Street, Southwark, 1969.
- **Nos 76-78 Montpelier Road**, Camberwell, 1969-73.
- **Wessex House**, No. 375 Old Kent Road, 1971-4.

Below: drawings of the interior foyer bar and the auditorium from the Official record of 1951 – designs for which Peter Moro bore significant responsibility.
***Bottom left**: Morro's own home in Blackheath Park.*

Moro, baptised as a catholic, was born in Heidleberg, and was at university studying architecture when it was discovered that his mother was Jewish and he was forced to leave. He moved to Zurich and later to London, where he went to work for Tecton.

In 1938 Moro worked on his first solo job, given to him by Laszlo Moholy-Nagy, to design the entrance screen to the 1938 MARS (Modern Architectural Research) Group exhibition held at the Burlington Galleries, London, and opened by Le Corbusier. During the war, Moro experienced six months of internment but in post-war years spent seven years teaching at the Regent Street Polytechnic. In 1947, he began to collaborate with the industrial and furniture designer Robin Day on a series of exhibition designs and in the following year was chosen by Leslie Martin as his associate architect on the Royal Festival Hall project – on which he was responsible for the interiors, including the auditorium. In 1952 he set up his own practice and undertook a variety of theatre projects. He also undertook public housing schemes, mainly for the London borough of Southwark.

Sir Colin St John Wilson
1922–2007

Extant London works include:
- **British Library**, St Pancras, 1962-97.
- **St Mary's University Library**, (with Kentish & Long, his wife's practice).
- **British Library Conservation Centre**, St Pancras, 2007 (with Kentish & Long, his wife's practice).

Sandy Wilson was born in Cheltenham as the son of a man known as 'the Red Bishop', because of his political leanings. In 1940 he went to Cambridge to study architecture and later studied at the Bartlett, then under the leadership of the rather reactionary Albert Richardson. After service in the navy during the war he went to the LCC, 1950, as many idealistic young architects did. At this time his interest in contemporary art led him to a group including Ron Kitaj and Eduardo Paolozzi, and he participated in the Sunday morning meetings of the Independent Group with the architects Bob Maxwell, Alan Colquhoun, Jim Stirling, Peter Carter, and others, at the house of his neighbour Peter Reyner Banham. He began writing articles for the Observer

and participated in the 'This Is Tomorrow' exhibition put on at the Whitechapel Art Gallery in 1956. Wilson then returned to Cambridge to teach at the University school and work for Leslie Martin, its Professor and Head. In this role he worked with Patrick Hodgkinson on Harvey Court and there began his worship of Alvar Aalto's work (then a friend of Leslie Martin), so evident within the hall of the completed British Library at St Pancras.

In 1965 Wilson was able to set up in private practice with a 'rent-a-crowd' of students giving visitors the impression of lots of work. Meanwhile, in 1962, Leslie Martin had been commissioned for a study to provide a new British Library – and Wilson worked for him. By 1964 Wilson was fronting and controlling the project – one that dominated his life and practice until 1999 (not helped by a change of site, to St Pancras, in 1974). Meanwhile, in 1975, he also took up the Chair of Architecture at Cambridge.

When the library building opened, Wilson declared: *"As a result of being the architect of what has been called the great British disaster I have no work and my practice, the actual partnership, has now dissolved."* He then worked with his wife's practice (Long & Kentish, who designed the Chichester Art Gallery that houses

The British Library

Prince Charles famously made rude remarks about the British Library, even as the steelwork was going up. And it is true: this is not the loveliest of buildings. But step into the lobby – Wilson's homage to Aalto – and one must surely be somewhat impressed. Aalto may have done better, and the glass box housing aged and valuable books may be a straight rip-off from SOM's 1960s Rare Book Library at Yale, but this building has its moments. It will always be monumental and derivative, but it deserves some respect. The project began as a Martin-Wilson consultancy intended to demolish half of Bloomsbury to house a library extension. Luckily, 1970s populist sentiment against such schemes helped

Wilson's notable art collection).

In true British tradition, Wilson was knighted in 1998, upon the Library's completion.

cut-back the project and move the site to St Pancras – where Wilson's problems continued (touches of Barry at Westminster and Street at the Royal Courts of Justice). The (latterly modified) external piazza is now a surprisingly pleasant space on a busy main road, and the public lobby areas may be derivative, but are successful and generous spaces. Externally, the façades suffer from heavy-handed sun-louvres and a manner of styling that anxiously prevaricates between choosing Aalto or vaguely Classical Post-Modernism. However, what you see is the tip of an iceberg that is mostly underground (see the section opposite).

Top left: overall view of the British Library. Scott's hotel building is on the right.
Left: typical section, indicating how the book stacks are deeply underground and Wilson made extensive use of top-lighting.
Above: view of the Aalto-influenced entry hall – perhaps one of the more successful of contemporary public spaces, although (as usual) already becoming cluttered.

Left: the British Library. In the background are the spires of George Gilbert Scott's Midland Hotel, at St Pancras Station, now home to the Eurostar trains. Wilson used the same brick on the Library.

Patrick Hodgkinson b.1930

Hodgkinson studied at the AA, spent some of his 'year-out' in Alvar Aalto's office, and then at the office of Felix Samuely before moving on to Leslie Martin (who was then working with Lionel March on issues of built form and density). As a Professor at Bath University, he made a career out of the building Martin handed over to him: the Brunswick Centre (the basis of Hodgkinson's practice, set up in 1962). It's recent refurbishment – involving its principal author – has turned a rather sordid 1960s megastructure into a glowing monument to that era, raising forgotten issues regarding urban form. Hodgkinson also taught at the AA and the Royal College of Art.

Extant London works include:
• **The Brunswick Centre**, 1959-72.

Hodgkinson worked on the Foundling Project (as it was initially known) as an ill-fated speculative development (of luxury flats) that went wrong and became social housing – then continued to go wrong, with a variety of compromises and cut-backs which included the sacking of the architect (in 1970). Nevertheless, this is a heroic scheme whose recent refurbishment illustrates just what can be done. The scheme had been intended as a demonstration project for Martin's low-rise/high-density message (an alternative to then prevalent tower blocks promoted by the governments of the day). However, apart from Futurist associations, the scheme reminds one of Hans Holleins famous drawing of an aircraft carrier set into a landscape and has been received in these incongruous terms up until its recent (and extensive) refurbishment. Strangely, but perhaps understandably, Hodgkinson strives to deny this is a megastructural scheme or that he ever was, in any way, a 'Brutalist' as opposed to a neo-Georgian man of sound tastes. "I don't care about hi-tech, brutalism or modernism," he once remarked, "They're all concerned with look. ... Too often this place has been written up as a megastructure, but there's no such word in my dictionary."

The basis of the development was a design for the Loughborough Road Estate in Lambeth by the LCC, where Sir Leslie Martin was the chief architect and Hodgkinson was employed. This was followed by a low-rise / high-density theoretical project by Martin, with Hodgkinson, for a site in West Kentish Town. In the background to both these schemes we are told was Hodgkinson's student work of 1953. The latter, however, was for largely four-storeyed maisonettes using a cross-over or scissor plan, while the section of the Brunswick Centre more closely resembles Harvey Court, 1957:

Martin's Cambridge project which employed Hodgkinson and Colin St John Wilson. (Martin was, by then, running the Cambridge School of Architecture.)

The first scheme was prepared during 1959-3 with Sir Leslie Martin; it was modified in 1964-5 (when Camden took over the scheme), and again in 1966-8 (when Hodgkinson was assisted by F.D.A. Levitt (of Levitt Bernstein, who handled the recent changes), A. Richardson, D. Campbell and P. Myers). However, the project hit difficulties and, in 1965, the contractor, McAlpine, took ownership, and the initial scheme of private housing, shops, car parking and offices was only saved when Camden council signed a 99-year lease on the housing and the architect was eventually forced out of the project (in 1970). The range of (single-aspect) flats was reduced from 16 types to three and the flats became smaller as the brick cross wall module reduced from 18 to 13 feet. Continuous winter gardens that would have slid open over one another were simplified and built to an alternative design with fixed balconies. However, Hodgkinson now had to work with Camden architect's department (under S.A.G. Cook) and it is here that architects such as Neave Brown (who designed the megastructural Alexandra Road project), and Benson and Forsyth (more oriented toward comparatively informal low-rise designs) were exposed to the ideas informing the Brunswick scheme.

Now (after a change of ownership in 1998), access to the 560 flats has been secured, 80 retail frontages renewed, the central deck bridges removed, and the whole entirely revitalised. However, fundamental conceptual flaws remain: in particular, there is a divorce between the aircraft carrier and its surroundings, particularly adjacent shopping and residential streets (despite protestations that the design sought to marry itself to local scales, celebrate Georgian architecture and Nash), and the flats are single aspect (making the west-facing ones particularly vulnerable to over-heating in the summer). In his 1976 book on megastructures, Reyner Banham described the Brunswick Centre as *"the most pondered, most learned, most acclaimed, most monumental, most bedevilled in its building history of all English megastructures – and seemingly the best liked by its inhabitants."* This is once again true. Certainly, young architects flock to try and live there.

Neave Brown b1929

Extant London works include:

• **Winscombe Street**, 1965; 5 houses (one which is Brown's home): a terrace designed and built for a group of young architects. Not being able to self-finance the project, Neave and Anthony Hunt approached Camden Council, which agreed to support them in forming a housing association to build what turned out to be five identical houses and shared spaces developed to suit five different briefs.

• **Fleet Road**, 1975; 71 houses, shops, etc. (for Camden). Also see references to Benson & Forsyth at nearby Lamble Street.

• **Alexandra Road**, 1972-8; 520 apartments, a school, community centre, etc. (for Camden); tight site bounded by major railway, seeking to reinvent the London terrace house as flats and maisonettes; in-situ concrete; 1,664 people at 210 p.p.a. Two celebrated community buildings are located at the east end of the linear scheme, designed by Eldred Evans & David Shalev. The northern of these two was briefly a children's home (and sorely criticised for its planning); the southern one (48 Boundary Road) was a home for the young and disabled (also sorely criticised; converted into a home for the elderly, 1996-7).

Above: the Brunswick Centre and, opposite page, its Futurist inspiration (from Sant'Elia) whose towers are, architectonically, reminiscent of many similar vertical gestures from church steeples to the Late Victorian / Edwardian fashion for similar prominent gestures giving presence to the architecture.
Below: the central area of the scheme, as it now is, after being refurbished, completed in 2007. Bridges between east and west wings have been removed, canopies added to the retail frontages, more upmarket leases promoted, etc. It all adds up to an imaginative revival of an ailing project.

Above: Brown's Alexandra Road scheme.

Brown was born in Utice, New York, came to England when he was three years old, went to Marlborough school, returned to the USA for the duration of the war, was in the military from 1948-50, and studied at the AA from 1950-56. In 1957 he was with Lyons Israel Ellis and later he became the chief architect at the architect's department of Camden Council. In 2000 he took up a course in fine art whilst also undertaking housing projects in Holland.

The Camden team on the Alexandra Road project included Gordon Benson and Alan Forsyth.

Peter Hugh Girard [Joe] Chamberlin 1919-78

Geoffrey Charles Hamilton Powell 1920-99

Christoph Rudolph Bon 1921-99

Extant London works include:
• **Golden Lane**, 1952-63, 557 flats and maisonettes designed for single people and couples working in the City. The sixteen-storey Great Arthur House dominates the scheme. The Goswell road part of apartments (above retail units) was the last phase.
• **Barbican**, 1956-81 (mostly to 1973): 140 plans; 6,500 people; 2,113 apartments; towers 125 m high.
• **Bousfield Primary School** in Kensington, South Bolton Gardens, 1954-6.
• **No. 30a Hendon Avenue**, 1956-8.
• **Geoffrey Chaucer School**, Harper Road, off New Kent Road, Southwark, 1958.
• **Vanbrugh Park Estate**, Greenwich, 1961-5 (90p.p.a).

This practice has two outstanding works to its name: the Golden Lane estate, and the adjacent Barbican, designs linked not only by authorship but by adjacency and the introduction of 'Brutalist' tastes to the later stages of the former development.

Chamberlin was born in Australia, son of an army officer. However, he was educated in England and at Oxford University who became a conscientious objector during World War II and later studied architecture at Kingston Polytechnic. Here, after graduating and becoming a lecturer, he met fellow-tutors Geoffrey Powell and Christopher Bon. The latter had been born in India, educated in England and studied architecture at the AA. Bon had been born in Switzerland, trained at the ETH (Swiss Federal Institute of Technology) in Zürich, and worked briefly for Ernesto Rogers (the uncle of Richard Rogers, see page 430) in Milan and for William Holford in London.

Of the practice, Kenneth Powell noted that, *"Chamberlin, Powell, and Bon's significance in the history of post-war architecture lies in the practice's bold enlargement of the vocabulary of modernism, including its frank exploration of historical sources, and its determined pursuit of a modern architecture which*

addressed real urban, as well as social, issues and eschewed the destructive philosophy on which so much development after 1945 was based."

Chamberlin was to die on a vacation in Egypt. His marriage of 1954 had been dissolved and Bon – with whom the Chamberlins had shared houses in London and France – later married Chamberlin's former wife.

In 1951 all three teachers submitted entries for a social housing scheme at Golden Lane, on the northern edge of the City, just outside the old Roman walls. Powell won, set up with his colleagues, and the project was completed in phases between 1957-63.

In 1956 they completed Bousfield Primary School in Kensington. Then came the Barbican scheme for 35 acres of land blitzed during World War II. Initial ideas were submitted in 1955 and the scheme, with over 2,000 apartments, was constructed between 1963 and 1983 (when the arts centre was opened). Pevsner found the

Barbican towers to be "*wild and wilful*".

Both residential schemes are impressive achievements, but it is the Golden Lane estate that, with hindsight, 'sings' in a manner that somehow eludes the more heavy keynotes of the Barbican design. The crucial difference between them is the latter's introduction of a deck as the beginnings of a 'pedway' system intended to separate pedestrians from cars. Each new building was to have a public deck at first floor level; bridges were to link one to another and the network was to slowly grow. Redundant pieces of it remain in various places over the City – monument to a concept of streets being given over to cars whilst people walked over or underground (a planning concept that then, and still today, ignores the potential of the City's aged network of alleyways and backlands that are rapidly being eroded by the progressive replacement of a number of smaller sites by single large buildings).

To get onto the Barbican deck pedestrians have to negotiate perimeter 'gateways' that self-consciously play with historical references to the adjacent ruins of the Roman's wall and the fortress once located at Wood Street – an intriguing PoMo perspective, well before its time. On that deck, three towers – then the tallest residential towers in Europe – dominate the Barbican skyline (and are exactly what contemporary bankers desire). Beneath them is a simple layout of large terraced blocks set around a central lake, with the cultural centre located at the northern edge.

The irony is that pedestrians find it so difficult to orient themselves on this deck that a yellow line has been set down to guide them from the 'gateways' to the cultural centre. But, on the whole, the planning is very good. Each flat runs from front to back of the block, has a terrace, etc., and occupants are fiercely proud of the place (now entirely privatised): a fact indicated by a summer bloom of flowers that graces most terraces (apart from on the windswept towers). However, one turns from the Barbican back to the Golden Lane estate for a lighter and somehow more joyful design of interplayed colours and proportions – and without a pedestrian deck. Together, they are without match.

A view of the Barbican. Terraces on the lower blocks also serve as fire escapes. Apartments are always double-aspect.

Above left: *the tower that dominates the Golden Lane estate, with its gestural 'tongue' that helps to visually terminate the stacked stories.*

Above: *a typical, elegantly proportioned Golden Lane block of maisonettes.*

Below left: *a later stage of Golden Lane, indicative of what was, by then, being designed for the adjacent Barbican estate.*

Below: *another Golden Lane block.*

Opposite page: *a typical Barbican view, with two of the three soaring towers set above long blocks of apartments. The concrete work is truly heroic.*

prickly brutalists

Peter Denham Smithson
1923–2003

Alison Margaret Smithson
(Alison Gill) 1928–1993

Extant London works include:
• **Economist group**, 1959-63.
• **Robin Hood Gardens**, 1966-72. Ten and seven storey blocks engendering a 'stress free' central area, designed according to the then new Parker Morris standards, built in the Swedish Sundh system; Jeremy Dixon as the job architect.

The Smithsons were odd heroes: architect's architects, intellectuals, brave and obscure, idiosyncratic and prickly, talented and arrogant, authors of one of London's worst housing estates (Robin Hood Gardens, Isle of Dogs) and one of its finest urban insinuations (the Economist group, in St James).

The 'everyday' is, paradoxically, a recurring theme in the couple's work that continually surfaces as a complex set of pretensions pretending to be otherwise, but with a nod and wink to the knowing. Their 'everyday' adopts culture with a small 'c', embracing it as what T.S. Eliot referred to as a taken-for-granted 'way of life'. This suggests architecture as a considered – but background – ornament to the city and its interactions; it draws attention to itself, but remains a mere accompaniment to social life. It ostensibly suggests the dumping of what Reyner Banham referred to as the 'black box' of architecture and an embrace of those insidious ideological bearings which constitute

the basis of society's 'common sense' (and thereby its standards of taste). Here is the late-nineteenth century sentiment of the Arts & crafts, and the voice of Adolf Loos celebrating vernacular wisdoms as a true manifestation of the Zeitgeist. On the other hand, in the hands of these architects, the everyday and ordinary leans toward a strangely élitist character that, as if personified, one imagines as some lone and prickly prowler in the cultural landscape, a Cultural flâneur who hopes, by merging into the background, to find himself backlit and thus starkly but paradoxically and enigmatically foregrounded. And that was the stance of Peter and Alison Smithson. Whilst expressing a sentiment of concern for the gritty and the everyday they strode across the cultural landscape of the 1950s wearing the sartorial proclamations of the art school and riding in an ex-army Willys jeep. Venturi did something similar, but without the style and wit. And the 'ordinary and everyday' continues as an architectural theme of fascination.

Kenneth Frampton describes Peter Smithson, in 1953, on the site of the couple's neo-Miesian, competition-winning Hunstanton School as 'a dashing figure'. This was the project (won in 1950) that pushed the couple to the forefront of the art and architecture scene and engaged them with the likes of Eduardo Paolozzi and Nigel Hendersen, Reyner Banham, et al, undertaking many projects and notable exhibitions such as Parallels of Art and Life in 1953, designing the 'Patio and Pavilion' at the This is Tomorrow exhibition, 1956, the House of the Future at the Ideal Home Exhibition of the same year, becoming involved with CIAM (Congrès International d'Architecture Moderne), forming Team X (a breakaway from CIAM, of 1956), teaching at the AA, etc.

For ten years or more they were busy but without lots of work by contemporary standards. And it is that period – the first fifteen years of their young practice – which left London with two significant buildings by this pair: the ill-fated Robin Hood Gardens social housing project at the north end of the Isle of Dogs (1968-72), and the sublime Economist group of buildings in St

James (1959-63). The 'streets in the air' of the former was never satisfactory and nowadays merely another monument to how badly architects with good intentions could get things wrong during that period. In contrast, the Economist group is Listed Grade I and remains a superb work. They should have stuck to Culture.

*This page and opposite: the Economist group. **Above** is a view from St James. **Below** is a view from the opposite side; the tallest tower is on the left.*

Peter Smithson was born in Stockton-on-Tees, son of a 'commercial traveller' in drapery. He attended a local grammar school and later went to study at the school of architecture at Newcastle (then a part of Durham University; 1939-42, and 1945-8). It was here that he met Alison. Then came the war, service in Burma and India, and more study in London, at the Royal Academy School (1948-9), marriage in 1949 and work for the LCC. Alison was born in Sheffield as the daughter of a graphic designer who became head of the South Shields School of Art, 1929-50. She was studying architecture in Newcastle from 1944-49, where Peter was a teaching assistant.

In the year of their marriage, the couple came to London and rented a flat in Bloomsbury Square, where their landlord was Theo Crosby, and it was at this time (in 1949) that they entered the Hunstanton School competition with a scheme that was a mix of Mies in Chicago and extensive employment of the Golden Section, no doubt from readings of Wittkower's influential work (*Architectural Principles in the Age of*

Humanism, 1949). In 1955, Peter Smithson started teaching at the Architectural Association where, among others, Peter Cook was a student (Peter Smithson ran the Fifth Year from 1957-60). Meanwhile, in 1952, came an entry in the Golden Lane housing competition in the City of London that introduced the concept of 'streets in the sky'. It was also during the early '50's that the pair proclaimed, "Belonging is a basic emotional need. Its associations are of the simplest order. From 'belonging' (identity) comes the enriching sense of neighbourliness. The short narrow street of the slum succeeds where spacious redevelopment frequently fails" (1953 CIAM statement against modernist orthodoxy). They had, in other words, moved from hard-edge Mies to an accommodation of the 'as found' nevertheless imbued with classical principles of proportion.

About this time they designed a house in Fitzrovia. It was designed with materials left 'as found', including a corrugated iron roof and unplastered internal walls. A weekend home – converted from a small farm worker's cottage to a dwelling of classical proportions – also manifest this same intermixing of culture and

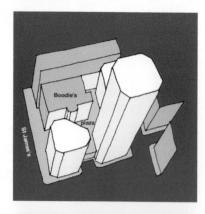

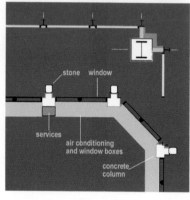

Top: diagram of the Economist group. St James' is on the left hand side.
***Above**: Mies' cladding at the Seagram Building, 1958, and how the Smithsons handled a similar problem (in a neo-Mies manner) at the Economist.*
***Opposite page top**: the cladding of the office tower.*

Culture (and a later trip to Japan in 1960 extended this direction of softened considerations).

It was while designing these houses that they are alleged to have conceived the 'New Brutalist' movement. Peter had christened himself Brutus at college – a name which stuck with his contemporaries although it was hated by Alison – and Mark Girouard tells us the joke that, at the time, 'Brutalism' equated to 'Brutus plus Alison'. Perhaps it was also a response to articles in the Architectural Review (1947-8) on Swedish architecture which referred to a 'New Empiricism' (or New Humanism). Whatever, the term 'Brutalist' first appeared in a feature on the Smithsons' design for an unbuilt house in Architectural Design of December 1953, and was widely adopted when Crosby published a manifesto by the couple in the same magazine, in January 1955 – not long after the Architects Journal of early 1954 (when Hunstanton was completed) had named them as 'the bright young hopes of the

profession'.

Their sentiments were manifest in the titles of books such as *Ordinariness and Light*, and *The Charged Void*, although *Without Rhetoric* expressed a sentiment not always fitting the stance and work of the couple, especially in their younger years: the Willys jeep, the Citroen DS, Liberty shirts, cravats and light suits of Peter, as well as the self-designed flamboyant dresses of Alison were hardly 'without rhetoric' and their architecture was voluble for those who turned to look and listen. But there was never a lot of work – a fact, noted Gavin Stamp, that may have come from "their reputation for being 'difficult', as well as a desire to keep their office small." It is commonplace for architects to declare such anti-commerical intentions of staying as small craft firms; perhaps the Smithsons meant it. Their later careers were marked by a little work abroad, much writing for AD, and teaching at Bath University.

As Girouard notes, it is sometimes difficult to imagine the extent to which, during the mid '50's the Smithsons considered themselves to be the natural leaders of the pack. But they had a reputation – justified or not – for a mixture of arrogance, prickliness, a forbidding bearing despite, in the case of Peter Smithson, of being (in Frampton's words) "a master of the repartee and the felicitous turn of phrase." Certainly, Alison does not come off well in biographer's essays. Girouard (in his work on Jim Stirling, who enjoyed considerable tensions with the Smithson's, particularly Alison, when the Smithsons led the field theoretically but Stirling, with his Ham Common flats of 1957-8, was already catching everyone's attention for what was built rather than spoken about), comments on Alison being "opinionated, outrageous, convinced of her own and her husband's importance, by no means without humour, yet in some fields quite humourless." No one denied her talent and intelligence, but the other side of this coin was apparently an outrageous capacity for self-styling and display that saw her self-made clothing the star attraction of parties (at one time, prompting Stirling to mockery, prompting Alison to throw a glass of wine over him).

358

Below: Robin Hood Gardens. There are 214 flats at 142 p.p.a. The 'streets in the air' (intended to link to later blocks, providing a network) included 'pause places' and recesses where, it was hoped, tenants would place flower boxes. These arrangements have been argued to deny private territory to tenants whose flats, in any case, turned their backs on the 'streets'. A three-metre high concrete wall surrounds the site to offset traffic noise, but this also helps to island the project. Despite the neglected condition of the place and, inevitably, the contributing guilt of the designers, there was a daring and bravery to design the intention. In another location, with less deprived tenants, better construction, properly managed, etc., this place might have been exemplary. As it is, it stands as a monument to the shameful state of some British social housing. It is likely to be demolished and a battle to List it possibly says more about the reputation of the Smithson's rather than the virtues of this project.

Their outstanding work – the Economist group – fits incongruously into this picture. It adopts the opposite stance to those ideological concerns with high-level walkways that characterised Smithson lectures and projects in the '50's. Here was the deck as a sensitive piazza that sought to reconcile old and new as a scene of repose counterpointing adjacent street movements. The scheme plays with the slope of St James' and sets four elements around the central area: a residential tower; an office tower (the tallest element); a bank building (now converted to a restaurant and bar); and a small extension to Boodles Club (of 1776), forming the northern flank wall of the development. The facings on the group are of Portland stone, but of a variety rich in fossils ('roach'). However, the idea for a centrifugal distribution of elements is attributed to a manager of the Economist, Peter Dallas-Smith; and the idea of varied heights is attributed to Maurice Bebb, a consultant architect to the contractors. Such notes may be irrelevant; they might also help to explain the peculiar success of the Economist group.

Eric Alfred Lyons 1912–1980

Extant London works include:
• **Oaklands**, 24 apartments, Twickenham, 1948.
• **Parkleys**, Ham Common, 1956 (169 Span apartments; the largest Span estate; Stirling & Gowan's ham Common flats are nearby).
• **Span** developments, Blackheath (nineteen in all), inc.: T2 House Type, the Hall II, Blackheath, 1957; Hallgate, Blackheath, 1958; T8 House Type, Corner Green, Blackheath, 1959.
• **World's End** estate, 1977 (with H. T. Cadbury-Brown).

Eric Lyons was born in Highbury and in 1929 began an architectural career articled to J. Stanley Beard whilst also studying part-time at the Regent Street Polytechnic. In 1933 he set out to work for other architects including W.E. Trent, Leslie Kemp, Andrew Mather, T.P. Bennett, and worked with Gropius and Maxwell Fry, who exposed him to Modernist ideology. Finally, in 1938, he started a partnership with Geoffrey Paulson Townsend, another student from the Regent Street Polytechnic (b1911). This was immediately followed by the Second World War and Lyons registered as a conscientious objector, somehow still managing to design factories and hostels for the cinema architect, Harry Weedon.

By 1948 Lyons and Townsend were designing furniture and building a block of 24 apartments on a site acquired by Townsend – the beginnings of an informal dimension to their partnership in which Townsend would find sites and Lyons would act as architect (architects were then not allowed to engage in formal relations with builders and developers since this was deemed to be a conflict of interest, despite a long tradition of speculation within the profession). It was now that Townsend acquired a company called Span (1957), which included Leslie Bilsby, a local builder and developer. Bilsby was also ex-Regent Street Poly, a painter who studied architecture and later went to work for a building merchant; in 1937 he had set up his own building company working for Connell, Ward and Lucas, Wells Coates, Denys Lasdun, Patrick Gwynne and Erno Goldfinger.

On the design side, Lyons was joined in 1955 by Ivor Cunningham – an ex-AA student who went on to study landscape; he became responsible for the landscape design and the detailing of plant layout for the Span developments; he was made a partner in 1963, creating the Eric Lyons Cunningham Partnership (which Lyons' son Richard joined as a partner in 1972).

The Span designs were outstanding private developments. Spread around housing around Twickenham, Putney, and Weybridge, as well as Blackheath, with other examples scattered in places such as Cambridge, Cheltenham, and Oxford. The team's most ambitious Span scheme was the creation of a new village in Kent – New Ash Green – where,

If Robin Hood Gardens is a late example of gritty, '60s inner London borough social housing values offering a sentimental nod toward the ostensible romance of packed, working-class East End streets (now raised in the air), then the speculative Span developments represented a middle-class counterpoint: the Outer Borough suburban dream for those enjoying the good life of Costa Brava holidays, the kids in a good local comprehensive school, a Morris car, Modernist tastes leaning toward the novelties of Heal's and Habitat furniture, and a lifestyle that was implicitly conservative (with, perhaps, a touch of liberality). The former was in the tradition of urban renewal, charitable housing trusts and the first LCC social housing estates which sought to address urban poverty and deprivation. The latter was in the tradition of middle-class Arts & Crafts values, middle-class growth and its affluence in the late Victorian period (engendering Queen Anne fashions), and also those gentrified cottages satirised by Osbert Lancaster, now urbanised as terraced town houses set within an 'urban village'. High density apartments in tall concrete was what the state provided; houses was what everyone – in every class – desired. Here was culture and Culture: one as a way of life, the other as pretension and aspiration; one addressed by welfare state policies and the other by the market. While the ill-fated Robin Hood has been layered with (usually)

beginning in 1966, Lyons designed over 500 dwellings and a town centre with fifty-seven shops (a scheme from which Lyons was forced to withdraw, in 1969, due to financial problems). From 1975-77 Lyons was President of the RIBA.

Opposite page left*: Span in Blackheath*
Opposite page Right*: the Setchwell Road, Neylan & Ungless.*

dysfunctional security devices, the Span developments are well maintained and quietly policed by a bourgeoisie intent on keeping strangers at bay. By the early 1970s fashions and funding in social housing had shifted away from tower blocks and hi-density /high-rise schemes toward high-density/low-rise schemes. Not only had so-called industrialised systems of construction been discredited, but so had the logic of point blocks as a way of achieving higher densities (e.g. by Leslie Martin and Lionel March's studies in the geometry of housing layouts, at Cambridge). The slogan was that space not 'owned' was space not maintained and that this was the only viable form of 'defensible' space. In a somewhat different world of Parker Morris standards (universally adopted in social housing by 1969) and sentiments more sympathetic to Span than Robin Hood, social housing design shifted its strategies toward low rise schemes – especially in the later generation of new town schemes such as Milton Keynes, where many Londoners continued to find themselves relocated into a continuation of the historic attempts to contain London's growth. But even the Inner London boroughs moved in a suburban direction. The end of an era came when Margaret Thatcher was elected to power in 1979 and immediately sought to end social housing programmes and wind down the new towns.

William Ungless b1931
Michael Neylan b1931

Extant London works include:
• 69 flats, Limewalk, off **Linden Grove**, Southwark, 1964-66.
• 312 dwellings, **Setchwell Road**, Southwark, 1972-78. 136 p.p.a.; celebrated in the Buildings of England as "especially attractive."

Neylan and Ungless represent the tail end of a long programme of social housing values in London: architects with an agenda distinctly different from the Smithsons, Neave Brown, Hodgkinson et al – even from Cullinan, and Darbourne and Darke, although all these architects shared an underlying set of concerns. Intent, however, was rarely the issue; it was how that intent was to be given form within a broader context of prevailing socio-economic values. And, with Neylan and Ungless, that meant a return to the neo-vernacular. Neylan was born in London (son of an employee of the Bank of England) and was to study architecture at the Wimbledon Art School and Kingston School of Art (1948-54). Ungless was born in Ipswich (son of a miner and master butcher) and became articled to Johns Slater and Haward (1952-54) and attended the Bartlett school of architecture (1957-9). He then worked for Chamberlin, Powell and Bon (where the met Neylan), Gnecchi Ruscone in Milan, Bernhard Hermkes in Berlin, and Denys Lasdun in London. Neylan worked for Chamberlin Powell and Bon, 1954-61, before starting his own practice, and later (in 1966) joining together with Ungless when they won a competition for 270 dwellings in Harlow New Town. Perhaps their best and most indicative housing schemes are in Southwark. With hindsight they suggest a suburban romanticism ('a homely feeling') arguably inappropriate to an inner London context. But that, in the '60s and '70s, was their point: the opposite of the Barbican, Keeling House, Alexander Road, Robin Hood Gardens, the Brunswick Centre, Lillington Gardens, Branch Hill, etc. Unfortunately, the N&U schemes have slowly transmogrified into a local DIY store vernacular undermining any vestiges of Modernist sentiment which Neylan and Ungless gently insinuated.

John William Charles Darbourne
1935–91

Geoffrey James Darke b1929

Extant London works include:

• **Lillington Gardens**, Pimlico, 1961-72; 780 dwellings, in three phases (210 persons per acre/150 dwellings per hectare). A pioneering scheme which includes Street's St James-the-Less, 1859-61, three pubs, a surgery, a library, shops and an old people's home (for 90 people) as well as considerable open space.

• **Marquess Estate**, 1966-76: 1,200 flats and maisonettes; 200 p.p.a (or 494 per hectare); large, dense schemes remained fashionable with local authorities. Renamed New River Green, after 463 homes were demolished, not all of which were replaced, following extensive social problems blamed on the design (failure to integrate with adjacent streets, networks of alleys, hiding places, etc). The layout was modified by PRP Architects but the issue of access control could hardly be addressed.

• **Athelstane Road Estate**, Charteris Road/Everleigh Street: a comprehensive scheme broken up at a time when large scale, comprehensive redevelopment went out of fashion in the mid-1970s and was replaced by many infill schemes.

• **Aberdeen Park** (east of Highbury Grove), 1979-81.

D&D got going in 1961 when John Darbourne won the Lillington Road competition (judged by Philip Powell) and was joined by Darke. Both had worked together with Eric Lyons on Span developments and hence landscaping was always a fundamental feature of their designs.

Darbourne was born in London and Darke (image left) in Evesham. Darbourne attended the Bartlett school at University College and graduated in 1958 and gained a masters in landscape design from Harvard in 1964. After his death, Darke carried on as Geoffrey Darke Architects.

Gordon Benson 1944

and

Alan Forsyth 1944

Extant London works include:
• **Maiden Lane**, 1973-82. 225 dwellings (mixed), 2-5 floors. Praised by architects such as Alvin Boyarsky and John Winter Maiden Lane was, a few years later, virtually uninhabitable. It remains an infamous scheme.
• **Lamble Street**, Gospel Oak, 1978-80. Split-level plan.
• **Branch Hill**, Hampstead, 1974-6. Remarkable scheme, tucked away.

Benson was born in Glasgow and trained at Strathclyde University and then the AA; Forsyth in Newcastle and trained at the AA, 1962-8. They set up in practice together in 1969. Between 1972-78 the couple completed four notable and infamous schemes for Camden Council. The couple practise what they refer to as 'enriched modernism" and have become a major international practice.

Above: *G.E. Street's St James-the-Less church at Lillington Gardens (its original intent and atmosphere somewhat buried beneath contemporary modes of usage that would probably have shocked Street).*

Below: *Branch Hill, Hampstead, inspired by Mediterranean hill towns and how other, contemporary Swiss architects were interpreting this theme on sloping sites. Hidden away, it is a fine scheme.*

Opposite page: *Lillington Gardens is D&D's most outstanding work and remains impressive: Span, as it were, facing the realities of inner city social housing needs. It is an attractive place. However, discussions with residents quickly reveal a host of problems common to estates and dense urban life. This is underscored by the police, who see the place as 'a fortress' – in other words, a place whose labyrinthian physicality intrinsically protects that antisocial element they seek to combat. Design gets blamed. However, to pursue this line of argumentation perhaps leads down a broad 'via negativa' of paranoia that acknowledges none of the pleasantries nevertheless enjoyed by the residents. Nevertheless, good design has a limited capacity to deal with bad neighbours, junkies, arsonists and 'me' generation values compounded by poor estate management, maintenance issues and the imperatives of privatisation that merely exacerbate the difficulties. It is for such reasons that social housing remains one of the more perennially difficult of design challenges. However, D&D's Lillington Gardens has admirably withstood damage infliction for nearly forty years. The potted flowers and shrubs nurtured by some residents are visible witness to a balance of satisfaction with a mode of provision that will never be repeated.*

Sir Denys Lasdun 1914–2001

*Lasdun, 1957: "... there are absolute and eternal
standards, valid and unchanging, challenging equally
and judging equally Corbusier and Icyinus, Mies van
der Rohe and Palladio, Butterfield and the builders of
Chartres."*

Extant London works include:
- **No. 32 Newton Road**, Paddington, 1937-8.
- **Hallfield Primary School**, off Inverness
Terrace, 1952-5.
- **Keeling House**, Claredale Street, Bethnal
Green, 1955-9. 'Streets in the air', converted to
private units by Munkenbeck & Marshall, with new
penthouse, 1999-2001. Another two blocks have been
demolished. Also
Sulkin House, Lansbury Square, Poplar, and
Trevelyan House, further east, both eight stories,
1955-8.
- **No. 26 St James' Place**, 1958-60.
- former Peter Robinson's store, **65 Strand**, 1958.
- **IBM** building, adjacent to the National Theatre, 1958.
- **National Theatre**, Southbank, 1967-76.
- **Royal College of Physicians**, Regents Park,
1960-64. The building was
designed just after the
momentous post-war years
that saw the formation of the
National Health Service and
a negotiated contract with the
College for the incorporation of
surgeon's services within the
framework of the NHS – what
was, surely, as significant in
its history as its founding and
Royal Charter. It was now that
it decided to move from the
Smirke premises in Pall Mall
East.
- **Institute of Education**, and
the library of the School of
Oriental and African Studies (SOAS), Bloomsbury,
1965-78.
- **Milton Gate**, Moor Lane, City, 1991 (Now with Peter
Softley (later the firm of Hurley Robertson; a peculiar
office building, clad entirely in frameless glass.

Denys Lasdun increasingly looks like
one of the larger talents of the post-
war period. He was born in Kensington,
within a family of Russian Jewish origins
and was educated at Rugby. He then
hesitated at the Royal College of Music (his mother was
a talented musician) before turning to the AA (1932-7).
Le Corbusier was already a strong influence and Lasdun
visited Paris, and met Corbusier. Nevertheless, his first
work (a house in Surrey), 1934, was very conventional.
However, by 1937 his design for a house in Newton
Road, Paddington exhibited a new, Modernist face.

At this time Lasdun was in the office of Wells
Coates, but had soon moved to Tecton where, although
he agreed wholeheartedly with Lubetkin (with whom he
shared a some background) that *"architects have only
one function: to produce the surroundings for a decent
life."* However, he apparently became increasingly
unhappy with Lubetkin's
approach and concern with
pattern-making.

When the war came Lasdun
was in the artillery and then the
engineers, landing at D-Day and
building airstrips. He returned
to Tecton in 1946, to be made
a partner in a firm that was
already breaking up. As a part
of this scenario Lasdun set
up a partnership with Lindsey
Drake and completed some of
the Tecton work, including the
Hallfield Primary School. This
kind of work continued during
the period 1952-9, when Lasdun
and Drake also managed the office of Fry and Drew
whilst they were in Africa.

The next key project was typical of post-war
housing projects in the East End, but handled in a
novel manner: the three 'cluster blocks' in Bethnal
Green, 1952-7. (By the 1990s Keeling, the best of the
three, was being emptied of tenants and converted to
private housing.) A more or less parallel project was a
contrasting block of apartments in St James' Place –
one of the first such blocks in post-war Britain. There
now came his most important commissions: for the

Royal College of Physicians, on a site in Regents Park. Lasdun was asked if he would produce a neo-Classical building. Instead, in Lasdun's words, he produced a building that *"accorded with the Nash terraces without imitating them."* Nevertheless the design betrays a deep concern with classical traditions and analogies between architecture and the body (a suitable allegory for such a building).

In 1960 Lasdun brought Alexander Redhouse and Peter Softley into partnership. There now followed the National Theatre project (*"a clever way of building a nuclear power station in the middle of London without anyone objecting,"* as Prince Charles derided it) and a 1965 project for London University in the megastructural manner of design then fashionable (cf. the nearby Brunswick Centre).

Kenneth Powell tells us that *"Lasdun found the changing ethos of practice uncongenial, disliking the competition system, valuing the process of collaboration with an enlightened client, and reluctant to work for commercial developers. He found the rise of post-modernism in architecture both distasteful and inexplicable, and was pleased when it proved to be a passing fad."* Before that fad, in 1977 he was awarded the RIBA Gold Medal. He was elected RA in 1991 and knighted in 1995 as one of the most talented of post-war British architects.

Above: the National Theatre.
Below right: the RCP, at Regents Park.
Below left: the University of London Institute of Education.

an organism in equilibrium

The Royal College of Physicians 1964

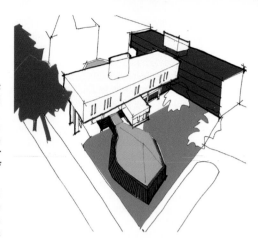

Lasdun believed the best buildings were *"the products of very specific study of very specific problems"* and not expressions of a universally applicable programme. However, he offered a rather traditional interpretation of what this meant: his work to be nourished, as he put it, by *"fantasies, feelings, attitudes ... a search for some kind of coherent system which is at the basis of all creation."*

On the one hand, this is a sentiment that could suggest a theme of water/promenade/building for the National Theatre's riverside site; on the other, it is one that was implicitly empathetic with a Neo-Platonic tradition and it is not surprising to find that, for this giant of post-war Modernism in Britain, both context and history were important to the design of the Royal College of Physicians, one of Britain's more historic and prestigious institutions. Lasdun enjoyed, for example, a real enthusiasm for Hawksmoor's work and it is with this in mind that one approaches the RCP and is not surprised to find that its plan and section can be, appropriately enough, read as an organisational allegory of the human body's architecture. This is, as William Curtis puts it, *"an organism in equilibrium."*

As an institution, the RCP has its roots in an era when alchemy and science could hardly be differentiated and experimentation had as much of a design content as an objectively scientific one in the sense that we now understand the term. It was established in 1518 and, during the early life of Sir Christopher Wren, became associated with Dr William Harvey, the King's physician who had discovered the principle of blood flow in the 1620s. During the 1640s the young Wren – a dextrous, highly skilled designer as well as a man of prodigious intelligence – was a part of a circle of experimenters

attempting to re-establish the data concerning blood flow (much of it apparently lost during the Civil War) and extend knowledge in this area. And the new building was designed at another interesting point in the College's history: just after the momentous post-war years that saw the formation of the National Health Service and a negotiated contract with the College for the incorporation of surgeon's services within the framework of the NHS – an event as significant in its history as its founding and Royal Charter. And now it had decided to move from premises designed by Robert Smirke, in Pall Mall East (adjacent to Trafalgar Square; the building still stands).

When the College's new building in Regent's Park was opened, in 1964, Alvin Boyarsky (who was to later run the Architectural Association for many years) discussed the movement planning of Lasdun's scheme in terms of blood flow, and a set of organs (Censors' Room as heart, library as head, laboratories as the feet, etc.

And it is true: the work that reveals itself to be a

Below: composite views to the street front and south (garden) side.

remarkable (and undeclared) interpretation of that masonic tradition in which architecture conceives of itself as a metaphorical human body and roots itself in that body's geometry and organisational principles. In simple terms, the *parti* of the building proceeds through piloti and entry porch beneath the Harveyian Library (serving as the equivalent of a columnated and pedimented porch, with a tri-partite vertical division), through to the cavernous double-height space of the central hall and gallery with its grand stair up to the Library and committee rooms, with the crucially important and symbolic Censors' Room off to the right (complete with wood linings from Robert Hooke's building of the 1670s, and views onto the garden and Nash buildings), through to the formal dining area and the kitchens, and finally – at the east end of the building on Albany Street – to a cross-axis administrative block housing the 'servants' of the College in quarters whose role and character continues the historic pattern of arrangements in this area, i.e. mews and servants accommodated in corridored spaces to the rear, along this street, behind the grand Nash terraces facing the Park.

To continue with the analogy, it is as if one enters through the mouth, beneath the brain of the institution, through to its heaving chest cavity (with the 'heart' off to one side), into the stomach and digestive tracts, down to the feet; the cleverly blue-brick, humped semi-underground auditorium off to one side (from the entry area) now reads, on plan, as a comic speech bubble. And each functional element is treated differently (brick, or concrete, or mosaic, etc.). The symbolism is at once crude and subtle, if somewhat incongruous to Modernist sensibilities. In any case, there appears to be no record of Lasdun discussing or referring to the building in these terms. Certainly, Boyarsky's reference to blood flows and organs touches upon the topic as a rather naughty dig at the architect's peculiar sensibilities. In fact, Lasdun's building is a fine ornament to this part of London and to the small *assemble* of pavilions planned for the Park and were only realised in part. Besides Nash, the spirit of Le Corbusier is here, but so is Frank Lloyd Wright and Louis Kahn. It is a masterful building that rewards study and experience.

Left: the entry level plan.

367

shadows on the promenade
The National Theatre, 1976

The National houses a hierarchy of three theatres: large, novel and thrusting; medium and conventional, with an adjustable proscenium; small and experimental, 'in the round'. These are so organised that the largest (the 1190 seater Olivier) sits on a dominant axis at 45 degrees to the Embankment approaches. The smaller, 890 seater Lyttelton sits slightly set back at 90 degrees to the river. And the 300 seater Cottesloe is even more 'deeply' buried, around the side and under the Lyttelton. These three auditoria form the heart of a complex that is otherwise physically divided between the foyer areas for theatre-goers, and the stage and support areas needed by staff and players.

Lasdun's design turns its back on a neglected and uninteresting backland; its orientation is entirely toward an embankment that came from the R.F.H. and ended here – what lay beyond, to the east, was a discovery to be made some twenty-five years later, as the embankment was extended, the Tate Modern opened, the river cleaned up, etc. Of course, a key issue for the public is access and the dominant 45 degree axis drives through the plan and points toward the principal entrance and an open area by the river, adjacent to Waterloo Bridge. (However, Lasdun's concept has recently been diluted by alterations that have enclosed his *porte cochére* arrival area and shifted the entrance off the diagonal.)

The Lyttelton has a separate entrance, to one side;

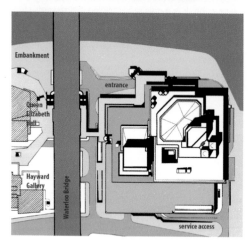

Below: the National Theatre today – an old lady being given a temporary make-over for a consumer carnival (the make-overs made inside are permanent). The umbrellas on the terrace are a thin parody of what Lasdun was ultimately suggesting for his river / promenade / building equation that has found it difficult to adapt to changing consumer notions of what it means to go to the theatre. Lasdun's vision was of "space, walls, light", with nothing between the theatre and people's experiences of the drama on stage. Changes at the entry area (by Stanton Williams) have not been kind to Lasdun's schematic concept.

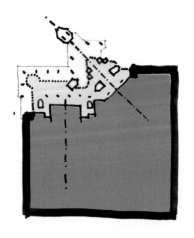

its true entry point was meant to be on the first level terrace, accessed from Waterloo Bridge, but this never worked properly. (In fact, it might be true to say that Lasdun's weakness was a lack of concern with formal entry points.) These entry arrangements dominate one corner of the building. The other two sides are secondary and wrap the main auditoria and their surrounding service spaces, with service access at the opposite side to where the public are.

The simplicity of this *parti* ends there, and Lasdun buries his concept within a deeply moody ambience of stratified layers, light and shadow. To linger in his foyers (admittedly ignoring some recent silting up that serves current visitor desires) is to engage in a drama of movement serving as a prelude to any drama on the stages themselves. In addition, the terraces which thrust out from the building to offer exciting views over the river are cut through, offering internal views between them. It's as if Lasdun was evoking some archetypal architectural experience: a ruined castle, perhaps, where one clambers around, discovering new low spaces and places; or a bombed building, its exterior blown away, but its monumental structure and staircases intact. One stands deep in shadow but looking toward the natural light, or moves from level to level on enclosed staircases (thick dark carpet and raw shuttered concrete) broken here and there by slotted and cross-cutting views. It's a sensual, playful and evocative architectural aesthetic.

On the exterior, the building reads as cantilevering horizontal planes projecting into space, at the same time wrapping the functional inner parts in a deep set of architectonic devices that defy any notion of 'façade' or neat boundaries between outside and inside (an effect underscored by the way similar concrete finishes are used both externally and internally). A contrast with the R.F.H. could not be more complete. From a distance, these strata are strongly dominated and stabilised by the concrete masses of the two fly towers. This effect is really only apparent on the Waterloo Bridge corner that diagonally faces on to Waterloo bridge. The other sides are more utilitarian. On the east, large diagonal struts prop a projecting deck level that cantilevers above a vehicle access road enabling taxis to come around to the river frontage (not Lasdun's original concept, but forced upon him by highway engineers). On the south side, the façade is taken up by a service wing of paint shops, rehearsal rooms, etc. All of this has been much altered by the changes that have taken place all around, especially by the changed nature and extension of the embankment walkway. And, internal changes may have served the viability of the National as an institution but have cluttered the interior and arguably compromised the architecture of one of London's finest buildings.

Except on sunny days, Lasdun's notion of a waterside promenade building is somewhat contradicted by the reality of a calm, charged, but almost foreboding building. There is no Lutyens-like frivolity. Nevertheless, if only Wilson's British Library had been like this.

Lasdun, in conversation with Peter Hall, about the design of the National Theatre, 1976:

"... it stands on the South Bank of the Thames [...] which turns through almost 90 degrees and picks up a panorama of the City of London that stretches from St. Paul's round to Somerset House and on to Hawksmoor's towers at Westminster Abbey. It's a magical position, probably the most beautiful site in London. The two main theatres are signalled on the outside by two large blank concrete fly-towers. The bigger one, the Olivier, is inflected at an angle towards Waterloo Bridge and the smaller one, the Lyttelton, acts as a sort of point of stasis and is pretty well touching the bridge. The two towers are then tied as it were by a series of terraces, which step down towards the river, and symbolically and physically connect to the bridge. I call these terraces, which are very horizontal in emphasis, 'strata' – it's a geological term that rather goes with concrete – and these strata are available to the public to just mill around in. They furthermore penetrate into the building. This is entirely made up in a pyramidal form of the fly-towers, the terraces, and the riverfront, and between these terraces is glass, so from the outside the people can be seen processing through the frame of the building. [...] There's one other aspect of concrete which is partly architectural, partly to do with the nature of theatre. I don't want anything to come between people experiencing the theatre and your drama. It must be space, walls, light. And the ornaments of the building are people moving around – they are a moving ornament in a big bare space that is beautifully lit and carpeted. It is the minimum. It is protected space and nothing else, with God's good light and sometimes electric light as well. But the rhythm of the building is interesting, given that it's also by the river. Because I want the feeling that the audience – like the tides of the river flow into the auditoria and become a community within them. Then the tide ebbs and they come out into the creeks of the small spaces that are made by all these terraces; because they're not vast terraces; they are very small, human little places for people to go to ... The National Theatre has come about ... when the language of architecture is non-existent, hence the unease, to put it mildly, which people express about modern architecture. [...] But the building, if I may say so, displays a classical order of a kind. It's an unfamiliar order but it's classical, with a lot of freedom within that."

Above: the Keeling House 'cluster block', now privatised.
Below: Milton Gates, all glass offices in the City (a very uncharacteristic scheme).

Above and below: the flats off St James.
Lasdun's East End cluster block of 1954 and the luxury St James' flats of 1958 are, of course, related designs, although their tenants and locations could not be more different. The somewhat implausible community concept of 'streets in the air' in the former were matched by a paid porter at the door in the latter. And, at St James', the section provides extensive balconies and grand double-height spaces unaffordable in Bethnal Green. It is somewhat ironic that the latter is now also private. Lasdun's characteristic stratification is an aesthetic theme of both designs.

Sir Basil Urwin Spence 1907–1976
and

Andrew Renton 1917–82

Extant London works include:
- **Sydenham School**, Dartmouth Road, Lewisham, 1957.
- **Swiss Cottage Library**, 1962-4 (was leisure centre).
- **Kensington Civic Centre**, Phillimore Walk, 1965-76 (executed by John S. Bonnington & Partners).
- **Knightsbridge Barracks**, 1959-1970.
- **Salter's Hall**, Fore Street (north of London Wall), 1972-6.
- **50 Queen Anne's Gate**, 1976.
- **Brent Cross**, (consultant to Bernard Engle).

former associate Bruce Robertson, being joined by R. Hardie Glover as an assistant in the following year (and partner in 1948). As an exhibition architect, Spence was leading the King and Queen around an exhibition at the V&A called 'Britain can Make it' (1946). In that same year he designed the Scottish equivalent, an Edinburgh event called 'Scottish enterprise' – an exhibition where Spence again took the Queen around. Other exhibitions followed, but his big break came with an opportunity to work on the exhibits of the Festival of Britain with Misha Black and James Gardner. The 'Sea and Ships' Pavilion (one of the more successful ones) is attributed to him.

And then the biggest break of all: winning the competition for Coventry Cathedral, in 1951 (the building was completed in 1962). Time magazine reported (in September 1951) that, *"Architect Spence, 44, 'nearly passed out' when he heard his design had been chosen. He had worked on it after hours, for relaxation from his chores as designer of the Festival of Britain's Sea & Ships Building and Glasgow University's new atomic-research laboratory."* As any architect knows, one is unlikely to work casually after hours 'for relaxation' on such a competition. Upon winning, he remarked, *"I could have done with some strong whiskey but all I got was dry sherry. It was but the first of many such drinks, as I found that Anglican clergy favour it above all others."*

But then came controversy, with criticism of the non-traditional (i.e. Gothic) design. Spence had to argue that he was, in fact, a traditionalist, but the controversy did not go away. The Royal Fine Art Commission offered to 'cooperate' in the detailed design and every detailed change was reported in the newspapers. Spence had received a poisoned chalice. However, it is interesting that a report on the 1953 Royal Academy summer exhibition should congratulate him on a masterly drawing of the Cathedral and not how comparatively rare such a draughting capacity was, even then. Meanwhile, Spence had to defend the construction and the criticism that the Cathedral would require bricks and bricklayers needed on rebuilding Coventry's war-damaged housing stock: *"It will not absorb one brick or use one bricklayer"*, wrote Spence. In a public address, he noted the apathy in Coventry and, on a note that is hardly imaginable today, especially given the controversy around the project, he suggested that the people of Coventry should not be the judges on the project. An unattributed comedian of Coventry is reported as saying, *"First of all, of course, we owe an enormous debt of gratitude to the German people for making this whole project possible in the first place. Second, we owe a debt of gratitude to the people of Coventry itself, who when asked to choose*

Basil Urwin Spence belonged to that famed body of Scots people enjoying the reputation of having built the British Empire, i.e. he was born in India, in Bombay, son of a civil servant. Aged twelve, he was sent back to Scotland to study and boarded at George Watson's College in Edinburgh, before attending the foundation course of the Edinburgh College of Art, studying painting and sculpture and then switching over to architecture (1925).

Spence was bright. He won a Pugin Studentship and travelled extensively in England in 1927; then in France and Germany in 1928. In 1929 he gained the College's certificate and exemption from the RIBA's intermediate examination and his skilled draughtsmanship secured him a place in the office of Sir Edwin Lutyens, in London (where, appropriately enough, he worked on designs for the Viceroy's House in New Delhi). While there he continued his studies at the University of London (the Bartlett School of Architecture). He returned to Edinburgh in 1930, became fully qualified and settled down to an Edinburgh career of practice (including ghosting presentations for others) and teaching before the war interrupted his career and took him off as a staff captain and later as a major, seconded to the Camouflage Unit at Farnham; later he was an intelligence officer in Normandy.

When the war was over, Spence returned to a city with little work. His former employer was unable to take him back and Spence turned to house extensions, furniture design, exhibitions and teaching. In 1946, aged 39, he became FRIBA and set up Basil Spence & Partners with

There is one London building that still sustains Spence's reputation: the Swiss Cottage Library (Sir Basil Spence, Bonnington and Collins), refurbished by John McAslan's practice in 2005. It is worth a visit, representing a lost tradition of well designed and stocked libraries that this nation has neglected in favour of things such as 'idea stores'. Spence first entered into relations with Hampstead Borough in 1958, winning the commission to design a town hall with some extravagant features that were pared down to a library and swimming baths. These were constructed, but the baths have now been demolished and replaced (2005). Only the refurbished library remains. The adjacent leisure centre is by Terry Farrell (2006); Rab Bennetts' Hampstead Theatre is nearby.

Above: the Swiss Cottage Library.
Left: Swiss Cottage Library as refurbished by John McAslan.
Below: 50 Queen Anne's Gate. Holden's Broadway building for London Underground is across the road. The Knightsbridge barracks are around the corner.

between having a cathedral and having hospitals, schools and houses, plumped immediately (I'm glad to say) for the cathedral, recognising, I think, the need of any community to have a place where the whole community can gather together and pray for such things as hospitals, schools and houses."

By 1967, relations between Spence and the Church had deteriorated to the point where local architects were employed to make changes and Spence resigned from the relationship. Midst such issues Spence received the commission for the sixteen-storey Thorn office building in St Martin's Lane, in 1956. Towering above all around it, in the middle of Covent Garden, this project was hardly less controversial than the Cathedral, although the Times' architectural correspondent considered the design exhibited at the RA to be lively and interesting (and without those 'unshapely' – presumably neo-Corbusier – structures on the roofs of other designs at the exhibition).

Spence's career was off, although controversy followed him everywhere that was indicative of Modernism's difficult acceptability to popular taste. Upon publishing a design for a building at Queen's College in Cambridge, it was noted by one commentator at the university that, in being backgrounded by a 'packing case' design, *"with what truth the willows weep."* Someone else wailed *"like a chorus of distressed Greek maidens."*

Nevertheless, more commissions came, including tower blocks in Glasgow and a share of the university building boom. By 1958 (just before Coventry Cathedral was completed) Spence was riding high as the newly elected President of the RIBA (giving Gold Medals to Mies and Nervi, and having Jacob Epstein create a bust in bronze). He was knighted in 1960, became the Royal Designer for Industry in 1960 and, from 1961 to 1968, was Professor of Architecture at the Royal Academy.

He was written up as an energetic (if sometimes imprudent) sailor, traveller and lover of good food and fine wine, as well as a persuasive, charming man who ensured that all the 'dashing' perspectives delivered to clients came from his own hand. His office was said to be subject to 'close personal control' (shorthand for discipline and authoritarianism, the hallmark of most notable offices), with Spence described as doing all the design work as rough sketches then handed over to his staff for development. But there appears to be a note of disillusionment. In 1960, just after his RIBA presidency, Spence was dissolving the partnership of which he was a part so that he could lend some smaller commissions his full personal attention – again, a characteristic and euphemistic way of describing a partnership break up. Around this time, in 1962, and after the opening of Coventry Cathedral to general approval, Spence was awarded the Order of Merit by the Queen (an award limited to twenty-four British members and seen as a gift of the monarch).

By now Spence had been awarded the commission to rebuild the Knightsbridge Barracks – but this was to turn out to be yet another controversial project, notable for the controversy over its thirty storey married officers' accommodation tower (95 m high) which rises up above all around it and oversees Hyde Park. Many voices joined in a chorus of anxious protest against what was happening to London and its skyline during a period when provincial cities across Britain were also tearing their historic cores apart – with Spence playing a significant role in this undertaking at places such as Glasgow and Newcastle. Sir Freddie Gibbert politely described the Knightsbridge Tower as an architectural gain and a townscape loss.

And so it continued. His British pavilion at Expo '67 was criticised by the Architectural Review as *"a shape designed for its own sake, with the means of construction decided afterwards."* And the next major building to hit the headlines was Spence's design for Queen Anne's Gate, where he had been brought in as a Lutyens-style design consultant to improve another architect's designs and was accused by the Architects Journal and by MP's of deceptive drawings (the AJ was miffed at being unable to access drawings and merely published early sketches, prompting controversy). Ironically, the building is now Listed.

As a man who had, ten years earlier, been awarded the Order of Merit, Spence claimed to be mortally wounded (even his obituary in the Times was to his sense of persecution). That was in 1972, but it was probably true: he died in 1976 in Eye, Suffolk and was buried at Thornham Parva, Suffolk – utterly out of fashion, despite all his awards. In the controversy over the Queen Anne's Gate building, even Vanbrugh's epitaph was, with irony and little humour, put before him: *"Lie heavy upon him, Earth, for he laid a heavy burden on thee."*

Andrew Renton, Spence's partner, was born in Dumfermline and also educated at the Edinburgh School of Art's architecture school. He worked in the Edinburgh offices of Sir John Burnet and Sir Robert Lorimor, and qualified in 1940 but the war took him off to Africa, Burma and India. He was Spence's London partner from 1949 to 1961, when the partnership broke up, and the designer of the Thorn building (he is also noted as the project architect for the Sea and Ships Pavilion). Renton then went on as Andrew Renton & Associates.

Ted Cullinan b.1931

Extant London works include:

• **Cullinan House**, Camden Mews, 1963-1964 (now listed).

• 16 Apartments at **Leighton Crescent**, Kentish Town, 1974-7.

• **Community Support Unit**, Lambeth, 1986–1988.

• **The Parish Church of St Mary's**, Barnes, 1978-84. Perhaps Cullinan at his best.

• 16 **Apartments** at Leighton Crescent, Kentish Town, 1974-79.

• **Lambeth Community Care Centre**, 1980-1985.

• **House** in Murray Street, 1982–1983. Again, Cullinan at his best.

• **Whittington Day Care Centre** for the Elderly, Streatham 1983–85

• 29 Flats for the elderly for Cecil Houses at **Chesterton Court**, Ealing, West London, 1984–89.

• **Charles Cryer Theatre and Arts Workshop**, Carshalton, Surrey 1988-91.

• **Docklands Campus for the University of East London**, Royal Docks, 1996-99. Interesting, but a questionable master-plan in such a flat, exposed area.

• **Office development for IBM/MEPC** at Bedfont Lakes, Middlesex 1989–92 (demonstrating that designs for corporate clients are not the Cullinan practice's forte). Hopkins also has a building here.

• **Greenwich Millennium School and Health Centre, Greenwich Peninsula**, 1998–2000. Late Cullinan with many enjoyable features, but whimsically playing the game of being a timber fortress.

Cullinan enjoyed the celebration of being the 2008 RIBA Gold medal winner as an architect who has done some outstanding work, especially in social housing and related social projects that, during the 1960s to '90's, demonstrated an architecture of humanist consideration and lack of pretence whilst remaining architecturally strong. In other words, his work is, at its best, within the Arts & Crafts 'free school' tradition and, in his own words, pursues a course midway between High-tech and Classicism – a stance which, in 1984 (at the height of Cullinan's creativity), prompted the Prince of Wales to remark that Cullinan was *"a man after my own heart"* *(1984) As a teacher, mentor and professional colleague he has the status that Ron Herron enjoyed of a 'dad' to many people. He was born in London and studied at the Cambridge University school from 1951-4 (where he "salivated over Le Corbusier's Unité at Marseille and the lovely hairy Maisons Jaoul"), before moving on to the AA (where his tutors included Denys Lasdun and the Smithsons; 1954-6). He then did a postgraduate degree at the University of California at Berkeley, briefly worked for Denys Lasdun (where he worked on the 'ziggurat' halls of residence at the University of East Anglia) and founded his practice as a co-op (which has always been one of its more notable features) in 1959. He claimed a lack of sporting prowess at school sowed the seeds of his architectural career. "I could not work out how to throw, or catch, or even to hit balls. So in my last two years I was let off cricket and tennis and put in charge of [building] a boathouse. It introduced me to the pleasure I've had from the slow process of building buildings myself, for all the rest of my life." He was elected RA in 1991.

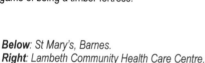

Below: St Mary's, Barnes.
Right: Lambeth Community Health Care Centre.

Top and above: the Docklands campus. (Photo: London Open House).

Left: the Greenwich Peninsula school. In both these projects there is a distinct Ralph Erskine influence (Erskine has housing adjacent to the school, but the influences bear reference to his Swedish work).

Below: Cullinan (**left**) and Hopkins (**right**) at Bedfont Lakes, bearing respective leanings toward the neo-vernacular and to the High-Tech still prevalent at this time. (Compare with the Millennium School and East London Docklands campus.)

Extant London works include:

• **Churchill Gardens**, Grosvenor Road to Lupus Road, Pimlico. 1947-62; the first English estate with tall slab blocks grouped with lower terraces' 16661 dwellings over 12.6 hectares (31 acres), built as 36 blocks in four phases at 200 p.p.a.

• **Lamble Street**, Gospel Oak (west end), 1951–4.

• **Mayfield School**, Putney, 1956.

• **Museum Of London**, London Wall, 1976.

• **Swimming Baths**, Dryburgh Road, Putney, 1968.

• **Queen Elizabeth Military Hospital,** Stadium Road, Woolwich, 1972-5.

• **Queen Elizabeth Conference Centre**, opp. Westminster Abbey, 1975-6. (*Photo **below**.*)

• **Dudley Court** housing, Endell Street, Covent Garden, 1983.

• **National Westminster Bank**, Shaftesbury Avenue, 1979-82.

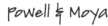

Above: *Phillip Powell and John Moya*

Powell & Moya

Sir Arnold Joseph Philip Powell
1921–2003

John Hidalgo (Jacko) Moya
1920–94

Powell & Moya began in practice in 1946 as young architects who had won a large housing competition. Powell had been born in Bedford, Moya in California. The two had met as students at the Architectural Association where Powell started in 1939 and Moya in 1938; both then worked for Frederick Gibberd before winning the competition for the Churchill Gardens project.

In 1951 the couple won the competition for the Skylon at the Festival of Britain: a symbol of hope when "*everything except hope was strictly rationed*", as Powell put it. Later work in the practice (what, in 1960, Banham described as 'gentlemanly' modern design: "*Nice, modern and British!*") was dominated by hospitals but included notable residential work in Cambridge. Young architects working in the practice included Richard Burton and Paul Koralek (later ABK), James Gowan, and Richard MacCormac. However, what Powell described as the practice's 'pragmatic modernism' was to become unfashionable in the 1970s when names such as Foster and Stirling were coming to the fore. Characteristically, neither Powell nor Moya was interested in pursuing commercial work, particularly speculative office schemes, and the Miesian office block located on top of the Museum of London was not a building of which Powell was proud.

Powell and Moya won the RIBA Royal Gold Medal in 1974 (the first occasion on which the medal had been awarded to a practice rather than an individual). Powell was appointed OBE in 1957, knighted in 1975, and appointed a Companion of Honour in 1984 and was elected RA in 1977.

Extant London works include:

• **Ackroyden** estate on Putney Heath, c.1950–54; the first of the LCC's post-war developments under the new architect's department of 1950 managed by Matthews.

• **Lansbury** neighbourhood, Poplar New Town (East India Dock Road to Limehouse Cut), scene of a 'Live Architecture' exhibition in 1951, including the first pedestrian market square (later parts are by the LCC Architects Department formed in 1950; architects for individual buildings included Frederick Gibberd, Geoffry Jellicoe, Norman & Dawburn, and Yorke Rosenberg & Mardall. The western part is by the GLC, 1970 on (near the market is David Adjaye's Idea Store, 2003).

• **Roehampton Estate**, 1951-8 (Alton East and Alton West), 'mixed', of high-rise blocks and low terraces on the Le Corbusier model of housing set in landscape (mixed with a touch of Scandinavian influences and an element of picturesque sentiment; garden city sentiments were now singularly unfashionable).

• **Royal Festival Hall** (see under Leslie Martin and with Peter Moro).

• **Commonwealth Institute**, Holland Park, 1958-62. Now disused; fate uncertain.

• **New Zealand House**, Haymarket, 1957-62. A fine example of the podium and tower equation imported from the USA; four lower floors; fifteen in the tower; roof terrace and bar; curtains as a novel way to combat solar glare.

• **Hillingdon Civic Centre**, High Street, Hillingdon, 1970-78. Brick and pitched roofs adapted to large and deep office spaces.

R-M-J-M

Sir Robert Hogg Matthew 1906–75

Sir Stirrat Andrew William Johnson-Marshall 1912–81

Top: Robert Matthew. Bottom: Johnson-Marshall.

Matthew was is another Scotsman who made good in London. He was born in Edinburgh, son of the architect John Fraser Matthew, partner of Sir Robert Lorimer. He graduated from Edinburgh University during the Depression and, without work, he studied slum housing. By 1936 he was advised by a family friend to work at the Department of Health for Scotland. Between 1940-45 he was working on the Clyde Valley regional plan, with Patrick Abercrombie and, by 1945, he was chief architect and planning officer to the health department for Scotland. He also became a member of the RIBA's reconstruction committee and, at its first meeting, was encouraged by Sir Charles Reilly (successor to the professor at Liverpool University school of architecture who had suggested he go into the Department of Health) to apply for the post of chief architect to the LCC.

In this new role he managed to bring housing projects from their place in the valuer's department to architecture and planning. He also rejected the traditional hierarchical organisational structure in favour of delegated responsibilities and group working, making his large office especially attractive to the young and in due course the most highly regarded urban housing authority in the world.

Together with Whitfield Lewis he scrapped all existing designs and substituted, under Scandinavian influence (he had visited Sweden in 1945), mixed developments of small towers and terraces whose prototype was the Ackroyden estate on Putney Heath (c.1950-56). Simultaneously, with his chosen deputy (and successor), Leslie Martin, he initiated the LCC's permanent contributions to the 1951 Festival of Britain – the charming Lansbury neighbourhood in the East End and the Royal Festival Hall. However, in 1953 he accepted the Forbes chair of architecture at Edinburgh University and moved back to Scotland – a career change explained as an outcome of a battle between so-called empiricists and Modernist intellectuals, at the LCC, with victory going to the latter. He now entered into partnership with Stirrat Johnson-Marshall (who had been at the Ministry of Education) and RMJM was born. (With Matthew in Edinburgh and Marshall in London.)

Matthew was knighted in 1962. In 1970 he received the RIBA Gold Medal when, it is fair to say, that era of public works which much of his career had concerned itself with was almost over.

Marshall was born in India, son of a civil servant. He was educated in England and, in 1930, entered Liverpool University's school of architecture. Not untypically for a young architect at that time, he became devoted to an ideal of service to the community fused together with a love of science and engineering. After graduating in 1935, local authority posts in Willesden and the Isle of Ely confirmed his conviction that public service was the right vehicle for the pursuit of social architecture. World War II found Marshall fighting the Japanese and narrowly escaping the fall of Singapore.

Back in England, Marshall was posted to the camouflage development and training centre at Farnham Castle, where he worked on the design and construction of decoy inflatable tanks and guns – apparently a seminal experience in the organisation of designing and manufacturing skills which remained fundamental to his dream of a revitalised building industry for the rest of his life. From 1945 to 1948 he was deputy architect of Hertfordshire County Council and, from 1948 to 1956, chief architect of the architects' and buildings' branch at the Ministry of Education.

His principal concern in these roles years was to promote economic, practical, and flexible schools which could be improved year on year in response to user needs and advances in technique and he was particularly interested in systems of prefabricated construction, which he saw as a key to reforming the building industry. The schools built in this period under his leadership gave Britain an international reputation for school-building. He was passionate about the basic elements of interaction between buildings and people, such as colour, light, sound, the control of temperature, and air movement, and the more tactile experiences from the ergonomics of furniture design to the feel of a handrail.

Andrew Derbyshire has noted that Marshall *"was fond of quoting the painter Fernand Léger: 'Architecture is not an art. It's a natural function of the social order.' He despised what he called 'hat fashion architecture' and was unhappy about architects who failed to take their clients' needs seriously and saw architecture rather as an opportunity for the monumental expression of their own egos."* It seems his ideal was a vernacular architecture created by the community, in which client and architect were almost indistinguishable – a kind of architecture of the Volk, a neo-Hegelian idea that has filtered through Modernism and characterised, for example, Nicholas Pevsner's historical perspective of the modernist *Zeitgeist*.

Marshall was even a leader of a movement to reform the RIBA, whose public architect members were in a majority for the first time in the institution's history (he was the RIBA vice-president, 1962-4). He was knighted in 1971, retiring in 1978 just as Post-Modernist ideology was determining architectural fashions. Matthew, meanwhile, became president of the RIBA from 1962 (whether as reformer or as a private architect and employer now reconciled to reality is unclear), when he was also knighted.

Above: Hillingdon Civic Centre – a 1970s work of emergent successors at the practice of RMJM during an era suddenly unsure of the Modernist idiom and returning to picturesque and Arts & Crafts themes, now on the level of civic design.

Opposite page: in contrast, New Zealand House, seen from Trafalgar Square. The 'Grand Trunk Railway' building in the foreground is by Aston Webb (1908).

Ronald Ward 1909–73

Extant London works include:
• **219 Oxford Street**, 1951, with reliefs celebrating the Festival of Britain. See page 336.
• **Millbank Tower,** (21-24 Millbank, adjacent to Tate Britain; formerly for Vickers), 1961-3. 118 m/32 stories. Some remodelling by GMW, 2001.
• **Other offices:** Astral House, London Road, Norbury, 1962-5; Park Lane buildings in Croydon, 1962-4 (St George House and Katherine House).

There is crude irony in the fact that a man five feet four inches tall should have been the author of the UK's tallest building at that time, and perhaps the tallest in Europe (at 370 feet). But was he the author? As an architect, he was nothing if not catholic: the Millbank Tower, the Oxford Street building, Holborn Viaduct Station, the Croydon Centre (1962-5), the neo-Georgian National Farmer's Union building in Knightsbridge and, of all things, Dungeness lighthouse (1960).

His practice was, as they say, without a house style. And, as one might expect, newspapers reported him as being 'well known in the City'. In fact, he got himself elected a Lloyds underwriter in 1963. He was a keen golf player and the office was the former Tsarist embassy in Knightsbridge (with his London penthouse upstairs). He was clearly a 'commercial' type and candidly said of his own success that it was the result of, *"being in the right place at the right moment and my face fitting ... and marrying the right woman"* (an actress turned secretary who married the boss).

Ward was born in Kings Worthy, educated at Peter Symonds School (Winchester) and at the Royal Academy schools. He was on the staff of the Essex, London and Surrey County Councils before settling down at Saxon Snell & Phillips, but then established his own practice in 1936. He had effectively retired by 1967, not long after the Millbank Tower was completed.

This page: Millbank Tower, seen from within its Lever House style punctuated podium.

Extant London works of GMW include:

• **Castrol House** (now Marathon House), Marylebone Road, 1955-60. Once a classic podium-and-tower equation; 15 floors. (In collaboration with Casson Condor. Later converted to apartments and partly reclad by others.

• **Commercial Union** (now Aviva Tower), Leadenhall, 1963-69; approx. 118 m high. Two clients both wanted to cooperate and use the same architects for a joint scheme; the overall site ratio was 5:1. This was in accord with the Holford and Holden 1947 planning report made for the City, which provided this ratio and encouraged open spaces and thereby a fracturing of the traditional 100ft height limit that was in place in London between 1894-1954 (prompted by Queen Victoria's wrath at the 151ft height of Queen Anne's Mansions – later replaced by Basil Spence's 50 Queen Anne's Gate – and reinforced by fire regulations). The two buildings were also originally linked at mezzanine level by the City's ill-fated 'pedway' system of decks and bridges. However, the former P&O building adjacent to the CU was demolished in 2008 to make way for a Rogers skyscraper (42 stories). The CU building suspends its floors: the 24 floors hung in two batches of 12; half are hung from the roof and half from an intermediate cantilever midway up the tower (plant rooms occupy the spaces created by large steel cantilevered beams). The building was reclad in modified form after the 1993 IRA bomb blast in St Mary Axe.

• **150 Leadenhall Street**, and **6-8 Bishopsgate**, 1974-81. The former is a particularly elegant eight storey block, in characteristic 1970s chocolate brown.

• **54 Lombard Street,** 1986-94 (Now 20 Gracechurch Street). Formerly the HQ of Barclays; 19 floors; extensively refurbished 2006-8, indicating how short a life some City buildings can have.

• **Minster Court**, 1987-91. London's only picturesque, neo-Gothic PoMo building (three linked buildings filling the urban block).

Also, 1-3 Clement's Inn, Westminster, 1983; Centurion House, Monument Street, City, 1984; 12-15 Finsbury Circus, 1991; 99 Bishopsgate, 1993-6, 26 stories / 104 m (also reclad after the 1993 IRA bomb blast).

on being 'commercial': GMW

Frank Gollins 1910–99
James Melvin b.1912
Edmund Ward 1912–98

From the left: Edmund Ward, Frank Gollins and James Melvin.

The City buildings designed by Gollins, Melvin and Ward make a particularly fascinating walk through the history of latterday architectural fashions, simultaneously exhibiting the history of a practice's passage from the post-war Modernism of its founders to the PoMo of their successors who continued as the acronym, GMW. Their buildings are notable for introducing to London two tall building equations that have been fundamental to urban developments around the world. The first was the podium-and-slab (or tower) equation introduced by SOM in New York, in 1955 (the Lever Building); the second was the piazza-and-tower equation (i.e. no podium) popularised by Mies van der Rohe in New York and Chicago. Their example of the latter – the Commercial Union building – remains one of London's more elegant tall buildings, even as reclad (much as before) after the damage wrought by an IRA bomb in the early 1990s.

Gollins was born in Birmingham, son of a landscape painter. He attended the local school of architecture. He then worked locally before entering the RAF when war broke out. Afterward, in 1945, he met with James Melvin, son of a wealthy Scottish stockbroker (born in Edinburgh; educated at various schools in Scotland, Switzerland and England) who had attended the AA (1930-35), and they started up in practice – later being joined by another of Melvin's colleagues at the AA, Edmund Ward. Initially, they had residential work for Lambeth borough and this led to educational work, later to university projects. This was also the area of their breakthrough: winning a national competition for a large university project (at Sheffield) in 1953 that was not completed until 1975, when Gollins retired. Other large projects followed, including an airport terminal in New York, and culminating in the CU building.

A former colleague in the office comments that, *"Common wisdom says that Frank Gollins and James Melvin started in 1947 and Edmund [Ward] joined them*

Above: 150 Leadenhall, with 6-8 Bishopsgate behind.
Below: the CU building seen from Lime Street, with the Lloyds '86 building to the left (what is fundamentally another standalone tower and piazza building, but with a residual piazza reduced to the status of a 'concourse').

two years later. Edmund {Ward} was the 'baby' and the 'design genius', eventually becoming a Royal Fine Arts Commissioner [...] He liked fast cars, beautiful women and his narrow gauge railway. James Melvin [...] was effectively the business brain and office manager. He was also the archetypal English [sic] gentleman. Frank [Gollins], by all accounts was the wheeler dealer who often brought the jobs in. I think, in the early days they would have worked quite closely together, though by the late sixties and early seventies they had a team of loyal assistants including Brian Mayes and Roger Goold and were probably becoming a bit less hands-on."

Another version tells us that Frank Gollins won lots of war-damage work and asked a 'well-connected' girlfriend about whom to team up with – having the outcome of he and Melvin setting up in Russell Square. Ward then joined them. At that time the office policy was not to employ women, but the trio did employ a young Jim Stirling. It seems that, in 1953, Stirling asked if he could join the team working on a Sheffield University complex competition (which GMW later won) and he was sacked when it was discovered he was already preparing a rival scheme. Stirling described GMW as *"the best of the safe, understandable moderns."* Such is oral history – but it is often what the academic version is indirectly founded upon.

By about 1980 (when the practice had 200 staff (no longer unusual twenty years later), work around the world and an expensive computer in the office, one of the first in London practices) GMW had decided that the approach to architecture that had made it famous (as the CU building) was no longer commercial – developers, according to a later partner, hated it. The Post-Modern phase of the practice's history had begun (exemplified by Minster Court and the Barclays Bank HQ buildings).

Latterly, it is recorded that younger staff in the office look longingly back at what Gollins, Melvin and Ward did. However, even the former P&O building adjacent to the CU has been demolished (2007-8) and is being replaced by a Richard Rogers skyscraper.

Skidmore Owings & Merrill's Lever House, on Park Avenue, in New York, was completed in 1950-52 and was a Modernist icon of enormous influence, seeing to satisfy two demands: the purity of a tower statement, seen at a distance; and a podium block that aligns itself with the street and provides architecture at, as they say, 'a human scale'. Two outstanding London buildings followed this typology: Ronald Ward's Millbank Tower; and GMW's Castrol House.

A few years later, Mies van der Rohe added another iconic typology to New York's Park Avenue: the Seagram Building, of 1954-58 – a design that threw away the podium block in order to establish a different form of purity and to leave an open piazza at the base of the tower (and, in the process, playing games with NYC's zoning laws that normally engender a series of setbacks).

GMW's Leadenhall conjunction of two London sites and projects arguably provides an interpretation on both, providing a low block (the former P&O; demolished 2007) to one side of a joint piazza with the CU. Another example is New Zealand House (see page 379). But Ronald Ward's former Vickers Tower (now Millbank Tower; see page 380) perhaps comes nearest to the Lever House game of a punctuated podium plus a tower block.

The alternative to these typologies was GMW's Minster Court, celebrated at the time as a 'groundscraper': filling the urban block, reinforcing street definitions and broken into linked blocks with dividing light wells and a large covered entrance court. (**Photo left**: Minster Court is to the right; the Gherkin is in the background; Arup Associate's Plantation Place – another block-filler – is to the left foreground).

YRM
Francis Reginald Stevens Yorke
1906-62
Eugene Rosenberg 1907-91
Cyril Mardall 1909-94
David Allford 1927-97
Brian Henderson b.1920

Extant London works include:
• **Gatwick Airport**, 1955-58 (now altered).
• former **YRM offices**, Greystoke Place, 1962.
• **St Thomas' Hospital**, Lambeth (at Westminster Bridge), 1966-76.

studying at the Birmingham School of Architecture – completing the course in 1930. That same year Yorke completed his first building – some agricultural workers' cottages – and also got married. The marriage didn't last, apparently because of Yorkes' propensity for flirtation and affairs.

1930 was also a bad time to set up in practice and Yorke initially turned to journalism, writing for the Architects' Journal as Assistant Editor on technical matters and publishing books on modern houses (e.g. famously, 'The Modern House', of 1934; as a journalist he shared an office off the Strand with Frederick Gibberd). He won a competition for some small houses in Essex, in 1933, with William Holford and Gordon Stephenson (Gidea Park). He was also a founding member of the MARS group in 1932 (with Wells Coates, Maxwell Fry, Morton Shand, and others, fronting the CIAM in Britain). This work also produced contact with Continental architects and, from 1935-37, Yorke was in practice with Marcel Breuer – a marriage of convenience for Breuer (as with Fry and Gropius), leaving both partners to practise separately (Yorke sometimes in conjunction with his father).

In 1939 Yorke and Holford joined together to act as the architectural arm of Sir Alexander Gibbs & Partners on the construction of factories, hostels and the like for the war effort (for the Ministry of Supply). Later, he became a researcher for the Ministry of Works on technical matters, and became interested in models for prefabricated housing. Then came the YRM partnership. While each partner in YRM took charge of particular projects, there was an intent to have a consistent outlook, with emphasis on efficient production, use of new building products, and a broad range of building types in the public sector. In addition, all three partners shared an interest in contemporary art. However, Yorke's approach to design often seemed casual. He was clearly an operator and enabler, spending little time in the office and delegating everything to talented young office staff (who before long began to rebel against the lack of new ideas). He has been described as a fisherman, a sportsman, a traveller, a lover of fast cars and good food, collected paintings, sculpture and drawings and books, a man with a sharp temper, and a farmer who bred pedigree cows on a farm in Oxfordshire.

The key moment of transition for the practice came with the commission for Gatwick Airport (1955–8), on which Yorke was joined by two talented and characterful newcomers to the practice, David Allford and Brian Henderson. Yorke had apparently always been ready to encourage his younger staff (and never wanted 'yes men'), and the commission for Gatwick was a crucial

That YRM rode to success on a wave called the post-war welfare state is a fact. How that came about has not been explained, although one can surmise that the success of the practice had a lot to do with 'K' Yorke, as he was called, combined with expertise from the foreign and Modernist expertise of his two partners: Rosenberg, from Czechoslovakia, and Mardall, from Finland. Rosenberg arrived first. He qualified in Prague and was there in private practice from 1934-38, having worked as a student in Le Corbusier's Atelier in Paris, from 1929-30. Escaping to England in 1939, he was sent to an alien camp in Australia before release in 1942. However, he had met Yorke in the '30's and the two joined in partnership in 1944. Mardall (formerly Sjöström) was born in Helsinki, came to England in 1927 and was taught at the Northern Polytechnic and at the AA, qualifying in 1933, learning expertise in timber prefabrication, joining the navy in 1940, and linking with Yorke and Rosenberg in 1945. Their first significant buildings were completed in 1947. Later work included the Susan Lawrence School that formed part of the Lansbury Estate in Poplar as a showpiece of 'live architecture' within the 1951 Festival of Britain.

The biography of Yorke reads like some eighteenth century country squire straight out of Fielding: a beer swigging womaniser of mischievous character and great persuasiveness who was born into a prosperous Birmingham family, was taught at Chipping Campden School, and followed his father (Francis Walter Bagnall Yorke; 1879-1957) into the architectural profession by project for the firm (and which was to feature largely in Henderson's career). The terminal, with its glass walling, marble floor, and crisp detailing (including white cladding tiles that became the YRM trademark, best seen on St Thomas' Hospital), showed English architecture catching up with international standards.

Allford was the son of a factory worker and had studied at Sheffield University from 1944-52 (a period interrupted by three years in the RAF) and came to YRM as his one and only job. He was made partner in 1958, Senior Partner in 1975 (after working for nearly ten years on the Warwick University project with Rosenberg, and Chairman in 1987, at which time Yorke Rosenberg and

in Smithfield (1961), with his penthouse on the top floor (where he kept his art collection and held office parties, from which wives were apparently excluded). He was awarded a CBE the next year but soon died in St Thomas' Hospital – which turned out to be another major YRM rebuilding project.

Under the leadership of Allford and Henderson the practice held up a high reputation throughout the period, having gone from 38 to 650 staff in Henderson's career, with offices in Venezuela, Australia, Hong Kong, the Middle East, Berlin, etc. But it all came to grief after an ill-fated flotation on the stock market in the hedonistic heydays of the late 1980s when architects

Mardall became simply YRM). He was made CBE in 1984, and retired a few years later. If Allford was the man in the duffle coat, Henderson (b.1920) was the man in the tailored suit, being the son of an Edinburgh banker who studied at the school of architecture there, did his 'year out' with Basil Spence and enjoyed the usual extensive European tours before starting work in London in the early 1950;s on housing projects in the firm of Armstrong & McManus. There followed National Service which included one year in Egypt (where he learned to sail, as well as travel in the Middle East), and a 'call-up' immediately afterward, going to Suez. Upon his return, he found work conditions still rather bad but managed an interview with Yorke. Allford had arrived a few months earlier.

In 1958, just before Yorke died (of cancer of the throat), and Rosenberg and Mardall retired, Allford and Henderson were made new partners taking the firm into a second generation and extensive international success. It was about this time that Yorke designed and completed new custom-designed offices for the practice

(after changes affecting their self-regulation) thought they could get rich by drawing in City investors. This all changed with the arrival of the recession. First Allford and then, two years later, Henderson, withdrew into timely retirement. Work-loads fell, returns could not meet shareholder's expectations, and a break up of the multi-disciplinary practice began, ending with a middle-management buy-out in 1997 that produced a third generation practice which still survives and continues the firm's name.

Above: the YRM offices in Clerkenwell – a six-storey building on a sloping site that includes a large car parking undercroft, which cleverly pretends it is a three storey garden pavilion. The area became dense with architects in the later 1980s and '90s, as a by-product of Fleet Street newspaper industry changes, the YRM building was refurbished by a fashion business and, was later occupied by the architects Wilkinson Eyre.

Richard (Rubin) Seifert 1910–2001

Extant London works include:

• **Tower 42** (formerly NatWest Tower), Old Broad Street; 43 stories / 183 m. 1960-80. Tallest unbraced tower in the world (i.e. all core, with a narrow perimeter of corridor and offices), marred by planing difficulties which delayed construction and completion into an era during which it was obsolete. Designed with a plan in the form of the client's logo – a PoMo gesture long before its time (a fun but rather silly architectural conceit guaranteed to please only the pigeons and the client). Present glazed base enclosure by GMW.

• **Centre Point**, Charing Cross/ New Oxford Street, 1967. 36 floors; 117 m. Wonderful landmark; not very economic as a building; dreadful piazza level gnarled by traffic engineers (resulting from a deal that gave the developer more space if he allowed the road works on the site). Load-bearing, pre-cast perimeter structure / cladding (built without scaffolding at the rate of one floor every five days), characteristic of much of Seifert's work. The building was deliberately and infamously not let until 1979.

• **Space House** (formerly Aerial House), Kingsway, 1962. Circular; ironically, now the home of CABE, a governmental design watchdog.

• Former British Rail offices, **Euston Place,** 1974-8. An early example of the employment of granite (which became ubiquitous in the later '80's), much as the late Victorians had turned to glazed tiles in order to deal with pollution.

• **Sheraton Park Tower** (originally Grand Metropole, Knightsbridge (1968–73)

• Other projects of note during the 1970s include hotels, the Wembley Conference Centre, houses, offices and a shopping mall in King Street, Hammersmith, London (1976-79); the Princess Grace Hospital, Nottingham Place, London (1975); the London Heathrow Airport Hotel (1976); the Wembley Conference Centre (1976); Orbit House, Southwark; Cutlers Gardens, City, 1978-82; Telstar House, Kensington; Planet House, Baker Street, etc.

• Numerous other works are around London: refer to the Buildings of England guide.

Poor Seifert: vilified in his life-time for being 'commercial', as a proverbial whore to developers, and an architect celebrated posthumously – in particular by those who denigrated him at the height of his infamy and now constitute the likes of those conservationist lobbyists eager to freeze London into an architectural museum. Perhaps worse (although one doubts if he would care): his most notable designs (such as the now listed Centre Point) are regularly attributed to his partner, George Marsh, although such arrangements are hardly unusual and the fact that this should be another way of denigrating Seifert says much about the vanity and hypocrisy that surrounds such issues of attribution. The alteration in assessments also indicates something of the change in attitude to 'commercial' issues before and after the early 1990s recession (as well as a degree of familiar nostalgia). But his practice's work now stands out as some of the last of British architecture that was genuinely tectonic in expression, notably exhibiting the influences of Marcel Breuer. We don't do it like that anymore, even with the digital tools that engender less robust and more 'mechanical' tectonics.

Seifert was born in Zurich but educated in London and entered the Bartlett school in 1928, where its head, Albert Richardson, soon told him to give up and be a doctor (like his father). He didn't. In 1934 he set up on his own, doing obscure work that was interrupted by the war, in which he served as an engineer in India, where he achieved the rank of lieutenant-colonel. He left the army in 1946 feeling very confident and, by 1947, was again in practice and beginning a new career of unswerving loyalty to clients, based on a thorough knowledge of the building regulations and planning law (the LCC had to introduce what it referred to as 'Seifert clauses' in order

Opposite page: Space House, now occupied by the government design watchdog, CABE. The building again adopts the podium and tower typology, but completely separates the one from the other and rather crudely links them by a bridge (to the right of the photo). However, the building is a good illustration of Seifert et al's concerns with tectonic expression (possibly inspired by the likes of Marcel Breuer) which the British profession as a whole (with few exceptions) has now forgotten. 2007, for example, saw the erection of a steel framed building in the City, designed by David Walker, pretending to a Seifert agenda but now as a theatrical façade exercise in a similar manner that a nearby Foster building pretends to a Mies van der Rohe theatrically (Mies' steel now as aluminium dressing).

to close the loopholes the architect discovered and exploited). The practice particularly benefited from the relaxation of construction constraints during the early 1950s and developers came to Seifert to maximise site profitability. He, in turn, learned to adapt his 1930s ideas to the novelties of pre-cast concrete construction techniques.

Over some forty years – as a man who was in the office by 7am, had three secretaries and shared designed kudos – Seifert designed some 600 works in London and at one time employed over 300 people. Denis Sharp wrote that, a long-serving assistant recalled *"that if a planner suggested that he was about to put an approval in the post Seifert would reply, 'Don't bother, I'll send my chauffeur'."*

He retired in 1988 (to a formerly modest north London home he had purchased, and hugely expanded, in 1946) and the practice's work (since 1984 run by his son, John) became PoMo and rather mediocre.

Above: *Seifert's turn to granite, at 19-22 Alfred Place (Whittington House; 1972), one of the best examples of his firm's work.*
Left: *the former NatWest Tower, with 150 and 6-8 Leadenhall to the right (the building on the opposite corner, left of the photo, is by Jestico Whiles, 1988, just after the nearby Lloyds building was completed by Richard Rogers).*

messages of good cheer

Ronald James Herron
1930–1994

Sir Peter Cook b1936
Warren Chalk 1927–87
Denis Crompton b1927
David Green b1937
Mike Webb b1937

Extant London works include:
• **Imagination**, Store Street, 1989.
• **Queen Elizabeth Hall** and **Hayward Gallery**, Southbank, with others while at the LCC.

Ron Herron and, below, Cook.

Archigram won the RIBA Royal Gold Medal in 2002, some forty years after they published 'archigrams' and upset the architectural establishment. They were an odd mixture of malcontents: initially Cook, Green and Webb, later joined by Chalk, Crompton and Herron (the latter all ex-LCC). Theo Crosby was responsible for bringing all six together to work on a project at Euston and, for some two years, the group of six made an energetic and polemical impact on the architectural world with a mix of pre and post-war influences (comics and consumerism). Their work – in the context of unworthy 'commercial' work and 'dreary' housing projects – was symptomatic of pro-American materialistic dreaming about a future of affluence, a maximisation of the available range of choice, and the conspicuous consumption of goods and services having lots of 'features'. Later, in 1971, Cook, Crompton and Herron formed an ill-fated practice that survived only a short while before the former pair withdrew into full-time teaching and Herron struggled on in order to build something as well as teach.

The influence of the group – coming from a corner of post-war architectural culture thoroughly oriented toward American consumerism, the newly discovered glamour of Los Angeles, of US pop art, pop music and jazz – was to be a crucial background ingredient of the High-Tech/Post-Modern rivalry of the '70's and '80's. The High-Tech, for example, was in love with a '60s mix of Buckminster Fuller and the insidious glamour of military hardware (this was, after all, the Vietnam era). The Rogers schemes for the Pompidou Centre and at Lloyds seemed to owe much to a compound of such influences, of 'West Coast cool' and Archigram imagery mixed with that of Cedric Price. There was also the influence of Reyner Banham, a witty historian and populariser eager to debunk Modernist traditions and argue for 'intelligent design' rather than merely seductive form. And the timing was perfect. Within this scene, Archigram, appeared to give architects a new kind of voice, to suggest a

value agenda that locked them firmly into the desires characterising the vital heart of the consumer economy and to promise a future of relevancy and legitimacy free from what Banham referred to as historical 'baggage'. Not that their agitation was intellectual: this was purely instinctive stuff. However, there is a (dreary) issue at the heart of celebrating Archigram: is expressive fantasy a legitimate basis for a Gold Medal? This is hardly a trite question and one sees it posed when comparing the two strongest members of the group – Cook and Herron.

Cook (knighted in 2007) proved himself as an outstanding educator, running the Institute of Contemporary Arts (ICA; 1969-71) and setting up Art Net (1972-79) before establishing himself as the charismatic Head of the University College school. Herron sought nothing less than to fulfil the ambitions of a youth who started in architecture articled at fifteen; attending night classes and struggling with an RIBA and appearing to be less than keen on working-class upstarts entering the profession. Cook came from a more bourgeois background: born in Southend and taught at the Bournemouth school of architecture. He later attended the AA, where his tutors included the Smithsons. Herron attended night classes between 1944-1956, first at the Brixton school of building and later at the Regent Street Polytechnic. Cook never attained meaningful practical experience, but Herron loved site mud on his boots. Cook was awed by his construction experience, although never inclined to follow him (his built projects, such as that in Graz, being reliant upon others to translate ideas into tectonic and realisable propositions).

Somewhat ironically, Herron had joined the LCC (1954-61) and worked with Chalk and Crompton on the South Bank's 'Brutalist' Queen Elizabeth Hall and Hayward Gallery. Yet it was Herron who was to do two things that sets him apart from the others. The first concerned fantasy: winning an international design competition in 1976 for a 'home fit for a superstar'. This was at a low point of his career: Archigram was effectively a memory; Post-Modernism was on the ascendent; its contrast, the so-called High-Tech was on the defensive; Punk was a sign of changing tastes. Herron's superstar – appropriately for an East End kid from a family of leather workers – was the Queen. His 'home' was, appropriately for a left-wing man in love with Hollywood, a film set located in open spaces outside Glasgow. The underlying theme – one of more import than most Archigram ideas put together (and taking us back to Inigo Jones) – was 'sets': the notion that architecture was fundamentally a form of thematic set design.

His second achievement was on similar keynote, but now a scheme for Imagination – an agency that, characteristically, would design outrageous press launches arousing jaded journalists to enthusiasms for familiar product launches (another touch of Jones). The outcome of the project was a building conversion opposite Cedric Price's office and hidden away from public view behind a vaguely Queen Anne façade. Even Foster admitted envy at Herron's remarkable achievement in separating out an 'H' plan into two wings linked by bridges and dressed in a protective, tensed fabric roof. It was a space and a place (a 'destination' as we now call such phenomena), painted entirely in white and prompting the unexpected which, for a while, became the heart of Imagination: a celebratory statement of its upbeat creativity and scene of all kinds of events.

Other Herron schemes followed – all intended to be built rather than consumed as fantastical propositions. But nothing significant was realised. In the background, among Herron's other practice experiences was a short stint with the office of William Pereira, in Los Angeles, in 1969, following a period teaching at UCLA, and, before that, working for the Halpern Partnership and Colin St John Wilson (1965-68). However, in 1970 the remaining Archigram members under Peter Cook (then teaching at the AA) won a large competition (*Features Monte Carlo*) and Herron returned to London. The project fell through, but the Archigram office had been established. However, it failed to win any significant work and faded away at the very time architectural tastes were shifting and the focus of attention was away from Archigram and divided between an American scene (to the likes of Venturi et al) and an emerging European scene (initially

*One of Herron's most famous proposals was for a 'walking city' (1964) – a marvellous fantasy of something like an aircraft carrier on legs stomping the planet. But its provocative contrast was to be the charged magic of something it perhaps inspired: the 'walking castle' of Diana Wynne Jones' novel (Howl's Moving Castle, 1986), made into a film by Hayao Miyzaki in 2004. As translated by Miyzaki this wonderful, magical, bumbling beast (**above**) arguably belongs to a tradition of the romantic, picturesque and mythic – certainly to a world of dreams that is alien to the mechanistic and consumerist heart of Archigram's architectural fantasies, speaking of an alternative set of values.*

***Opposite page**: the Imagination atrium roof – a realisation possessing its own kind of magic.*

to Paris, then Berlin and Barcelona). Herron was then briefly and somewhat unhappily with Pentagram (as an independent partner, but failing to win work) and then Derek Walker Associates before setting up his own practice in 1982 (interestingly, now with his two sons) and undertaking the Imagination project. Just as he was enjoying success, he died of a heart attack.

The 2002 Gold Medal award celebrated the inspiration of a group who broke through the profession's servile posturing into a fantasy world where necessity was banished, politics evaporated along with any form of realism, and architecture was an upbeat, hedonistic party. Herron, however, knew that Hollywood married its dreams to hard pragmatism – and that mix was perhaps where the real magic was to be found.

Cedric Price 1934–2003

Extant London works include:
• **Aviary**, London Zoo, 1961 (Fuller tensigrity inspired structure; with Lord Snowdon as client and Frank Newbury as engineer).

It is impossible to discuss the work of Archigram and '60s dreamin' without referring to Cedric Price, a monumental character whose intellect was as large as his prominent belly, an ever-present cigar on his lips and a glass of brandy in his hand, and whose values were as consistent as his uniform of striped shirt and separate stiff white collar. His work was arguably of more significance than Archigram's cheerfully articulated collages, and yet he failed to win (or perhaps desire) a similar degree of celebration. Oddly, his idea projects exhibited the concerns of a man of committed left-wing sympathies and what we would now interpret as right-wing free-market policies: a New Labour man before his time. And there was no Gold Medal for him.

Price was born in Stone, Staffordshire, son of cinema architect, Arthur John Price (who worked for Harry Weeden; d1953). He attended the school of architecture at Cambridge from 1952-5, and then the AA, 1955-57 (where his tutors included John Killick and Arthur Korn). Upon graduation he worked for Lasdun, Fry and Drew, and Erno Goldfinger (working on the 'This is Tomorrow' exhibition, where he met the engineer Frank Newby), before setting up his own practice. Price even applied to the LCC for a job, was turned down, and turned to illustration as a source of income, producing drawings for the mail-order catalogue of a big department store. He started part-time teaching at the AA in 1958, and met Bucky Fuller in 1959 before setting up in practice in 1960. Stephen Mullin was his principal assistant from 1964-69; later, he was assisted by Peter Eley, Paul Hyett, Will Alsop and John Lyall, the latter two subsequently setting up in partnership before later separating (with Alsop imitating the physical characteristics of Price).

There followed a series of remarkable projects. First there was the Fun Palace (1961-4), a collaboration with the radical theatre director Joan Littlewood (1914-2002), founder of the Theatre Workshop and scourge of middle-class theatre. The 'palace' was seen as *"a people's workshop or university of the streets"* by reviving the tradition of the 18th-century Vauxhall Gardens – the Thames-side entertainment promenade. Its form and structure were to resemble *"a large shipyard in which*

enclosures such as theatres, cinemas, restaurants, workshops, rally areas, can be assembled, moved, re-arranged and scrapped continuously."* (Price's words; the description reads as the basis of Peter Cook's concept for the 'Features Monte Carlo' proposal, 1970.) *"It was well into the detailed design of the project that, at an alcohol-inspired brain-storming session off Times Square in 1962, we decided on the name Fun Palace for our short-life conglomerate of disparate, free-choice, free-time, voluntary activities, planned as a public launching-pad rather than a Mecca for East London"* , said Price, in Buckminster Fullersque language. In Littlewood's words, *"the essence of the place will be its informality; nothing is obligatory, anything goes. There will be no permanent structure."* A site was proposed in the Lea Valley but, by 1966, this had fallen through.

In the meantime, there was the Potteries Thinkbelt Project (1964), a scheme addressing the issue of the death of Britain's older heavy industries in the north of England, about which Price famously wrote, *"Education, if it is to be a continuous human service run by the community must be provided with the same lack of peculiarity as the supply of drinking water or free teeth."* There was also Non-Plan, 1969, with Peter Hall and Paul Barker – a project that questioned the conventions of British planning policies.

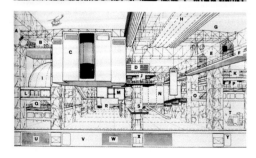

Above: the Fun Palace, as drawn in 1964

Cedric Price's Aviary in London Zoo (here straddling the Regent's Park Canal) has lasted what its author would, no doubt, have found to have been an embarrassing length of time. It is one of London's more remarkable and taken-for-granted works of architecture and engineering, now with a well-established foliage within its netting and an almost Frank Lloyd Wright touch to some of the landscape design. Sadly, the London Zoo long ago became an assemble of cheap, unambitious structures silted up with bad graphics and ad hoc gestures pandering to an audience (and set of inhabitants) who deserve better. The Aviary remains a strange project for such a man, but one that indicates the promise of someone who preferred the ambiguities and temporary status of service to the ostensible permanence of formal architectural gestures.

The implicit message in all these projects concerned change, choice, consumer services, indeterminacy, so-called 'built-in-obsolescence', and the idea – prevalent at the time – that what was important in architecture was what it *did* for you rather than what it *looked* like (at the time, no self-respecting young architect drew an elevation if they could avoid it). But there was always (in contrast to Archigram's stance) an implicit political basis to Price's propositions. His work was, almost invariably, intellectually challenging within a framework of Buckminster Fuller inspired practice postures, and yet idiosyncratically offbeat.

Rem Koolhaas noted that: *"I don't know a single person who doesn't believe that the Pompidou was not derived from or intimately connected with the Fun Palace in some way. ... I think Cedric Price ... was an ideologue but not a theorist. In general, I am very sceptical that you can be theoretical in architecture, because there is really no theory. There are precedents, directions and movements which generate forms: it's very important to separate that from theory. [...] he was, in a certain way, an arch nostalgic and conservative. Ultimately, his most radical and innovative contribution was his relentless and endless questioning of the claims and pretensions of architecture and architects. He was a sceptic torturing a conservative discipline. So, the 1960s are very compelling in two ways. On the one hand there's the scale and the sincerity and earnestness of the effort, and, on the other, the ruthlessness of the questioning of that very effort by people such as Price. Presumably, there is an internal connection between the two: he could only be ruthless because the period produced strong and compelling forms."*

Later projects of the '70s and '80s failed to enjoy the same radical content in an era when the PoMo/High-Tech debate had left the 1960s as an historic period of polemical gestures in which no one any longer had much interest. The formalities of 'what it looked like' were, by then, again a principal issue and even the High-Tech school – which construed its roots to be within a tradition of Modernism stretching back through European heroes to the Arts & Crafts, etc. – accepted compositional aesthetics as a prime project issue. A provocative concern with strategic relevance and intent – rather than the form and style that expressed such intent – was out of place in the 1980s and never found a place in the 1990s. Price's lasting monument remains a rather large bird cage in London Zoo, now almost fifty years old, but it hints at what might have been achieved by a modification of Price's attitude to architecture and its practice.

The man himself remains somewhat of an enigma: what were the influences upon a twenty-six-year-old who created the Fun Palace? What was the interest in theatre that took Price from running the Cambridge University arts society to Joan Littlewood and then his partner of many years, the actress Eleanor Bron? What was the intermix of values that married a left-wing sentiment with right-wing market policies? Why

the sartorially disciplined uniform and posturing which bizarrely included a cigar and brandy for breakfast? How was an office with little work sustained? What drove a need for independence that underlay the practice and what some people have read as a deliberate avoidance of building commitment? We await a biography.

Price on architecture: *"It's a way of imposing order or establishing a belief, and that is the cause of religion to some extent. Architecture doesn't need those roles anymore; it doesn't need mental imperialism; it's too slow, it's too heavy and, anyhow, I as an architect don't want to be involved in creating law and order through fear and misery. Creating a continuous dialogue with each other is very interesting; it might be the only reason for architecture, that's the point. In the 17th century, Sir Henry Wotton's translation of Vitruvius' Latin text defined architecture as "Commodotie, Firmness and Delight." Commodity is good housekeeping, money. Firmness is structure. The delight factor might be the dialogue. They've served me well – commodity, firmness and delight – because I can hang anything on them."*

The sentiment is profoundly anti-architectural in the sense that the French writer Georges Bataille (1897-1962) voiced a suspicious counter-architectural fear of its ordering, and imposed ideological reassurances. In all Price's work he sought to avoid such expressivity and, in this sense, his notion of architecture as 'what it does for you' bore within it an instinctive profundity of concern that was entirely missed by a whole generation of functional materialists of the Hi-Tech ilk. Whilst the latter sought to essentially continue familiar architectural traditions in a novel stylistic guise, Price's stance was rooted in an ambivalence that sought to build without ideological formalism, to avoid that issue altogether and provide architectures that, as he said, compounded delight with dialogue. There is here a democratic openness that perhaps begins to explain a left-wing leaning married to right-wing market sentiments oriented toward consumer choice, as well as Price's apparently peculiar attitude to practise commissions. In this, he was a truly exceptional architect fated to straddle a line that defined the boundary of being in or out of the profession. And this, of course, was to be his career weakness as well as his strength.

...scenes of
ideological import

Sir Nicholas Grimshaw b.1939

Sir Terry Farrell b.1938

Robert Venturi b.1925

Peter Foggo 1930-93

Quinlan Terry b.1937

John Outram b.1934

Sir Michael Hopkins b.1935
Lady Patty Hopkins b.1942

James Gowan b.1923
Sir James Frazer Stirling 1924-92
Michael Wilford b.1938

Sir Richard MacCormac b.1938

Sir David Jeremy Dixon b.1939
Fenella Mary Ann Clemens b.1938
Edward David Brynmor Jones b.1939

Lord Richard Rogers b.1933

Lord Norman Foster b.1935

... scenes of ideological import

Below: the 'suburban strip' in Los Angeles, with the cheap sheds plus expensive signs celebrated by the likes of Banham and Venturi. Beyond the drive-in, 'strip' aspect of West Coast architecture, architects on their Grand Tour (such as Farrell, Foster and Rogers) would travel from the east Coast via Chicago to seek out the works of Eames, Soriano, Schindler, Ain, Lautner, Ellwood, Neutra, Jones, and the California Case Study houses promoted by John Entenza.

Bottom: MacDonald's in its architectural heyday (Buffalo, mid-1960s) – all signage, wrapping and disguising a cheap 'n' cheerful shed, as opposed to merely juxtaposing sign and shed.

The 1970s should have been a fulfilment of the 1960s. And they were, but not in a manner one might have expected. The creativity of Archigram found its fruition in a competition win – 'Features Monte Carlo' – but their energies seemed to evaporate the moment some of the group established a practice and found their victory had been taken away from them by a competing American practice. That was to be the story of the 1970s and '80's: continuing American influences arriving as an energetic import and filling an ideological vacuum on the British scene. However, whereas those influences in the immediate post-war period had been in the form of Mies, SOM and even Paul Rudolph's brand of Modernism, they were to be quite different for a subsequent generation.

The shock of Archigram was born in an era when one could offset bebop against 'trad jazz' and a vibrant folk scene (each to be respectively shocked by an electrified Miles Davis and Bob Dylan). But along with 1969's Woodstock festival in upstate New York came the replacement of bohemian 'cool' by hippiedom, which arrived in the UK as the home made architecture of 'wood-butchers' and alternative life-style publications such as The Whole Earth Catalogue and Domeworks. The talk was of 'thinking small', of geodesic maths, domes, zomes, and of 'life-raft earth'. Buckminster Fuller had become a folk hero. For almost everyone. Archigram's hedonistic consumerism with its roots in immediate pre and post-war American mass culture now seemed somewhat irrelevant to values that were as politically concerned as Archigram had been politically apathetic, as committed to an alternative life-style as Archigram had been bound to the fringes of a bourgeois British architecture and art scene. Long hair, denim, dope, talk of 'vibes', of 'street-farms' and squatting, and of a spiritual dimension to life and architecture was alien to all they stood by and enjoyed.

While such things marked the transition from the late '60's to the early '70's, they were without a relevance to the core of the architectural profession. Nevertheless, what remained as a common denominator was reference to what was happening on the other side of the Atlantic. The traditional 'Grand Tour' undertaken by architects had, especially in the post-war period, become study in an established East Coast university followed by a cross-continental tour – one that was to be crucially important to the likes of Foster and Rogers.

In the context of an oil crisis and an ensuing 'three-day week' in the early 1970s, Archigram struggled to find

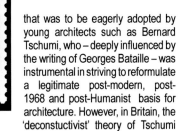

Left: U.S. stamp celebrating the legendary Woodstock Festival that prompted many British imitations.

patronage and work for their small office. It was all too late. Into the ideological vacuum there arrived yet another American import: a set of values and concerns that, on the one hand, addressed free-wheeling formal and compositional values that were to become labelled Post-Modernism and, on the other hand, a view of all things 'Pop' that grounded design perspectives in popularised semiology and a typological understanding of 'strip' architecture that left Archigram's collages as little more than upbeat optimism devoid of everyday pertinence and valued only by those who identified themselves as a so-called High-Tech lobby defensively countering the nightmare of Post-Modernism.

Robert Venturi – a man who could not be further removed from the likes of domeworks and the sentiments of Fuller – now featured saliently in both these aspects of a new architectural direction (and was later to be rewarded with a commission to design the Sainsbury extension to the National Gallery).

As an ideologue, practitioner and populariser who viewed architecture and mass culture from an East Coast high-ground of intellectuality, Venturi was able to ride the shoulders of a post-war tradition that had become habituated in looking across the Atlantic for inspiration. He thought he had found a way to appropriate the energies of mass culture in a manner that had not suggested itself to those radicals of the 1960s who – within a framework of the 'angry young man' ethos manifest in the 1950s – simply rejected architecture's established traditional pretensions. But Venturi went down to the culture of the strip; he drew and analysed what was going on and came back to the Cultural high-ground with the message that it was all about an equation of cheap sheds plus a lot of loud signage. Archigram may have intuited this, but they didn't know it in intellectual terms. Venturi had arrived as the brightest kid on the block, with a message that spoke about architectures and could be absorbed by the mainstream of the profession.

But not all architects looked across the Atlantic. 1968 was not just a year of riots in Grosvenor Square (against Vietnam and the policies of the American Establishment), but of student riots in Paris. Here was the home of a distinctly un-American and un-English brand of intellectuality concerning language and texts that was to be eagerly adopted by young architects such as Bernard Tschumi, who – deeply influenced by the writing of Georges Bataille – was instrumental in striving to reformulate a legitimate post-modern, post-1968 and post-Humanist basis for architecture. However, in Britain, the 'deconstuctivist' theory of Tschumi et al was to find itself thrown on stony ground. The formalist dimension of deconstruction was to find little favour in the UK and zero potential for built realisation.

But while a divide (on both sides of the Atlantic) was deepening between theoretical discourse and actual practice – one whose outcome could only be theory's transmogrification into grist for the mill serving a keen appetite for formal gestures that pretended to novelty but worked soundly within a traditional framework of cultural power – it was Paris that was to serve as the common denominator to all these groupings, bringing itself to the architectural foreground once again. At the heart of this reorientation was the programme of 'grand projet' that had Richard Rogers' Pompidou Centre at its heart. This had been won in 1971 and completed in late 1976, by which time London's brief period of mild-mannered hippiedom had given way to the aggressivity of Punk.

In fact, European architecture as a whole was about to realise a strength not known since New York had challenged and then stolen cultural supremacy. It was Paris first, then Berlin, after that Barcelona, and later London – each adding to the leverage shifting the attentions of younger architects away from the USA and toward western Europe. (And, at that time, it must be added, to Japan – then the world's economic and architectural giant whose wealth drew in European and American architects as novel 'strawberries' of their cultural scene.)

The context of all this – in terms of the construction industry – remained one of boom and bust. But then came the 'Big Bang' of banking deregulation in the City and, in 1986, many incoming American banks brought their US architects with them, hoping to jump off from a base in London to new markets in Europe. London was suddenly enjoying a unique boom. If, in this context, there was to be theory, then it was to be convenient as well as legitimating. And Post-Modernism admirably fitted the bill. Developer's appeared to love it, perhaps as a release from the arcane (and implicitly socialist)

Right: Buckminster Fuller – hero of hippies and the High-Tech school. He would come to London to give lectures lasting four hours or more about his life's work about, for example, his World Design Science Decade (1965 to 1975), concerned to do 'ever more with ever less', thus avoiding a Malthusian global crisis: "The present top priority world problem [...] may be summarised as how to triple, swiftly, safely and satisfyingly the overall performances per kilowatts and man hours of the world's comprehensively invested resources of elements energy time and intelligence." At the time, his message was largely ignored.

Below: an elliptical geodesic dome – a typical experiment in dome-making of the late 1960s/early '70's which extended Fuller's investigations and, in some ways, is at the beginnings of the distorted mathematical building shapes that have now become so familiar (see the Gherkin in the photo opposite, a building whose form strangely compounds such geometries with military and erotic associations).

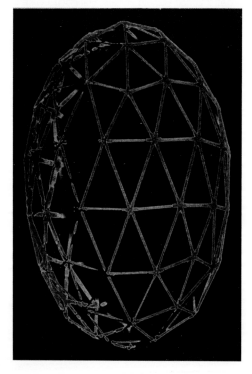

demands of Modernism.

The City now underwent historic cultural change. It was no longer such a tight English club (socially similar, in the post-war period, to what it had been one hundred years previously) bound within a largely invisible physical framework with one cardinal rule: a respectable address that was to be 'ten minutes walk from the Bank of England', i.e. within the Roman walls once surrounding the City. The City of London now looked to expand outward – especially into the problematic and empty Docklands (Canary Wharf, although the particulars of this example of expansion are filled with irony), into the vacated plots of Fleet Street (the newspapers having moved out to Docklands), to the north in order to redevelop railway lands (Broadgate), and even across the River Thames to south London (as at London Bridge City and More London). And, after horizontal expansion, there was only one way to go: upward – a direction the City is still exploring.

The London docks (from St Katherine's, through Limehouse, to the Isle of Dogs, the Surrey Docks and the Royal Docks) progressively, but rapidly, closed from about 1970, presenting London with enormous socio-economic and redevelopment problems. After that – and for the next thirty-five years – the area was to enjoy the initial phases of a redevelopment undertaking that will, undoubtedly take another thirty-five years before it all becomes a distant memory for historians to pore over. This development was a story of optimism rising from ground-zero and an inappropriate eagerness to reinstate manufacturing employment, to huge enthusiasm for offices, financial services and expansive (and often expensive) new housing.

As the flagship of redevelopment, Canary Wharf (once so detested by, and shocking to, a London architectural profession that received the development as a wake-up call) arose as an almost entirely North American phenomenon and, by the early years of the new millennium, was maturing into a diversified pattern of ownership and tenancy, i.e., islanded, but nevertheless (slowly) becoming a more organic part of the metropolis. Meanwhile, the 'Big Bang' had established firms such as SOM, Swanke Hayden and HOK in London, and prompted a building boom that briefly lasted from the mid-1980s to the dark years of a recession that had become sorely manifest itself by about 1990 and was not to evaporate within the architectural profession until

The City viewed from Butlers Wharf (at high tide). On the left, a 1930s warehouse converted to flats (note the glass balconies), with restaurants on the ground floor. In the near distance, Tower Bridge, Seifert's former NatWest Tower, and Foster's 30 St Mary Axe ('the Gherkin'); in between is the GMW Commercial Union Tower, and blue cranes on the top of the Rogers' iconic Lloyds '86 building are just visible. On the right, the 1960s hotel built at St Katherine's Dock, on the eastern edge of the City. This is the skyline that is projected to dramatically change as the City expands upward as well as outward during years of phenomenal, globally recognised success in its financial services businesses.

Left: view across the River Thames to early Millennium housing adjacent to St Katherine's Dock. Note the glass, terraces, penthouses, etc. – all features unsuited to most English tastes before the recession of the early 1990s and uncharacteristic of what was provided in Docklands before the early '90's recession.

four or five years later. During much of that period some many British architects were unemployed. Typically, for some, employment was to be found in a vibrant Berlin (or Hong Kong, or even Japan), not London.

As the recession receded, the economy and British architecture soared into another boom period all over again. But what was most peculiar about this new era was the disappearance of Post-Modernism: it had evaporated, without debate. Everyone was now practising some form of 'Late Modernism'. The likes of Lord Rogers and Lord Foster, Sir Nicholas Grimshaw and Sir Michael Hopkins were the established masters of the British profession, but their former High-Tech posturing was now irrelevant; Farrell had to reinvent himself (which he managed to do rather well).

All this was taking place at a time when digital technologies were beginning to have a significant impact on architectural practices and design possibilities – and to be exploited by Foster and his then partner, Ken Shuttleworth, at London's new City Hall (2000) and for the St Mary Axe building (2004). And, perhaps equally significantly and at the level of culture rather than Culture, the mass of Londoners began to exhibit – for the first time – a novel taste for the same Modernism that many architects had rejected. Ordinary people now wanted open lofts, expansive terraces, big glass windows and to live in the heart of the city at the top of a tall building by a newly discovered and de-industrialised River Thames. London began to eagerly provide itself with new apartments rather than houses. From the mid-1990s architecture was everywhere: most 'broadsheet' newspapers had a permanent architectural correspondent with a weekly page; TV wanted to discuss it. Everyone seemed to know an architect and wanted to employ one for a back-extension.

However, architecture was everywhere at just

at the time project managers and contractors were taking full control of professional outputs, arguably emasculating the British profession as never before. Architects were simultaneously at once more glamorous and less powerful than ever. And their attitudes had changed.Before the recession they still suffered a post-war prejudice that divided the body of profession into those able to enjoy supposedly non-commercial work and those whose reputation was deemed to be sullied by commercial and, especially, speculative work. But now – after the recession – most architects seemed to appreciate that they were either in business or out of practice. They were now all 'Late Modern' in a strangely post-modern way. Foster's practice, in particular, produced a spate of London works during this period that self-consciously posed in some thematic architectural sartorial attire – using aluminium sections, for example, to lend one City office building a pseudo-Mies appearance; concrete was used to give another a 1960s SOM look; and canted redundant props gave character to a curved façade on another, as if Jim Stirling had been a ghostly architectural consultant. History and gestural theatricality were now as much evident as they had been in Venturi's work, but the historical reference was now Modernism itself.

Simultaneously, as the art paradigm insinuated itself ever further into architectural practices, the tectonic concerns of Seifert largely disappeared – joining the disposal of any architectural skill with a numerate or engineering basis. Instead, we had the emergence of narrative (Geoffrey Scott's 'literary fallacy') and the employment of artists on almost every project with any serious pretensions to cultural import. In fact, after the millennium, some developers started to go to art schools for artists to establish a project theme before going to the architect to develop that theme into a building – who, in turn, would be restricted to the shell and core, with others undertaking the building fit-out.

If the hero of the twenty to thirty years after World War II was Denys Lasdun then, in the next period (however defined) it was 'Big Jim' Stirling. Sadly, London enjoys only two significant works by Stirling: the Clore extension to the Tate Britain and No. 1 Poultry, in the City. Other examples are small, less significant and belonging to his earlier career. One (an office building at Carlton Terrace) is more characteristic of his partner, Michael Wilford, and was completed after Stirling's death (as, in fact, was No. 1 Poultry).

Norman Foster has had a major impact upon

Terry Farrell: " I have always said Post-Modernism is a way of seeing things and recognising that Modernism is over. [...] The importance of the Post-Modernist era was to change the rules, to question the rut that Modernism had got into, and the idea that Modernists had that contemporary architecture could only be good if it was socially based or concerned with construction as product. In both cases these were only limited truths and I think that the eighties changed all that, in particular the understanding of the city and of urbanism, which Modernism had no grasp of at all. It did not have the scope to associate itself with urbanism, because urbanism involves context and context involves the past which was the very tenet Modernism set itself against in the 1920s."

London's fabric in the post-Millennium period, but his practice's output enjoys none of the consistency of the Rogers' output, reflecting its huge size (over 400 chartered architects) and, the challenges of control. The practice's most impressive London work is perhaps projects where new has to be married to old (as, for example, at the British Museum Great Court). Rogers' practice, on the other hand, even with the pensionable head man strongly committed to politics and a consulting role in London planning, and with most older partners (such as John Young) now retired and replaced by a new generation, has enjoyed commitment to long-standing Modernist values of truth, honesty, readability and the like: theatricality there may be, but is hardly artificial or constructionally redundant. Similar values inform the works of Michael and Patty Hopkins (Foster's former partner).

Two other fascinating figures of the period are Sir Terry Farrell and Sir Nicholas Grimshaw – partners during the 1970s (until 1980) and, in the 1990s, respective and opposed representatives of Post-Modernism and the High-Tech. These architects are now the old, established men of the profession. They remain prominent London architects, but each is in that transitional stage during which a younger generation is taking over the reins and having to do battle with other practices who sometimes enjoy the continuity of acronyms or are now themselves established mainstream figures such as Bob Allies and Graham Morrison, Will Alsop, Zaha Hadid, and David Chipperfield – the latter two without any (or any significant) London work.

Perhaps the outstanding architect – and practice – of these recent decades has been an ageing Lord Richard Rogers and the group of partners with whom he so readily shares the limelight. Their body of work (in this country and abroad) has been, on the whole, remarkable. In contrast, there is a younger generation for whom the High-Tech is merely historical – the latter a generation flattered by a ubiquitous awards industry and mostly lucky enough to be unfamiliar with a five to eight year economic cycle. After an inevitable downturn the profession will, undoubtedly, continue its obsession with Survival, Success and Significance – added to which will be those two and ever-more

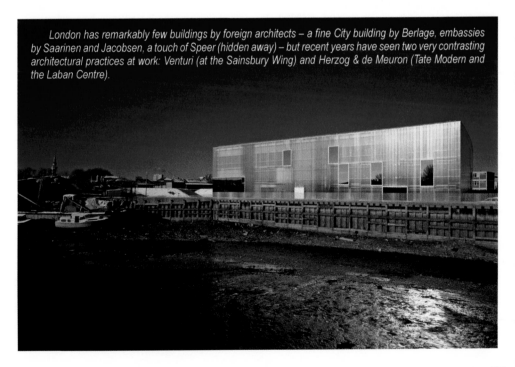

London has remarkably few buildings by foreign architects – a fine City building by Berlage, embassies by Saarinen and Jacobsen, a touch of Speer (hidden away) – but recent years have seen two very contrasting architectural practices at work: Venturi (at the Sainsbury Wing) and Herzog & de Meuron (Tate Modern and the Laban Centre).

urgent imperatives that established themselves in the early years of the Millennium and begin with the same letter of the alphabet: Sustainability and Security for a body of inhabitants who serve and feed the strange and complex phenomenon that is London itself.

In 2008 that beast continues to enjoy a unique metropolitan metabolism. It has been, for example, the envy of New York in terms of the liveliness of its financial services sector and enjoys a massive reputation for creativity. Whether the latter is fact or myth is a contentious issue, for it is self-evident that the boom years of the '80s and since the ending of the early '90s recession have, surprisingly, produced few notable buildings of international standing or merely passing novelty. In fact, one of London's most notable buildings of that period is the Laban Centre, by the notable Swiss architects Herzog & de Mueron – a building that strives to orient itself toward one of the only other architectural works of any standing in the area: Thomas Archer's church of St Paul Deptford. Certainly – against a background of project management and health & safety concerns – there has been no significant shift within architectural theory, ideology or tastes within recent years, apart from a variety of digitally-driven enthusiasms for patterned surfaces and new shapes that perhaps express familiar values and concerns in a novel formal guise. The Millennium still awaits its architectural heroes.

Meanwhile, London is ever more large, dense and culturally diverse. And, although it scandalously fails to provide decent and affordable housing for its younger, more poor and deprived inhabitants it is perhaps on the brink of accepting physical growth by again building tall and querying the merits of the constraining 'green belt' which surrounds the capital and separates it from a hinterland. That historic struggle currently adopts the form of an attempt to switch London's westward orientation into a second phase of Dockland's regeneration (the Thames Gateway project). But it possibly has odds stacked against it: brown sites and flood plains do not make an attractive proposition. However, London at last (since 2000) has a city mayor to champion the capital's civic cause. Together with proposals for a giant mosque in the East End, recent changes at Heathrow (Rogers' Terminal Five) and, in the heart of London, at St Pancras Station are aspects of London self-consciously striving to understand whether its multi-racial nature means it is also multi-cultural. This may imply further work for architects from our European neighbours and, perhaps, from much further afield. One can imagine the busy Continental equivalent of George Gilbert Scott leaving the Eurostar train, sitting in the station's long champagne bar and, like that famous Victorian, wondering why he is there. It will be because London continues to call for more ornaments to its fascinating mix of the banal and the scintillating.

the brightest boys on the block ...

The Farrell Grimshaw Partnership (FGP)

Terry Farrell and Nick Grimshaw were, for over ten years, partners who graduated from the AA in 1965 and immediately entered upon a professional career together. In 1980, they were 'divorced', Farrell then embarking on a remarkable ten years that saw him established as Britain's premier Post-Modernist and Grimshaw, on the other hand, standing shoulder to shoulder with the High-Tech group that included Foster, Rogers and Hopkins. These contrasting stances hardly helped the Farrell / Grimshaw stand-off during an era and boom period in which these two camps gave one another nightmares. A lot seemed to be at stake. The outcome, as already noticed, was that the battle of values and styles evaporated during the recession of the early 1990s and both terms – Post-Modern and High-Tech – became moribund. However, both architects enjoyed successful careers and both were knighted.

The practice began with a conversion of terraced Victorian buildings in Paddington that were serviced by a 'bathroom tower' of prefabricated fibre-glass 'pods' (the Louis Kahn 'served' and 'servicing' concept of architectural articulation) arranged along a spiral ramp – students simply walked up or down in order to find a free bathroom. The project (the tower is now dismantled) made it to the magazines, especially the trendy Architectural Design, then edited by the remarkable Monica Pidgeon. Grimshaw was photographed with Bucky Fuller standing beside him, with the tower in the background. The boys had arrived: they were immediately in a club of witty, inventive high-tech practitioners who adopted that radical approach to architecture – a club that flew a flag with the slogan 'It's what it does for you that matters.' They were among the brightest kids on the block.

The reality was that, during the early to mid-1970s Grimshaw was designing what was then the novelty of business parks populated by sheds with long spans and slick cladding. In the meantime, Farrell was tackling housing association projects that addressed a rather different set of issues and often ended up using bricks rather than gaskets.

At first, however, the two stood on common ground. The bathroom tower project was soon followed by 125 Regent's Park Road: another remarkable site and project, carried out in a brief era when architects were being encouraged to establish housing societies, find land and design dwellings to be let on a cooperative basis. The pair set about designing 125 as a stack of apartments topped by four penthouses – including one for each of them (and in which, briefly, John Young, then working as assistant to Richard Rogers', was a sub-tenant of Farrell). Other housing projects followed, taking up Farrell's interest. Meanwhile, Grimshaw's

clients and their sheds became more sophisticated, often employing a Kahnian served/servicing concept.

It is this divide of workload and interests that one finds the roots of the work each partner undertook independently in later years.

Below and opposite: the Gresham Street speculative office building is a rare example of a City building with an informal entrance, one that has been cleverly design in relation to an existing former graveyard that fronts the site. Much of the architectural presence and expression of the building is also at this front end – particularly in the form of a typical acrobatic structural gesture that is again without precedent on such an office building (the entire front end is suspended). The outcome is a mix of the gestural and the considerate that produces a simple (but again rare) entry sequence: street/lobby/glass lift/ view out to the City from the floor lobby/office area. It is simple and it works.

404

Sir Nicholas Grimshaw b.1939

Extant London works include:
• **125 Park Road**, 1968-70. See Terry Farrell.
• former **Financial Times** printworks, Blackwall, 1988. Now converted to offices, with the high printing room given additional floors.
• **Sainsbury's** supermarket, Camden Town, 1988, (with a terrace of housing along the canal to the north).
• British Airways Combined Centre Of Operations, (The **Compass Centre**), Heathrow Airport, 1993.
• former **Eurostar** terminal, Waterloo Station (1993; until late 2007). There is also an Operations Centre, completed 1991, which sits above some of the platforms in another part of the station. Extensive work was also carried out at Paddington Station, 1999.
• Lord's **Grandstand**, 1998 (complementing similar work by Hopkins).
• offices, **25 Gresham Street**, London (2003). 10,750 sqm.
• **University College London Cancer Institute**, 2007. Architecture with clarity and a (now) rare exercise in sophisticated tectonics.

Nicholas Grimshaw was born in Hove and educated at Wellington College. It seems he inherited an interest in engineering (one of his great-grandfathers was responsible for overseeing the installation of Dublin's drainage and sanitation system, while another built dams in Egypt). However, from 1959-62, he studied at the Edinburgh College of Art before winning a scholarship to attend the AA School of Architecture in London (entering the Third Year), where he won further scholarships to travel to Sweden in 1963 and the United States in 1964. He graduated from the AA in 1965, and entered into partnership with Terry Farrell.

However, by the mid-1970s the office was effectively being run as two separate teams and the partnership was dissolved in 1980, with each former-partner setting off in opposite directions, spending the next fifteen years or more as self-conscious rivals.

While Farrell designed TVAM and the like, Grimshaw designed the Sainsbury supermarket, also in Camden. After designing Britain's pavilion for the Seville Expo in 1992, he was appointed a CBE. He was later elected President of the RA and remains internationally famous, especially for the Eden project in Cornwall (2005). Most of the practice's London buildings are worthy of viewing. In almost all of them, an acrobatic play with structure features as a strong part of the overall architectural schema, as does an intense focus upon detail and product design.

Below: the Grandstand at the Lords cricket ground equals its Hopkins precedent (directly opposite) in structural virtuosity, providing structure-free views of the action on the pitch.

Left: the Sainsbury supermarket in Camden epitomises some of the merits and demerits of Grimshaw's architecture. Overall, the scheme 'does' a lot for its client: providing a structure-free hall, served by an adjacent yard and above an underground car park. Urbanistically, it strives to counter the problem of a shed in such an urban situation by stacking offices above the shed along the street frontage – and by scaling the height and the bay rhythm to the traditional Georgian town-house terrace opposite. Similarly, the townhouses bounding the service yard and along the Regent's Canal strive for an urbane presence and, by design, counter a northern orientation. Characteristically, the supermarket principal street frontage achieves its ends with structural acrobatics. However, the whole – in being metal and grey – self-evidently exhibits the enthusiasms of the High-Tech school for all things military. A client reluctant to pay for maintenance and some strange design decisions have resulted in the supermarket being painted baby-blue.

Below: the cancer research labs designed for UCL are an expert insinuation into the existing urban fabric and a building enjoying architectural clarity and carefully considered detailing (including a street frontage that, once again, exhibits this practice's penchant for structural acrobatics and the display of technical virtuosity, as well a classical bottom/middle/top hierarchy. At its completion in late 2000 the building was a rare London example of contemporary architecture that was both tectonically knowledgeable and expressive – what is becoming a lost dimension of modern architecture.

125 Park Road, opposite Regent's Park: a low-cost co-operative with characteristic Farrell customised floor plans, clad in characteristic Grimshaw strip-windows and aluminium.

survival, success, and significance . . .

from London's premier Post-Modernist to its premier urbanist . . .

Sir Terry Farrell b.1938

Extant London works include:

• **125 Park Road**, 1968-70. Housing society venture; 40 apartments inc. four penthouses, two for the FGP partners. Now listed.

• **The Colonnades**, Porchester Square, 1974-76. Mixed-use development: 240 dwellings plus shops, pub, etc.

• **Claudia Place**, Wimbledon, 1974. Two four-storey terraces.

• **Charles Jencks' house**, Lansdowne Walk, Holland Park, 1979-82. Conversion and extension.

• Former TVAM, now **MTV**, Hawley Crescent, Camden Town, 1981-82. Once crazily themed interior and 'rising sun' façade. Egg-cups decorate the canal-side elevation.

• **Comyn Ching Triangle**, Covent Garden, 1978-85. A fine integration and reinvention of three, triangulated terraces.

• **Tobacco Dock** (1811-14), 1984-90. Marvellous historic building and skilled conversion to shops; now deserted but accessible.

• **Former Midland Bank**, Fenchurch Street, 1983-86. Corner building illustrating Farrell's Otto Wagner period.

• **Embankment Place**, Charing Cross, 1987-90. Some 62,000 sqm of offices, with side service and access towers. More neo-Wagner details on the Embankment side.

• former **Allied Irish Bank**, Queen Street, City, 1982-85.

• **Alban Gate**, London Wall, 1988-92. Twinned towers. 65,000 sqm. of offices.

• **MI6**, Vauxhall Cross, 1989-92. 42,000sqm, mostly in some nine stories underground. Clever design with vaguely 1920s New York tower details.

• **Farrell studio**, Hatton Street, NW8, 1985-88.

• fomer **Home Office**, Marsham Street, 2004.

• **Paternoster** master plan (with Thomas Beeby and John Simpson; later taken over by William Whitfield). Also, the masterplan for Paddington Basin and Chiswick Park.

When Terry Farrell set up practice on his own, in 1980, he started again upon a path that should have been, in part, already behind him: a sought-after progress from Survival to Success and on to Significance. Survival and success were not much of an issue; it was the pursuit of Significance that was to haunt this architect's career ambitions. Latterly, he is unique in imaginatively pursuing this ambition by taking the initiative on major urban projects of relevance to the whole capital – an undertaking that is comparatively rare. In these terms one also thinks of Rogers, but the latter tends toward *grand projets*, while Farrell adopts a quite different approach that seeks to achieve the grand outcome by a process of original thinking and heterogeneous acts of urban 'healing' influenced by his post-graduate work in Philadephia with Ian McHarg and others.

One of his first projects in the new, post-Farrell Grimshaw guise was for Charles Jencks, who adopted the role of mentor and needed an executive architect to make a major house conversion – a role in which Farrell grasped every opportunity to promote his own ideas and learn from an association with the man who liked to claim he had coined the term 'Post-Modernism'. Another notable client concerned a garden centre in which Lord Rothschild had a stake – resulting in the highly publicised and soon demolished Clifton Nursery projects in Paddington and Covent Garden. Yet another outstanding PoMo work was the now radically altered MTV building in Camden Town (one of London's finest lost façades, in the true Venturi manner).

Farrell had re-established himself as this country's leading Post-Modern architect – a role in which Jencks was eager to promote him. But he was always a shrewd, intelligent and inventive designer and he was soon in demand from developers as the '80's rose into its boom years, notably completing a large project of speculative offices straddling Charing Cross Station. He even came to the attention of Margaret Thatcher's government and designed the bizarrely prominent MI6 building at Vauxhall Cross, arguing that the building (like that at Charing Cross) belonged to a series of historical river-side palaces. He even took on the High-Tech establishment (rather less than successfully), designing a building standing over London Wall that strove to prove that he, too, could be technologically acrobatic. And he designed notable buildings abroad, e.g. in Hong Kong. Success had been firmly re-established. But with the subsequent and abrupt closure of the door on Post-Modernism Farrell found himself in the unenviable role of being fashionably unfashionable, despite a change of design stance that adapted to the realities of a post-recession world (and in spite of extensive vanity publishing exercises).

It was a curious fate. Developers, however, were convinced of Farrell's worth and he remained in much demand as a master-planner (for example, at the controversial Paternoster development and the Chiswick Business Park development built on by Rogers, as well as at Paddington Basin, where both he and Rogers have office buildings). And he continued to add to London's buildings, skilfully replacing the so-called 'Three Ugly Sisters' of Marsham Street (a hated 1960s development) with a considered replacement of government offices and housing. That scheme was rooted in its master-plan, but when it came to the actual building architecture it was insisted that Farrell bring an artist on board the project to cheer-up his elevations – surely a particularly uncomfortable position for the architect to be in. Meanwhile, significance had at last arrived: Farrell was knighted in 2001 (one year ahead of his rival, Grimshaw).

In the final analysis Farrell will be remembered as both a notable Post-Modernist and urbanist – an architect possessing talents surpassing those of others who eagerly adopted this set of values during the 1980s (his key decade of creativity) and who has self-consciously emulated John Nash in his contributions to London planning. However, significance is a rich scenario of preoccupation, demanding a kind of hegemony that is difficult to satisfy. No doubt 'added-significance' will one day come Farrell's way in the form of historical narratives able to adopt a more kindly perspective on issues of this architect's outstanding talent and ill-fated unfashionability.

Farrell was born in Sale, Manchester, later moving to Newcastle where he studied architecture at the university (1956-61) and won scholarships that financed trips to Scandinavia. In 1961 he came to London and joined the architect's department of the LCC, where he designed the Blackwall Tunnell ventilation shaft that now (much to Farrell's evident amusement) intrudes through the Millennium / O2 done designed by Rogers. Herron, Crompton and Chalk were also there at this time (whom Farrell met on the one day he worked with the Southbank team); it was also here that he met Nicholas Grimshaw.

After only six months Farrell left the LCC to join the office of Stillman and Eastwick-Field. He now applied and won a Harkness Scholarship for study in the USA, travelling to New York and on to Philadelphia in 1962 (where Grimshaw came to visit him). At the University of Pennsylvania Farrell studied urban design under Louis Kahn, Paul Davidoff, Denise Scott Brown and Robert Venturi. During 1963 the Harkness fellowship allowed Farrell to travel extensively in the USA (as Foster and Rogers were also to do). Further scholarships allowed Farrell's 'Grand Tour' to continue on to Tokyo, Hong Kong and Delhi.

Upon returning to the UK Farrell went to work for Colin Buchanan but, within months he had decided to set up in practice with Nick Grimshaw, who was still in his final year at the AA.

The first office was in the basement of Farrell's Canonbury home. The second was in Fitzrovia, where Archigram briefly rented a room. (This was before everyone went to Clerkenwell; John Winter and Foster had an office up the street; Cedric Price was a few blocks away.) Both partners taught part-time at the Bartlett, Farrell also at the AA. The first significant job – the student hostel – came through Grimshaw's uncle. Grimshaw worked on the add-on tower of bathrooms and Farrell on the main building conversion – a pattern that continued through the fifteen years of their partnership.

Above: *the interplay of a remarkable historic structure and Farrell's equally remarkable shop fronts at Tobacco Dock. The development currently stands moth-balled and unloved.*

Embankment Place

The Embankment Place building straddling Charing Cross Station was a remarkable constructional feat and, as a design, stands as a clear strategic diagram. Expressionistically, the architecture plays with its massiveness with a Baroque stridency offset against the pedestrianised scale of adjacent streets and alleys. Only under the railway lines themselves does Farrell's uncertainty turn toward the incongruous inspiration of Otto Wagner's station work in Vienna. Other structurally demanding details are similarly poorly handled – somewhat in the manner they are dealt with on the contemporaneous Alban Gate building.

Farrell's work of this Post-Modern period invariably has some historical theming, as if to make a claim to legitimacy founded upon academic knowledge and the wit with which this is applied to whatever design challenge is at hand. However, Farrell rarely resorted to Scott's 'literary fallacy' of substitutive narrative – he is too conscious of the concrete substance of an architecture. Most positively, he was among the few architects who strove to reorient architects toward overt compositional issues – something that was contrary to his former partner's contention: what a building did for you was all important, and not what it looked like. This was particularly evident at Alban Gate, but was considered a veritable act of treachery with regard to Modernism for which Farrell has hardly ever been forgiven and rarely complimented.

Above: *Villiers Street side of Embankment Place.*
Below: *Embankment Place.*

Top: the former TVAM façade (now having roundels covering the 'TVAM' signage, etc.) The interior has been stripped and remodelled.

Above: Alban Gate, London Wall – two interlinked buildings, one spanning across the road.

Top right: MI6, one of the few post-war buildings along the River Thames that adopts a positive relation to the River Thames. The step-backs and façade detailing have distinctly New York undertones.

Right middle: the Marsham Street offices – divided into three blocks, with housing to the opposite side of the urban block.

Bottom right: Farrell's Soane-esque exercise at the Comyn Ching development in Covent Garden – an interesting and unusual attempt to reinvent an urban block.

411

Robert Venturi b.1925

Extant London works include:
• **Sainsbury Wing**, National Gallery, 1985-91.

Venturi is not a London architect in the sense of everyone else mentioned here, but he is among the more important of late C20th architects and was a huge influence upon many London practitioners – especially Farrell. He also gave London an example of authentic US Post-Modernism with the Sainsbury Wing addition to the National Gallery and is a rare example of the foreign architect undertaking work in London (one thinks of Herzog & de Meuron, Saarinen, and Arne Jacobsen, making comparatively rare contributions over a long period). For this, he has been mocked rather than celebrated – in part because the design of this extension became a notorious project underscoring the interferences of Prince Charles in planning and architectural matters during the 1980s. That he had been awarded the commission after much controversy was surely to have been handed a poisoned chalice. Nevertheless, the obtrusion of Sainsbury into the affair of an extension to the National ended funding controversy and introduced to London an eminent architect 'of the moment'. What Venturi and his partners (including his English wife, Denise Scott Brown) designed was a demonstration exercise that laid claim to an intellectual high ground even as it served the masses who came to the National Gallery. What resulted was a fascinating mix of intellectuality and sensuality, of the palpability of affect and effect employed in conjunction with traditional claims to knowledgeable legitimacy.

Venturi first of all realises a considerable relation of the new pavilion to the Wilkins (not very good) building. This is epitomised by two gestures. The first concerns an act of gamesmanship that Jim Stirling was also to employ at the Clore: picking up the material and forms of the original and repeating them in the new addition – only to quickly drop them, or lightly absorb them into the new architecture. The second gesture is internal, direct and daring: a bold extension of the central, access corridor that reaches from one end of the National to the other, pushing it directly through and out, into the new pavilion and, with a flourish, conjoining its physicality with the perspective of a major medieval painting that adorns the new pavilion's end wall. It is masterful. There is more, but it falls short of this almost brutal 'pinning' of the old to the reality of the new.

In turn, this 'more' has three principal aspects. First,

there is the stair (modelled on the example of the Scala Regia, in Rome) accessed from (a rather dreary and far too low entry hall), complete with a reverse perspective and, above, a heavy structure that marvellously hangs and turns out to be made of plywood and without any actual structural role. Secondly, there is a section schema within the various rooms of the gallery that refers itself to John Soane at the Dulwich – except that this is now entirely a conceit determined to exclude light rather than bring it in. Thirdly, and more interestingly, cross-axial relations are set up that seek to draw the visitor's eye to important art works as they pass between the rooms through their connecting arches. All these aspects of the architecture command attention but fail to be totally convincing: intellectuality now plays a problematic and irritating relation to the substantial facts of space, concrete form and actual experience. The net result – the expression of intent – bears a ponderous, self-important note that undermines the sound, strategic nature of that intent. Nevertheless, the building outshines most of what London architects were giving to the city in those days.

Venturi was born in Philadelphia. He studied architecture at Princeton, briefly worked under Eero Saarinen in Bloomfield Hills, Michigan, and later for Louis Kahn in Philadelphia before completing his studies at the American Academy in Rome, 1954-1956. He became a key figure in articulating what became called Post-Modernism. In a famous first book, *'Complexity and Contradiction in Architecture'*, 1966, Venturi posed the question, *"Is not Main Street almost all right?"* He argued for *"the messy vitality"* of the built environment: *"an architecture that promotes richness and ambiguity over unity and clarity, contradiction and redundancy over harmony and simplicity."* This was followed by another famous work of 1972: *'Learning from Las Vegas'* (Denise Scott Brown and Steven Izenour). One imagines a host of architects from Vitruvius to Blomfield telling him to theorise less and build more.

His architectural voice continues on the London scene through practices such as FAT and AOC. And his pioneering concerns with ornament and decoration (hardly evident at the Sainsbury) become every day more fashionable.

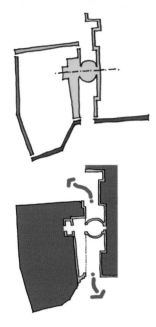

This page: *the Sainsbury Wing to the National Gallery. (Photos below courtesy of VSB).*

Above: *diagrams indicating Venturi's strategic intent with regard to issues of the Sainsbury façade and the passage in between the new pavilion and the old building. The former's glass wall was intended to effect the grand stair as a part of the outside architecture; of course, it doesn't, as Venturi has admitted. Nevertheless, this and other aspects of the architecture make the Sainsbury one of the most intellectually attuned works in London (which makes it interesting – 'almost all right', as its author would say – rather than good).*

Peter Foggo 1930–93

Extant London works include:
• **Finsbury Avenue** 1, 2, and 3. 1984. Site was previously empty for forty years (after World War II).
• **123 Buckingham Palace Road**, Victoria, 1990.
• **Broadgate**, City, 1983-90. 129,000 sqm.
• **Buildings B5 and B7**, Stockley Park, Heathrow, 1987.
• **60 Queen Victoria Street**, City, 1999.

Peter Foggo was, for many years, the lead designer of Arup Associates – the architectural design arm of Ove Arup's firm of engineers, a group that had been founded in 1953 and later formalised as Arup Associates in 1963.

Foggo was born in Liverpool, where he worked as a bank clerk before the impressiveness of his Victorian surroundings in the city prompted him to begin studies at the Liverpool University school of architecture. Upon graduating he briefly worked for the Architects Co-Partnership and set up a partnership with David Thomas, with who he had been a student at Liverpool, before entering Arup's in 1959.

By 1970 he was a partner in Arup Associates and, by 1984 (the year the No. 1 Finsbury Avenue building was completed), a senior Director in the Ove Arup Partnership. He enjoyed substantial professional respect, although he was a firm believer in adopting a background role and being a team player. He designed a number of notable and large buildings, all for private clients and none of them speculative before the Finsbury Avenue project for Godfrey Bradman and Stuart Lipton, of Stanhope. (These include famous buildings at Basingstoke, which were the basis of the Finsbury Avenue design.)

This characteristically late '70's design (chocolate brown) was a huge success and the first of City office buildings to be targeted at a specific user group (at that time a novel concept). This led to the master-planning of the Broadgate development on the adjacent railway lands, a scheme that had Arup Associates designing the master plan and one half of the buildings, and SOM – in full Chicago Beaux-Arts, PoMo mode – as designers of the other half. The common denominator was granite cladding, which the developers insisted upon and which Foggo's team strove to 'float', indicating its Modernist, non-loadbearing role (and, by the time the façades reached the attic stories, the granite was thrown away and replaced by aluminium).

Broadgate is a remarkable City development, completed in the later, post-Big Bang years of the later 1980s. Its prompt was not just local demand, but competition from a rival development going on in Docklands: Canary Wharf. Before this, the City planners had been complacent, thinking only about foreign competition. Canary changed their tune and Broadgate obtained planning development in the unheard time of some six weeks.

Foggo's master-plan comprises three squares defined by perimeter office buildings, all with atria: one square by SOM, with vaguely Henry Richardson touches along with the Beaux-Art architecture; one (with No. 1 Finsbury Avenue along a principal side) that was, originally, rather understatedly English in how its landscaping was dealt with (before changes in the later '90'); the third was mixed and, strangely, romantic.

The work was undertaken at a demanding, furious pace for a notoriously demanding client (who came to architects not to learn how to build, but to, tell them how they were to do it). In 1989 – when the final building designed by Arup almost began to match SOM in its strange manner of 'floating' heavy slabs of granite – Foggo threw in the towel and started up on his own.

Four years later he was dead of a brain tumour. In the meantime, he had designed 60 Queen Victoria Street under his own name – a unique design that appears to owe something to Jean Nouvelle's work in Paris and the nearby Bracken House by Hopkins (however, the posthumously realised building suffers from a chemically attained patina that refuses to mellow). Broadgate, still impressive (if you like mainstream office buildings) remains his claim to fame.

Overall, these are some of the City's most successful civic spaces.

The latter square has, at its centre a Rockefeller Centre inspired ice-skating rink that, in the summer, facilitated operatic performances and the like as lunch-time entertainment for workers (long before the fad for Xmas temporary ice-skating rinks arrived in London). This is surrounded by what was originally an architectural assemble that resembled nothing less than a Modernist version of some ruined Roman amphitheatre, now overgrown with vegetation. Below it, and within its framing, was retail content (bars, restaurants, etc.). This was an intrinsically PoMo, historicising scheme that seemed to play SOM at its own game, but with a Modernist flourish and a more poetic richness. Unfortunately, these qualities have now largely gone, thanks to a significant expansion of Broadgate's retail content, which has filled up most of Foggo's 'ruined' stone-clad concrete framework.

Top right : 40-66 Queen Victoria Street, in the City.
Below: Arup Associate's management tower at Broadgate.
Bottom right: two images of the Broadgate Arena as it was and now is. The original concept of a ruin has now been overbuilt and thus suffocated.

Quinlan Terry b.1937

Extant London works include:
• **Dufours Place**, Soho, 1983-4. Offices and 25 apartments.
• **Richmond Riverside**, 1984-87.
Two retained listed buildings and new offices, flats, shops, two restaurants, community facilities, two underground car parks, and riverside gardens.
• Six **Regent's Park villas**, 1988-2004.
• **St Helen's**, Bishopsgate, 1994-7, (restoration).
• **offices**, 2-36 Baker Street, 2001-2.

To Terry the practice of architecture is 'glorified tailoring' and a client is to be fitted up with something suitably fitting. This quip comes from a man with the reputation of being serious to the point of being humourless, a reputed misogynist and anti-Modernist who believes that neo-Palladianism is God's true direction for architecture, as if there had been no intervening period between the mid-eighteenth century and the 1920s and '30's – the latter being the period during which Terry's later partner, Raymond Erith (1904-73), founded what was to be their joint practice. Terry, in other words, is a talented but idiosyncratic figure on the English architectural scene, and one who continues to attract publicity and clients (including the Prime Minister's office in Downing Street) to his serious form of neo-Classicism.

He was born in Hampstead, son of a City solicitor and his artistic wife, both with communist leanings who, nevertheless, felt it necessary to send their son to Bryanston public school – which Terry left with decidedly reactionary sentiments. These were subsequently reinforced by a conversion to Christianity while at the AA – where, he says, "I was sworn at by the masters and told, you will fail if you do another classical scheme". He left the AA and – incongruously – briefly worked with Stirling and Gowan before moving on to Raymond Erith in 1962, the latter being a respected architect who, as if continuing an inter-war enthusiasm for all things Georgian, was successfully practising all that Terry aspired toward.

The Regent's Park villas sum up Terry's values, further Nash's original intentions and are worth examining (if only to see what kind of architecture many of London's rich prefer). On the other hand, the Richmond Riverside office development was sorely criticised as inappropriate and picturesque neo-Classical disguise of a thoroughly modernist internal reality. However, the scheme put Modernists on the spot and brought old and thorny issues such as authenticity and integrity back to the foreground of debate.

Terry now practises in partnership with his son, Francis, and wife, Christine (who attended the AA with him).

Opposite page top: the Ionic Villa, one of a set along the Regent's Canal, Regent's Park. (Note the security devices – high-tech has no stylistic loyalties.)
Centre: *the Gothik Villa.*
Bottom: *Richmond Riverside.*

John Outram b.1934

Extant London works include:
• **McKay Trading Estate**, Kensal Road, 1981.
• **Pumping Station, Stewart Street, Isle of Dogs**, 1987-8.

Outram is a paradox: a verbose, theoretically-oriented architect quick to quote ancient texts who is as equally and profoundly committed to practical construction and the virtues of direct architectural experience. His polychromatic and allegorical pumping station on the Isle of Dogs remains without equivalent in London and is a masterful exercise that defies easy categorisation. It is simultaneously inspired by Aalto, the temple form, prefabrication and expressive functionalism, whilst offering a façade akin to some child's drawing of an airplane. Disturbing and frequently dismissed as trite, it is anything but that.

Outram attended the Regent Street Polytechnic 1955-8 (where he was one of the editors of the Polygon student magazine), and then the AA. His practice was established in 1973.

Sir Michael Hopkins b.1935
Lady Patricia Ann Hopkins b.1942

Extant London works include:

• **Hopkins House**, Downshire Hill, Hampstead, 1976. In the California Case Study house tradition.

• **Hopkins Studio**, 27 Broadley Terrace, 1987 on. A fine 'village' of pre-fab 'Patera' sheds with patios and tensed fabric roofs in between.

• **Mound Stand**, Lords cricket ground, 1985-7, built on top of a stand of 1899 (a remarkable design that retained an existing stand at the lower level) and extended the existing brickwork arches, providing a tensile structure above.

• Lords **Compton & Erich Stand.** One of an assemble of notable pavilions, beginning with that of Frank Verity (1890), Louis de Soisssons (Warner Stand, 1958), Grimshaw (Grandstand, 1998, replacing a stand by Herbert Baker), and Future Systems (Media Centre, 1999) and buildings by David Morley (cricket school; TCCB building; shop; 1994-8.

• **David Mellor building**, Shad Thames, 1991. Terence Conran's penthouse on the top. Elegant small building; exposed concrete frame, with lead faced panels.

• **New Square**, Bedfont Lakes (south west of Heathrow Airport), 1992 (**IBM** building). The building opposite, on the north side, is by Cullinan.

• **Bracken House**, 1992. An expert reinvention of the former printing hall of the Financial Times building's (Albert Richardson 1955-9.

• **Portcullis House**, Victoria Embankment, Westminster, 1998-2000, (offices for 210 MP's), and **Westminster Underground Station**, 1999 (a veritable Piranesian exercise).

• **Haberdasher's Hall**, Smithfield, 2002. Buried in the urban block and arranged around a hidden cloistered quad.

• **Evelina Children's Hospital**, St Thomas', Battersea, 2005. 140 beds. Large atrium.

• Wellcome Trust **Gibbs building**, Euston, 2006. Spectacular atrium (with a remarkable suspended sculpture by Thomas Heatherwick) inside a literally grey exterior fronting Euston Road. The old Wellcome building immediately to the east was refurbished (2007) by Hopkins as a museum.

• **Inn the Park** restaurant, St James' Park, 2004. Larch structure; 120 seats sheltered; 100 seats inside; rear part submerged beneath a mound; grand central, covered court.

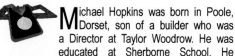

Michael Hopkins was born in Poole, Dorset, son of a builder who was a Director at Taylor Woodrow. He was educated at Sherborne School. He attended the Bournemouth School of Art (1952-4), then worked for Frederick Gibberd 1954-56, the Church commissioners 1956-57, and Basil Spence, 1957-59 , before attending the AA in 1959, graduating in 1964. He then worked for Leonard Manasseh and Tom Hancock 1964-1968, before entering partnership with Norman Foster, 1968-1976

Patty Hopkins was brought up in the Staffordshire countryside; both parents were doctors. She was educated at Wycombe Abbey School and went to the AA aged seventeen (1959-68, working for Frederick Gibberd in her 'year out' (from 1962). Fellow students included Ed Jones, Jeremy Dixon and Nicholas Grimshaw. Here she met Michael Hopkins. Her final project employed the Californian SCSD system; Foster was on the jury and this meeting apparently led to the Foster-Hopkins partnership. She was in private practice from her graduation in 1968 until 1976 (while raising a family), and the partnership with Michael began, after he left the Foster practice. (Hopkins was apparently responsible for the IBM Cosham building.) Their first office inhabited the top floor of the Downshire Hill building (their home was below). They then moved the office across the road before moving to Marylebone and erecting a series of 'Patera' sheds. Their first work was the conversion of the Port of London Authority building for Will Faber, and the Greene King Brewery building at Bury St Edmunds.

Michael Hopkins was elected to the Royal Academy in 1992, awarded the CBE in 1989, and knighted for services to architecture in 1995. Michael and Patty together received the RIBA Gold Medal in 1994 (the only husband and wife team to win the award since Ray and Charles Eames).

Former Hopkins staff include Chris Wilkinson, Bill Dunster, and John Pringle.

Opposite top: the former Financial Times building, now Bracken House.
Opposite page bottom: the Inn the Park restaurant

Above: Bracken House. The Hopkins team had decided to keep two old brick wings, convert them and add to them. And he played strange games with the façade of the new parts. Fans were shocked. It was confusing: why wasn't it all new? Why was the façade not slick glass? Why did it play hierarchical and overtly contextual games? The scheme was received as a form of heresy. If fact, it is distinctly within the Modernist tradition. There is, for example, no 'front' and 'back' in the sense that Post-Modernists were then enjoying (a more traditional architectural approach that dispenses with the need for sartorial show once one turns a corner from the principal façade); the loading bay is as well designed as any other part. And its principal parts (especially the elaborate, load-bearing façade game that was an answer to Prince Charles' complaints about thin-skin buildings) is eminently 'readable'. However, later work, such as Portcullis and the restaurant in St James' Park, merely seemed to confirm the impression that – no matter how impressive the detail was – there was a lapse at issue: a loss of intent and nerve; no longer a concern to surprise and even shock, to gesturally demonstrate novelty. The Hopkins', it seemed, had matured.

Left: the Wellcome Gibbs building appears more conventionally 'techy' than Portcullis House (**opposite page**). However, both enjoy light-filled atria that, in the case of the Euston Road building, is in contrast to its grey exterior. Its atrium terminates at the upper level in a large staff restaurant area. And it includes a remarkable Thomas Heatherwick sculpture (**bottom**).

Opposite page: Portcullis is a palzazzo, like its neighbours: Norman Shaw's Scotland Yard buildings. It, too, is a square plan employing a double-loaded corridor around a central court, all topped by a steep roof with characteristic Queen Anne tall chimneys set into a steeply pitched roof with dormers. The Hopkins design even realises a horizontally striped affect, similar to Shaw's design. And it also has the same weight of Shaw's architecture, contributing to that fortress-like quality affected by Shaw and a natural aspect of the ostensibly bomb-blast proof façade of Portcullis. The latter also has dormers and a steep, dark-coloured roof – now leading to heat reclamation chimneys which terminate the façade ducting that draws air out of the offices, up and over the roof.

On the other hand, Portcullis also makes reference to the spikey, narrow and repetitive perpendicularity of Pugin's detail to Westminster Palace. Thus, overall, the design is deeply contextualist. All of this stands in contrast to the central courtyard of Portcullis: covered with a stainless steel, oak and glass structure, and edged by a veritably Piranesian arched structure that picks up the weight of the massing above so that the loads can be threaded through and in between the Underground tubes that lie deep underground.

Internally, there is not one painted surface to this almost entirely precast and prefabricated, readable and thoroughly Modernist building. In fact, overall, Portcullis is a masterful building, although it disturbs many architects. This is possibly for the same reason that Hopkins design for Bracken House surprised an earlier generation by its readiness to engage and make reference to older buildings, to indulge in respectful reinvention and intrinsic celebration when the common expectation was that he would do exactly the opposite. Similarly, perhaps the criticism that Portcullis is ugly fails to appreciate that the Hopkins' team have put their finger on the essential cultural quality that characterises the Houses of Parliament: it is an intrinsically conservative gentleman's club, with a few ladies tolerantly allowed in. To counter this would, perhaps, have courted the danger of a culture of inhabitation and a culture of design in conflict, i.e. exactly the problem suffered by Rogers at the Lloyds '86 building. There may be a lobby to List the latter, but this comes from architects and architectural conservationists, not the brokers at Lloyds.

James Gowan b.1923

Gowan began in partnership with Jim Stirling in 1956, when the latter, frustrated at being unable to get a scheme of houses at Ham Common through the planners, called upon Gowan's advice. They were in partnership until 1963, the year the engineering faculty building at Leicester University was completed. The partnership was then dissolved, with Stirling becoming an international celebrity and Gowan fading into the background as the architect's architect of those in the know – a man of immense talent and remarkable precision in his work.

Gowan was born in Glasgow and had studied at the Glasgow School of Art (1939-42; described by him as "very beaux art and traditional in the worst sense"). He then worked for Brian O'Rourke, did war service and later attended the Kingston School of Architecture (1946-48) before going to work with Powell & Moya on the famous Festival of Britain Skylon. In between his architectural studies he was in the Royal Air Force, where he was taught radar at the Bomber Command HQ.

In 1952, he went to Lyons Israel Ellis (a place where, he remarked, "you either survived or blew up"). It was here that he later met Stirling. The association deepened when, in late 1955, Stirling won the Ham Common commission and Gowan obtained a commission for a house on the Isle of Wight. They joined together and the former job established the pair's reputation (and, soon, Michael Wilford arrived in the office). However, after the Leicester Engineering block success the two parted ways, rather bitterly and partly on the basis of a difference of opinion over Gowan's designs for the Schreiber House and Stirling's for the Cambridge Library (which sought to continue on from Leicester in a manner Gowan considered technically inappropriate).

Extant London works of Stirling & Gowan include:
• **No 17A Grenville Place**, 1957-9.
• **Langham House Close**, Ham Common, 1955-58.
• **Brunswick Park School** dining and assembly hall, Benhill Road, Camberwell, 1958-62.
• **Perrygrove** old peoples' home for the LCC, Rectory Fields Crescent, Charlton, 1960-64.
• **Houses** (quad of four-storey maisonettes), Trafalgar Road and Creek Road (for the LCC), 1965-8.

Extant London works of Gowan include:
• **Schreiber House**, No. 9 West Heath Road, 1962-4. Nearly demolished in 1986 after its owner had died and the inheritors could not sell it. The house was hugely admired by other architects upon its completion, notably as an exercise in control over detail.

Below: the Schreiber House, adjacent to Hampstead Heath, described by Gowan as having "a Scottish puritanical exterior and a concentration of effort on the interior which is preoccupied with the tiniest detail."

Sir James Frazer Stirling 1924–92
Michael Wilford b1938

Extant London works of Stirling include:
- **Nos 37-41 Gloucester Avenue**, Camden, 1963-4.
- **Clore Gallery**, Millbank (Tate Britain), 1981-87.
- **No. 1 Poultry**, Cheapside, 1986-98.
- **Offices**, Carlton Gardens. 1988-99.

Big Jim as he was popularly known became one of Britain's most internationally celebrated architects, particularly after the completion of the Stuttgart Art Gallery (1977-84). However, he left little in London, among two works stand out: the Clore Gallery and No. 1 Poultry. The former was problematic at the time and has been somewhat altered internally; the Poultry office building took so long to be realised that, when completed, it left its audiences bemused by its idiosyncratic and rather PoMo character.

Stirling (who never used his middle name or initial) was born in Glasgow, son of a marine engineer, later attending Liverpool School of Art and the University of Liverpool School of Architecture, finishing his education at the School of Town Planning and Regional Research in London (1950-1952). Before that, he had served as a lieutenant in the paratroops, 1942-1945, and even participated in the D-Day landing in France. After war experience Stirling began a course in town planning – which he soon left – and spent five weeks at the LCC before moving to the office of James Cubitt and Partners.

Later (on the recommendation of Peter Smithson), he began three years as an assistant with Lyons, Israel and Ellis (1953-56, an office in which, at that time, everyone wore white smocks), subsequently entering private practice with James Gowan as a partner (1956-63) and then with Michael Wilford as a partner (from 1971). Wilford, born 1938, had joined Stirling & Gowan in 1959 and was their first assistant.

It was with Gowan that the

Below: No. 1 Poultry is a difficult design on a problematic site. It began as a set of Belcher buildings that were to be replaced by a Mies van der Rohe scheme which, characteristically, replaced the small buildings by a large tower rising out of a piazza. That may have been alright in 1965, but was hardly so in the 1980s when Lord Palumbo resurrected the scheme. Enter Stirling: an architect who was also to die while designing a scheme for the site.

pair shot to fame with the Ham Common flats and the Leicester engineering building of 1959 – the latter a scheme that, ironically, marks the date of their separation (Gowan had set up the basis of the scheme during Stirling's absence and the pair completed it). Wilford (who had been laid off after Leicester was completed) came back to Stirling, to work on the Cambridge Library (commissioned just before the Leicester building was complete).

Stirling went on to become internationally celebrated but with little further work in the UK. The Clore is probably the last building that strongly has his fingerprints upon it. Internally, it has been somewhat altered, but the river façade and the entry sequence demonstrates Stirling at his most gameful and perhaps epitomises this period of his work. No. 1 Poultry and the Carlton Gardens buildings were both executed after his death by Wilford.

In 1992, after Stirling's unfortunate demise (during a routine operation that went wrong) Wilford set up Michael Wilford & Partners with other Stirling staff. This practice later collapsed in mysterious circumstances and Wilford set up a new practice.

Above: the Clore. The meeting between old and new, where Stirling clearly enjoys the game of picking up selected aspects of Sidney Smith's 1897 building as informants of his own façade design. A similar game is played at the other end of the façade, now in relation to the only remaining building of the hospital once here.
Below: the garden view to the principal façade (with the foreground area modified by Allies & Morrison from soft to hard landscaping). Here, Stirling is perhaps an architect frustrated by the political machinations of internal gallery arrangements, withdrawing to a place where he can get on with what he wants to do and play games no one can object to: after all, this is Stirling the genius at work.

Sir Richard Cornelius MacCormac b.1938

Extant London works include:

• **Shadwell Basin** housing, London Docklands, 1987. 169 dwellings around a former dock basin. The challenge was to provide a semblance of larger scale to terrace housing.

• **Vining Street**, Brixton, 74 flats, 1989.

• **Strathleven & Mauleverer Road**, housing, 42 dwellings of ten variable types for the elderly and disabled, 1991.

• **Sandmere Road**, special needs flats, Brixton, 1989.

• **Southwark** Jubilee Line station and **Waterloo East** station, 1999.
Note: the above, apart from Shadwell Basin, or not on the MJP web site.

• **The Wellcome Wing**, The Science Museum, 2000. Acrobatic structure to house exhibits.

• **Queen Mary & Wesfield College**, Mile End Road. 96 student flats along the canal. Also, Ifor Evans Place, 16 six-person units in two blocks, around a courtyard; Informatics teaching Laboratory. Projects completed 2002.

• **Wellcome Wolfson Building (Dana Centre)**, The Science Museum, 2003. More in the collegiate style one associates MacCormac with.

• **John Watkins Plaza**, London School of Economics, 2003. The forecourt to Foster's Library building.

• **Friendship House**, Belvedere Place, 2003. 170 low-rent bed-sits adjacent to a railway line.

• **Warwick Court**, Paternoster Square, 2003. The 'odd man out' of the Paternoster office buildings, displaying an attempt to modify the conventions of the type.

• **BBC**. Works at New Broadcasting House, 2006-10. A large project from which MJP was divorced after the first phase.

• **10 Crown Place**. Medium size offices (6 storey), north of Broadgate in the City, 2007. Similar to Warwick Court and also determined not to provide the stereotypical office building forms.

MacCormac was born in London and studied architecture at Cambridge and the Bartlett school (then considered a very dull neighbour to the AA), qualifying in 1963. He worked for Powell & Moya in 1963, and for Israel Lyons & Ellis from 1965-7 before going to the London borough of Merton, 1967-9. He then set up in practice and, in 1972, was joined by Peter Jamieson. Since then the practice of MacCormac Jamieson Prichard have built over 2,500 homes, founding the reputation of the practice on low budget social housing in the 1970s and 1980s, but particularly on work at Cambridge University and at Queen Mary & Westfield College, London (where the housing is on a significantly smaller budget than provided at Cambridge). MacCormac enjoys what he refers to as 'proto-classical' Elizabethan architecture, as well as the work of his great hero: Frank Lloyd Wright and his own London home is an exercise in these enthusiasms in a rather Soane/Farrell manner. The practice is particularly keen on suburban housing and low-rise solutions. But perhaps housing no longer allows for the poetic expression he desires: *"the concept comes through if the detail gives it rhetoric."* (Corner windows are a practice trademark.) He was RIBA president from 1991-3, during the dark years of recession and was elected RA in 1993.

Right: Warwick Court, Parternoster, looking toward St Paul's Cathedral.

Below: view into the Wellcome wing at the Science Museum – a highly serviced box with floating platforms, as if a multi-storey version of Foster's Sainsbury Gallery. Each side wing houses access stairs, services, lifts, etc. The interior is highly coloured by the (mainly blue) lighting.
Right: housing at Shadwell Basin, Wapping. The height variation was originally argued as a means of bringing wind down into the basin, where leisure sailing takes place.
Centre: Friendship House.
Bottom right: the Dana Centre, adjacent to the Wellcome (and Imperial College).

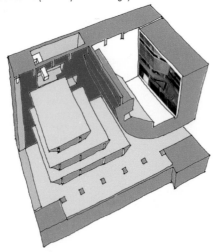

grunting a path to success ...

Sir David Jeremy Dixon b.1939
Fenella Mary Anne Clemens b.1938
Edward David Brynmor Jones
b.1939

**Extant London works
include:**

• **Plough Way** housing,
Rotherhithe, 1966-71 (for
Frederick McManus).
• **St Mark's Road**, North
Kensington, 1975-9. A return
to streets, made up of a series
of twelve semi-detached villas
containing two maisonettes
sitting above a flat. (Described
as a Modernist version of the
Queen Anne.)
• **Lanark Road** housing, Maida
Vale, 1981-83. Five linked
1820's 'villas' that are actually
blocks of seven flats. At this time all social housing had
been stopped by Margaret Thatcher.
• **Ashmill Street**, Maida Vale, 1983-85. A terrace of
mews houses over flats.
• **Compass Point**, Isle of Dogs, 1984-87. Riverside
housing, with a Dutch flavour, but again founded upon
the notion of a tradition in London housing.
• **Tate Britain** basement restaurant, 1981-84
• Clifton Nurseries Shop, Little Venice, Paddington,
1984-5.
• **Royal Opera House**, Covent Garden, (with BDP),
1984-89. A huge and complex scheme that seeks to
find disparate ways to address its place in the city
whilst it resolves issues of internal programme.
• **Ondaatje Wing**, National Portrait Gallery, 1994-
2000. A clever reinvention of circulation, in the manner
of Foster at the Royal Academy.
• **National Gallery** access and lobbies, 1998 on.
• Cafes, bridges and fountains, **Somerset House**,
1998-2000.
• **Kings Place**, Kings Cross, 2008.

Ed Jones and Jeremy Dixon represent a very post-
Festival of Britain generation of architects who
attended the AA: old enough to remember the war and
its immediate aftermath, as well as to share in its anti-
commercial sentiments and be in favour of all things
progressive and socialist; young enough not to be
eligible for the disruptions of National service.

Jones was born in St Albans, son of a man who
had studied sculpture and ended up styling cars for
General Motors, and a mother who is described as an
accomplished portrait painter. Dixon, born in Bishop's
Stortford, also attended a
conventional public boarding
school and his mother was also
an artist. Both came to the AA
when, as Dixon describes it, the
school was *"a wonderful place
... it offered a new landscape of
opportunity and freedom."* It was
*"an old-fashioned world, in a way,
elitist but with a radical tinge."*
Its tutors during their time there
included Alan Colquhoun, Peter
Smithson, John Killick, Arthur
Korn, Kenneth Frampton, and
Robert Maxwell. The prevailing
values were not only anti the
so-called Swedish effeminism
of the 1951 Festival, but also Le Corbusier's high-rise,
megastructural aspirations as well as the Architectural
review's pursuit of 'townscape' (as illustrated by Gordon
Cullen). As might be expected, their musical taste was
for cool jazz, early white Corb, Terragni et al.

Fellow students at the AA (where housing was
the key topic of concern) included Mike Gold, Chris
Cross (later to run the school of architecture at Oxford
Brookes), and Chris Woodward. Dixon studied at the
AA from 1957-64 and found his first wife in Fenella
Clemens (1964; she was born in Portsmouth), with
whom Jones shared a flat. She was to be Dixon's
professional partner until 1989.

*Right: St Mark's Road housing. Oddly, this housing
by Fenella and Jeremy Dixon is possibly a more
significant contribution to London's architecture than
their largest work, the Opera House.*

427

Above: The Royal Opera House project (which lasted sixteen years) confronted Dixon Jones with innumerable problems, not only in terms of the brief but also in terms of a rationalisation of new and old, and quite disparate urban conditions around the building. The Covent Garden façades prompted a reinvention of Inigo Jones' arcades as a shopping occasion (with the addition of an upper loggia), and each of the other façades (including E.M. Barry's of 1858) was dealt with in a different manner. The net result – filling an entire urban block – is inventive, clever, hugely impressive and has its moments, but possibly bears the weight of its long gestation period (as the British Library). Later, Wilkinson Eyre added a rather acrobatic twisting bridge between the old building and an adjacent block (below).

Jones started a year later, but completed the course in 1963, including a 'year-out' in the USA, with Eero Saarinen. Upon graduation he worked with Douglas Stephens for a year, where his fellow employees included Kenneth Frampton, David Wild, Elia Zenghelis and Birkin Haward (once famous as the author of the Foster practice's characteristic drawings; later in practice with Jo van Heyningen). Later, he worked with Colquhoun & Miller, together with Chris Cross. He then left with Cross and both he and Dixon entered the office of Frederick McManus & Partners, where Jones stayed for five years, also teaching at the Regent Street Polytechnic, and the AA (1970-2). Meanwhile, Dixon had briefly worked for the Smithsons on the Economist building, then for Castle & Park, before also moving to McManus, together with Mike Gold.

Dixon, Jones, Gold and Cross now formed a creative group colloquially known as 'the Grunt Group' – a grunt, Peter Cook noted, of seriousness and asceticism that embodied a neo-purist horror of all that was arbitrary, wilful and picturesque: a return, noted Gold, to the basics of Modernism (and one that was criticised as being essentially nostalgic). It was, in any case, quite the contrary to Archigram's then-current concerns and the group of four took their values to the new Milton Keynes Development Corporation in 1971 – one of the last of the new towns intended to promote a depopulation of London and a rehousing of its poorest inhabitants (to a plan modelled on Los Angeles, translated to an English context, but subsequently compromised under the leadership of Roche and Walker). The group's Netherfield scheme stands out – a last gasp of Modernist purism in social housing programmes that flew in the face of all that Terry Farrell, for example, was to attempt in his housing projects of the 1970s and was, ironically, to become the first of the new town's slums. The group also completed a notable exhibition, 'Art and Revolution', at the Hayward Gallery (1971), at a time when the Russian avant-garde was being rediscovered.

In 1973 the group won a competition (bizarrely, if brilliantly, in the form of a pyramid) for a new county hall in Nottingham and together left MKDC (now with Birkin Haward and Adrian Sansome). The partnership of Cross Dixon Gold Jones Sansome resulted. But the collapse of the project led to the break up of the team: the Dixons practising alone, Cross briefly practising with Sansome (before the latter's death), Jones doing a scheme with Gold and Cross but mostly teaching at the Royal College of Art (1973-82, with Kenneth Frampton, Su Rogers and John Miller) before leaving for Canada after winning the Mississauga City Hall competition together with Michael Kirkland, an architect practising in Toronto.

It was also at this time that the experiences of Milton Keynes were producing a counter-Modernist sentiment in the minds of the Dixons. This change was manifest in the St Mark's Road, Lanark Road, Ashmill Street

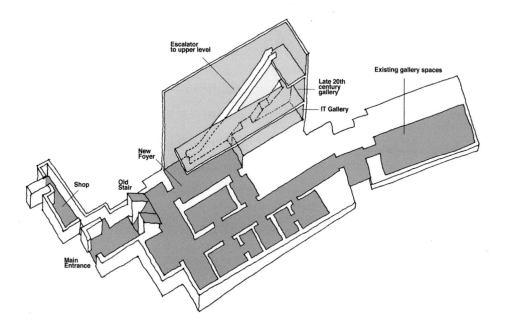

Escalator to upper level

Late 20th century gallery

Existing gallery spaces

IT Gallery

New Foyer

Shop

Old Stair

Main Entrance

Above: *the Dixon Jones scheme for the National Portrait Gallery bears distinct similarity in strategic intent to what Foster achieved at the R.A. and was similarly inventive and daring, transforming the potential and the reality of the institution by reforming its circulation and thus the conception informing the whole.*
Right: *Kingsplace. Kings cross, 2008.*

and Compass Point housing schemes of 1975-87 that stand in stark contrast to Netherfield and its values. In all these schemes the label 'PoMo' was resisted. They were, says Dixon, merely trying to repair the city on the basis of a model of 'texture and monument' (the latter making bad housing).

Similarly, Jones – now teaching at a variety of international schools as well as the RCA – had turned toward the monumentalism of a Stirling, Aldo Rossi and Leon Krier variety. Key differences in the approach of the two had emerged – one more soft, the other more hard and explicitly derivative (rather like Michael Wilford without the strident colour). However, in 1984 the Dixons won the competition for works at the Royal Opera House (in conjunction with BDP) and, in 1989 (after the Jeremy and Fenella relationship had broken up; also the date of the Darwin College Study Centre, in Cambridge, 1989-94, one of Dixon's finest designs), Jones rejoined Dixon in partnership. In the meantime, the latter had, as he put it, *"shaken off the mood of the 1980s."* Both

had returned to the spirit of Post-Modernism, but now purged of socialist and functionalist content as well as indiscriminate historicist sentiment.

In latterday housing boom, the housing designs of the Dixons have remained a neglected topic, but they are possibly the most considered and valuable aspect of the Dixon's and Jones body of work.

Lord Richard Rogers b.1933

Extant London works include:

- **No. 22 Parkside**, Wimbledon, 1977. Two houses (for Rogers' parents).
- **Rogers Studio**, Rainville Road, Hammersmith, 1984. Comfortable, unpretentious conversion of former warehouses at an oil depot; wife's famous River Café next door.
- **Lloyds '86** building, Lime St, City, 1978-86. Still an iconic building, although now self-evidently betraying the agenda and values of the era in which it was designed.
- **Pumping station,** Royal Docks Tidal Basin Road, 1987. A minor work to be compared with John Outram's contemporary work on the Isle of Dogs – between them summarising the contrasts between Hi-Tech and PoMo.
- **former Billingsgate Market,** Lower Thames Street, City, 1988. An ill-fated conversion with some fine parts to it.
- **Reuters**, St Lawrence Street, 1989. A gigantic housing for digital equipment.
- **Montevetro**, Church Road, Battersea, 1999..
- **Channel Four**, 124 Horseferry Road, 1994. Also see the K2 building for a similar approach to lending identity to a building by concentrating the 'architecture' at the entrance.
- **Paddington Waterside**, Paddington Basin, 1999 (currently the HQ of M&S).
- **Chiswick Business Park**, Chiswick High Road, 2000 on. Master plan by Terry Farrell. A masterful set of buildings which belie the fact they were designed to very tight budgets.
- **88 Wood Street**, City, 2000. A characteristic approach to developing a site and providing a 'readable' modern office building.
- **former Millennium Dome** (now 02, Greenwich Peninsula, 2000. Still a fine design, whatever its content.
- **Lloyd's Register of Shipping**, 71 Fenchurch St., City 2000.
- **15 Broadwick Street**, Soho, 2002.
- **Mossbourne Academy**, Downs Park Road, opp. Hackney Downs, 2004.
- **K2** (London Bridge House), Tower Bridge north side, 2005. Similarities of strategy to the Channel Four design.
- **Terminal Five**, Heathrow Airport, 2008. A masterful work.
- **Maggie's Centre**, Charing Cross Hospital, Fulham Palace Road, 2008.

Richard Rogers – a man who has turned out to be one of Britain's more outstanding post-war architects – was born in Florence as the great-grandson of an English dentist practising in Italy. His father was a doctor and his mother was an artist, both and mother preferring to escape fascist politics by emigrating to England in 1938.

By all accounts young Rogers had a challenging and somewhat adventuresome upbringing that served him well by not only moulding his character but exposing him to two disparate cultures – an affluent one in northern Italy and a distinctly more lean (although cultivated) one in southern England – within a family framework leaning distinctly toward the former. It was later, while unhappily serving in the army and doing a final year stint during his National Service, that Rogers spent a rather pleasant time escaping army rigours (in, appropriately enough, Trieste) by visiting the studio of his uncle, Ernesto Rogers of BPR, an architect who aroused the ambition of returning to England and studying architecture at the Architectural Association. This he did, after attending a foundation course at Epsom School of Art (1953-4).

As a dyslectic, Rogers graduated after six years of mostly poor student reports (possessing, it was said, a combination of bad drawing skills but significant *savoire faire*) as an unlikely prize student (his tutors included Peter Smithson, Alan Colquhoun and John Killick). He then worked briefly for the LCC under Bill Howell (later of Howell, Killick and Partridge). Rogers then married and obtained a place and scholarship to Yale, where he and Su Brummel studied from 1961-2. It was here that Rogers met Norman Foster, also on the course. Upon its completion Rogers and his wife set off to California, where Rogers briefly worked in the San Francisco office of SOM. They then returned to England to set up Team Four.

T4 (see page 434) lasted until 1967 and, after the split with Foster, Richard and Su Rogers was set up. It was around now that Renzo Piano wrote to Rogers about his admiration for the practice's work (by then including the Zip-Up House proposal). Marco Goldschmeid now joined the practice (1969). But work dried up and, at the same time, the Rogers' marriage broke up. Rogers, and his new partner (Ruth), now went to Cornell University to teach.

Then onto the scene came Renzo Piano. He had a practice in Genoa and, in the late '60's, had contacted Rogers admitting his admiration for the latter's work.

Opposite page: perimeter detail at Terminal Five, Heathrow. The concourses are to the right.

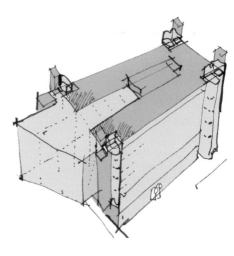

Left and below: Tower Bridge House at St Katherine's Dock.

Above: Tower Bridge House (former K2), a building that fits into a family of designs produced by the Rogers practice. It bears a marked similarity to the strategy of identity given to Channel Four, but the general design strategy of these buildings, at 88 Wood Street and the Lloyds Register of Shipping (below right) is rooted in what was established for the Lloyds '86 building in the mid-1970s. In essence, a typical schema seeks to establish a rational constructional heart at the centre of the site, taking up the residual site geometry (around the perimeter) with lifts, escape stairs, and services. At Lloyds Register this strategy is contained within a perimeter of surrounding buildings and even by a former graveyard that forms the entrance courtyard.

Below left: external lifts and escape stair at the Lloyds Register of Shipping building on Fenchurch Street.

Above: *the once derided, now celebrated Lloyds '86 building remains an iconic design that – intended to last at least 125 years and enjoy all kinds of change – was in fact so customised and costly that it has hardly changed at all and, within eight years of completion, was sold to a German developer. The top photo shows the piazza between Lloyds and GMW's C.U. building (in turn, adjacent to Foster's Gherkin).*

    Right: *like the K2 building, C4 similarly concentrates its acrobatic architectural action around a principal façade.*

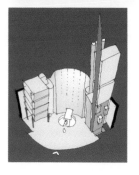

They became great friends. In 1971 he and Rogers began to enter competitions together. They had been introduced to Ted Happold (of Arups, late of work on the Sydney Opera House) who, in early 1971, asked the pair to enter a competition for a building in Paris. Rogers resisted, but the rest of the team made a commitment. By June that year – despite improbable but real difficulties in getting a submission to Paris – they learned they had won the Pompidou Centre competition.

'Beaubourg' was, of course, a huge success. However, by 1977 the practice had very little work and Rogers was about to close it and withdraw to teaching when he won the commission to design a new building for Lloyds, in the City. Since then the practice has enjoyed nothing but significant international success. Among many awards and honours, Rogers was knighted in 1991 and made a life peer (as Baron Rogers of Riverside) in 1996. He was awarded the RIBA Gold Medal in 1985 and the celebrated Pritzer Prize in 2007. Also in 2007 the partnership became Rogers, Stirk, Harbour, & Partners, acknowledging the roles of Stirk (b1957; joined in 1983 and responsible for the London office buildings) and Harbour. (b1962; joined in 1985). A visit to the partnership's website reveals who worked on which project – something rarely exposed by other practices.

Lord Norman Foster b.1935

Norman Foster has no biographer like Appleyard, as Richard Rogers has enjoyed, or Girouard, as Jim Stirling had, or an enthusiasm for self-publication that has given us much personal information about Terry Farrell. In fact, one can hardly imagine anything but a well-engineered and expertly stage-managed equivalent. Instead, we may have to await the passing of this notable architect before a sound biography will assist in penetrating his personality and weighing his achievements. That he stands as one of the twentieth century's more influential architects is without doubt, but his London work may – with a few exceptions – cast him into the city's history as a late twentieth century George Gilbert Scott. It is unlikely he will be a Lutyens (whose affability and playful and masterful exuberance colours that man's remarkable architectural work), and Foster's memory may live on in the problematic manner of, for example, Lubetkin. Such is the uncertainty that crowds about salience when it concerns the titular head of an exceptionally large, established and successful international practice.

Until comparatively recently, there was little of Foster's work in the capital apart from Team Four's meagre output. Those penetrative exercises that established his reputation tended to be elsewhere. However, all that changed in the period from the early '90s onward, beginning with Stansted (London) Airport (1991); his own riverside studio (a project with

Team Four

T4 was made up of Richard Rogers, Su Brummel, Norman Foster and Georgie Cheeseman (later Georgie Wolton, whose sister Wendy, was also a former-girlfriend of Rogers and was to marry Foster). The practice (set up in Wendy Cheeseman's flat) was formed upon the return of the first three from the USA to London in 1963 – except that Cheeseman left after one week (with her name still on the letterhead, because she was the only one who was fully qualified and a member of the RIBA). Rogers and Foster had met doing the same post-graduate course at Yale and the practice had its first job as a house for Brummel's parents.

At Yale (1961-62), Rogers and Foster (two unlikely partners, being quite different characters) had been exposed to teaching from the likes of Paul Rudolph, Eero Saarinen, Louis Kahn, Philip Johnson, Vincent Scully and Craig Ellwood. Stirling was also doing some teaching there at the time and the foursome of Rogers, Foster, Brummel and Stirling would make weekend trips together to New York. Similarly, Foster and Rogers went off together to discover the works of Mies and Wright.

The office was immediately a trendy addition to the London scene. Three of the first employees in the office were Frank Peacock, John Young and Laurie Abbot – all ex-AA students. But life was hardly comfortable: ill-suited to Foster's life-style preferences that were less tolerant of an intermixing of home and office, and fraught with project difficulties that led Rogers to consider suicide (the expensive Brummel house was planned to take six months and actually took three years to build, although it immediately won an RIBA prize).

The work that finally established the practice was Reliance Controls, in Swindon (using Anthony Hunt as engineer; now altered) – a simple, taut steel-framed shed in the manner of Saarinen, Ellwood, Soriano and Eames (an image, as Rogers' biographer Bryan Appleyard, puts it "of naked technology and engineering." Again, prizes were won by a building that seemed to evoke, as an assessor put it, "a lost vernacular." After this, work dried up, differences surfaced and the practice broke up (1967).

Extant London work of T4 includes:
• Nos 15-19 Murray Mews, Camden, 1984-5.

a dramatic double-height studio, initiated during the speculative boom of the late '80s); the Sackler Gallery at the Royal Academy; the redesign of Trafalgar Square's relationships to its surroundings (an idea for which Rogers makes a claim); the Willis building in the City; and the self-effacing success of the Great Court at the British Museum. Some of these are public works in which Foster's partner, Spencer de Grey, played a lead role. Other such projects, the Millennium Bridge (engineered by Arup) and the Wembley Stadium (with HOK) also stand out, as well as the series of academy schools. Foster's other two notable London works – City Hall (at More London) and 30 St Mary Axe (aka the Erotic Gherkin) – became the subject of a row over authorship resulting in a divorce between Foster and his partner, Ken Shuttleworth (who left to set up Make as a practice

Extant London works include:
• former **IBM** Technical Park, Greenford, 1977-79; also 1985.
• Riverside **studio** (1986-90) and **Albion** apartments (2003), Chelsea Reach. The Albion's rather fine social housing terraces are again neo-SOM or Mies in character. The dramatic principal block suffers an incongruously blandness to its bulbous backside.
• **Sackler Galleries**, Royal Academy, 1985-91. Still an outstanding exercise in 'heart surgery', reinventing one part of the RA behind and on top of Burlington House.
• **Canary Wharf Jubilee Station**, 1991-2000. With Hopkins' Westminster Station, this is possibly the best of the Jubilee extension stations.
• Redevelopment of the **Great Court** of the British Museum, United Kingdom, 1999. The roof and other structural works by Buro Happold are remarkable (they are the true heroes of this project, on an equal basis with the Foster team).
• London **City Hall**, 2000, and **More London**, London Bridge, 2003 on.
• **Millennium Bridge**, London, (1996-2000). To be compared with the Lifschutz Davidson design at Hungerford Bridge (a quite different but contemporaneous exercise). Foster gave us the 'bridge of light' concept; Arup engineers realised it.
• **J. Sainsbury** HQ, Holborn Circus, 2001.
• **British Library of Political and Economic Science**, London School of Economics, London, 1993-2001.
• **Citigroup** building and **HSBC** Tower, Canary Wharf, London, 1997-2002.

Below: *the Foster pre-digital studio (with his penthouse on the top), born in the late 1980s boom. And the later, post-digital curves of the Albion development, born in the following boom (2003).*

- **100 Wood Street**, 2000. Offices with interestingly different east and west façades, on what was once the north-south axis of the Roman fort. The Rogers 100 Wood Street building is nearby.
- **Citygate House**, Finsbury Sq., 2001 (The offices of Bloomberg).
- **No.1 London Wall**, 2003 (west end). Offices reinventing the wavy glass façade, but having to cope with a location on the edge of the 1950s Barbican deck.
- **Capital City Academy**, 2000-3.
- **10 Gresham St**, 2003. Block-filling office building with a large central atrium.
- **HM Treasury** refurbishment, Whitehall, 2002. A transformation hidden behind Bryden's Baroque façade in Whitehall.
- **Tower Place**, Tower Hill, City, 2003. An unusual, 'look-no-hands' atrium that stops short of the ground whilst maintaining a local microclimate without a divorce from surroundings. The building itself is less interesting.
- **Trafalgar Square** pedestrianisation, 2005. First proposed by Rogers.
- **30 St Mary Axe**, 1997-2003. Remarkable tower-and-piazza building. Note the Aalto touches to the entrance lobby walling.
- **Asprey** Store, Bond Street, 2004. Another outstanding work with older buildings (a set of former Georgian houses).
- **Faculty Building**; **Flowers Building**; and **Tanaka Building**, Imperial College, 2004 to 2006. Buildings that seek to insinuate themselves into the complex Imperial circulation networks.
- **National Police Memorial**, The Mall/Horse Guards Road, 2005.
- **Offices**, **Spitalfields**, 2006. Integrating with the market buildings; rather forbidding and somewhat bland. (The City creeping eastward toward Brick Lane.)
- **Moorgate House**, London Wall, 2006 (east end). Sculptural shaping.
- **Bexley Business Academy,** Yarn Way, Erith. 2001-3
- **Capital City Academy**, Doyles Garden, Willesden, 2000-3
- **London Academy**, Spur Road, Edgeware, 2006.
- **West London Academy**, Compton Crescent, Northholt, Ealing, 2002-6
- **Wembley Stadium**, 2007 (With HOK Sport, who also did the Emirate's Stadium). A new landmark arch helping to cope with an incongruous slab that is the building's sliding roof.
- **Willis** building, Lime Street, City, 2007. On the site of Terence Heysham's 1958 Lloyds building, opposite the Rogers' building - enjoying a fine, genuflecting relation to its neighbour.
- **Silken Hotel**, Aldwych, 2008.

contriving to be everything the Foster practice was not; the fallout bizarrely resulting in Foster being accused of exercising a Stalinesque Photoshop elimination of Shuttleworth from office photographs). Foster's London office buildings (as at Canary Wharf and More London) have, on the whole, been formulaic – with the exception, perhaps, of interesting ones such 100 Wood Street (exorcised from the practice's web site, possibly because of a lack of purity and the blatant theatricality of one façade), and the nearby Gresham Street building that strives to make homage to Mies (except that the 'steel' cladding sections are now aluminium looking like steel). The Jubilee Line station at Canary Wharf remains, despite a degree of 'silting up' to which Foster designs are particularly vulnerable, a very pleasant way to enter and leave the development.

Overall, however, Foster's London schemes commonly enjoy success at the strategic level compromised by less success at the level of tactile experience. And, ironically, unlike Baron Rogers of Riverside or Sir Terry Farrell, Lord Foster of Thamesbank has not been known for contributions to public life or to London's planning during a period of his own success and London's marked change, expansion and densification. Perhaps his most overlooked achievement has been to engender and run a large practice culture that has, on the whole, enjoyed a remarkable internal consistency as well as the high standards that have resulted in a outstanding body of international work. However, in the final analysis his reputation rests upon the early years of his career as a leading figure of the Hi-Tech movement, and as the leader of a firm capable of realising some very satisfying marriages between old and new.

Foster was awarded the RIBA Gold Medal in 1983. The '90s were also a significant time for other honours: he was knighted in 1990, awarded the AIA Gold in 1994, made a life peer in 1999, and became the 21st Pritzker Architecture Prize Laureate in that same year.

Norman Foster was born in Manchester, in 1935; his father was manager of a furniture and pawn shop who also supported the family by working night-shifts in an aircraft factory. After a brief stay in the Manchester Treasurer's office the young Foster did his National Service in the Royal Air Force and left after two years (in 1961) to do miscellaneous jobs before, at the age of twenty-one, attending the Manchester University School of Architecture. Upon graduating he did what every young post-war architectural graduate dreamed of: he went to the USA on a scholarship to Yale, where he met Richard Rogers and undertook a version of the 'Grand Tour' around the USA. On return to England, he set up Team Four with Rogers, Su Brummel (Rogers' then wife), and Georgie Cheeseman. However, the relationship did not last beyond the notable Reliance Controls building of 1967 (since altered). He, and his late wife Wendy Cheeseman (Georgie's sister), set up partnership alone and the practice later designed works such as the IBM building in Hampshire (1971), the Willis

Faber building in Ipswich (1974), the Fred Olsen Line terminal building in the London docklands (1975), and the Sainsbury building at East Anglia University, the Hong Kong and Shanghai Bank (1986), and Stansted Airport (1991; serving London but actually some fifty miles away from the centre).

By late 2007 Foster had withdrawn from a strangle-hold on practice ownership (structured in marked contrast with the culture of the smaller Rogers' practice). External investors had been brought in and the partnership extended. Foster was perhaps exiting to live as a tax-exile in Switzerland and fly gliders and the 747's he is qualified to make airborne - what he once referred to as his favourite building.

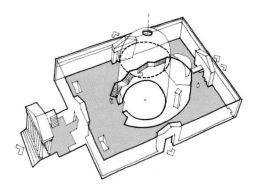

Above: The transformation of the British Museum took place around the Victorian British Library drum that sits at the heart of the building's central court; circulation was entirely reorganised by the new court roof and additional space was provided beneath the court and around the drum. This was the Foster team at its best, but (under their leadership) it is arguable that the real heroes of the project were the engineers, Buro Happold.

Above: 100 Wood Street – not the finest of Foster's works, but one of the more interesting simply because of its inconsistencies and mix of strategies on different façades. The east façade is top (with diagrid roof); the west façade is below (note the redundant and theatrical huge steel, canted 'props'). Both work in their disparate contexts (Wood Street as the eight-storey north-south axis of the old Roman fort; the other side adjacent to a former graveyard).

Opposite page: the office building at 10 Gresham Street, in the City, at the bottom of Wood Street (which was the north-south axis of the Roman fort). This rather elegant and well proportioned building fills the urban block and has a central atrium, with escape stairs at each outer corner (in addition to internal cores). It is conventional steel frame, with permanently shuttered decks. The interesting thing is the cladding: Mies in New York and Chicago, reinvented as aluminium profiles that look as if they might be steel. The reflection in the façade is Terry Farrell's Alban Gate building at the other end of Wood Street (adjacent to other buildings by Rogers and Parry).

Above: the spectacular stair at the Asprey shop.
Below: the grand hall of Canary Wharf Jubilee Line station (Arup engineers).
Right: Foster's 'blade of light' concept that served as the basis of Arup's engineering for the Millennium Bridge.

Left: City Hall – the 'strawberry' of the More London development, designed for 400 people, currently housing about 700 (with hot-desking); a curiously admirable and yet seriously flawed design (mostly concerning security, access and internal movements).

Above, below and opposite page: 30 St Mary Axe, a building whose context (Lloyds '86, the CU, PoMo, medieval and other buildings all around it, including Foster Willis building), with a remarkable (not accessible, except to tenants) top level having views all around London. However, the building's 'green' credentials have a significant 'spin' content.

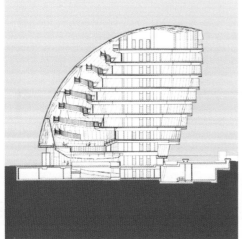

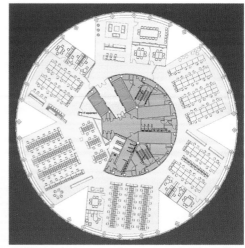

Access to the Gherkin – penetrating the steel diagrid structure – is well-handled (with a touch of Aalto to the lobby detailing). Typologically, the building is a piazza-and-tower equation, as is its neighbour, GMW's C.U. building.

past and future generations . . .

In Ibsen's drama a successful middle-aged architect/master-builder entrenched in an interplayed mix of commercial success and domestic difficulty is confronted by a femme fatale in the shape of one Hilda Wangel – a precocious young woman who comes to call in a promise, to free Solness (the master builder) from his bourgeois entrapment and draw him into a refound heroism, a basis of stature upon which he will build 'castles in the air' and once again enable Hilda to hear his defiant voice as the sound of harps in the air. Determined to transfigure his life and elope, Solness demonstrates his rebirth with a daring act, only completed once before in his life: to fearfully climb to the towering summit of a new building in a ceremony of 'topping out'. To Hilda's wild excitement he does, and then falls to his death. The onlookers – including his wife and the employees of Solness – are horrified; but Hilda remains ecstatic and protests: "But he mounted to the top. And I heard harps in the air"!

This summary of London's architects and their London architecture suffers no other choice than to close abruptly. One steps, as it were, from an on-going stream of activity going on all around. Since the mid-1990s that stream has been quite lively and well-established, although always threatened by a variety of potential crises (of the kind that emerged in late 2007 and early 2008 in the world of finance). Economic crises or not, we can, of course, be certain that architecture in the near future is unlikely to be what it is now. To some extent this is self-evident – as this review demonstrates, architectural fashions change rather frequently and sometimes abruptly. However, there is an underlying theme that emerges: while everything appears to change, perhaps the underlying challenges do not. There is mutation, but it is the less salient continuities that become interesting. Among the most notable of these are those personal and situated aspects of the architect's challenge to realise survival, success and significance. These vocational criteria serve as eternal parameters of undertakings that merely have their situational terms of reference constantly and circumstantially rewritten. Jones and Wren (even Vitruvius and Palladio) would, no doubt, have recognised the pattern.

Self-evidently, a huge number of architects *survive* in their adopted vocational role. Those who don't become lost in a historical fog and quietly disappear from view. And yet a city such as London is nevertheless peppered with fragments of interesting work by anonymous or forgotten architects.

Many find more or less notable *success*, although every practice name is a façade with an inner reality of many working parts and true authorship can be, as earlier noted, an ambiguous and contentious issue of attribution. However, a practice would hardly be viable without the pretence of heroic endeavour by at least one leading figurehead. It is then interesting to find that one acquires a generalised impression that the *vital* part of practice success is sustained for a comparatively few number of years. There is a run-in – sometimes (but not always) quite rapid, followed by a period of acknowledged promise: a strange compound of talent, aspiration, character, place, time, and opportunity. Then, if it happens, there is a relatively short period of true success. This is followed by a period when that success might be sustained, but a vitally creative period has already become history. For no arguable reason, something like eight to ten years of real vitality comes to mind.

Salience is, of course, the essential ingredient of a subsequent stage of achievement: *significance* Only a few architects realise this status. And, like survival and success, its terms of reference are problematically dependent upon standpoint: the lists of Gold Medallists and Presidents of the RIBA, as earlier noted, are littered with once influential and significant figures whose status has been eroded almost to the point of erasure. Apparently, and perhaps contrary to expectation, significance is hardly more durable than survival.

The context of salience is, of course, an ever shifting one characterised by perceived legitimacy and relevancy of stance, as well as issues of birth, talent, upbringing, opportunity, experience and so on. But one doubts if the basic issues of aspiration and challenge ever change. Nevertheless, in writing about the most notable of London's architects whose work remains in some manner extant and vital, this author is conscious of having ignored a large body of individuals whose work has been lost, forgotten or transmogrified. And about everyone's pertinent biographical detail there is, almost invariably, uncertainty and ambiguity. Anyone addressing such complex issues has two principal guides: one academic and the other oral. The former tends to enjoy a sometimes abstracted and necessarily interpretative basis. And the oral record is, by definition, hugely subjective. To hear the latter – as one's own voice or that of friends and colleagues, perhaps handed down as reportage or gossip – is to stir up anxiety concerning the academic perspective – a concern that parallels one's suspicions regarding the wealth of supplementary oral records that technology now makes available. Perhaps the truth concerning our ostensible heroes is somewhere in between. Certainly, it is here that one finds admirable biographical works on the recently deceased that grasp at a career, warts and all: works such as Girouard's on Jim Stirling, and Appleyard's on Richard Rogers (written at the height of Rogers' career).

Such examples are all too rare, but they can possess a controversial vitality that reverberates in a manner no academic work on Jones or Wren or Pugin can hope to parallel. Invariably, one finds these narratives to be imbued with a note of contingency and precariousness: events might not have turned out that way. But there is also a recurring keynote that concerns individuality and a strength of character from which arises a notable acting in the world that impresses now as it once did in the days of the Greek polis. Now, as then, the core issue informing an architect's individual endeavours is one of social context and answers to the situated questions of What should I do? and, How should I do it? There are, of course, many subsidiary and nuanced dimensions to those interrogatives. Vitruvius dealt with them in the rather abstracted semiotic terms of what is signified and what signifies, or what we might term intent and the expression of intent - all of which is elusively dependent upon 'hitting the mark' in a manner that bears the strange quality of being self-evident. That challenge is, by implication, fundamentally as moral, ethical and civically oriented as it is situated, formal and unique.

It is from this perspective that we should understand the truth in Fernand Léger's comment that, "Architecture is not an art. It's a natural function of the social order", as well as appreciate ideological anxieties such a conclusion prompted in the mind of Georges Bataille. The Greeks dealt with the issue as action within the public realm and a demonstration of that practical sense they referred to as phronesis. The Romans made reference to a sensus communis – later a keynote of the eighteenth century's Rule of Taste. In the modern period the issue has arisen in terms of what the Germans called Bildung and the French le bon sens. However, the architect acting in a public realm might understand the core issue very simply in terms of the above interrogatives. These questions call upon a Ruskinian 'penetrative' understanding and creative vision, as well as compositional talents and customary appreciations that also refer to his criterion of 'flourishing'. But whatever terms are employed, they embody a familiar note of Apollonian homogeneity set in opposition to potentially disruptive heterogeneous Dionysian counterpoints. Here, in all their manifold aspects, are the juxtaposed mythic keynotes of order, necessity and contingency which continue to inform architectural practice and its scenes of action. Architecture always has, and will have, a role and meaning embracing such issues.

Our historical scene of architectural action has been London: a splendid example and a body, as it were, with either a strange life of its own or, at least, a peculiar collective metabolism that is somehow not quite in our control, despite best intentions. And yet its life and history is as patterned as that physicality noted by the likes of Summerson and Farrell. And so, knowing its tomorrow will be, in terms of particular situated challenges, paradoxically familiar and yet entirely unique, one raises a metaphorical glass: to the next generation of architectural heroes; to their survival, success, and significance. May they do the right thing and do it well. And may it make them - and us - happy.

Index of architects